DATE DUE

DEMCO 38-296

BY THE SAME AUTHOR

STRAVINSKY IN PICTURES AND DOCUMENTS   *1978*
(*with Vera Stravinsky*)

CURRENT CONVICTIONS   *1977*

PREJUDICES IN DISGUISE   *1974*

CHRONICLE OF A FRIENDSHIP   *1972*

STRAVINSKY

SELECTED CORRESPONDENCE

ALFRED A. KNOPF   NEW YORK   1982

STRAVINSKY

SELECTED CORRESPONDENCE

VOLUME I

EDITED AND

WITH COMMENTARIES BY

ROBERT CRAFT

This is a Borzoi Book published by Alfred A. Knopf, Inc.

Copyright © 1982 by Robert Craft.

Pan-American Copyright Conventions.

Knopf, Inc., New York.

rk. Originally published

don.

ritings by W. H. Auden

he correspondence between

l here corrects the versions

s and Commentaries.

Not to be reprinted without written permission of Professor Edward Mendelson.

Library of Congress Cataloging in Publication Data

Stravinsky, Igor, 1882–1971.   Stravinsky, selected correspondence, volume I.

Includes index.

1. Stravinsky, Igor, 1882–1971.   2. Composers—

Correspondence.   I. Craft, Robert.   II. Title.

ML410.S932A395   780'.92'4   [B]   81-47495

ISBN 0-394-51870-5   AACR2

Manufactured in the United States of America

First American Edition

Igor Stravinsky

*. . . You play an enormous role in music, and this role
was appreciated by another of my unforgettable
friends, Nicolai Andreyevich [Rimsky-Korsakov], who
doted on you, as you well know. Despite the miserly
grip he kept on his favorable opinion, he continually
recommended your new works to me, and I recall that
he once pronounced to me adamantly: "Igor Stravinsky may be my pupil, but he will never be my or
anyone else's follower, because his gift for music is
uniquely great and original." (Letter from
V. Belsky, Belgrade, November 15, 1928)*

*Il me semble que vous avez atteint et exprimé l'une des
forces élémentaires de l'homme, son besoin profond et
organique du rythme et la libre expansion de toute la
musicalité qui est en lui. (Jeanès, June 1913)*

*Stravinsky, qui était entré avec fracas dans la gloire,
pénètre, solitaire et sereinement, dans l'éternité musicale. (Francis Poulenc, 1941)*

*Pour vous, cher Igor Stravinsky, sur ce versant d'un
siècle où vous faites, et de haut, toujours face à
l'avenir. (St.-John Perse)*

CONTENTS

When Paul Collaer, the Belgian musicologist, sent Stravinsky the completed manuscript of his monograph, the result of a study of the music guided by the composer himself and of extensive correspondence, Stravinsky replied: "Nowhere in the spirit of your book do I recognize myself, not in the 'life' and not in the 'work.' " This statement, more than any other consideration, was responsible for directing my own work away from a Stravinsky biography and toward the editing of his correspondence. The spirit of Stravinsky has been captured in a few moments on film, but not in any writing about him.

For a variety of reasons, a sufficiently complete "life" and an adequate examination of the works still cannot be written. Obviously a biography must follow, not anticipate, a presentation of at least the principal events, a task that the three volumes of selected correspondence now being published only begins to accomplish. The chief obstacle to a study of the music is that the larger portion of the sketches and drafts, as well as all but two or three manuscript full scores, has already been dispersed—in such repositories as the Library of Congress; the Pierpont Morgan Library; the British Museum (the J. & W. Chester manuscripts); the Bibliothèque Nationale (Symphony in E flat); the Museum of Israel (*Abraham and Isaac*); the New York Public Library (Symphony in Three Movements); the Koussevitzky Music Foundation (*Symphony of Psalms, Ode*); the Dumbarton Oaks Library (Concerto in E flat, Septet); the Rychenberg Stiftung (*Histoire du soldat, Les Noces*); the libraries of Princeton (*Requiem Canticles*), Oberlin (*Threni*), Stanford (*Danses concertantes, Scènes de ballet*), Southern California (*The Rake's Progress*), California at Berkeley (*Orpheus*); the private libraries of André Meyer (the sketchbook of *Le Sacre du printemps* and the first full score of Part One); Paul Sacher (the manuscripts of a dozen major pieces); Luc Gilbert (Duo concertant); M. L. Kasper-Ansermet; Adriana Panni; Serge Lifar; Theodore Stravinsky (the Kireyevsky books of Russian poetry with the composer's annotations); and Boosey & Hawkes, for the composer's publishers are in possession not only of the manuscripts of *Petrushka, The Nightingale,* and *Oedipus Rex,* but also of hundreds of pages of his corrected printers' proofs.

To attempt a biography would be premature until the crucial information is made available about Stravinsky's formative years through the time of *Firebird*. Apart from music, what most occupied his mind—painting? politics? law?—and what were his social and religious beliefs during the decade before the creation of his first masterpiece? Moreover, which friends exercized the greatest influence on him? In *Chroniques de ma vie*, he singles out a certain Ivan Pokrovsky, but the name occurs nowhere else. Who is the Troitsky who appears in the photographs of the young composer with Rimsky-Korsakov's sons; V. V. Yuzhin, the dedicatee of the 1918 piano transcription of *Firebird;* and A. F. Yelagin, who gave the composer a medal "in commemoration of April

14–15, 1908"? Who is Mitya Rublyov, whose death, in Leningrad in 1932, provoked his brother Andrei to write to Stravinsky from Viborg, December 31, 1932? In the 1930s, Stravinsky corresponded with a former teacher, Alexander Vasilievich Efimov (then living at Pirogovsky Ulitsa, Kiev), but what was his subject? And what became of Stravinsky's love affair with Ekaterina Mitusova, to whom he sent money in Leningrad as late as the 1930s?

Even the relationship between Stravinsky and the Rimsky-Korsakov family remains obscure. In Leningrad, on July 15, 1932, Andrei Rimsky-Korsakov, the composer's son, wrote to Stravinsky in Paris asking him, in French (!), to contribute to a volume honoring the twenty-fifth anniversary of the death of the composer of *Shéhérazade,* and asking, as well, for copies of Rimsky-Korsakov's letters to his pupil. Did Stravinsky answer, and did he send copies of these letters, if he still had them? Though Andrei's style is formal (*"Cher maître . . ."*) and the request makes no reference to the families of either, he uses the intimate form (*"tu"*). Stravinsky would probably not have ignored Andrei's statement, "Recalling the profound impression that this death made on you, I believe that you will be inclined to associate yourself with a manifestation of this kind," yet the present writer was unable to find any trace of a reply in the Rimsky-Korsakov Museum (Leningrad) on a visit there in September 1981.

No less surprising, though Stravinsky attributed a considerable role in his early development to his uncle A. F. Yelachich, the *Chroniques* barely touches on this branch of the family. (The Yelachich correspondence contains intriguing asides, such as this reminiscence in a letter from Stravinsky's cousin Gavril A. Yelachich, Belgrade, March 26, 1936: "To me you are the dear, kind older brother with whom I went turtle-hunting in the thistle bushes, and in whose room we developed our first, childish ideas about Art.") As an indication of the vagueness surrounding Stravinsky's background, all that has been made known in the West about his paternal uncles is that one of them, a colonel in the Tsar's army, witnessed the future composer's baptism.

Presumably these lacunae will be closed by the family correspondence from the 1880s until World War I, still in Leningrad. (The primary document for the composer's first twenty years is his father's extensive diary, 1877–1902, now in the possession of A. A. Yacovlev, Stravinsky's niece's widower.) But the composer's own archives do not contain a single line referring to progress on *Firebird,* nor any "eureka" such as he was to exclaim while at work on *Le Sacre du printemps.*

Only in this centenary year are books from the USSR finally appearing in English translation, notably Boris Asafiev's 1929 classic and the monograph by M. S. Druskin.[1] Still more valuable publications, such as Irina Vershinina's work on Stravinsky's use of folk material, and Igor Blazhkov's two-volume edition of letters, have been promised.

Volumes II and III of the *Selected Correspondence* offer far larger tracts of

---

[1] Mikhail Semyonovich Druskin met Stravinsky in Berlin and, after coaching by the composer, played his Piano Concerto there in January 1932.

unknown territory than Volume I, and Volume II is almost entirely new. But in all three books, Stravinsky's wit and overwhelming charm are unfortunately less evident than less desirable qualities, partly, no doubt, for the reason that he always wrote under pressure and in a great hurry.

Before Stravinsky's death, I was familiar with only small portions of his archives, namely the French letters and the Russian correspondence that he translated for me. Since 1971 I have discovered views and statements by him that would be scarcely conceivable coming from the Stravinsky I knew, a very different, incomparably more likable human being than the author of a great many of the letters of the 1920s and 1930s. My thoughts about him have changed, but not my feelings.

Each chapter of Igor Stravinsky's correspondence presented in this book is self-contained, each focuses on a different period of his life, and in each the relationship between writer and addressee is radically different. The contents are complementary, the overlapping is minimal. Most of the Delage and Derzhanovsky letters precede the Cocteau correspondence, which centers, first, on his aborted *David* (1914), during which time Stravinsky wrote only a single postcard to Ernest Ansermet, and, second, on the creation of *Oedipus Rex* (1925–27), which did not involve the conductor. The letters to Nadia Boulanger, and those to myself, help to fill a gap—that of the 1940s—in the letters to Ansermet, while the correspondence with Lincoln Kirstein and with W. H. Auden brings the chronicle to the 1950s and early 1960s, when, after long absences, Cocteau and Ansermet reappear, thus rounding out and giving continuity to the story.

The selection inevitably suffers from the near silence on Stravinsky's side in his correspondence with Catherine, his first wife, and with Derzhanovsky and Delage. Stravinsky rarely kept copies of his extensive personal correspondence—he did not preserve so much as a draft of any letter to his closest associate, Arthur Lourié—and he seems to have written more rapidly in Russian and to have had even less regard for making carbons when writing in his native tongue. This explains the absence of the Lourié and Pierre Suvchinsky letters that the reader would naturally expect to find in a first volume of Stravinsky's correspondence. Only the recovery of Stravinsky's side of the exchanges with both men could provide an adequate view of the composer's intellectual life in the 1920s. Suvchinsky, Mirsky, and Efron, with the collaboration of Shestov, Remizov, and Tsvetaeva, edited the émigré periodical *Versti,* whose first issue featured an essay by Lourié on Stravinsky and an article by E. M. Forster (translated by Mirsky) on (largely) Eliot and Joyce. Since Rozanov's *The Apocalypse of Our Time* appeared in the second issue, with an essay on the author by Suvchinsky, and since Stravinsky's *Poetics of Music* quotes from this publication, the leading émigré reviews, including *Sovremmeniya Zapiski,* with its bias toward Berdayev, must be examined for similar connections.

The opening chapter of the present volume provides the most important material so far to appear for an understanding of Stravinsky the man. This introductory segment does not contain the composer's side of the correspondence, which is apparently in the possession of his elder son, but is based entirely on Catherine Stravinsky's letters to her husband. They reveal much about him, nevertheless, both background and foreground, the child as well as the mature composer, and this though the texts are limited to fragments. (That the letters could ever be published in their entirety is doubtful, and in any case the results would belong as much to medical as to musical history.)

The originals of the excerpts from Catherine Stravinsky's letters (and from the letters of her sister and mother-in-law) are in Russian, as are those to and from the publishers N. G. Struve, E. A. Oeberg, G. G. Païchadze, F. V. Weber; the magazine editor V. V. Derzhanovsky; the concert agent Zereteli; and such colleagues as Maximilian Steinberg. French is the original language of the Delage, Cocteau, Ansermet, and Boulanger correspondence. Stravinsky's usage is not idiomatic, and his propensity to invent new words and new forms of words, noted by Paris interviewers, is evident in his written no less than in his spoken communications. According to *Paris-Soir,* December 7, 1932: "Stravinsky's singing Russian accent and extraordinary knowledge of our language permit him, if he cannot find a word, to turn the difficulty around, and, with authority, to forge a felicitous neologism."

No doubt I shall be criticized for not giving the texts in the original languages, but a book that is part Russian, part French, and part English is unlikely to find a publisher and would have few readers if it did. The translations include a few silent corrections of grammar, spelling, and punctuation, which, for intelligibility, has been added in telegrams. In certain instances in which Stravinsky's meaning remains obscure in the most literal English rendition, a word, or words, has been interpolated in an attempt to make his intentions clear. Most of these emendations have been bracketed. Such license would be inexcusable in translating the letters of a literary artist, but Stravinsky cannot be so classified in the French letters that make up most of his correspondence in this volume. For all of the losses in translation—as well as, I hope, some gains—his telegraphic style survives. The typical Stravinsky letter, direct, terse, blunt, and exquisitely polite, begins *"qq [quelques] mots: suis très pressé,"* followed by a flood of requests, often itemized by number and letter, and ending with a demand for an answer by return mail. Regrettably, the texts of many of his letters have had to be transcribed from copies from which the signature, often revealing, is missing.

English (and some Franglais) is the language of Stravinsky's letters to W. H. Auden, Lincoln Kirstein, and myself. These have been reproduced exactly as written, including slips in spelling that would be routinely righted by an editor but are left uncorrected here in order to determine the exact state of the composer's command of the language in 1947–48. His communications to me were written exclusively by him, I should add, whereas one or two to Auden are partly the work of Stravinsky's son-in-law and secretary, André Marion, and they are easily identifiable as such.

Even in translation, Stravinsky's Russian correspondence is so different from the French and English that the Russian letters could not be successfully juxtaposed in the first volume. Those to Derzhanovsky are the exception, for they are an isolated unit: the two men never met, the period of their exchanges is very brief, and the musical life described is of Moscow, not of St. Petersburg. In other Russian correspondence, Stravinsky coins words, puns, performs syntactical tricks, plays with the language, and draws on a richer and more scurrilous vocabulary than is found in his foreign-language communications. Some of his Russian allusions are obscure, at least for those of us whose knowledge of the culture is slight.

I did not attempt to supply commentaries for the Auden chapter, having already done so elsewhere. The Auden-Stravinsky letters represent a friendship that was immediate and steadfast; Auden, in the week before the composer's death, was his last "outside" visitor. Nor have I added more than a few personal notes to the Cocteau, Ansermet, and Boulanger chapters, since I was present at too few of the composer's meetings with these friends. But the Auden and Cocteau correspondence includes both sides and should be self-explanatory. Cocteau's letters reveal that he failed to understand Stravinsky initially, but that by the time of *Oedipus Rex,* great strides had been made in the two collaborators' apprehension of each other. The Cocteau correspondence, and the Ansermet, provide a unique inside view of the music and ballet worlds, especially of the final decade of the Diaghilev period. Diaghilev himself appears, too, though less frequently than in much of the correspondence included in the later volumes, which also contain his own correspondence with Stravinsky.

Ansermet's letters to Stravinsky are not included, because they devote a disproportionate amount of space to matters that have no place in a book on Stravinsky and because they greatly outnumber the composer's letters to the conductor. I have tried to compensate for the omission by extensively annotating Stravinsky's side of the correspondence. As for the Delage letters, these suggest a very different Stravinsky, but as yet I have not been able to learn anything about the friendship beyond what is given in these texts.

Nadia Boulanger worshipped Stravinsky, but not "simply," and his letters to her show that she was well aware of the threat he posed to her working time. Stravinsky's communications with Nadia Boulanger present a special problem in that her closest association with the composer belongs to a time—the decade before his first letter to her in this book—that is not documented in epistolary form. As early as 1931, his trust in her musicianship was such that he instructed his publisher to ask her, without consulting him, to resolve all questions in the proofs of the *Symphony of Psalms* (letters to Païchadze, March and September 1931). Her chapter in the eventual Stravinsky biography will have to be constructed from the letters and memoirs of others.

Ernest Ansermet deserves a special word, since the letters to him make up so large a share of this first volume, and since conductors tend to be forgotten. The association with Stravinsky was the most important in Ansermet's life, and the thirty-year-old conductor was, with Debussy and Ravel, one of the first musicians to recognize the young composer's true stature—that of the greatest creative musician of his generation. From 1915 through the mid-1920s, Ansermet was not only the principal conductor of, but also the most intelligent spokesman for, Stravinsky's music. And Ansermet conducted more Stravinsky premieres—*Histoire du soldat,* the 1919 *Firebird* Suite, *The Song of the Nightingale, Pulcinella, Renard, Les Noces,* the Capriccio, the *Symphony of Psalms,* the Mass—and continued to give more performances of the music than anyone other than its composer.

A phrase in a letter, January 8, 1914, from one of Stravinsky's publishers in Moscow suggests that the composer and Ansermet were not on very close terms before this date: "If you can rely on the bandmaster in Montreux, we will send the Symphony to him on credit." The reference is to Stravinsky's Symphony in E flat, which Ansermet wished to perform, and for which he must have sought Stravinsky's permission and aid in obtaining the score and parts. The word "bandmaster" must have been Stravinsky's, since the publisher would hardly employ this pejorative description unless the composer had used it first. In any case, the earliest written communication between composer and conductor is dated March 1914; the rarity of the letters during the four years of the war indicates no more than that the friends saw each other regularly and had no need to correspond. In 1915, as a result of Stravinsky's recommendations to Diaghilev, Ansermet became chief conductor for the Ballets Russes, replacing Pierre Monteux, who was serving in the French army.

Stravinsky and Ansermet were coevals, and the conductor had aspired to compose. Perhaps because of this, Ansermet suffered from a sense of being in a secondary position, which was aggravated when Stravinsky began to conduct his own music, thereby challenging Ansermet as its most authoritative inter-preter. The question of authority led to a never-resolved conflict between them, which began in 1937 and was exacerbated after World War II, when Stravinsky continued to explore new paths while his former champion grew increasingly antagonistic toward developments in music that Stravinsky considered the most vital of the age. I was present at Stravinsky's post–World War II meetings with Ansermet (in New York and in Geneva), and I remember the conductor as an amusing mimic of his colleagues, and, whatever his views, as a perceptive and intelligent musician. By this time, Stravinsky did not share my respect for Ansermet, but the composer's pre-1937 letters reveal his genuine feeling for the man he once called "my guardian angel" (letter of March 14, 1927).

Finally, it must be said that Stravinsky would not have approved of the publication of his letters. When Edward Lockspeiser, the Debussy scholar, requested permission to use one of them addressed to the French master, Stravinsky replied, through an intermediary (November 4, 1964):

> I am not keen on the idea of publishing the letter to which Lockspeiser refers. . . . I do not consider the letter interesting. It is banal and does not contribute anything to the other letters that he is planning to publish. . . . Also, I see that this business is taking place without my permission, though when I published Debussy's letters to me, I obtained permission from his heirs, through my English publisher. . . . Answer that I have not given my permission to publish my letters to Debussy. . . . [Original in Russian]

ACKNOWLEDGMENTS

With a different title and in abbreviated form, "Igor, Catherine, and God" appeared in the *New York Review of Books,* November 22, 1979. "Letters to Robert Craft (1944–1949)" was published, not quite complete, in the *Musical Quarterly,* July 1979, and Appendices C, E, F, and G were written for, and first published by, the 1979 Stravinsky Festival, London. I am grateful to the editors of these publications for permission to reprint. I am also grateful to Mme Jean Seringe, niece of Francis Poulenc, for permission to publish the facsimile signatures, "Igor Stravinsky" and "Vera" (Sudeikina), with frame drawn by Stravinsky, that appear on the dedication page. They are taken from a group letter to Poulenc, written on stationery of the Restaurant du Petit Louvain in Brussels, January 13, 1924, which is St. Sylvester's Day in the Russian calendar.

The translations from the Russian, including Catherine Stravinsky's letters, are by Mary Brown and Malcolm Macdonald, with the help and expert advice of Franklin and Helen Reeve. The translations from the French are the work of several hands: my own, in the first stages, and those of my sister Phyllis Crawford and, principally, of her daughter, Kristin. Sara Nelson contributed. Susan Godfrey then revised the translations of the whole of the Cocteau and Ansermet chapters, after which Eva Resnikova again revetted and revised all of the translations from the French.

Above all others, I thank Vera Stravinsky for sharing her memories and for the use of her diaries, letters, and other personal papers. For numerous improvements throughout the manuscript, thanks are due to Edwin Allen, Elbert Lenrow, Lawrence Morton, Phyllis and Kristin Crawford. Patrick Carnegy and others at Faber & Faber, and Robert Gottlieb and Eva Resnikova at Alfred A. Knopf, have also improved the text in countless ways and are hereby gratefully thanked.

IGOR, CATHERINE,

AND   GOD

Catherine Nossenko Stravinsky, first wife of the composer, is not mentioned by name in the three references to her in his Chroniques de ma vie (1935). *Yet any full study of Stravinsky must include the stories of both of his marriages, and while Vera Stravinsky's place in the composer's life has been partly established, Catherine's remains almost unknown. If the deficiency is not rectified by the excerpts presented here from Catherine's letters to her husband, these passages should at least help to give some sense of her personality, as well as to contribute to an expanded and intimate view of his character.*

Stravinsky more than once testified to the unhappiness of his childhood and youth. Not only was he apparently the least favored of the four sons—at any rate by the mother—but he hated school, where he was taunted because of his short stature. One exception to this unsympathetic treatment was the kindness, affection, and encouragement shown to him by his cousin Catherine Nossenko, eighteen months his senior, who may have perceived the genius not yet visible to others. Like Igor, she had a talent for painting and calligraphy and made copies of some of his earlier manuscripts, notably Renard, Histoire du soldat, *and the Octet. Before showing his newly composed music to anyone else, Stravinsky played it for Catherine,[1] as he did in later years for Vera.*

Catherine must have been aware of Igor's explosive and tyrannical nature, and of the will that could crush any obstacle.[2] But she seems to have understood him, and during the summers of their late adolescence, these first cousins were as close as siblings, the more so, no doubt, because the "brother" had only brothers, the "sister" only another sister. Stravinsky's letters to his parents in July 1901 show that he both enjoyed Catherine's artistic companionship and was grateful for her goodness and generosity. In retrospect, it seems almost inevitable that she and Igor should marry (which they did in 1906).[3] She soon assumed a maternal role, addressing him in all her letters by the childhood nickname "Gimochka," occasionally adding the endearment "dunik." This marriage within the family was apparently practical and successful, until Firebird (1910) *took him into a new, lionizing world and tuberculosis made her a chronic invalid (from 1914).*

---

[1] "I am so happy when I think about your present composition [*Jeu de cartes*]. I liked what you played for me immensely." (January 17, 1936)

[2] On his return from America in 1935, Igor received a letter from Catherine, in which she says that her sister, Lyudmila Beliankina, and Irina Terapiano, sister of Stravinsky's sister-in-law, "have written to me that you are somehow completely changed—even-tempered, calm, and kind." Lyudmila attributed the transformation to an improved liver condition; Irina, who was typing the composer's *Chroniques,* spoke of "a spiritual cause." But the new character seems not to have been long-lasting, for Catherine begins a letter on August 23: "Forgive me for having been all wrong about [the] telegram. . . . I know how such things make you angry."

[3] Since parallel-cousin marriage was forbidden in Russia, the Stravinsky-Nossenko ceremony was performed in secret. For the genealogical chart of the Stravinsky family, see *Stravinsky in Pictures and Documents,* New York and London, 1979 (hereafter referred to as *S.P.D.*).

Fifteen years after wedding Catherine, Stravinsky met and became infatuated with Vera de Bosset Sudeikina. Telling Catherine that he could not live without this other woman, he expected his wife not only to accept the triangular relationship but also to join him in admiring and befriending the younger woman. Since Catherine had always subordinated her wishes to her husband's, he correctly anticipated that she would do the same in this new situation. It may be said that she had no alternative, for her illness precluded a full participation in his life, and divorce between two people so closely united was unthinkable. But these pragmatic explanations are less important than that of her absolute devotion to Stravinsky and to what she saw as his divine creative gift.

The new relationship does not seem to have altered Catherine's feelings for her husband. Her letters suggest instead that she, who always coddled him, regarded Mme Sudeikina as a partner for his help and protection.[4] Many of Catherine's letters begin with expressions of anxiety about the effect that the bad news of her illness may have on him:

All I did was think of you and how my letter must have upset you. . . . (October 30, 1937)

I would so like to write something comforting, but I only distress you with all that I say. (January 8, 1938)

She shielded Stravinsky in other matters as well. One of the themes of her correspondence was that he should spare his energies for composing, and to that end she urged him to travel less and to ignore comments about himself in the press:

So you plan to go to America again next winter. . . . When will you ever have time to rest and to compose?[5] (March 11, 1935)

---

[4] Both women made and kept for Stravinsky the copies of the letters he wrote when he was without a typewriter, and both performed other errands. G. G. Païchadze, of the Edition Russe de Musique, wrote to Stravinsky in New York, January 13, 1937: "In accordance with Ekaterina Gavrilovna's instructions today, we sent the *Mavra* and *Baiser de la fée* piano scores, and, as Vera Arturovna telegraphed, we added the scores of your three church choruses." Two weeks later, Païchadze wrote again saying that "Vera Arturovna" had relayed Stravinsky's instructions concerning *Apollon* and *Fée*, which ballets, it had been decided, were to complete the program, with *Jeu de cartes*, at the Metropolitan Opera in April. Païchadze added that the score of the *Fée* had to be copied from the original manuscript.

[5] That Stravinsky's concert tours did affect his composing, both in quantity and form, is indicated by his letter to Ernest Alexandrovich Oeberg of the Edition Russe de Musique, September 23, 1925, saying that three parts of the Serenade are finished and that "in all probability there will be six parts." Two weeks later he had written the fourth movement, which was destined to be the final one, arguably because of interruptions for concerts.

I understand why you are indignant, and how unpleasant all of this is for you, especially now with these silly newspaper articles. . . . If I were in your place, I would withdraw the candidacy.[6] [What matters] is that this should not disturb your work. (January 18, 1936)

Mika[7] wrote that Schloezer[8] has published another unpleasant article about your [*Chroniques*]. But this is not worth getting excited about, since it is plain that he's always going to write unpleasant things. It's impossible to get away from this. There will always be such people. But, then, there are others. (February 3, 1936)

Stravinsky had arranged for Vera and Catherine to meet, in Nice in February 1925, while he was far away in America. "If there has to be another woman, I

---

[6] For election to the Institut de France. A law was passed, May 19, 1934, barring the candidacy of any naturalized citizen for a period of ten years (see Appendix B). Stravinsky was not aware of this, however, and thus of his ineligibility. His candidacy had been proposed by Gabriel Pierné, to whom Stravinsky wrote, July 8, 1935, that Jacques-Emile Blanche had told him of Pierné's ". . . very gracious intention; I do not need to tell you how happy and honored I would be to become a part of this illustrious company." But six months later, Stravinsky wrote to Blanche and Pierné: "Your letter awaited me upon my return to Paris tonight, after my obligatory visits to Maurice Denis and Le Sidaner. My candidacy was a result of your insistence and because you assured me, dear Pierné, that to do otherwise would be disastrous. Now it seems that I must withdraw in order to avoid 'humiliation and scandal.' The legal question . . . is not my affair. . . . In order not to derogate the custom, I submitted, reluctantly, I admit, to all of the formalities which the position demands. I did not lack encouragement from you until tonight, when suddenly you ask me to withdraw. . . . To withdraw for reasons that are beyond my comprehension would perhaps be a noble gesture in the eyes of some, but the majority would certainly interpret this as an indication that I fear rejection. My dignity prohibits me from exposing myself to this. . . ." (January 15, 1936)   On January 22, 1936, Stravinsky wrote to Yakov Lvovich Lvov, San Remo: "On the subject of my 'dignity' . . . I fear that you are in for a bitter disappointment: it is not likely that the old-timers at the Institut will choose me. The newspapers and the public . . . want me to be chosen, but the Academy is very far from exhibiting the enthusiasm or unanimity necessary for me to have any serious chance of being elected. In fact, the old-timers have done everything to try to eliminate my candidacy—which, in the first place, I had proposed against my own wishes, to avoid offending certain members who had asked me to enter my name. The voting this Saturday will determine who was right." See "Stravinsky and the Institut de France" in *Stravinsky: Selected Correspondence*, Volume II (hereafter referred to as *S.S.C.* II).

[7] Lyudmila ("Mika," "Mikusha"), Stravinsky's elder daughter (1908–38).

[8] Boris de Schloezer (1881–1969), brother of Alexander Scriabin's second wife, was the author of *Igor Strawinsky* (Paris, 1929; English version by Ezra Pound, *The Dial*, 1929). Schloezer's estheticizing irritated Stravinsky, who once wrote to Nicolas Nabokov: "What rubbish the Russian intelligentsia [Schloezer] represents." (December 15, 1949) .

am glad that it is you," Catherine told Vera on that occasion. Improbable as it
may seem, the two did become fond of each other. Most of Catherine's letters to
Igor in the 1930s mention Vera (or "Verochka"):

I was at Vera's recently. We sat and talked and then she drove me to the Beliankins'.[9] On Christmas, her birthday, I congratulated her over the telephone, and sent some azaleas to her. (Paris, January 8, 1935)

I wrote to Vera before I left [for Sancellemoz], and she answered with a very nice letter. . . . (March 21, 1935)

I am writing these lines while you are still sailing on the *Ile de France*. . . . Vera will meet you in Le Havre on Saturday morning. . . . (April 1935)

How did you like Bologna, after driving out of Venice? . . . I kiss Vera warmly and wish her a lot of pleasure from this trip. . . . (Sancellemoz, May 21, 1935)

Yesterday all of the children and Yuri[10] were at Vera's, where they had tea. Perhaps Vera has already written. . . . (Paris, October 2, 1935)

How is Vera? Has she given up her flowers, or is she still working on them?[11] How does she feel in this gloomy and foul weather? (Sancellemoz, January 31, 1936)

---

[9] Lyudmila ("Milochka") Beliankina (1880–1937), Catherine's sister; her husband, Grigory ("Grisha") Beliankin, a retired naval officer; and their two children, Ira ("Irusha") and Ganya. When the Ukraine was invaded by Germany, early in World War I, the Beliankins moved from Kiev to Odessa. After the armistice, they fled from Russia, through Germany, to the Swiss border, where, after Stravinsky posted a bond and René Auberjonois and an official in Bern, Louis Ador, intervened in the composer's behalf, the refugee family was admitted to Switzerland.

[10] Yuri Mandelstamm (1908–43?) was employed in Paris as a film critic by the Russian émigré paper *Vozrozhdenie*. Early in February 1935 he met Stravinsky's daughter Lyudmila, who introduced him to her mother on February 14. By the end of April, he and Mika planned to marry—after his conversion to the Russian Orthodox Church. Before taking this step, he wanted "to discuss theological questions with Bulgakov"— Sergei Nikolayevich Bulgakov (1871–1944), a friend of Berdyaev and of Biely, and the author of several books on theology—"but Bulgakov told him to go directly to Father Vassily, who is the one who will baptize him." (Catherine's letter of May 11)   Catherine later reported that "Yuri is somewhat disturbed by the dryness of the catechism," but the baptism took place on September 12, the marriage on October 23. Mandelstamm ghosted Stravinsky's essay on Pushkin: "Yuri has just written your article about Pushkin, and tomorrow is coming here to dictate it to Ira, who will type it on your machine as you asked." (Catherine's letter of January 3, 1937)   Mandelstamm remarried after Mika's death, but, as late as April 1939, Anna Stravinsky (the composer's mother) wrote to Igor that "Yuri comes by on Saturdays when he is free from the editorial office." An article on him by Yuri Terapiano appears in the book *Vstrechi*, New York, 1953.

[11] Vera Sudeikina was self-supporting during the years between her Sudeikin and Stravinsky marriages. The reference here is to her boutique for artificial flowers, but

Advise Vera about this medicine [*Extrait d'ail*]. . . . After all, she likes to try all sorts of medicines, doesn't she, and this one is harmless and promising. . . . (July 29, 1936)

. . . Right now Milene[12] is buying slippers for Vera. . . . [Vera] said that she has so much to do that she has not written to you yet. . . . (Paris, December 12, 1937, to Stravinsky in Tallinn)

But when Catherine expresses gratitude to her husband for his considerateness toward Vera during his absence in South America for concerts, the reader can scarcely believe that the intention is not ironic:

How good that you have decided to make it possible for Vera to move to another apartment. Does she already have something in mind? . . . Apparently, otherwise you would not have decided so quickly. . . . This is very good for Vera in many ways, first, for her health . . . and, second, for her spirits, since a change of apartments somehow always brightens one's mood. As she will be doing this while you're gone, the process of settling in will keep her busy and make the time of your absence seem shorter. . . . (Sancellemoz, February 22, 1936)

This will remind some readers of Graham Greene's story "Mortmain," in which a newly married man is bombarded by his former mistress with such messages as "All I really wanted to say was: Be happy both of you."
    As might be expected, Stravinsky wrote more frequently to Vera than to Catherine:

This morning . . . I talked with Vera on the phone and she already had a letter from you. She said that you had described the storm. . . .[13] (January 11, 1935)

Vera received a letter from you today but I still haven't gotten one. She received one before I did the other time, too . . . now I wait impatiently for my letter. . . . (January 18, 1935)

Yesterday, I received your letter of the 4th, but Vera received one from St. Louis two days before that. . . . (February 16, 1935)

I wait for news from Lisbon or Madeira. Perhaps you wrote only to Vera from Lisbon, but I hope that when she receives the letter, she will call me. . . . (April 14, 1936)

---

her most substantial sources of income were from a fashion accessories shop, the "Tula-Vera," and from the designing and making of costumes in an atelier that she supervised. Catherine wrote to Igor, May 25, 1936: "Because of the political developments and the change in the Ministry, everyone is afraid about the future . . . and Vera writes that the number of her orders dropped immediately, but she has probably written to you about it herself."

[12] Milene, Stravinsky's younger daughter (b. 1914).

[13] Stravinsky had written from New York after a rough transatlantic crossing on the S.S. *Rex*.

Not having received a letter from you in 15 days, I asked Vera if she had gotten one. . . . Vera wrote to me that you had written. . . . (May 25, 1936)

Neither Vera nor I [had] received anything since the letters of March 7 that you wrote on the train outside Los Angeles . . . [but] Svetik[14] has just come in and informed me that Vera has received a letter from you. . . . (March 30, 1937)[15]

I spoke to Vera on the telephone. She told me that she received a letter from you three days ago. . . . (April 20, 1937)

Since Stravinsky's letters to Vera from North and South America reached her in Paris before his letters to his wife arrived in Sancellemoz—where she was confined for long periods during his 1935, 1936, and 1937 transatlantic tours— Vera often telephoned his news to Catherine.

Stravinsky was in the United States in February 1937 when Milochka, Catherine's sister, suffered a brain hemorrhage, and her husband, Grisha, instead of informing Catherine first, telephoned Vera, asking her to get a doctor. Catherine wrote to Igor that "dear Vera . . . helps the family in everything. Because of my lack of health I cannot be useful to them. . . ." (February 3).   On February 9, the day before Milochka's death, Catherine wrote, "Vera is there all the time," and, on February 19, "Vera is still making arrangements for the family."

On April 10, Catherine wrote that she and Vera had received letters from Stravinsky on the same day, sent from Tacoma,[16] and went on to say that "on Monday I arranged with Vera that I'll be with her." (Vera's diary records that she received Catherine at home on April 12.) By the summer of 1937, Catherine's health had deteriorated and her marriage had become almost purely vicarious:

I really hope to receive something written from you. . . . So far you've told me very little about how you are spending your time [in Italy with Vera]. (September 23, 1937)

I imagine that Vera would want to come before you left, but perhaps she's going with you to Naples?[17] (November 6, 1937)

---

[14] Sviatoslav-Soulima ("Nini") Stravinsky (b. 1910), the composer's younger son.

[15] Stravinsky received this letter from Catherine at the Sulgrave Hotel in New York, May 3, two days before his departure for Europe.

[16] On March 29, Stravinsky and Samuel Dushkin were in Tacoma, where they gave a recital, one of thirty concert and ballet programs in which the composer participated on the tour, a large number for the era of train travel, especially since the orchestral and ballet performances required rehearsals.

[17] Returning from Naples, Stravinsky went to Sancellemoz. A letter to Willy Strecker, Stravinsky's publisher at B. Schotts Söhne, sent from there on November 17, reveals that the composer had just added the last six measures of the first movement of the *Dumbarton Oaks* Concerto.

Some of Catherine's references to Vera contain the most revealing statements so far published about Stravinsky's relationship with his mother, who did not know of his association with Vera:

Mama already noticed Vera in church, and that means she still remembers her. She's already talked to me about her and she could begin to ask questions. . . . (January 18, 1935)

I'll write to Vera tomorrow. [The letter was actually written August 6.] How long will she be there?[18] It occurred to me that if you will be receiving letters from her frequently, then Mama, who probably has morning tea earlier than you do, will notice that the handwriting on the letters is all the same. She always looks very closely at the mail lying on the table. . . . (August 3, 1936)

I called Vera twice and would love to see her . . . but it is always difficult for me because of Mama, since it would have to be after dinner. . . . Vera and I have arranged to meet between 11 and 12 o'clock somewhere in a café. . . . (January 10, 1937)

I will telephone Vera early tomorrow morning from bed; it's unlikely that I'd reach her right now, and, what's more, Mama might come in. . . . (Paris, December 14, 1937, to Stravinsky in Riga)

For more than sixteen years, the composer lived in dread of his mother's discovery of the liaison, and, though the secret was kept, her suspicions were aroused—once, apparently, when a photograph album with pictures of Vera on the same page with family groups had not been spirited away in time. Such friends as Samuel Dushkin and Baron Fred Osten-Saken, who knew Catherine, Vera, Igor, and his mother, have affirmed that he was intimidated by "Mousechka," as she signed her letters to him, and that the two were constantly quarreling. Catherine writes:

I'm afraid that an argument and conflict may arise between you and Mama. . . . It's better to give in to Mama. (August 3, 1935)

. . . You usually spend Sundays with Vera, but I do not think that you should leave Mama alone today, her birthday. (August 11, 1935)

---

[18] Vera spent August 1936 at Kurhotel-Wolf, Wiessee, a resort south of Munich. Stravinsky remained in Paris, composing *Jeu de cartes* and taking English lessons from a Berlitz instructor. The previous summer Catherine had written, "You are studying English in the evenings, but is it possible to do this on your own, especially the pronunciation? Don't overload your already so overloaded mind." (August 14, 1935) Stravinsky's English was evidently much improved by the time of his next American tour, in 1937. His friend Alexis Kall, a Greek scholar and philologist, wrote to him, May 13, 1939, advising him to read his lectures at Harvard in English: "No more than 5 or 10 will understand you in French. You spoke English wonderfully when you were here [Los Angeles] last."

In other words, it is quite possible that Stravinsky did leave his mother alone, and the story that he refused to attend her funeral (she died on June 7, 1939) until Vera persuaded him to go was well known to intimates. That Mama was indeed dour is substantiated by Catherine:

I begged the children to be a little more affectionate to Mama and indulgent of the hard side of her character, which always gets her into arguments, and because of which she concludes that the children do not love her. They do not communicate in any way, since she cannot understand them in their youthfulness. That is where the conflict lies, and, in my absence,[19] it is very difficult for her. (Undated)

Catherine understands both sides. But between her husband and her children, she appears to be more protective of the former. Nor do the difficulties inherent in being the children of Stravinsky seem to evoke any special sympathy from her, as if she had expected them to augment his glory and was disappointed after they failed to do so. When her pianist son, Sviatoslav, wrote from Barcelona that he had made a mistake in a performance of the Capriccio under his father's direction, her concern seems not to have been for her inexperienced child, and the possible traumatic consequences to him, but for her husband, to whom such incidents must have been routine:

Svetik writes that he managed to get through this uncomfortable moment, but did his doing this frighten *you*? (November 20, 1933)[20]

Nor does Catherine refrain from criticizing her son's playing to his father, though she takes into account some of the circumstantial difficulties that beset the younger Stravinsky, remarking, for example, that the real disadvantage of a forthcoming recital in the Salle Gaveau is that on the following week

Rachmaninov[21] will have a recital, and many people, especially Russian, will spend their money to hear him, rather than Svetik. . . . (March 5, 1935)

---

[19] Stravinsky's mother, wife, and children had lived together in Biarritz (from December 1922), Nice (from September 1924), and Voreppe (from September 1932). But after the move to Paris (October 15, 1933, first to 21 rue Viète, then, on June 20, 1934—the date of the lease—to 25 rue du Faubourg St.-Honoré), Catherine spent most of her time in the sanitarium at Sancellemoz, which her mother-in-law could not visit because of the altitude. Stravinsky lived alone with Walter Nouvel in the rue du Faubourg St.-Honoré apartment until October 1, 1934, when the family arrived there from Voreppe.

[20] Barcelona seems not to have been the younger Stravinsky's lucky city with the Capriccio. On March 18, 1936, Catherine wrote: "Yesterday I received Vera's letter of the 14th from Barcelona, and today I received Svetik's of the 15th. . . . I already know from Mama how he, poor thing, lost count and got out of phase [in the Capriccio]."

[21] Though Stravinsky ended a letter to Nicolas G. Struve, April 6, 1919: "My regards to

(Stravinsky himself had changed the date of a concert in Prague in 1930 because Rachmaninov was scheduled to play on the same evening.) On January 14, 1935, Catherine wrote that "poor Svetik was disappointed with Holland. There was a very small and cold audience and the reviews were bad." Ten days later she observed that "Svetik very much needs a few lessons from Philipp[22] *before the recital," and on February 11:*

At my insistence he took a few lessons from Philipp. . . . On his return he'll study with Philipp again, but this time [he should concentrate on] technique, which, in my opinion, he has neglected.

Two years later Catherine noted to her husband that their son, in a Salle Chopin recital, "got a little lost in the Bach Suite and in an Etude by Liszt." (February 19, 1937)

Catherine's mother had suffered from tuberculosis. In January 1914, following the birth of Milene, Catherine had to be treated for the disease, and Lyudmila died of it in November 1938.[23] *Stravinsky himself had it in an active form in*

Rachmaninov," by the 1930s the two composers were not on good terms. Surprisingly, however, until the 1940s Rachmaninov's royalties were not vastly greater than Stravinsky's. Païchadze wrote to Stravinsky, April 8, 1930: "Columbia Records paid us $1,200 in American recording rights for *Petrushka* and this year they are paying us $2,000 for Rachmaninov's Second Concerto." In Los Angeles, in 1942, Rachmaninov telephoned to his biographer, Sergei Bertensson: " 'I know how much Igor Fyodorovich has always disliked my compositions. . . . I am not sure whether I could invite him and his wife to my house—which I'd love to do—because I don't know how he would receive my invitation. Would you be so kind as to send out a feeler? . . .' I called Vera Arturovna [Bertensson reports], and her immediate response was 'Delighted!' Before dinner and during it . . . they talked about managers, concert bureaus, agents, ASCAP, royalties. Both composers were glad to have the old barrier broken down. The Stravinskys later returned the invitation. At the first dinner, Stravinsky mentioned that he was fond of honey, and within a few days, Sergei Vasilyevich found a great jar of fine honey and delivered it personally at the Stravinsky door. Rachmaninov played at Hollywood Bowl on July 17 and 18 [and dined] the following night with the Stravinskys and [Artur] Rubinsteins. . . ." In Baden-Baden, in October 1951, Stravinsky dismissed a request to contribute "a statement or article about Rachmaninov" with the remark, "I knew Rachmaninov very little."

[22] Isidor Philipp (1863–1958), pianist and professor at the Paris Conservatory from 1903 to 1934.

[23] On August 18, 1935, after consulting doctors on the medical consequences of Mika's forthcoming marriage, Catherine reported to Igor: "She cannot have children for at least three years." Mika gave birth to a daughter fifteen months after the marriage, and died the following year. In the same letter, Catherine says, "I am certain that I also had a tubercular infiltration when I got married." On September 5, 1935, she told Igor that "Dr. Tobé attributes Mika's lung condition to a very long-range

1937, in 1939—in which year he spent six months at Sancellemoz—and from July to December 1969. Catherine was continually ill with pulmonary disorders in the 1920s and early 1930s,[24] and tuberculosis was diagnosed in May 1925 when, in a disastrous attempt to accompany her husband to Rome, she became ill and had to return home, the last part of the way in an ambulance. In 1935 she was obliged to write to her husband in New York:

Dr. Lipschitz, Dr. Sobesky, and Dr. Parisco all emphatically denied that there was any trace of the disease, but Dr. Rist immediately made an X-ray, which determined the tuberculosis and the lesion. He expressed great amazement that, until now, and with such a long history of illness and repeated pleurisy, a radiograph had never been done. He thinks that I never had influenza of any sort. . . . He said that I should go to a sanitarium immediately. Even before they took the X-ray, Milochka realized that my lesion is the same as in 1914, since she well remembers the place on the picture that Dr. Demiéville pointed out in her presence. (March 17, 1935)

Rist sent his patient to Sancellemoz, where she had first stayed two years before. "It will be cheaper there than at Leysin," she says in the same letter, "and more convenient for you to visit me, since I will be there for several months." Her sister stayed with her a short time, and wrote to Stravinsky on March 23, reminding him that "pulmonary tuberculosis is a serious thing" and that "Katya will stay in the sanitarium for several months, and, after that, must remain in the mountain air, which reminds me of early spring in the North." (This letter also mentions the tendency of Stravinsky's mother "to give severe criticisms" of piano playing.)

All of Catherine's letters from February 1935 until her death on March 2, 1939, contain detailed medical reports, including almost hourly tabulations of her temperature, expectorations, and descriptions of treatments ("Lipschitz gave me some foul stuff extracted from the liver of an unborn horse"; "the eucalyptus injections have had to be stopped"). Some of this correspondence is almost too painful to read:

I hope that, just as at Leysin [in 1914], I will soon stop coughing and spitting up blood. . . . Dr. Rist told me that I won't be able to have pneumothorax induced because of my pleurisy, but they have another method, operating on one of the nerves near the collarbone and thereby raising the diaphragm and compressing the lung. . . . (March 21, 1935)

---

aftereffect of a case or cases of pleurisy, but we know of only one instance of her having had pleurisy, when she was ten years old, whereas I have had such a condition all my life."

[24] In a letter to Païchadze, July 25, 1927, Stravinsky refers to the "unexpected illness of my wife," a surprising choice of adjective, since, from her letters, it seems that illness could never have been unexpected in Catherine's case.

Dr. Tobé examined me. . . . He remarked that the infiltration began to progress after my first cold, and even more after the second. Also, the cavity began to open again. He said that though I've gotten worse, I will recover. . . . (January 15, 1936)

But Catherine's loneliness must have been as hard to bear as her physical suffering. She begins a letter on her twenty-ninth wedding anniversary:

At the very time I am writing this, you and I were going to the Finland Station. . . . It feels like a very, very long time ago, much longer than all those years. . . . (January 24, 1935)[25]

Here are passages from other letters from Sancellemoz:

What is most difficult for me is that you will return home and I won't be there. . . . Perhaps you could come and see me, if even just for a bit. . . . How wonderful it was when you were with me in Leysin and composed *The Nightingale*. . . . (March 17, 1935)

How I long for the Fourteenth of July to be over[26] and then you will come and, if possible, stay for at least two whole days. (July 8, 1935) . . . After the 14th, I'll be waiting for you to tell me the date that you are coming to see me—only if this won't disturb your work. Please don't interrupt your work just to set your mind at rest about me. . . . (July 12, 1935)

. . . I saw some gorgeous hyacinths, and I began wanting to have some in my room. But there's no pleasure in buying them for oneself. And then I said to myself that if you were to write to me and say that I should buy some flowers, then I'd feel that this would be your present, and I would buy them happily. . . . (February 22, 1936)

I hope that God gives me the consolation of seeing you. . . . I'll spend three days with you, and I'll be home when you leave for Argentina, so I won't have to say good-bye from afar . . . but will actually hug you. . . . (February 22, 1936)

I must bear this cross of continued separation from you which God is sending me. . . . At first there is always a prick of pain in the heart when I find out that another separation is at hand. . . . (April 5, 1937)

Occasionally the letters describe macabre events in the sanitarium, but so matter-of-factly that the effect verges on black humor:

---

[25] Catherine was born on January 25, but, as she wrote to Igor on January 11, 1935: "Since the day of our wedding, I always associate my birthday with the 24th." She also celebrated the day of her engagement, August 15 (Old Style)—the Feast of the Assumption—1905.

[26] Catherine seems to have known that Igor regarded July 14 as the date of his "marriage" with Vera.

It turns out that while you were still at Sancellemoz, some poor young woman died, which I had already begun to suspect since we could not hear her anymore. . . . (October 6, 1937)

Small wonder that in California, in the 1940s, free of ill and dependent in-laws, and of the daily threat of morbid and depressing family letters,[27] *Stravinsky seemed radically different to friends who had known him in Europe during the previous decade.*[28]

Whether or not in reaction to Catherine's letters, Stravinsky seems to have kept her informed about his own most minor ailments, including a spell of high-altitude dizziness. She wrote, "I received your postcard from Texas. What a shame that you had to be at such heights in Colorado . . . and it has already irritated your sympathetic nervous system." (March 17, 1935)   And on July 10, 1935: "You write that you are feeling very nervous. . . . But you are always more nervous when you compose. . . ." One letter begins, "What's this? Have you caught cold again?" (October 4, 1935), and another, after she received his first communication from South America, "I am sorry that you had a sty." (April 27, 1936)   On one occasion she acknowledges that "you are feeling poorly in general and you had a headache for two days" (July 27, 1936), but, though fatally ill herself, she says,

With me it's all *"des ennuis"* and *"des petites misères,"* nothing serious, thank God. As for the unpleasant peculiarities from which you are constantly suffering, and which are distressing—better this than something serious. . . .

"Unpleasant peculiarities," indeed. She is obviously aware of his hypochondria but dares to allude to it only through a reference to the same affliction in her daughter-in-law Denise:

She looks for illness in herself, and this very thing *is* her illness, just as is the case with you. If it's not one thing that's bothering her, it's another, and she's always suffering from something—at age 23! (Sancellemoz, September 9, 1937)[29]

---

[27] During a short vacation with Vera, in Positano, in 1937, he received no fewer than ten lengthy communications from Catherine, containing such information as: "Yesterday I coughed up 19 times"; "Since it's cold at night I put on wool socks over my stockings"; "Don't lie on the beach in the sun, as it could be very harmful to your lungs, liver, and nerves."

[28] On February 17, 1947, Stravinsky wrote to his sister-in-law Elena, widow of his brother Yuri, in Leningrad: "I have enjoyed good health since I moved to California, and I compose and travel a great deal."

[29] On September 1, 1937, Catherine returned to Sancellemoz, after a few weeks at the Château de Monthoux. Stravinsky accompanied her to the sanitarium, then left for Venice on September 7, Positano on September 13, and Sancellemoz on September 27.

The most puzzling feature of the correspondence is Catherine's lack of money, and the frugality of her existence in a provincial sanitarium contrasts strikingly with the comfort of her husband's life while on concert tours[30] or in the family's rue du Faubourg St.-Honoré apartment. She realized this disparity, and that, for example, his sartorial tastes (his tailor's bill in May 1932 had been 3,000 francs) must have been changing:

I would like to knit a scarf for you before your departure for South America, but if you don't like it . . . I won't be offended. . . . (February 8, 1936)

Yet when she wrote that "Now with my sickness, we have overloads on the budget" (March 21, 1935), it was also true that his earnings from concerts, broadcasts,[31] recordings, royalties, and commissions were substantial. In 1936, furthermore, he seems to have had a surplus. In a letter dated March 6, she says that "Svetik just wrote to me that you had extra money in Italy and that you bought silver."

No doubt Catherine had a desire to arouse feelings of guilt, but this comes into the open in these letters only once, when she reports a conversation with a doctor, in dialogue form and in French, as if she feared to use Russian: "I told him, 'Je suis une personne sacrifiée.' " (October 9, 1937) Many of her statements make the reader wonder about Stravinsky's control of the family purse strings:

Fedik[32] [and his fiancée] are here. . . . I'm sure that you've already forgiven me for the money spent on their food (June 11, 1935) . . . Tell Mama that I

---

[30] In 1935, writing to his wife from Indianapolis, Stravinsky complains that good wines are not available in the United States. By the time of his next tour, two years later, he apparently expected a change in the American standard of living, but, disappointed, arranged for N. Malayev, who had helped draft the scenario for *Jeu de cartes,* to bring twenty-four bottles from France. On January 14, 1937, Catherine wrote: "Malayev was here. . . . He said that he'll probably set out on the S.S. *Paris* on the 27th, and he will carry out your errand. He's confused about how he'll deliver the wine to you, but will in any case send a message by radio before he gets to New York. Either you must call yourself or send someone for it." In France, Stravinsky purchased his red wine—Marquiset 1929—by the *barrique,* directly from Louis Eschenauer in Bordeaux. On January 26, 1937, Stravinsky's younger son wrote that Malayev would not be making the trip, but that the violinist Jeanne Gautier would be sailing on the *Paris* the next day, and that she had promised to bring the wine.

[31] Fees for broadcasts started to become important to Stravinsky in 1930–31. A letter from Païchadze, February 13, 1932, reveals that the League of Composers (New York) paid $800 to perform *Oedipus Rex* and an additional $400 for the radio transmission of the work. On February 11, 1932, Païchadze sent 50,000 francs in performance fees, many from broadcasts, to Stravinsky's bank in Geneva.

[32] Theodore ("Fedik," "Fedya"), Stravinsky's elder son (b. 1907).

am without money and can't even buy stamps. . . . When is Vera going to Italy? (August 1, 1935)[33]

I have already accumulated three bills. . . . Please send money now before a fourth is added. . . . God and the Holy Mother keep you. I kiss Vera. (March 13, 1936)   . . . In the light of your departure, what about the next bill? . . . Who will send money to me for the trip? (March 21, 1936)   . . . I will return the money to you that I don't spend, but it is better not to be caught short. (September 10, 1936)   . . . I'm afraid I won't be able to manage with just the 15 francs that remain. (October 26, 1937)

Perhaps your trip to Riga was sent by God, since it was unexpected and came just at the time when poor Fedya has no money and it's imperative to help him. . . . (Paris, January 7, 1938, to Stravinsky at the Hotel Excelsior, Rome)

But the most astonishing remarks of all are Catherine's pleas on behalf of Stravinsky's mother, then in her eighties:

I understand [Mama's] fear of not being able to manage with the sum you gave her. I also understand *you* but I think you are burdening her. . . . It seems to me that you've cut down a great deal on the money for expenses. (June 26, 1935) . . . The poor thing barely manages, borrowing from [the housekeeper], giving it back to her, and borrowing again. (July 6, 1935)

Mama is dreadfully worried about her hair, which is completely falling out. If she needs to get a wig, since she can't stay bald, perhaps you would pay for it and then she could pay back 100 or 200 francs a month from the household money. That's been worrying her a great deal. (May 16, 1935)

Catherine was intensely religious, perhaps more so as her illness progressed:[34]

You say that you look forward to a normal life, but you won't find one, and we will bear this cross [TB] that God has sent us and we will not stop praising Him and thanking Him for everything. . . . In your heart you know that what is important for you is how you stand before God. Temptations and trials are good for the soul. . . . (March 17, 1935)

---

[33] In this same letter, Catherine says that during the brief absence of Mlle Svitalski, the governess, "all the servants will be home," and that Marcel "never leaves [Mama] alone and watches over things in the evenings, while you are gone." In October, no doubt frightened by the danger of contracting tuberculosis, Marcel, Thérèse, and Raymonde departed, leaving only the maid, Emma, and the new cook, Céline.

[34] "Since I turned to God," she writes, March 11, 1935, "this is the first time that I've begun Lent without going to church."

In letter after letter she says that she is happier in church than anywhere else. When describing the consecration of a church in Paris, in March 1937, she expresses some of the homesickness of exile:

The walls are painted in light ochre with a pinkish tint, like some of the old buildings in St. Petersburg. There is something very Russian and ancient in the form and the color. There were about 500 people and [one's] heart rejoiced as the *Mnogiya lieta*[35] was sung. . . . Our names were mentioned among the donors.

She quotes from the Dobrotolyubiye,[36] *an essential book for anyone interested in Stravinsky's theological beliefs—in the Docetic Resurrection, for example. Catherine drew a Greek cross at the head of each of her letters to Igor, and ended each one with blessings ("May the prayers of St. Nikolai Chudotvorets keep you safe," or "May God's holy servants [ugodniki] protect you"), sometimes adding, "I will light the icon lamps[37] now and go to bed." She invokes a saint for every occasion and difficulty, beseeching St. Expedite when her brother-in-law, who was in charge of Russian cuisine at the Café de la Paix, urgently needed money, and praying for "la sainte indifférence, about which St. François de Sales talks so much." (May 28, 1935)   She lives according to the observances of the Orthodox calendar—"I am glad to be eating meat during these great days of the* sedmitsa"[38] *(April 25, 1935)—and is constantly reminding her husband of forthcoming ones:*

[35] The meaning is roughly equivalent to *l'chaim.*

[36] This is the Russian version of the *Philokalia*, the writings of the early Fathers, compiled on Mount Athos by Macarius of Corinth and Nicodemus of the Holy Mountain, and published in Venice in 1782. The book was translated into Slavonic in the eighteenth century; in the 1870s a five-volume Russian edition was published, and a three-volume edition appeared in Moscow in 1905. (In 1951, Faber & Faber published a selection in English, *Writings from the Philokalia*.) On August 20, 1936, Catherine wrote to Igor: "I am reading the *Dobrotolyubiye* every day and comparing how these people with great souls and faith, who lived only in God and for God, talked and measured, and thought about life. How simple and clear everything was to them." And on October 9, 1937: "I'd like to have another volume of the *Dobrotolyubiye*, since I have already reread everything and am rereading everything again." And in one letter, she asks him to bring Viktor Ivanovich Nesmielov's little book (probably on Gregory of Nyssa). To judge from Stravinsky's extensive annotations in his copy of Nesmielov's *The Science of Man* (3rd edition, Moscow, 1905, 2 volumes), this philosopher exerted a major influence on the composer's thought.

[37] On January 24, 1935, Catherine wrote, "I went to church. The holy wonder-working icon was there. Father Vassily and Deacon Pyotr will bring it home with us tomorrow and we will pray." Three years later, she wrote, "Tomorrow Father Vassily is bringing a marvelous icon to me." (December 14, 1937)

[38] Holy Week.

Tomorrow there will be a service for the Archangel Mikhail's day. (November 20, 1935) . . . Do not forget to kneel to the holy Plashchanitsa[39] and leave a candle. (April 13, 1937) . . . Do not forget that Mama's name day is the 22nd. (September 18, 1937)

And she tries to comfort him with the thought that prayers are constantly being said for him on his concert tours:

On the holy Mount Athos, the humble elder, the Hieromach[40] Gabriel, prays for you as you travel. . . . (February 11, 1935)

Father Vassily will be here on Friday to lead a *molyeben* service to pray for you on your journey. . . . (April 14, 1936)

To his wife's deep disappointment, Stravinsky neglected the formal require-ments of his religion.[41] Once she complained to him, "You have for so long been leading a vain life, with your work, business, and people, completely without the church." (March 27, 1935) But all who knew him closely were aware of his deep faith—Païchadze, for one, who wrote to him after the death of his sis-ter-in-law: "Your strong faith will help you through this time of grief." (Febru-ary 20, 1937)

Catherine's kindness is apparent throughout her letters. To give just one ex-ample, her sons, her younger daughter, her niece Ira Beliankina, and her cousin Dr. Vera Dimitrievna Nossenko all opposed Mika's marriage to Yuri Mandelstamm.[42] But when he first visited Catherine in Sancellemoz, she wrote to Stravinsky:

---

[39] Good Friday shroud. An effigy of St. Plashchanitsa was carried from the church on Good Friday. "Here in Paris they bring her out later than in Nice," Catherine wrote to Igor, April 26, 1935.

[40] A monk who is also a priest.

[41] Religion was never far from Stravinsky's thoughts, nonetheless, as is shown in the following passage from a letter to Païchadze, after seven years of silence: "Aged? Of course you have aged. We all have aged in these seven years. . . . But, speaking for myself, it is difficult to say whether I have aged or not, since I do not think much about it: I do not have time. I live from year to year, as everyone does, in the emotional after-math of events. But I am unlike everyone else because of the pressure I have been under from composing: a lot has been created and a lot performed in my concert tours during these years. I work independently of *reality* for, after all, music goes on inde-pendently of it as well. People say, of course: 'He is against the expression of feelings in music and has made it so dry that it has no more spirit.' When you encounter such judgments, it is impossible not to remember the distinction that the Apostle Paul drew between *emotional* and *spiritual,* a distinction that people continue to ignore after 2,000 years. . . ." (April 11, 1946)

[42] Catherine's letters contain many glimpses of "traditional" Russian antisemitism.

Despite all that the children were telling me, I immediately felt in him not just the niceness, but also the complete goodness, of the man, to whom we can entrust our Mikusha not simply without fear, but rather with total trust. The impression that I got from my eyes is confirmed through meeting him. He is obviously intelligent and kind, and loves Mika with a genuine love. (May 21, 1935)[43]

Catherine's patience was tried almost beyond endurance but, in these letters at least, she seems never to have lost it,[44] or her courage and hope, and, outwardly anyway,[45] she continued to believe in an improvement in her condition, even in a cure.[46] So, far from despair, her letters radiate joy in the gift of life, even in a life of pain, and gratitude for any alleviation. Some of this feeling might be attributed to the euphoria said to characterize certain stages of tuberculosis, but surely the larger part of it is in the transcendence of adversity—and, in that, she can be described as saintly.

She wrote to Igor that her cousin Vera refused to visit Mika because "she is going to marry a Jew. You see what Vera Dimitrievna's attitudes will be for the future. . . . It is really even funny. . . . I feel sorry for her that her ways of thinking with respect to Jews are what they are." (August 11, 1935)   Ironically, Yuri's daughter was to be reared, from infancy, by Dr. Nossenko. Since Ira, the bride's cousin, and a professional couturier, had the same prejudices, Mika ordered her wedding dress from someone else.
[43] Later, Catherine decided that Yuri had questionable taste: "He even wanted to look [for an apartment] with his sister, who also, no doubt, has bad or mediocre taste." (August 2, 1935)
[44] "Patience and more patience, that is what is essential. . . . I think that this is all that God wants from us." (October 6, 1937)   "The doctor told me: 'You will always have bronchitis, but you have a good nature, and will bear it.' " (October 28, 1937)
[45] Once Catherine did refer to another woman at Sancellemoz, "who, poor thing, considers herself a lifetime patient, like me." (September 8, 1937)
[46] Catherine's death was hastened by that of her elder daughter. In Paris, February 1, 1939, Stravinsky wrote to Willy Strecker: "My wife is not at all well. Since our terrible unhappiness, her lungs have become much weaker, and the lesion is larger. She never leaves her bed and is further debilitated by a cough that tires her in the extreme. In three weeks she has not been able to recover from an exhausting grippe. We were to have gone to Pau, where the air is supposed to calm the nerves and soothe the irritation in the bronchial tubes, but in her state it is impossible to move. What can I do? I wait, I hope, and I am full of anguish. . . . A huge discouragement strikes me every hour, every day. I wait, I wait, I wait."

CORRESPONDENCE WITH

MAURICE DELAGE

1912 ~ 1923

STRAVINSKY TO MAURICE DELAGE[1]

Ustilug[2]
October 14, 1912

Cher vieux,

I sit before your letter with that familiar and very dear signature, "Maurice" (judge for yourself whether I have copied correctly), and those four words, "3 rue de Civry": I can't express to you how precious they are to me! *Oh, I have such a desire to come to your house*[3] to spend a few autumn days with you again in that little pavilion which silently guards the memories of our compatible life of a year ago. Far from the brouhaha of the high season of the Ballets Russes, [we were] calm and intimate there in that little pavilion with its little rooms which I so wish to see again. My old friend, we absolutely must see each other soon! Is it impossible to hear some word of what you have done and undergone during our separation of nearly five months? Paris is two cities: one of them gives me glory and money, the temptation for which gnaws relentlessly at my entrails; and the other is Maurice, 3 rue de Civry, who, without being aware of it, takes away all of the filth of the "Grand Saison des Ballets Russes." Continue writing to me, and do not forget to keep your sincere friendship for me always, although I hardly merit it to the extent that you and others would testify. In a few days we will move to Clarens, Hôtel du Châtelard, and it is from there that I will send you the 150 francs to be delivered to the lawyer.[4]

I embrace you cordially.

Forever, your Igor

---

[1] Maurice Delage (1879–1961), French composer, pupil and friend of Ravel. Delage and Stravinsky met at the time of *Firebird*, June 1910, and immediately became friends. Delage's papers, in the Bibliothèque Nationale, include Stravinsky's corrected second proofs of the orchestral score of *Petrushka* with the concert ending inked-in on the last page. The last eight measures of trills, in red ink, are identical with the published original score, but the ninth measure is scored for the lower strings only, timpani, brass (no bassoons). This score is dated Berlin, 1911, and was composed after Stravinsky's visit to Benois in the summer of that year. Since Stravinsky did not keep copies of his personal, or at any rate non-business, letters, his side of the correspondence is missing, except for his letters of October 14, 1912, and December 15, 1913 (fragment). Some of it was sold at auction, but probably all of it was preserved in private collections. The two friends saw each other only once after World War I.

[2] Stravinsky's summer home in Volhynia. He had just returned from St. Petersburg, and, having interrupted work on *Le Sacre du printemps,* composed a song, "Akahito," dedicated to Delage, a part of the cycle *Three Japanese Lyrics.* Delage had made voyages to the Orient and was a collector of Japanese prints. Stravinsky's lyrics were undoubtedly inspired by this friendship and influence.

[3] The emphasis is by Delage, who wrote in the margin next to the passage, "If it were true!"

[4] Maurice Fanet, who, in Stravinsky's name, was suing Mme Miquel Alzieu, a pianist who had borrowed 3,000 rubles from him and had not repaid the loan.

A thousand best wishes to everyone I love and who loves me. I expect to arrive in Berlin[5] on Saturday, October 19. Write a note to me care of my publisher: Russischer Musik Verlag, Dessauer Strasse 17, Berlin. *A bientôt,* my good one!

DELAGE TO STRAVINSKY   *October 23, 1912*

Thanks, friend, for your delicious long letter. The little pavilion and its guardian are ready and await you; you must come. I will go so far as to tell you that you ought to see your lawyer during your visit, even if it does not prove very useful. Do you remember the wonderful pear that we shared that night while taking Argutinsky[6] home? I am still moved when I think of that delightful fortnight. We have to start doing that again. You will see that I have been working and I will make you listen to the Hindu records, a kind of music of which you have no idea.

Ravel returned from St.-Jean-de-Luz. Always the boaster, he did absolutely nothing there. He is so lazy that I wonder if he even bothered to sleep.

Thanks also for the photograph which reunites the two greatest artistic revelations that I have had. My God, can it have been so long already!

I am in a hurry for you to be here, so that I can play something for you that I feel you would like.

Just received a letter from the Caucasus, from Bakst.

To say that we have hardly had time to see each other during this awful season is true. Your Japanese prints are still lying in a dresser awaiting you. Quickly, a word from you, four lines that will tell me what to expect.

I like to hope that I am the first to welcome you to Switzerland. I couldn't write to you in Berlin, having received your letter only last night; the mail has played tricks on me.

My respects to Madame Stravinsky and best wishes to the children. My parents send their best friendship.

Je vous embrasse tendrement,   Maurice

DELAGE TO STRAVINSKY   *Thursday, November 7, 1912*

Lausanne

Friend,

I could not confirm the telegram that Godebski[7] sent to you yesterday at my request, having had to run to your attorney and to the Palais de Justice.[8] I expect that all is explained and that you have received the money from Ballot. That is

---

[5] Stravinsky was returning to Switzerland by way of Warsaw and Berlin.

[6] Prince Vladimir Argutinsky-Dolgurokov (1874–1941), of the Russian Foreign Ministry, Stravinsky's close friend.

[7] Cipa Godebski, brother of Misia Edwards Sert.

[8] See n. 4 above.

the issue. In order to avoid paying bail (a cash deposit) to the French court, you must establish by birth certificate that you are a legal Russian subject. Can you send a certificate, obtained from your [Russian] Consul, that is to say, a proof of birth authorized by him? I will return it to your lawyer. If I must, I will go to see Argutinsky, so write to him about it.

Next, I was not able to see Sechiari,[9] who still has not materialized at rue du Rocher. He probably does not live there. I am going to request a meeting, but tell me what to do with the piano score of your [*Zvezdoliki*] when I have it—simply keep it, or send it to you?

How I would like to introduce you to the Hindu songs that I have brought back. Some of them are magnificent. After the three songs that I am now composing (one is finished), I will begin a poem for orchestra on *Les Bâtisseurs de ponts* by Kipling. I have such an urge to do this that I have nearly stopped everything else. It would be splendid!

You know that the Astruc theater is finished.[10] It seems quite promising, and good things ought to be played there. I think I have nearly maneuvered them into taking Schmitt's *Salomé,* which makes him very happy.[11] When are we going to see you? I am kept in Paris at the moment, aside from work, by the marriage of my sister, which will take place in three weeks.

What is this little object that you have made for me? Thank you in advance.

My best regards to Madame Stravinsky. Everyone says to send his love (one dares not speak of you out of jealousy, but *not* professional).

Je vous embrasse,   Maurice

DELAGE TO STRAVINSKY   *Paris*
                                        Tuesday, December 17, 1912

Mon bien cher petit,

I have intended to write to you for so long! First, do you know that I have been very ill with a cold and all kinds of fevers? I spent fifteen days wrapped in flannel, suffering nightmares and furious at being able to work only a little, and badly. Imagine that five days after your departure, stimulated by your magnificent courage, I had already written close to three minutes of music for *Les Bâtisseurs de ponts*. Now I have doubled that amount, starting again six days ago. What I am able to play of it attracts many compliments and some astonishment too. You have no idea how frustrated I am that you do not experience my work as I am doing it. I know that I will see you within a month, but how long that is! And the weather here is so horrible that I probably will leave

---

[9] Pierre Sechiari, a choral conductor who wished to present Stravinsky's cantata *Zvezdoliki.*
[10] The Théâtre des Champs-Elysées.
[11] See the correspondence with Florent Schmitt in *Stravinsky: Selected Correspondence,* Volume III (hereafter referred to as *S.S.C.* III).

for the Midi. You are no longer in Beaulieu, as you were two years ago![12] I would have been able to orchestrate under your eyes. I always think about the instrumentation while composing, but I am terribly anxious about it nevertheless. And you? Is *Sacre* finished? How I envy you. It always seems to me that you must work in a state of joy.

Life in Paris is full of ridiculous prattle. How I would like to be far away! I know that I am ignoble, but I ask you to write another short note to me soon. Having discovered that Diaghilev is in Paris, I have been continually hoping that he will need you here (not as much as I do).

My dearest affectionate respects to Mme Stravinsky and caresses to the children.

Yours tenderly,   Maurice

DELAGE TO STRAVINSKY

Paris
December 27, 1912
[Telegram]

Stravigor
Clarens
Montreux

Will arrive Sunday morning train as usual. Affectionately,   Delage[13]

DELAGE TO STRAVINSKY

Clarens
January 4, 1913

Hotel Hungaria
Budapest

En bien, mon cher petit,

What are these desolate thoughts that disappear before Oscar Wilde? I hope that you have regained your good humor in the arms of that horrible fiend Diaghilev.

[You should] behave in the same manner as Madame Stravinsky, who, with terrible heartlessness, spent an excellent night, after a similar evening, in the company of your friend (I refer only to the evening, of course).

It is 11 o'clock in the morning, and the children continue their desperate screaming in the form of "Monsieur Delage." Let's see. I cannot answer all the children at once, and I give you preference.

Today I plan to translate your second Japanese song and to add several stones to my Hindu bridge. Soon we will discuss you, of course, and will order from Kern's the photographs that I want to bring with me. You have already forgiven me. I thought I had chosen such a great number, yet Mademoiselle Vera [Nossenko] remains unconsoled. Why?

---

[12] Delage stayed with Stravinsky in December 1910 in Beaulieu-sur-Mer.
[13] Delage arrived in Clarens on December 28 for a short stay with Stravinsky and his family.

I have not yet warned the gallant Aubert[14] that all is changed. He will be disappointed that you did not hear his work. Moreover, if it is postponed again, will I hear it myself? One never knows.

Good-bye, *vieux très cher.*

Kisses from your   Maurice

DELAGE TO STRAVINSKY

Hotel Bristol
Vienna

*Clarens
January 7, 1913
[Postcard with a view
of the Hôtel du Châtelard]*

Bien cher ami,

I am leaving right away for Geneva, carrying with me one of the best memories of my life, my stay in Clarens. I feel like a new man and am ready to work ceaselessly to justify our common love of "Belles Musiques." But do not tell me that you are coming to Beaulieu only for two days. . . . Would you like to shake Diaghilev's hand for me?[15]

Yours tenderly,   Maurice

DELAGE TO STRAVINSKY

Clarens

*Paris
January 10, 1913*

I wrote to Mme Stravinsky about how good I thought *La Forêt bleue.* It is a charming piece of music, as is Perrault's tale. [Aubert] really regretted your absence. He reported an excellent success—three curtain calls in the last entr'acte, quite unlike the usual complacency of the Geneva public. He was terribly tired, at the last moment having had to replace the conductor, who had pneumonia. He had all the bad luck.

And you? How is *Sacre?* What is Nijinsky doing? I saw Roerich's costumes, which are splendid. Send the songs for the translation (composed up to the last measure) to me at my Nice address, simply putting word for word, unless this becomes too obscure. I think that you will be pleased with the translation of No. 2, which I left in Clarens. I am impatient to be settled in Nice, to be able to work well. I want so much to do something that pleases me.

See you very soon, I think, at Beaulieu or in Nice. I saw Ravel yesterday. It seems that he has just written a very forceful article about d'Indy's *Fervaal.* I also saw Calvocoressi,[16] who told me that he continues to like the piece. You know that d'Indy was one of his first loves.

---

[14] Louis-François-Marie Aubert (1877–1968), composer of *La Forêt bleue,* an operatic fairy tale, first performed in Geneva, January 7, 1913.

[15] Stravinsky had joined the Ballets Russes in Budapest, then gone with the company to Vienna.

[16] M. D. Calvocoressi (1877–1944) translated several of Stravinsky's Russian texts into French.

I will keep you informed of my whereabouts until Nice. Give my best re-membrance to Diag.

Yours tenderly,   Maurice

What a good memory of Clarens.

DELAGE TO STRAVINSKY   *Nice*
                                          [Postmark: January 25, 1913]
Mon cher vieux,

I have just been ill again. No sleep for three days, except for two hours, sitting in a chair. It is frightful. Finally a new treatment. I slept last night and am going to take advantage of it and work. When will you arrive? Mme Stravinsky made me hope for news from you. I have a feeling you were not very pleased with your trip to Vienna. What happened?

We had a remarkable trip through the Alps. Too bad you were not with us. *A bientôt.*

With best wishes to all,   your Maurice

DELAGE TO STRAVINSKY   *Savoy Hotel*
                                                    London
Mon cher petit,   *[January ?] 1913*

Had an excellent trip, and spent the evening with Evans,[17] a splendid fellow.

I left the *Sacre* page at Monteux's, but he was not home. I hope to see Diaghilev today. London is still an admirable city.

Best regards to the two Madame Stravinskys.

Kisses from your   Maurice

DELAGE TO STRAVINSKY   *March 3, 1913*

Mon cher vieux,

I'm so happy that you have returned to Clarens and so proud of your success in London. So you found Scott Evans[18] very nice? What does he think of your work? I expect that one of these days he will send an indignant article that he has written about you. The *Bâtisseurs*? Hardly moved.

Crises, illnesses. It's awful. I received a charming letter from Siloti,[19] in-viting me to conduct the Hindu symphony in Russia, too. As soon as it is fin-

---

[17] Edwin Evans, music critic for the *Pall Mall Gazette*.

[18] Probably Edwin Evans, although Stravinsky had spent an evening in London with both Cyril Scott and Evans. See the correspondence with Evans in *S.S.C.* III.

[19] Alexander Siloti (1863–1945), pianist and conductor. He led the first performance of Stravinsky's *Fireworks*.

ished. My God! When? Maybe I am affected by the perpetual cold gray weather here. The sun goes farther and farther away. That is not a cure for neurasthenia, nor are the music students who never cease, from morning until evening, practically under my window. At this very moment, there is a horrible accordion with a squinting B-natural. Ugh!

I hope that the family is well. I look regularly at the nice photos that I took in Clarens (Kern's). Give everyone my love. I leave in two weeks, finally almost contented, and truly anxious to see you.

Yours tenderly,   Maurice

DELAGE TO STRAVINSKY

Paris
May 9, 1913

What must you think of my silence, dear old friend? You know that after my arrival in Paris I underwent intensive treatment that has finally cured me. I feel marvelous at present, and *Les Bâtisseurs de ponts* is well too, naturally. I saw Bakst recently; he brings letters from Siloti, some of them five pages long. Will the Hindu symphony be finished soon, etc., in time for me to play it in Petersburg? You see, it is excellent for conductors to be foreign, or unknown. Bakst was excited about the idea of *Bâtisseurs* and he envisages two magnificent sets. What do you think about it?

We will soon see, as you wrote from Clarens. What a pity that my own little Châtelard is not large enough to accommodate Madame Stravinsky comfortably. You live in a bouquet of lilacs. It is magnificent. What is more, it is now winter here, and I am furious at having to describe the warmest part of India with a wool shawl over my shoulders. Grotesque.

I think that you arrive on the 13th.[20] Drop me a note and I will come and fetch you.

Best regards to Mme Stravinsky. Kisses to the children, and my apologies to poor Theodore, who sent me such a beautiful Tunisian flag.

Toute l'affection from your   Maurice

DELAGE TO STRAVINSKY

Sunday, October 18, 1913

Hôtel des Crêtes
Clarens

Mon cher petit,

Very happy to have received your card, more so than you realize, for we were all very anxious. I am writing to you from my bed, where I have been for several days, having finally resigned myself to the indispensable surgical intervention. I

---

[20] In Paris, for the first performance of *Le Sacre du printemps*.

know that you have been working well. So have I, but, having been ill again, not as much as I would have wished. I hope that it is over now. Give my best regards to Madame Stravinsky and kisses to the children.

Je vous embrasse,   your Maurice

Ravel has been in Paris since yesterday. I am frustrated at not having seen him yet.

DELAGE TO STRAVINSKY   *November 10, 1913*

Dear Igor,

Here I am, completely recovered and at work. I am doing three Hindu poems for small orchestra. I would love to play them for you. When will we see each other? The little Auteuil pavilion still awaits you for as long and as often as you wish. Won't you come to Paris this month? I plan to visit you in Clarens around December 10 for about two weeks.

I had all sorts of problems with Fürstner,[21] and, Durand[22] having made me some serious offers, I am at the point of going into total seclusion. I will tell you all about that, but when?

I must also go to London to see Rudyard Kipling after making an agreement with his agent on the material questions of collaboration.

Tell Mademoiselle Vera [Nossenko] that we took great pleasure in learning of her medical triumphs. Embrace the children for me; I hope they are well.

And Madame Stravinsky? Well also, I hope. Give her my respects.

Je vous embrasse,   Maurice

Until when? Soon? Yes?

DELAGE TO STRAVINSKY   *London*
                                          [Postmark: November 26, 1913]
Clarens   *[Picture postcard showing*
                                          view from London Bridge]
Vieux,

Here for the meeting with R. Kipling. I don't like London, all alone. Evans owes you a letter, and I have much to tell you. When will we see each other? I return to Paris in a few days.

Je vous embrasse,   Maurice

---

[21] Adolf Fürstner, the Berlin music publisher.
[22] Durand & Cie was the leading French music publisher.

DELAGE TO STRAVINSKY   *Paris*
                                                    December 9, 1913

Mon cher petit,

I return from London, utterly discouraged. No way of obtaining 10 minutes of Kipling's time for a meeting, he having been summoned by his agent for that very purpose. They have done everything possible to put me off. Imagine this brute, who has taken four weeks to understand that there are no words in a pantomime.

Since I undertook this unlucky business no one has helped me with anything. Neither Fürstner nor anyone else. I think that I am going to abandon the project. I am constantly offered batches of idiotic librettos, but I want to do something better. . . .

Fortunately, I did four Hindu songs for small orchestra this summer. Ravel maintains that they are good. So much the better.

Enough complaints. I came back this evening from the S.M.I.[23] The program for January 14 is settled. Your three Japanese songs will be performed. If you come, as I hope, I will accompany you to Switzerland for a while.

Now, do you agree to being sung in Russian, since this would have the advantage of breaking the possible monotony of the concert? I have proposed Andreyev for you. Do you have a better suggestion?

I have become neither a lunatic nor an anarchist, but my green pen is empty.[24]

Ravel has already retained Bathori[25] for himself, and I don't know any others. Anyway, I am so discouraged that I don't give a damn.

What am I going to do? I have no taste for work. When I see you, I think that we should chat about the way to end this Kipling matter.

I hope that Madame Stravinsky and the children are well. My parents send you their greetings.

Je vous embrasse,   Maurice

Ravel leaves for London tomorrow morning for two weeks.

DELAGE TO STRAVINSKY   *Saturday, December 13, 1913*

Thank you, friend, for your wonderful letters. I have also received the December 9 letter. But you do not say anything about Andreyev and the concert. I assume that it is all right, and I shall tell him so.

Owing to all this and to my latest efforts in the Kipling affair, I cannot leave Paris at the moment, but I would be so happy if you came here. I will not insist

---

[23] The Société Musicale Indépendante, founded by Ravel, Koechlin, and others.

[24] The writing switches from green to red ink at this point.

[25] Jane Bathori (1877–1970), mezzo-soprano, who sang the premiere of Ravel's *Trois Poèmes de Stéphane Mallarmé* at the January 14 concert.

too strongly, because I want to respect your work. But I will definitely spend the second half of January with you.

Ravel went to London the day before yesterday, I think for two weeks. Three days ago, they played two of his pieces composed "in the manner of" Borodin and Chabrier. Casella[26] also gave three new ones, of which "Vincent d'Indy" was the most perfect success that he could have hoped for, since an old lady in the first row of the stalls fell asleep.

I am starting to work again, with great courage, but I do not know what to do. My best regards to Mme Stravinsky and kisses to the children. Also give my best to Mesdames and Monsieur Beliankin.

Je vous embrasse,   Maurice

STRAVINSKY TO DELAGE

Clarens
December 15, 1913
[Fragment of a letter]

What can I say about the music of this German *Kolossal Werk*,[27] with its 800 performers, 600 in the chorus and some 200 in the orchestra? Imagine that during two hours you are made to understand that two times two is four. . . .

DELAGE TO STRAVINSKY

Paris
January 6, 1914

Clarens[28]

Mon cher petit Igor,

Do not think that I have forgotten you! Good God! I have been running around for eight days to find a singer, since Andreyev is in Petersburg, Allchersky in Marseille, and the others who knows where? I have finally settled on Nikitina, because of the very high register. Don't dream about French tenors (good musicians are rare).

---

[26] Alfredo Casella (1883–1947), Italian composer, pianist, conductor. He performed these pieces in the Salle Pleyel, December 10, 1913. Casella was the author of a monograph on Stravinsky published in Italy in 1926. See the correspondence with Casella in S.S.C. III.

[27] Stravinsky had just heard Mahler's Eighth Symphony in Zürich. N. G. Struve wrote to Stravinsky, March 16, 1914: "In Leipzig I heard Schoenberg's *Gurre-Lieder* (138 men in the orchestra and 600 people in the chorus and, in addition, soloists). But what a remarkable piece of work it is. He has taken everything that he feels inside of himself and turned it into music! And for ten years this work remained unfinished." Struve was the first director of the Edition Russe de Musique (the Russischer Musik Verlag), founded in Berlin in 1910 by Serge Koussevitzky (1874–1951). A photograph of Struve is included in Bertensson's *Sergei Rachmaninov,* New York, 1956.

[28] Forwarded to the Clinique Mont-Riant, Avenue de la Gare, Lausanne. Stravinsky's

The worst of it is that I had to learn your Japanese lyricism on the piano in order to rehearse with Mme Nikitina. I would have preferred to have worked with the voice, but all will be well in the end.

I count on you to return the favor. When? You must be present at this concert,[29] first of all. Come, come, it is so long since we have seen each other, and the concert will be better than hearing Mahler.

I am worried about my small orchestra, because I was trying to find those Hindu sounds that send chills up my spine.

I think that this note will arrive in time to wish you a good Russian Christmas [January 7] as well as, on the part of all of your friends in Paris, a belated French New Year. So many friends! Unless he comes one of these days, I shall think that the small pavilion at [rue de] Civry is no longer sumptuous enough for Prince Igor. . . ?

You never give me any news of Mme Stravinsky. I hope she is well. All best wishes for her, as well as for the three children and Mademoiselle Vera [Nossenko] and Madame and Monsieur Beliankin, and all those whose names I forget. Thanks.

I am now published by Durand, you know. I even obtained permission to dedicate one of my songs to you, orchestra included. You are in company with Ravel and Schmitt, as I am in the *Japanese Lyrics.*[30]

Send news soon, and come and see me.

Je vous embrasse as strongly as in 1913.

Your   Maurice

In the meantime, the *Bâtisseurs* goes more and more askew. Good for them! I am furious.

DELAGE TO STRAVINSKY   *January 14, 1914*
                                                  (2 a.m.) [15th]
Hôtel du Châtelard
Clarens[31]

Très cher petit,

I returned to the little pavilion, alone, after the concert. My first success, and you were not with me. I am distraught! It is not because, apart from a few good friends whom you know, an unknown audience, like all audiences, has ap-

---

wife had been confined to this hospital for the birth of her younger daughter (January 15), for which reason the composer did not go to Paris for the premiere of *Three Japanese Lyrics.*

[29] In the Salle Erard, January 14. Struve wrote to Stravinsky from Berlin on January 6, 1914: "The score and parts of the *Japanese Lyrics* were sent off today by express mail to Casella. Please tell us how the performance goes."

[30] The songs are dedicated to Delage, Florent Schmitt, and Maurice Ravel.

[31] Forwarded to the Clinique Mont-Riant.

plauded my songs until they were repeated. For that, I do not give a damn. What matters is that I did almost what I wanted to do, at least in my orchestration, and you did not hear it. Oh well! I would have loved the pleasure it would have given you. What pain this gives me.

I should have begun by telling you that your three *Lyrics* went very well, sung by Nikitina, whose transparent voice suited them so well, and that they were a great success with the audience—with some hissing, naturally, but do not catch typhoid over that.[32]

As for Ravel, a success.[33] Bathori is as always. I find that the third piece, *Surgi de la croupe,* is an incredible thing, beyond any music that he has composed. A sad and abused splendor!

Do you agree with me in thinking that the second of your songs is the most magnificent?

I confess that the blow was hard for me to take. What company to be in. I must have benefited from being placed at the beginning of the program. People will recall everything now, the warm room after the rue du Mail, and that [my] India was better than the noises of a bus, etc. . . .

I am going to bed. I will send my songs tomorrow. Embrace the children for me, and hurry and give me good news of Madame Stravinsky.

Tenderly yours from the bottom of my heart,   Maurice

DELAGE TO STRAVINSKY   *164 rue de Courcelles, XVIIe*
                                        February 5, 1914
Clinique Mont-Riant
Avenue de la Gare
Lausanne

Mon cher vieux,

I apologize for not having answered earlier. I was ill again, and not sleeping, etc. I will reply to first things first. Jean Cocteau, 10 rue d'Anjou, Paris. I no longer recall the slightly mysterious commission with which you entrusted me with regard to Casella. Write a little note to him.

Fanet.[34] It seems that the Miquel sale produced very little. I have no news of the proceedings and, above all, would really like to have done with father Alzieu. That is all. But how?

Other news. I have a great urge to finish the winter working under you. Moreover, the doctors would like to send me somewhere for the air, to a country with *good milk,* since that is all I drink and water is all I eat! Only with that sacrifice will I be able to work without suffering too much. Otherwise I ought to stop all work. It is frightful. So, could you please tell me the price of a room in

---

[32] Stravinsky caught typhoid after the stormily protested premiere of the *Sacre.*

[33] The *Trois Poèmes de Stéphane Mallarmé.*

[34] See n. 4 above.

Clarens, one that would be near you *without* impeding your composition. I would rent a piano, which is very important, too. Is it possible to rent a gramo-phone-phonograph, or some kind of gramophone? I have a lot of records with which I must work, not having done the transcriptions of the themes that I need. I think it can be arranged. Soon you will see me catch up.

Does this idea please you? I hope that Madame Stravinsky is better and better, and that you will return to Clarens quickly. Mme Delage was supposed to have sent a little package for the children yesterday. Have you received it?

I await your answer impatiently. This plan would allow us really to live to-gether, which we have never done. Tell me soon. Kiss the children and give my regards to all.

Je vous embrasse,   Maurice

Ravel has gone to St.-Jean-de-Luz to orchestrate some things.

DELAGE TO STRAVINSKY   *Auteuil*
                                                          Paris
Grand Hôtel   *February 11, 1914*
Leysin

Cher petit,

I received your letter, the one written before you left for Leysin. That country, so far away and so high, deeply frightens me. Do you really think you will stay there? I assume that the children stayed at Clarens. At the moment I am work-ing like a crazy man—without ever eating—and my work goes well. I should like to play for you what I have already composed, a thieves' dance with the song of a gentleman who is pursued and who whines. He continues the dance with a stick across his shoulders. There is also a tiger's dance, performed while lying down, running to grab his lemon. How funny it all is!

Tell me in your next letter if you have to stay in Leysin for some time, be-cause that country would not correspond to the vacation that I have in mind for Switzerland.

My warm embraces.
My respects to Madame Stravinsky.

Your   Maurice

DELAGE TO STRAVINSKY   *3 rue de Civry*
                                          Wednesday April 28 [?], 1914
Hôtel du Châtelard
Clarens

Dear Igor,

Again deeply moved by your great triumph in Paris, my friend, and above all that the master did not forgo the little pavilion where I kept watch while he slept.[35] You see. In April, my soul wraps itself in a romantic turban, and I am the Toddy devoted to his Sahib.

Have you returned from Kiev? I think so. I received a letter from E. Evans, who is preparing the Russian season by means of a book in which he is supposed to speak about you at length—at any rate, something more than a birth notice, he says.

First of all, will you send a letter telling me everything you would like to see published about *The Nightingale,* in a telegraphic style if you wish, to save time, since it is for translation? I ask you to write to me, first, so I may be certain of what you think, second, because I could complete it myself (have no fears, since I will cut myself loose from the claws of my colleagues, and will send the proofs to you).

Also, *as soon as you can,* send the score to E. Evans, 31 Coleherne Road, Earl's Court, S.W.

Like last year, I will come and see the new works in Paris, on the 9th or 10th of next month.

Returning from the station at Lyon, on Sunday night, I ran into poor [illegible]-Offenbach, and I could read bitter reproaches in his eyes. He still awaits the score of *Petrushka.*

Send news as soon as possible, my old friend, it is urgent.

Hug all of the children and give my best respects to Madame Stravinsky and Madame Beliankina, to whom, figuratively, I send all the lilies of my little garden.

Je vous embrasse, your devoted   Maurice

DELAGE TO STRAVINSKY   *Friday [Postmark: June 20, 1914]*

Villa Bel-Air
Salvan (Valais)

Dear Igor,

I was very surprised last night at the Marigny, where I was playing the piano in a revue, to hear sizable excerpts from *Petrushka,* the Dance of the Wet Nurses and of the Coachmen, the Russian Dance, etc., played by a greatly reduced orchestra. I hope that you will be like the man with the "wooden leg"[36] and that

---

[35] Stravinsky stayed with Delage at the time of the first concert performance of the *Sacre,* April 5, 1914, in the Casino de Paris. The letter may refer to the repeat performance, April 26, since Stravinsky told his friends that he planned to go to Ustilug and Kiev in mid-April, a trip he postponed until July.

[36] Stravinsky had been sued for incorporating the melody "Elle avait une jambe en bois" into *Petrushka,* and, until the 1950s, he was obliged to pay the publisher a percentage of the *Petrushka* royalties. Delage refers to the "man" with the wooden leg, but it is a woman.

you will send Bernstein[37] to claim your author's rights. These could amount to something, since revues of this kind sometimes last for a long time. The sets and costumes are very Russian, and more Bakst than Benois.

Durand was enchanted with *Ragamalika,* which Ronfeart sings admirably. Durand gave me 500 francs, orchestration included.

Hug all of the children, and give my best wishes to Catherine and to Madame Beliankina.

Je vous embrasse,   Maurice

DELAGE TO STRAVINSKY

164 rue de Courcelles
March 23, 1915

Dear Igor,

I am happy that a word from me suffices. You are less demanding than the Parisians who would like to receive a Zeppelin every evening. I am very tired, between the frequently long missions, but I have been able to survey almost our entire front. Many things to tell you. And the poor little pavilion, covered with dust, sad with many beautiful memories and with hopes tenderly caressed. I want so much to compose at this moment. It seems to me that I was at last writing something good before this unspeakable war!!!

Will we not see each other before the end? In any case, I have a feeling that this is not far off. My parents send you all good wishes. The fighting has been going on so long that it seems to me that your children ought to be, I don't know, married, perhaps? Embrace them in any event, and Catherine too.

Kisses for you,   Maurice

The German bombardments no longer dumbfound me; they will have to come up with something new.

---

[37] Léon Bernstein, *"Agence littéraire et théâtrale pour la Russie,"* was Stravinsky's representative in Paris. Someone from this firm wrote to the composer in Ustilug, July 28, 1913: "Dear Igor Fyodorovich! I have only just returned from London today. . . . I met with Sergei Pavlovich [Diaghilev] there, spoke with him at length, and, of course, met with energetic resistance on his part. What is of particular concern to you is that Sergei Pavlovich has declared that he is not prepared to pay you anything for performances outside Paris and Monte Carlo. . . . I pointed out that it is hardly fair to pay Russian authors only in those instances in which, because of the peculiar conditions of the Société des Auteurs [et Compositeurs Dramatiques], it is impossible to avoid doing so. The unfairness of this becomes even more obvious when one considers that Sergei Pavlovich is obliged to pay non-Russians, like Debussy. . . . Sergei Pavlovich will be in Paris in a few days, but in the meantime, please write a letter to me in French giving the terms that you established with Sergei Pavlovich for each of your works. . . ."

DELAGE TO STRAVINSKY   *3 rue de Civry*
                                                    January 23, 1919
[Morges]

Dear Igor,

I embraced you for the last time in Versailles, many centuries ago! Since then, I
have been carried along at random by the whims of the military, and have lost
more than fifty pounds during six months in many different hospitals. Finally,
in October, I became a civilian again.

I am writing to you from the little pavilion, restored, at last, and I am being
roasted to the marrow by a fierce fire (a good imitation of Liberia, these three
days).

I cry above all for the beautiful projects grown old under four years of dust.
Understand, my old friend, that all the building materials gathered in 1914
have become useless, like plaster left out in the rain—wasted. And to take up
the strands of work, and find confidence in a personality debased by the many
platitudes of the army. One's fantasy is wounded, murdered, at every moment
of a life spent as a mindless servant: you see all that. Look at this paper on
which I am writing. We bought it together in Montreux; Robert Seinet-Laillard,
at the Laiterie Bazaar, 2 Grand-Kère. I see both of us there so clearly. . . . Place
me at the feet of Madame Stravinsky for as long as is necessary to be forgiven
for this long silence. Send news of the children, too. I learned, after a delay so
long that it was ridiculous to write to you, about the death of your kind
brother,[38] and since then I have so often thought of him. What horrors and
what poor results!

You recall the Théâtre du Vieux-Colombier? They have asked me if I want
to orchestrate *The Marriage* by Mussorgsky, for about twenty instruments.
Didn't you begin to do this yourself once? Do you still intend to work on this
score? I won't disguise from you the little confidence I have in my abilities as an
orchestrator—though recently much improved. Answer me. Ravel, with a
slight pulmonary affliction, is taking a cure in the Haute-Savoie, at Degère, near
Chamonix. He is incapable of work. And you?

Spread my affection all around you, and believe in the tenderness of

                                                    Maurice Delage

DELAGE TO STRAVINSKY   *Auteuil*
                                        Tuesday [Postmark: October 6, 1920]
Villa "Bel Respiro"
Garches

Vieux Iglg,

I learned that there should be an apartment for rent at St. Germain, 25 rue de
Lorraine.[39] That is what is commonly called a miracle. In the same district,

---

[38] Gury Stravinsky, the composer's younger brother, had died in Iasi, Rumania, in the
summer of 1917.

[39] Stravinsky was apartment-hunting. The Villa "Bel Respiro" belonged to Chanel, and

there is a Professor Jaraud who would give lessons to your children, if it is time yet for all that.

Are you settled and working? I am. I finished the Schumann, according to our agreement, and I am working on the Apsaras dances (Deradattys, a kind of Amazon, excited by the old, beloved Krishna). When you are a little more settled, I think we could look at it together.

Embrace your wife and the brats. Affectionate rubs to you, those in B minor.

Maurice Delage

DELAGE TO STRAVINSKY   *Auteuil*
                                                  June 21, 1923
Mon cher petit,

I had [a] great joy yesterday. . . . I heard *Les Noces*. . . . I searched every corner of the theater looking for you afterward, and all the way to the rue Réaumur. I expect to have the same difficulty in finding you tonight, for which reason I am sending you this note.

One day I shall share some things with [you], in front of a green boxwood vase. . . . I have some portraits of [you], who are ever present, and loom above the orchestra score I am now composing (which is giving me a great deal of trouble).

Nelly sends you best wishes, and the two of us await you with great affection.

Maurice Delage

DELAGE TO STRAVINSKY   *Auteuil*
                                               November 6, 1923
Mon vieux,

Thank you for the reserved seats for the Soldier and his Tale, as well as for the Octet, which we will be delighted to hear again.

But even before your festival, my concert will be rehearsed, tomorrow morning (Wednesday). I will be there at 10 o'clock. And since I truly need your advice—I accept advice from very few—let me remind you that you promised to come, if you don't have a rehearsal of your own at that time. Is it possible? I would be very happy. We will rehearse at the theater, of course. My wife and I embrace you as we love you.

Maurice Delage

My score is played on an anvil weighing 72½ kilos. . . .

---

was a temporary residence—until the spring of 1921, when he moved his family to Biarritz and rented a two-room studio in Paris, at the Maison Pleyel.

CORRESPONDENCE WITH

V. V. DERZHANOVSKY

1912 ⟞ 1914

Much respected Vladimir Vladimirovich!

I apologize very much for not having answered your kind letter of May 15, 1912, before now. I am only partly to blame, however, because the letter, addressed to Clarens, did not find me there—I was in Paris. It was forwarded to Ravel's, where I direct all my correspondence, and then it lay there for about ten days. Ravel asks me to tell you that he assumes all blame for the delay.

After such a long introduction I shall get down to business.

First, about *Petrushka:* I have not granted the Pavlovsky Concerts permission to perform *Petrushka,* nor have I forbidden it. I also do not know whether they have approached my publisher or not. As for Saradzhev,[2] I will gladly give him permission to do *Petrushka,* only I must warn you that the parts are not yet ready, and that we will perform in Paris, as they will in London, from the galley reprints. The parts will be ready at the end of the summer. Thus if you have the opportunity to present *Petrushka* at the end of the summer season, that will be a good time. I am concentrating on the correction of the orchestral parts, for until now I have been excessively busy with composing. I have not made a suite from *Petrushka*—it can be performed as a symphony, with all four scenes in succession. In the event that one of the organizers of the concerts is bothered by the pantomimic nature of the last pages, then a special ending (after the "mummers" scene), attached to the score and the parts, can be substituted in a concert production of the work.[3] My frank opinion, though, is that *Petrushka* should be performed from beginning to end without a single cut, change, or the special ending. I have long considered using this composition for the concert stage and have now reached this conclusion.[4]

With regard to the Symphony, I actually do not know what to tell you. I am not at all ashamed of it—it is my first opus. It has a few nice sections, but most of it is crude, in the Glazunov-Tchaikovsky style, and the instrumentation is academic. In itself the work is not interesting, but it serves as one more document illustrating how not to compose. If all of this does not frighten you, then play it. Consult with Steinberg[5]—he knows where the score is, and

---

[1] Vladimir Vladimirovich Derzhanovsky (1881–1942), editor of *Muzyka,* Moscow, 1910–16.

[2] Konstantin Solomonovich Saradzhev (1877–1954), conductor.

[3] See n. 1 on p. 23.

[4] See Appendix C.

[5] Maximilian Oseyevich Steinberg (1883–1946), Russian composer and son-in-law of Nikolai Rimsky-Korsakov. The tone of Steinberg's letters to Stravinsky changes from condescension to supplication—for help in appealing to Diaghilev. On October 15, 1912, Steinberg, in St. Petersburg, wrote to Stravinsky in Ustilug: "Dear Igor! Yesterday I played my ballet at Diaghilev's, who told me that you had written to him of its existence. I hasten to thank you for your friendly assistance. Bakst, Nouvel, and [Nicholas] Tcherepnin were there." In the same letter, Steinberg has notated the re-

the parts are either in Petersburg or on the way to Ustilug, where I am now living.[6] If the July date for the Symphony meets with your approval, then I'll send the parts to you myself. By then their whereabouts will have come to light.

Forgive this careless letter and its familiar style. When people of the artistic world approach me, I am uncomfortable in maintaining an official tone, and I tend to go to the opposite extreme.

With sincere regard,   Igor Stravinsky

I await your answer to this letter.

---

peated chord of the "Danse des adolescentes" from *Le Sacre du printemps*, adding, "this is all I remember from the first time." On November 2, he wrote to say that he had "given the *Firebird* score to N. G. Struve, who took it to Berlin. . . . I still do not have any answer from Diaghilev, and I am distraught." In December, Steinberg wrote that Diaghilev had not yet made a decision about the ballet, and "Since I am in the dark as to the state of my composition, and since I am reassured by your second telegram, I have set to work to complete [Rimsky-Korsakov's] *Foundations of Orchestration.*" The remainder of this letter is concerned with questions regarding the availability of a "timpano piccolo," for *Le Sacre du printemps,* which Stravinsky had asked Steinberg to investigate, and with Steinberg's story that Bessel, the publisher, had asked him to orchestrate Mussorgsky's "Flea," even though Stravinsky's orchestration was still in print: "Bessel complains that he could not wait for a reply from you." Steinberg wrote to Stravinsky from the Hotel Russischer Hof in Berlin, January 11, 1913, supplying information about the possibility of constructing a timpano with high notes and explaining the choice of piccolo trumpets: "They are available in St. Petersburg in E flat but not in D, though the D trumpet can be ordered. . . . I have not heard a whisper from Diaghilev." After sending wedding anniversary greetings to the Stravinskys, in January 1913, Steinberg wrote, April 17, saying that he had arranged to meet with Diaghilev in London at the beginning of June, and that "I am very glad that I shall finally get to hear *Firebird, Petrushka,* and maybe even the *Sacre.*" In this letter, he also asks Stravinsky about proper attire for London, and states his complete disagreement with Stravinsky's high opinion of Strauss's *Elektra.* (In spite of the "present insignificance of German music," Steinberg remarks, "Schoenberg is a very kind and talented man.") Steinberg urges Stravinsky to decide about the small timpano that he wishes to order for the *Sacre,* and, on May 7, says that "the trumpets and the mutes have been ordered and will be sent off to Paris in a week, I hope in time for the first performance of the *Sacre.*" On May 31, Steinberg wrote: "Diaghilev and I have arranged to meet in London at the beginning of June so that he, Bakst, Nijinsky, *you,* and I can discuss the details of the production of my [*Metamorphosis*] . . . . I would very much like to show the score to you personally before turning it over for printing. . . . I hope all the instruments arrived in time for the *Sacre* production. . . . P.S. I've just found out about the enormous success of the *Sacre* from Gury's telegram. . . ." On hearing that Stravinsky had contracted typhoid Steinberg wrote to Catherine: "I received a telegram from Igor on Sunday, and the same day sent a telegram to Diaghilev, to which I have had no reply. . . . I hope that . . . Igor will see Diaghilev and will get an answer to what I asked." On June 21, Steinberg wrote to Stravinsky at the Villa Borghese, Neuilly, deferring their "musical discussions" until

DERZHANOVSKY TO STRAVINSKY

Moscow[7]
May 12, 1913
[Postcard]

4 avenue Carnot

Paris

(c/o M. Ravel)

My dear Igor Fyodorovich,

I have received Ravel's article on [Mussorgsky's] *Khovanshchina*, and will, of course, publish it. How could he doubt that?! The mere fact of our having run

---

Stravinsky's health had improved. The next letter, July 9, continues with the same story—Diaghilev does not answer—and in the one after that, October 15, 1913, Steinberg is still begging Stravinsky to arrange a meeting with Diaghilev. On November 17, Steinberg says that Diaghilev has finally spoken to him on the telephone. The next-to-last letter, February 9, 1914, says, simply, "I'm not writing about the *Sacre* because we will have to talk about that and talk about it quite a bit." The last letter is a rather pathetic request for tickets to *Pulcinella* and *Le Chant du rossignol* at the Ballets Russes, Paris, June 16, 1925.

[6] Nikolai Rimsky-Korsakov's widow wrote to Stravinsky from St. Petersburg, October 20, 1912: "Dear Igor Fyodorovich, I received your letter three days ago. You and I did discuss your Symphony when we met at Max's, but you never told me to give your autograph score (a gift to Nikolai Andreyevich) to any engraver. What is more, to have asked that of me would have been absurd. I said at the time that we would not allow an engraving to be made from that unique copy, and you said that you would give [G. P.] Jurgenson your orchestral parts. In my view, if Jurgenson is demanding a copy of the score from you, he is in the right and you are in the wrong. There was no copy of the score for the author to present to the publisher, and with which to sell the composition to him. If you want a copy to be made from the score that I have, I will immediately send it to the copyist, in your name, and send the second copy to the publisher. If Jurgenson is prepared to spend his own money for the copying, then have him send confirmation to me that he would like to have the original from me in order to make a photocopy, and that he is responsible, once the copy has been made, for returning the original to me immediately, clean and intact. I do not believe the promises of any publisher that his engraver will not soil the manuscript. I know from my own experiences the condition in which manuscripts are returned, and, for that reason, I will not surrender the original for engraving. Scold me as much as you like, be angry with me, but I still say that I am completely within my rights to refuse to give a manuscript to a publisher, above all, a manuscript that has become my own property and that I value very much, first of all because I love the music in it, secondly, because it was your gift to Nikolai Andreyevich and testifies to the warm feelings that you had for my husband. The best solution would be the following: I will give the score to a copyist here in St. Petersburg for him to make a photocopy, charging either you or Jurgenson, as you prefer, and concerning which I hope you will give me instructions. . . . I hope that all is now well with your family. My regards to Ekaterina Gavrilovna; I shake your hand affectionately and send my best wishes to you. Until you are next in St. Petersburg . . . Love, N. Rimskaya-Korsakova   P.S. Andrei sends you a kiss."

   On October 31, 1912, Boris Petrovich Jurgenson, brother of Gregory Petrovich, wrote to Stravinsky promising to write to Andrei Rimsky-Korsakov "today, asking him

A.R.I.'s[8] article does not indicate a hostile attitude toward Ravel (whom *Mu-zyka* loves and appreciates, incidentally), much less toward you, but rather a desire to present this interesting event as clearly as possible.

Ravel's article will appear in issue No. 129, since the coming issue is devoted entirely to Wagner.

I have been meaning to write to you for many months now, about several things, but I have been bogged down in all sorts of cumbersome affairs. Today I am finally getting around to it.

I wish you the greatest success, and please give my warm regards to Ravel.

Yours,   V. Derzhanovsky

DERZHANOVSKY TO STRAVINSKY   *Moscow*
                                                              May 13, 1913
4 avenue Carnot
Paris
(c/o M. Ravel)

My dear Igor Fyodorovich,

Knowing of your goodwill toward *Muzyka,* to which our magazine responds in kind with unfailing enthusiasm for your work—I would like to solicit your support and assistance, because *Muzyka,* alas, remains totally impoverished. For

---

to send the score. . . . Your suggestion that we engrave straight from the parts is quite impossible. . . . Saradzhev promised to give me his parts for the Symphony." On January 11, 1913, Jurgenson wrote that "We have only started to engrave the Symphony because we have just received the first part of the score from the copyists." On February 16, 1913, the publisher wrote: "It is a great pity that you do not have time now to read the proof of the Symphony, since I hurried to have it engraved, and the engraving will probably be completed within a week. . . . [Andrei] Rimsky-Korsakov was displeased because we kept the score of the Symphony for so long." On May 19, when Stravinsky was in Paris for the premiere of the *Sacre,* Jurgenson wrote that the score of the first part of the Symphony had been typeset, that the other parts would soon follow, and that the work would be released in August if Stravinsky would take the time to proofread it. A letter of July 23 reveals that Stravinsky had not yet done this. Another letter, August 30, implores him to finish the task, since "the parts are being engraved from those used by Saradzhev." On September 23, G. P. Jurgenson wrote that Karagichev had finished proofing the score, except for the slow movement, which was still in Stravinsky's hands. (Boris Vasilievich Karagichev, 1879–1946, was a composer.) On November 21, Stravinsky wrote: ". . . I ask you not to forget to print the dedication to N. A. Rimsky-Korsakov. Best of all, place it on a page in large type as it was in the manuscript: To my dear teacher, Nikolai Andreyevich Rimsky-Korsakov." On November 27, Jurgenson wrote that this had been done, but on December 22 he informed the composer that the parts would not be ready before January 13, 1914.

[7] All of Derzhanovsky's letters were sent from the offices of *Muzyka* on the ruelle Troitsky in Moscow.

[8] Unidentified music critic.

one thing, we still have no foreign correspondents, and probably shall not have any for some time to come, since that would involve expenditures which we are hardly in a position to make.

Were it simply a question of a few isolated German, English, or other musical personalities, then it would not be crucial to have foreign correspondents, but so much is going on abroad: Diaghilev's enterprise, for example, is under way, and, finally, France has such remarkable artists as Debussy and Ravel. Neither *Muzyka* nor any other publication specifically devoted to new ideas and current events can afford to ignore all this. So what are we to do?

If you would help us, the situation could be remedied, at least to some extent. I would like you to persuade M. Ravel to write for us occasionally about the more important events in Paris, such as, at the moment, the production of your *Le Sacre du printemps,* of Debussy's *Jeux,* of Florent Schmitt's *La Tragédie de Salomé,* and *Khovanshchina.* For the magazine to carry articles about these works is absolutely essential, and, moreover, serious articles, written by a specialist, someone with a fresh and progressive mind. No one is more qualified for this than Ravel. As I have already said, however, we cannot pay anything, and of course it is not feasible to use someone's work without paying, just as it is disagreeable even to request such work from an artist who already has plenty to do. After all, the artist is not a patron of the arts, and not a Croesus. . . . I have invented a recompense of sorts that Ravel might accept, should my proposal interest him at all: we will pay for his articles by advertising his works in *Muzyka*. This type of payment we could easily extend to him, and it would undoubtedly be helpful in the dissemination of his works throughout Russia. You could be of invaluable service to us, Igor Fyodorovich, if you would discuss the affair with Ravel and convince him to agree. And, finally, it is the avant-garde that will gain by the propagation and popularization of the new precepts dear to us all. If this could be arranged—and how wonderful that would be—I would anxiously await articles on the great news items of this spring season.

For your part, send me, if possible, whatever you can in the way of set sketches, pictures, photographs pertaining to the production of *Le Sacre du printemps,* and anything else that might be useful to illustrate articles. If Ravel, in the event that he does agree to write for us, would like to complement his articles with musical examples, he should not hesitate to do so, and we would be very grateful for any technical-analytical contributions.

B. P. Jurgenson informed me that he is rushing the printing of *Zvezdoliki*[9]

---

[9] Jurgenson realized that this opus could not be exploited commercially and offered Stravinsky only 300 rubles for it (letter of December 23, 1912). Stravinsky refused this at first (Jurgenson's letter of January 1, 1913), but accepted a counter-offer, and on January 11, Jurgenson acknowledged the receipt of the manuscript. On April 8, Jurgenson wrote that the score had been given to the engraver, that a copy of the proof would be sent to Calvocoressi, who was to prepare the translation, and that "Scriabin's Etudes are being sent to you." In a letter of April 23, Jurgenson says that he is sending the proofs of the piano score and, "in a day or two, those of the full score, so that this and the choral parts can be printed in time for the performance that you wrote about."

in order to be in time for the concert, either the one in Paris or the one in London, where your cantata will be performed along with the works of all the ultra-innovators. *Muzyka* should review the premiere, but if the performance is in London, I see no possible way. If it were in Paris and Ravel refused to review it, that would be a great pity.

But even if Ravel were in perfect accord with my proposal, his own works would still be neglected, for of course he could not write about them himself. I would therefore ask you to do this, though I know how much you dislike writing. Perhaps you could write in letter form, unofficially, and I could concoct something from this correspondence, as I did for this year's first issue, after your last letter. Maybe Calvocoressi will reply, but it seems that he has completely forgotten us recently, though *Muzyka* itself, or, rather, its status as an "impoverished lady," is to blame.

Alas, Igor Fyodorovich, two more requests. The year before last—and earlier, while the original "Evenings of Contemporary Music"[10] were still going on—Durand's publishing firm used to send us its news briefs. For some reason, we have not received any in the past year, and we are no longer able to list French news in our bibliography, which we regret immensely. Aside from that, it is vexing, since the present editors of *Muzyka* and the former administration of the "Eve. of Contemp. Mus." did a great deal to popularize Debussy, Ravel, and others in Moscow, and as a result of our Moscow concerts, interest in these composers has increased steadily. Perhaps Ravel will be kind enough to take it upon himself to speak with Durand and arrange to have news of current events—including last year's—sent to us, beginning with the *Valses nobles* and the piano score of *Daphnis et Chloé*, neither of which has arrived yet. Durand continues to receive *Muzyka*. In any case, he ought to remember me personally, since he is indebted to me and to Saradzhev because we sent them some extra money when we wrote out the notes for the Falconer concerts. I am sure that they will remember. We will review everything that they send.

On May 19, Jurgenson complains that Stravinsky has not corrected the proofs, "sent long ago. I cannot print because, as you say, the French title will have to be changed."
[10] The "Evenings of Contemporary Music," organized in St. Petersburg by Walter Nouvel and A. Nurok, lasted from 1901 to 1912, but the group of musicians had already begun to meet during the 1900–01 season, before the start of the open concerts. In all, fifty concerts, five or six a season, were given in the period indicated. They took place in various Petersburg halls, among them the auditorium of the Reformate School and the Lenishevsky Gymnasium. The proximity of the concerts to the "World of Art" group determined the orientation of the "Evenings" toward the work of contemporary composers. The concerts presented works by Debussy, Ravel, Dukas, Chausson, Franck, d'Indy, R. Strauss, Mahler, Wolf, Reger (who participated on one occasion, December 1906), Schoenberg (March 28, 1911, when Prokofiev performed two of the piano pieces Opus 11), Scriabin, Medtner, Gnesin, Steinberg, Akimenko, Tcherepnin, Stravinsky, and Prokofiev. Concerts were also dedicated to little-known works of Mussorgsky, Borodin, and Rimsky-Korsakov.

A final request. It seems that you are on good terms with Debussy. I wonder if you could ask him to consent to appear in, or at least to attend, a concert of "Evenings of Contemporary Music," which will be given in his honor, when he comes to Koussevitzky's in Moscow next year, and after his appearance with that famous and wealthy gentleman.

I fear that I have tried your patience to the utmost, so I shall leave off here; my warmest regards and best wishes to you. I would be very happy if you could do at least some of what I have requested. All the best.

Devotedly yours,　V. Derzhanovsky

In your last letter, you said that you had sent *The Faun and the Shepherdess*[11] score to me to give to Konstantin Solomonovich Saradzhev, but it never arrived. Are you receiving *Muzyka*?

[*Handwritten*] Please let us know if you compose anything new.

P.S. I've just had a complaint from the office that you have not subscribed to *Muzyka* this year. I explained that you probably had just forgotten or did not know how to transmit the money to us. Since our office is very strict and scrupulous about figures, I will tell them that they can settle the subscription fee through Jurgenson and have him send the fee directly to the accounting office of *Muzyka*, Moscow, Ostojenka, Troitsky 5, which would be the most convenient way.

P.P.S. Yesterday I sent a postcard to you stating that, because of the Wagner jubilee, Ravel's article on *Khovanshchina* will be featured in the following issue (No. 129).

DERZHANOVSKY TO STRAVINSKY

Moscow
June 1, 1913
[Picture postcard with
a photograph of Wagner]

Splendid Hôtel
1 bis, avenue Carnot
Paris

My dear and most esteemed Igor Fyodorovich,

I am overjoyed at the brilliant success of *Le Sacre du printemps,* and most grieved that we in *Muzyka* will not be able to review it or *Jeux.*

Keep well and happy.

Devotedly yours,　V. Derzhanovsky

---

[11] Suite for mezzo-soprano and orchestra on three poems by Pushkin. Composed in Imatra and St. Petersburg in 1906 and dedicated to Catherine Stravinsky, the work was published by Belayev, Leipzig, 1908.

DERZHANOVSKY TO STRAVINSKY   *Moscow*
                                              June 12, 1913

Villa Borghese[12]
29 Boulevard Victor Hugo
Neuilly-sur-Seine
Paris

My dear Igor Fyodorovich!

What is new and good with you? I am very impatient and cannot wait for you to remember me, once you have won a respite from all your troubles.

I see nothing in the newspapers about *Le Sacre du printemps* or *Khovanshchina.* . . . What a pity! The piano score of *Sacre* and the *Japanese Lyrics* finally arrived. I have a few questions. Is it true that the full score of the *Sacre* will *not* be for sale? That would be scandalous! How could we write about it then?! More to the point, Koussevitzky is terribly vulgar.

I have a puzzling question for the author of the *Japanese Lyrics*. The music is rapturous, really quite marvelous, but what is the meaning of the persistent and systematic correspondence between the musical meter and that of the text? The accents seem to fall either on the eighth or on the quarter. Since your declamation is always ideal, it must be intentional, some subtlety in the meter modulation. But *what* is your intention, precisely? Please tell me, otherwise it will be impossible to interpret the work properly. And once again, the score will not be published!

These are the matters that are on my mind, apart from my former worry.

                         All the best to you,   V. Derzhanovsky

P.S. One more thing. For *The Nightingale* production, *Muzyka* will need a detailed analysis with music examples and the like. How are we to accomplish this without the score? It is splendid that Saradzhev will prepare and conduct the opera. He will do it all in a masterly fashion and with his usual absorption.

DERZHANOVSKY TO STRAVINSKY   *Moscow*
                                              July 11, 1913

Villa Borghese[13]

My dear Igor Fyodorovich,

I was very glad to receive the letter about your improving health but was unable to answer because I am completely out of touch. My wife underwent an operation and was in the sanitarium.

Soon I shall write to you in a proper fashion, but for now I wanted simply to

---

[12] Stravinsky was confined with typhus to this sanitarium.
[13] Forwarded from Neuilly, July 15, to Ustilug ("via Warsaw") and postmarked "Ustilug, July 24."

find out where you are (at the Paris sanitarium or in Ustilug), and whether you have recovered completely. My warmest regards to your wife, and I thank her for her mediation in our correspondence.

Devotedly yours,   V. Derzhanovsky

P.S. I have not had a letter from Ravel.

DERZHANOVSKY TO STRAVINSKY

My dear Igor Fyodorovich,

Since you are already in Ustilug, you must already have made a significant recovery, which pleases me. I found out that you were in Ustilug because an issue of *Muzyka* was returned here from Paris. It is interesting that the French post looked for you there and in Neuilly, and finally sent the issue to Ustilug. But no sooner did the parcel land on the Russian border than our postmen were unable to think up anything cleverer than to return the issue to the editor's address. Everything is muddled here.

I have been so busy with bothersome personal as well as professional errands that I could not really answer you, so I limited myself to a postcard expressing my gratitude, sent to Neuilly. I do not know if you received it.

I read your explanation of the *Japanese Lyrics* with interest, and my guesses, which I was already prepared to employ in defense of the work against the critics' arguments, were confirmed. And yet I am somewhat anxious at the thought of that eventuality. Your idea is simple enough, though still intricate and subtle; but it is somewhat theoretical. All in all, the positive is consumed by the negative. Is that not where the trouble lies, in that nothing really comes across in the declamation? I fear that nothing does. True, there will be accents, but timid and limp ones. Of course, we will have to wait for a performance to tell. Perhaps my wife is right that it would be interesting to provide the original Japanese text in the edition, transcribed phonetically and as closely as possible. What, then, would be done with the syncopations? Their whole system, of course, is for non-Japanese texts. The problem remains unsolved, and I think it will not be solved simply by a regular count of the accents.

Here your *Sacre du printemps* is being cursed to hell and beyond, by both Sabaneyev—which is not really surprising, since Scriabin considers himself God, making Sabaneyev his prophet—and A[ndrei] Rimsky-Korsakov. I do not know what is happening with the latter, but a certain personal enmity is evident in his writing, which in fact is shallow and evaluates very little of the *Sacre*, even negatively.

In the light of this, it is a great pity that Ravel did not send an account, and a *musical* analysis of the work. But I have a critic who understands your work probably better than any other: Miaskovsky.[14] He was not able to see the ballet,

---

[14] Nikolai Yakovlevich Miaskovsky (1881–1950), composer.

however, and no score is available here. Without the score, of course, one cannot write about the work. Here is an excerpt from his letter to me, in answer to the articles by [Andrei] R.-Korsakov and Sabaneyev that I sent to him:

> I have read R.-Korsakov and also looked at this Sabaneyev of yours, and I think that there is a grain of truth in what each one says. At the same time I must say that Stravinsky is a more considerable musical phenomenon than they admit, and I think that I will soon pick up the scent and be led logically and naturally to the *Sacre,* which, so far, I have not found. I feel that I am gradually beginning to comprehend this latest stage of Stravinsky's work.

In a previous letter, Miaskovsky wrote:

> In the music of the *Japanese Lyrics,* there is a great deal that is personal, "linearly" intimate, harmonically fresh, and thank God, *non-Scriabin.* . . . All the music of *Sacre* is characteristic and consistent, which, to me, is the principal retort to criticism of Stravinsky for lack of organization and thoughtlessness.

These excerpts characterize M.'s unfailing and serious interest in your music. And on the basis of this, I want to ask you, Igor Fyodorovich, to make regular gifts to *Muzyka,* just as [Nikolai] Rimsky-Korsakov used to do with Yastrebtsev,[15] by sending the superfluous first proof-sheets of each of your works to Miaskovsky, and the second proofs to the publishers. This will be a nuisance in the sense that it represents still more correspondence for you to tend to, but, on the other hand, Miaskovsky will always be ready to write a critique of any new work of yours. As a result, *Muzyka* will not be in such a ridiculous state of ignorance. What do you say, Igor Fyodorovich? Or am I going too far in asking this of you? If you find this feasible, it would be most desirable if you could send the printed proofs of *Nightingale.* Then, before the premiere, we would publish a comprehensive article, which would prepare the public appropriately, and the critics, too. And it goes without saying that such gifts would remain Miaskovsky's secret and mine.

---

[15] On June 12, 1961, Stravinsky wrote to Pierre Suvchinsky: "Of course I knew Yastrebtsev. He was a blockhead." On February 7, 1963, Stravinsky wrote again: "What an interesting letter you have written to me about Yastrebtsev's book. I had completely forgotten what he looked like, and, to tell the truth, I had confused him with Belsky, Rimsky-Korsakov's librettist, whom I had seen in Paris 30 years ago, and for whom I arranged the payment of author's rights for his Korsakov libretto to the Société Dramatique. Your observations on Yastrebtsev's second volume—and what about Volume 1 (you have never mentioned it)?—are probably true, but I have always regarded the book as just the usual obscurantism of the Korsakov entourage. The only fresh element in all that world was Stepchka Mitussov. All of the others constitute the principal reason for my flight from St. Petersburg. I will procure both of the Yastrebtsev volumes."

I await a reply from you on this matter. Incidentally, at one point there was some mention of a printing of some of your compositions. Neither I nor Saradzhev has received the score of *The Faun and the Shepherdess,* which, if I recall, you were to have sent in my name so that I might give it to K. S. Saradzhev. Perhaps it has been lost; with the state of affairs here, that certainly is possible.

If you happen to write to Ravel, perhaps you would let him know that I would be happy to have his analysis of your masterpiece, of Debussy's ballet [*Jeux*], and the text of the announcement of his compositions to print in *Muzyka.*

I do not want you to become fed up with me, so I close on that note.

Get well and conserve your strength.

Sincerely yours,   V. Derzhanovsky

P.S. My respectful regards to your wife.
P.P.S. I've typed this letter so as not to tire your eyes with my handwriting.

DERZHANOVSKY TO STRAVINSKY   *Moscow*
                                              July 28, 1913
My dear Igor Fyodorovich,   *[Postcard]*

I was very pleased to receive your letter, and I hasten to answer your questions.

Of course Miaskovsky will be delighted to have the orchestra score of the *Sacre* for a sense of the whole ballet. His address, until August 6, is as follows: Nikolai Yakovlevich Miaskovsky, Snt., Sadovaya 8.[16] After that he will be here with me as a guest. It is better to send it to him immediately, so that he will be *"au courant"* upon his arrival here.

I have the piano score of *Zvezdoliki,* but I still have not received the *Faun,* which must be lost.

Yours as ever,   V. Derzhanovsky

---

[16] Stravinsky sent the score to Miaskovsky in St. Petersburg, and the latter acknowledged it from that city on August 7: "Dear Igor Fyodorovich, I was very touched by your parcel to me containing the score of the poems of the *Japanese Lyrics,* which I have come to like very much. I want to express my sincere gratitude for this gift, as well as for the score for Part One of *Le Sacre du printemps.* I hope that when I have become acquainted with the execution of these new ideas of yours, striking to me in their originality, I will finally be able to master the music of *Le Sacre,* which even now, though I know it only through transcriptions, I find increasingly fascinating. Once again I thank you with all my heart. You will have the score back, as you have requested, no later than August 14 [27]. Most devotedly yours, N. Miaskovsky.   P.S. Forgive me for the slight delay in replying to you: your letter came while I was away and I opened it only yesterday.   N.M." (See Appendix D.)

DERZHANOVSKY TO STRAVINSKY

Ustilug

My dear Igor Fyodorovich,

Thank you very much indeed for *Zvezdoliki*, with the autograph. Oh, for more of this kind—and any other kind—of "nonsense"! Actually, I had already seen this piece: *Muzyka* gets everything new from Jurgenson immediately. Koussevitzky's and Belayev's publications are another matter. They send nothing, and nothing can be done about it!

Thank you also for *Montjoie!*[17] This is curious. Of course they have be-

---

[17] Stravinsky's article on *Le Sacre du printemps* appeared in this review on May 29, 1913. *Montjoie!* was a periodical, edited by Ricciotto Canudo, and published in Paris. In his letter of August 25, 1913, Stravinsky says that he is changing the *Muzyka* translation of his *Montjoie!* article on the *Sacre*. He did so as follows (his revisions are in capital letters above the line):

It has been several years now since the French public first graced my *Firebird* and *Petrushka* with kind attention. I do not think that my friends could have failed to notice the conceptual evolution that carried me from the fantastical fables
OF THE TWO WORKS MENTIONED   SECOND
of my first works to the strictly human character of the latest. I am afraid that *Le Sacre du printemps,* in which I no longer invoke either the magic of fairy tales or the more real human emotions of joy and sorrow, but in which I appeal instead
                                    ANTAGONIZE
to a greater abstraction, might create a certain confusion among those whose sympathy I have enjoyed until now.

In the prelude, before the curtain is raised, I let the orchestra convey the terror that inhabits every feeling soul that comes into contact with secret forces—forces that can grow and develop infinitely. The delicate sound of a flute
SOLO FLUTE   CONCEAL WITHIN ITSELF
by itself can describe this secret force, though subsequently it will per-
                                    TURBULENCE
vade the whole orchestra. The resulting sense is one of dimness, vagueness but also of power, born of the renewal of all of Nature's forms; it is the turbulence profound and great, of worldwide blossoming. I wanted to convey this sense in
THE VERY
my orchestration. . . .
THAT IS WHY   THE
Therefore I excluded strings from this melody, for with their crescendos and diminuendos, they are too sensual, too much like the human voice. Instead I
                                    "LIGHT"
brought out the woodwinds, which are more dry, more distinct, less rich in light
PRECISELY
expression, and,∧because of this, I find, more moving.

In general in the prelude I wanted to convey the panic and terror of Nature
BEAUTY,
at the birth of its sacred horror before the midday sun, something like a
SUBSTANCE OF THE MUSIC ITSELF
scream from Pan. The musical material grows, swells, widens. Each instrument
AN INDEPENDENT
here is a part of the great whole.

trayed their own principles. . . . We would be interested in even a simple description of the Paris editorial on *Khovanshchina*. We have heard only that the Sanine[18] *Nightingale* project is extremely interesting, but apparently they are unable to carry it out.

Have you sent the score of *Sacre* to Miaskovsky?

Yours as ever,   V. Derzhanovsky

STRAVINSKY TO DERZHANOVSKY   *Ustilug*
                                                    August 25, 1913

Highly Esteemed Vladimir Vladimirovich!

I've certainly caused you enough trouble with my telegram to Miaskovsky! Forgive me, for God's sake. The fact is that I have got so much work that I alone cannot make the corrections. Therefore I decided to appeal to Miaskovsky, knowing of his ability to find his way quickly in other people's scores. I would very much like to get to know him personally and speak to him about this, for I would like to entrust to him not only the task that I now have in mind, but several others as well. At present I have to proofread the first, second, and fourth parts of my Symphony; after that I'll have to proofread the orchestral scores of *Holy Spring* [*Sacre*] and *The Nightingale*. Perhaps he will still decide to pay me a visit, for there is much to discuss—it is difficult to write about everything in a letter.

Now to another matter. I read in *Muzyka*, No. 141, an unauthorized translation of my letter to *Montjoie!* I must say that it is highly inaccurate, full to overflowing with incorrect information, especially in the part concerning the subject of my work. I have decided to change this translation and send the revised version to you for inclusion in *Muzyka*. The style of this letter disturbs me a great deal. It was written practically on the run for *Montjoie!*; they asked me to give them at least a few words about *Sacre*. Even in French the letter was more decent and coherent than the translation that you published in *Muzyka*. In a few days I shall send the new translation to you. Meanwhile, I ask you not to be angry with me for these complications and to understand that I am very upset with and even blush at the translation from *Montjoie!*.

I am sending Florent Schmitt's long-promised article about the *Sacre*. He sent the article to me a few days ago, and it must be returned to me as soon as you have finished with it. This is the most factual article to appear about the *Sacre* in the current season. Tell Miaskovsky not to be angry with me for not writing to him. Indeed, there is no time.

Always yours truly,   I. Stravinsky

Somewhere or other you asked me about the final chorus to *Khovanshchina*. It was played with great success in Paris three times. The critics, present *in corpore* at the premiere of the opera and thinking that my chorus would be per-

---

[18] Alexander Aksimovich Sanine (1868–1956), theater director.

formed on that occasion (actually Rimsky-Korsakov's was played), denounced it thoroughly.[19] Then they were intentionally absent when my chorus was presented, so as not to become involved in an unpleasant story, for my chorus had been given a special announcement by Diaghilev.

If you wish to familiarize yourself with the music of my concluding chorus to *Khovanshchina,* I will send it to you shortly.

DERZHANOVSKY TO STRAVINSKY   *Moscow*
                                                  August 29, 1913
My dear Igor Fyodorovich,

I was just getting ready to write you when your letter arrived. Let me begin with the question that concerns you most.

Miaskovsky has come to my house primarily to rest and entertain himself, but his visit is opportune in that he will enlighten Saradzhev and me with respect to *Le Sacre du printemps,* at least the first part.[20] He knows it "through and through," and he can present it in a truly delicious way, for he is "mad" about it. All of us here are "mad" about him as well, and because he really came for only a short time, we did not want to surrender him to you. Besides, he is a "touch-me-not," a sweet character with a kind of "mimosa" nature, who will withdraw into his shell very easily. Because of this "misanthropic" temperament, he generally does not like new acquaintances, for they represent a threat to his sense of security. Despite his truly exceptional and great love of everything that comes out of your musical laboratory, he—and of course this is between us—was slightly shocked at your request that he come to Ustilug, for he saw in that circumstance a certain threat to his complete security and independence. Those few words with which I have attempted to characterize Miaskovsky's "personal nature" explain, to some extent, why he was "shocked." I hope, Igor Fyodorovich, that you will not take offense; in turn, I have convinced our dear Nikolai Yakovlevich that in fact there is no reason to "cringe" or sulk. I trust that the sincerity with which I am writing to you about this whole tragicomic affair will persuade you likewise to regard it lightly, forgivingly, and perhaps even humorously.

Now for the practical side of the question. Miaskovsky is above all a composer and by nature, in my opinion, a highly gifted one. Because he is also an extremely prolific author, he has very little time to spare. Despite his love and affection for *Muzyka,* it is only with great difficulty that he manages to give us

---

[19] The premiere of *Khovanshchina* was originally scheduled for May 31, then postponed to June 5, by which time Stravinsky was ill with typhoid. The Paris newspaper *Le Gaulois,* June 9, announced that the first performance of the final chorus ("composed by Stravinsky on themes by Mussorgsky") would take place the same evening. On June 16, however, both *Le Gaulois* (p. 3) and *Le Figaro* (p. 5) announced the first performance for that evening.

[20] Stravinsky had sent his second orchestra score (of Part One only).

some of the little spare time that he does have. But in addition to these charitable undertakings, he also earns his living in the service of the Tsar's chancellery, where he "passes certain simpletons on to the following rank." He actually enjoys this service, if it can be called that, precisely because it does not involve *music*. He cannot stand any kind of lessons, transcriptions, or any other such "musical" work, and he will never do it. But such work takes on a wholly different character in his eyes if it involves your music. In that case he can and, despite grumbling, will do it, and with ill-concealed delight. The only doubtful factor is time. In my opinion, if you entrusted *Le Sacre du printemps* and *The Nightingale* to him (and even more, if you wish), thus freeing him from your Symphony, he would find the necessary time, and do the work as no one else could; I can guarantee that. From then on nothing would get in his way, since there would be no more pile-ups like the present one—which can be attributed to the fact that he is not making progress on his symphony. I can recommend an excellent person to proofread your Symphony, a certain B. V. Karagichev, who is also one of *Muzyka*'s employees. In addition to being a good musician, he is a superior theoretician, and he knows the Symphony because he played it in Saradzhev's orchestra. Saradzhev, who has the greatest affection for you and for all of your creations, also felt, when I conferred with him on the matter, that Karagichev would do a magnificent job. Finally, Miaskovsky knows and respects Karagichev. So if all of these recommendations mean anything to you, you will consider the Symphony question resolved. As for Karagichev, he will be in Moscow in a few days and will stay at my house as usual. I do not know how long he will be here because it seems he has been invited to teach at the Saratov Conservatory, but I doubt that this will happen before the second half of September. In any event, his class will be small, since there are other theoreticians at Saratov.

Now that I have finished with the Miaskovsky proofreading business, let me turn to the *Montjoie!* incident. The man who translated your article speaks French like a native Parisian, is a Professor of Philosophy at the Sorbonne, and a former musician. Anything is possible, of course, and evidently the translation is a poor one. I am very glad that you wish to correct it, but I want very much to avoid any embarrassment to *Muzyka*, and publishing a new translation *of the same article* would be embarrassing. Is no other solution possible? Something, for example, in the nature of a paragraph on the inexactly translated *Montjoie!* letter, in which you correct what is incorrect and perhaps even add a little new material?

What you have told me about the final chorus of *Khovanshchina* is both curious and malicious. Can something be published about that? Thank you very much for your intention of sending the vocal score to me for a short period, I await it; only it is a pity that Miaskovsky is leaving for service in Petersburg and will not be here when the manuscript arrives.

More about your compositions: couldn't you send me the *Japanese Lyrics* with the Japanese text written in, even if only in French letters?

Koussevitzky's performance of *Petrushka* was promised in the summer concerts here, but was not forthcoming. And thank goodness, because this conductor, though knowledgeable, is utterly ungifted.

Well, Igor Fyodorovich, for now I wish you all the best.

Sincerely yours,   V. Derzhanovsky

DERZHANOVSKY TO STRAVINSKY   *Moscow*
                                                      September 7, 1913
Ustilug   *[Postcard]*

My dear Igor Fyodorovich,

Karagichev (Boris Vasilievich) is now here at my house, but for how long is uncertain. In any case, send the proofs in my name, and if he has already gone off to Saratov, then I'll forward them to him there immediately. But when the work is done, should he return the proofs to you or directly to Jurgenson?

I will write to you again, but for the moment I want only to scribble these words about the Symphony on a postcard.

Yours as ever,   V. Derzhanovsky

DERZHANOVSKY TO STRAVINSKY   *Moscow*
                                                     September 22, 1913
Hôtel du Châtelard   *[Postcard]*
Clarens

My dear Igor Fyodorovich,

Where are you now? Is this your correct address? When you confirm this, I'll send you the "Shintovsky" review, which I now have. I sent the returned issue of *Muzyka* to Ustilug, but, of course, I did not include payment.

Karagichev took the proofs with him to Saratov and, in all likelihood, will soon have them done, and done well, I think. G. P. [Jurgenson] feels reassured now, especially since Cooper[21] has taken the Symphony off of the program. Nevertheless, there are still things to discuss, and I intend to do so as soon as possible. All the best.

Yours,   V. Derzhanovsky

DERZHANOVSKY TO STRAVINSKY   *Moscow*
                                                     September 24, 1913
Hôtel du Châtelard

My dear Igor Fyodorovich,

For God's sake, let me know your exact Clarens address, as I'm afraid to send off the manuscript of the chorus without being certain. There are a lot of things

---

[21] Emil Cooper (1877–1960), Russian conductor, friend of Stravinsky from the early Diaghilev years.

about which I would like to write to you. Karagichev has already sent the corrected proofs, but Jurgenson is worried about the Andante and grieved at your silence. Incidentally, I asked Jurgenson about the cost of the proofs, and he told me 40–50 [rubles] for the page. Of these two figures, B. V. Karagichev settled on the first, i.e., 40 per page.

All the best. I am waiting.

Yours,   V. Derzhanovsky

P.S. My wife arrived and sang the *Japanese Lyrics*. It turns out that, in practice, you are right, not I.

DERZHANOVSKY TO STRAVINSKY   *Moscow*
                                                 November 3, 1913
My dear Igor Fyodorovich,

I have not written to you for such a long time, not because I have been busy (for I am always busy), but because I have been ill and burdened by all kinds of worries and errands for *Muzyka*.

Let me begin with a request, an extremely important one to me, and I do not think that it will be difficult for you. On November 24 we are going to have an "Evening of Contemporary Music" here, the program of which you may have noticed in *Muzyka*. Besides two of your songs, among some other works, my wife will be singing several pieces by Debussy. I wish to take advantage of some connections: firstly, mine with you, and secondly, yours with Debussy. Write to him that the organizers of the Evening would be very pleased to have him attend this soirée as a guest, if only for the first part of the concert, during which his songs and yours will be performed. Not without justification, my wife considers herself the best female performer of Debussy in Moscow, or, at any rate, an excellent one. She was also the first one to do Debussy, and after her 1909 performance, people here started to become acquainted with him, so in a general sense our "Evenings" played a decisive role in getting Debussy on Moscow programs. Of course Debussy began to be popular in Moscow only after it could no longer have any significance for him personally, for it was already plainly shameful not to be familiar with Debussy. Nevertheless, he may appreciate our sincere enthusiasm and our efforts. It would be marvelous if he would also consent to play two or three preludes from his new notebook at this soirée, but we would be happy if he would simply come as our guest. This depends entirely on you, Igor Fyodorovich, and on your solicitations on behalf of your Moscow friends. Thus I ask you to do us this kind favor and to write to Debussy immediately, acting as mediator in the affair. Our concert will be on *the day after* Debussy's appearance in Koussevitzky's concert. Along with this letter, I send programs of our "Evening," one copy of which I ask you to transmit to Debussy, since I do not know his address.

What you tell me about Scriabin and your compositions does not surprise me at all, because in general, Scriabin doesn't know anyone else's music. Perhaps this is not due to any particular reluctance on his part as much as to the tenor of life that has developed at home under his wife's influence, and outside the house, under the influence of flatterers and obsequious types. . . . But what is still worse is that the people who write about your compositions do not know them at all. And unfortunately, my close colleague L. Sabaneyev distinguishes himself with particular shamelessness in this respect. *Muzyka* will not have anything to do with these little adventures of his, but everywhere else he blows up a storm. Not long ago I sent a specimen of his writing to Miaskovsky and this was his reaction:

> Your Sabaneyev and our Bernstein[22] would make a wonderful couple; you have sent me his pitiful little exercise in vain; it is boring, disgusting, and nothing more. M. Ivanov[23] himself could not display as much short-sightedness, naive self-satisfaction, and thoughtlessness. Damn him anyway; you did not really think, did you, that his attack on Prokofiev and Stravinsky would mean anything to me?! I find his *"grand-seigneur"* blindness amusing, and it is the sole thing that his writing evinces. . . .

That is what one famous musician has to say about the critical writings of another. I, of course, am completely in agreement with Miaskovsky's opinion. And since I have mentioned him, let me get to the question of the proofs.

N. Y. Miaskovsky absolutely and categorically refuses to do the proofs, but, it turns out, this has nothing to do with the "shock" you gave him; indeed, it is doubtful that the memory of the "shock" even entered his head. The simple truth of the matter is that M. has very little time, so little that he cannot even make order of his own compositions; his symphony has been lying around untouched for God-knows-how-long, and he does not write for *Muzyka* at all anymore. The service is what has worn him out! Furthermore, he informed me that if he were to consent to do the proofs, he would become so engrossed in the work, as he usually does in such cases, that everything else would go to rack and ruin. You cannot be angry with him about this, and to press the matter would be senseless. Would it not be better to try Karagichev, who apparently did the proofs of the Symphony very well, and who, in general, is grossly underestimated? (Karagichev wrote to me, incidentally, that he had not received anything from you. His address is: Saratov, the Conservatory, Boris Vasilievich Karagichev.)

Concerning the Free Theater—it is a curious business to begin with, but for a musician, it is virtually unheard of, since the only musician involved, Saradzhev, is drowned in the dilettantism of the other directors. Saradzhev called me today and told me that he plans to demand that the management give him more power and autonomy, and that if they do not meet his demand, he will leave. Then their musical value will be nil. What makes things worse is that the troupe they have assembled is very weak. Even if *The Nightingale* is three

---

[22] Nikolai Davydovich Bernstein (1876–1938), music critic for the *Petersburg Gazette*.
[23] Mikhail Mikhailovich Ivanov (1849–1927), music critic.

times easier and more primitive than the *Japanese Lyrics,* it is still too difficult for their vocalists. The art of singing is in a slump here in general, but at the Free Theater the vocalists are still on the level of students, and students with very dubious *musical* training at that. You would never manage Tchaikovsky's harmonies with such singers, and they probably could not even sing [Rimsky's] *Kastchei.*

Is it true that *The Nightingale* will not be ready for this season? So the theater itself (Sanine, I think) has reported; the implications for the theater are grave because *Kashchei* (which was dropped because of the conflict with Bessel[24]) and *Nightingale* were the only operas that they had prepared. And the *Fair at Sorochinsk*[25] in its present state is practically an operetta (*"malorossikaya"*[26])! You really must finish *The Nightingale.*

And why is it, anyway, that *Muzyka* and its editors always find out about everything to do with the composer Stravinsky only at the last minute?! That is how it was with the news about *Nightingale,* too!

I should also say that the discrepancies in the translations of the *Montjoie!* article about the *Sacre* amount to *absolutely* and *positively nothing,* and everyone apparently read it with great interest. . . . Wouldn't it be unwise, therefore, to call attention to those discrepancies? They will be covered up in time (in your eyes) by a special *Muzyka* article, and others will never notice the difference.

Tomorrow I shall go out for the first time since my illness, and I plan to see Jurgenson and tell him about *Zvezdoliki.*

Forgive my filthy handwriting; I ought to have typed this letter because I have completely forgotten how to write with a pen.

Don't forget us, and our hopes and aspirations.

Yours as ever,   V. Derzhanovsky

P.S. The *Muzyka* issue about the "Evening of Contemporary Music" contains a picture of you and Debussy together.
P.P.S. I have heard absolutely nothing from Ravel.

DERZHANOVSKY TO STRAVINSKY   *Moscow*
November 8, 1913
My dear Igor Fyodorovich,

If you still have not written to Debussy, perhaps you would be so kind as to tell him the following as well.

Koussevitzky made a mistake with the dates and has now postponed his concert until December 13 (it had been scheduled for the 6th). If Debussy wishes to attend our soirée, have him inform us of exactly which days he will be

---

[24] The publisher.
[25] Mussorgsky's opera.
[26] "Little Russian" (Ukrainian).

in Moscow. We will try to postpone our soirée so that he can be present. Also, will he be alone or accompanied by his wife? We would like to know whether to reserve one seat or two.

Dear Igor Fyodorovich, do not be angry and do not refuse us this favor. We will be deeply grateful. Jurgenson says that he sent you the rights to *Zvezdoliki.*

Yours as ever,   V. Derzhanovsky

P.S. And if your kindness and good-naturedness lead you to act on our behalf, please bear in mind that time is of the utmost importance in arranging this affair.

DERZHANOVSKY TO STRAVINSKY   *Moscow*
                                                    November 16, 1913
My dear Igor Fyodorovich,

I thank you enormously for the various kindnesses you have extended to me and to the "Evenings of Contemporary Music."

Turning now to current problems, let me begin with a few words with respect to the article about the *Sacre.*

Of course I am not advocating that the matter be completely hushed up. You and I agreed that you would write something new in reference to the inexact translation of your article from *Montjoie!,* and you, Igor Fyodorovich, have not yet sent me this new article and, I suspect, do not plan to send it. You are always terribly busy. So what is to be done? Perhaps you could simply make a note of the inaccuracies and clarify the true sense of certain phrases in a letter to the editor. This would be a bit unpleasant for *Muzyka,* but we must also keep your interests in mind. Your most recent suggestion, to run a new translation of the article, would be curious, even comical, and would really make us a laughingstock. So I would like to see the problem solved in one of the two ways first proposed, and not in this last way. I shall await your final decision on this matter.

Now concerning Debussy and everything related: I was not surprised by what you told me about Koussevitzky. I think that in all of Russia you will not find a more absurdly impolite and utterly obtuse character. Koussevitzky is always that way—i.e., a cad from head to toe—toward everyone to whom he "pays money": what an abomination! If we lost the opportunity and satisfaction of seeing Debussy in Moscow because of him, it would be simply awful. My own relations with Koussevitzky are so hostile that we do not even greet each other, but I immediately called Sabaneyev, with whom I am on very good terms, at least outwardly. Sabaneyev is in Koussevitzky's good graces (even participates in his concerts) and will take measures to bring a little decorum to this whole epic.

As for the program of this Evening, it will not be published separately this time but rather in the issue of *Muzyka* that precedes the Evening. For this reason I was not able to send it either to you or to Debussy. Please inform Debussy, to avoid a misunderstanding, that the Evening, which was planned a long time ago, will be devoted to new Russian composers connected with Petersburg. In the past, as you know from programs you have received, we were the hosts for two evenings of French composers—both of which included Debussy—and an evening of Moscow composers. Counting on Debussy's participation, however, we are putting a series of his songs in the program to honor him, *Ariettes oubliées* and *Fêtes galantes,* which should be considered as something outside the program, something special. Incidentally, Igor Fyodorovich, please tell Debussy this as well. Perhaps he will find it interesting to listen to the young Russians, including the wonderful "Forget-me-not" and "The Dove."[27] To feature the *Japanese Lyrics* with piano accompaniment did not make sense, and we did not have enough money for the instrumental accompaniment.

We have postponed the concert until December 11, but it turns out that Debussy will be in Petersburg on the 10th, if I am not mistaken. In order to attend our concert, therefore, he would have to leave Petersburg right after the concert there. This is so inconvenient for him that we dare not count on it. If Belusov can stay in Moscow one more day, then we will put our concert off until the 12th. By tomorrow we will definitely have fixed the date, and I hope to include it as a postscript to this letter.

The Free Theater rehearsed *Pokryvala Peretty* ["Stolen Veil"] this afternoon. This production made a more favorable impression; apparently Saradzhev has attained more independence in that organization. Moreover, the pantomime and singers are not involved in this piece. In spite of having a gifted conductor and a good, though small, orchestra, the problem of poor acoustics remains, for the orchestra cannot achieve a sound of compactness, and unfortunately the orchestra groups cannot blend the sounds into one, each group emitting *its own sound.*

Well, I imagine that I have bored you to tears by now.

All the best.

Yours,   V. Derzhanovsky

P.S. It has been finally and irrevocably settled that our soirée will take place on *December 12, i.e., the day before* Debussy's appearance at Koussevitzky's (which is on December 13).

P.P.S. Would it not be preferable to wait until next season to present *The Nightingale,* when the situation will be better, all the nonsense will have stopped, and the troupe will have been improved—if the theater survives, that is?

---

[27] Stravinsky's Balmont Songs (1911), which were performed for the first time anywhere in this concert.

DERZHANOVSKY TO STRAVINSKY   *Moscow*
                                                November 26, 1913
Hôtel du Châtelard   *[Postcard]*

You are the kind one, Igor Fyodorovich, not I! Thank you for Debussy. His at-
tendance will be very important to us. But will he be turned against us if he
stays at Koussevitzky's mansion? It is too late now to write to Paris, so perhaps
you would speak with Debussy once more in Petersburg (the concert there is
on the 10th).

   Saradzhev has said that he will present *The Nightingale* as soon as you
send it to him.

                         Yours as ever,   V. Derzhanovsky

STRAVINSKY TO DERZHANOVSKY[28]   *Clarens*
                                                December 26, 1913
My dear Vladimir Vladimirovich,

I have just read the latest issue of *Muzyka,* containing the article by your venerable colleague L. Sabaneyev. If it had been the *Petersburg Gazette*, through
its own Mr. Bernstein, welcoming, in such a refined manner, the arrival in
"Belokamennaya"[29] of "the West's greatest contemporary musician" (*Muzyka*'s description of Claude Debussy in its preceding issue), no true musician
would have been surprised. But such an attack in *Muzyka*'s own pages is most
perplexing to the magazine's readers, considering it is the magazine best versed
in life behind the scenes. What is it to me if this article by a *Muzyka* employee is
written in more proper and careful language—and thus, in outward appearance, by a more learned individual—than that of some mediocre reviewer from
the *Petersburg Gazette*? Does this change the essence of the matter? I contend
that it makes it even worse, and the situation becomes all the more dangerous
when characters like Bernstein learn to throw sand in your eyes.* But even
taking Mr. Sabaneyev's article seriously, its unparalleled one-sidedness and un-
disguised partiality are just too obvious for anyone not to notice. Its evaluation
of Claude Debussy's work is not ostentatious but refined, even if negative. Yet
this wonderful piece of writing appears in *Muzyka*, the review which greatly
admires this famous French artist who has recently arrived in Moscow. Of
course, the fact of a complete, impartial evaluation of ONE artist's musical
achievements (Scriabin's) does not serve as a guarantee of such an evaluation
of another's work (Debussy's). *Muzyka* knows this all too well, and that is why
it is twice as difficult to understand: first, why Sabaneyev was allowed to write
about Debussy at all; and second, how such a risky affair managed to find its

---

[28] Stravinsky wrote, in red ink, at the top of this letter: "A copy (Katya's) of my letter
to V. V. Derzhanovsky in Moscow concerning L. Sabaneyev's article in the December
7, 1913, issue of *Muzyka*, No. 159."

[29] "White stone city," the Muscovite's expression for Moscow.

way into the pages of *Muzyka* at a time when Moscow is holding a "Debussy celebration." If only the editors had run other articles in the same issue reflecting contrary views, or else said something to the effect that they were featuring the article, which reflects the opinions of its author, despite the fact that the editors do not share this opinion. But unfortunately nothing of the kind was done, and Sabaneyev will not be the one who will have to answer for this scandalous piece, but the editors, and you, too, Vladimir Vladimirovich. In conclusion, let me express my doubts that with such articles, and with Sabaneyev's contributions in general, your *Muzyka* will win any durable or solid sympathy from the educated musical public of Russia or the West. Keep in mind that in Paris itself there are two individuals, Laloy and Calvocoressi, who speak Russian and read *Muzyka*. At any moment I expect a letter from Calvocoressi lodging "a protest against *Muzyka*." It is an open scandal, for you can be sure that Calvocoressi will not hesitate to discuss "Mr. Sabaneyev's homage" with Debussy. What is he going to think of you, of *Muzyka*, and of those organizations and individuals who are closely connected with *Muzyka*?! I discussed it with Debussy, of course, when he was preparing to leave for Moscow.

No, it will not be easy to extricate yourself from this. I considered myself, not without reason, a friend of your magazine, the welfare of which is of genuine concern to me. That is why I take this awkward and rash step of *Muzyka*'s so much to heart. Forgive me the stern and perhaps too sharp tone of this letter, but rest assured that I am not hiding a stone behind my back.

Yours,   I. Strav.

*This is part of their "learnedness."

DERZHANOVSKY TO STRAVINSKY   *Moscow*
                                                          May 15, 1914
My dear Igor Fyodorovich,

I am just now getting around to writing to you, though I really should have answered you as soon as I received the letter in which, quite rightly, you gave me and *Muzyka* such a "tongue-lashing." I was unable to answer at the time because I was mentally and physically exhausted: my wife had become very ill (and we had the concert to get through, if you recall), and then there were all kinds of problems to cope with, large and small, personal and professional, so that in general it was a difficult time. But, then, is it possible for the editor of *Muzyka* to have an easy time of anything?!

Now it is all in the past, and I will tell you what a blow your letter was to me. Not because it was undeserved (you were quite right), and not because it *was* deserved, for I do not suffer from false pride, but only because it arrived at a very difficult time. But, again, I do not want to go on about all that. I will say only this, that although you were stern and did not take into consideration (how could you, if you were unaware?) the quite exceptional conditions under which our little enterprise makes its weary (limping!) way, yet your letter had a profound effect on me and led to positive results. I explained to Sabaneyev that in a certain sense, and under given conditions, he should maintain the "direction" of the magazine, and that he cannot assume that everything that he writes is his *personal* responsibility. We decided in the end that he will write only on theoretical questions and about Scriabin. This development is a direct result of your letter, and I must now thank you for it. It had this effect on me because I was firmly convinced that, as you wrote, you were not "hiding any stone" behind your back, and that, on the contrary, your intentions toward *Muzyka* were friendly.

Now that I have taken care of this question, let me get on to other things. I never wrote to you about the artistic results of our "Evening of Contemporary Music," and of course you will learn very little from the reviews. The best thing would have been for Miaskovsky to describe the concert, but some of his own work was being performed! Here, briefly, are my impressions. The *Japanese Lyrics* were performed very well,[30] though not perfectly, because it was impossible to go through one more rehearsal with the singer (and even so, the orchestra cost us over 100 rubles). But, I repeat, for a first performance it was very, very good. Praising my wife, some reviewer (I think it was Rizeman) upbraided the instrumental accompaniment: this was completely unjust. I knew the score beforehand, listened carefully, and am satisfied that everything (with the exception of a single slipped harmonic on the cello) sounded exactly as it had been written, and the character of the performance as a whole was subtle and poetic. The musicians (from the Czech orchestra of the former Free Theater) were also the best, and all the talk is no more than the usual grumbling of critics. When something so new is performed, it is not easy to take it in the first time around. I would also like to see how the performers will treat the string harmonics in a natural acoustic [*"zvukoriad"*] when the thing is performed by other groups. The musicians declared right away (I remember that the viola

---

[30] Struve wrote to Stravinsky from Berlin, February 28, 1914: "Saradzhev, Derzhanovsky and company performed your *Japanese Lyrics* in Moscow, having extracted the instrumental parts from the score. Did they communicate with you about this, since they would not have the right to perform this work without your permission, or to copy anything? The new laws governing performance rights contain a clause which states that a piece can be performed without the permission of either the author or the publisher if the program in which it is performed is for non-profit purposes. But even if Saradzhev had this [loophole] in mind, he still had no right to extract the parts. These have now been sent to be engraved, then to be printed, and our proofreader is checking them with the score. . . . Evans, in London, writes that he has made an English translation of your *Japanese Lyrics,* but we did not ask him for one and are not planning to publish them in that language. An English edition is not needed in any case, because demand for this composition has been negligible: in almost a year, since May 1913, eight copies have been sold in England and twelve in France. After the Paris performance there were no more requests or orders for it."

player was very stubborn) that "this is impossible to play." But with Saradzhev, everything can and should be played. The *Japanese Lyrics* apparently had a very profound effect on the public. At least a few people were stunned by the first song, and the audience asked that the second and third ones be repeated. Of course our public is on a somewhat higher level than the usual, but even given that fact, I consider these results extremely good.

Koussevitzky was a bit cold with the *Sacre,* but not nearly to the extent implied in the newspapers. True, it was somewhat spoiled by some unbearable pounding in the percussion section, for which Koussevitzky has a weakness.

As for the "Forget-me-not" and "The Dove," they were evidently less popular. I attribute this solely to the fact that they have not appeared on the program before, and until our concert, the Moscow public had not heard Stravinsky vocal music, except for the two poems by Gorodyetsky[31] and *Faun*—which are a lot easier, of course. However, they asked to have "The Dove" repeated, which has a very difficult tessitura; before there were some very low, almost contralto songs of Miaskovsky's, and my wife was afraid of accustoming her voice to a high register. In short, I think that we can be satisfied with the performances and with the concert as a whole. Of course the critics were dissatisfied, or not wholly satisfied. But critics, with only rare exceptions, always have a hard time of it, both with the works themselves and with the right interpretations of them. By the way, do you know Prokofiev,[32] who was so shocked by Sabaneyev, and how do you like him?

---

[31] Stravinsky's two songs to texts by the poet Serge Gorodyetsky were sung by E. Petrenko in the Evenings of Contemporary Music concerts in 1907. At the premiere of one of them, "Monastery Spring," July 27, 1907, the piano part was played by M. Tovanovich (*not* by Stravinsky, as he stated in his later years).

[32] Derzhanovsky seems to have forgotten that he referred to Prokofiev in a letter of November 3, 1913. Stravinsky and Prokofiev were together in London in February 1913 and again in June 1914. In April 1915 Prokofiev had been with Stravinsky in Milan and heard what had been completed of *Les Noces.* A note about the new piece appeared soon after in the Russian newspaper *Birshovka,* and Stravinsky had been told that Prokofiev was the author. Stravinsky wrote to Prokofiev, May 12, 1915. Prokofiev's answer is postmarked Petrograd, June 3: "I have not seen the column in *Birshovka,* and have had nothing to do with this business. I related certain information to Derzhanovsky, on the basis of which he threw together the *Muzyka* article, as if he had just returned from the first performance. *Russian Musical News* reprinted this in its own botched-up style, which is as idiotic as the paper itself." The letter goes on: ". . . Your Symphony was played here by Malko, very handsomely, and the second movement especially pleased me, as well as many things in the finale. . . . Occasionally I meet Benois, Nouvel, and the aging Nurok, but I have not played the draft of *Chout* for them, nor am I going to. Recently I played the *Sacre* and *Petrushka* 4-hands with Karatygin. . . . My regards to Sergei Pavlovich, Massine, and the Khvoshchinskys. If you are in touch with the Edition Russe de Musique, and if you are as kindly disposed

Next season we are giving three or four concerts, and we naturally do not intend to ignore your work. But how do you regard us? My wife already sings your wonderful children's songs at home, but they are off-limits because of their author's prohibitive inscription.[33] Does it pertain to *Koposova*? We have to know this, and we would also like to know if you plan to give us anything for the coming season. Perhaps you have something in manuscript form? To tell the truth, all of the "contemporaries" here have the impression that our performing efforts have become a matter of complete indifference to you, although my silence may also play a role.

And now, Igor Fyodorovich, a request, if, that is, you are disposed to hear me out in my requests.

At the first performance of *The Nightingale,* a certain Petersburg musician, Asafiev,[34] will be present. I have asked him to write a detailed and thorough account of the opera, even an analysis, for *Muzyka*. Would you find it possible to cooperate by allowing him to attend the rehearsals and by letting him have the piano score and the full score, if only for a short time? Since Emil Cooper needed it recently (perhaps you have a second copy?), I will write to him, too. I would be extremely grateful to you.

Now it remains for me to wish you the fullest success with *Nightingale* and to hope that last November's events will not have put an alienating distance between us.

---

toward me as before, please mention my name to this firm. I have a whole pile of manuscripts, including the Second Concerto, but Jurgenson is jewing and bargaining, and I find him downright repulsive." Nikolai Malko (1883–1961), the conductor, was a lifetime friend of Stravinsky's. Vyacheslav Karatygin (1875–1925) was a writer on music. Basil Khvoshchinsky was attached to the Russian Embassy in Rome.

[33] Stravinsky forbade public performances of his *Souvenirs de mon enfance* when this work was first published.

[34] Boris Asafiev (1884–1949), who wrote under the name Igor Glebov, was a pupil of Rimsky-Korsakov. (*Prokofiev by Prokofiev,* New York, 1979, includes a photograph of Asafiev.) Stravinsky's sister-in-law wrote to him, March 23, 1935: "I've just read Igor Glebov's book about you [*Kniga o Stravinskom,* Leningrad, 1929] which Beveridge [Webster] brought back from Petersburg. Glebov discusses *Pulcinella* . . . and *Mavra*. It's amazing that someone who has had no personal contact with you understood your work so well, and without your help. He explains everything, and he warmly and intelligently defends you before your adversaries, the academic circle in Russia." An invoice from the Edition Russe de Musique, Paris, shows that Stravinsky purchased a copy of this book on October 4, 1930, and his extensive marginalia were probably written soon after. It should be noted that the same invoice lists other books on music sent to Stravinsky between that date and May 30, 1931, as well as several volumes of Bach's organ music, 20 volumes of the Bach Gesellschaft, scores of the *Missa Solemnis, Die Zauberflöte, The Creation,* and a number of works by Brahms, Palestrina, and D. Scarlatti. (Stravinsky purchased many more Scarlatti volumes on October 28, 1935.) All his life, Stravinsky kept his invoices from music dealers and his publishers. He also charged books to his publishers—for example, a copy of *Faust* on November 10, 1930.

Do write a postcard so that I might know how you view me and *Muzyka* now. Did you know that, beginning in the fall, a new magazine will be coming out in Petersburg, [Andrei] Rimsky-Korsakov's *Musical Contemporary,* which, incidentally, has as its task to battle "extreme trends"[35] (but which ones?! that's the question!).

Yours as ever,   V. Derzhanovsky

---

[35] Andrei Rimsky-Korsakov's hostile appraisal, "The Ballets of Igor Stravinsky," appeared in the magazine *Apollo,* No. 1, 1915. The same author had attacked *Petrushka* in the newspaper *Russian Talk,* June 27, 1913. *Firebird* is dedicated to him.

CORRESPONDENCE WITH

JEAN COCTEAU

1913 ∽ 1962

JEAN COCTEAU TO STRAVINSKY   *Paris*
                                      January 1, 1913[1]
Hôtel du Châtelard   *[Telegram]*
Clarens
Lac de Genève

I embrace you[2] and Delage.[3] Friendly regards to your wife.   Jean Cocteau

COCTEAU TO STRAVINSKY[4]   *10 rue d'Anjou*
                                                 Paris
My dear Igor,   *[1913]*

What you call arrogance must correspond to what I call "lucid pride," without
which you would not be aware of my tender disposition toward your work. Enthusiasm is one of the highest manifestations of pride. The stronger it is, the
more it evinces the value that we instinctively attach to our judgment. Besides,
a just pride is the most noble of all honesties, and I detest falsehood.

                            Your friend,   Jean Cocteau

COCTEAU TO STRAVINSKY   *10 rue d'Anjou*
                                                 [1913]
My dear Igor,

You will encounter bad, childish passages in this book,[5] as well as others in
which only your ingenious perspicacity could discover our flame.

    Give my kind regards to your wife. I embrace you, joyful to know that you
are young and lively. Never having known the deceased is a poor consolation for
the death of great men.

                                    Jean Cocteau

---

[1] According to Cocteau, he met Stravinsky for the first time in Monte Carlo in April
1911. Cocteau was there to design posters for *Le Spectre de la rose.*
[2] The "vous" form of address is used by Cocteau until the telegram of December 27,
1913.
[3] Maurice Delage was visiting Stravinsky in Clarens.
[4] A different translation of this note appears in *S.P.D.*, p. 110. Efforts to discover the
letter that provoked Cocteau's reply have been unsuccessful. Stravinsky did not keep
copies of his letters to Cocteau, except those concerning business matters.
[5] *Le Potomak,* written in 1913–14 but not published until 1919, is dedicated to
Stravinsky.

COCTEAU TO STRAVINSKY   *Paris*
                                                    December 27, 1913
Hôtel Châtelard   *[Telegram]*
Clarens

I embrace you, and to hear *The Nightingale* is what I would like for Christmas.   Jean Cocteau

On January 22, 1914, during a visit to Paris, Stravinsky played the first two acts of The Nightingale *for a group of friends, including Cocteau, Jacques Copeau,[6] Maurice Delage, André Gide, Maurice Ravel, Jacques Rivière, and Erik Satie. A day or so later, Stravinsky went to Lausanne, where his wife was in the hospital. He returned to Clarens,[7] but was back in Lausanne on February 3,[8] then left with his wife and family for Leysin, where they installed themselves in the annex of the Grand Hôtel.*

COCTEAU TO STRAVINSKY   *Paris*
                                                     February 4, 1914
Clinique Mont-Riant
Lausanne

My dear Igor,

Amidst the gloomy Kléber orientalisms,[9] I was not able to express my profound pleasure to you. Like the Emperor of China, I had tears in my eyes, and I was proud to inhabit the same world as you.

    Our plan enchants me.[10] The dance *must not express anything.* The [dancer's] body must arouse itself in a burst, becoming another instrument of the orchestra. The anatomy must comprise a visual curve among the sonorous curves, and serve the ensemble.

---

[6] Jacques Copeau (1879–1949), of the Théâtre du Vieux-Colombier, had asked Stravinsky to compose a dance suite, but had not yet offered a commission. Copeau was close to Stravinsky in the 1920s and 1930s, especially when performing in and directing *Histoire du soldat* and when staging *Perséphone.*

[7] On January 26, Stravinsky wrote to Struve from Clarens, not from Lausanne, as is incorrectly stated in *S.P.D.,* p. 106.

[8] Stravinsky wrote to Andrei Rimsky-Korsakov on this date, not on the 16th, as is incorrectly stated in *S.P.D.,* p. 57.

[9] This refers to Misia Sert's Chinese room on or near the avenue Kléber, in which Stravinsky had played *The Nightingale.*

[10] *David,* a projected ballet, for which Cocteau was to write the scenario and Stravinsky the music. The "*David* Notebooks"—four cloth-bound notebooks, 13¼ x 10 inches—are now at the Humanities Research Center of the University of Texas, at Austin. Cocteau inscribed in various colors of ink an (incomplete) maquette of the projected work. In these, one is labeled "*David*—Ouverture," the second and third, "Premier Tour," the fourth "Deuxième Tour." The last notebook contains a page of pen-and-ink and wash drawings—perhaps for a title-page—but no text.

Thévenaz[11] accepts that very humble role with great emotion.
I am going to arrange everything with Copeau tonight at 6 o'clock.

> With love,   Jean

STRAVINSKY TO COCTEAU   *Leysin*
                                                  February 8, 1914

Mon cher petit,

Write to me now in Leysin (it is in the mountains, not far from Montreux),
where I will probably stay until May, my wife having fallen ill with tuberculosis
just after my arrival from Paris. I was obliged to take all possible measures to
arrest the horrible disease at the start. I have been through some very distressing moments. . . .

> Your   Igor Stravinsky

COCTEAU TO STRAVINSKY   *Paris*
                                          [Before February 12, 1914]

Mon cher petit Igor,

Your letter staggered me. I am very much with you in my thoughts. But I cannot believe that there is a real danger, *with the pains that you are now taking,
with your wholesome existence,* and with the gentle air of Clarens and Leysin to
cauterize the illness.

  Mon cher petit Igor, I was so exhausted. I wanted to come and see you and
work with you, but Leysin is too cold for my lungs. Let me know right away
which village on the shore of the lake is the nearest to Leysin.

  I will send my work to you nonetheless, because activity relieves everything. I embrace you with all of my admiration and brotherly affection.

> Jean

Remember me to your wife and children, whom I look forward to seeing again.

---

[11] Paul Thévenaz (1891–1921), painter, musician, pupil of Emile Jaques-Dalcroze. On
December 2, 1919, Thévenaz wrote to Stravinsky from 134 East 22nd Street, New
York: "*Mon cher ami* . . . In a month or two you will probably receive a visit from Cole
Porter, American musician, composer especially of ragtimes. He has a certain talent
and wants to study with you. I told him that I was not at all sure that you would accept
a pupil. But this could be interesting. He will pay anything you ask. He is a very nice
boy, intelligent, gifted, and a multimillionaire."

STRAVINSKY TO COCTEAU   *Leysin*
                                                  February 12, 1914
Paris

Cher petit Jean,

Come soon to Leysin! What a joke that your lungs could not tolerate the air of Leysin, which is designed specifically for the lungs! Come! We must discuss various matters. But remember that I must finish *The Nightingale* first. The *idea* of *David* is too seductive for me to allow myself to become absorbed in it without first having completed my *Nightingale,* which seems at the moment to be coming along well. He sings in the snow and in the sun. If everything goes well, he will finish his song in another month.

                                          Your   Igor Stravinsky

P.S. Not a word *to anyone,* do you understand? Not even that you are coming to my house!

COCTEAU TO STRAVINSKY   *Paris*
                                                  [February 13, 1914]
Mon cher petit,

I have not spoken to anyone, except, of course, to Delage (who will no doubt be with us in Leysin), Gide, and Copeau. Thus even the thing itself is not conscious of itself, only knowing as much about itself as you wish. This is to say that I am evasive in answering the interrogations of those types from the *Nouvelle Revue Française* milieu. To say nothing at all seems preferable to me.

As for Leysin, it is a way of fleeing the telephone and the rest, [to obtain] total silence. Precise answers, please:

1. Is it cold?
2. On what date should I come with the work?
3. Do you want the text immediately, or shall I bring it with me to explain it to you?
4. Is there snow?
5. Could you write to me soon concerning the size of the orchestra and chorus that you plan to use, so that I may inform Copeau?
6. Recent news about your wife.
7. If Serge [Diaghilev] asks about me?

I have a sore throat. I gargle, imitating the nightingale of the Emperor of Japan (what a charming affectation!).

I am finishing my (your) book [*Le Potomak*] and dreaming of salubrious repose in Switzerland.

                                          I embrace you,   Jean

STRAVINSKY TO COCTEAU   *Leysin*
                                                  February 15, 1914

Paris

Vieux,

Before answering your questions, I would like to pose one of my own to you, the
reply to which I need urgently. I have just received an offer for a commission
that, financially speaking, could be very advantageous. Since I am now in a
state of considerable poverty, I must know immediately if the Théâtre du
Vieux-Colombier, in commissioning my work, would be willing to give me a
sum of six thousand francs. In exchange, the Theatre would acquire the exclusive rights for theatrical performance of the piece in France (including Monte
Carlo) for two years. To rent the parts, the Theater would simply have to ask my
publisher, whose address you know.

Now, in regard to these questions, I ask you to act as my representative
with the administration of the Theater and to let me know as soon as possible
whether you can do this. . . . You understand that my answers to your inquiries
about *David* depend entirely upon this new question.

Your   Stravigor

COCTEAU TO STRAVINSKY   *Paris*
                                        [Postmark: February 17, 1914]

Leysin

Mon cher petit,

All hope of escaping my sorrow and ill-health rested upon our meeting in Leysin: your letter torments me. I can only answer you feebly because I have tears
in my eyes. The Vieux-Colombier is the theater of the young, of the contemporary movement. Like the *Nouvelle Revue Française,* it manages to operate
courageously and skillfully without a sou. The Vieux-Colombier was only hoping to revive some old work of yours, or to have two or three short dances, which
you could write like three melodies for a concert. There was no question of an
"oeuvre," but only of a few measures with your name on them.

Mon cher petit, I shall not even attempt to read your letter to them. Never.
[I would be] too afraid of doing you a grave disservice before a group of young
people who themselves are partly responsible for your present glory.

Mon cher petit, if I had the 6,000 francs, I would send them to you immediately, without mentioning the matter to the Theater: such has been my desire,
the hope that sustained me, for the past fortnight or a month. I could already
envisage [Leysin,] the hotel, the skating rink, the snow, *The Nightingale,*
and the piano, etc. . . . I cannot even discuss it; it makes my heart sink
terribly.

Mon cher petit, I beg you to write to me *as to whether you can see any
possible way to arrange it,* to compose, out of benevolence, just a tiny little

something for this enthusiastic and disinterested company, or, if that's impossible, just to convince Serge not to obstruct our project and this marvelous trip. I embrace you in all confidence and grief.

Jean

COCTEAU TO STRAVINSKY

Grand Hôtel
Leysin

Paris
February 19, 1914
[Telegram]

Difficult to see each other right now. I was counting on coming in seven or eight days, and for two weeks. Telegraph or write what I should do. I remain hopeful because I know of your marvelous kindness. With all my heart,   Jean

Stravinsky must by now have received the letter of February 17 and telegraphed a positive reply.

COCTEAU TO STRAVINSKY

Leysin

Paris
February 20, 1914
[Telegram]

You could not disappoint me. I am happy and embrace you. When shall I come? With all my heart,   Jean

COCTEAU TO STRAVINSKY

February 21, 1914

My dear Igor,

So I will be there on March 2. What joy! I will bring the notes for *David*, and doubtless Thévenaz, too, if Dalcroze doesn't detain him, because I would like to indulge in some winter sports with him (if there is still enough snow).

A female theosophist described one of David's dances to me, according to the Magi: it is prodigious. He danced before the Sacred Ark: *The Dance of the Planets*!!! Imagine the music!! What an exalted thing we could create [with that theme], forceful and rugged, as in the era when Jehovah was the ogre and the church sacrificed 2,000 lambs to *please* the Good Shepherd.

With love,   Jean

P.S. I have heard that your wife is feeling better.
P.P.S. Tell me the prices of the "most modest" hotels and which one is the best.

COCTEAU TO STRAVINSKY   *Paris*
February 23, 1914
Grand Hôtel   *[Telegram]*
Leysin

People warn me about a scarlet fever epidemic. Is this true? Would like to know exact date when you will be able to begin [working] with me. Endearments. Joy at seeing you.   Jean

STRAVINSKY TO COCTEAU   *Leysin*
February 23, 1914
Paris   *[Special-delivery postcard]*

There is no scarlet fever here and no Black Death either! *The Nightingale* will not be finished for a month, and I would prefer to see you before then. Why not come now? There is snow, which you would find delightful. Rooms are available in the villa (*pension* is 10–15 francs, I think).

COCTEAU TO STRAVINSKY   *Paris*
February 24, 1914
Leysin   *[Telegram]*

Reply quickly dear Igor. I am impatient. *A bientôt.* Would the 2nd be all right?   Jean

COCTEAU TO STRAVINSKY   *Paris*
February 25, 1914
Grand Hôtel
Leysin

Cher petit,

What luck! So I will leave on Monday. Dalcroze is lending Thévenaz to me; it is still impossible for me to travel alone. I am looking forward to introducing you to this ingenuous intelligence.

I leave Paris, fleeing: the telephone, the world, the papers, the migraine, the fever, the tango, the devotees of Sarah Bernhardt, and a female who has begun to pursue me.

I dread encountering the little scarlet germs. Being a fusspot, I prefer to stay in the hotel. Telegraph if you find a hotel near you, and reserve two very simple rooms.

                        I embrace you.

STRAVINSKY TO COCTEAU
February 26, 1914
[Special-delivery postcard]

Leysin does not have hotels in the proper sense of the word, but only sanitaria, with medical attendants, etc. This should not necessarily deter you from coming, and getting away from pestiferous females, migraines, the telephone, and God knows what besides 606[12] that may be bothering you in Paris. Although I will ask at the "hotel" if they have two vacant rooms, I repeat that it is not really a hotel but a sanitarium. Do you understand that? Go to hear Pierre Monteux's *Petrushka* concert at the Casino de Paris on Sunday. He thinks it will be interesting, this first concert performance.

Embrace you,   Stravinsky

P.S. Two telegrams have just come, pressing me to complete *The Nightingale.* I think it would be wiser to postpone our meeting for a bit, three weeks or so. I fear, *mon petit,* that you do not realize how little time I have; I work on *The Nightingale* all day long. There will be a real scandal if I do not complete it on time.

COCTEAU TO STRAVINSKY
Leysin
Paris
February 27, 1914
[Telegram]

I am coming even though too tired. Will go to Aigle if you prefer and then return [to Leysin] later. Bringing *David* despite everything. Idea too exciting not to apprise you immediately. Telegraph if family *pension* has comfortable bath and rooms for fusspot like myself. Arriving Tuesday. Reserve two rooms right away. Endearments,   Jean

STRAVINSKY TO COCTEAU
Old fusspot,
February 27, 1914
[Special-delivery postcard]

What a peculiar idea to go to Aigle. Go, rather, to the Hôtel Byron in Villeneuve (10 minutes from Aigle and the first station beyond Territet). You will be comfortable there, and for quite modest rates will find all that you need: rooms, baths, hot and cold water, lukewarm women, boys from 8 to 13. . . . Follow this advice and you will be comfortable.

COCTEAU TO STRAVINSKY
Grand Hôtel
Leysin
Paris
February 28, 1914

I take the 9:30 train Monday night with Thévenaz. I must escape, regardless. Reserve us two rooms in your *pension,* at least for a start. We can always switch

---

[12] Arsphenamine, a specific remedy for syphilis discovered in 1909 by German bacteriologist Paul Ehrlich.

[hotels]. I imagine that they would be more indulgent of you than of a transient like myself. *Telegraph the name of your* pension *to me.* What a pleasure to see you and to hear *The Nightingale* again! I often see the theosophical Magi and old Fabre, who knows everything about *David.*

I embrace you,   Jean

P.S. If I arrive too early, don't worry. I'll [leave and] return [when you are ready].

STRAVINSKY TO COCTEAU

February 28, 1914
[Special-delivery postcard]

I must leave for Berlin tomorrow and will not be back until Thursday or Friday, so delay your trip until the end of the week.[13] And consider this fortunate, since we are having frightful weather now, fog so thick that it is impossible to distinguish a goat from the sanitarium housekeeper. Be fair, and don't mistreat the poor woman you mention in all your letters.

Stravinsky went to Berlin on February 29 to discuss the preparation of the score and parts of The Nightingale *with the Russischer Musik Verlag.*

COCTEAU TO STRAVINSKY

Paris
March 6, 1914
[Telegram]

Leysin

I have decided with all the sorrow in the world to surrender to circumstance. Bringing Tartar costumes, for I strongly doubt the Alpine snows [will be] helpful to my fatigue. Places are reserved. Will not interrupt your work on *Nightingale;* I am bringing skis and a book to finish. Will see you during recreation hours. Rooms are provisional, just so that I have a place to go. Will change afterward if it inconveniences you too much. Will be there Saturday morning. Affectionate good-byes,   Jean

Grand Hôtel
Leysin
March 7, 1914[14]
[Hand-delivered note]

COCTEAU TO STRAVINSKY

Pardon my abrupt entry into your room, but I thought that you were alone. Offer a thousand apologies to your wife for me.

---

[13] Struve wrote to Stravinsky, March 16, 1914: "Diaghilev asked about the reasons for your coming to Berlin. I told him it was on publishing business." Stravinsky was back in Leysin on March 2.

[14] On March 11, Stravinsky and Cocteau sent a postcard to Misia Edwards. The composer wrote: "I will send you a [music box] chalet that plays *William Tell* if you will send me a large, very large box of shellfish [oysters]. Igor or Stravigor." Signed, "Stravinsky at Leysin above Aigle."

I came to Leysin with Thévenaz, hoping to find enough snow for winter sports, and though I have taken rooms at the hotel, I will undoubtedly go on to Villeneuve. Be in touch to let me know when I may embrace you. The joy of saying hello to you and of discussing *The Nightingale!* Don't scold me for having come. Paris was too painful for me in that rain, and I was sick at heart. I saw Serge the day before yesterday. He asked me to remind you that he is alive and said that you work like a slave.

Until very soon,   Jean

Writing to Gide, Cocteau described the intensity of Stravinsky's work, and revealed that Jacques Copeau was expected to present David. *Cocteau must have left Leysin after a few days. In any case, Stravinsky wrote to Copeau on March 15:*

Dear Sir,

Jean Cocteau was supposed to write to you on the subject of our *David.* Many things have happened since then, and, consequently, I feel that I should have a meeting with you.[15] I will be coming to Paris for the Monteux *Sacre* concert (around April 5).[16] Would you please be so kind as to inform me whether you will be in Paris at that time? I rejoice at the thought of a collaboration with this group [the Théâtre du Vieux-Colombier] which has supported me so generously.

---

[15] A letter from Copeau to Stravinsky, March 17, proposes a meeting in Paris to discuss *David* "around April 5," the date of the *Sacre* concert there. The present writer doubts that this meeting took place, since Copeau wrote on April 4, from Paris: ". . . I waited for you yesterday. Jean Schlumberger [1877–1962, writer and friend of Gide and Copeau, etc.] telephoned to say that you would definitely be coming then. . . ." On March 18, Cocteau wrote to his mother that Thévenaz and Juliette Wherle had played the *Sacre* arranged for piano 4-hands, adding that *"David* will be something very very important . . . I doubt it will be necessary to join Igor at Jersey this summer." Cocteau also wrote to his mother, in an undated letter: ". . . Stravinsky played something of the future *David* and it is impossible to say how beautiful it was. . . . Spring is forcing its way from beneath the last snow. In the evenings I go to bed at 9, dead tired. . . . *David* will be short (20 minutes) but, as Igor says, this drop will poison an elephant of five acts."

[16] Though Monteux's performance of the *Sacre* on April 5 had been scheduled since January, Stravinsky probably would not have attended if he had not finished *The Nightingale.* On February 8, he wrote from Leysin to Lucien Vogel, 182 rue de Rivoli, Paris: "I doubt that I will come to Paris before May, but if you have occasion to pass through Switzerland, I will always be glad to discuss the affair with you." Vogel wanted to commission a work from Stravinsky (as another of the composer's letters to him from Leysin, dated February 24, 1914, indicates), but nothing else is known about the project, for Stravinsky did not keep Vogel's side of the correspondence.

I hope for a rapid and affirmative reply and beg you to be assured of my ardent artistic sympathy.

Igor Stravinsky

COCTEAU TO STRAVINSKY   *Paris*
                                                    April 27, 1914
Clarens   *[Telegram]*
Lake Geneva

Was unable to bid you a proper farewell. I was worried about your difficulties and so anxious about our dear *David*. I embrace you now, on the shore of the lake, and wish you every success in your Kiev affairs.[17] Your old one who loves you,   Jean

COCTEAU TO STRAVINSKY   *Paris*
                                                    May 11, 1914
Clarens   *[Telegram]*
Montreux

When will you come? Telegraph me [so that I may] meet the train. Have serious advice to give you in secret, from Misia [Sert], even, about *Nightingale*. Embraces,   Jean

COCTEAU TO STRAVINSKY   *Paris*
                                                    May 14, 1914
Clarens   *[Telegram]*
Montreux

Madly want you to come. Just had a serious disagreement with Serge. Crucial (for you) that I speak to you before anyone else does. Above all, do not fail to telegraph arrival. Will take all measures to be able to meet you.   Jean

COCTEAU TO STRAVINSKY   *[Probably May 15]*

Dear Igor,

Thus *Joseph*[18] has been presented. I prefer to tell you about it in person.
    David *will be the great work of the era*. The "Montjoies!"[19] can no longer

---

[17] Stravinsky had planned to go to Kiev for business reasons and to procure books of Russian folk poetry, but he postponed the trip until July. See n. 35 on p. 36.

[18] Richard Strauss's ballet *La Légende de Joseph* was presented by Diaghilev's Ballets Russes, at the Paris Opéra, on May 14 (also on May 17, 19, 21, and on June 4 and 6). Stravinsky seems not to have been present at any of these performances, even though *Petrushka* was also on the May 21 program. *The Nightingale* was performed only twice, on May 26 and 28.

[19] See n. 17 on p. 54.

restrain their curiosity. Canudo has made excuses about his old attitude toward me (prodigious scene).

David *is essential. One awaits* David *as the sand thirsts for fresh, heavy water. I am completing the second* [illegible]. [Illegible] perilous on his own. He works with all his heart and I think that Serge has received a severe lesson in respect to the *"fastes tralalas."*

Be strong. Don't overextend yourself. I have confidence in you.

Jean

COCTEAU TO STRAVINSKY   *Paris*
May 26, 1914
My dear Igor,

The reason I did not go with all of you this evening is that audiences disgust me and that Serge is intolerable. Misia, too, subjugated by him, becomes offensive. I was [hiding] at the back of a loge, overwhelmed by your precious music and by all the memories of Leysin which surround it. The more I witness, the more I detach myself, for the sake of my work, from that which crawls after the Ballets Russes. Poor, divine little *Nightingale* in its oversized cage![20] I embrace you. I admire and love you.

Jean

P.S. I learned, too late, alas, that Madame Stravinsky was in the theater. There is no consolation for having missed her, but she knows what feelings I hold in my heart for her and for you.

COCTEAU TO STRAVINSKY   *Sunday [end of May 1914]*

The misunderstanding between us is stupid. You are a long way from *David,* and I am too, because of the proofs of my book. The matter is this simple. We should have been frank with each other. Silence always complicates. Misia told me about her conversation with you yesterday. Since my book was dedicated to you from its conception, I did not want it to be published while there was a cloud between us. I will come tomorrow morning at about eleven and embrace you among the tennis courts, the roses, and the cockatoos.

Jean

---

[20] Cocteau is referring to the Paris Opéra. A smaller hall would have been more suitable.

COCTEAU TO STRAVINSKY

My dear Igor,

I saw Madame Edwards [Misia Sert]. There is just one thing which you did not understand and which she did not understand. Thus it is important that I insist: *David* does not matter to me. Never speak to me about *David. David* is already banished from my head. *David* is you, the *Sacre,* the *Noces villageoises.*[21] *David* is a moment of us, which was no doubt necessary to our union. What must be retained of *David* is a pact of long and fraternal friendship.

Jean Cocteau

COCTEAU TO STRAVINSKY   *[Before August 11, 1916]*[22]

My dear Igor,

Here are a few much-needed words to put an end to this uneasiness. I have heard that you think I am hostile. My sorrow surpasses my astonishment, for I love you, and I love you in such a manner that I must declare it *once and for all.*

I am not going to discuss *David:* a youthful excess, a fogginess [of vision] brought on by city life and a series of inopportune circumstances, all culminating in the bungling of my first attempt at a work of which, undoubtedly, I was not yet worthy.

I blame myself, and the time, when it was impossible for me to comprehend your attitude. Today, slightly matured and free, I recognize that you were right and that, perhaps without realizing it yourself, you [were able to] perceive a [true] idea by ingenious instinct.

My veneration for you is well known. It will become more so chiefly by my work, which, at the threshold, expresses gratitude for two things: first, for hav-

---

[21] Misia had written to Cocteau at the end of the summer of 1915, from Ouchy: "... Stravinsky provided me with an overwhelming experience. Imagine the most beautiful work of our greatest musician.... Yesterday he played *Les Noces villageoises* for me.... He has opened yet another door, and there everything is permitted, everything is sonorous, joyous, and each note takes you by surprise ... and overwhelms you. He is preoccupied at this moment with another work ... and he will not commit himself to *David* just now.... I delivered your letters, which were not read in my presence. Stravinsky seemed to be very much affected by them and he told me that he would write to you."

[22] *Misia,* by Arthur Gold and Robert Fizdale, New York, 1980, contains a letter from Misia to Cocteau, dated Paris, Sunday, June 1916, saying that "Igor passed through Paris on his way to Spain to see Serge, [who] went to Spain where he has been with Stravinsky ever since. Therefore I asked Stravinsky to support Satie and he was so enthusiastic that he even thought of combining this project with a new work that was commissioned from him by Polignac...." But except for the spring season of the Ballets Russes in Madrid in May 1916, Stravinsky visited Diaghilev in Spain only very briefly in September of that year.

ing detected what lies beneath the surface, despite appearances; and second, for having accelerated my period of moulting with your incomparable dynamism.

You are the one I admire and respect the most. Nietzsche's lines come to mind: "I spare none of my relations with other men, but not for any price would I erase from my life the days spent at Triebschen, days of intimacy, gaiety, of sublime happenings, of profound moments. I do not know the experiences of *others* with Wagner, but no cloud ever passed in *our* sky." I do not recall ever approaching the annex of the hotel in Leysin without experiencing Nietzsche's excitement at the gate of Triebschen: and you see that I reserve a seemly role for my pride. Leysin remains with me as [though it were of] the self, the divine, the fecund, the fatal, the invincible. It was in its warm snow that I shed an old skin, that I began afresh. I think that from this [declaration] all should be healed.

My somnambulism increases in proportion to my task, as I impel myself toward the eye of the mind, as I raise myself toward the unbreathable. The dangers and solitudes are worthwhile only because I shall encounter you. There is no longer any question of human misunderstandings. Everything begins anew. I listen to you and you love me.

My dear Igor, I had to write to you. Never have I addressed you with anything but the voice of a disciple. Alas! No one is worth the effort involved in clearing up these misunderstandings. But you! To think that we would never again be at one, though even at a distance, mars my awakenings and my work.

With love,   Jean

COCTEAU TO STRAVINSKY   *10 rue d'Anjou*
                                                                Paris
My dear Igor,   *August 11, 1916*

I am taking advantage of a leave[23] to write to you. If I were free, I would meet you in Switzerland so that we might re-establish our precious contact. As I was saying to my old friend Errazuriz,[24] "On ne m'a pas brouillé avec Stravinsky, on m'a embrouillé avec Stravinsky," which is at the same time both less and more serious. Gide took me to hear your little chamber pieces[25] at Darius Milo's [Milhaud's],[26] a sort of Beethoven in sheep's trotters. The first piece agitates

---

[23] Cocteau was in the French army.

[24] Eugenia Errazuriz, the Chilean patroness of both Picasso and Stravinsky. The composer had met her in Paris in May 1916.

[25] The Three Pieces for String Quartet. See Appendix E.

[26] Darius Milhaud (1892–1974). Stravinsky was surprisingly hostile to Milhaud in the 1920s, as the letters to Ansermet reveal, yet the diary entry of Jean Hugo (grandson of Victor) for July 5, 1923, mentions Stravinsky—along with Brancusi, Radiguet, Cocteau, Cendrars, Diaghilev, and others—among the guests at a house-warming party for the

and haunts me like certain phrases of the Bible (I thought about the Jewish wedding in Leysin).[27] The second and third evoke Rimbaud: "Cauchemar de Chinoises" and "Après le Déluge." Excuse me for comparing the incomparable, but geniuses can address each other as "my cousin" across the centuries, like kings across Europe.

Nothing is more amusing than the women in beautiful crinoline dresses: Picasso has nicknamed them "women from another world" or "women from beyond." Accustomed to Wagner's leitmotivs, to Schumann's refrains, to Debussy's air currents, and even to *Shéhérazade,* which these women found interminable: they arrived during No. 1; brushed their skirts during No. 2; adopted commanding poses during No. 3 and, finally prepared to understand, *understood nothing.* Even our smart Misia *understood nothing.*[28] She rejects the era and judges impressionistically, with verve but without form, in the same way as Bonnard and Vuillard paint. This highly colored disorder seems strange to our milieu, to us who seek to reconstruct, to concentrate, to put a *book* into a telegram.

I speak frequently about you with Satie and Picasso. Picasso, tender mandolinist and fierce picador: you would like him! Satie, the old angel, who hides his twenty years and invents marvelous music while his friend Claude [Debussy] proves his youth again and "has had enough of these Russians"!!!! Satie and I are collaborating together for Serge, since Serge, from whom I feel separated by an *abyss,* is still the only impresario with genius. Our work [*Parade*] will be ready in October. Will it capture that involuntary emotion which circuses, alhambras, carousels, public balls, factories, ports, cinematographers, etc., emit? The work is too short to be developed in depth.

Milhauds in their apartment on the boulevard de Clichy (see Cocteau's letter of July 24). In their California years Stravinsky and Milhaud became close friends. As described in *S.P.D.,* Milhaud performed a great service for Stravinsky during the war in transferring money to his children in France, and it was to Milhaud that Stravinsky turned when his younger son was accused of collaboration. (Stravinsky wrote to Milhaud, May 23, 1945: "A long letter from [Soulima]. At the moment all is still the same, but I have hopes that this is not going to last forever, and that, once passions have cooled, people will understand that they have gone too far in their zeal.")

[27] This spectacle may well have been one of the inspirations for *Les Noces.*

[28] The concert took place at Poiret's art gallery on July 18, and the program included Satie's *Gymnopédies* and *Sarabande.* Misia wrote to Stravinsky on July 19, criticizing his pieces. He replied on July 24 as follows (in part): "Your letter caused an abscess that I shall pierce with these few lines. . . . I do not understand your rage against my little quartet pieces. Really, my dear, you should be able to understand before falling upon this poor little quartet, composed, do you remember, for you, to be played in your Chinese room. . . . My works are always difficult and demand my personal supervision . . . before they can be played. I can imagine what was played for you?!!! Your brother spoke to me about it, since the pieces had already been performed last winter, and he did not recognize them when I played them for him on the piano."

From left and right (especially from the right) I obtain scraps of information about your work, through airtight compartments of incomprehension, or what is misconstrued as comprehension. [For instance,] a certain anecdote about a urinal in Madrid enchants Picasso and myself: a perfect image of the rococo, clandestine, impudent, and de luxe, but it has been reported to us as if it were a scandal, "to make us laugh." Fortunately, true artists are linked together from one part of the world to another despite a thousand dense layers [in between].

In eight days I return to my post on the Somme where the big cannons, camouflaged by Bakst and the Cubist school, make all of Picardy tremble. We create, we create: there is nothing to console one in this huge factory of destruction but to create, to know that the musicians and painters are creating.

Good-bye, dear Igor. The idiots and the blind change nothing in my heart: it remains intact. I [kiss] your wife and children and embrace you.

Jean

COCTEAU TO STRAVINSKY   *10 rue d'Anjou*
                                                              Paris
Morges   *December 21, 1916*

My dear Igor,

I think of you every day, so happy to have *found you again*, maintaining a definite contact between our hearts, of course. Come quickly. Send news of your wife and children. I embrace you and entrust you with my loyal endearments to the lady Catherine.

Jean

P.S. You had promised me Ramuz's text and a manuscript page of the *Sacre*, which I would like to include in my [*Potomak*].

COCTEAU TO STRAVINSKY   *10 rue d'Anjou*
                                                              Paris
Morges   *January 29, 1917*

My dear Igor,

Serge tells me that you are better, back at work, and sporting a big moustache. The gallant Igor whom we love must quickly reconvert himself into the masterpiece-making machine. Serge looked like a nineteen-year-old, with admirable strength and enthusiasm. You can imagine my joy at seeing him understand all our group's endeavors and winning Misia's support for the *"grand galop."* Misia is slender, very pretty, and very nice. This would be the golden age if it were not for the Boches and for your illness.[29]

---

[29] Intercostal neuralgia.

I embrace you, a thousand tender regards to your wife. I would like you to become acquainted with the Eugènes.[30]

Your old brother   Jean

P.S. *Le Potomak,* like all books, is waiting for Mercury.[31] It is full of you and of the Eugènes. The young people have taken measures so that it might appear; I tried, but of course it is impossible, owing to a list that includes Gide, Maeterlinck et al. They are also waiting. Thus I accumulate manuscripts for posthumous publication. You had promised me Ramuz's text and a manuscript page of the *Sacre.*

Bakst has the appearance of a good, fat snail with his new yellow half-boots; I take him to the Cubist vanguard where he is adored.

I am here now, less sick than after [illegible], but full of rheumatism.

COCTEAU TO STRAVINSKY   *[February 1917?]*

My dear Igor,

Every time it rains I think of Leysin. I was still a bumpkin, but those are some of the most beautiful memories of my life. Send a letter with news and with Ramuz's text. I have finished my work with Satie. Picasso is working. Serge announces his arrival and Misia is fresh as a rose.

The trenches in the north must be beautiful in the snow. My comrades write to me about the heat, while here it is freezing, a coal shortage. I am tempted to join them, but the rheumatism persists and I would be bored in the bureaucracy.

Embrace the children for an old friend whom they do not know. Kiss your wife's hand.

Your loyal   Jean

I am working on *Le Potomak.*

COCTEAU TO STRAVINSKY   *Hôtel de Russie*
Rome
Dear Igor,   *[March] 1917*

I am working with [Diaghilev's] troupe. We speak of you every day. Rome basks in the sun, and the Marchesa Casati emerges from between the old stones like the serpent of the terrestrial Paradise, with an apple in her big mouth.

Bakst pursues the fat women.

I embrace you,   Jean

---

[30] In *Le Potomak* there are two clans, the Eugènes (Cocteau's baptismal name), who are monstrous, and the Mortimers, who are boring.

[31] Cocteau is also referring to the *Mercure de France,* whose director at this time was Alfred Vallette (see Cocteau's letter of July 2, 1917).

COCTEAU TO STRAVINSKY

Morges

10 rue d'Anjou
Paris
July 2, 1917

My dear Igor,

Be an angel and send *by return mail and in your hand* the first two lines of page 64 of the *Sacre,* [*Evocation des*] *Ancêtres,* and, separately, the first phrase of the *Sacre.* These are for *Potomak;* they will be better [in your hand], more alive than if printed!

Dead tired and sick. What is the weather like at the lakeside? If I can obtain permission, perhaps I will come and greet you.

I will write a long letter about *Parade* and the storms. I embrace you. A thousand best wishes and respects to your wife.

Jean

Misia and Eugenia [Errazuriz] entrust me with their kind regards. You will do me a great service in sending the above requested pages to me immediately, because Vallette will now decide whether to publish *Potomak* along with Apollinaire's book.

COCTEAU TO STRAVINSKY

Les Fougères
Diablerets

Paris
July 16, 1917

Very dear Igor,

Did you not receive my last letter? *Le Potomak* is urgent. I am correcting the proofs despite my fatigue and my eyes, which hurt dreadfully. You are not unaware that *Le Potomak* opens and closes with a letter to you, that the Eugènes were mysteriously born out of the music of the *Sacre,* and that in the book I outline what I plan to write about your work one day. I would like to include a line in your handwriting in facsimile. For example, the first notes of the *Sacre,* the first phrase of the *Evocation des ancêtres.* You would do me a great favor by answering quickly because the printers drag on endlessly and do such a poor job.

I feel ill. Perhaps I can get a furlough, but I cannot come to Switzerland, because of difficulties with my passport, which also prevent me from accompanying Gide there, near Jacques Rivière. Perhaps I can come to the shore of the lake, to a neutral zone, near Annecy.

Work—I work. WE WORK. That is the only important thing.

I am so moved, so impatient to hear *Les Noces.* A thousand best wishes to yours. I embrace you as I admire you.

Jean

COCTEAU TO STRAVINSKY   *September 16, 1917*
                                                           [Telegram]
Morges

Learned of cruel waste[32] through Misia. Think of you with all my heart and embrace you.   Jean Cocteau

COCTEAU TO STRAVINSKY   *February 20, 1919*

My dear Igor,

Yesterday I brought your *Ragtime* to Madame Gulon, the engraver. The work will be started immediately. I also saw Picasso, who will do the cover. Come soon to see us all.

                                                With love,   Jean

                                                           La Réserve
COCTEAU TO STRAVINSKY   *Nice*
                                                     September 23, 1922
My dear Igor,   *[Postcard]*

I have an answer to your colored semaphore. How do you like Misia's salon, painted by Sert, on the reverse side?

    I am going to send you some "vocabulary" that you will know how to understand, vocabulary which—as in *Mavra*[33]—leads my best friends astray.

    The "secret" is ours—yours, mine—*people will never know.* Let's keep it.

    Is Eugenia [Errazuriz] in Biarritz? Give me her address. [Georges] Auric is at the Hugos'.

    I would like you to read my article in this month's *Vanity Fair.* I tell the story of *Mavra,* for young Americans who have enthusiasm but are greatly askew in their understanding. Get a copy at the bookshop in Biarritz. In the same issue, [Robert] Delaunay's portrait of you appears in an article by Tzara.[34] I will inscribe the issue to you in Paris.

    I embrace you. Remember me to those close to you.

                                                                Jean

---

[32] The death of the composer's brother Gury.

[33] Ansermet wrote to Stravinsky on September 10, 1921: "I can no longer promise the translation of *Mavra.* Why not ask Cocteau, who has a great facility in versification, and who can work closely with you for fidelity to the music?" Stravinsky apparently did ask Cocteau, but Ansermet repeated his suggestion in a letter of October 13: "I counted on Nouvel to help me place the words of my literal translation [of *Mavra*] under the corresponding Russian words, but during his stay we were always too busy. [Why not] ask Cocteau, who has verbal imagination and a melodic sense?"

[34] Tristan Tzara (1896–1963). From Zürich, in February 1918, Tzara sent some issues of the magazine *Dada* to Stravinsky, in Morges, together with a request for two

COCTEAU TO STRAVINSKY   *Piquey-par-Arès*
                                                              Gironde
My dear Igor,   *July 24, 1923*

I enjoyed the bird festival at Milhaud's but was sad to say good-bye to you. Radiguet[35] dictates his novel to Auric, who turns his back to the sea and types on the
machine. Poulenc and Auric describe the Octet to me. I burst with jealousy. I
would like not to work. Alas, work *loves us* and there is no defense against it.
Are you working? I wanted to send the sketches to you, but the printing was a
failure and will not be begun again until October.

Send a card: tell me things.

The Hugos, Gouy, and Greeley have given me a thousand tasks. Gouy will
come and see you in Biarritz. I am sending you the *Revue Hebdomadaire* containing my brief words for the students of the Collège de France. Your name
was hailed with a salute. *Mavra* should definitely have been written after *Les
Noces.*

I love you, I embrace you.

                                                              Jean

Needless to say, these terribly "modern" types are sulking about *Plain-Chant*. I
haven't finished disfiguring them.

COCTEAU TO STRAVINSKY   *Piquey-par-Arès*
                                                              Gironde
Dear Igor,   *August 2, 1923*

Here is the gentleman who owns the enormous parrot that bit the typewriter.
Auric plays *Les Noces* every night. It is his only exercise. We nag him on with
the typewriting. Since your typed letter, the typewriter is triumphant. It makes
an infernal noise. I embrace you. You must come and see us.

                                                              Jean

COCTEAU TO STRAVINSKY   *September 1923*

My dear Igor,

I must tell you that I plan to go to Bordeaux tomorrow with the Hugos, to dine
at the Chapon Fin. I shall [no doubt] become very ill and repent too late, as you

---

pages of an unpublished manuscript for facsimile reproduction. Stravinsky wrote on
February 12 inquiring about the "pecuniary terms." (See his letter in the Bibliothèque Jacques Doucet, Paris.)

[35] Raymond Radiguet (1903–23), author of *Le Diable au corps* (1923) and *Le Bal du
Comte d'Orgel* (1924). In an article entitled "Thirty Years Ago" (*La Parisienne*, December 1953), Valentine Hugo describes the month of August 1923, spent in Piquey
with Jean Cocteau, Radiguet, and Georges Auric: ". . . Between walks, our young nov-
elist Radiguet carefully corrected the proofs of the *Bal du Comte d'Orgel*, sometimes
aided by Georges Auric, while our musician composed the ravishing ephemeral operas

did. Auric described your menu at Biarritz and your visit to Mme Errazuriz. I am writing this backwards because I don't have a typewriter.

Jean

P.S. Over and over we sing [from *Les Noces*] "Chez ma Nastasie la démarche est légère. Sa pelisse est un drap d'or, Avec un col de castor."

COCTEAU TO STRAVINSKY *Paris*
December 1, 1923

Biarritz

Petrushka with Marcelle[36] at the piano is a marvel. You may rejoice.

Embraces,   Jean Cocteau

COCTEAU TO STRAVINSKY *[1924?]*

Dear Igor,

Run to see the Chaplin film. It is an *incredible marvel.*
   Poor Gautier-Vignal!

I embrace you,   Jean

Until Friday

COCTEAU TO STRAVINSKY *Paris*
[1924?]
[Telegram]

167 bvd Carnot
Nice

Thinking of you all. Marcelle [Meyer] played me her part of the Concerto. She is marvelous. Embrace Catherine, yourself, and children. Ask Theodore [Stravinsky] to be in touch.   Jean

COCTEAU TO STRAVINSKY *Villefranche-sur-Mer*
October 1924

My dear Igor,

I have a slight fever and have not dared to defy the germs. I will be nearby on Friday or Saturday and will give precise news by telephone.
   Many of my prayers have been for the *Gones.*[37] I believe they are well.

Jean

---

that he played for us every day on the piano that came expressly for him by boat several days after our arrival."

[36] Marcelle Meyer (1897–1958) played one of the piano parts in the premiere of *Les Noces*. She was a close friend of Vera Sudeikina.

[37] Nickname for the "Eugènes."

*Cocteau told a friend that in the summer of 1924 he had had a "reconciliation"
with Stravinsky, when they met by chance in a sleeping-car. (Stravinsky
"broke" with Cocteau after the publication of* Le Coq et l'Arlequin, *in the
spring of 1918.) But Stravinsky's letter to Ansermet, August 11, 1922, proves
that the friendship had been reinstated by then. Stravinsky had left Nice for
Paris on May 10, 1925, and, on July 20, he purchased a car. On August 22, back
in Nice, he played his Sonata for his family and a group of friends, and on the
next day, Cocteau came for dinner. In September, Stravinsky played the Sonata
in Venice. On his return to Nice, he heard Cocteau read his play* Orphée,[38] *was
impressed by it, and wrote to Cocteau soon after, inviting him to collaborate.
Yet Stravinsky later wrote on the cover of a file of papers concerning* Oedipus
Rex:*

> *Annoying and useless correspondence with J. Cocteau* concerning the
> first performance of* Oedipus, *in which many people wanted to have their
> say, and which greatly frayed my nerves.*

> **And many others*

STRAVINSKY TO COCTEAU   *Nice*
                                                                October 11, 1925
Villefranche

My dear Jean,

For some time now I have been pursued by the idea of composing an opera in
Latin on the subject of a tragedy of the ancient world, with which everyone
would be familiar. I would like to entrust the verbal aspect of this work to you,
as I proposed the other day. The scenario as well as the setting would be realized through our intimate collaboration. I write these lines to you, impelled by
the desire to establish with the utmost clarity the terms for anything that might
arise from such a collaboration.

    Leaving aside in this letter all questions of division of authors' rights, pub-
lication, etc., which will be the object of a special meeting between us, I would
like these lines to stand as a testimony to our promise of mutual agreement to
keep our collaboration a secret, not only for as long as it lasts, but even after the
piece is finished, that is to say, never to speak of it in any form (books, letters,
articles, interviews, lectures).

    In the case, improbable, I hope, that we do not reach an accord on the
aforementioned business aspect (authors' rights, publishers, etc.) and that the

---

[38] Cocteau wrote to Valentine Hugo, September 9, 1925, saying that he would read his
Orphée to Stravinsky "tomorrow night," but Stravinsky was in Florence on the 10th.
Cocteau had completed the first version of the *Oedipus* libretto by October 28 and sent
it to Jean Daniélou for translation into Latin. A letter from Cocteau to Daniélou dated
January 8, 1926, indicates that the translation was not yet complete, but Stravinsky
must have had the opening lines, since he began to compose on January 3.

collaboration does not occur, I reserve the right to realize my idea in any form. I guard my idea of a musical piece with a Latin text very jealously.

I embrace you,   I Strav

[*At the bottom of the carbon, in Stravinsky's hand*] Voreppe, Feb. 4, 1932. The original of this letter, on which Cocteau has written his name and "read and approved" beneath my signature, is probably at the Edition Russe de Musique, along with Cocteau's contract and other documents concerning the business side of our collaboration.

COCTEAU TO STRAVINSKY

Welcome Hôtel
Villefranche
[*Between January 1 and 27, 1926[39]*]

Let me know as soon as you return: you will have a nice surprise. I have found the trick and finished all of the

masses
boxes

I also have the Gloria and the various greetings of the chorus for each character. Mysterious silence from Monte Carlo [Diaghilev].

Jean

COCTEAU TO STRAVINSKY

Villefranche
[*February 1926*]

[Stravinsky on tour]

Dear Igor,

Catherine must have written to you about the sets. We perceived, with Theodore,[40] that the ensemble looked like a funeral. We all examined it and finally realized that the mistake was in Oedipus' pedestal, which suggested a catafalque. I proposed (and Theodore is trying it) an Acropolis, a rock. This has a double advantage:

---

[39] On Tuesday, January 19, Cocteau wrote to his mother from Villefranche: ". . . Stravinsky makes music in which, he says, each note will be 'curled.' The Golden Fleece, he says. But how difficult! For the third time he has obliged me to begin my work all over again. The only good that comes out of this is that it forces me to relearn Latin. I leave the coast for 8 days (to Paris and Biarritz), during which I must rewrite the ending and correct the beginning. I will perform myself. . . . I will be the speaker who tells the story of each scene. Probably Igor will conduct the orchestra; thus we would pay for [the performances] with our own appearances. Above all, do not show this letter to any living soul. Stravinsky hides our work even from his mother and children. . . . If he knew that I am speaking to you, he would become wild. Diaghilev has begun his season with a 'Festival Igor.'"
[40] Stravinsky had wanted his elder son to design the sets and costumes for the first performance.

1. It is more regal, more savage, less visible than a box, and more normal, thanks to the column that Oedipus climbs and which forms (with him) a temple on the mountaintop.

2. The movements of the rocks and their irregular shadows contradict the architecture, giving it depth and making the chorus lose the appearance of a puppet show.

The white horses were good but too reminiscent of the statue in the Place de la Concorde. I suggest that they be black and outlined in white, like the temple in the sets of Act Two. Thus in the second set, Creon becomes recognizable and the ending unfolds as if prepared in secret.

I think that the innovations will please you. There, the horse is like the sea. Orpheus will jump on the wave as on a wild horse. The secret of our work gives me strength.

With love,   Jean

[*In the margin*] I am making a "mystery" bust for Tiresias, something savage, like the moon. A bearded old man would simply be one more bearded old man—a dead spot.

COCTEAU TO STRAVINSKY   *Villefranche*
                                                        March 6, 1926
Villa des Roses
Montboron
Nice

Dear Igor,

I am happy with Theodore, who has progressed enormously and made the corrections (in which one can best perceive the value of his work) with perfect intelligence. I am starting to work on the details without losing sight of the whole. The King's daughters are exquisite and [Theodore] himself had the idea of the treacherous hand on the shoulder, a superb find.

I have not mentioned what you gave me to understand. I must employ a vocabulary that is constraining. At such times one can respond only with the eyes, a glance, and silence.

Your work is a column which curls itself naturally.

Next to God, only our collaboration could save me from my phantoms. I embrace you with all my heart.

Jean

Before leaving Villefranche at the end of March 1926, Cocteau completed the following rough notes for the sets of Oedipus.

Decor

In the center is a high fountain, symbolizing the head of the old man Tiresias. The arms of the singer go through the orifices and his hands grasp the edge of the basin. The fountain will sing Tiresias' part.

The fountain forms a pedestal and a column rises out of it. Oedipus stands on the top of the capital, dominating all. After the interrogation scene, the column is slowly lowered into the basin and Oedipus disappears. He appears again only in the final scene, blind, wearing a black mask and red gloves.

The chorus stands below and to the right, on three tiers, each higher than the other. The singers remain behind a mass constructed of costumes and masks. Above the chorus, on one of the palace balconies, Jocasta sings. A curtain covers and uncovers her. Creon appears and disappears on the left, facing Jocasta, behind a carriage with prancing horses. The horses, reaching the platform where Oedipus stands, form a staircase, which the Shepherd and the Messenger climb. The Speaker, dressed in evening clothes, moves forward to the foot of these steps. A dark cloud crosses the sky from left to right during the Shepherd-Messenger scene. Another staircase, hidden behind the fountain, allows Oedipus' daughters (represented by one character with two heads) to move close to him on the platform. The masks of the King and his wife look barely human. They are regal attributes.

NOTES ON DECOR FOR *Oedipus Rex*

The advantage of this set is that it has no depth, thus preventing the voices from being lost. All of the action takes place in the foreground.

The decor of the first act is bathed in blue light, adorned with white curtains. The second act is the same, except that the draperies are removed and the new backdrop is black. The Acropolis, which is sketched lightly in chalk on the first-act backdrop, to show off Creon's curtain, appears again on the curtain for Act Two. During the entrances and exits of the protagonists, the curtain is drawn.

Aside from Tiresias, the Shepherd, and the Messenger, the characters remain in their constructed costumes and masks, moving only their arms and heads. They should have the appearance of living statues.

The exit and re-entrance of Oedipus in the second act is effected on the spot by a trap door, as in a fairy tale. When Oedipus reappears, he is wearing another mask, indicating his misery: he is blind.

Jocasta stands on a balcony between columns. A curtain covers and uncovers her. After the flight, one niche remains empty, and the Messenger presents himself in that niche, singing: "Divum Jocastae caput mortuum." He carries a long double trumpet which he raises to his mouth before singing, and during the ringing of the bells, which interrupts the Speaker's lines.

Creon appears at the summit of the rocks. A curtain is drawn back to reveal him near his chariot and horses, pictured on the curtain. He remains there until the end of Act One.

Tiresias is the spirit of truth, the spirit of the fountain of truth. Night falls. The rock beneath Creon becomes clear; it opens, revealing a cave. Tiresias emerges from the cave, a vague statue with veils floating around him which the spotlight follows everywhere. After singing, Tiresias returns to the cave, the rock closes again, and the light is restored.

The Shepherd carries a young lamb around his neck. The lamb, the mask, and the costume form a carapace which obscures the singer, leaving only the arms and legs visible. The Shepherd enters from the left and sings at the foot of the steps, indicated in the drawing. Likewise the Messenger, who has moved, finishes his part from Jocasta's balcony.

The chorus in the foreground is concealed behind a sort of bas-relief on three tiers, made of sculptured draperies. The Speaker, in evening clothes, enters from the left wing and moves forward on the proscenium. He exits after having spoken. He sounds like a lecturer, describing the events in a detached tone of voice.

Prologue

Speaker: Spectators. You are about to hear a Latin version of *Oedipus the King*. In order to spare your eyes and your memory all effort, and because the scenes maintain a monumental, static aspect, I will recall Sophocles' plot for you as the drama progresses.

Unwittingly, Oedipus is in the grip of forces that watch over us from the other side of death. They have set for him, since his birth, a trap which you will see ensnare him.

1. Subject: Thebes is demoralized. Following the Sphinx, the plague. The chorus beseeches Oedipus to save the city. Oedipus has conquered the Sphinx. He promises. (Speaker exits.)

2. Creon, Oedipus' brother-in-law, is introduced. He has just consulted the oracle. It demands that the murderer of Laius be punished. The assassin, hiding in Thebes, must be found at any cost. Oedipus boasts that he will penetrate the mystery, that he will find the assassin and banish him.

3. Oedipus questions Tiresias, the soothsayer, embodied by the fountain of truth. Tiresias avoids answering. He knows that Oedipus is manipulated by the heartless gods. The silence irritates Oedipus. He accuses Creon of wanting the throne and Tiresias of being his accomplice. Angered by this unfair accusation, Tiresias makes a decision. The fountain speaks. Here is the oracle: the King's assassin is a king.

4. The dispute between the princes draws Jocasta's attention. You will hear her calm them and then shame them for raising their voices in a pestilential city. Jocasta does not believe in oracles, and proves that they lie. For example, it had been foretold that Laius would die by the hand of one of her sons, but, instead,

Laius was murdered by thieves at the junction of the roads to Daulis and Delphi.

5. The trap is ready. [Here Stravinsky wrote in the margin: *"Trivium!* Cross-roads! Remember well that word."] Oedipus is terrified. He recalls that on his return from Corinth, before encountering the Sphinx, he killed an old man at the crossroads. If that was Laius, what was going to happen now? The oracle had threatened that if Oedipus returned to Corinth, he would kill his father and marry his mother. He is panic-stricken.

6. The gods' trap is working. The witness of the murder emerges from the shadows. The Messenger announces the death of Polybus to Oedipus and reveals that he was only the adopted son.

Jocasta understands. She tries to push Oedipus back. She stops her ears and covers herself. Oedipus thinks that she is ashamed to be the wife of an up-start.

O Oedipus, so proud to have resolved the mystery! He is in the snare. He is the only one who does not perceive it. Now the truth strikes him. He falls. He falls from on high.

[Cocteau's draft for the Speaker's last narration]

Trumpet. And now you are about to hear the illustrious monologue "The divine Jocasta is dead," the monologue in which the Messenger recounts the demise of Jocasta. *Trumpet.* He can hardly open his mouth. The chorus assumes his part and helps him to explain how the Queen hanged herself and how Oedipus put out his eyes with her gold clasp. *Trumpet.*

Suddenly the atrocious thing becomes clear: Oedipus' trap. The snare worked. Oedipus is his own downfall. Oedipus encloses Oedipus. Oedipus is alone in the night of Oedipus. The gods do not care. The King is consumed.

Then comes the epilogue. Epilogue: the King is caught. He wants to show himself in his trap. He wants to reveal himself to everyone, to reveal to all the filthy beast, the incestuous patricide, the madman. He is banished. He is banished with great tenderness. Good-bye, good-bye, poor Oedipus. Good-bye, Oedipus; you were loved. *Trumpet.*

COCTEAU TO STRAVINSKY   *10 rue d'Anjou*
                                                         May 1, 1926
Dear Igor,

I feel very sad, exiled far from our work. Ask Theodore to send me news, and if there are any new designs, to send the sketches.

Paris tires me. *Orphée* will be done at the end of May or beginning of June. Still more fatigue at the thought of that.

The *Lettre à Maritain*[41] and his reply will go out on Monday. You will be

---

[41] Cocteau inscribed his *Lettre à Jacques Maritain* to Stravinsky, as Maritain did his *Réponse à Jean Cocteau.* During the period 1923–38, Cocteau inscribed at least six of

sent a copy. I hope with all my heart that my letter will please you and that in it you will find renewed proof of my admiration and boundless affection.

No one in the world doubts *Oedipus*. What is amusing is that the Comédie Française has now asked me to write an *Oedipus Rex* for them. I will do it after ours.

Have you been vaccinated? Since yesterday I have experienced atrocious aftereffects (of the Mistral type) from the vaccine.

I embrace you and entrust you with my tender wishes for Catherine and the whole household.

Tell our little artist-painter that I will come to fetch him around July 15!

Jean

[*In the margin*] Could you make it clear to the gentleman that Auric awaits the costumes impatiently?

COCTEAU TO STRAVINSKY   *Paris*
                                                     [December 1926]
Villa des Roses
Montboron
Nice (across from the ancient Octroi)

Very dear Igor,

1) The photo is a masterpiece—we are exalted to the sky; the earth is already distant. 2) Vera's telephone number is lost—send it. 3) The Princess[42] came to see me. She is happy about our collaboration, but it will be impossible to make her sign by New Year's Day. She shows a true affection for both of us. She would like to be in touch with Aron,[43] or with Serge's lawyer, to determine the cost of the staging. She anticipates a drama with Serge because he was counting on a piece that he could parade everywhere and that would enhance his programs. I said that since London he has known what kind of surprise [to expect] : a homage. I also told her about the work, but she understood obliquely,

---

his books to the composer: *Les Parents terribles; Essai de critique indirecte; Les Chevaliers de la table ronde; Plain-Chant; Poème; Picasso*. In May 1979, these were offered for sale by the Massachusetts bookdealer G. B. Minkoff, but without any statement concerning the provenance of the volumes. (Stravinsky did not have any books from his European library with him in California.)

[42] Princess Edmond de Polignac (1865–1943), born Winnaretta Singer, was the daughter of the inventor Isaac Singer, who left her an immense fortune. She married twice, the second time to Prince E. de Polignac, who was thirty-one years her senior and died in 1901. Apart from her long career as a patroness of Stravinsky (from 1912 until World War II), she is best remembered as the dedicatee of Ravel's *Pavane pour une Infante défunte*.

[43] André Aron, artists' agent.

thinking that my Speaker's text would be projected on a screen. I supposed that you must have said to her that our style was cinematographic, and from that she had muddled everything, as is usual with even the most agreeable people of this world. She left me, saying: "It is the principal musical event of our era, thus we will succeed and we will put it on, but not without some back-stabbing" (allusions to Serge, Misia, and company). The Princess did not know about your departure, the beginning of your flu, etc. . . . Send a card to her. She is dying to hear *Oedipus*. The prospect of work and quarrels rejuvenates her and puts a sparkle in her eye.

I am very weak again. I weigh 50 kilos (!) and I'm beginning the Carton diet.[44]

I embrace you. Give my affectionate regards to Catherine, Theodore, Nini, and the girls.

Your   Jean

COCTEAU TO STRAVINSKY   *Paris*
                                                      January 19, 1927
Villa des Roses
Montboron
Nice

Dear Igor,

How is Catherine? I would like *recent news*.

Serge asked me if the work I was writing with you was religious. I assumed my most candid attitude and answered "no." Then he said: "I asked Igor, and he answered 'no,' but I thought that perhaps he wanted to keep it a surprise." Reply quickly and give your opinion of this interrogation. Until further orders, I will continue to deny tenaciously.

With love,   Jean

STRAVINSKY TO MME GEORGES COCTEAU[45]   *167 bd. Carnot*
                                                            Nice
R.P. 10   *[February 9, 1927?]*
10 rue d'Anjou   *[Telegram]*
Paris

Not knowing Jean's address, beg you cable him to come Nice without delay, given my departure soon. Respectful greetings,   Stravinsky

---

[44] Dr. Carton, a celebrated Paris physician. Stravinsky was his patient for many years.
[45] Cocteau's mother.

COCTEAU TO STRAVINSKY   *[February 9, 1927?]*
                                                                [Telegram]
167 bd. Carnot
Nice

Physically dangerous to stop injections and morally dangerous to leave under Serge's intrigued surveillance. Besides am broke and trip very expensive but will come despite all if presence deemed indispensable. Give latest date. Hurry to decide. Affectionately,   Jean

STRAVINSKY TO COCTEAU   *Nice*
                                                          February 10, 1927
My dear Jean,

I am stupefied by Diaghilev's behavior. What indiscretion! He tried at all costs to unveil the surprise I had promised him, an incredible attitude to take before a homage being prepared for him, and a homage is not a business enterprise!!!!, as he well knows. I beg you to tell him exactly what I have just written.

In questioning you about the subject of the work he gives the impression of knowing precisely that you are the one with whom I am collaborating—unless that was simply a provocation. I hope that you did not allow yourself to be taken in. Also tell him that he would do better to answer the letters written to him instead of attempting to uncover the surprise behind my back. I wrote to him in Monte Carlo and received no reply.

And you, Jean, I am astonished that you question the silence. Silence is natural. Do you not feel the necessity for it yourself?

Just this instant I received your telegram. I will send one to you; thus everything will be arranged correctly. I must see you in order to settle certain questions about the general organization (committee, Polignac, etc.), as well as about various publishing details (I have just received the proofs of Act One), the Latin text, Speaker, etc.

Take your injections calmly and recover quickly. Catherine is better and better and sends her kind regards.

I embrace you. Your   I. Stravinsky

COCTEAU TO STRAVINSKY   *[Paris]*
                                                         [February 12, 1927?]
Villa des Roses
Montboron
Nice

Dear Igor,

I confess that I found Serge's conniving very unpleasant, the way that he insisted, telling me: "I know nothing except that the work is purely Russian." I answered that I knew nothing, and that even if I knew I would hold my tongue because I found it in very bad taste to botch a surprise and to show a child the contents of his Christmas stocking beforehand. *He is all Serge.* His niceness: to consider only that; his terrible childishness; and his female side: to destroy a surprise. There is no question of my saying anything. This silence frames your work and greatly amuses me.

I embrace you. A thousand best wishes to all, and to Catherine my great joy to know that she is recovering.

J.

P.S. I succeeded in stopping the cuts in [a periodical] . I said that it was already too short.

STRAVINSKY TO COCTEAU	*167 bd. Carnot*
	Nice
10 rue d'Anjou	*March 14, 1927*
Paris	*[Telegram]*

Zereteli[46] communicates that in view of the increased cost of singers, sum 70 insufficient. Try obtain 15 more. If money left over will return it.   Stravigor

COCTEAU TO STRAVINSKY	*[No date]*
	[Telegram]
167 bd. Carnot	
Nice	

Must await Chanel's return. Embraces.   Jean

STRAVINSKY TO COCTEAU	*167 bd. Carnot*
	Nice
10 rue d'Anjou	*[No date]*
Paris	*[Telegram]*

Zereteli communicates uneasiness concerning delay engagement singers and impossibility of reaching Aron. Telephone him. Cable me news.   Stravigor

---

[46] Prince Alexis Zereteli was the director of Zerbason, the Paris concert agency with which Stravinsky had entrusted the organization of the *Oedipus* production. On March 19, Stravinsky wrote to Zereteli: "Dear Prince, Thank you for your letter of the 17th. I accept in principle, but in fact, as I told you in my last letter, you must address yourself to M. André Aron, who is in charge of examining the contracts and of making the necessary payments. I see that according to the fixed rates for the solo singers and the chorus, the round figure will come to 20,000 francs. We must not exceed that amount. Thus I beg you to see M. Aron as soon as possible, telling him that I am in agreement with the budget that you have presented to me, and that if he is already in possession of the necessary sums, the contracts can be drawn up and signed. In awaiting your good news, I send you, dear Prince, my friendliest greetings.   I. Stravinsky."

COCTEAU TO STRAVINSKY   *[March 22, 1927?]*

Dear Igor,

I have taken so long in writing to you because every day I wait for Chanel. They called last night to say that she would not return for ten days or so; she is in London. I feel that it would be a grave imprudence to write to her. Either she would not answer at all or she would not do so quickly enough, pondering and discussing it with M [isia] S [ert] instead.

The delay is annoying but does not spoil anything. In making this statement I must concede that she could still refuse, or give only part of the sum. I will see Aron and knock on some other doors. You may see that there has been no mistake on my part and that you would also find yourself in front of the same wall.[47] I will arrange things for Theodore this week. It will be necessary for him to send the sketches to me.

I have ascertained with pleasure that if the whole little world of the Ballets Russes knew our secret, it would still remain a secret to the musical world and to all those who do not frequent the Misia–Diaghilev circle.

I embrace you. Affectionately, to all.   Jean

STRAVINSKY TO COCTEAU   *167 bd. Carnot*
                                                        Nice
10 rue d'Anjou   *[Late March?]*
Paris   *[Telegram]*

Urge retain immediately singers who will cost 20,000 [francs], chorus 10,000, four orchestra rehearsals 10,000. If sketches really indispensable telegraph immediately. Will send. Am wary of Chanel. . . .   Stravigor

COCTEAU TO STRAVINSKY   *[March 24, 1927?]*
                                                        [Telegram]
167 bd. Carnot
Nice

Write Princess yourself explaining why immediate sum would be useful.[48] I will see her but a move from you would have a good effect on her.   Jean

---

[47] Stravinsky wrote to Païchadze, March 31, 1927: "Unfortunately Cocteau still has not succeeded in overtaking the people he was counting on for the moneys needed to perform *Oedipus* with Diaghilev's company. I am very anxious about this, given the little time left for the engagement of singers, which cannot be done without the guaranteed sums."

[48] Stravinsky did write, but he must have done so reluctantly, since the year before he had asked the Princess for a large loan in order to reconstruct his house and garden in Nice (his letter of August 14, 1926). She responded from Venice, August 29, 1926: ". . . How well I understand your desire to have a home to your taste in the Midi where

STRAVINSKY TO COCTEAU

10 rue d'Anjou
Paris

167 bd. Carnot
Nice
March 28, 1927
[Telegram]

Polignac replies will give money when other sums have been found. Circumstances creating danger losing singers. What to do? Stravigor

COCTEAU TO STRAVINSKY

167 bd. Carnot
Nice

Paris
[April 1, 1927?]
[Telegram]

Saw Chanel. Asks [that we] consider ways [she might] help us. See her again tomorrow. Am confident. Letter follows. Jean

---

you will find the calm necessary for a musician. I would like to help with your project."
To the new request, the Princess replied promptly from Vichy, March 20, 1927: "Dear great friend, Your letter touched me deeply. Be assured that it is a pleasure for me to contribute to the performance of your great work. . . . Since your departure from Paris I have heard nothing from Jean Cocteau nor of the result of his proceedings. I do not know if M. Aron would handle the practical organization of these beautiful events, or if Cocteau found in his friends the cooperation for which he had hoped. . . . My role would be limited to the guarantee of the $1,500 which you would like to receive for the three performances, and which I would be happy to deliver directly to you, and a sum of 20,000 francs to the office of the committee as a contribution. Diaghilev indicated the dates of the performances to me. You know how proud and happy I would be if the advance premiere could be given at my house. . . ." Stravinsky's answer of March 23 exists only in a draft: "I thank you sincerely for your kind lines which I just received. At the same time as your letter I received one from Cocteau which informs me that Mlle Chanel, absent from Paris for some time, is due to return in a week. I suppose that for this reason the business will drag on a little longer. Cocteau prefers not to write to her but to explain the affair in person. What is especially pressing at this moment is to engage the soloists and the chorus, which, happily, can now be done thanks to your generous guarantee. I should be very grateful, dear Princess, if you would send to the lawyer, M. André Aron, that sum of 20,000 francs which you have had the great kindness to offer us. . . . It is with the most passionate joy that I would seat myself at the piano to perform *Oedipus* with the soloists and the chorus for an advance premiere at your house. I plan to be in Paris the first days of May. . . ." The Princess then wrote to Stravinsky: "Dear great friend, I have been in Paris for a few hours and I want to thank you for your letter of the 23rd. I will give M. André Aron's address to an accountant who will take care of the whole affair. But it would be useless to engage the artists without being certain that the production will be possible. I have still heard nothing from Jean Cocteau. . . ."

COCTEAU TO STRAVINSKY   *Paris*
                                                    April 2, 1927
Villa des Roses
Montboron

Dear Igor,

I saw Chanel—perfect. Misia had told her, "They wait for you, my dear, you hold the purse strings (*sic*)." [Chanel] was disgusted. "Who told you that?" "The Princess de Polignac."

You can well imagine that Madame de Polignac did not say such a thing.[49] I told Chanel that it is precisely because we mistrust the types who indulge in this sort of gossip that we have addressed ourselves to her. She thought the sum very large and asked to think it over until tomorrow. Anyway, she will have Serge establish the exact amount. If you had been there, it would have been like a game of roulette.

You promised to send Theodore's sketches. I have taken care of everything, but I can only speak vaguely about them, and you know how precise Chanel is. Can you say what the singers, orchestra, the whole musical part will cost? I will determine the rest from the sketches as soon as I receive them.

Misia was *atrocious*. She advised Serge not to present a work that has nothing to do with his ballets. She herself admits that Serge replied with grace that his point of view differed from hers and that he would always be proud to present us together. Chanel does not want to see her anymore. I will write to you the day after tomorrow, after my visit to Coco's.

I embrace you and I am confident.   Jean

STRAVINSKY TO COCTEAU   *167 bd. Carnot*
                                                            Nice
10 rue d'Anjou   *[April 3, 1927?]*
Paris   *[Telegram]*

Astonished receive only now reply my telegram of [March] 28. Have explained situation precisely Polignac. [Her] reaction expected. Dare not insist given her reasonable desire to await participation others. If Chanel[50] takes too long afraid affair definitely compromised.   Stravigor

---

[49] Polignac wrote to Cocteau on April 2: "My dear Jean, Finally some news about your projects. . . . I can only participate in this manner: by giving $1,500 and an additional 20,000 francs, but my accountant will not advance any funds [until the remainder is guaranteed, on the grounds that] the project might be unrealizable. You will easily understand this. I know that Madame Sert will give nothing. It is a question of finding 80 or 90,000 francs."

[50] Chanel telegraphed Stravinsky from Monte Carlo on April 7: "Just received your telegram. Leave tonight by boat for Spain. Will be in Paris in 10 days. Think you will be there. Write to Paris. Kind regards.   Coco."

COCTEAU TO STRAVINSKY   *Paris*
                                                April 3, 1927
Villa des Roses
Montboron
Nice

Dear Igor,

I see Coco again tonight. In the meantime I have written a long letter to the Princess so that she will give you the guarantee. (I have been trying to meet with her for four days now.)

As for Theodore's exhibition, the most pleasant and least expensive gallery is still the Galerie Percier at the corner of avenue Percier and rue de la Boëtie. I spoke with M. Leven, the director. He usually asks 1,500 francs, *but to make you and me happy he will settle for less.* (In all the galleries it is customary for the artist to pay for the catalogue.) The two free times are the fifteen days ending May 30 or the fifteen days beginning June 12. Tell me what I should do and send me some photos that he would like.

I will write to you tomorrow after seeing Coco. Be assured that I am preparing myself for the worst and that I act as you yourself would act. To approach Coco, after the frightful business undertaken by Misia Sert against us, requires the utmost delicacy.

I embrace you.   Jean

STRAVINSKY TO COCTEAU   *[April 4, 1927?]*
                                           [Draft of a telegram]
167 bd. Carnot
Nice

Explain Zereteli we await definitive answer this week. Received third letter from him urging we settle with singers.

COCTEAU TO STRAVINSKY   *[April 4, 1927]*
                                                  [Telegram]
167 bd. Carnot
Nice

Dear Igor, Advise you engage singers. Polignac guarantees sum and you will take honorarium from second sum of money. Let me know.   Embraces

COCTEAU TO STRAVINSKY   *29 rue du Faubourg St.-Honoré*
                                                    Paris
My dear Igor,   *[April 5, 1927?]*

I am writing to you from Coco's house; she leaves Monday noon for Cannes (Hôtel Carlton). She would like to see you immediately and will tell you herself the way she thinks this affair should be handled if it is to succeed. She adds that the work will certainly be presented in the form you wish, and that first of all a detailed and exact budget must be drawn up.

For this reason I advise you to send the sketches to me quickly. Attached is the Princess's answer.

I embrace you.   Jean

COCTEAU TO STRAVINSKY
167 bd. Carnot
Nice

Paris
[April 10, 1927?]
[Telegram]

Galerie des Quatre Chemins willing to postpone another exhibition to show Theodore from June 1 to 15. No expenses besides catalogue. Reply.   Jean

STRAVINSKY TO COCTEAU
10 rue d'Anjou
Paris

167 bd. Carnot, Nice
[April 11, 1927]
[Telegram]

Thanks. I beg you reserve Quatre Chemins. Given absolute impossibility of arranging projected *Oedipus* performances I refuse to worry about it and reinstate first promise to Diaghilev.[51] He will present it exactly according to established design. Letter follows.   Stravigor

STRAVINSKY TO COCTEAU
Paris

Nice
April 11, 1927

My dear Jean,

I have just sent a telegram to you from which you will learn that things do not always go as planned and that I have had to surrender *Oedipus* to its own course. In short, whoever wants to play it now has only to address himself to my publisher, who is the owner of the piece.

Since the premiere was promised to Diaghilev a long time ago, and he was arranging his program around that promise, I had to ask him, before anyone else, if he still intended to give the premiere. He answered that he would do it with joy. He will use Theodore's decor and realize the piece exactly as it was conceived.[52] For my part, I renounce my plan to conduct it, not wishing to

---

[51] On April 11, Stravinsky telegraphed Zereteli: "Kindly make agreement with Diaghilev who will present my opera.   I have decided not to stage it myself.   Stravinsky." Diaghilev in Monte Carlo telegraphed Stravinsky in Nice on April 18: "All arranged with Polignac in concert form. I have telegraphed Zereteli to engage the singers and beg you to inform Païchadze."

[52] Within the next two or three days, Diaghilev ruled out all plans for a staged performance. As Stravinsky wrote to Zereteli on April 17: "My dear Prince, I received your let-

weigh down the budget. Diaghilev will engage the performers of his choice (conductor, singers, speaker, chorus, etc.), as any theater would have done it. My role will be limited to the guidance which I always offer when a work of mine is performed. There you have the official report on the affair.

The unofficial report is that I saw that it was clearly impossible to devote myself to the very complicated enterprise of raising the necessary sums, engaging artists, etc., during my pressing work on the instrumentation. On the other hand, and I will not hide this from you, it is really too painful for me to hear nothing but gossip (instead of enthusiasm) accumulating around this work, which, for me, is particularly intimate.

As for Chanel, who wanted to see me "as soon as possible" (according to your letter), she answered my telegram only last Friday, saying that she was going to Spain. She will return to Paris in ten days and asks me to write to her there. Thus you misunderstood her; she did not have the slightest inclination to make decisions that were of great urgency for us. Frankly, I have nothing more to write to her now, except to thank her for having wanted to involve herself in the realization of *Oedipus,* and that, given the lack of time for making decisions, I have had to surrender the production to Diaghilev.

I will write to Mme de Polignac, thanking her for having offered funds for *Oedipus,* but stating that I cannot conduct it. I shall ask her to give these funds to Diaghilev, who, not having planned to stage *Oedipus* himself, certainly will lack the necessary means. A thousand thanks for Theodore's show; he is happier about that than anything.

See you soon, and I embrace you.

Stravigor

COCTEAU TO STRAVINSKY   [April 22, 1927?]

My dear Igor,

I have done *the impossible* in order to serve you. Chanel asked me to see you, and I wrote the letter *before her very eyes.*

You are right. Diaghilev wanted to stage the work, and he has in hand a set

---

ter of the 15th. Diaghilev tells me that he sent you a telegram at the same time so that you would engage the singers and chorus. It is now a question of performing *Oedipus* in concert form, a change undertaken abruptly because Diaghilev does not have the time required for staging this important work in theatrical form, nor do I. Having found the necessary funds for the three performances of *Oedipus* in concert form (which will be spent on these productions), I have given Diaghilev charge of the affair. Thus for you nothing has changed, except that instead of addressing yourself to me, you must address yourself solely to Diaghilev. . . . I do not think that I will be able to go to Russia this year because I have undertaken too many things for next season. A bientôt, dear Prince, I will be in Paris at the beginning of May. Your sincerely devoted   Igor Stravinsky."

painter, a painting studio, etc. I will be the Speaker if he asks me. If he wants an actor, I will look for one.

Madame de Polignac is behind the gossip. She was telling everyone (including Misia) that "Stravinsky wants the money for himself first. I gave the money for him. Cocteau said that Chanel would do the rest" (*sic*). You see how clever that is. I do not reproach her for it: *mondain* people are all the same.

For myself, I do not see anyone, except Maritain and several very young poets. I find this situation marvelous, and I never have to listen to any nonsense. The little that I know about the *Oedipus* gossip came through Chanel, who took it very grandly, and was only interested in the work.

It was very difficult to find a gallery for Theodore. All the dates were already reserved. I did my best, and I think the Galerie des Quatre Chemins is perfect.

I embrace you.   Jean

COCTEAU TO STRAVINSKY   *[April 23, 1927?]*

Dear Igor,

Coco summoned me yesterday, asked me if you were in Paris, and asked how she is to come to an agreement with us about the delivery of the sum. I told her that the arrangement no longer holds and that Diaghilev is organizing it. She told me that she was ready to give the money to you immediately, in case you misunderstood the mix-up with the telegrams (your telegram having been sent to her from Cannes to Monte Carlo by regular mail). Agreed for the Quatre Chemins.

With love,   Jean

COCTEAU TO STRAVINSKY   *Paris*
                                                          April 24, 1927
Villa des Roses
Montboron
Nice

Dear Igor,

I was at the Quatre Chemins yesterday; they are going to write directly to you. Send a note to Chanel. Even before I announced the Diaghilev arrangement to her, she asked when you were coming so that we could *meet and receive the 80,000 francs.*

When she found out about the change, Chanel asked me to tell you that the post office was responsible for the Cannes mix-up, and that, furthermore, you could not possibly think that it was a [illegible] since [you know] that would be unlike her. She thought that the 17th in Paris was not too late. She believes, however, that the presentation by Diaghilev will be advantageous for the work,[53] given the imbeciles elsewhere. As always, her conduct was flawless.

> I embrace you.　Jean

COCTEAU TO STRAVINSKY　　　　　　　　　　　　　　　*Paris*
　　　　　　　　　　　　　　　　　　　　　　　　April 26, 1927

Villa des Roses
Montboron
Nice

Dear Igor,

You had no reason to beg my pardon. Besides, it was only that I find Theodore's sketches admirable and Serge's victory annoying, as he does not want them at any price.

　　I find the oratorio form very noble and abstract. But the entire balance depends on the Speaker. Watch closely to see that I make the actor rehearse at the same time as the orchestra. In his desire that the work have the appearance of a cantata in his honor, Diaghilev is capable of anything.

> I embrace you.　Jean

P.S. Demand that Theodore's *maquettes* be shown and you will poison Serge and justice will be done.

STRAVINSKY TO COCTEAU　　　　　　　　　　　　　　　*Nice*
　　　　　　　　　　　　　　　　　　　　　　April 28, 1927[54]

Dear Jean,

You are wrong if you think that I was begging your pardon in my last letter because I felt myself to be in some way at fault concerning *Oedipus*. I have no

---

[53] This was Polignac's opinion as well. She telegraphed Stravinsky on April 16: "Happy you approve new arrangement, canceling old one. Delighted proposed rehearsal. Am here until 20th [of May]. Polignac." The "rehearsal" refers to a private reading of *Oedipus* in her house. Soon thereafter, Stravinsky telegraphed Diaghilev at the Hôtel de Paris, Monte Carlo: "Cocteau writes that Chanel, returned from trip, offers necessary sums if you would like to stage *Oedipus*."

[54] On the same day, Stravinsky wrote to Zereteli: "Dear Prince, Received your kind letter of the 26th. . . . I will be in Paris at the beginning of next week. . . . As to the question of changing the soloists' terms because Diaghilev is now in charge of the performance, the artists must understand that it is still I who did the necessary groundwork for that performance. Diaghilev has simply undertaken, as a friend, to relieve me of all the organizational troubles which are too time- and energy-consuming while I am laboring to complete the orchestra score. Explain that to them clearly, my dear Prince, and assure them that no trickery is involved, either on my part or on Diaghilev's. Diaghilev comes to Paris any day now, and Nouvel, just arrived there, will relieve your concern about the vocal scores. My publisher and I are doing all we can to prepare the

reason to reproach myself in regard to you. I asked your pardon simply because I was on my way to Communion at the time that I wrote.

And your remark, "Serge's victory is annoying, as he does not want Theodore's sets at any price," must be a supposition on your part, since Diaghilev spent all yesterday evening with Theodore examining his sets, finding them quite good, and giving him advice for the next production. Serge also felt that it is time for Theodore to have an exhibition, and Theodore showed the pictures that he intends to exhibit, as well as the sketches for *Oedipus*.

See you soon. I go to Paris next week.

With love,   I. Stravinsky

P.S. I received the letter from Walter of the Quatre Chemins, and I beg you to give him a call, thank him, and tell him that Theodore will write.

COCTEAU TO STRAVINSKY   *[April 1927?]*

Dear Igor,

I am happy to know that Serge understood the beauty and novelty of Theodore's work, which will stupefy those imbecilic inhabitants of Paris who propagate false news. I am glad to be confronted once again with the nobility that Serge keeps buried at the bottom of himself and which obliges him to [illegible] his heart.

Pardon me, love me well, and pray for me. This afternoon I will arrange the lights for the revival of *Antigone,* but the lighting will not be complete without all of you in the hall.

I am impatient to hear *Oedipus* from beginning to end, and I regret that my work does not take me on the Villefranche-Montboron route. Do not forget to tell Serge that he can count on Coco in case of emergency.

I embrace all of you, and I rejoice at the prospect of seeing you soon and of helping Theodore to hang his canvases.

Jean

The first performance of Oedipus Rex *took place at the Théâtre Sarah-Bernhardt, May 30, 1927. A note in Stravinsky's hand on an envelope containing clippings and articles pertaining to the event states: "Chorus on stage before the curtain, solo singers in the orchestra pit." Stravinsky conducted and Pierre*

---

parts as soon as possible. Have patience a little while longer. . . ." With Diaghilev presenting the work, Lanskoy, the tenor, had asked for a higher fee, but as early as April 19, Zereteli assured Stravinsky that "the agreement with Diaghilev does not change anything so far as the artists are concerned." Answering Stravinsky's letter of April 28, Zereteli said: "I wrote to Lanskoy, who initiated the difficulties, and I explained Diaghilev's role, as you explained it to me. I am certain that all will be in order and that the study of *Oedipus* will begin soon."

Brasseur was the Speaker. Stravinsky also conducted the first part of the program, which consisted of Firebird, *with Alexandra Danilova in the title role, Georges Balanchine as Kastchei, and Serge Lifar as Ivan Tsarevich.*

COCTEAU TO STRAVINSKY

Paris
September 1927

My very dear Igor,

Thank you. Your publisher just gave me the check. [Thus] ends the material side of an adventure of which the spiritual aspect is eternal.

Can you believe that I am going to have a car?!!!!!! Moyses owes me a large sum, and I'd rather he paid me in the form of a modest B 14 Citroën which runs well, and in which you will one day see me arriving at Montboron.

I am very happy to learn that numerous cities are doing *Oedipus*. Daniélou and I both sent our texts. I hope that by consulting both, people will learn something.

I am beginning to find Paris a bit sad. The people are returning. *Americans flood the streets,* among them, old women in police helmets with leather and bundles.

No news from Auric or Poulenc. Honegger's *Antigone* will be done first in Essen, Germany, since the Opéra-Comique was afraid, expecting a repetition of [his] *King David*. Nicolas Nabokov[55] wrote a cantata that I found very touching. Dima D.[56] took such big roses to London that he was invisible behind them. One sees a rose. It opens: Dima D. appears.

Give news of Catherine, whom I love and respect with all my heart. If you have too much work, entrust Theodore to write to me. I embrace you and your whole little world.

Your   Jean

COCTEAU TO STRAVINSKY

9 rue Vignon
May 1934

Dear Igor,

Foolishly, I have again suffered one of those attacks of rheumatism from which I thought I was free. This deprives me of everything and especially of the immense joy of seeing you. The doctor wants me to live in the country, and I am going to hunt for a corner for myself. I hesitate to settle in the Midi because of my mother. I have been lent a car. Perhaps we could meet next week? I want to so much that I would go as far as the sun.

---

[55] See Stravinsky's letters to Nicolas Nabokov in *S.S.C.* II.

[56] Vladimir Dmitrievich Filosofov. See Richard Buckle, *Diaghilev,* London and New York, 1979 (though Buckle seems to have made two Filosofovs into one: Vladimir Dmitrievich and Dmitri, i.e., uncle and cousin, indexed as one).

Madame Ida Rubinstein and her troupe[57] have the air of a family of nouveaux riches in a Phantom Rolls.

I embrace you.

COCTEAU TO STRAVINSKY   *9 rue Vignon*
                                                          June 1934
My dear Igor,

I will definitely be there next Saturday or Sunday. I will telephone. I learned with deep joy that you have become my compatriot.[58] [Illegible]

With love,   Jean

COCTEAU TO STRAVINSKY   *Hôtel de Castille, rue Cambon*
                                               January 1, 1936[59]
My very dear Igor,

I read with emotion the pages of your *Chroniques* that form the monument to our friendship and collaboration. The high tone of the book gives something very special to even the smallest facts that you cite. For me, the number and dates of these are in my heart and the rest must be imagined, like the missing landscapes in *La Princesse de Clèves* . . . and in La Fontaine. In short, your books are not pleonasms to your music, rather they provide a frame for it. This is marvelous.

Happy New Year to Catherine and the whole family.

I embrace you.   Jean

---

[57] In *Perséphone,* Stravinsky's melodrama with a libretto by André Gide, which had just been staged at the Opéra. Ida Rubinstein (1885–1960) had scored a tremendous success in leading mime roles in Fokine's *Cléopâtre* in Diaghilev's first Paris season in 1909 and in his *Shéhérazade* the following year. She left Diaghilev and in 1911 commissioned from Debussy the music for Gabriele d'Annunzio's *Le Martyre de Saint-Sébastien.*

[58] Stravinsky became a French citizen in June 1934. (See Appendix B.)

[59] Later in 1936, Stravinsky sought Cocteau's help in constructing the *Jeu de cartes* libretto. Catherine Stravinsky's letters to her husband reflect his desire for the collaboration. She wrote to him on July 2: "When will you see Cocteau? I so wish that he would fix your subject and would think up what is missing so that you could go on composing freely." On July 25, she wrote: "I hope to receive a note from you tomorrow to find out if you met with and spoke with Cocteau." On July 27, she wrote once again: "What of Cocteau? Mama writes that you doubt that he will prove useful to you or help you in your difficulty. What are you thinking of doing then?" Samuel Dushkin, in Ohio, wrote to Stravinsky on August 2: "I hope that Cocteau is helping you and that the ballet is progressing." There are two further letters from Cocteau to Stravinsky, dated September 20, 1935, and July 14, 1936. (See the chapter on *Jeu de cartes* in *S.S.C.* II.)

COCTEAU TO STRAVINSKY

1260 N. Wetherly Drive
Hollywood, Cal.

Best wishes and endearments.   Jean Cocteau

STRAVINSKY TO COCTEAU

Hugo Gallery
26 E. 55th Street
N.Y.C.

Dearest Jean, Welcome to America. Hope to see you in N.Y. in February while conducting concerts there. How long are you staying in N.Y.? Affectionate thoughts,   Stravinsky

COCTEAU TO STRAVINSKY

1260 N. Wetherly Drive
Hollywood, California

My Igor,

It is quite awful to be so far from and so close to those one loves. I am staying only twelve days in New York, and this quick visit is nearing its end. It would be a dream to see you, and it may just be possible for me to do something about this dream, for the universities have invited me to return, and I shall organize my itinerary in such a manner that I might embrace you in your home.

All my old affection,   Jean

COCTEAU TO STRAVINSKY

1260 North Wetherly Drive
Hollywood

My very dear Igor,

I am working on [*Oedipus*]. I think that the spectacle should not be given too much prominence. The eyes should not distract the ears; the action on stage should simply underscore certain of your grandeurs.

This spectacle demands a visual assault, punctuated by an Italian curtain, which will close when the visual effect has been achieved, allowing the music to continue alone. I do not think that the spectacle (a variety of living tableaux) should correspond to the music. The music . . . should be the reality, the spectacle the dream. The background should be a slumbering imagery. It is essential not to weaken your work . . . ; only the aggressive classicism must be accentuated. I have noticed, as you yourself must have, . . . that the audience [yields] only to force. That force may be expressed in any form and is unpredictable.

Thus the question is not one of a theatrical oratorio, but rather of a spectacle which imposes itself upon the oratorio.

I would like to be certain that you agree with my concept. We [must] address our work to the innumerable spectators and listeners who unite to protest the stupidity of the present. I now live in St.-Jean–Cap-Ferrat, facing Villefranche, which is to say that, little by little, I ponder our youth.

I embrace you,   Jean Cocteau

STRAVINSKY TO COCTEAU   *March 17, 1952*

"Santo Sospir"
St.-Jean–Cap-Ferrat

My dear Jean,

Thank you for the very interesting letter. Needless to say, I was thrilled to learn that you intend to mount *Oedipus*.

Your ideas are perfect, and I support you entirely. The only thing we must avoid, as a consequence of the abstraction, is to go too far, making it difficult for the audience to follow us. But I trust that you will be wary of that potential snag.

I suppose that by "Italian curtain" you mean the one which conceals Creon (the statue), Tiresias (the fountain), and Jocasta (the Queen on the balcony), exposing these characters only when they sing, and closing again when their arias are over.

Will you also do the sets?

Send me a note in reply.

A *bientôt,* I embrace you affectionately.   Igor Stravinsky

COCTEAU TO STRAVINSKY   *St.-Jean–Cap-Ferrat*
                                                   March 21, 1952
1260 North Wetherly Drive
Hollywood

My very dear Igor,

The idea was not explained to you correctly, and undoubtedly I myself did not understand it clearly. . . . I think that the oratorio style must be left to oratorio. Behind the orchestra, I plan to put a narrow platform to be obscured by a curtain which rises (I have abandoned the Italian curtain idea). A rather violent image [will be painted] on the curtain. I will show seven (a sacred number) *comtes scènes,* in the form of living tableaux, which will be unveiled at the moments determined by the music. The illustration will only be allusive, because . . . to repeat the action of the ear for the eye would be a grave error. You know of the attentive and maniacal seriousness with which I approach these things—indeed, I owe it to you. Three dancers and mimes will complement the work . . . along with several strange items of decor. I would like to work on [the opera] night and day from April 20 until the performance. I have reserved all of the material by contract, but if you need it elsewhere, it will of course be at your disposal. . . .

Write and tell me immediately whether my style suits you, because it is too late to conceive of a different one, so we would have simply to modify mine if it is not to your liking.

I embrace you.   Jean

Very dear Igor, a P.S. to my letter to tell you and tell you again that your work is so forceful that it cannot be accompanied by visual pleonasm. Several images must serve to underline the grandeur with a calm violence. No one could comprehend better than you that for us to subordinate ourselves to the same public which condemns us to "galas" is unthinkable. The *Sacre, Parade,* and *Mercure* must not be lost. Neither you nor I myself should descend from the grand epoch.

I love you and embrace you.   Jean

STRAVINSKY TO COCTEAU   *April 2, 1952*

"Santo Sospir"
St.-Jean–Cap-Ferrat

My dear Jean,

A thousand thanks for your letter of March 21, to which I am replying only now because I have been concertizing in Mexico.

Your specifications are very interesting. My only fear is that you will overshoot your initial aim of not distracting the audience from the music.

I agree that the oratorio style must be left to the oratorio; precisely for that reason I feel that to introduce dance or pantomime will detract from the music and, instead of helping the audience to listen to it, will capture all their attention.

Thus I advise you to avoid all dance or mime, which I never envisaged while composing this opera-oratorio.

Be nice and arrange that.

Affectionately, *à bientôt.*   Igor Stravinsky

COCTEAU TO STRAVINSKY

Tuesday, April 29, 1952
[Flight message TWA 922-28]

My dear Igor,

I am in the process of working for you, which is the reason for my absence.[60] I embrace you with all my heart.

Jean Cocteau

COCTEAU TO STRAVINSKY

May 6, 1952

Dear Igor,

You cannot imagine my perfect joy last night at the Vefour.[61] It was like finding oneself again.

I embrace you and Vera.   Jean

To Igor
  with my
    old love
      Jean
        1952
(Athena—column of Oedipus the King)
[*Drawing of Athena*]

COCTEAU TO STRAVINSKY

May 22, 1952

Plaza-Athénée Hôtel
Paris

My Igor,

I did not want to leave your side before my departure,[62] but I must pack my bags and put my affairs in order here in the country.

---

[60] At Orly Airport, where Stravinsky had a short stopover on his flight to Geneva (to attend a performance of *The Rake's Progress* on May 2). Cocteau was working on his staging of *Oedipus Rex*. Of this staging, Cocteau wrote in his *Journal d'un inconnu:* "I have not disturbed the oratorio by Igor Stravinsky by a spectacle or by dances. I have contented myself with seven very short apparitions during my speeches. These apparitions take place on a dais above the orchestra. . . . The masks were constructed to be seen from below, and they became incomprehensible when seen from the audience eye level. Most of the masks were ovoid, with the eyes protruding from their sockets, and, in the final mask, popping like ping-pong balls painted red—what is called *semble-sang* in the Midi."

[61] On May 5, Stravinsky and Cocteau dined at the Vefour, joined later by Mrs. Stravinsky and by Robert Craft and his sister, Phyllis.

[62] Cocteau went to Vienna to read the part of the Speaker in *Oedipus Rex*.

Our recent encounter . . . was one of the most profound joys of my life. I will carry it to Greece with me like a treasure. I will try to see you before Orly. And I entrust you to embrace those close to you.

God keep you. I love you.   Jean

COCTEAU TO STRAVINSKY

Vienna
May 27, 1952
[Telegram]

Palace Hôtel
Brussels

Magnificent singers and orchestra. Performance tonight. Will telegraph tomorrow. Embraces,   Jean Cocteau

COCTEAU TO STRAVINSKY

St.-Jean–Cap-Ferrat
June 2, 1952

1260 North Wetherly Drive
Hollywood

My Igor,

Oedipus Rex, performed in Vienna in an enormous (and absolutely full) hall, enjoyed an *incredible* triumph. After thirty curtain calls, I took the liberty of thanking the audience myself in your name. An aristocracy of the soul pervades Vienna, and a certain grace exists there, something tragic and joyous. I would like to know how your concert went in Brussels[63]—very sad that I was not with you. Did you receive Hindemith's drawing and card? In short, I have barely stopped thinking of you since our encounter. I love you, embrace you, and ask you to relay my best wishes to your wife and the whole family.

Jean

It must be said that the spectacle was [illegible] because the [illegible] of soloists had the power of the masks. Conductor, orchestra, chorus [were] all perfect, noble, and forceful.

COCTEAU TO STRAVINSKY

"Santo-Sospir"
St.-Jean–Cap-Ferrat
Alpes-Maritimes
July 2, 1952

Hollywood

My very dear Igor,

I arrive by chariot from Daulis and Delphi: there I dreamed for a long time of you, of us, of that *sweetest and most beautiful* collaboration *of my life.*

The success of the oratorio in Vienna surpassed the imaginable. I would have had time to take a second bow for you and then another for myself before

---

[63] Stravinsky conducted *Oedipus* in Brussels without a Speaker.

the standing ovation in that immense hall stopped. Send a note to let me know if everything went as well in Brussels as in Paris and Vienna.

Endearments to Vera and to your entourage. I embrace you from the bottom of my heart.

Jean

I have had the masks and sets moved in order not to lose or to destroy them. Tell me about the *Odyssey*.[64]

STRAVINSKY TO COCTEAU   *Hollywood*
                                                      July 28, 1952
"Santo-Sospir"
St.-Jean–Cap-Ferrat
Alpes-Maritimes

My dear Jean,

My long silence following your kind letters and telegrams was due to my return trip here by car, which took fifteen days,[65] and after which I had to catch up on everything that had accumulated during my 2½-month absence.

I was delighted with the triumph of *Oedipus* in Vienna. Musically, it went very well in Brussels and Amsterdam. In Amsterdam the singers were particularly splendid.

I have heard nothing in regard to the *Odyssey* and interpret the silence as a delay or a fiasco. I believe that Powell's last film [*The Tales of Hoffmann*, 1951] was not very successful and perhaps this is thwarting the project.

Also no news of the television film of *Oedipus*. If I learn anything, I will let you know.

Let's not lose touch anymore; send news from time to time. I was so happy to see you again, and in such good form.

Affectionately, as always,   Igor

COCTEAU TO STRAVINSKY   *St.-Jean–Cap-Ferrat*
                                                      Alpes-Maritimes
Hollywood, California   *August 1, 1952*

My dear Igor,

I was overjoyed to receive your letter. I have become reaccustomed to our contact, to hearing and admiring you intimately again. The loss of that treasure

---

[64] This film project, never realized, had been discussed with Stravinsky by Michael Powell, and, on January 12, the composer had read the script, by Simon Harcourt-Smith.

[65] The Stravinskys had purchased an automobile at Flint, Michigan, and they, Alexei

would be disastrous for me. Even more than in my new book, I think of the era of Villefranche and of *Oedipus Rex*.

Francine has stacked up all the manuscripts and set designs on one shelf. I was afraid of the disorder becoming [comparable to that] of a theater. They

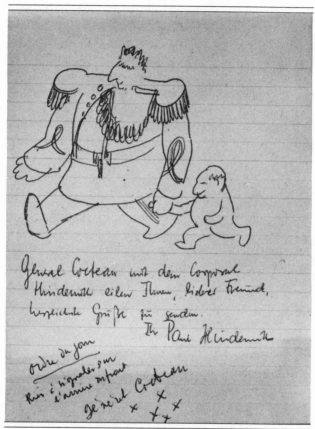

Hindemith's drawing of himself and Cocteau at the time of the performance of Oedipus Rex *in Vienna. (See letter of June 2, 1952.)*

are anxiously waiting to be revived, and if you have no news of the television [project], I will think of some other way.

[*At the foot of the letter*] In the margin of this strange era, I love and embrace you.

Endearments to Vera and the family.   Jean

Haieff, and Robert Craft drove to Los Angeles via northern Minnesota, North Dakota, British Columbia, Washington, and Oregon.

COCTEAU TO STRAVINSKY

1260 N. Wetherly Dr.
Hollywood 46, California

St.-Jean–Cap-Ferrat
Alpes-Maritimes
October 3, 1952

My very dear Igor,

Here we are very much with you through the medium of recording, but I am disconsolate at being so far away and no longer living near the Plaza-Athénée. I would love a few lines of news of you, your work, and your family. The winter has begun its upward climb in a very benign fashion, and we are still swimming. Do you have a new agreement on the *Odyssey*? I have finished my book and a poem. I have made mosaics with profiles here; they have a touch of *Oedipus Rex* about them. But it is impossible to forget our dinner at Vefour and the dinner jacket in which I found you at the hotel, just as you were in Villefranche. Give me the pleasure of seeing your handwriting on an envelope.

I embrace you and Vera.   Jean

STRAVINSKY TO COCTEAU

St.-Jean–Cap-Ferrat
Alpes-Maritimes

Hollywood
October 11, 1952

My dear Jean,

Thank you for the affectionate note. Like you, I am always at work: composing, concert tours (I am just back from Vancouver), and correspondence.

Unfortunately, no news about the *Odyssey*. The promoters are silent. . . . I have heard nothing and I fear that this may be one of those innumerable schemes that fade into oblivion. But I hope this will not in turn silence you. I am always so happy to hear from you.

Have you read Charles-Albert Cingria's[66] very nice article about your stage setting for *Oedipus* in Paris? Theodore sent it to me, having clipped it from "*Carreau,* August/September 1952." It is probably a Swiss publication.

I embrace you affectionately.

COCTEAU TO STRAVINSKY

My very dear Igor,

St.-Jean–Cap-Ferrat
Alpes-Maritimes
October 15, 1952

In a few minutes I am going to take a plane to Germany, where Gründgens[67] will stage and play *Bacchus*. I have been fortunate enough to receive your letter and I leave armed with this token of luck in my pocket. Blind Homer, the mute

---

[66] Charles-Albert Cingria (1883–1954), one of Stravinsky's closest friends. See the correspondence with Cingria in *S.S.C.* III.

[67] Gustaf Gründgens (1899–1963), one of the great directors of the German theater.

[illegible]: all of that seems to me to be in order. A project may fail, but it will always propel another. I am at ease so far as you are concerned. Would you be able to send the article by Charles-Albert? I consider his command of the French language to be incomparable.

Endearments to all of you. I embrace you. I will write to you upon my return.

Jean

STRAVINSKY TO COCTEAU   *Hollywood*
                                         October 25, 1952
St.-Jean–Cap-Ferrat
Alpes-Maritimes

My dear Jean,

Enclosed is a duplicate of Charles-Albert's article—so you may keep it.

I hope that you have had a good trip to Germany, and I do not doubt that, once again, you experienced your habitual and deserved success there. Hope to hear from you soon.

I embrace you.

COCTEAU TO STRAVINSKY   *Beaulieu-sur-Mer*
                                         Alpes-Maritimes
Hollywood   *October 29, 1952*

Very dear Igor,

Thank you, but our Charles-Albert gives a lot of importance to three miserable hisses. . . . Every day I gain proof that the spectacle has deeply excited the people who count.

I presented *Bacchus,* with Gründgens, in the fiefs of German Catholicism. We had 38 encores and a veritable victory. Gründgens was prodigious.

There is the news. Give news of your work, which is alive in my heart.

Jean

COCTEAU TO STRAVINSKY   *Milly*
                                         Stoïse
Very dear Igor,   *May 16, 1953*

I would love to have one of your kind letters. I heard that *The R [ake's] P [rogress]* triumphed in New York. I am exhausted after presiding over the Cannes Festival and the ballet *La Dame à la licorne,* for which I had to do the sets and the costumes in Munich.

It is terrible to live so far from each other, and yet endlessly to be traversing that same Montboron, my memories of which contrast with the [present] distances.

The radio and the recordings do not suffice. This is the anniversary of our meeting long ago in that Paris of the Printemps, in the theater where [last year] I felt so honored to work for you.

    Embrace your wife as I embrace you and the whole family.

Jean

P.S. As soon as the records of *Oedipus Rex* are released, send them to me at St.-Jean–Cap-Ferrat. I will be there in 8 days.

COCTEAU TO STRAVINSKY
Milly
Stoïse

Very dear Igor,
June 2, 1953

I am writing to you now after having listened to the recording of *Oedipus Rex*. It has renewed memories in the service of Villefranche (from where, moreover, the record was sent): Villefranche, Montboron, the Champs-Elysées, Vienna. For the first time I heard you, I heard us, from a distance. I embrace you and entrust you to distribute my loyal endearments around you. The record came to me here, like a treasure.

To you, forever,   Jean

COCTEAU TO STRAVINSKY
St.-Jean–Cap-Ferrat
August 14, 1954

My very dear Igor,

I have been very ill. The death of Charles-Albert [Cingria] stunned me. That of Colette is like a little blue flame that has run out of fuel. She suffered. She will not suffer any more. Charles-Albert's death was a terrible surprise. It is difficult to imagine such an eye closed. This must have given you much pain—Gagne-bin,[68] Charles-Albert—all of our Swiss friends returning to the water of the lake. I do not stop thinking of you and of them.[69]

I embrace you.   Jean

COCTEAU TO STRAVINSKY
Claridge's
London
November 19, 1959

Hotel Ritz
London

Very dear Igor,

You gave me great joy with the *Oedipus* at Festival Hall. I am very sad to see so little of you, but I must finish the frescoes of Notre Dame de France and I must be in Paris, where I have proposed Jean Rostand for the Academy.

    I embrace you and Vera with all my heart . . .

Jean

---

[68] See n. 198 on p. 192.

[69] Stravinsky answered on August 18, but did not keep a copy of his letter.

COCTEAU TO STRAVINSKY   *"Santo-Sospir"*
                                             St.-Jean–Cap-Ferrat
My dear Igor,   *August 12, 1962*

By a gross error, the drawings [for the 1952 *Oedipus Rex*] were left in Neuilly. As soon as I return there, I shall send them to you, and if someone can locate them for me, I will have them delivered here [beforehand] in order not to make you wait. Every day augments my affection and respect for you.

                                             Jean

COCTEAU TO STRAVINSKY   *St.-Jean–Cap-Ferrat*
                                             December 28, 1962
Tender wishes. Faithfully,   Jean Cocteau   *[Cable]*

On December 21, 1963, Stravinsky answered a request from Paris to write a paragraph on the death of Cocteau:

For some time we have been aware that Jean Cocteau's life was endangered by a heart condition, yet his death, though not a complete surprise, was a terrible shock, nevertheless. I grieve the passing of this old friend, this incomparably brilliant being, brilliant in his conversation, in his books, drawings, extraordinarily penetrating in theater and film. It is hard, very hard for me to accept his death.

The composer recorded his message and it was broadcast in France on January 20, 1964.

LETTERS TO

ERNEST ANSERMET

1914 ❧ *1967*

STRAVINSKY TO ERNEST ANSERMET   *Leysin*
                                              March 28, 1914
Montreux   *[Postcard]*

Dear friend,

I have finally finished *The Nightingale* and would like you to copy the last pages
(21–27) so that I can get them on Monday morning when I see you. I will leave
for Paris on Monday at 2:00. I will be happy to see you at the *Sacre* dress rehearsal on April 4, concert on the 5th.[1] I will take care of the piano.

                                      Your   Igor Stravinsky

My sister [-in-law][2] will deliver the last pages of *The Nightingale* to you.

STRAVINSKY TO ANSERMET   *Morges*
                                             February 14, 1916
[New York]

My dear Ansermet,

Thank you for the telegram. And what a success, triumph, etc.!!![3] Here in Europe, too. So much the better. I have just received a letter from Madame
Khvoshchinskaya[4] in Rome, telling me that Toscanini conducted *Petrushka*
there, at the Augusteo, with great success.[5] Can you imagine, that enormous
room, seating an audience of thousands, was so full that to find a single seat
was impossible! I do hope to go there. To hear Toscanini conduct my work

---

[1] The concert performance of *Le Sacre du printemps* conducted by Monteux on April
5, 1914, at the Casino de Paris. On April 24, Ansermet wrote to Ramuz: ". . . I had
hoped to see you in Paris, where I leaped at the opportunity of hearing Stravinsky's *Le
Sacre du printemps* conducted by Monteux, but I passed through so quickly that I did
not find time even to cross the Seine. I want only to recommend that you go to the second performance, this Sunday. Make reservations in advance (very good bargain at 50
centimes . . .), because there will be a mob. It is at the Casino de Paris, rue Clichy."
(From *C.-F. Ramuz, ses amis et son temps*, Volume V, 1911–18, Paris, 1969.)
[2] Lyudmila Beliankina.
[3] Ansermet had cabled from Boston on February 10: "You had colossal success. Send
piano pieces and terms publication." The success in America to which Ansermet refers
is of the Ballets Russes performances of *Firebird* and *Petrushka*. In a letter to the Edition Russe in Moscow, June 27, 1916, Stravinsky says that Diaghilev had performed
Petrushka in America "approximately thirty times from January to May 1916," and
that he had "agreed to the conditions quoted to me in your telegram of April 13 concerning the extension of exclusive rights to *Petrushka* for one year."
[4] The wife of Basil Khvoshchinsky, of the Russian Embassy in Rome.
[5] Toscanini conducted *Petrushka* at the Augusteo, Sunday, February 6, on a program
with Beethoven's Sixth Symphony, a symphonic poem by Sibelius, and the Overture in
C by Foroni. Toscanini repeated *Petrushka* on February 9 at the Augusteo, on a different program.

would interest me immensely. He has stated that he plans to present the *Sacre* next year, but we shall see what happens.

Now, apropos of the edition of my little pieces for piano.[6] Was it the Marche, Valse, and Polka that you heard? If so, please inform the publisher that these pieces are for 4-hands (hence the "2da"*), [and are not] composed for "someone who plays the piano badly" (!!?). I will send the 2-hand versions as well. Also, tell the publisher that these pieces were intended for the atmosphere of a music hall or café-concert, and because of this I have orchestrated them for a small ensemble (as you know), and I will send these scores as well. I ask 25,000 Swiss francs (if the Swiss franc is higher than the French franc at the time that the money is paid) for the right to perform these pieces in a music hall, café-concert, or another public place.** I must explain that the rights that he buys from me do not include those of mechanical reproduction. This will have to be dealt with separately.

For the moment, I close my letter with best wishes for your success and thank you warmly and fraternally for all the work that you must have done with my music.

Cordially yours,   Igor Stravinsky

*Left hand in the bass
**Within the limits provided by the law—i.e., if the law entitles the publisher to some of the author's rights, then of course the publisher must take them.

When do you return?

And the trip to South America?[7]

I will send my pieces with Mrs. Bolm,[8] who leaves for America on the *Lafayette* March 12. It would be very kind of you to send the most important newspaper clippings.

Tell Diaghilev that he should send the money for the month of March *directly* to Switzerland, and cable beforehand. It is really distressing to lose on the French-Swiss exchange. Bolm sends money to his wife through the Bank of Zürich. Ask him about it, since this is the only bank that receives money by cable from America. The money that you mentioned has also diminished appreciably. Your wife should be aware of this.   I Str.

---

[6] The Three Easy Pieces for piano 4-hands, composed 1914–15, published by Adolphe Henn in 1919, then by J. & W. Chester. On April 7, Ansermet cabled acknowledgment of the receipt of the music.

[7] This Ballets Russes tour took place in the summer of 1917. Diaghilev did not go but entrusted the direction to Serge Grigoriev, the company manager, and to Ansermet. The contract for the engagement specified that the corps de ballet must make the journey to Rio de Janeiro on an English boat, but Diaghilev, fearing submarine attack, chose a neutral Spanish boat, which sailed to Buenos Aires. Many difficulties resulted from this decision.

[8] Beatrice Bolm, wife of the dancer and choreographer Adolph Bolm (1884–1951). She was Stravinsky's secretary in the early 1940s.

Also give Diaghilev best wishes from Jurgenson, publisher of *Firebird*. Try to arrange to send the money for March, as Diaghilev promised, through the Bank of Zürich, adding, if you wish, the money for your wife.

STRAVINSKY TO ANSERMET   *[Morges]*
                                                 [After March 14, 1916]
[New York]   *[Postcard]*

My friend,

Do not give anyone the three music-hall pieces that I sent through Madame Bolm. If someone asks to examine these pieces with an eventual production in mind, I want you to ask for my authorization first.

I embrace you.   I Stravinsky

STRAVINSKY TO ANSERMET   *[Postmark: Morges]*
                                           Friday [December 28, 1917]
19 avenue Druey
Lausanne

My friend,

I am in bed. The doctor suspects pleurisy, but this has not yet been confirmed. I would very much like to see you. If you have a free afternoon, take the 2:35 train. You can always return on the express at 6:00.

Have you spoken to Bartholoni?[9] You have told me nothing.

Yours,   I Stravinsky

[*Note in Stravinsky's hand on a letter from Ansermet*]

Accounting of payments according to the contract of July 1917.

	15–20 August	8 thousand
1917	1–5 October	4 thousand
	15 December	2 thousand
	1 March	8 thousand
1918	1 May	2 thousand
	1 June	2,500

All in Swiss francs

[Diaghilev's signature]

---

[9] Jean Bartholoni, oil millionaire, whose family founded the Geneva Conservatory of Music. He purchased the full-score manuscript of *Firebird* from Stravinsky for 8,000 francs. See *S.P.D.*, p. 623, n. 288.

STRAVINSKY TO ANSERMET   *Morges*
                                                      April 12, 1919
Dear friend,

Now, after the dress rehearsal of the new *Firebird* Suite,[10] which happens to
coincide with the end of the concert season of the Orchestre de la Suisse Romande,[11] I must tell you of my appreciation for the admirable spirit of understanding which you have demonstrated in the performance of my new score, as
well as for your *general comprehension of contemporary music.* I wish that
more people were aware of the effort behind the execution of a work such as the
one you have succeeded in realizing this winter. I also wish that people were
aware that the kind of sensibility which contemporary music demands is in no
way contradictory to that required for music of the past. On the contrary, the
misunderstanding of contemporary efforts is actually injurious to comparable
ones attempted under similar circumstances in the past.

Be confident, dear friend: neither music nor you will be stopped. I am very
sure that you know this yourself; but, thinking that the disinterested testimony
of a professional would be significant to you and to your musicians, I take pleasure in making use of the present occasion to address myself to you.

Let me give you a more tangible gift: allow me to dedicate this new *Firebird* Suite to you, to the Orchestre de la Suisse Romande, and to its committee.

Be assured, my dear friend, of my warmest sentiments.

                                                      Igor Stravinsky

STRAVINSKY TO ANSERMET   *May 11, 1919*
                                                 [Draft of a telegram]
London

Letter received. Ask Diaghilev send immediately first advance *Noces* for payment performance my ballets. Would like reach agreement with him fixed sum
each performance.   Stravinsky

STRAVINSKY TO ANSERMET   *Morges*
                                                      May 16, 1919
Stage Door   *[Draft of a telegram]*
Alhambra Theatre
London

Received your second letter. Tell Diaghilev not to put himself out for me anymore.[12]

---

[10] Ansermet conducted the first performance of this Suite in April 1919. The manuscript score, dated February 1919, is now in the Bibliothèque Nationale, Paris.

[11] Founded by Ansermet in 1918, and conducted by him until 1966.

[12] The same day, Stravinsky telegraphed to Misia Sert: "Thank you for everything but
please address yourself to Diaghilev. Some day I will tell you about the way he treats
his friends. Happily my situation has improved.   Stravinsky."

STRAVINSKY TO ANSERMET   *Morges*
                                                  Saturday, May 16, 1919
My dear,   *[Draft of a letter]*

I must say two things to complete yesterday's telegram. I have your May 7 letter, and I really appreciate Diaghilev's attitude toward me, toward these obligations, etc. It is useless to tell you that his statements are without a word of
truth. The fabrications are completely conscious and calculated, and your sup-
positions (as to the reasons for the brusque change in his attitude toward me)
are perfectly correct. I know the *gaillard* too well to be mistaken.

All that I ask you to do is to mark on the top of the page each of the performances (and the dates) of my works as they are given.* This is for later, so
that I may confront Diaghilev with the list after what he tells me. I leave him
in peace, and, happily, I can do without him. But the day will come when he will
need me, and I will remember. . . .

I hope that you have transmitted my telegram "textually."

                              Faithfully yours,   I Stravinsky

Write me everything.[13]
And my piece for pianola.

*Or better still, bring all the official notices of the performances.

STRAVINSKY TO ANSERMET   *May 24, 1919*
                                                  [Draft of a telegram]
Stage Door
Alhambra Theatre
London

Your May 17 letter received. All my conditions author's rights also for *Noces*.
Letter follows. Regards,   Str

STRAVINSKY TO ANSERMET   *Morges*
                                                          May 26, 1919
My dear Ansermet,

Here are the guidelines to follow in your negotiations with Diaghilev. But before
I outline them, two words.

You can understand how painful it would be for me to write to him personally. His "moral integrity," about which he speaks incessantly, is not worth
much,* when you consider the enormity of his contention that, "since *Petrushka* was published in Germany and *Firebird* in Russia," he is not obligated
to pay me anything, but that, being good and generous, he would pay a *very
small* sum anyway for these two works already performed a *great* number of

---

[13] In 1919, the Ballets Russes, at the Alhambra Theatre, performed *Petrushka* twenty-
seven times between April 30 and July 29, and *Firebird* thirty-five times between May
8 and July 26.

times ("No big thing," he would claim). I was really ill when I learned of all this, not so much from his taking refuge in these "legal" rights, as from his alluding to them,** especially at a time when a friend finds himself in a difficult situation. A strange way to express friendship! But since it is this way, and since the various means by which I could obtain what is due me due are equally repugnant, I advise you to cable him that I will wait until the moment he needs me. Only then will my rights be valued. For this reason, too, I henceforth renounce all moneys that he might decide to send me without acknowledgment of my rights, moneys that I consider gifts and refuse to accept. And he should not complain about my behaving in this manner, for he provoked it.

I embrace you, dear Ansermet, very sadly, your friend,   Stravinsky

P.S. You can let me know if Diaghilev wants the following papers (with my terms).

*In my opinion
**If they are imaginary (as Diaghilev has claimed)

My dear Ansermet, here are the points concerning which I telegraphed to you on May 24:

Firebird

a. Exclusive property* of S. Diaghilev from June 25, 1910 (date of the premiere at the Paris Opéra), to June 25, 1915.[14]
b. Extension of these exclusive rights for three more years, on June 25, 1918. The money for these eight years of exclusive rights was paid to me.

*For theater performances

Petrushka

a. Exclusive property* from June 13, 1911 (date of premiere at the Châtelet, Paris), to June 13, 1916.
b. Extension of these exclusive rights for one more year, to June 13, 1917. The money for these six years of exclusive rights was paid to me.

N.B. The essential questions are: did the Ballets Russes perform *Petrushka* after June 13, 1917, in South America, Spain, or elsewhere, and if so, how many times?

*For theater performances

While the Ballets Russes were in South America in July 1917,[15] Diaghilev came to see me in Diablerets, and, on the train that was taking him to Italy, the following agreement was concluded between us:

---

[14] In an interview in the *Petersburg Gazette,* October 10, 1912, Stravinsky says that the Imperial (Maryinsky) Theater had not performed *Firebird* and *Petrushka* because of Diaghilev's five-year exclusive performance rights to both works.
[15] Stravinsky and Diaghilev did not see each other, or communicate directly, between this date and September 1919, when Stravinsky went to Paris to discuss the commission for *Pulcinella* and to receive from Diaghilev the music on which the score would

a. Diaghilev promised to pay me 20,000 Swiss francs for the exclusive right to present *Les Noces villageoises* in all countries for two years.

b. It was understood that he would not have to pay any other author's rights to me during this two-year period except in countries controlled by the Société Dramatique (which automatically collects these rights in the French-speaking countries, France, Belgium, Switzerland, Monte Carlo, and perhaps others), where I will collect as I do for all my other works.

c. In my declaration on the contract with the Société Dramatique, I give a half of a third of my author's rights to the choreographer, or, five-sixths to me, one-sixth for the choreographer, as in the case of my other works with Fokine and Nijinsky.

d. Diaghilev assumes the responsibility of having the parts copied at his expense.

e. When *Les Noces* is published, Diaghilev must deliver the parts to the publisher in exchange for printed parts, and the publisher must reimburse Diaghilev for his expenses in preparing the work. From that time, Diaghilev must pay the publisher 100 francs rental for each performance.

That was the agreement for *Les Noces*. At the same time, we agreed to prolong the right to perform *Petrushka* for another year (June 13, 1917, to June 13, 1918) for the sum of 7,000 Swiss francs (or 10,000 French francs). The terms of payment for *Noces* and the additional year of *Petrushka* were established (always by common agreement) at the top of the paper which is now before me, complete with Diaghilev's signature. A similar piece of paper would be found in his files with my signature (if he shows you a copy).

We separated at Aigle, he going to Italy, I to Diablerets. On the train I reread the terms of payment and realized that it was almost a thousand francs short (27,500 is the total). We made a mistake in our figuring of this apportionment of the payment. I suppose that he would not take advantage of this error. Yet if he does insist on it, I can do nothing. I am in the wrong because I signed. There is the background, dear Ansermet. Now, here is my proposal:

Although this contract has expired, I agree to extend it under the following conditions:

1. The agreement is followed strictly, starting with the first performance of my ballets in the current year in London.[16]

---

be based. At the end of September he wrote to Diaghilev agreeing to compose the ballet. At the beginning of October, Massine sent the libretto, adding a note: "Seryozha and I are delighted that you have been so taken with Pergolesi. . . ." Writing to Struve on October 16, Stravinsky referred to "a work that Diaghilev has asked me to compose based on Pergolesi's music (from various unpublished—in the main—and little-known works by that master). This will take up all of my time until January. . . . Then I was planning to conduct some chamber and symphonic concerts of my music in Paris."

[16] "April 30, 1919" (Ansermet's marginal note).

2. The terms of payment for the year 1919: monthly. I shall not repeat the agreement (20,000 Swiss francs for *Les Noces,* 7,500 Swiss francs for the new year* of *Petrushka*), since the conditions are itemized on the preceding page.

I noticed that *Firebird* does not figure in this agreement—a new one concluded between us for the year June 25, 1918, to June 25, 1919—and I want to add this work as well, asking 7,500 Swiss francs for the performances of this year. If, for one reason or another, Diaghilev breaks this pact, I propose another to him as follows:

1. For one year, from the premiere of the present London season, 250 Swiss francs for each performance of each of my works.
2. I give *Les Noces* to him for two years from the day on which I deliver the piano score to him**—not later than December 2, 1919—this being agreed only in the event that, until this date, he has paid the money in accordance with our present contract (he will pay the monthly sum of 25,000 Swiss francs to me, the figure that he proposed to me, according to your letter of May 17). As for the orchestra score, I will give this to him no later than March 2, 1920, on condition that all of the money due to me under the present contract will have been paid. All of the other agreements, such as those concerning the eventual publication of *Noces,* author's rights ("Dramatica"), division of rights with the choreographer, terms of payment, are the same as those of the agreement of July 1917, subject to the conditions indicated above.
3. For performances of *Petrushka* after June 13, 1919 (in South America, in Spain, or elsewhere), I want to receive 250 Swiss francs each, and, in any case—which is to say, no matter which agreement is chosen—the last point holds.

For the moment, this is all I have to say.

Your   I Stravinsky.

*Beginning with the first performance of my ballets in the current year in London
**At the post office, where I keep the receipt

STRAVINSKY TO ANSERMET   *Morges*
                                                              May 30, 1919
My dear Ansermet,

I received your letter of May 23. Tomorrow or the day after you will receive mine of May 26. You have done well in faithfully transmitting all the details of your conversations with Diaghilev, just as they occurred. I know now what I must do, and how to defend myself, since it is really a question of self-defense. That is my feeling about the whole matter.

I suppose it is true that at first Diaghilev felt friendship and kindness toward me, and, as he thought about it, probably realized that I might gain an advantage by creating precedents. This, at any rate, is what he has always repeated: morally he owed me money for the performances of my works, but legally nothing (!!!). At the bottom of his heart, he found nothing wrong with the fact that a composer—who is his friend and whose works, which certainly earn money, Diaghilev plays—is literally obliged to beg left and right, while in the meantime Diaghilev benefits from the success of the works. If Diaghilev finds this situation abnormal and unfair, would it not be more logical for him to protest against this injustice, created by *laws,* declaring openly that he would never make use of similar "rights"? Would he ever be logical enough to take this sort of action rather than the action he is now taking? For the moment, he is doing just the opposite. He does not protest against these "rights," with which the law so generously endows him, but, on the contrary, finds them perfectly convenient, since they provide a means for displaying his generosity. He agrees that he feels morally obliged to pay me, and "accepts this obligation"*; but I would like to know exactly how much this moral obligation amounts to per performance in Swiss francs. So, it becomes amusing: the morality of the affair is agreed upon because Diaghilev feels all this injustice and the cruelty of these "rights" that he believes to be his. But if this is so, then who is holding him back from acting morally? Not me, anyway. Are those scruples what prevent him from following the "laws" (which permit him not to pay me)?

Let's be serious! Frankly, what rights is he talking about? When my last letter is before you, you will see for yourself that it is always a question of agreements for one or more years of performances, and that the question of the right of nonpayment for my works cannot even be raised. Diaghilev always dealt with me, *never with my publishers.* For that reason, he found it timely to explain to you that I had been published in Berlin and Moscow.** First, this is wicked, and second, it could turn against him, because he has never fulfilled his obligations to these publishers. Let us also not forget that *Firebird* is played from copied, *not printed,* parts. The orchestra score is my personal property, and I am asking you to bring it when you come back, as you promised. He happens to have *Petrushka* because of my intervention with Struve, who on many occasions demanded the return of the parts to the Edition Russe de Musique (the Edition not having been fully paid).[17] Now judge for yourself how many of these dealings are honest.

Well, one method of defense will be the publication of a letter in the Paris and London newspapers, in which I will ask the public to judge between us.

I cordially shake your hand.

Your   I Stravinsky

P.S. As I was finishing these lines, I received some very advantageous proposals for *Les Noces* and *The Nightingale* in New York and Chicago. I would like to

---

[17] As late as May 31, 1922, Ernest Alexandrovich Oeberg (d. 1925), director of the Russischer Musik Verlag in Berlin, wrote to Stravinsky: "I wonder if you would remind Diaghilev that he owes 1,000 francs to the R.M.V. for *Petrushka.* . . ."

know whether or not Diaghilev would buy out the interest on these future productions, since, out of moral obligation to him, I must give him first option, that
is to say, ask if he wants to reserve the rights to produce these works in North
America.

*I quote his phrase from your last letter.
**The day will come when Moscow and Berlin will demand money from him;
he should not forget that this was settled by the Bern Convention.

STRAVINSKY TO ANSERMET   *Morges*
                                                         June 6, 1919
My dear Ansermet,   *[Fragment of a letter]*

Thank you for your note of May 1.[18] You have fully understood the role of this
decent (but naive and not very intelligent) Evans in the matter of the piano
rolls. But you must be absolutely clear, so please make careful note of the following: no one commissioned the Etude for Pianola. Evans, having learned
from my letter to him (autumn 1917) that I had written a piece for pianola (*the
first in the world!*), offered to find a publisher for me, which he succeeded in
doing. Soon after that, he had the strange notion of building a whole pianola
repertory in a short time, in order to give lectures about it, eventually, and to
present himself to the public as the founding spirit, or initiator, of this "business." I swear that no one ever commissioned pieces for pianola from me—as
my Aeolian contract proves. Casella's participation in this business clearly
shows Evans's "finesse" (because this much is certain: Evans arranged the
commission of a piece from Casella for Aeolian).

               I embrace you and thank you. Your   Stravinsky

Tell Diagh. that I have long ago given up the idea of doing the music for
Liturgie.

STRAVINSKY TO ANSERMET   *Morges*
                                                        June 18, 1919
Stage Door   *[Draft of a telegram]*
Alhambra Theatre
London

Cable me if Kling[19] would undertake to represent England to collect net author's royalties *Petrushka* and *Firebird*. Reveal to him details situation.   Stravinsky

---

[18] Actually June 1; at least, the June 1 letter is the one that Stravinsky answers here.
[19] Otto Marius Kling (d. 1924), director of J. & W. Chester, Ltd., London, Stravinsky's
publisher.

STRAVINSKY TO ANSERMET   *Morges*
                                                         June 24, 1919
Stage Door   *[Draft of a telegram]*
Alhambra Theatre
London

Understood except for number of years determined. Ask Kling send forms in French if possible.[20] Regards,   Str

STRAVINSKY TO ANSERMET   *Morges*
                                                         June 27, 1919
Stage Door   *[Telegram]*
Alhambra Theatre
London

Please go see M [isia] Edwards Savoyhotel for me and tell her frankly about my differences with Diaghilev.

STRAVINSKY TO ANSERMET   *Morges*
                                                          July 2, 1919
Stage Door
Alhambra Theatre
London W.C.2

Friend,

By the same post, I am sending (1) *Ragtime* (score and parts), (2) complete music of *Histoire du sold.* (score and parts). Understand that *these are for you only,* which is to say that I am giving the right to perform this music to you alone and am asking you not to let go of it or to *lend it to anyone.* About the songs dedicated to Mme Pechich,[21] I still do not have a copy, and I put the question aside for the moment. I received your June 26 letter. Thanks. [I] telegraphed to Kling asking him to send another contract covering all my works as a unit (those which cannot be protected are not included, of course).[22] When would [Sir Thomas] Beecham like to play *The Nightingale*? I have made and sent a copy of it as he requested. And M [isia] Edwards? Let me know quickly if she has succeeded in convincing D [iaghilev].

                                        I embrace you.   Stravinsky

When do you plan my lecture-concert?[23]

---

[20] This telegram answers Ansermet's letter of June 20, 1919.

[21] Stravinsky had dedicated the *Quatre Chants russes* to the Croat singer Maja Strozzi-Pečič. (For a discussion of one of these songs, "Sektanskaya," see Appendix I.)

[22] I.e., compositions not protected by copyright in certain countries.

[23] In June, Ansermet had suggested to the director of the Aeolian Company Ltd. that he organize a "recital-and-talk," with Edwin Evans, about the recent works of Stravinsky performed in Aeolian Hall.

STRAVINSKY TO ANSERMET

Morges
July 2, 1919
[Postcard]

Stage Door
Alhambra Theatre
London, W.C.2

I was told at the Morges post office that the package (declared value of 1,000 francs) would reach you in eight days.[24] I add on this card that you must take care to return to me all the music that I have sent. The *Soldat* score is unique, since it incorporates all the changes that I made during the past winter, and these are not in my wife's copy.

Tell me again, my friend, what special courier will bring Beecham (for whom I wait every day, in accordance with his telegram)? Will he have the authority to conclude arrangements for *The Nightingale*? He does not breathe a word about terms. Speak to Kling about all of this. I really do not know what one should ask. In 1914, Beecham paid me about 1,000 francs a performance.

Your   Stravinsky

I had just written these lines when a postal employee told me that I must go to the British Consulate to get permission to send something of this declared value; I have therefore divided the manuscript into two packages. How convenient!

STRAVINSKY TO ANSERMET

[July 11, 1919]

My dear Ansermet,

I have received your telegram[25] and am reassured about the music that I sent: *Ragtime,* score and parts (the piano score was sent in June), and *Histoire du soldat,* score and parts.[26]

I wanted to come to London, see Mme Edwards, talk to her, and insist that she do everything possible regarding Diaghilev, since, despite his promise (your letter of July 2), and hers to obtain from D. all that he owes me within three days, it is now the 11th and nothing has happened. Also, the second contract that you sent is no better than the first, because I must protect *all my published works* for three years. Those which cannot be legally defended are lost, of course, and I do not want to pay the expenses for an eventual lawsuit, because I would risk losing everything. Tell all of this to Kling; I have already told his son,[27] who is here.

I went to the British Consulate in Geneva—very bad impression: I am without protection and nothing can be done. Would it be better to come in the

---

[24] On June 30, 1919, Ansermet asked Stravinsky to send several works, one of which was *Histoire du soldat,* for the July 18 concert.

[25] Of July 9, 1919.

[26] Stravinsky's postcard of July 2, 1919.

[27] Harry Kling, who succeeded his father in 1924.

autumn, when they will play my opera? It is a disappointment not to hear your lecture-concert.

Your   I Str

STRAVINSKY TO ANSERMET

[Morges]
July 15, 1919
[Draft of a telegram]

Stage Door
Alhambra Theatre
London

Thank you but cannot go to London now. Still awaiting results interview Misia Diaghilev.

STRAVINSKY TO ANSERMET

Morges
July 15, 1919[28]

My dear Ansermet,

It is understood: I reserve the premiere of *Le Sacre* for you, for the autumn concert in London that we discussed. Too bad that your lecture-concert on the 18th of this month was canceled. It would have been one of the reasons for my eventual trip to London, since everything else could be arranged through Kling's son, who is returning there in a short while. I will not come now, but perhaps in the autumn. What does Mme Edwards say? I find it extraordinary that she cannot obtain anything from Diaghilev, and she would already have told me if she had. I am very upset. Ask [Kling] what I should do. If he sets the business in motion, all that he will obtain is payment for *Petrushka,* which is to say 25 performances at about 250 fr. each. But if Mme Edw [ards] could arrange the business amicably, I would be pleased. Will she be able to do it? Kling just wrote to me that nothing can be done about *Firebird* (which is considered to have been published in Russia). In this case, why that figure in the contract? Bring the orchestra score, which is mine, *without fail!*

Your   Stravinsky

STRAVINSKY TO ANSERMET

Morges
July 22, 1919
[Telegram]

Kling, Chester
11 Great Marlborough Street
London[29]

Consent payment from Diaghilev 10,000 Swiss francs for performance rights *Petrushka, Firebird,* number unlimited. Agreement valid for three years starting August 1, 1919, not April 30, 10,000 payable each August 1, reserving my rights collected by Société Auteurs. Letter follows.   Stravinsky

---

[28] This letter is in response to a cable from Ansermet dated July 13, 1919.

[29] Forwarded to Ansermet at the Alhambra Theatre.

STRAVINSKY TO ANSERMET   *Morges*
                                                      July 23, 1919
My dear Ansermet,

Thanks for your very interesting letter of July 18. Yesterday I telegraphed to you my reply to Diaghilev's proposed conditions regarding my author's rights for *Petrushka* and *Firebird,* and addressed the telegram both to you and to Kling. As you see, I have changed the date of the beginning of our agreement from April 30 to August 1. You can guess the reason: I want to receive my rights collected by the "Dramatica" in Paris and the advance money. I am recounting the above circumstances to Kling and ask you to see him and to have him *read you the letter* that I am sending him (at the same time as this one). Talk seriously with him and tell him *absolutely everything,* while reading my letters to him (if necessary). Give him all the notices—which you sent to me—and inform him of all changes (the substitution of one ballet for another) that concern me, as you have done in the notices that I have.* *This is very important.*[30]

What interested me in the conversation that you and Diaghilev had with Mr. Capell[31] was the subscription fund in my favor started in the New York press. This is the height of cynicism. When in my letter to Kahn[32] I challenged his moral right to rob me, he answered very amicably that he had not meant to do so[33] (pretending that he did not know my address). The affair embarrasses him, and thus he sent money for five performances at the rate of 250 Swiss francs each,[34] the same amount that Diaghilev owes me. Moreover, being a sharp Jew, Kahn has situated himself at the head of a committee formed to come to my aid.[35] You will agree that this last attitude is different from Diaghi-

---

[30] Underlined twice in the original.

[31] Richard Capell (1885–1954), music critic for the *Daily Mail,* later for the *Daily Telegraph.*

[32] Otto Kahn (1867–1934), banker, Maecenas. One of the directors of the Metropolitan Opera in New York.

[33] On April 3, 1919, Giulio Gatti-Casazza, director of the Metropolitan Opera of New York and friend of Otto Kahn, wrote to Stravinsky that the circumstances of the war had slowed the payment of performance fees for *Petrushka,* but that these sums would be sent.

[34] On May 22, 1919, Stravinsky wrote to Kahn to acknowledge the receipt of the sum of 1,245 francs, the total of the rights for five presentations of *Petrushka.*

[35] In May 1919, Stravinsky received $100 from Mrs. Marie Brooks of 600 West 114th Street, New York, and he promptly wrote to thank her for her "généreux appui." On June 5 he received 1,912.40 French francs through Mr. Blair Fairchild, who was in Paris at the time, and was the president of the Society of American Friends of Musicians in France. The money was sent by order of Mrs. G. M. Tuttle, the secretary of the Society, and the check came through Mr. Lewis W. Haskell, the United States Consul in Geneva, via the Bank of Lombard and Odier. The money was transmitted with the help of Lieutenant A. Raymond, Mrs. Brooks's son-in-law. Stravinsky wrote a lengthy reply on June 7, addressing it to Mrs. Daniel Gregory Mason and asking her to express his gratitude and explain his circumstances to the other committee members (particu-

lev's. The latter has stolen (or wishes to steal) from me in a more disgusting way than Kahn—more disgusting because Diaghilev was my friend until now, and it is therefore wrong [for him] to invoke laws that legalize theft.

More amusing still is that since *Petrushka* was published in Berlin, it is protected in England by the rules of the Bern Convention, in which England participated. Unfortunately, this is not the case with *Firebird*, which was published in Moscow.

So I am considering the following idea. Could I not, through the intermediary of Mr. Capell in the *Daily Mail*, reply to certain letters to the editor which ask, "Why is it that a subscription has had to be opened for Stravinsky in America when his ballets are performed so often at the Alhambra?" The explanation could then be put in print: Diaghilev contests my author's rights from this triumphant season. What do you and Kling think of that? I consider it a capital idea. I also think that if Diagh. were seriously faced with the possibility of such a reply in the *Daily Mail*, he would change his mind on the question of my author's rights in England (though perhaps not in Italy). Diaghilev must be made aware that I am seriously tempted to do this.

Hearty thanks for the concerts,[36] too. (I also sincerely thank [Anthony]

---

larly Mrs. Tuttle, Mrs. Brooks, Mrs. Raymond, and Mrs. Hill). He stated that because of the political situation in Russia, he now considered his personal fortune to be definitely lost. He expressed his special appreciation for the delicate manner in which the committee was treating this act of charity. Evidently they had asked him to compensate in some way, since he explained that most of his works were not protected by copyright in the United States and offered a solution: "I wish that you would consider this sum (1,912.40), and those which may follow, as advances toward the moneys which I would receive from future concerts devoted to my music." He goes on to say that in exchange for these generous gifts, he would like to offer Mrs. Mason and the others the premieres of: (1) the new *Firebird* Suite, (2) *Pribaoutki*, (3) *Berceuses du chat*, (4) the Eight Easy Pieces, and he sent these scores, requesting that *Firebird* be returned when no longer needed. He wrote again to Mrs. Brooks on July 25, thanking her for the 10,540 francs received. On August 26, he wrote to Mrs. Noemi Pernessin Raymond, saying that he had sent the manuscript of Piano-Rag Music and the orchestra score of the *Firebird* ballet to her mother, entrusting her to pass them on: "Please tell Adolph Bolm that you have received the score, the only one in existence and my personal property, and that if he decides to stage the work this season, he must understand that all rights are mine, absolutely. . . . He must return the parts immediately." As for *The Nightingale*, Stravinsky said that he could send the orchestra score, the string parts, and the chorus parts, but that the other parts must be copied from the full score. He thanked Mrs. Raymond for providing him with cigarettes (by way of Paris and London). On September 26 he wrote again to Mrs. Mason thanking her for a check for 2,581 francs and saying that he had received a proposal from Mr. Morris Gest of the Century Theater to come to New York and to compose something, all expenses paid, but that the project could not be realized at the time.

[36] Stravinsky refers to two planned concerts of his works mentioned by Ansermet in his letter of July 18.

Asquith for his patronage.) I will gladly go with you to London. But they must pay me well: trip, lodging, and honorarium. As for the rental of the parts of these three works,[37] you must talk to Kling (henceforth the representative of my author's rights in England). It would be even less delicate not to speak to him about it since he receives 10% commission on every deal.

Is Mme Edwards still in London? I imagine that Diaghilev planned to use my last communication[38] as proof that he was justified in introducing me to Mme Edwards as a man who wants to rob him, etc. While he, Di., proposes the most "advantageous" arrangements for me, I, Str, want still more, etc.

Please ask Picasso if he has finished my vignette for the [Editions de la] Sirène *Ragtime.*[39] And as for the *Rag,* please leave the cimbalom part (what luck in having found the instrument in London!) with the player and the rest of the parts—like *Soldat*—at Kling's. Bring only the score for the ensemble. Do not forget the large printed score of the *Firebird* ballet. *That belongs to me. Be sure you do not forget it.*

Show Kling my new piece for piano solo called Piano-Rag Music, which I composed recently for Art. Rubinstein.

I don't know what to do with *Les Noces.* It is absolutely ridiculous to put on this *divertissement* (for it is *not* a ballet)[40] without a set, just because the set does not represent anything, and with pianola, harmonium, 2 cim[baloms], percussion, singers, conductor on the stage, and dancers who come and go. The set is there to decorate, *not* to represent something. I tell you, it's idiotic to perform it at the Paris Opéra at all. Maybe Diagh. ought to know all this so that he doesn't make needless preparations. What do you think? The design of the Gheusi theater is certainly much better for the *Soldat.*

When does Diagh. leave London? Kling must have time to act while Diagh. is still there.

I embrace you as a brother.

Your   Stravinsky

I enclose an article by M. Gust. Doret on the role of music in the cinema. This music criticism compromises everything that it touches.[41] Can you imagine

---

[37] *Firebird* Suite, *The Nightingale,* and *Le Sacre.*

[38] Telegram of July 22, 1919.

[39] See the correspondence with Blaise Cendrars in *S.S.C.* II.

[40] Writing to Struve, April 6, 1919, Stravinsky refers to *Les Noces* as a "Russian song (cantata or rhapsody, what?!)."

[41] This article, "Music and Cinematography," appeared in the *Journal de Genève,* Saturday, July 19. Doret wrote, in part: ". . . Cinematography is a process which could one day have the potential (as in its documentary role), not to replace dramatic art—we know that—but to create a new form of expression. And since music is indispensable to it, we are certain that it will become free, and will enter into an unexplored area.

what music would become if it were to underscore films? This gentleman has never understood the charm of music played concurrently with the development of a film. He still has this anxiety about expression, even in cinema. God, what an ass he is! *Don't forget to bring my orchestra score for the ballet, Firebird!*

*I am missing: (1) those of the first performance of June 2; (2) from June 21 to 30; (3) the very last—after July 10. Please send them to me or bring them with you.

STRAVINSKY TO ANSERMET   *Morges*
                                                              July 25, 1919
Stage Door
Alhambra Theatre
London W.C.2

Friend,

I received your letter of July 20 describing the conversation you had with Diagh. that resulted in his sending his terms for my author's rights. Thank you. Now I understand, according to your letter, that the phrase *"rights collected by the Société des Auteurs without prejudice"* means that he will pay me more than 10,000 Swiss francs per year (collected automatically, in any case). I await your reply to my telegram.[42] Thus I am guaranteed 30,000 Swiss francs for the 3-year period. [Diaghilev] does not mention a word about the terms of payment. It is a good thing that I was careful to note this in my reply. He must pay 10,000 to me at the beginning of each year, or else the money will be added to the cost of the other contracts (*Noces, Soldat, Sacre,* etc. . . .).

                                                        Your   Stravinsky

STRAVINSKY TO ANSERMET   *June 25, 1920*
                                                         [Draft of a telegram]
Berners Hotel
London

Distressed at not being able to come. Letter follows.   Stravinsky

---

Music will no longer be a humble and docile servant, but will be the intimate collaborator, with, perhaps, a hint of tyranny."
[42] Ansermet wrote on July 25, 1919, answering Stravinsky's telegram of July 22, 1919.

STRAVINSKY TO ANSERMET

Carantec
June 28, 1920
[Postcard]

Berners Hotel
Berners Street
London W.1

My dear,

I beg you to answer immediately by return post as to whether you need the Suite[43] or the original score of the *Soldat.* [Otto] Kling spoke to me about it, but not clearly. Both [scores] are at my house. I await your reply.

Your   Stravinsky

STRAVINSKY TO ANSERMET

Carantec
July 1, 1920

Berners Hotel
Berners Street
London W.1

Cher vieux,

Thanks for your letter. If you are playing the complete *Soldat,* I must make some changes (enlargements) in the Devil's last dance. Do I have time before the 20th? (I have the orchestra score here.) If not, you can cut this dance, along with the Devil's couplets. In that case you would finish with the other dance of the Devil (the Suite), playing the chorale after the 3 dances (Tango-Waltz-Rag), which would be preceded by the Pasodoble. Two words by return mail, please.

Your   Stravinsky

Do you want *The Song of the Nightingale?*[44] If so, how will it be done? Your Stravinsky

STRAVINSKY TO ANSERMET

July 5, 1920
[Draft of a telegram]

Bernershotel
London

Am sending score *Soldat* with changes.[45] Do not take definite steps program before receiving my letter.   Stravinsky

---

[43] This refers to the arrangement for violin, clarinet, and piano of five pieces from *Histoire du soldat.* Ansermet performed the original version for seven instruments in Wigmore Hall, July 20, 1920, in a concert he gave of Stravinsky's chamber music.

[44] Ansermet's letter of June 28, 1920, mentions the possibility that he will conduct *The Song of the Nightingale.*

[45] This telegram is in reply to Ansermet's postcard of July 3, 1920.

STRAVINSKY TO ANSERMET

July 8, 1920
[Postmark: Carantec]
[Postcard]

Berners Hotel
Berners Str.
London W.1

My dear Ansermet,

Along with these lines, I am sending the Violin and Clar [inet] parts of the *Soldat* Suite (for piano, viol., and cl). Acknowledge receipt of this as well as of the (bound) orchestra score which I sent a few days ago.

Your   I Stravinsky

Before going to Switzerland, come to see me in Carantec with Clark.[46]

STRAVINSKY TO ANSERMET

July 21, 1920
[Postmark: Carantec]

Berners Hotel
Berners Street
London W.1

Cher vieux,

Your telegram has given me immense pleasure. I embrace you with all my heart for this concert, and for your love of my music. After such presentations of my music, and with a friend like you, one can do the most unbelievable things. You cannot imagine the degree of joy that you have given me. Write a long letter and write out the lecture (for Kling). They are going to publish it along with the program. Send some copies.

Your   I Stravinsky

[End of July 1920]
[Postcard]

STRAVINSKY TO ANSERMET

I expect to be in Paris with my wife and Madame Beliankina at the end of the month and at the beginning of August to look for an apartment. Try to see me during your trip through Paris. I dare not ask you to come to Carantec, having received a letter from your wife entreating me not to monopolize you. The separation from you was apparently very painful for her, but this time it would be for

---

[46] Edward Clark (1888–1962), English conductor, pupil of Schoenberg. After directing the orchestra of the Ballets Russes in London during the 1924–26 seasons, he became chief of the BBC Orchestra. Clark and his wife, Elizabeth Lutyens, were close friends of the Stravinskys from 1956.

only one day. Answer quickly. When are you leaving? I hope that your illness was not serious. I received a very nice telegram from Clark.[47] Give him my best wishes and keep at least half for yourself.

Your   Stravinsky

Write the approximate address of the Paris copyist who you think is the best, the one you spoke about.

STRAVINSKY TO ANSERMET

Villa "Bel Respiro"
Garches (Seine-et-Oise)
September 22, 1920
[Postcard]

Dear Ansermet,

Thank you for your kind letter. I would like to write to you at length, but my nerves are in poor condition these days, and I limit myself to answering only your most urgent questions: (1) *Petrushka,* the parts are with Chester. See M. Desbaillets[48] in Geneva and find out if they are complete. If not, ask the firm in London and be sure that the terms for the rental are the same, 125 francs per performance. Tell Desbaillets that, according to *his letter of July 31, 1920,* I will not bother him about the rentals of my works published by the Edition Russe de Musique and, consequently, that you must deal directly with me. You should pay them only for the cost of mailing, if the parts come from England. If you take the *Petrushka* packet, which should be in Geneva, pay attention, for it is not complete. (2) The *Firebird* Suite: this too is in la Place de la Fusterie; what you tell me proves it because, when leaving, I sent it to Chester with the address (to the Bibliothèque, etc.), begging him to forward it; please tell Desbaillets this. (3) About the *Soldat,* ask Chester, who has our contract with Ramuz, and then do not forget that our friend Reinhart[49] will support you with all of his power. The March is orchestrated, but not the Galop. I am in the middle of finishing a concerto for string quartet (Flonzaley),[50] Debussy[51] later.

Embrace you.   I.S.

---

[47] Clark wired Stravinsky, July 21, 1920, congratulating him on the success of the *Soldat.*

[48] J. & W. Chester's Geneva representative.

[49] Werner Reinhart, the Winterthur industrialist, amateur clarinetist, friend of Stravinsky, Schoenberg, Berg, Webern, Rilke et al.

[50] Concertino for string quartet, composed in Carantec during the summer of 1920, commissioned by and dedicated to the Flonzaley Quartet.

[51] The *Symphonies of Wind Instruments,* dedicated to the memory of Debussy.

STRAVINSKY TO ANSERMET   *Garches*
                                                    February 11, 1921

My dear Ansermet,

I see that you never received the letter in which I informed you that Diaghilev and Massine had a falling-out (in Rome).[52] Diaghilev is coming to Paris in a few days, and I will have all the details of the separation, as well as his future plans.

Concerning the concert, I also asked you to take all steps with the Paris musicians because time is running out! And the chamber concert? If *Renard* cannot be given, what will you conduct?[53] Pleyel took my cimbalom to construct a mechanism of the pianola genre, but I doubt that there will be time to do all that between now and April. My God, how I would like to have you in Paris for just two days to determine what is possible and what is impossible. Has Kling given the order to copy the *Renard* parts? Has he spoken to you? That should have been done first, *mon vieux*. I have withdrawn under the pretext that I do not want to hear Golschmann[54] do *Histoire du soldat* in the Salle Gaveau, so you can do it here. I do not believe that you should mix Mozart, Schubert, and Haydn with my works in the concerts. And I will do my concert with Chanel alone—nobody else*—[for reasons] too long to explain. Have you answered Goossens,[55] and what are your projects for London?

I ask you very seriously to come, since I guarantee that you will accomplish nothing by correspondence. Answer all my questions quickly.

                                              Your   Stravinsky

*All the others turn it into a lot of babble.

STRAVINSKY TO ANSERMET   *[End of July 1921]*

Just a word, *mon cher*. I forgot to tell you that, unless I am mistaken, you can easily replace the basset horn by a bass clar[inet].[56] Consider, *mon cher,* what can be said in the English press against Koussevitzky's letter.[57] Artur [Rubinstein] says that Koussevitzky has even discredited himself with my enemies, thanks to this letter. But how can it be that none of my friends has answered him? Are they all cowards? And what about my enemies? You I thank with all

---

[52] In 1920, Diaghilev had criticized Léonide Massine (1895–1979) as a choreographer, and in January 1921, while the Ballets Russes was in Rome, dismissed him.

[53] Whether Stravinsky is referring to technical difficulties, such as finding a competent cimbalomist, or to contractual ones—the performance rights belonged to the Princess de Polignac—is not clear.

[54] Vladimir Golschmann (1893–1972), conductor.

[55] Eugene Goossens conducted a concert performance of *Le Sacre* in London, June 7, 1921.

[56] In the *Symphonies of Wind Instruments*.

[57] Published in *The Times* of London, July 24, 1921. In *S.P.D.*, p. 223, Diaghilev's letter to Stravinsky, apropos of Koussevitzky's letter, is wrongly dated June 29 (for July 29).

my heart for the *Symphonies*. And why doesn't Goossens put it on his programs? The score of the opera *The Nightingale* was delivered to Oeberg, 3 rue de Moscou.

I embrace you.   I Stravinsky

STRAVINSKY TO ANSERMET   *Biarritz*
August 23, 1921
c/o Dr. Blanchod   *[Postcard]*
Bière (Vaud)

Very dear friend,

I must look into the affair of *The Nightingale* with Kling and Oeberg, because the latter now has possession of the parts and score from Chester, complicating the business. I will do what is necessary.

Your   Stravinsky

Anglet
STRAVINSKY TO ANSERMET   *September 10 [1921]*

Thank you for your letter,[58] my very dear one. What you write surprises me, but I am sure that all will go well and work out for you: I am convinced of it. Now to business: (1) *Symphonies:* fortunately Koussevitzky has nothing to do with this; *it is mine.* The score is with Chester in London, and I ask 150 Swiss francs (if that is expensive, tell me what you can pay). (2) Address of A. Rubinstein: Hôtel du Palais in Biarritz. He is leaving at the end of the month and is not coming to London. (3) The composition of the opera is going well, very well even, and *you will like it.* It is quite different from anything that I have done. I have finished [Three Movements from] *Petrushka* for Rubinstein, a very virtuoso transcription. No more room.

I embrace you.   I Stravinsky

STRAVINSKY TO ANSERMET   *[September 10, 1921]*

My dear Ansermet,

I received your letter, and despite my expectations, what you write has deeply shocked me.[59] I sent your letter to Artur [Rubinstein], whom I haven't seen since, but will see soon. I shall write to you again next week,[60] but I did not want to leave your letter without an immediate reply and am writing you these lines to tell you that you can *always* count on me no matter what the circumstances in your life.

---

[58] Of September 7, 1921.

[59] Ansermet had written that he would have to leave his job and Switzerland, but he does not give the reasons.

[60] Letter of October 15, 1921.

I have settled in Biarritz as a permanent residence. For the moment, write to me at the Cottage l'Argenté, Anglet near Bayonne, Basses-Pyrénées.

With you wholeheartedly,

Your   Stravinsky

STRAVINSKY TO ANSERMET   *Paris*
                                                      [September 1921]
Very dear friend,

Yesterday I received the score that you have written so well. Thanks, *mon cher.* At the moment, I do not have the time to answer your good letter. I return to Biarritz on Friday. I sent *Mavra* to you yesterday: *I beg you to translate it.*[61] I will see Oeberg in Biarritz and will discuss with him everything that interests you.

I am happy that you have recovered from the leg trouble. I embrace you with all the affection that I have for you.

I Stravinsky

P.S. Just finished the revisions for the Three Pieces for String Quartet (Ed. Russe de Musique), which is dedicated to you.[62]

---

[61] Pleading lack of time, Ansermet did not make the French translation (see n. 33 on p. 91), which, instead, was done by Jacques Larmanjat (1878–1952). Larmanjat and his wife were in charge of the recording of Stravinsky's music for the Pleyela, under the direction of Gustave Lyon's Pleyel Company. The relationship between Stravinsky and Larmanjat deserves some space in Stravinsky's biography. Stravinsky entrusted Larmanjat to make piano arrangements and vocal scores, as is shown by the following excerpt from a letter from Nice, September 29, 1924: "I am in the process of reviewing your work on *The Song of the Nightingale* transcription, which seems to conform to my desires. Certainly there are things which I am modifying (simplifying), but the whole seems simple enough. I am not going to review the Chinese March (not out of laziness but because of a complete lack of time), which I believe is the same reduction as mine in the opera. Tell me if this is so: I have told Oeberg that it should be that way. I do not entitle the sections but simply begin each part (which corresponds to a Pleyela roll) using Roman numerals, as in a symphony: I, II, III. I have just sent a few explanations to Oeberg, but, to be sure, I beg you to go see him when he receives your manuscript from me, probably at the end of this week or the beginning of next." What Stravinsky had written to Oeberg, from Nice, September 28, 1924, was that "a copy must be made of Larmanjat's manuscript because I fear that the printers will not be able to read his writing, especially with my corrections. . . . It seems to me that Larmanjat has introduced my reduction into his manuscript, but I cannot confirm this categorically, since I have not yet unpacked my music (because of the complete disorder here), and I do not have the opera *The Nightingale* at hand. If this supposition proves to be true, do not forget to add a note: 'Piano 2-hand arrangement by the composer.'"

[62] The Three Pieces for String Quartet, composed in 1914 and dedicated to Ansermet, was published by the Edition Russe de Musique in 1922.

STRAVINSKY TO ANSERMET   *Biarritz*
                                          Monday [September 1921]
My dear friend,

Barely returned from Paris (Friday), I promptly caught the flu and am staying
in bed. I am anxious to know if you received the piano score of *Mavra* that
Pleyel was supposed to have sent to you. Answer me, *mon cher,* as soon as you
have received this note.

How is your leg? Are you up yet? It is cruel on my part, but I do not want to
hear anything about any other translation of *Mavra* but yours. Do the impossible, but translate it.

Do you think you can still reach an agreement with Diagh. to go to
America for Jan., Feb., and March? He has already spoken to me about it. I
don't know if I will be compelled to accept this time, but I would so like to go
with you.

I am finished, and a little tired.

Yours, affectionately,   I Stravinsky

                                                      [Biarritz]
STRAVINSKY TO ANSERMET   *October 15, 1921*

Excuse my great haste. I am moving and doing a thousand other things all at
once. Returned to Biarritz, *mon cher,* and eager to answer your main questions.[63] (I) For the *Symphonies,* I just gave the order to Chester (London) to
send the score and parts to you immediately, saying that I would fix the rental
with you right away. You are obliged to reimburse him only for the cost of mailing and insurance. (II) For *The Nightingale,* write directly to Musique Russe,
3 rue de Moscou, Paris, explaining to M. Leonardi[64] that you would like to have
a fair price for everything that interests you. He must finally have received from
Kling all the parts of *The Nightingale* (opera). (III) As for Diagh. and all that
concerns you, I shall speak to him soon, since I am going to London Oct. 24 or
25 for the premiere of *La Belle*[65] and will stay for about a week, at the Savoy.
Finally, will Goossens, or Fitelberg,[66] be conducting? I imagine the scandal

---

[63] In Ansermet's letter of October 9, 1921.

[64] Leonardi was a music dealer specializing in the works of Russian composers. He had
an office at the Edition Russe de Musique in Paris in the early 1920s.

[65] *"La Belle"* has a double meaning: Stravinsky was going to London as much for the
debut of Vera Sudeikina in the role of the Queen in *La Belle au bois dormant* as for the
ballet. On October 10, 1921, he completed his orchestration of the "Variation of the
Lilac Fairy" and a few days later composed some measures for a transition in the finale
of the first act. *The Sleeping Princess* had its premiere on November 2. On November
19, Sudeikin, in Paris, telegraphed Diaghilev asking him to send his wife back: "Is she
receiving the best possible care? Should I come?" She did not leave the company, however, until mid-January.

[66] Gregor Fitelberg (1879–1953) was the conductor.

that poor Diagh. will have to endure there. My new address: Chalet [*sic*] des Rochers, rue la Frégate, Biarritz.

I embrace you. I Str

STRAVINSKY TO ANSERMET

Paris
November 22, 1921

Hôtel Continental
3 rue Castiglione
Paris

Two words, friend, to let you know that Diaghilev is there! A joke! I must finish the instrumentation of *Noces* for the May–June season in Paris.[67] I have a studio at Pleyel, where I will settle down to do this job. But nothing has changed in the plans for your concert. On the contrary, I have entered into partnership with Diaghilev for it, and I await you impatiently. As for Racz,[68] the cimbalomist, I would like to hire him full-time and pay him by the month. He would be a kind of secretary, assisting me in the copying and in all sorts of things in my musical work. He will also play the cimbalom in *Noces* if we do not succeed in mechanizing the instrument, which we are now trying to do. Ask him how much I must pay him a month. I must know this right away. I think that he is the man I need.

Write to me immediately at the Hôtel Meurice. I go by there to pick up my mail, which is *care of Madame Sert,* but write my name very large so that she does not open the letter by mistake and see that you are discussing a concert about which she knows nothing and, for the moment, should know nothing.

I embrace you and wait eagerly for your response.

I Stravinsky

STRAVINSKY TO ANSERMET

[December 1921]
[Postcard]

Bien cher,

I thank you thousands and thousands of times for your letter, which greatly moved me. My heart and thoughts are always with you, and I wish everything for you that I would wish for myself. Ah, if wishes were as sure as checks.

I have been composing[69] for two months now without a break and believe that I have done a good job. I beg you, send news about yourself as often as possible.

---

[67] The first performance of *Les Noces* took place on June 13, 1923, at the Théâtre de la Gaîté-Lyrique.

[68] Aladar Racz (1886–1958). See *S.P.D.,* p. 620.

[69] *Mavra.*

La Belle au bois: did you like it?

The 100 Swiss francs finally received. Thank you.

I embrace you heartily. Your   I Strav

STRAVINSKY TO ANSERMET

Biarritz
Friday, December 2, 1921

Thank you, *mon cher*, for your kind letter.[70] Thank you for the *Symphonies*[71] (not the "Symphony"), a good performance, I am sure, despite the small accident that you describe.[72] How did the public receive it? You do not say a word.

As for Diaghilev, I am at a loss to give you advice;[73] he is secretive and so sly! While in London, I spoke to him about you and your offer to conduct in December. He answered, "Yes, I know, he mentioned it to me." Then he added, "But you see all the problems that I already have with two conductors, Goossens and Fitelberg," and he truly does have a problem, although these two musicians conduct the ballet very well. What can be done? Perhaps you will see more clearly when you are there; I have not seen anyone for three weeks. In any case, give me your address (and dates) in England. As for myself, I plan not to budge, in order to work without pause on my opera, which it seems will be a "masterpiece."[74]

I embrace you strongly.   I Stravinsky

STRAVINSKY TO ANSERMET

This Thursday [no date]
[Postcard]

Dear,

Still nothing received (revision of *Le Sacre*) despite your little note, which, apart from the questions, informed me that the pages have been sent. I think that this card will find you still in Geneva and, if necessary, you could see what the problem is at the post office. Very anxious about this package, above all if it is not found.

Yours,   I Str.

---

[70] Of November 27.

[71] Underlined twice in the text.

[72] The "small accident" described in Ansermet's November 27 letter was that the bassoons missed their entrance and one of the oboe players did not turn a page fast enough.

[73] On November 27, Ansermet had written, "I am going to London around December 10. Tell me what you want me to do about Diaghilev."

[74] *Mavra.*

STRAVINSKY TO ANSERMET   *[End of February 1922]*
                                          [Draft of a telegram]

32 bd. des Tranchées
Geneva

Diaghilev accepts your terms.[75] I beg you to conduct *Sacre* and *Noces,* whose new instrumentation will comprise only 4 pianos and percussion. They are not playing the Tchaikovsky with Fitelberg; *Renard* will replace it.[76]

STRAVINSKY TO ANSERMET   *Villa "Les Rochers," Biarritz*
                                          July 22, 1922
Dear friend,

A business letter! Rudolph Ganz,[77] who is connected with the Hammond publications,[78] is in Zürich at the moment. I was obliged to return* to Paris specifically to see Hammond and Ganz, with whom I had a long meeting. They have no idea that I returned expressly to see them, Poulenc having told them that my trip was in connection with the emigration of my mother.[79] Young Hammond has now left for America; he arrives there about the 26th and plans immediately to discuss the future publication of my works with his committee. I proposed three alternatives: (I) Annual payment for my entire life: everything that I compose will be theirs; (II) For 5 years; and, (III) Purchase of works at hand that have not yet been published: A) *Symphonies* B) Concertino C) Orchestra score of *Pulcinella* D) *Mavra.* All of these solutions seem to place me in some danger because I am Russian and can be protected neither by the Europeans nor by Hammond himself; I mean, I cannot obtain copyrights. The only thing for me to do is to be naturalized and to become a French subject. Before

---

[75] Ansermet wrote to Stravinsky on February 19 that he had received no word from Diaghilev about his terms for performing *Le Sacre,* although he had promised to answer by the end of January.

[76] Stravinsky is referring to the premiere of *Renard* at the Paris Opéra on May 18, 1922.

[77] (1877–1972), conductor, pianist, and composer.

[78] Richard Hammond (1896–1980), Stravinsky's neighbor and one of his closest friends in California in the 1940s and 1950s. Hammond wrote to the present writer, January 27, 1979: "I went with Rudolph Ganz in [1922] to call on Stravinsky. He then had a studio at Pleyel. At that time I was on the board of the Franco-American Music Society which was connected with the Composers' Music Corporation in New York, and later joined the League of Composers. When Ganz told me that there might be a chance of obtaining a Stravinsky work for publication, I was interested in the idea and went with pleasure to meet a man I so admired. . . . I do not know who was publishing Stravinsky at that time, Schott, Jurgenson, Chester. Anyway, Ganz said he would take up the matter. Stravinsky himself was warm and gracious. I did not hear from Ganz for a little while, but for some technical reason the matter couldn't go through. . . . Later, I met Stravinsky at Nadia Boulanger's and subsequently saw him there a number of times."

[79] Anna Stravinsky was to sail from Petrograd to Stettin (Berlin) in November 1922.

talking to these gentlemen, I had never imagined such a possibility, but since then I have seriously considered it, and it is the only way out for me, the only solution. And so, my dear, I ask you to write immediately to M. Rudolph Ganz (Ganz & Co.), Bahnhofstrasse 40, Zürich. Tell him (diplomatically, since I do not want to appear to be chasing after them) that, finally, I have decided to become a naturalized French citizen to protect myself, and suggest that it would be wise to cable Hammond on this matter. My decision will shock his committee, and this sudden blow could help us obtain something from them which, it seems to me, might be very difficult under normal conditions. I know that Ganz likes you very much, also that you are in a good position to ask him. Say that you want to pay for the cable (I will pay you back). Hurry! Answer me quickly.

I embrace both you and Marguerite.[80]

Your   I Stravinsky

*A week ago

STRAVINSKY TO ANSERMET   *Biarritz*
                                                        August 11, 1922
Dear friend,

1,000 thanks for your kind letter.[81] I am enclosing your questions with my answers to them. I once again thank you many times for your work on *Le Sacre.*[82] Tell that good Oeberg, who is now in Berlin (Russischer Musik Verlag, 17 Dessauer Str.), that you will soon be ready, and that he absolutely must print the *Erratumblatt* of the *Sacre,* and insert it in both the large and small orchestra scores.

I received an enthusiastic note from *Melos* about your article,[83] expressing their gratitude for my having recommended you.

Thrilled about your project to conduct *Le Sacre* at the Berlin Philharmonic in November. Very probably I will go.

No news from Wiéner;[84] he is in Salzburg. Why didn't you go there?

---

[80] Ansermet's wife.

[81] Of August 9, 1922.

[82] In the August 9 letter, Ansermet had said that he was planning to conduct *Le Sacre* on November 19 and 20.

[83] Ansermet's article, "On Russian Music," appeared in the July issue of *Melos,* published in Berlin. He wrote, in part: ". . . Stravinsky is simplifying his style more and more, reducing it to the most common, direct, and frank elements, recalling the most exceptional forms without losing any of the new-found freshness in his manner of expression. He is beginning to use instruments as groups (*Pulcinella, Symphonies of Wind Instruments*) without returning to the orchestral system. And he returns to tonality, or, rather, he no longer needs to be atonal, his tonality exercising no constraint in the game of polyphony. He reduces himself everywhere because in poverty he finds wealth. The opera *Mavra* is the beginning of a new period, one in which music is divested of everything that has cramped it. . . ."

[84] Jean Wiéner (b. 1896). In the autumn of 1921, he founded the Wiéner concerts, specializing in contemporary music. He and Clément Doucet became a famous

Wiéner received 5,000 francs from Mme de Polignac for my concert. She is delighted not to be bothered with it because she is working very hard on Golschmann's behalf (!). In any case, I'm delighted that she gave a considerable sum for my concert without imposing a single condition; moreover, she advised him to appeal to other people and ask them to give the remainder of the necessary money by promising to play at their homes. I find that very *chic*, and I have high hopes for the month of Dec.[85] I will send the piano score for your draft of the French translation of *Mavra* as soon as possible. Cocteau asks me to say hello to you; he writes to me often now, and we are on good terms. And I must say that the attitude of the Cocteau gang is much more *chic* than that of the band of Ecole Normale pupils of *La Nouvelle Revue Française,* and of poor [Henry] Prunières (who seems to be completely lost). It seems that there is an article (twice as violent as the one in the Russian paper) by Monsieur de Schloezer[86] in the current *La Nouvelle Revue Française.*[87] Poulenc warned me, but I haven't read it yet.

---

team of duo-pianists, and the Wiéner-Doucet name still evokes the club Le Boeuf sur le Toit. Between 1925 and 1939, Wiéner gave more than 2,000 concerts.

[85] Stravinsky alludes here to the concert of his works organized by Jean Wiéner on December 26, 1922, at the Théâtre des Champs-Elysées. The program consisted of the *Symphonies of Wind Instruments* (first time in Paris), Concertino (played by the Pro Arte Quartet), Piano-Rag Music, *Mavra, Pulcinella.* The performances, which featured the Modern Society of Wind Instruments, were conducted by Ansermet.

[86] Boris de Schloezer became the editorial secretary of Henry Prunières's *La Revue Musicale* in 1921, and in this same year began to contribute to the *N.R.F.*

[87] The article by B. de Schloezer, "Les Ballets Russes," appeared in the July 1922 issue of the *N.R.F.* (No. 106, pp. 120–25). He wrote, in part: "In *Mavra* Stravinsky did not succeed, and the general impression is that of a pastiche, of a sort of musical joke that is not sufficiently amusing. Stravinsky's idea is probably involved with the question of renovating his forms, of creating a new comic-opera style. In this case, the subject is too thin, too fragile, and the Italo-Russian and black-American styles do not mix." Schloezer wrote to Stravinsky from Dieppe on June 27: "Dear Igor Fyodorovich, my article on *Mavra* came out on the same day that I left Paris. I read it only when I was already en route, and I found to my horror that one particular sentence that I considered very important had been cut: 'It is entirely possible that I am wrong in my evaluation of *Mavra,* but if, after a year, I see that I *was* wrong, I want to be the first to admit it and shall be very glad to say that I made a mistake, critics' mistakes (there have been so many) being much less significant than those of artists and authors.' Probably none of this is important to you. But you know what exceptional value I place on your work and how much I love it, and I would also like you to know that, if I take the liberty of expressing myself openly about what is not to my liking in your music, I do so with the tremendous respect which all artistic geniuses deserve, fully aware of the possibility that *I* may be wrong, not you. . . ." Stravinsky drafted a reply: "Dear Schloezer, I, too, am of the opinion that critics' mistakes are far less significant than the mistakes of authors-artists, but I must admit that I do not entirely understand what conclusion I (or the public) am supposed to draw from this. Nor do I understand your phrase, 'if, after a year, I see that I was wrong . . .' Why after a year, why not after

I embrace you, *mon bien cher,* and, with my wife, send all the best regards to you and to your wife.

STRAVINSKY TO ANSERMET   *[Postmark: Biarritz]*
                                                       August 5, 1922
Marecottes /Salvan (Valais)
Please forward

My dear,

I am sending *Les Feuilles Libres* with Poulenc's article (on *Mavra*) for you to read and return to me, please.[88] Tell me when I must send the piano and vocal score of *Mavra* for translation, because time is pressing. A word of reply by return mail. How did "Les Ballets" go in Geneva?[89]

---

two or even five years? And, more generally, if you allow the possibility of a mistake in your evaluation of *Mavra,* then you should have waited before writing your review, or at any rate refrained from such categorical statements as: '*Mavra* is Stravinsky's first failure . . .' Unless this phrase was distorted by the editor, it would seem to me that the phrase that *was* cut would not have changed the sense at all; on the contrary, had it been printed, *it* would have made no sense. . . ." Schloezer first met Stravinsky in Paris in June 1923. (In a letter to the composer dated July 7, Schloezer refers to the "fond memories of the two hours I spent in your company.")

[88] See *Les Feuilles Libres* (June–July 1922), especially the passage "Many people consider *Mavra* a parody of the style of Rossini and Verdi. Nothing could be more false. Music contains operatic forms, just as it does the sonata form and the rondo form, and [they are] free for everyone to use. Stravinsky has used the tradition of Glinka-Tchaikovsky, and is hoping that our musicians will follow the line Gounod-Bizet. Finally, it is *Mavra*'s harmony that has been attacked whenever Stravinsky has been reproached for his *originality*. It is amusing to respond to this, since the musicians of the post-Debussy generation, with their hair turned gray by rare harmonies, have become accustomed to regarding the resolution of chords as banal. Since we live in an age of leveling, where all chords appear to be on the same plane, we must look, for novelty, to a composer who has reintroduced the dominant in our harmony. *Mavra* uses the system of modulation, and it is through horizontal juxtaposition and elongated notes that Stravinsky achieves precise music, bouncing and eminently tonal (rare today). No critic has mentioned this. . . ." Poulenc might have referred to Chabrier, a composer who continued to attract Stravinsky to the extent that in Paris a Chabrier-Stravinsky Festival was given in 1938. Stravinsky's library of Chabrier's music was greatly increased at that time, beginning with the purchase of a score of *L'Etoile* on November 4, 1936. It should also be said that, curiously, Stravinsky did not have any orchestra scores by Glinka while composing *Mavra,* the instrumentation of which owes something to the earlier composer. An invoice from P. Jurgenson in Leipzig, dated October 12, 1922, shows that he purchased the full score of *Ruslan and Lyudmila* in July 1922, and that of *A Life for the Tsar* in August.

[89] On Wednesday, August 2, and Thursday, August 3, 1922, the Ballets Russes performed at the Grand Théâtre in Geneva. The program consisted of *Les Sylphides, Carnaval,* and *Shéhérazade.*

A thousand good wishes to Marguerite from both of us and also to you, *mon cher vieux.*

Your   I Str.

STRAVINSKY TO ANSERMET   *[No date]*

Dear friend,

I have verified, added to, and corrected everything in the "Errata [for *Le Sacre*] ." I beg you to copy all of this *very carefully* because we are working with Germans who do not know, or pretend not to know, French. The directions for the conductor must be printed separately, for which reason I ask you to make a special sheet for them. A third special page would contain the changes in the *Danse sacrale,* which must be marked only in those instrumental parts that have been changed, and also the small sheet for **58** to **59** that I have added in red ink. Make certain that I haven't made a new mistake in the timpani at **57** and **58–59**, since I could easily have slipped up there. Please send it to Oeberg well copied and clear, since you have the parts containing your numerous comments and consequently are the only one who can put everything in place and *coordinate the parts.*

The page with the "Roster of the instruments in *Le Sacre*" must precede these "Errata," "Directions," etc. I hope you will not be too angry that I have returned these sheets for more work, but this is much more expedient than to send them all to the Germans before you see them again.

Good-bye, *mon cher,* and thanks with all my heart.

I Stravinsky

Better simply to send the pages to Ed [ition] Russe de Musique, since Oeberg wants to come to Biarritz, and because Mr. Schmitt [?] will do the corrections.

STRAVINSKY TO ANSERMET   *Biarritz*
                                                          August 15, 1922
My dear Ansermet,

I have just sent to you by registered mail my pocket score of the *Sacre* with the corrections (not all of them!) marked in red ink and pencil—to make your work easier, in case you have any doubts. I beg you to hurry, and to send the corrections on to Berlin and to ask the editor there to send the results to me as soon as his work is finished. By what date must I send *Mavra* to you with your summary translation, which is still at my house?

According to Kochno,[90] it seems that the Ballets Russes were successful in Ostend. I have just received a letter from Wiéner, who is back from the interna-

---

[90] Boris Kochno (b. 1904), Diaghilev's secretary and the librettist of Stravinsky's *Mavra.*

tional musical festivities in Salzburg.[91] He tells me that since the *Soldat* Suite (violin, clarinet, and piano) could not be rehearsed, my name was simply removed from the program of this "big international congress" (Wiéner's phrase). He says that he importuned these people to play my Piano-Rag Music, because the total absence of my name seemed to him, as he writes, "a bit excessive. I insisted so vehemently, and, with me, Poulenc,* that we convinced the festival organizers that it was an excellent idea. Thus the performance of Piano-Rag was an *enormous* success."[92] Reading all that, I wonder what it means. Here I am at the head of modern music, so it is said, and as I willingly believe. Here I am, forty years old, and ignored in the grand prizes of the "Great International Congress" of Salzburg—the capital of Mozart, who is for me what Raphael was for Ingres and is for Picasso. Is it true, all of this? Certainly it is true that the committee reserves important places on the program for Darius Milhaud, Ernest Bloch, Richard Strauss, probably Korngold,[93] Casella, even Varèse—all musicians of "international" stature. But we should not ask too much of them—the poor people are spent. They invite the queen of singers, Marya Freund herself (also very "international"). What is to be done (as Ramuz asks)? Nothing, nothing can be done! That is what is difficult, for it is completely true. Oh, the *cons*. The only satisfaction is that one becomes inured to it . . . which is what must happen with *cons*. That is all they deserve. I send you, *mon cher vieux,* all my great friendship.

Your   I Stravinsky

P.S. Have you sent the telegram authorized by Ganz? No news yet from Hammond. What do you think? I'm nervous.

*Poulenc, if one believes *Comoedia,* "accompanied Marya Freund," who was certainly there and sang some Ravel.[94]

---

[91] In an article, "The Salzburg International Festival," *Comoedia,* August 14, 1922, Gabriel Monferrat wrote that Wiéner "carved a lively success for himself in a piece by Stravinsky."

[92] On August 18, Stravinsky wrote to Wiéner: ". . . Thank you for your kind words, which touched me greatly. I am thrilled to know that you had such a great success with my Rag Music, and I am flattered by the passionate interest in me shown by the illustrious 'International Congress' of Salzburg. . . ."

[93] Erich Korngold (1897–1957), composer of *Die Tote Stadt,* settled in America in 1934, and in the 1940s and 1950s was on friendly terms with Stravinsky.

[94] Marya Freund (1876–1966), soprano, participated in the premieres of many contemporary works. In his Comoedia article G. Monferrat wrote: "During the Festival, Mme Marya Freund, accompanied by M. Poulenc, earned applause for Ravel, and also for young Italian and Spanish composers. . . ."

STRAVINSKY TO ANSERMET   *Biarritz*
                                                    August 19, 1922

Mon vieux,

Our letters have crossed, as you see. I received your card and, in a hurry to reply, am returning a part of your last letter, with my answers in red ink and pencil.

Once again, all my gratitude for your *invaluable* work that saves so much of my time.

Your   I Stravinsky

I am reading with interest the biography of Haydn,[95] in which I find very significant things:

> . . . the secondary and late contribution of Haydn to the *Lied* repertory demonstrates that no real penchant, no special faculty, directed him toward the German song. The development of the *Lied* was parallel to that of German lyric poetry, in which there is no evidence that Haydn was interested.

Amazing, isn't it?

STRAVINSKY TO ANSERMET   *August 27, 1922*

Dear,

Give me a quick answer to the following questions: (1) Is it necessary to send your provisional translation with the piano score of *Mavra,* since time presses? (2) Can I answer the enclosed letter (which I beg you to return to me immediately) in the affirmative? I mean, is it serious?

Write to me in Paris (Pleyel, 24 rue Rochechouart), where I'm going tomorrow. I await news of my mother, who is supposed to leave Petrograd very soon; I will meet her in Germany and then take her to Biarritz.

[Waiting] impatiently for your reply.

I remain your faithful   I Stravinsky

I. P.S. Have you cabled to Hammond for Ganz's authorization?[96]
II. P.S. To save time and if you find it convenient, I authorize you to answer M. Gabellers.[97]

---

[95] Michel Brenet, *Haydn,* Paris, 1909, p. 105.
[96] Stravinsky had written to Ganz on August 22: ". . . Have you heard from Hammond? Me—nothing. Is this a bad sign? . . ."
[97] The writer of the letter that Stravinsky encloses.

STRAVINSKY TO ANSERMET

Dear friend,

Pleyel, Lyon & Cie
22, 24 rue Rochechouart, Paris
September 2, 1922

What bad luck![98] I was stupefied on learning what had happened to you. I hope that by now it is no more than a bad memory, and that your poor foot is completely healed. Two words on this subject, I beg you.

I am still here awaiting news of my mother.

I enclose a sheet of music for the conclusion of the Prelude to the second tableau of *Le Sacre*. I think that you will understand it, but if something is not clear to you, ask me immediately.

I embrace you. Your   I Str.

STRAVINSKY TO ANSERMET

My dear Ansermet,

Biarritz
December 31, 1922

I am thinking of you, this evening of December 31, and I wish you all that one can wish a true friend. Hoping that this new year will bring you much happiness in your world, as well as all the other joy you desire that will stimulate your work. I left you (or, rather, you left me) with the impression that your morale, which was so strong at the beginning of the work, was rudely shaken. Is *Mavra* the cause?[99]

Send me a word on this subject; I think about it all the time, and that torments me.

A thousand good things for you,

Your   I Str.

STRAVINSKY TO ANSERMET

Bien cher,

[Paris]
[January or February 1923]
[Fragment of a letter]

I have received your second letter (with the program of *The Song of the Nightingale*). Thank you and please excuse me for not having written sooner.

---

[98] On August 29, Ansermet had written that he burned his foot while lighting a lamp. The burn became infected and an operation was performed.

[99] The reference is to Ansermet's concert performance of *Mavra* in Paris, December 26—as well as to the poor reception of *Mavra* at its premiere. On May 29, 1922, *Mavra* had been performed at the Hôtel Continental, Paris, for an invited audience, with Stravinsky accompanying the singers at the piano and Fitelberg conducting them. Since the opera was sung in Russian, Ansermet gave a résumé of the plot in French. Stravinsky seems not to have played the overture on this occasion, and his 2-hand reduction of it was evidently not finished until March 1924; his manuscript (R.M.V. 411) was received in Berlin on March 28. The opera buffa was enthusiastically received in the piano performance but was "a fiasco" at the Opéra on June 3, as Léon Bakst delightedly informed Diaghilev a few days later.

I saw Hanson, who has now left for Berlin, in order to examine with him what must be done. This business is evidently not very clear to me, yet I think that Antheil has considerable power, for, if not, Hanson would not give the impression of wanting to do what the boy desires.[100] And Hanson gives that impression rather strongly. I am waiting; that is all I can say for the moment about the publication business.

As for the concerts, I do not know the reasons for Antheil's delay, but they are probably related to the negotiations with Hanson. Moreover, you will see Hanson soon because he took your address, to meet you in Geneva. He will be going to Zürich, then will pass through Geneva on his way to France.

You are right about repeating *Le Sacre;* now is the time to play the *Soldat.* The *Pulcinella*[101] parts are in Biarritz, and I will send them as soon as I return there—without the orchestra score because this is for the complete ballet. You would be an angel if you looked for the missing third and fourth horn and the English horn parts for the *Symphonies.* . . .

Biarritz
[January or February 1923]
[Fragment of a letter]

STRAVINSKY TO ANSERMET

. . . *It is absolutely necessary to arrange a concert of my chamber music in February*. I am counting on it firmly, and I hope you will light a fire under Antheil.

Oeberg, who has just arrived at my house, wants me to ask you if you need these parts.[102] If so, he will send them to you immediately. Write a note to him. The rental will cost 50 Swiss francs.

I saw Diaghilev, who spoke enthusiastically about what you told him concerning the Octet. Since it was understood that you would not talk to him about it, I told him that you had never heard it. He then said "what a liar that Ansermet is." *Mon vieux,* you have put me in a very sad situation, making me an unintentional liar.

With love,   I Stravinsky

---

[100] Martin Hanson was an American impresario of Danish origin who began representing the American composer George Antheil (1900–59) in 1922, organizing a European tour for him in that year.

[101] Ansermet conducted excerpts from *Pulcinella* at the tenth subscription concert at Victoria Hall, Geneva, February 24, 1923. The program also included the Overture to *Euryanthe*, Debussy's Nocturnes, and the Goldmark Violin Concerto, with Joseph Szigeti as soloist. An article about the concert appeared in the *Journal de Genève,* February 26, 1923.

[102] For the premiere of Stravinsky's arrangement of the Prelude and an aria from *The Nightingale* as a concert piece.

STRAVINSKY TO ANSERMET

[January or February 1923]
[Fragment of a letter]

. . . Of course I am very touched by your story of Wiéner, who is even incapable of guaranteeing not to lose the orchestra parts which I had rented to him.[103]

About the beginning of *The Nightingale,* make the request directly to Oeberg, who is at 3 rue de Moscou (8ᵉ) until the 26th, then in Berlin.

Try to arrange a good rental for *Pulcinella,* the author's rights being completely insignificant everywhere and especially in Switzerland.

STRAVINSKY TO ANSERMET

Monday
[January or February 1923]

Dear,

I am answering your questions about the *Soldat*[104] in a great hurry.

1. As for the mutes, remove all the indications for them. Not having the orchestra score at hand, it is difficult for me to answer your question about the trumpet mute in the Triumphant March, but it ought to be made to conform to the *new piano* score. It would be kind of you to arrange it.

2. As for the placement of the 3 side drums without snares:

large

medium

small

I remember that I placed them this way on purpose. Unfortunately I do not have the orchestra score. The only ones in existence anywhere are 1. the manuscript, which Werner Reinhart has, and which belongs to him; and 2. the copy at Chester's, which they have not taken the precaution to have copied. In any case, the placement of the drums at the end must be changed to conform to the piano score, in which all three lines are indicated.

You will see Antheil and Hanson. Explain to them, without revealing that I have talked to you about them, that my principal objective is to publish the works that I compose. I will go anywhere, with you and with them, but they must find a way to arrange for publication. This matter is of the utmost importance, and if I am satisfied with their arrangements, they can then count on my participation in the trip to America with you (which would be the point of their visit to you). Pay attention to what I am saying, my old friend, and *be persistent enough* to convince Antheil. He seemed to understand me in Berlin but now appears to have given in to pressure from Hanson; he is evidently interested in *displaying* me in America, and getting his hands on some more or less considerable sums. . . .

---

[103] For the Stravinsky concert of December 26, 1922, at the Théâtre des Champs-Elysées.

[104] The Geneva performance of the *Soldat,* announced for Thursday, February 8, 1923, at the concert of the "Nouvelles Auditions," was postponed to February 22 because Ansermet was ill. The program also included the Sonata for clarinet and bassoon and an extract from *Le Gendarme incompris* by Poulenc.

I'm really counting on you, and, as much for your sake as for mine, I want you to understand the full importance of the interview you will have with these gentlemen.

Send a telegram to "Strav. Pleyel" as soon as you have seen them.

I embrace you.   I Stravinsky

STRAVINSKY TO ANSERMET

[February 1923]
[Fragment of a letter]

Instructions on the instrumentation of the *Soldat*
 I. Replace "horn," which is absurd, with "cornet."
[For *Les Noces*:]
II. 2 side drums without snares, large

and

small size

   1 drum without snares.
   Bass drum.
At the beginning of *Les Noces,* this same nomenclature should replace the old one, in which three sizes of side drums were listed.

STRAVINSKY TO ANSERMET

Paris
February 10, 1923

12 bd. des Tranchées
Geneva, Switzerland

My dear,

Why this silence? Received a teleg[ram] from Prelat on the success of *Le Sacre*[105]—very nice of him to have cabled. And the *Soldat*? I waited to receive a note from you, too. No news from Antheil. What does that mean? Write to me quickly, I beg you.

Your   I Str.

Diagh. is in Monte Carlo, confirming with Kochno [the proposed] South America [n trip] and a short season in Milan in May.[106]

---

[105] This benefit concert for the musicians of the Orchestre de la Suisse Romande took place on February 5 at Victoria Hall, Geneva. The program included *Le Sacre*, Bach's Concerto for two violins (with Fernand Closset and Jean Lacroix as soloists), Beethoven's Fifth Symphony, and the Overture to *Tannhäuser.*
[106] Neither of these projects was realized. Instead, the company returned to Monte Carlo after the Paris season, passing through Switzerland and presenting *The Sleeping Princess, Cléopâtre, Shéhérazade,* and *Pulcinella.*

STRAVINSKY TO ANSERMET   *Pleyel, Lyon & Cie*
                                     22, 24 rue Rochechouart, Paris
My dear,   *February 11, 1923*

Oeberg has entrusted me to have you send to him—*here in Paris, 3 rue de Moscou 8e*—the score you used the last time you played the Prelude to *Le Sacre*.[107] I hope that this score was of the Prelude and not of something else, since Oeberg is certain that you have no scores other than the Prelude at your home. He also wants to know the price you fixed with your committee for the rental of the score.

Otherwise, Oeberg would like to know if you need the scores of the Prelude, Song of the Fisherman and of the Nightingale, because Koussevitzky needs them for his concert. Since communications with Germany are very difficult, you will understand the anxiety of your friend Oeberg.

If you come to Paris soon, or pass through Paris on your way to Nantes (will you go there, finally?), bring with you, *cher,* the score of the *Sacre* Prelude. You will be a love.

I send all my affection and await your news with great impatience.

                                   Your   I Stravinsky

At the Théâtre-Lyrique at Trianon, I heard a marvel of music: *Philémon et Baucis* by Gounod, together with *Isabelle et Pantalon* by Roland-Manuel,[108] a work about which, unhappily, I cannot say enough.

STRAVINSKY TO ANSERMET   *March 5, 1923*

12 bd. des Tranchées
Geneva, Switzerland

Eh bien, cher,

Why this silence again? I have been in Biarritz since March 1 and have not yet heard anything from you. How did *Pulcinella* go? I sent word to you from Paris explaining why it was impossible to get the orchestra score of *Pulcin* [*ella*] to you in time. Did it arrive?[109]

                                   I embrace you.   I Str

---

[107] Ansermet had written to Stravinsky on September 15, 1922, telling him of a desire to conduct the Prelude to Part Two of *Le Sacre,* and requesting Oeberg's permission to perform it in Zürich on October 31. On May 8, 1923, Oeberg wrote to Stravinsky: "While I was still in Paris, Ansermet sent the orchestra parts for the Prelude to the second part of *Le Sacre,* but did not send the score. I do not know whether he made any corrections or left everything unchanged. Would you please ask him about this and send a quick reply to me here?"

[108] The premiere of *Philémon* had taken place at the Théâtre de la Gaîté-Lyrique on February 18, 1860, and that of *Isabelle et Pantalon* occurred on December 11, 1922. "Roland-Manuel" was a pseudonym of Alexis Manuel-Lévy (1891–1966).

[109] See p. 163.

Were you present at the recitals of my pleyelization rolls at Foetisch's,[110] organized by Gagnebin?[111]

STRAVINSKY TO ANSERMET   *March 15, 1923*

My dear Ansermet,

When you read these words, it will have been three weeks since you played *Pulcinella* in Geneva (if you did play it), and, except for your telegram* of a week ago, no other news! What is happening? Why do you not write to me about anything? There are so many urgent things to tell you. I receive letter after letter from Antheil, who always asks me to inform him by telegram where I am or where I will be, so that he can come to see me. But he fails to give me his address, and my telegrams do not follow him, because I just received one returned from Budapest with the notice that Antheil had *left*!! Yet this intelligent boy is astonished at my silence! I do not count on these people, although it might interest me if Hanson represents Fischer and wants to see you. Answer me eventually. Starting on Tuesday I will be in Paris for a week.

                                   I embrace you.   I Stravinsky

Diagh [ilev] is going to Monte Carlo today.

*Announcing the arrival of Hanson

STRAVINSKY TO ANSERMET   *Pleyel, Lyon & Cie*
                                    22, 24 rue Rochechouart, Paris
My dear,   *May 14, 1923*

Enclosed is Hanson's letter, which I took the liberty of opening. I just saw Adams[112] and Kahn,[113] and also Artur Rubinstein, who leaves immediately for a month-long tour of Spain and then returns to Paris. That trip will be arranged, and I beg you, if necessary, telegraph Hanson that I will come to America next winter.*

    Have you seen Reinhart? And, since my finances right now are in a critical state,[114] have you discussed the question that interests me?

                        I embrace you and yours.   Igor Stravinsky

---

[110] Foetisch Frères, Swiss music dealers.

[111] Henri Gagnebin (b. 1886), Swiss composer, was named director of the Geneva Conservatory in 1925.

[112] A. F. Adams, director of the Wolfsohn Musical Bureau, New York, the oldest concert agency in America, founded in 1884 by Henry Wolfsohn.

[113] Alexander Kahn (1872–1942), American concert agent, director of publicity for many opera companies, including those of Boston and Chicago, European representative of the Wolfsohn Musical Bureau.

[114] In a postcard dated November 20, 1923, Werner Reinhart asks Stravinsky if he will come to Switzerland for the performance of the *Soldat*.

*A telegram may change things in the wrong direction, which is to say that Hanson or Fischer might think it more practical to await my arrival to deal with the affair. In that case is it perhaps better not to telegraph?

STRAVINSKY TO ANSERMET

Bien cher,

Pleyel, Lyon & Cie
22, 24 rue Rochechouart, Paris
Tuesday, May 22, 1923

Until now nothing received, in spite of your promise that a "letter *will follow.*" I understand that you have an enormous number of things to do, but you will understand my nervousness and impatience if I tell you that the Adams affair, which appeared to be progressing, seems at this moment to be in jeopardy. I have been seeing Stokowski[115] every day and had reached an agreement to tour with his orchestra in several cities. This was to serve as the basis of my engagement with Adams. But Stokowski has just received a flat refusal, telegraphed by Judson[116] (with the agreement of Adams and the manager of the Committee of Philadelphia). Well, in order not to lose all hope, I brought up the question of a similar tour with [Walter] Damrosch, who is here; he is going to study the possibilities with Kahn.

I beg you to say *nothing at all* to Diaghilev. He knows only that I am negotiating with Stokowski, *that is all.*[117]

I have just received a letter from G. Antheil, as idiotic as the others, and since it concerns you in part and your business with Hanson-Fischer, I am sending it to you; return it to me in Paris.

Answer me, *mon cher.* Is there some hope on the Reinhart front?

Your   I Strav

The Octet is finished.

---

[115] Leopold Stokowski (1882–1977). (See Appendix J.)

[116] Arthur Judson (1881–1975), American impresario. In 1922 he became manager of the Philharmonic Orchestra of New York, and in 1928 the Judson Bureau absorbed the Wolfsohn Musical Bureau, later becoming Columbia Concerts.

[117] In April 1931, greatly agitated by an announcement in the American press that Stokowski was presenting *Oedipus Rex* at the Metropolitan Opera on the 21st of the month as a *"film sonore,"* Stravinsky in Nice telegraphed to Païchadze in Paris asking for an investigation and an answer at the Excelsior Hotel in Trieste. Stravinsky had written to Païchadze on the 15th: "I am here until Sunday, the day of my departure for Trieste, for a week or ten days. Reinhart comes tomorrow and will stay with me until then, but I do not feel well these days; there is something very disagreeable in the atmosphere which upsets my nerves."

STRAVINSKY TO ANSERMET

My dear Ernest,

As you see, I am typing my letters better and better all the time, which is to say, more quickly. Wiéner showed your letter to me and said that you are suggesting the following program:[118]

    1. *Noces*
    2. Octet
    3. Songs (with the *Noces* singers)
    4. *Noces*

instead of:

    1. *Soldat*
    2. Octet
    3. *Noces*

saying that the reasoning behind this preference was the economy in rehearsals. He asks my opinion and, to tell the truth, I am sorry that the *Soldat* is missing, the more so because Paris has not yet seen his beautiful uniform of the Vaudois country. I understand the argument about economy in rehearsals, but am seeking a way to include the *Soldat* anyway. Couldn't you arrange *two* concerts with these *two* programs?

1st concert	2nd concert
1. *Soldat*	1. Octet
2. Songs	2. *Ragtime*
3. *Noces*	3. *Noces*

If you feel that *Ragtime* is too short to fill No. 2, perhaps you could add a fragment of *Renard,* which also requires a cimbalom, and which I will arrange for concert performances. What do you say?

I also have a letter from Collaer,[119] who says, among other things: "the concert with Ansermet is definite for January, with *Pulcinella* in its entirety, and, if you would like, the Octet, and *Mavra.* I would have added the *Symphonies,* but since the instrumentalists who are playing for us are Prévost's,[120] I can hardly take them from him, especially since he is conducting the piece in our first concert."

Here is what I think: 1. *Pulcinella* should not be played in full but in the

---

[118] The program was for a concert organized by Jean Wiéner that took place on November 7 at the Salle des Agriculteurs, eventually with the following works: *Histoire du soldat,* Aria from *Mavra* (soloist Madeleine Caron), Octet, *Berceuses du chat* (Madeleine Caron). Stravinsky conducted the Modern Society of Wind Instruments.

[119] Paul Collaer (b. 1891), Belgian musicologist, author of a book on Stravinsky published in 1929.

[120] Germain Prévost, violist of the Pro Arte Quartet, and a friend of Stravinsky in the California years. He gave the first performance of Stravinsky's Elegy for solo viola.

large Suite (given last year at Wiéner's); 2. the *Symphonies* certainly should be played, and Prévost's performance of it in his first concert is not a drawback; 3. *Pulcinella,* the Octet, *Mavra,* and the *Symphonies* seem to me to be a little too much for one concert. What to do therefore? Give a second concert? Tell me what you think.

What are you doing up there? Give me news of Marguerite, of her health, of Jacqueline,[121] of Monsieur C. F. Ramuz, who does not like to come to Paris when *Les Noces* and *Renard* are being performed, and finally of everybody in whom I am interested.

I embrace you.   Igor Stravinsky

I am composing a piece for piano and many other instruments, and the work is coming along well. I also do gymnastics every morning and sunbathe from noon to 1:00.

STRAVINSKY TO ANSERMET   *August 31, 1923*
                                                   [Postcard]
Jolimont
Marecottes/Salvan (Valais), Switzerland

Dear,

I have just arrived in Biarritz after my trip to Weimar[122] and my short stay in Paris. One of these days I will write a long letter with my impressions and answer all your questions. I slept badly on the train last night, so this is all for today.

I embrace you.   I Stravinsky

STRAVINSKY TO ANSERMET   *Biarritz*
                                             September 9, 1923
My very dear Ansermet,

I spent all this week in the company of Auric, who came to visit me in Biarritz. He stayed at my house, and we played rather a lot of music. He played a great duo for two women that he has just composed for an opera with a libretto by Cocteau. I like it very much, for it is good-humored.

What are you doing, *mon cher*? Are you staying a long time in Marecottes?

As for me, I don't regret having made the trip to Weimar: (1) Scherchen did the *Soldat* music[123] well; (2) the German public received the piece very

---

[121] Ansermet's daughter.

[122] Stravinsky and Vera Sudeikina had gone to Weimar to see the Bauhaus production of *Histoire du soldat*.

[123] Hermann Scherchen (1891–1966) had conducted the first performance of the *Soldat* in Germany, in Frankfurt, on June 20, 1923. A year later, Stravinsky wrote to his publisher: "I never wrote to Scherchen about the Octet, or about granting permission

well, giving me an ovation, which is *always profitable for the future,* when Germany resumes its former life; then (3) I saw with my own eyes the enormous abyss that separates me from this country and from the inhabitants of the whole of Middle Europe. The *Kubismus* there is stronger than ever and, absurdly, it moves arm in arm with the *Impressionismus* of Schoenberg. I heard concerts of the interminable *Lieder* of Hindemith, which bored me a great deal:[124] it is a kind of H. Wolf! Too bad, I had hoped for something else. Scherchen said that Hindemith composes too much. Perhaps. I also heard an *Abteilung* of Busoni's piano works played by Petri,[125] a good pianist from Berlin. Among these compositions were brand-new pieces for piano that were not bad at all.[126] I met the *"maître,"* who was sitting next to me, and who, with his wife, cried real tears during the *Soldat,* the story so moved them.

Now something else. Big news: Kling is going to print the orchestra scores of (1) *Renard,* of (2) *Soldat,* and of (3) *Les Noces!![*127] You must agree that this is progress. He is moving so quickly, O. M. Kling, that it would no longer surprise me to learn that M. Jean-Aubry[128] himself was sent away, after a violent discussion on the subject of new acquisitions of works by Malipiero. Add to that the orchestra score of (4) *Pulcinella* (or of its Suites) that is probably going to be published by Hansen in Copenhagen,[129] and (5) the orchestra score of *The Nightingale.*[130] I will have a year of proofreading.

So long as we are undecided about *Mavra,* don't mention it to anyone. As for what you wrote to me about the Pro Arte and their desire to keep the parts of the Concertino[131] permanently, it should be easily arranged because Hansen will probably sell instead of rent. You see, *mon cher,* that I can tell you nothing about the score of *Mavra* because of these negotiations with Hansen. Anyway, do you think that the small overture of *Mavra* would fit with the Chinese March as (a) and (b) of one number of the program?[132]

I advise you, rather, to play the Overture with Parasha's aria, which I plan

---

for anything . . . all of that is a brazen-faced lie. I implore you to take the parts away from him." (Biarritz, August 21, 1924)

[124] *Das Marienleben,* Opus 27, composed in 1922–23 on Rilke's cycle of poems.

[125] Egon Petri (1881–1962), assistant to Busoni in Berlin in the 1920s. From 1932, Petri taught at Cornell University, and later at Mills College.

[126] *Fünf kurze Stücke zur Pflege des polyphonischen Spiels,* composed in 1923 and dedicated to Edwin Fischer, and published by Breitkopf & Härtel the same year.

[127] Chester published the *Soldat* and *Les Noces* in 1924.

[128] Georges Jean-Aubry (1882–1949), French musicologist.

[129] The Copenhagen firm of Wilhelm Hansen had published Stravinsky's Concertino for string quartet.

[130] *The Nightingale* and *Mavra* were both published by the Edition Russe de Musique.

[131] See nn. 50 and 85 above.

[132] Performed on October 27, 1923, under Ansermet. The program consisted of Beethoven's Sixth Symphony, Mendelssohn's Violin Concerto, the overture to *Mavra,* the Chinese March from *The Nightingale,* and Three Symphonic Episodes from *Antoine et Cléopâtre* by Florent Schmitt.

to enlarge as follows: after the actual aria, there will be several measures connecting it to the duo (G minor), which Parasha will sing alone (the tenor part having been placed in the instruments), and finishing with the short repetition of the song, as in the score. In my opinion that would go quite well! What do you think?

I am in despair about Wiéner. He will never make up his mind to do two concerts, and I don't really know what to answer him; he is still waiting for my reply. What shall I tell him?

Koussevitzky is here. The other day I saw Zederbaum,[133] who described a new association whose aim is the performance of chamber music, and whose *president* (!!—*sic*) is Koussevitzky. These Jews understood my Octet, as you may well have guessed, and will even invite me to conduct it. I will see Koussevitzky one of these days and find out just what this business is about.

On my return from Weimar, I saw Benois,[134] who had just arrived from Petersburg. He will do costumes and sets for Diaghilev's *Le Médecin*[135] but, un-

---

[133] Vladimir Zederbaum, a doctor of medicine, was Koussevitzky's secretary.

[134] Alexandre Benois (1870–1960) has never received due credit as the originator of the musical conception of *Le Baiser de la fée*. He wrote to Stravinsky, December 12, 1927: "I was overjoyed to learn that you have reached an in-principle agreement with Ida Lvovna [Rubinstein], for thus my great wish for us to enter another artistic venture together will be realized. Obviously to describe this dream to you . . . in person would be easier, but since there is no hope of meeting much before February, I will try to give you an idea, in very general terms, of what we have in mind. . . . We wish to present Tchaikovsky as seen by Stravinsky. For quite a while I have wanted to do something with Uncle Petya's music, something not necessarily based on his ballet music. . . . Nor is my inclination in the direction of the symphonies, for the inflexible symphonic form might interfere with the creation of an original and integral work. This would not be the case if we were to choose certain piano pieces, which, together, would constitute a subject, or, better still, a base on which a subject could then be imposed, since the pieces would already be linked by purely musical affinities. Let me mention a few 'candidates' (I think that you will agree with me on many of them): from 'The Seasons'—nos. 7 and 11 (July and November). From the Six Pieces Op. 51—no. 1 Valse de salon (perhaps), no. 2 Polka peu dansante, no. 3 Menuetto Scherzoso, no. 4 Natha-Valse, no. 5 Romance. From Six Pieces Op. 19—no. 1 Rêverie du soir, no. 2 Scherzo humoristique, no. 3 Feuillet d'album, no. 5 Capriccioso. From the Twelve Pieces Op. 40—no. 2 Chanson triste, no. 5 Mazurka, no. 7 Au village, no. 10 Danse russe, etc., etc. . . . To continue is senseless; let me ask you point-blank: Do you like the idea of fixing up Uncle Petya's music and making something new of it? If so, . . . then simply say 'splendid,' and the matter will be done. If you do not like it, I know there is no way that I will be able to win you over. . . . I would like to add a prayer: 'God grant that this proposition will prove interesting to you and that this dream that I have been nurturing might, thanks to you, really come to pass.' . . ." Stravinsky used seven of the pieces on Benois's list.

[135] Gounod's opera *Le Médecin malgré lui*, with recitatives by Satie, decor by Benois, and choreography by Nijinska, was performed by the Ballets Russes in Monte Carlo, January 5, 1924.

happily, will not stay long in France, for he is obliged to keep his post as Director of the Hermitage.[136] Even so, I have conceived of several vague projects of collaboration with him for *Mavra* and *The Nightingale,* since he is firm in his intention to return to Paris. Do you find it absolutely impossible to stage these pieces in Switzerland with him? Don't you think you could manage to interest Reinhart in that? In what form and where should the operas be performed? In Zürich? Winterthur? Perhaps even in Geneva? Although Benois is of a different generation, I am convinced that his work will make a thousand-times-better impression on the public than that of another painter whom I may admire much more than I do him. Unfortunately, it would be impossible to realize my project under Diaghilev because: 1. Diaghilev will never do a second set for *Mavra,* having already done one (in a Galeries Lafayette Cubism);[137] 2. *The Nightingale* opera does not interest him at all, chiefly because he has Matisse's set (of which he is so proud) * for *The Song of the Nightingale.*[138] In a few days, these "old friends" will see each other. Diagh. arrives September 12; right now he is in Antibes at Picasso's, returning to Milan, while Benois is beginning to wonder if Diagh. really needs urgently to see him. . . . I am convinced that there will be some obstacle, especially because Benois is unenthusiastic about Picasso, which bothers me a great deal. This lack of enthusiasm I attribute with some certainty to a very understandable jealousy, a jealousy that Diagh., being himself a jealous person (we know it, do we not?), will interpret completely differently. I can foresee it.

I see that my letter will never be finished if I don't stop in time. The time has come and I put down the pen.

I embrace you, *mon vieux,* and your family. Tell Ramuz, if he still exists, that I often think of him and that we would have had fun together at Weimar, despite the fact that it was not at all funny to see a young idiot from Frankfurt mime the role of the Princess. She assumed oriental postures and wore a transparent costume!!! In contrast, the Reader, the Soldier, and the Devil, but especially the first two, were very good. Even so, Auberjonois's set was beautiful! Unfortunately the little theater was placed on a horrible background, a very vulgar blue, somewhat in the style of Larionov's decor for [Tchaikovsky's] *The Snow Maiden.*

I will definitely never finish with this. Good-bye.

Your   I Stravinsky

* Matisse's name is desirable, by Jove!

---

[136] Benois was the chief curator of paintings at the Museum of the Hermitage in St. Petersburg. He published *Treasures of Russian Art, A History of Russian Art in the Twentieth Century,* and *A History of Painting of All Time.*

[137] These sets were by Léopold Survage.

[138] The premiere of *The Song of the Nightingale* as a ballet took place at the Paris Opéra on February 2, 1920.

STRAVINSKY TO ANSERMET   *Biarritz*
                                                               September 15, 1923
Cher vieux,

Our letters have crossed.

Oeberg is here in Biarritz and begs you to write to him at my address; he is staying until September 25. Here are the answers to the questions that interest you, point by point:

I. *Mavra.* As I have told you, it is better to play the Overture together with Parasha's aria (in the just-finished arrangement that I spoke to you about),[139] in the version for voice and piano, at least for the moment. Since this makes a very short number, you will also be able to play the Chinese March, so that my music will be divided a. and b. on the program:

> a. Overture and Parasha's aria from the opera *Mavra.*
> b. Chinese March from the opera *The Nightingale.*

I can send my manuscript orchestra score of the Overture immediately and also start work on the orchestra score of the Aria. To save time, I am sending the score of the Overture by registered mail (to Geneva). You must get to work on copying.* Quickly send word by return mail as to when you must have the orchestra score of the Aria.

II. *Pulcinella.* I have just given my rights for the orchestration (not sold to Chester) to the Edition Russe de Musique, which, coincidentally, is also the owner of the *Pulcinella* Suite. Oeberg will send this Suite to you as soon as he returns to Paris and establishes the terms. Is this the Suite that you have already played at Wiéner's and with your orchestra? Oeberg asks me to warn you that he will be able to rent it to you only on the condition that you return it before December 1, because he will need it, and so will I, for my concert at Antwerp.

III. The Octet.[140] This will probably be published by the Edition Russe de Musique, but since the question is not pressing, let us postpone it until another time.

---

[139] In the actual arrangement, Stravinsky goes from **6** (rehearsal number in the full opera) to the first three measures of **21**, where, however, he stays in B-flat minor (i.e., Parasha's part in the opera, a half-step lower). Instead of the several connecting measures referred to in his letter of September 9, the composer simply transfers the three measures of the vocal duo that follow to an oboe and bassoon, he adds an accompaniment of two clarinets, and he does not change the tonality. In the G-minor duo, the tenor part is assigned to oboes, alternating with bassoon. The piece concludes with the reprise of the B-flat minor aria and a final B-flat minor triad sustained by three horns. The orchestration of the arrangement (R.M.V. 458, published in 1925) is for pairs of oboes, clarinets, and bassoons, four horns, tuba, and the same combination of strings used in the opera.

[140] The Octet was on the program of the Wiéner concert, December 26, 1923.

IV. For my rental conditions, see what you can get for me—for *Mavra*, since, on all other works, Oeberg decides.

I will probably conduct the Octet myself for the Dixtuor Society, about which I spoke to you.

I am in a big hurry, which explains the tone and dryness of my letter, for which please excuse me.

> I embrace you.   Igor Stravinsky

*The parts, which, as you so kindly promised, will become my property.

STRAVINSKY TO ANSERMET   *Biarritz*
                                                   September 21, 1923

My dear Ernest,

Here again is a point-by-point reply to your two letters, that of Sept. 17 to me, and of Sept. 15 to Oeberg (who asked me to answer for him, to save time, and because he does not know French very well).

I. Diagh. still has the same (old) parts for *Petrushka*. He will have the right to play *Petrushka* only if he agrees to Oeberg's terms as set forth in his last letter from Germany. Did Diaghilev receive it? If so, he has not answered, and Oeberg interprets the silence as an acceptance of his terms. If by chance the letter has not reached Diaghilev, he should inform Oeberg (3 rue de Moscou), who will repeat the terms. If everything is settled, and *Petrushka* is to be played,[141] Oeberg asks you to keep the piano score; if not, return it to him at 3 rue de Moscou.

II. For 100 Swiss francs, Oeberg will send the *Sacre* score to you from Paris, with the additional string parts, in accordance with your letter.

III. *Pulcinella*: if you play it many times, the price is 50 Swiss francs per performance. At the beginning of October, Oeberg will send the number of supplementary orchestra parts indicated in your letter. Unfortunately, there will not be sufficient time to copy the full score.

IV. It is all right to play the Overture to *Mavra*[142] with Parasha's aria, which I am in the process of adjusting. I will send you this score, and you will be responsible for having the parts extracted. The Edition Russe de Musique, which

---

[141] The Ballets Russes performed *Petrushka* in Geneva on October 3 and 4, with the Orchestre de la Suisse Romande conducted by Ansermet. The program for October 3 also included *Cléopâtre* and *Soleil de nuit;* that for October 4, *Pulcinella* and the Polovtsian Dances from *Prince Igor.*

[142] The Overture to *Mavra* was in the program of Ansermet's October 27, 1923, concert with the Orchestre de la Suisse Romande.

now owns *Mavra,* as well as the *Symphonies* and the Octet (do not tell anyone about this yet), will authorize you to play this excerpt and the Overture, at no cost, on condition that you return the parts to them. So, no *Mavra* in the subscription concerts, but, on the other hand . . .

V. The entire *Song of the Nightingale* as you requested. Oeberg will send the complete score to you from Paris for 100 Swiss francs per performance.[143] Let him know the number of additional strings.

VI. Oeberg asks me to tell you that Prokofiev has the parts for his Concerto,[144] and Oeberg will send the full score to you from Paris.

Those are all of the answers. Now something else. Tell Diagh. that if he plans to perform *Les Noces* in Paris before the New Year, he must do so before October 15, since our solo singers (except D'Arial) are all going to Barcelona at about that date and will stay there until the end of the year. Another question arises about *Les Noces* in regard to the Wiéner concert (this poor soul cannot even fix a date!!!):[145] where, I ask you, will he get the parts? Diaghilev has the only set in existence, and Kling had only one extra score, which, for the moment, is at my house being prepared for printing. If Diagh. is unwilling to lend his parts to Wiéner, what can be done? Still, there is this question of the Octet. Koussevitzky invited me to conduct it at the end of October or the beginning of November for the Dixtuor Society, about which I spoke to you; they will pay a rather estimable fee, which I could still refuse. Even if Diagh. agrees to lend the *Noces* parts to Wiéner, I still do not agree to a double performance in the same concert. I propose to do the *Soldat,* Octet, and *Les Noces,* if Diagh. were to lend the parts.

There is no more room, I am finished, and I embrace you affectionately.

I Stravinsky

STRAVINSKY TO ANSERMET

My dear Ansermet,

Pleyel & Cie
22, 24 rue Rochechouart, Paris
November 15, 1923

Et voilà! The Wiéner concert is over and it was a great success, due as much to my guidance in the conducting as to my works. I hope that this does not make you jealous, and that you will rejoice with all my friends and with Catherine, who was also there. I frankly confess that I greatly missed you that night.

Send news, I beg of you. I am staying here ten more days, awaiting the signing of the contract for next year in the United States.

---

[143] This was performed in Ansermet's October concert.

[144] Prokofiev was the soloist in his Third Concerto for piano and orchestra on December 8, 1923. The program included Schubert's last C-major symphony and *Thamar* by Balakirev.

[145] *Les Noces* was not performed at the November 7 Wiéner concert.

And Brussels? Will the January 5 concert take place?

Have you forgotten to return to Ramuz a certain paper that he rightly de-clares uninteresting, but that he must sign for the authors' rights [for *Histoire du soldat*] ? Do it, *mon cher,* because I have already been annoyed with this paper for several weeks.

I embrace you and yours.

STRAVINSKY TO ANSERMET   *Biarritz*
                                                  February 23, 1924
My dear Ansermet,

I have just received your letter and am very happy finally to have news directly from you, because I have already heard some things about the *Soldat* in-directly.

Unfortunately I cannot write at length, being very busy with: the composi-tion of the last part of my Concerto; the orchestration of the first part (the sec-ond is finished); the piano reduction; the correction of the proofs of the *Soldat* (Chester's orchestra score); preparations for my concerts in Barcelona[146] (I go there via Paris on March 4), etc. etc. etc. It is enough to drive one crazy!

Thus I answer you quickly on two important questions:

1. Diaghilev—I have spoken to him about the necessity of having you conduct the Paris season, especially in view of his restaging of *Noces.* He told me that he would see, that perhaps Monteux will come round, and that he always quarrels with you, though he recognizes your value. Thus, indecision: that was the state of things in Paris, where I was a week ago. Vera writes to me in Biarritz about what is happening in general. I conclude that Diaghilev is afraid that if he does not engage you, you will work with me on the *Soldat,* be it with Beaumont[147] (whose organization includes: (1) Satie, who is furious about my criticism of his recitatives in *Le Médecin malgré lui* in Monte Carlo, (2) Massine, (3) Pi-casso, (4) Cocteau, (5) Picabia,[148] (6) Tristan Tzara) or with Beriza, a rich singer who will rent a theater in Paris for the high season and will play *Mavra* and probably *Soldat.*[149] Madame Picabia, the ex-wife of the painter, is actively involved with the *Soldat,* and she went to London yesterday to make an agreement with Kling.[150] She wants to acquire the exclusive rights for staged presentations and then sell them to various enterprises.[151] She is a

---

[146] These concerts, under Stravinsky's direction, took place on March 11, 13, and 16 at the Teatro Liceo.

[147] Comte Etienne de Beaumont (1883–1956), organizer of the "Soirées de Paris."

[148] Francis Picabia (1878–1953), French painter and friend of Stravinsky.

[149] Marguerite Beriza did present *Histoire du soldat* in Paris in April 1924.

[150] Gabrielle Picabia was Stravinsky's agent for *Histoire du soldat,* and she shared an apartment with Vera Sudeikina, 1922–25.

[151] On February 13, Stravinsky had written to Gabrielle Picabia: ". . . I possess the complete rights of scenic presentation of the *Soldat,* in respect to my music. In respect

very nice person; I like her very much. She lives with Vera. As for Diaghilev, I advise you to be firm about the fee which you want to ask (5,000 fr.)—it is certainly childish—but it seems to me that his season, though short, will be more significant than those of Beaumont or Beriza, for which nothing has been decided yet except *Mavra*. There are also plans for South America. I suppose it would mean leaving at the end of May. If you were to find a way of arranging things for yourself in Paris (still with Beaumont or Beriza) after the Ballets Russes season, I would advise you not to go [to South America].

2. *Soldat*—I think you are right about the percussion at the end, and I beg you to render me this service: I will send you the proofs of the final Dance and ask you to correct it and to send it directly to Chester by registered mail. I am happy to know that the *Soldat* is recognized in Switzerland, because there are many things which are not yet in order. But who will conduct it if you go with Diaghilev?

I embrace you warmly.   Igor Stravinsky

P.S. I will go back to Biarritz at the end of March, then to Paris around the middle of April, remaining there for the whole season.

STRAVINSKY TO ANSERMET   *Palace Hotel*
                                                                       Madrid
Cher,   *March 24, 1924*

Two words to give you my news and to ask for yours.

I spent two weeks in Barcelona, where I conducted three enormously successful concerts at the Liceo: *Firebird* (Chester); *Fireworks; The Song of the Nightingale; Pulcinella;* Prelude with 2 arias (Fisherman and Nightingale); some short, newly orchestrated pieces (again for Antwerp-Janacopulos);[152] "Tilimbom"[153] (lengthened to twice its size); "Pastorale"[154] (accompanied by 4 woodwinds); and *The Faun and the Shepherdess,* which is not bad at all.

You were discussed often and in the most enthusiastic terms. At the mo-

---

to Ramuz's text, Chester owns the material. You must therefore deal with all three of us, beginning with Chester. But you must know that a ten-year term is, in my opinion, excessive, given the difficulties, in the times in which we live, in trying to foresee what could happen: I am thinking primarily of finances. Thus you will have to make a proposal in dollars (I am speaking only for myself) and for five years. Furthermore, I would like to be involved, even in a small way, in the returns for the performances."

[152] Vera Janacopulos, Brazilian soprano.

[153] "Tilimbom," composed in Morges, May 22, 1917, originally as part of the *Three Stories for Children* (1915–17), translated by Ramuz, published in 1920 by Chester, and twice instrumentated, in 1923 and 1954.

[154] "Pastorale," song without words for soprano and piano, composed in Ustilug in 1907, dedicated to Nadiezhda Rimsky-Korsakov (Mrs. Steinberg) and published by Jurgenson in 1910.

ment, I am in Madrid, where I conduct a concert tomorrow at the Teatro Real with the Philharmonic Orchestra of Pérez Casas.[155] The local aristocracy[156] organized the concert, and I am playing *Firebird* and *Pulcinella.* Wednesday I return to Biarritz. And you, what are you doing? And why does no one hear from you? Are you going to South America or not?[157] Is Ramuz really in Paris? On receiving these lines, I beg you, *mon cher,* to send back those pages of the *Soldat* (printer's proofs) that I recently sent to you. I shall attend to them immediately because Chester is on the verge of threatening to reclaim them.

I embrace you and yours.   I Stravinsky

STRAVINSKY TO ANSERMET   *Biarritz*
                                                       March 28, 1924

Dear friend,

I am in Biarritz and beg you to send immediately the proofs of the Triumphant March of the Devil. I wrote to you about it from Madrid; did you receive my letter?

Do you know that Beriza is giving three galas at the Champs-Elysées, April 24 to 26, in which she will play the Berners[158] opera [*Le Carrosse du Saint-Sacrement*], my *Soldat,* and something by the very young Sauguet?[159]

Tell me if you are free to come to Paris around April 15 to conduct the rehearsals of these three galas. They are asking me to conduct the *Soldat,* which is impossible because of the absolute lack of time. Imagine that I must finish the last part of my Concerto, learn to play the whole piece on the piano, and perform gloriously at the premiere on May 15!

Awaiting your reply by return mail and also the requested proofs. I send you all my friendliest wishes.

I Stravinsky

---

[155] Bartolomeo Pérez Casas (1873–1956), Spanish composer and conductor who founded the Philharmonic Orchestra of Madrid in 1915.

[156] The Marquise of Salamanca. Pérez Casas conducted the first and third parts of the concert, Stravinsky the second. The program began with *Shéhérazade,* and ended with the Prelude to *La Princesse lointaine* (Tcherepnin) and the *Capriccio espagnol* (Rimsky-Korsakov).

[157] Ansermet describes his trip to Buenos Aires in a letter to Stravinsky, September 21, 1924.

[158] Lord Berners (1883–1950), composer, painter, writer. Stravinsky and he were good friends before World War II. See the correspondence with Berners in S.S.C. III.

[159] Henri Sauguet (b. 1901), French composer, pupil of Koechlin and Satie.

STRAVINSKY TO ANSERMET

12 [bd. des] Tranchées
Geneva

Believe able to come Berlin June 6 or 7. Honorarium 5,000.[160] Regards.   Stravinsky

STRAVINSKY TO ANSERMET

Dear,

Received your letter and am in a hurry to answer that the most convenient time[161] would be the end of November, since we are moving from Biarritz to Nice at the beginning of that month. With all my heart I wish you success in Argentina and *bon voyage*!

I embrace you.   I Stravinsky

Diaghilev has just sent Messager[162] as conductor. You will see the articles by Monsieur Doret.

I would like you to know that I will come to play my Concerto in Switzerland only if I have *three* engagements, at a minimum of 1,000 Swiss francs a performance, and, since this would give us an opportunity to be together, do not waste time. Tell me what you think.

STRAVINSKY TO ANSERMET

Letter to my friend Ernest Ansermet

What a joy, my dear friend, to know that you are back and to have such good news about your interminable trip![163] I cannot write at length, being too busy with all that I am doing and will do this winter, which includes the following:

1. I am moving, which is to say that I have already moved to Nice, Villa des Roses, 167 boulevard Carnot; I am in the midst of settling in, and you know what that is like![164]
2. I am composing a sonata for piano,[165] and you don't know what that is.

---

[160] This project was never realized.

[161] For a concert in Geneva.

[162] André Messager (1853–1929), a minor opera composer.

[163] The trip to South America referred to in n. 157 above.

[164] The Russian refugee population in Nice was even larger than that in Biarritz. Perhaps Stravinsky's closest new friends of this period were the Vinogradovs. A letter to Stravinsky in New York, March 22, 1946, from N. Vinogradov recalls trips together in Stravinsky's car, and many social evenings.

[165] Sonata for piano, dedicated to the Princess Edmond de Polignac and published by the Edition Russe de Musique in 1925. Stravinsky reserved exclusive performance rights for five years.

3. I am correcting proofs of the orchestra score of *Les Noces* and revisions of Larmanjat's work on the 2-hand piano version of *The Song of the Nightingale*.
4. I am still practicing the piano.
5. I am typing, and damaging my fingers, on my "Continsouza," waiting until I have a secretary who can do it for me.

And here, God willing, is what I shall be doing this winter:

1. A tour of Europe—Three concerts in Holland (November)
   Three   ″   ″ Switzerland (November)
   Three   ″   ″ Germany (December)
   One   ″   ″ Marseille[166]
2. A tour of America—I leave on December 27 and will give a total of twenty concerts between Jan. 7 and March 11. The tour is guaranteed by Mackay, the manager [*sic*] of the New York Philharmonic, and organized by Bottenheim, Mengelberg's secretary.[167]
3. Returning from America, I go directly to Barcelona, where I will give three concerts (March 24 to April 5). When I am in Switzerland, I shall tell you what I did during your trip. For the moment, and until Nov. 1, I will not budge, so write to me here. Oeberg will send the Concerto parts to you; it is now being printed. Write to Oeberg: Les Grandes Editions Musicales, 22 rue d'Anjou, Paris, 8ᵉ; you must write to that address now, instead of to 3 rue de Moscou.

My family, in the largest sense of the word, is, thank God, in the best of health, and I wish the same for you and yours, my dear Ernest.

With my faithful affection. Your   Igor Stravinsky

STRAVINSKY TO ANSERMET

Geneva

167 bd. Carnot
Nice
My cable address: STRAVIGOR NICE
October 10, 1924

Two words, *mon vieux,* to ask if you still intend to play the *Scherzo fantastique;*[168] I find in my datebook "*Scherzo* for Ansermet—Oct. 5." Since I am playing the piece myself at the end of November in Holland, after my tour in

---

[166] The concerts took place in Amsterdam (on November 23, at the Concertgebouw, Stravinsky played his Concerto under the direction of Willem Mengelberg [1871–1951]) and The Hague; in Winterthur, Lausanne, and Geneva; in Leipzig (on December 4, Stravinsky played the Concerto under the direction of Wilhelm Furtwängler [1886–1954]) and Berlin; and in Marseille (on December 21, Stravinsky played the Concerto under Pierre Sechiari and conducted the *Firebird* Suite).
[167] Salomon Adriaan Maria Bottenheim (1880–1957), Dutch musicologist. On July 22 Clarence H. Mackay, the Philharmonic's board chairman, confirmed Stravinsky's engagement and informed him that the contract had been sent to Bottenheim. (Mackay's daughter married Irving Berlin.)
[168] Ansermet telegraphed on October 13: "No need for *Scherzo* now. . . ."

Switzerland, I would like to coordinate this with you because I have the only set of parts. Be an angel, then, and telegraph the address to which I must send the parts, if you need them for Oct. 25. I seem to remember a kind of office in Paris, through which, occasionally, I have already sent things to you. Let me have that address, and if the score must be sent, I will do so immediately. You must know, however, that the Concertgebouw of Amsterdam, where I have played and conducted many times, already awaits the *Scherzo* score, though it is difficult for me to give the exact date by which they must have it.[169] For this reason you must oblige me by sending it, immediately after your Oct. 25 performance, to Mr. Sam Bottenheim, 68 Reijnier Vinkeleskade, Amsterdam; he is Mengelberg's secretary, and I signed my American contract with him.

Have you received my letter of Oct. 2? I await your telegram then, and embrace you.

Your   Igor Stravinsky

STRAVINSKY TO ANSERMET

Geneva

167 bd. Carnot
Nice
October 22, 1924

My dear friend,

Thank you for your kind letter.[170]

We have spent some terrible moments here, all four children falling ill on the same day with a very dangerous form of diphtheria! Imagine, poor Theodore just escaped asphyxiation. The vaccine saved them; and all of us, ourselves and our servants, were vaccinated immediately. Happily, the danger has passed. We will be out of bed tomorrow, and the disinfection of the house will take place in a week. A great start, no?

Now to business:

1. Today, I sent my manuscript orchestra score of the Concerto[171] to you by registered mail. Oeberg asked me to do this urgently.
2. I would really like to conduct my Octet, but I do not want to deprive you of this pleasure either, the more so because I would also like to perform the *Symphonies*. But to conduct and to play my Concerto would be too tiring, while to conduct only the Octet would seem peculiar. What about the following solution: I play my Concerto and you accompany me, then you do the Octet and the *Symphonies* (replacing the alto flute with the alto saxophone). This program, or at least the part that concerns me, will be representative of what is called the

---

[169] Probably for the November 23 concert. On July 3, Stravinsky had written to Ernest Giovanna, secretary of the Orchestre de la Suisse Romande: ". . . between the Winterthur concert, November 26, and my Amsterdam concert, November 23, there are only two days."

[170] Of October 20.

[171] For the November 30 concert in Geneva.

direction of my music today, whereas *The Song of the Nightingale* would be a bit jarring.

3. As for Winterthur, a rehearsal at your house is impossible! I come straight from Amsterdam[172] and rehearse the same evening. That will be Nov. 25. The 26th is the concert, with the dress rehearsal in the morning.

4. Catherine* will come to Lausanne Nov. 23, spend the night at the home of her cousin, Mme Schwartz, and join me in Winterthur the next morning. From there we will go to Lausanne or Geneva, depending on where you rehearse. I must know where immediately.[173] Answer by return mail, because I am leaving next Wednesday, October 29, for Warsaw, where I have two concerts.

I thank you very much for your hospitable offer to put us up, but I think that two people would be too much.

I finished my Sonata and am now practicing the piano. Maybe I will play the piece on my tours if I feel able to do it at that time.

Write immediately and tell me if it's agreed about the *Symphonies*. If so, get the parts from Oeberg immediately, since he has only one set and someone has already asked for it.

Your   Igor Stravinsky

In the confusion of leaving and of pressing work, I typed the copy on the wrong side, and so am sending you this horrible letter, half-original, half-copy.

*She is coming only for the few days that I am in Switzerland. There was never any question of a month!

Nice
October 8, 1925
[Postcard]

STRAVINSKY TO ANSERMET

Thank you, *cher vieux*, for your letter. I was very happy to have your good news and thank you for having thought of me. I hope that Jacqueline's illness is [by now] nothing more than an unpleasant memory.

One of these days, I will write a little more to you. For the moment, I embrace you sincerely.

Your   I Stravinsky

STRAVINSKY TO ANSERMET   *December 20, 1925*

My dear,

I am writing these few words to you on the train to Nice, returning from my tour after having spent ten painful days in Paris. The pain was due to the death

---

[172] Stravinsky was obliged to leave Amsterdam on the morning of November 24.

[173] On October 27, Giovanna wrote to Stravinsky on Ansermet's behalf that the rehearsal would take place in Geneva and informed the composer that Ansermet had had to replace the *Symphonies of Wind Instruments* with *The Song of the Nightingale*.

of Oeberg, whom I loved very much, as you know. A short illness of three days took him from me. My poor friend suffered terribly: first, a liver attack, immediately thereafter a ruptured appendix, peritonitis, an operation, and death.

We were constantly together during my concerts in Berlin and Frankfurt, and you should have seen how active he was. I feel almost orphaned without him. Vera—who also loved him very much—and I were near him these last three days of his life.

Here, for the moment, is the sad news that I have to give to you. I pray to God that the new year will start off better than the end of the old one—1925—as much for me and those around me as for my friends, who are not so numerous, and among whom you, dear old friend, occupy a very sure place, always.

Your   I.S.

You have also had problems, as I have heard, and I sympathize with you very much.

STRAVINSKY TO ANSERMET   *Nice*
                                                          December 26, 1925
Dear friend,

Your letter received. I am so eager to see you. I would be very happy if you were to spend a few days at my home. You can sleep on the couch. The trip here is not much longer than one to Paris, where I won't be coming until the end of February, on the way to Holland[174] for a series of concerts. Say yes, I beg you, and come, any time starting tomorrow. I too am very hungry to see you. In great haste,

Your   I Stravinsky

I do not say "Happy New Year" in this letter, because I want to tell you that in person. But greet your family for me.   I Str

STRAVINSKY TO ANSERMET   *[Postmark: Nice]*
                                                          January 5, 1926
10 rue Toepffer
Geneva, Switzerland

My dear friend,

Did you receive my note of nine days ago?[175] Or is "no news good news," which is to say that you are coming to Nice? I will be extremely happy if this is the case.

Your   Stravigor

---

[174] In Amsterdam Stravinsky was to conduct *Le Sacre* himself for the first time.
[175] Letter of December 26, 1925.

STRAVINSKY TO ANSERMET   *Nice*
                                                  January 30, 1926
Geneva

With no news from you, I am wondering if everything is all right. Don't be so
lazy: answer these lines with a few words.

   In three weeks I am going to Holland, where I will conduct one of the concerts. I want to ask you for this very important piece of information: have the
[*Sacre*] parts really been changed according to the groupings of measures indicated in your "Note for the Conductor"? What interests me above all about this
is the end of the *Danse sacrale,* since at the beginning—and when the same
music occurs a half-tone lower, a little farther along[176]—I have succeeded in
grouping the measures while redoing the instrumentation. This needed
strengthening in the bass, which determines the accentuation and the dialectic
structure of the musical phrase. As for the end,[177] nothing in the orchestration
is to be changed, in my view, and there is no question about the grouping of the
measures.

   Another thing—tell me which Mozart symphony you played a year ago at
the Pasdeloup,[178] along with the *Sacre.*

   So, take up your pen and answer quickly.

                               I embrace you. Your   Stravigor

STRAVINSKY TO ANSERMET   *Nice*
                                                  November 1, 1926
Geneva

Dear friend,

Thanks for your kind letter.[179] Of course, one can always rearrange the details
of the chamber-music program. Here it is: (1) Trio from *Soldat;* (2) a. Sonata,
b. Serenade; (3) Violin Piano—a. Khorovod and Berceuse from *Firebird,* which
I must transcribe for Kochanski, b. Suite based on the fragments of Pergolesi.[180]

---

[176] Rehearsal number **167** in the Edition Russe de Musique edition of 1921.

[177] Rehearsal number **186** in the same edition.

[178] It was the "Linz," K. 425. The concert took place on Saturday, March 21, not at the
Pasdeloup but at the Théâtre Mogador. The program consisted of the Third Brandenburg Concerto, the "Linz" Symphony, the Piano Concerto No. 5 by Saint-Saëns, excerpts from *The Tsar's Bride* and *The Snow Maiden* by Rimsky-Korsakov, and *Le Sacre
du printemps.* André Schaeffner reviewed the concert in *Le Ménestrel,* March 27,
1925.

[179] Of October 19.

[180] The pieces listed are: the violin, clarinet, and piano transcription of *Histoire du soldat;* the Sonata (1924) and Serenade (1925), both for solo piano; transcriptions for
violin and piano of two sections of *Firebird*—the Khorovod (Dance of the Princesses)
and the Berceuse—both dedicated to Paul Kochanski (1887–1934, Polish violinist)
and published by Schott in 1929; and the 1925 transcription for violin and piano of

But *Mavra* would be infinitely more interesting: is it absolutely impossible to introduce the work (piano + 4 singers) in this program? If only we could have the same singers that I had last year at my Frankfurt festival! They were so good (except the alto). True, they sang in German, but apart from the alto, who really was a pure German (although good enough, she had a very small voice), the others were foreigners who knew French very well.[181] They could relearn the music in French very easily.

To realize this project, we must certainly have the approval of Reinhart and do a concert in Winterthur for him (I ask for nothing better). I know that you would not want to bother doing it this year. Besides, Reinhart has not yet returned from his trip to Japan. I could easily ask this of him, my conscience being relieved by the fact that my fees in Switzerland were and are so little— close to one-third of what they are elsewhere.

Vera would be pleased to see you; her address is 22 rue du Ranelagh (16ᵉ arrondissement), between the Seine and the rue Raynouard. Her telephone is Auteuil 24-79. Call her in the morning to be sure to reach her. She is very busy right now because Diaghilev has commissioned some costumes for *Firebird* from her. He is performing it with Goncharova's sets in London in a few weeks. I wonder, which score is he using to play the music?

Give me news of yourself, you know how much pleasure your letters always give me. Would it be quite impossible for you to make a small detour before Antwerp, where you must play to the Belgas, and come see me here, where you will not even pay any Francas?

I embrace you. Your Stravigor,   Igor Stravinsky

STRAVINSKY TO ANSERMET   *Nice*
                                                        December 28, 1926
10 rue Toepffer   *[Postcard]*
Geneva, Switzerland

Good and Happy New Year, my dear Ernest, to you and yours. I await with pleasure your arrival at the beginning of February, as you promised in your last letter. I was very ill with the grippe and left Paris with a 39° [102° F.] fever in order to be ill at home. I am well now and work like three mules.

I embrace you. Your   I Str.

---

some movements from *Pulcinella*, dedicated to Kochanski, called Suite italienne. Stravinsky made an entirely different version with Dushkin in 1932 but kept the title.

[181] These soloists were Marya Freund, Maria Pos-Carloforti, and Bertha de Vigier (sopranos), Ruth Arndt (alto), Antoni Kohmann (tenor), and Karl Rehfuss (bass).

STRAVINSKY TO ANSERMET

Thanks for your letter and telegram. I am very nervous about the fate of my score.[182] I insured it, but even if I were reimbursed for this value, it cannot be replaced and does not exist anymore, even in Russia. I'm sorry that I did not answer you immediately. I have been very busy lately with Catherine, who has just undergone an operation for appendicitis and is now under ice packs. Having frequently suffered threatening symptoms, she decided to have [her appendix] out. Fortunately, all is well now.

In two weeks, I will answer your questions on the subject of my new work. I want to conduct it myself. Do not think that this reflects a lack of confidence in you: that remains unshakable. But I do not want to deprive myself of this great joy. And I am certain that it will be in good hands, because the good God has endowed me with performing talent. I know and feel this, like so many other things; and just as I do not fail in my estimations of the performances of other artists, I am not mistaken in appreciating my own talents. Your performances and talent, for example, testify to the justice of my powers of appreciation.*

Excuse these few words. I am in a great hurry. I await you with pleasure on Feb. 3.[183] Telegraph your arrival time.

Your   I Strav

*Especially at a time when no one was paying attention to what you were doing

STRAVINSKY TO ANSERMET

Cher vieux,

Thanks for your letter, which I received in Paris. Now I am in Nice again, working to finish the full score of *Oedipus*.

I have been irked by the people who cling to this *Oedipus*, though the work is no concern of theirs, and its meaning completely escapes them, as it will surely continue to do in the future. But no matter. I am working and have stopped thinking about it. I repeatedly beg God to protect me from these people, which makes me calmer.

Now, something else. The score of *Firebird* has finally been found, to my great joy!

I have a proposal for you. Since you are not going to Argentina this spring, and since I suppose that you have the time and the desire to hear *Oedipus*, I invite you to come to Paris. I will pay for your hotel and for the trip, and ask you to give me a hand with the chorus (the same as for *Les Noces,* but larger) and a few other things that I will need. These "little things" include having one's guardian angel present in the flesh.

---

[182] In a letter of December 31, 1926, Ansermet had asked Stravinsky to send his score of *Firebird,* which Ansermet was conducting for the Ballets Russes at La Scala, Milan. On January 20, he wrote again to inform Stravinsky that the score had still not arrived.
[183] Ansermet had announced his arrival date in his letter to Stravinsky of January 20.

Answer by return mail if the project is possible.

I embrace you affectionately and congratulate you on your award[184] (so late, unfortunately).

Your faithful   Igor Stravinsky

STRAVINSKY TO ANSERMET

Chalet des Echarvines
Talloires, Haute-Savoie

My dear Ansermet,

July 31 [1927]

Why this silence? Especially between neighbors, as we are right now. If I were free and not working regularly every day, I would not hesitate to run over to see you, but my work keeps me even from inviting you to my house.

What do you think about the Pleyel fire? That is really something. Robert Lyon[185] wrote that "it would be improved," which means, I suppose, that the hall will not be so ugly, but I think Robert was implying something else. What is displeasing to him, I think, are the acoustics. Delgrange[186] wrote that all of the concerts at the beginning of the season will be held at the Théâtre des Champs-Elysées.[187] Will you have repercussions there?

On what are you working? The mountain that is before me and that separates us prevents me from asking questions aloud. And your situation is the same as mine. Let's go on through letters, therefore.

I embrace you, good things to you.

Your   Stravinsky

STRAVINSKY TO ANSERMET

[Nice]
[c. December 20, 1927]

I am sending you these few words, my very dear Ansermet, to tell you what great pleasure your letter gave me, especially the part that concerns Jacqueline and the course of action that you are following (without, as yet, daring to admit it to her).[188]

---

[184] In a letter of March 3, Ansermet had said that he had received the award of "member of the French Legion of Honor" for "services rendered to French music abroad."

[185] Robert Lyon (1884–1965), director of Pleyel until about 1930.

[186] Félix Delgrange, cellist, impresario, and concert agent. Writing to Oeberg on August 21, 1924, Stravinsky characterized Delgrange as "a conniver, always pestering me with stupid propositions, from which I have concluded that he knows nothing. . . . Answer this scoundrel in the way in which I have asked you."

[187] The inaugural concert for the new Salle Pleyel, on October 18, 1927, included the *Meistersinger* Prelude, Franck's *Symphonic Variations*, Debussy's *Nuages* and *Fêtes*, Falla's *Nights in the Gardens of Spain*, the *Firebird* Suite, Dukas's *The Sorcerer's Apprentice*, and Ravel's *La Valse*. The orchestra of the Society of the Concerts of the Conservatory was led by Philippe Gaubert. Ravel and Stravinsky conducted their own pieces.

[188] Ansermet's daughter had contracted tuberculosis.

That is all I have to say on the subject.

My children are going to Lausanne on Monday. Their arrival coincides with the performances of the Ballets Russes,[189] which they will not attend there, since they will see all of that here. You will probably speak with Diagh. about my *Musagète*.[190] But here is the result of my frankness with him; read this masterpiece by M. Georges-Michel[191] and draw your own conclusion without my drawing you a picture. I was so upset and disgusted that I had to clarify it for the public, hence I exposed the truth of the matter in an interview* at the intermission during my last trip to Paris three weeks ago. I beg you to *send the clippings back to me.* I am guarding them carefully because they are the only copies that I have.

I send my children, who will see you, and through them I send my faithful regards,

Your   Stravinsky

P.S. I am staying here until January 20; then I play my Concerto with Klemperer[192] in Berlin, attend the [stage] premiere of *Oedipus*,[193] and return to Paris to conduct *Le Sacre* on February 10 and 18.[194]

*Which is also enclosed

---

[189] The Ballets Russes gave a series of performances in Geneva on Monday through Thursday, December 19–22, 1927. On the first two evenings, the works performed were *Les Biches*, *Les Matelots*, and *Firebird;* on the last two, *Cimarosiana*, *Le Tricorne*, and *La Boutique fantasque*. Ansermet conducted the Orchestre de la Suisse Romande.

[190] *Apollo* (1928).

[191] This article, entitled "A New Work by a Great Musician of Today: *Apollon Musagète,* by Igor Stravinsky, and the unpublished concepts of the composer," appeared in *Excelsior,* October 27.

[192] Otto Klemperer (1885–1973) was one of the few conductors whom Stravinsky liked. Early in the summer of 1929, the composer wrote to his Berlin concert agents, Wolff & Sachs: "In June, during my last sojourn in Berlin, I expressed to Mr. Klemperer my desire to play my new piano concerto . . . with him. He received the idea with enthusiasm and immediately spoke to me about the Gewandhaus and about Berlin, where he will conduct next year. . . ." Stravinsky wrote again on August 6: "I do not want to deprive myself of the pleasure of playing my new concerto with Klemperer in the first year of its existence." On September 8, Stravinsky wrote directly to Klemperer: "My new work is not called Concerto but Capriccio for piano and orchestra. . . ." (Stravinsky played the Capriccio with Klemperer in the Stadttheater, Berlin, in a concert that began with *Le Baiser de la fée* and ended with Mozart's G-minor Symphony.) F. V. Weber wrote to Stravinsky on March 7, 1932: "The *Symphony of Psalms* enjoyed a truly exceptional success in Vienna. Klemperer says that the only place where it has had equal success is Russia. . . . Klemperer told me that the mask of Beethoven that you saw [and wanted] has been broken, and that he does not know where to find another like it. . . ."

[193] Stravinsky attended the first performance of his *Oedipus Rex* at the Kroll Opera,

STRAVINSKY TO ANSERMET

Bien cher Ernest,

Bracks Doelen Hotel
Amsterdam
April 20, 1928

Catherine forwarded your letter,[195] and I read it with the avidity that you must have anticipated. Vera gave me your news upon my arrival in Paris, and I regretted having missed you. I hope, however, that we will see each other in a week, for I will be in Paris from April 26 to May 7. Unfortunately, it is hardly possible, as I had wished, for me to come to Brussels to hear *Noces* and the

---

but according to a letter from F. V. Weber to the composer following the second performance, March 2, 1928, the tenor in the title part "sang as badly as at the premiere, and in fact he made the same slips as before, in the same places. . . . The applause was great, much greater than at the premiere and would have been many times greater still if the following had not happened. When the piece was finished, Klemperer left the stage immediately. The audience clapped for at least five minutes before the Jocasta came out alone and with a very embarrassed expression. Then she came with the Messenger and the Shepherd, which was funny, because they have such small parts. She came out a third time, alone, and then, despite the continuing applause, the curtain was lowered, which means here that the artists will not appear anymore. The audience understood that something was not right backstage, since neither the Oedipus nor Klemperer emerged, though both had been called out by the enthusiastic audience. It seems that Klemperer became furious with the tenor, forbade him to go on stage, and, out of malice, would not go out himself. Since the theater was packed, it was a great mistake on Klemperer's part not to come back."

[194] On February 10, 1928, Stravinsky conducted the Straram Orchestra in the first of two concerts in the Salle Pleyel; the program consisted of *The Song of the Nightingale, Le Sacre,* and *Petrushka.* The second concert, on February 18, included the first performance in France of the orchestral versions of the Eight Easy Pieces (Andante, Napolitana, Española, Balalaika, March, Valse, Polka, Galop).

[195] In this letter, Ansermet gives his impression of the musical life in Leningrad and tells about meeting Stravinsky's brother Yuri there. Soon afterward, Stravinsky began to send money to Yuri. An invoice from the Russischer Musik Verlag in Berlin, dated February 15, 1929, shows that 250 rubles were sent to "Jurig Strawinsky, Leningrad" on June 13, 1928, 250 rubles (547 marks) on August 27, and 614 marks and $136 on December 31. In January 1935, Yuri's wife and one of his daughters, Tanya, wrote to say that he had developed angina pectoris. Catherine Stravinsky forwarded this news to her husband in America, explaining that "[Yuri's] work [as an architectural engineer] is strenuous, and he often does it at night." (January 11, 1935)   At the beginning of August 1936, Stravinsky received a postcard from Yuri explaining that the coffins of their father and younger brother Gury had been removed to another cemetery. Catherine wrote to Igor on August 4, 1936: "Mama is undoubtedly very distressed by this news, so I will tell her that it is not a matter of blasphemy or of disregard but rather of a humanitarian desire to honor the memory of famous people and of artists, and to bring all their graves together [in a poets' corner]. It happens, after all, that the Lord allows even worse to be done to the remains of His holy servants, which are blasphemously destroyed or displayed in [Soviet] museums. . . ." Yuri Stravinsky died on May 12, 1941. His widow, Elena Nikolayevna, wrote to her brother-in-law in

Symphonies under your baton (the only one that I like).[196] The trains do not suit me, with five hours one-way, after getting up at 6 in the morning, and a five-hour return trip,* meaning ten hours altogether.

In an hour I will start to rehearse *Oedipus,* which I am playing on the 24th, along with the Suite from *Petrushka.* Mengelberg will begin the concert with Chester's *Firebird* Suite.

Last night I went to the second part of a Strauss program conducted by Mengelberg. It is so many years since I heard the *Heldenleben* that I could no longer understand a single measure by this German composer. What horrible music! And how much care and certainty Mengelberg put into its performance.

I was shocked by the enthusiasm for Boris Asafiev[197] with which you returned. I do not know him personally, but I have often had the opportunity to read his writings on music; if you were to read them, you might change your mind. I read him on Rimsky and Tchaikovsky and discovered that he belongs more to the Andrei-Rimsky and Steinberg clan than to the one opposing that nest of old wasps. This greatly surprised me, since I have always been told that Asafiev is the only one who really counts in Russia today.

That's all for now. I embrace you and rejoice at seeing you again soon.

Your   I Str.

*Immediately after the concert

February 1946 (the envelope is postmarked Moscow, March 3, 1946): ". . . He's buried in Okhtensky Cemetery; Novodevichy is closed. . . . Our family consists of Tanya and her husband and their son Roman, who's already 17, Xenia and her 13-year-old daughter Elena. I live with Xenia. From apartment No. 66 we moved into 42 and now live in the supervisor's apartment where everybody died and where it's much better. It has only four rooms! and we have two of them. We live on Xenia's earnings; as you know, she's an architect. She and her husband separated long ago. I don't feel too badly, and do the housework and the shopping. Tanya has finished art classes, and helps take care of the house. Her son is a wonderful, able boy, hard-working. He's at the university, studying chemistry, for which he shows exceptional interest and enthusiasm. My granddaughter, Alyonushka, is also a very able girl. . . . We all left Leningrad during the siege and lived near Kostroma. Fortunately, the apartment was spared, but the library suffered. Yuri had sold a lot of books, but, still, there were some left, and now there's nothing. In the public library, we inquired if there wasn't some correspondence with you, from your letters, manuscripts, your compositions, but, unfortunately, all of this has been lost. . . . Do you know the music of our Shostakovich? He's our very best and most talented composer. His music is very successful. Is it played in America? I see the R.-Korsakovs from time to time. Mikh., Nik., and Vladimir are alive. They live with their grandchildren and great-grandchildren. . . ."

[196] This concert of Stravinsky works, conducted by Ansermet on April 21 at the Théâtre de la Monnaie, Brussels, was repeated the next day. The program consisted of the Overture and Parasha's aria from *Mavra* (Mme Smirnova, soloist), *Les Noces,* the *Symphonies of Wind Instruments,* and *Petrushka.*

[197] See n. 34 on p. 68.

STRAVINSKY TO ANSERMET

My dear Ansermet,

Chalet des Echarvines
Talloires, Haute-Savoie
August 7, 1928

My children and I are going to Thonon this Friday, the 9th, at about noon. I have written to Elie Gagnebin,[198] who will now entreat you to descend from the heights, where, in my opinion, you have lingered too long.[199] I hope that Ramuz and Auberjonois will come, too, since I have also invited them. I am taking two days' rest: tomorrow we are going to Combloux, near St. Gervais, to see Païchadze,[200] who is at Koussevitzky's. Koussevitzky has been resting here all summer, and for that reason I hope to have a spiritual communion with him for at least two days. Come, don't be lazy.

Your Stravinsky,   I Str

Nini is typing this letter; I type in red.

STRAVINSKY TO ANSERMET

Dear Ansermet,

Chalet des Echarvines
Talloires, Haute-Savoie
August 11, 1928

How happy I was to have received a letter from you and how sad not to have seen you. Only Auberjonois was waiting for us in Thonon; he alone had time to answer our call.[201] I am awaiting you here, because I no longer have the time to move. I do not know if you are up-to-date about my obligations to Ida Rubinstein,[202] to whom I must send three-quarters of my ballet[203] (piano 2-hand score) on September 1. I am working like a dog from morning till night. The only time that I can rest is during supper and in the moments before falling asleep. I have just written to Ramuz that I could be with him only at this time of day. So, come with Jacqueline before August 31, the date on which I am going through Paris to Scheveningen.

As for the programs of my concerts, I don't recall if in my most recent letters I mentioned my plan to play my Concerto with you in Paris. I suppose that I

---

[198] Elie Gagnebin (1891–1949), Swiss geologist, member of *Les Cahiers Vaudois* (founded by Edmond Gilliard in 1914), and the Narrator in the first performance of *Histoire du soldat*, September 28, 1918.

[199] Ansermet was in Diablerets.

[200] In 1925, G. G. Païchadze succeeded Oeberg as the director of the Edition Russe de Musique. On July 28, 1927, Stravinsky wrote to Ramuz: ". . . I had to give control of my business with Kling-Chester to my friend M. Gabriel Païchadze."

[201] Ansermet wrote on August 7, 1928, to tell Stravinsky that he was in Diablerets, and that he was thinking about him but could not go to Thonon.

[202] See n. 57 on p. 114.

[203] *Le Baiser de la fée*, allegorical ballet in four tableaux, composed in 1928 and performed, with choreography by Nijinska, at the Paris Opéra under Stravinsky's direction on November 27 and December 4 of that year.

said nothing about it, though, since you sent a proposal to me for two (concert) programs of my music. So, I propose it again: in one of the concerts, I will be appearing as a pianist, playing my Concerto with you, and in the other conducting a program of my own works. The latter program would be the one that you chose for the Friday concert: (1) Etude (5 minutes),[204] (2) Symphony (from 45 to 50 minutes),[205] (3) *Apollo,* (4) two small suites. In my opinion, the order of the program ought to be changed slightly: I will begin with the Symphony, then intermission, the Etude, and *Apollo.* The timing of the two suites, which should end the concert, is 12 to 15 minutes. I would be very grateful to you for doing whatever is necessary to arrange it definitely just as I want it, in regard both to my appearance as pianist and to the program. I will explain to you in person why I stick so firmly to this demand. That's all for today.

I embrace you affectionately.

STRAVINSKY TO ANSERMET

Chalet des Echarvines
Talloires, Haute-Savoie
August 16, 1928

L'Etoile
Les Diablerets

Dear,

It is agreed for Friday and Saturday November 16 and 17. But since it is no longer on the 18th and, consequently, I will have no time to rehearse the orchestra on the 16th and 17th, I ask you please to arrange definitely that my participation on the evening of the 17th be [only] as soloist in my Concerto. Unfortunately I will not have time to prepare the piano part for *Petrushka* and will be able to play only the Concerto. Thus, in short: I will conduct the first concert, the program of which I gave to you in my last letter, and in the second concert I will play my Concerto and you will conduct the rest of the program. I would really like you to do the *Symphonies of Wind Instruments* and the "Song of the Volga Boatmen"[206] before the Concerto, and to finish with *Petrushka.* Between the Concerto and *Petrushka,* there should be a 15-minute intermission.

Come quickly to see us.

I embrace you.   Igor Stravinsky

---

[204] The orchestration of the Etude for Pianola; the duration is actually about 2½ minutes.

[205] The Symphony in E flat.

[206] Stravinsky had orchestrated this for an ensemble of wind instruments and tympani in Rome in April 1917, and this version was used as the Russian national anthem by the Ballets Russes in Rome, Naples, and Paris after the abdication of the Tsar.

STRAVINSKY TO ANSERMET

Paris

167 bd. Carnot
Nice
October 1, 1928

Dear,

Very satisfied by your kind letter,[207] embrace you with great friendliness.

Have examined your programs with satisfaction, happy to find that the Free Masonic music of Darius Milhaud is absent.

The following is the order for the program of my second concert: 1. "Volga" 2. *Scherzo fantastique* 3. First *Firebird* Suite. Intermission. 4. *Apollo* 5. Suite from *Petrushka*.

The parts can be obtained from Païchadze, except for the "Volga," which I will bring (it is my own set).

In a great hurry, I embrace you.

STRAVINSKY TO ANSERMET

Geneva

Paris
December 11, 1928

Dear friend,

Back from Brussels, where I heard the *Fée*,[208] and now leaving for Nice. Brussels was very painful: the curtains between the four tableaux rose only after five- to eight-minute intervals. Thus the music designed for continuing—with the whole play of modulations with which you are familiar—was totally lost, the score completely sabotaged.

I was warned that it would be the same in Geneva. Is this possible? That makes me very unhappy.

[Ida] Rubinstein should have sent the parts to you with my orchestra score this morning, by the most rapid means possible. Païchadze telegraphed her yesterday.

Reassure me, *mon cher*.

I Str

---

[207] Of September 29.

[208] In December, the Ballets Ida Rubinstein gave a series of performances at the Théâtre de la Monnaie. Stravinsky attended the first evening, December 7. Besides *Le Baiser de la fée,* the program, conducted by Corneil de Thoran, included *Les Noces de Psyché et de l'Amour* by Honegger, Ravel's *Bolero,* Nocturne by Borodin, and "Princesse Cygne" (extract from *Tsar Saltan*). The program was repeated on December 10 and 12.

STRAVINSKY TO ANSERMET   *January 4, 1929*

Très cher,

The note you sent the other day gave me great pleasure. I also send heartiest
wishes for the New Year, even though it is already January 4.

Yes, you are right to say that this year, with *Apollo* and the *Fée,* was one of
the most fruitful ones of my life, where my work is concerned, and one of the
most significant in terms of development. As I interpret it, this is what is meant
by fecundity. And I accept with deep gratitude your wish for its continuation.

Aside from the same thing you wished for me, what should I wish for you,
egotist that I am, but the continuation of your superb activity in the publicizing
of my music? This does not mean that I do not appreciate the great worth of
your performances of the classics of other composers. You know my opinion of
that: but, on the other hand, it is not by chance that we speak the same language. In sending you this kind of egotistical wish, however, I would like to af-
firm to you once more not only my confidence, but also my admiration, *mon
vieux;* yes, ADMIRATION, believing always that the admiration I have for what you
do with my music will be shared by many others (and not like the sharing Vuillermoz[209] did to bore them).

I am sure that *Le Sacre* was magnificent the other day; Vera gave me news
of it with very enthusiastic comments. I am completely in agreement about re-
establishing the $\frac{2}{16}, \frac{3}{16}$ etc. at no. **192,**[210] but on the condition that the orchestra
be similar to yours. Otherwise not. I think that you cannot disagree, unless you
are hiding a surprise from me with the little exercise you have prepared for the
conductor that "makes the transition certain." Very curious to know what this is.

Best wishes to yours and a brotherly kiss to you, *mon bien cher.*

STRAVINSKY TO ANSERMET   *[After February 19, 1929]*

My dear Ansermet,

Very saddened by what you tell me;[211] I can only answer it by saying that I, too,
am *"full of immense disgust."*

I have just sent a telegram informing you that you have my sympathy (and
not Robert Lyon and Monteux), but that, despite my wishes, it is absolutely
impossible for me to come to Paris before Tuesday morning.

I am asking Vera (who is very fond of you) to stop by at your house so that
you might give her all the information about this dirty business in detail; then I
will be au courant and, if necessary, able to lend a hand. I beg you, cooperate

---

[209] Emile Vuillermoz (1878–1960), French music critic, one of the founders of the
Société Musicale Indépendante.

[210] In the *Danse sacrale.*

[211] Writing on February 19, Ansermet had told Stravinsky that Robert Lyon "behaved
like what the French call a cow," trying to replace Ansermet with Monteux.

with Vera and give her all the dates (your return, your concerts, trips abroad if any, etc.). When will you come back from Milan? In any case, I plan to stay on in Paris for a week after my concert on the 5th.

In great haste, your faithful   I Stravinsky

P.S. Thanks for the news about Kiesgen.[212] He wrote to me that all the rehearsals are arranged.

STRAVINSKY TO ANSERMET   *Nice*
                                                    March 28, 1929
Geneva   *[Postcard]*

Dear,

When are you going to Russia? Why have I received no news from you? Nothing since your last letter from Milan. Perhaps you are no longer in Geneva; it is a week since you were to have left Paris.

I address this note to you and to Marguerite, so that she may answer me if you are far away.

I embrace you.

Your   I Stravinsky

STRAVINSKY TO ANSERMET   *Paris*
                                                    June 11, 1929
Fürstenhof
Berlin

Cher vieux,

Before I go to London tonight (via Dunkirk-Tilbury), I wanted to warn you that Païchadze and I are not managing very well here with Diaghilev. After your departure and our conversation with Païchadze on the subject of cutting *Apollo,* he sent a registered letter to Diaghilev. Païchadze said he heard that Diaghilev still had not given up the idea of making that cut[213] in *Apollo,* and that as the representative of my author's rights, Païchadze forbids him to do this. If the cut is made, Païchadze will consider the contract broken and will take steps to prevent the work from being performed. Thereupon a reply came from Diaghilev, saying that he would not go back on *the promise* that he gave me (?) to replace the cut, and that he is surprised to learn that a simple "joke" (*sic*) during a luncheon had given his go-between a chance for criticism. He was astonished that we are so strict with him while we are so indulgent toward the Staatsoper, where he said *Pulcinella* is horribly abused, even with the order of the numbers in the ballet changed—without protest from me.

---

[212] Charles Kiesgen, Bureau of Concerts.

[213] Terpsichore's variation.

Païchadze answered with a letter of thanks for having alerted him to this situation, and saying that measures will be taken to rectify it. Keep this to yourself. But that is not all: the other day, Prokofiev and Païchadze were served with a summons to appear in court this Wednesday (tomorrow) to respond to charges formulated in the complaint of "Boris Kochno" (i.e., Diagh.). He is suing both of them for having published *The Prodigal Son*[214] (entitled *The Prodigal Child* on the published score) without the permission of the author of the scenario, despite the existence of an agreement between Prokofiev and Kochno that joins them together as collaborators.[215] Both Païchadze and Prokofiev are accused of having murdered the "book," that masterpiece of literature (in the complaint Kochno calls himself a "man of letters"), by publishing the titles in a form that renders the meaning of this "work" completely different from what Kochno had conceived, etc. etc. (I must admit that Païchadze and Prokofiev did not put Kochno's name on the score.) In short, yesterday they consulted a lawyer who, unfortunately, foresees trouble, because, as a preventive measure, the document threatens the confiscation of all ballet editions by Prokofiev.

There, *mon vieux,* is what's happening with these gallant gents of the Ballets Russes, so genteel, and so devoted to the cause of art!

See you soon, *mon cher.* I arrive in the Friedrichstrasse-Bahnhof at two or three o'clock in the afternoon of the 17th, and go directly to the Fürstenhof. Please, advise the hotel and *Mr. Weber* of the Russischer Musik Verlag (Dessauer Str 17).

I embrace you. Your   I Stravinsky

STRAVINSKY TO ANSERMET

Dorn Hotel
Cologne, Germany

Paris
June 19, 1929
[Postcard]

Dear friend,

Returning from Paris, I realized that I had forgotten to ask you to intervene discreetly with regard to Diaghilev or his entourage, informing him that I will be in London at the same time as he is, and that I will stay at the same Albemarle Court address to which he always goes. I think that it would be best if he knew this now, since, for reasons that are clear only to him, he has been

[214] *The Prodigal Son*, ballet in three acts by Prokofiev, based on Kochno's scenario. The premiere had taken place on May 21, 1929, at the Théâtre Sarah-Bernhardt, Paris, with choreography by Balanchine and sets by Rouault.
[215] Prokofiev did not consider Kochno—author of the libretto—as a co-author of the ballet. Kochno insisted that the title be changed on publication (*The Prodigal Child* was used, instead of *The Prodigal Son*), and Kochno's name did not appear. The court forced Prokofiev and the Edition Russe de Musique to pay a fine.

avoiding me for a long time.[216] How did the premiere and subsequent performances go?[217]

I embrace you. Your   Stravinsky

STRAVINSKY TO ANSERMET   *Les Echarvines (Talloires)*
                                                   Friday, July 16, 1929
Dear,

We came here a week ago. Since then, we have received from Petersburg the
sad news of the death of our old aunt Sophie, my mother's sister. I think that
things are bad there from all points of view, and it would probably improve the
situation if they were to attempt to finish the war with the Chinese. Can these
Soviets really believe that in their condition they will be able to win?

I received your note today.[218] In six days you will be going to the mountains. If I possibly can, I will visit you before your departure for Geneva. Are you
home in the mornings? It will be difficult to let you know in advance, even by
telegr[am], because this is not a very reliable means of communication in
France, unless sent a week ahead. I have not yet answered the Orchestre Symphonique de Paris because I myself await answers concerning my other engagements next winter. I think that it would be dangerous to accept the
December 6 date, since some very important business may be arranged for the
end of November, and this would require three weeks. I won't know until
around August 15.[219]

About Lourié, his address is 53 rue La Fontaine, Paris XVI, but I doubt
that he will still be in Paris.[220] Consequently, perhaps he could send the re-

---

[216] When the Ballets Russes opened its spring season in Paris, May 21, 1929, with a
program that included *Renard,* Stravinsky and Diaghilev did not meet. In Berlin, in
mid-June, Stravinsky stayed in the Fürstenhof, Diaghilev in the Bristol, and again the
two men did not meet. In London, they lived in adjoining rooms at Albemarle Court
from June 23 to 28 but still did not meet. On June 27, at Kingsway Hall, Stravinsky
conducted *Apollo* and *Le Baiser de la fée.* Diaghilev's season, in Covent Garden, took
place between July 1 and July 26, and the programs included *Apollo, Petrushka, Renard,* and *Le Sacre.*

[217] Of *Le Sacre* and *Apollo,* in Charlottenberg (Berlin).

[218] Of July 15.

[219] The concert with the premiere of the Capriccio did take place on December 6, in
the Salle Pleyel.

[220] At this date, Arthur V. Lourié (1892–1966) was still Stravinsky's most trusted con-
fidant in Paris. Two days after the "Festival Stravinsky" in the Salle Gaveau, January
27, 1926, a chamber concert sponsored by *La Revue Musicale,* Lourié wrote to Stravinsky: "Vera told me today that you are interested in my impressions of the Festival. I
do not want to hurt you, but I must say that the concert was most absurd, and that
those who organized it do not even suspect this. . . . The premiere, profiting from the
use of your name, drew a full crowd. . . . Of the performers, Safanova was better than
the others, at least in the *Quatre Chants russes.* . . . She can be faulted for much, but

quested manuscripts to you. Write to him, and to me, too, telling me if it would be possible to spend a day with you, Ramuz, and Auberjonois. We would leave early with my children and go to 10 rue Toepffer in the morning. I await your reply and sign myself,

yours, affectionately,   I Str

STRAVINSKY TO ANSERMET

Echarvines (H-S)
Friday, August 16, 1929

Well, have you returned? No news from you since your visit here. Since then, I have had a request from the O.S.P.,[221] which I answered by telegram that, having in the meantime cleared my calendar for the beginning of Dec., I accept the engagement for Dec. 6.[222] Probably you already know this, though I am not entirely sure, since the O.S.P. has not yet answered me on the subject. Would you come to see us here? I would like that so much!

My children and I have been to Lausanne twice. Mika is still there (at Prevorange, near Morges, at her friends', the de Mestrals) and will spend Monday and Tuesday at Ramuz's. Next week Mermod[223] will bring [Mika] and [the] Ramuz [family] here with him. Come with them, and if there is no room, we will come to fetch you. Do you want to?

One word of reply, please.

Your   I Str

STRAVINSKY TO ANSERMET

Friday, October 3, 1929
[Postcard]

Dear Ernest,

You must have received the requested parts a few hours after sending the cable; I learned this by telephone from Rabenek,[224] since Païchadze is in London again. Meanwhile, I have written to Païchadze that you are waiting for the promised reply. He is very busy in London, and it is not surprising that he is making you wait.

---

she was conscientious and thoughtful. Everything else was worse. Guller played both the Sonata and Three Movements from *Petrushka* poorly, the Sonata at quite unbelievable tempos and with a smothered sound, *Petrushka* loosely and carelessly, and, what is more, only the first two movements. Instead of the third movement, she played the second movement again! (I heard Borovski play *Petrushka* a few days ago, and there was no comparison even with him!) The Octet was very disappointing, . . . but disappointing and torturous only to us. The audience and the musicians thought that everything was fine and they were very pleased with themselves and with each other. . . ."

[221] Orchestre Symphonique de Paris.

[222] For the premiere of the Capriccio.

[223] Henri-Louis Mermod (1891–1962), publisher.

[224] Arthur Lvovich Rabenek was an assistant to Païchadze at the Edition Russe de Musique.

[Nicolas] Nabokov just played his Symphony for me. He really has a gift that I find pleasant. I advised him to show the score not to Monteux, but rather to you, and I promised to insist that you do the Symphony (3 parts, 20 minutes long) with the O.S.P. So be in touch with him at the Maison Pleyel,[225] at Pincherle's,[226] where he earns his living. I will be in Paris for another week, then in Nice. Nini is coming one of these days to take lessons at Nadia Boulanger's; she will choose a piano teacher for him.

Your   I Strav.

Was anything decided between you and Mermod?

Nice
                                                    October 21, 1929
Geneva

Dear,

No news from you since your letter describing little Markevitch's[227] visit, a letter which crossed with the one from me recommending young Nabokov's Symphony. It is true that in the meantime I have received your prospectus for the Orchestre [de la Suisse] Romande and your beautiful article, but my business

---

[225] From 1928 to 1930, Nicolas Nabokov collaborated in editing the magazine *Musique* (formerly *Le Pleyel*).

[226] Marc Pincherle (1888–1974), French musicologist and critic, author of a fundamental study of Vivaldi, was artistic director at Pleyel from 1927 to 1955 and editor-in-chief of *Musique*. In October 1933, Pincherle helped Stravinsky to move from his studios at Pleyel to his apartment at 21 rue Viète. The composer wrote to him on October 10: "As for the removal of the piano and furniture to my new domicile, I beg you to add the following three pieces of furniture from studio number 35: the two small armoires (chiffonières), one yellow and the other red; and from studio 36, a second small red armoire chiffonière, in addition to the large picture over the sofa."

[227] Igor Markevitch (b. 1912), composer and conductor of Russian origin. He was introduced to Diaghilev by Mme A. Trusovich, a friend of Stravinsky mentioned in his correspondence with Païchadze. Markevitch published an article on *Le Sacre du printemps* in *Le Jour*, 1934, which offended Stravinsky, who wrote to Markevitch on March 13: "In many of your compositions I have detected the influence of this work, from whose aesthetic tendencies I have been moving further and further away in what I have been doing for more than fifteen years. To my mind, the kind of statement that you make is illogical coming from you, because you have contradicted it elsewhere, as if the statement were not yours. I think that you will find yourself inextricably caught in a lie in *Jour*, a lie whose initiative will rest with you; this seems quite logical to me. Furthermore, these speeches emanate not from a professional journalist, but from a young poet who is able to play a part in a certain artistic milieu of some prestige. . . . That is all that I can say to you in response to your kind letter of March 10. I send you, my dear Markevitch, my friendliest greetings."

Three years later, Ansermet sent Stravinsky yet another article by Markevitch,

with you is something different. In your last letter you asked me when I would be able to come to Switzerland for the concerts that Mermod intends to organize. I replied that I could be in Geneva from March 25 to April 1, leaving for there the day after my concert in Barcelona, which is to say, after the 24th, because I am busy in Barcelona on the 20th and the 23rd.[228] After that I will probably go to Holland,[229] where I said I could be at the beginning of April. I would be so pleased if the "Swiss combination" did work out, and I would also like, if possible, to hop over to Winterthur to play my Concerto under your baton at Reinhart's. But I strongly doubt whether we will be able to arrange this, since all the [other] dates were set a long time ago. I have never heard from Werner Reinhart,[230] who must certainly in the meantime have received my letters, one of which was even registered.

Conclusion: I await your reply. Write to me if you are going to America, and if not, what would you like to substitute in place of that trip? Tell me whether you have drawn up the contract with the record company[231] that you mentioned, because I have no idea what you are doing, except that you are shaping your muscles, for which the O.S.P. trembles in anticipation of its *chef eminent* (Monteux's official title), supposing that your exercises must have a completely different motivation from the ones that you make known to people. I have just learned (by a letter from [Elie] Gagnebin to Theodore) that Mermod "thinks that he will be able to organize the concerts *for February*" (!?). But I never said anything about February!

"La Réponse du musicien," from the July issue (No. 9) of *La Lanterne,* a review published in Vevey. Ansermet advised Stravinsky to ". . . arm yourself with irony and read this. . . . The reading of this opus has delivered me from any trace of doubt or scruple in regard to M. This really is not permissible. Without mentioning the abominable style, the mixture of sycophancy and lack of constraint, of puerility, of nonsense and of impudence, the stammering and feebleness of thought and [above all the] profound improbity. . . . How can anyone who thinks or talks in this way make authentic music?" (Letter of August 29, 1937)

[228] Two concerts of Stravinsky's works, conducted by the composer, were given at the Teatro Liceo in Barcelona. The program of the first consisted of the Symphony in E flat, *Apollo,* and the *Firebird* Suite; the program of the second, of excerpts from *Pulcinella,* the Easy Pieces for small orchestra, *Le Baiser de la fée,* and the Suite from *Petrushka.*

[229] Stravinsky was mistaken; he means Belgium. On September 19, 1929, he negotiated with the Joseph Torfs agency for a concert project there, and proposed the beginning of April.

[230] On August 16, 1929, Stravinsky wrote to Reinhart proposing to play the new Concerto in Zürich and Winterthur under Volkmar Andreae's direction. Reinhart (who was traveling) did not reply until November 15 that the programs were already fixed.

[231] Columbia Records. On January 23, 1930, Vera Sudeikina wrote to Ansermet on behalf of Stravinsky: "He plans to record the Capriccio, under your baton, for Columbia."

Awaiting the pleasure of your letter, dear sir, I beg you to accept that, etc. . . .

Igor Stravinsky

How did *Apollo* go?

STRAVINSKY TO ANSERMET   *Nice*
                                                              October 26, 1929
Geneva

Dear friend,

Thank you for your note and for sending the clippings. What it comes to is a disarmament, as you say, but at what a price!!! And Moser's compliments are as inane as his insults. Fortunate¹ ,, the one being as bad as the other, they leave me completely indifferent.

As for my concerts, if they cannot be given at the end of March, we must see if arrangements can be made to do them immediately after Germany: I mean after Feb. 6, the day of my last concert in Düsseldorf. You see that I am talking about *two* concerts, not just one; as I have made clear to Mermod, a single concert involves too much expense and trouble for me to accept without hesitation. Therefore, when I refer to these concerts I mean Lausanne and Geneva, one after the other. For the program, it seems to me that you could do *Apollo* again, the Capriccio—Intermission—and the *Fée*. I do not want to play anything but the Capriccio in this concert. To prepare the Sonata and the Serenade well would take too much time, which unfortunately I do not have this year.

I embrace you. Your   I Str

Send the dates after my German tour, up to February 15.
Answer please.

STRAVINSKY TO ANSERMET   *November 16, 1929*

Paris

Dear,

You probably know that I had a concert with the Philharmonic at the Salle Pleyel on March 5.[232] Anyway, just as I was leaving Paris I received the enclosed letter from Kiesgen. I also enclose my answer to this brilliant French orga-

---

[232] On March 5, 1929, the Philharmonic Society of Paris presented a Stravinsky concert in which the composer played his Sonata and Serenade, and conducted his Octet and *Histoire du soldat*. Jacques Copeau read all three parts in the *Soldat,* the Narrator, the Soldier, and the Devil.

The last photograph taken of Stravinsky in St. Petersburg, October 1912.

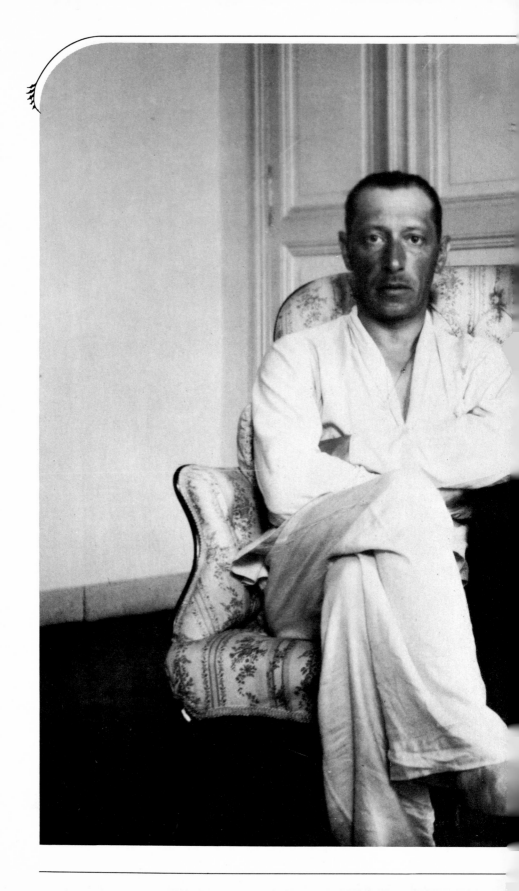

Igor, Anna, and Catherine Stravinsky, Nice, 1925.

Catherine and Igor Stravinsky, Biarritz, 1922.

Vera de Bosset Sudeikina in the Royal Gaillac, Paris, 1923. Photograph by Stravinsky.

Madame Sudeikina, Paris, February 1921.

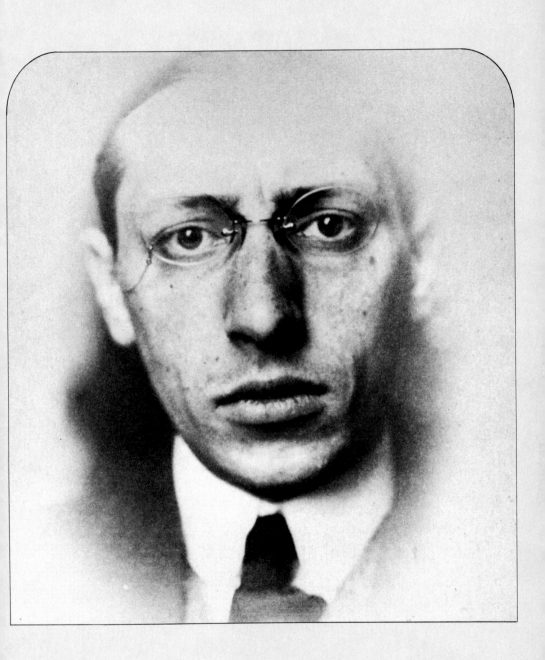

At Beaulieu-sur-Mer, January 1911.

With Ernest Ansermet at "La Pervenche," 1915.

Jean Cocteau at Leysin, 1914. Photograph by Stravinsky.

With Ansermet, Geneva, October 1951.

Vera Stravinsky at home in Hollywood, September 1945.

J.I.St. Honoré
Dec 1936

…avinsky's
…u Faubourg St.-Honoré
…ment, with Nadia
…nger, Ruth Kimball,
…tanley Bate,
…mber 1936.

With Lincoln Kirstein
…t a rehearsal of *Jeu de cartes*,
New York, April 1937.

The Stravinskys leaving the Excelsior Hotel, Naples, for the train to
Milan and the rehearsals of *The Rake's Progress* at La Scala, August 1951.

With W.H. Auden
during a rehearsal
at La Scala.

With George Balanchine
in the Stravinskys' living
room in Hollywood, 1947.

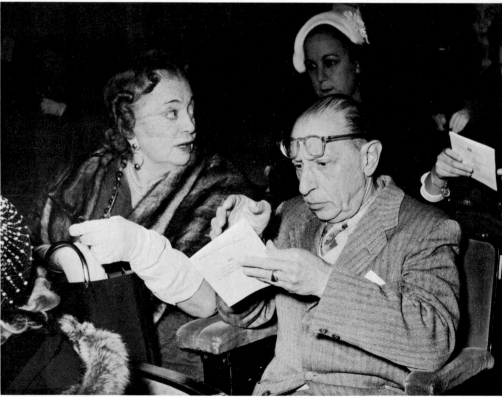

Robert Craft on the front lawn at 1260 North Wetherly Drive, summer 1950. Photograph by Stravinsky. At the Teatro Eliseo, Rome, before the European premiere of Stravinsky's Septet, conducted by Craft, April 14.

With Craft at a rehearsal of *The Flood*, Hamburg State Opera, May 1963.

Hollywood, March 1952. Photograph by Sanford Roth.

nizer. The point of my letter to you is to beg your assistance in this matter, for it concerns your first violin, and if possible, the musicians would be taken from your orchestra to replace those who, for one reason or another, cannot come.

I am disgusted by all these organizations, or rather, dis-organizations. They are never precise and they take off their clothes in public. In this case, they make an appeal to goodwill and mouth vague phrases, as if that were the way to put on a concert!

How did *Les Noces* go? *Oedipus* went admirably well in Dresden, and I conducted very well, or so I think, to judge by the very special compliments from Busch,[233] who is extremely reserved, not to say severe, with regard to his colleagues. He esteems you very highly, as an exception, for which reason I believe that his judgments are not always the result of jealousy. Busch is an excellent musician and conductor himself (very good performance of *The Queen of Spades*), rather hostile to all new tendencies, which is somewhat rare in our time for a man of thirty-eight. I would be the first to welcome this mentality with open arms, but on condition that it had passed through the ideas of our time. It is not enough to disapprove of Darius Milhaud or Alfredo Casella,[234] for though this is a good sign in the development of a musician, I ask still other things of a strong and good man.

Your   I Stravinsky

STRAVINSKY TO ANSERMET

Linz
February 7, 1930
[Postcard]

10 rue Toepffer
Geneva
Switzerland

From Düsseldorf to Bucharest, passing through Linz, one thinks of Mozart, and also, as is evident, of you.

Very happy to play my Capriccio with you at Winterthur. And the O.S.P.? Will that take place? My address until the 16th is the Athénée Palace, Bucharest,[235] then to Prague, where I will play my Capriccio with Talich[236] on Feb-

---

[233] Fritz Busch (1891–1952) conducted the Dresden Opera from 1922 until he left Germany in 1933 to become director of the Glyndebourne Opera.

[234] Stravinsky seems never to have had a good word for Casella, who continued, however, to champion Stravinsky's music. After the premiere of Stravinsky's Piano Concerto, Casella wrote to him: "I think constantly of the joy of hearing your Concerto, and I can hardly wait to have the score on my piano." (July 27, 1924)   When Stravinsky conducted a chamber-music concert in Rome for the Accademia Santa Cecilia, April 24, 1925, Casella played the piano part in the *Japanese Lyrics.*

[235] Stravinsky gave two concerts in Bucharest, February 14 and 16, conducting his Symphony in E flat, *Fireworks, Scherzo fantastique,* and *Petrushka,* and playing the piano part in the Capriccio.

[236] Vaclav Talich (1883–1961), Czech conductor.

ruary 25 or 26. Would it be possible to find out whether or not I am playing at the O.S.P. on March 7?[237]

Your   I Str

In Prague, Hotel Ambassador.

STRAVINSKY TO ANSERMET   *167 bd. Carnot*
                                                                          Nice
Geneva   *March 5, 1930*

Thank you for your two letters,[238] *mon cher,* and also for the photo. The placement of the performers in *Les Noces* is very good, and I'd like to print it in the orchestra score as a direction for its conductors.

Yesterday I sent a letter to [Edward] Clark telling him, regretfully, that I prefer the two Courtauld concerts[239] to the one at the BBC, mainly because the dates that you gave me in January unfortunately are not convenient. At the same time, I accepted the Courtauld engagements almost reluctantly, because this will prevent me from doing the premiere of the Capriccio in London with you. I still would have hesitated if the thing were being done in October.

Here are my projects: I must finish my work for Boston by October 1, then a week of rest and [then] en route for a long tour of concerts that I would like to begin in Holland, from October 10 to 20. After Holland, I would like to do Cologne, Hamburg, Copenhagen, Oslo, Stockholm, Helsinki,[240] Riga, Revel, Warsaw, Berlin (with Bruno Walter[241] conducting the Capriccio and Ernest Ansermet the First Concerto at the Rundfunk), Prague, Vienna, Munich, and Zürich.[242] After all these cities, I shall be in Brussels on December 13 and 14, as

---

[237] There is no contract with the Orchestra Symphonique de Paris for this date showing Stravinsky's participation.

[238] March 2 and 3.

[239] These two concerts took place on March 2 and 3, 1931, in the Albert Hall in London. The London Symphony Orchestra was directed by Malcolm Sargent and by Stravinsky. The program, the same at both concerts, consisted of Beethoven's Eighth Symphony (Sargent conducting), Capriccio (Stravinsky as soloist), and *Firebird* Suite (Stravinsky conducting). Elizabeth Courtauld, the founder of the Courtauld-Sargent concerts, arranged for Stravinsky's engagement.

[240] Stravinsky was not to conduct in Helsinki until September 1961.

[241] Bruno Walter (1876–1962), pupil of Mahler, director of the Vienna Opera orchestra, conducted frequently in France, and, from 1931, in the Salzburg Festivals. He emigrated to the U.S. during the war and conducted at the Metropolitan Opera.

[242] Before his departure, Stravinsky had established the following schedule for his autumn tours (in the programs that included Capriccio, Concerto, and Sonata, Stravinsky did not conduct but only played the solo piano part):

OCT. 14 Zürich: Capriccio (Conductor, Volkmar Andreae. *Song of the Nightingale, Sacre du printemps*)

      17 Lausanne: Capriccio (Ansermet. *Baiser de la fée?* and 3 encores)

arranged yesterday with Cuvelier.[243] By the same mail, I wrote to Monteux and am now awaiting his reply. If this vain, petty individual and conductor stands by his refusal, I will be grateful to him, for I will then be able to do the Brussels concert with you.[244] In the letter to Cuvelier, I explained the whole business about Monteux and about you, including our conversation of the other day, which is to say that if Monteux accepts my invitation to conduct the concert, you will voluntarily surrender the baton to him.

It is understood about the Columbia arrangement (you with O.S.P. as counterpoint to Monteux-H.M.V. [His Master's Voice]). I am writing to Couesnon[245] today to ask him to fix the recording date of the Capriccio with the O.S.P. under your direction for the week of May 5 to 11.

In order to play at your rehearsal on the morning of March 18 at Winterthur, I must be at the Reinharts' on the evening of the 17th.

I await your news on this subject and beg you to tell me when you are going to Prague,[246] and whether you will then go directly from there to Winterthur.

I embrace you. Your   I Str.

---

18 Geneva: same program

25 Mainz: I conduct *Fireworks, Apollo,* Eight Easy Pieces, and *Firebird* Suite

31 Wiesbaden: I conduct *Apollo,* Eight Easy Pieces, and *Le Baiser de la fée*

NOV. 4 Bremen: Capriccio (Conductor, Wendel. *Petrushka* and *Le Sacre du printemps*)

6 Berlin: Sonata (Studio Rundfunk)

Capriccio (Ansermet at the Philharmonic. Program unknown)

13 I conduct a program of which I am not yet sure

23

24 Frankfurt a [m] M [ain]—Sudwestdeutscher Rundfunk: Capriccio (Conductor, Rosbaud. Progr. for the moment unknown)

29 Vienna: Capriccio (Conductor, Spanjaard. Program unknown)

DEC. 4 Nuremberg: Capriccio (Conductor, Wetzelberger. Program unknown)

9 Mannheim: I conduct *Firebird* Suite, *Fireworks,* and the *Fée*

13

14 Brussels: Capriccio (Ansermet. Premiere of the Symphony [of Psalms])

18 Amsterdam: Capriccio (Mengelberg, program unknown)

20 Paris: Concerto

[243] Marcel Cuvelier, founder of the Jeunesses Musicales Belges.
[244] See the correspondence with Monteux on this subject in *S.S.C.* II.
[245] Jean-Félix Couesnon was the French representative of Columbia-Couesnon, the English branch of Columbia Records.
[246] Stravinsky and Ansermet were together in Prague, and it was at this time that F. Dolbin made his drawing of the two musicians with Alexander von Zemlinsky.

STRAVINSKY TO ANSERMET   *167 bd. Carnot*
                                                    Nice
Geneva   *March 24, 1930*

Won't you find out, dear friend, whether there is a way to change our Brussels concerts from December 13/14 to November 15/16 (the date that you had indicated to me, and that you also state in your letter)? I ask you this even though I am not able to fix the date immediately (if you answer in the affirmative), since that depends on my manager Sirota,[247] who is supposed to arrange a Scandinavian and Baltic tour for me between October 20 and November 20. In the past month he has given me no date. I sent a telegram warning him that unless I receive the outside dates of my Scandinavian tour immediately, I cannot say that I will accept his proposals when he finally makes them.[248]

No further word from Couesnon. I fear that our recording with O.S.P. will not succeed, because of Monteux, who does have a voice in the matter and will refuse to give "his" orchestra (such an obvious probability that it has only now come into my head). Then what? The so-called Straram Orchestra? That would require several extra hours of rehearsal. My God, my God, nothing but difficulties!

I embrace you. Your   I Stravinsky

STRAVINSKY TO ANSERMET   *167 bd. Carnot*
                                                    Nice
Dear,   *March 27, 1930*

Having [as yet] received no answer either to my letter or to my cable to Sirota, who was bothering me with his Scandinavian project for October 20 to November 20, I decided to send him on his way.[249] Consequently, I would like to change certain concert dates in this period that are inconvenient for me, primarily the one of our Brussels festival, if it is still possible: transfer it from December 13/14 to November 15/16. I beg you to take these steps with the Philharmonic, explaining to them that it is upon my request.

After I have waited three weeks for a reply from Couesnon about your recording of my Capriccio, these idiots tell me that they have nothing against your conducting, and they prefer that I arrange your emoluments directly with you. Because of their obligations in London, they cannot pay different fees for the same work. Nothing could make me more furious than these negotiations. I answered that during this year of my contract with Columbia, I am going to

---

[247] Peter Sirota, impresario and concert organizer.

[248] Stravinsky telegraphed Sirota on March 24, 1930: "Confirming letter March 16. Please telegraph dates Scandinavian tour otherwise cannot accept, being obliged daily to fix different engagements." Sirota answered on March 25: ". . . For the Scandinavian and Baltic tours, I want to set aside the dates from October 15. I can pay 2,000 dollars net for five concerts. You do not have to pay either the commission or taxes."

[249] Stravinsky should have received Sirota's reply.

record *Apollo* and fragments of the *Fée*. When I am in London, I shall see Sterling and speak to him as I should. But for now it is futile, a waste of time. It is these malevolent bureaucrats of the Maison Couesnon (Cannu & company) who answer me, instead of Bérard, of whom they wish to dispose.[250] How lovely!

Still no reply from Reinhart or from Basel,[251] despite their promise to write to me last Saturday. Could you call Reinhart again?[252]

Your   Stravigor

STRAVINSKY TO ANSERMET   *167 bd. Carnot*
                                                            Nice
Brussels   *April 1, 1930*

Dear,

My sharp letter had its effect. Bérard wrote to me that "there was a misunderstanding," and that they are "thrilled" to record the Capriccio. Rather an inappropriate answer, since it was not a question of my Capriccio, but of your salary. I replied yesterday, telling him what I thought of their first letter, and proposing that if they do not want to pay you a special fee, they should pay you what the second violins would ordinarily receive. I have that right, since the orchestra is engaged as a complete unit, and the ensemble of the Capriccio does not include second violins. I gave Bérard your address at the Grand Hôtel in Brussels, in the hope that he will write to you. It is perfectly idiotic to lose a month on something which could be cleared up in four days by a letter.

Why do I have nothing from this Clark? His style is to send a cable demanding an urgent reply, then after you capitulate, he is not heard from again.[253] I beg you, write to him and see what is wrong.

As for the Rundfunk of Berlin, I am waiting for Brussels to give me a definite date, and then I will be able to collate my engagements. I would have kept December 13/14 free had I known that Bottenheim would succeed in arranging Holland for me from the 15th to the 23rd. Today's cable says that the dates for my tour with Mengelberg will not be definite until next week.

---

[250] The English branch of Columbia Records was headed by Louis Sterling. Philippe Parès and Jean Bérard were directors of Columbia-Couesnon. Cannu was named artistic director while Parès took charge of publications at the Couesnon office.

[251] On April 3, Paul Sacher, conductor of the Basler Kammerorchester, wrote to Stravinsky that he thought he would be able to organize an October performance of the Capriccio and asked the composer to specify his conditions.

[252] This correspondence with Reinhart is concerned with a concert in Winterthur during the next season.

[253] On March 14, Edward Clark had sent Stravinsky the following telegram: "We plan two programs your compositions January 28, February 1, Ansermet conducting. Let us know if you accept these two dates to play the Concerto." Stravinsky agreed to the concerts but with the Capriccio, not his Concerto. He also proposed the first English performance of the *Symphony of Psalms*.

Still nothing, not from Andreae, not from Winterthur, not from Basel! They're in no hurry.

To our success. Your   Istr

STRAVINSKY TO ANSERMET   *167 bd. Carnot*
                                                              Nice
Brussels   *April 3, 1930*

Here, *mon vieux,* are the photos from Winterthur; they came out pretty well. I have just received a letter from one of my agents in Germany who is fixing my concert at Stuttgart for November 16/17. It is therefore impossible to change the dates of our concert in Brussels from December 13/14 to the proposed November dates.

And finally a letter from Monteux!!![254] He tells me he was profoundly touched by my letter and the confidence that I gave him by choosing him to conduct the Brussels festival. He also told me how sad he was that I no longer trust him with the premieres of my works, and complained that I no longer approve of his interpretation of *Le Sacre,* as he learned from my publicity letter to Columbia. But, wishing to put an end to these misunderstandings (?) and to show that he has forgotten it all, tomorrow, on his birthday (*sic*), he is going to play *Le Sacre* with the O.S.P.!!! And not a word about Brussels. I answered immediately, point by point, beginning the letter by explaining that after such a long silence, Brussels had concluded that Ansermet might as well be the one to do it, and that the Philharmonic had invited Ansermet "as soon as you had made known your refusal to conduct the concert." I added: "Unless you received my lines of March 4 and entered into direct correspondence with Ansermet or the Philharmonic, something about which I am ignorant."[255]

And now, I await news from you.

Yours,   I Stravinsky

STRAVINSKY TO ANSERMET   *167 bd. Carnot*
                                                              Nice
Grand Hôtel   *[After April 3, 1930]*
Brussels   *[Telegram]*

Let's keep December dates.[256]

---

[254] Dated March 31, in reply to Stravinsky's of March 4.

[255] Monteux wrote to Stravinsky on April 17, and noted in the P.S.: "As for the Brussels concert, it is announced in the program of the concert that I just gave in this city, 'Under the direction of Ansermet.'"

[256] That same day, Ansermet wrote to Stravinsky saying that the concert originally planned for November 15/16 could be changed to December 13/14.

STRAVINSKY TO ANSERMET

Geneva

Dear,

Two words in a great hurry! Why don't I have any reply from you—to my last letter sent by express mail on the 3rd (with photos of Winterthur), and to my cable ("Let's keep December dates")—concerning our conversation in Brussels about my festival?

Meanwhile, Couesnon wrote to me that they have already reached an understanding, but that the O.S.P. still has not given him an answer. After that, I received a telegram from Monteux asking me to play my Capriccio with him on May 2, at the concert that the O.S.P. is dedicating to contemporary music!!!!!! I answered by telegram: "I accept your proposal willingly, also asking you to speed up arrangements for my recording of the Capriccio with the O.S.P. with Ansermet as requested by Couesnon." And an hour ago I received a letter from Schaeffner[257] telling me that Monteux had a lot of trouble deciding to give his consent for my recording, that he was very nervous and jealous, and that he, Schaeffner, would do all he could to convince Monteux during the course of their present trip to Belgium and Holland, etc. If I wait for Monteux's consent, I could easily lose all the dates. That's why I cabled Couesnon: "If impossible to obtain O.S.P. consent, ask immediately for the Straram Orchestra, week May 5–11, to prevent risk being left without musicians. Telegraph, Stravinsky." In any case, having the name of O.S.P. on the record would not affect you one way or the other: it would be just as good whether it was O.S.P. or Straram. Answer.

Your   I Str

STRAVINSKY TO ANSERMET

I don't know what to do anymore. I received your letters;[258] thank you. Yesterday I received two telegrams from Couesnon, the first saying that there has been no answer about the O.S.P., the second telling me that the Straram Orchestra is free only on the mornings of the 8th, 9th, and 10th. I cabled Couesnon about this, asking them to telephone me, which just happened, but to no avail for us. I wanted Couesnon to get an additional rehearsal for you because the Straram Orchestra has never played the Capriccio. They answered that in the entire month of May those are the only dates on which the orchestra is free! That's lovely! Under these conditions, there is no question of recording my

---

[257] André Schaeffner (1895–1980), French musicologist. He was artistic secretary of the O.S.P. and, from 1929, custodian of musical instruments at the Musée de l'Homme. In 1931 he published a biography of Stravinsky.
[258] Two letters of April 15.

first Concerto (which is what I wanted to do). The Capriccio might be done on six sides (three two-sided records) and recorded in three sessions, but I doubt that we will have enough time to rehearse before. What do you think? Telegraph whether I should keep these three dates anyway.[259] I have just written to Andreae. A few days ago Reinhart let me know that the October 15 date for Winterthur was not convenient, and that he wanted another date later on in the season.[260] I have not yet answered him, but I will do it one of these days, probably proposing Wednesday, November 5.[261] I await your cable.

Your   Stravigor

Listen, if you find it possible to do the Capriccio in these three days with Couesnon, indicate to him by cable the number of musicians you will need.

STRAVINSKY TO ANSERMET   *167 bd. Carnot*
                                                               Nice
Geneva   *April 17, 1930*

Series of events: 1. Hardly had your letter been sent when I decided to send a telegram to Couesnon: "Keep May 8, 9, 10. Musicians required for Capriccio. Stravinsky." 2. This morning: a telegram from Monteux in reply to mine expressing my astonishment at not having had an answer from him. This is what he telegraphed: "Thrilled to have your agreement May 2. Hope to be able to do Capriccio with you soon. Have found solution for recording. Letter follows. Monteux." I can well imagine what this solution will be![262] For this reason I do not regret having reserved May 8, 9, and 10 for the Straram Orchestra. Although this orchestra has not yet played my Capriccio, you could probably manage in the three sessions that they are giving us—eight hours in all!—

---

[259] The recording of the Capriccio took place on May 8, 9, and 10, with the Straram Orchestra under Ansermet's direction, Stravinsky as soloist. The Columbia recording number is LFX 81-3.

[260] Reinhart had telegraphed: "October 15 unfortunately impracticable. Other dates still possible are November 19, December 3 or 17, January 21, February 4, March 18. Please telegraph Musikkollegium."

[261] Stravinsky answered: "Agreed for January 21."

[262] On April 16, Stravinsky sent a second telegram to Monteux: "Astonished your failure reply to my cable Friday." Monteux wrote to Stravinsky on April 17: ". . . What delayed my reply to Columbia was that it seemed to me unflattering that this company asks for my orchestra without me. There is no such thing as recording an orchestra with a conductor other than its own. I still don't see a record from the Concertgebouw without Mengelberg, from the Berlin Philharmonic without Furtwängler, from the Concerts Colonne without Pierné, from the Concerts Pasdeloup without Baton!! etc. etc. You must understand that [being obliged to take] Ansermet is disagreeable to me; he is making a recording with the O.S.P. without me. Anyway, I am prepared to allow you to have my orchestra for this recording on condition that the name of the orchestra is not mentioned."

to teach the music to the players and to record it. 3. A cable from Winterthur gives the dates from which to choose; I picked the only one that is convenient for me, January 21.

I embrace you.   I Stravinsky

STRAVINSKY TO ANSERMET   *167 bd. Carnot*
                                                          Nice
Geneva   *Easter Sunday [April 19, 1930]*

First of all, Happy Easter, *mon vieux!*

I have received your letter of the 18th, and thank you for all the condolences. What a dreadful atmosphere of hatred, envy, and chi-chi vanity surrounding such a simple and natural event.[263] Above all, this should make people understand that if these things are part of the foundation of this world, the opposite will necessarily be the domain of the other.

I am not totally in agreement with the division you propose in the Capriccio; we will do it like this: *1st side:* from the beginning to the 3rd measure of **21**; *2nd side:* from the 4th measure of **21** to the end of the first part; *3rd side:* from the beginning of the Rhapsody to **46**; *4th side:* from **46** to **54** (finishing with the measure before this number); *5th side:* I agree with your divisions, and we shall proceed as follows: from the beginning of the last movement, it ought to be from **52** (but this time without holding the long G in the flute from the conclusion of the preceding movement) to **76**; *6th side:* from **76** to the end. The division into five sides, though possible, is not commercially feasible.

As for the make-up of the orchestra in the wind section, you are wrong only concerning the trumpets: there are three, not two. I prefer the combination 10, 8, 6, 4 for the strings.

Besides the Capriccio, I want to do my Concerto, but with which orchestra? And when? Yesterday Monteux deigned to inform me by letter that he has "found a solution." If the name of the orchestra does not appear on the records, he will let me have it. He prefaces this great "solution" with a long explanation, telling me that one does not ask for the Concertgebouw Orchestra without Mengelberg, for that of Colonne without Pierné, for the Berlin Philharmonic without Furtwängler,[264] etc., etc., etc., all the way to Rhené-Baton, thoroughly

---

[263] I.e., the use of Monteux's orchestra.

[264] In March 1931, when Furtwängler asked Stravinsky's Berlin publisher which excerpts from *Petrushka* were customarily performed in the concert suite, Stravinsky wrote to Païchadze: "Furtwängler is beginning to worry, sensing, on the one hand, that serious representatives of contemporary music—the first culprit being myself— are hostile toward his notorious conducting, and, on the other, that he cannot simply cling to Brahms just to please the German (and international) lower middle class." (March 24, 1931)   When asked to contribute to a memorial album for Furtwängler, Stravinsky refused, saying that his reasons "were too long and too complicated to explain in a letter."

enumerated. I answered that I am of the same opinion on the matter because it had not even occurred to me to put the name of the O.S.P. on my records, never having done so on my other recordings. I went on to say that in asking to use the O.S.P. I had not thought it would be a gaffe to invite Ansermet to conduct, since he had founded the orchestra and consequently would not be considered a stranger there. I did not go on to say whether or not I will use the orchestra. That is the whole business, and I urgently need your help. We have [May] 8, 9, and 10 reserved for the Straram Orchestra. Should we do the Concerto with [them]? In reserving the dates with the O.S.P., should we do the Capriccio with them, since they already know it? Come immediately to an agreement with Couesnon on this subject and settle it all yourself. If necessary, I could be free until May 17. Anyway, here is the makeup of the orchestra for the Concerto: 3 picc [olo] and f [lutes], 2 ob [oes] and English horn, 2 clar [inets], 2 bassoons (and contrabassoon), 4 horns, 4 trumpets, 3 trombones, tuba, timpani, and 6 contrabasses.

In great haste. Your   I Stravinsky

Telegraph if you arrange everything with Couesnon, or if I must also get mixed up in this affair.

I am waiting for a telegram from Monteux to find out if he accepts my terms. He asked me in his letter to take into consideration the difficult situation of the O.S.P., since he is now responsible for the whole business. I answered him by telegram: "My unalterable conditions are 500 dollars each appearance payable morning of concert rental of orchestra parts at expense of organization."

Lourié's article has not pleased me much this time. I am somewhat of your opinion.

STRAVINSKY TO ANSERMET   *167 bd. Carnot*
                                                                      Nice
Geneva   *April 22, 1930*

Thank you for your affectionate Easter note.

I return the enclosed letter from Monteux and the draft of your reply to him, of which I totally approve. Schaeffner, who came to see me here during his Easter vacation, had some knowledge of these letters. His attitude was like Gehret's; I suspect that they share a disgust for Monteux that they are afraid to admit.[265]

Monteux is back in Paris tonight after a pleasure trip in the company of his

---

[265] On May 4, 1930, Schaeffner wrote to Stravinsky: ". . . It is unfortunate that we must take into account the sensitivity of a Monteux, since this same sensitivity no longer comes into play when it is a question of aesthetic as well as egotistical evaluation of certain music. . . ."

wife and Gehret (!!), which explains why I still have no answer either to the cable about my terms or to my letter.

Yesterday I sent a telegram to Couesnon: "Monteux accepts proposition to lend O.S.P. for my recordings on condition not to put orchestra name on records. Will record Capriccio with O.S.P. and Concerto with Straram Orchestra. Retain O.S.P., arrange dates with Ansermet, and respond immediately about rental parts from Edition Russe."

Since the post offices are still closed for the Easter holiday, I cannot expect news from Couesnon until after tomorrow. Païchadze wrote to me that he is going to London, which is very inconvenient in respect to the conversations about the rental price. Although he promised not to create obstacles for me, they are asking more for the rental this time. My God, when will we have finished with the history of this recording, which to me seems complicated and annoying in the highest degree?

Schaeffner told me that you are moving. Is that true? What address?

Your   I Stravinsky

Just received an absurd cable from Couesnon. . . .

Zürich is set for October 14, Winterthur for January 21. What dates do you foresee for Geneva or Lausanne?[266]

STRAVINSKY TO ANSERMET   *Nice*
                                                April 24, 1930
Geneva

Thank you for your two letters.[267] Since my last letter to you (22nd of this month), I have received the following reply from Couesnon: "We regret infinitely but cannot record the Capriccio May 8, 9, 10 as arranged with Ansermet Strarem Orchestra. Cordially, Jean Couesnon." I answered as follows: "Astonished your cable, having the right by contract to make six two-sided records and Capriccio constituting only three. Insist recording first Concerto. Stravinsky." They replied: "London affirms contract fulfilled, thirteen records having been released in two years. Capriccio will make up part of your recordings for third year. We will arrange to record Concerto before end of contract. Couesnon." So, all is clear concerning this affair, and everything corresponds to what you wrote to me.

As for Monteux, who asked me to lend my support to his concert of May 2

---

[266] These two concerts of Stravinsky's works took place on October 17, 1930, in Lausanne (under the auspices of the Committee of the "Soirées de Lausanne"), where Ansermet conducted the O.S.R. in the Suite from *Pulcinella*, *Le Baiser de la fée*, and the Capriccio (Stravinsky as soloist), and in Geneva on October 18, where the program consisted of *Le Baiser de la fée* and the Capriccio.

[267] Of April 21.

and begged me to help as to terms (and you know the telegram that I had sent to him on that subject), Gehret answered yesterday: "Concert May 2 canceled, bad date, does not permit us to risk high costs. Regrets, Gehret." This morning, a telegram from Monteux: "Conditions unacceptable. Regrets, Monteux." The uselessness of this telegram after that of Gehret (who was obviously acting on orders from Monteux himself) seemed to signify a wish to be frankly disagreeable to me. What a sad person, that Monteux!

God willing, I shall be in Paris on the morning of the 7th and begin work at eight or nine o'clock.

Your   I Str

I will be in Winterthur January 16 to 21. I am telling you this in case the period in October will cause problems for Lausanne or Geneva, or [both] Lausanne and Geneva, as Gagnebin thinks possible. He is here these days, at our place, with Olivier. Schaeffner also comes by our house these days. After Monday, I will be alone and can begin my regular work again.

STRAVINSKY TO ANSERMET   *167 bd. Carnot*
                                                                    Nice
Geneva   *April 28, 1930*

Dear,

Received your telegram. Unfortunately, I think it is impossible for me to be free the first week in December. I will be in Nuremberg at that time, playing my Capriccio with the Nuremberg Philharmonic on December 4.

Weber,[268] who just saw von Benda,[269] of the Berlin Radio, wrote to me that he will soon see to it that the dates of the engagement and rehearsals are fixed definitely. Von Benda asks me to play my Concerto, *which he likes so much* (that's touching!), but I obtained his consent to play the Capriccio, which I have played only once in Germany, versus many times for the Concerto. And besides, the Concerto, which requires a special technique, could take a lot of time to prepare, and to keep it in shape during a long trip of two months is neither convenient nor practicable, since the performance would be the only one on this tour.

Have you finally had news from Clark? What is happening to him there?

When are you coming to Paris, and to which station? Myself, I leave on the 6th, and, consequently, will be in Paris on the morning of the 7th, working at my piano at Pleyel.

Is the first week in December the only time you can be available for the Rundfunk? What dates do you anticipate for Lausanne or Geneva?

Your   I Str

---

[268] Fyodor Vladimirovich Weber of the Russischer Musik Verlag.
[269] Hans Robert Gustav von Benda (1888–1972), German conductor, became artistic director of the Berlin Philharmonic in 1934.

STRAVINSKY TO ANSERMET
167 bd. Carnot
Nice

58 chemin de la Roseraie
April 30, 1930

Geneva

Dear,

Thank you for your lines (budget for the concert). Certainly I agree to the proposed reduction. I do not want to decide anything on this subject. I entrust myself to you, and beg you to fix my fees yourself and to arrange these two concerts[270] immediately after the one in Zürich, since I fear that connecting them with the one in Winterthur at the end of January would be less convenient for me; but let us keep this last solution in reserve.

On the one hand, and much as I want your help on the question of the fees, I am firm in my wish to play only my Capriccio in this concert.

I envy you, hearing Toscanini,[271] whom I still have never heard. But be careful to get a seat in advance. According to Schaeffner, everything is taken.

A bientôt, mon cher, I embrace you very affectionately.

Your   I Str

STRAVINSKY TO ANSERMET
Charavines-les-Bains
Isère

Geneva
September 3, 1930

Welcome home, dear!

I received your letter written on several very pretty postcards,[272] from which I learned that tomorrow you will disembark at Genoa. I hope that you will find Jacqueline completely recovered, and that you will begin the season with your heart relieved of these cruel torments, which paralyze one's work. I would like to hear from you immediately upon your arrival. You would be kind to write to me here at Villa Waddington, Charavines-les-Bains, Isère, where we have spent the best summer we have ever had, despite unpleasant weather at the beginning of our stay.

Two weeks ago I finished my *Symphony of Psalms* (I have titled it thus).[273] I already have a photocopy of the orchestra score, which I have writ-

---

[270] Lausanne and Geneva.

[271] On May 3, at the Paris Opéra, Toscanini conducted the New York Philharmonic in Beethoven's Third Symphony, Brahms's *Haydn Variations,* the Nocturne and Scherzo from Mendelssohn's *A Midsummer Night's Dream,* and the Prelude and Liebestod from *Tristan und Isolde.*

[272] Of July 28, 1930.

[273] Stravinsky first chose the title *Symphonie psalmodique.* On August 12, 1930, he answered Schaeffner's question about the meaning of the word *"psalmodique"*: "Then would it be *Symphonie psalmique?* Frankly, that is not at all what I wanted. To me the word 'psalmique' indicates only that the symphony contains some psalms sung by soloists or choirs; that is all. I was looking for a brief title which would seize the special

ten in such a way as to make the best calligraphers envious (!). Païchadze is making several copies for our European performances. The vocal parts are printed, the orchestra score is copied by hand. This symphony is in three parts, which are linked to each other: I. Prelude; II. Double Fugue; III. The Symphonic Allegro, with which you are familiar. I am impatient to show the first two parts to you.

Ten days ago I went with my sons to Koussevitzky's in Plombières-les-Bains. Païchadze came with his wife,[274] and Lourié (who brought Koussevitzky the terrible book that he had commissioned, thinking that Lourié's pen would know how to immortalize his "genius").[275] With Nini's help, I played the entire

---

character of my *Symphony*. In short, this is not a symphony into which I have put some psalms which are sung, but on the contrary, it is the singing of the psalms which I symphonize, and that is difficult to say in two words."

[274] Stravinsky had telegraphed to Koussevitzky at the Villa Charmilles, avenue Lorraine, Plombières-les-Bains, on August 18 or 19: "Telegraph me Stravinsky Charavines-les-Bains if I may come with my sons at the end of the week. Best wishes." And on August 20, Stravinsky wrote to Païchadze: "Today I am sending the manuscript of the orchestra score of the first part of my Symphony to you. Tomorrow I will return the corrected proofs of the [vocal score]. I just received Koussevitzky's reply to my cable, saying that he awaits me with joy at the end of the week. My sons and I plan to go there on Saturday. We will leave in the morning and hope to arrive around the time of the evening meal. Try to come too; it would give me great joy. Better still, come to Grenoble (take the Friday night train from the Gare de Lyon and you will be in Grenoble at 7 or 8 in the morning), and we will drive the 300 kilometers together in the car. I beg you to afford me this pleasure and to telegraph to me if you accept. In that case we would pick you up at the [Grenoble] station around 8 a.m. Include in the telegram an acknowledgment of the receipt of the manuscript. I am waiting for the English contract to be returned. I embrace you."

[275] Lourié had been commissar of music in Petrograd until emigrating to France (1923). He was Stravinsky's closest musician friend, as well as his assistant, from 1924 to the mid-1930s. Stravinsky tried to help him find a music publisher, as a letter to Stravinsky from Willy Strecker, May 19, 1932, indicates: ". . . The works really interest me, especially the *Concerto spirituale*. But I have the impression that . . . the recasting of religious thought into symphonic expression does not quite succeed. He remains stuck in a neo-liturgical style and . . . he is often very much influenced by your music, but . . . though he attains places of unusual effectiveness . . . he still lacks scope and the smaller form would suit him better. [He] uses the Gregorian style but does not actually experience it and translate it into the idiom of our time. . . ." The publication of Lourié's book *Serge Koussevitzky* (New York, 1931) strained, but did not destroy, the friendship with Stravinsky, to whom Lourié wrote, September 20, 1930: "I am a little disappointed that the book, which contains many reminiscences, and in which I touch upon many serious questions, has to revolve around Koussevitzky's biography. Actually, I say very little about him and write in more general terms. Still, this dolt stands out like a statue among a number of important figures. I could not avoid talking about you, of course, but I tried to say very little and . . . I wrote quite candidly about his performance of your music, saying that, despite all of his love for your com-

Symphony in the casino at Plombières-les-Bains, on a casserole in B flat, because Koussevitzky has no piano at his house (!). Do not be astonished at this, since this contrabassist never needs to play the piano, having become the American star purely through his conductor's baton. His genius frees him from the necessity of studying at the piano the scores that he deigns to conduct. For that inferior function, someone is always ready to play the music until this star has his ass full of it. That, as he claims, is his system.

At the same time as these lines, you will receive a letter from Schaeffner about which he spoke to me recently. A few weeks ago, Monnet[276] and Gehret

---

positions, he is fundamentally at odds with them. I foresaw this particular point becoming something of an issue. [But] I ought to have my say about *something* in this project of his which was never designed to be anything more than fuel for his outrageous ambition, that being the only thing in the world that motivates him. . . . It has turned out to be a funny book, full of wicked irony for those who know how to read it. . . .'' Lourié wrote again a fortnight later, describing how he was made to read the book to the Koussevitzkys: "We would break for an hour or so for lunch or dinner, only to begin the ordeal all over again afterward. It boiled down to a veritable duel between Natalia Konstantinova [Mrs. Koussevitzky] and me. She took exception to any unambiguous statement and any clearly delineated judgment, and she was incredibly stubborn in her efforts to convince me that everything should be expressed in a vague, noncommittal, and harmless way with regard to events and facts, while the figure of Koussevitzky himself should somehow appear all-knowing, learned, and all-understanding. . . . Serge was passive throughout all this. . . . He was obviously embarrassed and, for the most part, he remained silent. Occasionally, however, even he would say: 'After all, what he's saying is true, Natalia.' . . . Koussevitzky wants to establish a link among the three of us. 'Take me into your circle; there is a great deal that we can do together.' "

Here it should be said that Lourié was one of the two or three most important associates in Stravinsky's life, and that the correspondence may well be the most valuable of all, though Stravinsky's side of it has not been made available. Lourié's letters attest to his superior powers of discrimination. Thus, in 1930, he wrote to Stravinsky about one of Byron's notebooks: "It is marvelously written but the nicest thing about it is that it is without a trace of 'Byronism.' . . . I had always thought of him as affected, pompous, and old-fashioned. Not at all! He is a true gentleman, bright, unusually modest, and plagued by the same fears and worries that have always plagued all thinking people." In another letter, commenting on a biography of Napoleon, Lourié reminds Stravinsky, "It is difficult for us to realize the phenomenon that Napoleon really was because his name represents a period of history, and because he has been galvanized, which is to say rendered harmless, by bourgeois-intelligentsia culture and civilization." In one letter, from the Engadine, February 8, 1931, Lourié reports that "many stupid people are prepared to serve the 'cause' of Russian art . . . and they have hushed up old man Glazunov, who has taken a professor's post in Berlin. . . . In Paris I saw the dress rehearsal of *Boris,* in which the much-aged Chaliapin spent a great deal of time teaching the chorus to sing the Requiem in church Slavonic, which violates all opera rules."

[276] One of the board members of the O.S.P.

asked me if there were any possibility of my playing my Capriccio with you at the O.S.P. I replied that it was not up to me to change your plans, since, as organizer of the two galas, you had firmly engaged me for two appearances, not one, even proposing that I sign the contract, which I thought was needless. Finally, I advised them to await your arrival and to speak directly to you, not to me, as I have nothing to say in this affair. Although I understand them very well and share their reluctance to see themselves put aside in this very important event, I nevertheless foresee nothing of importance for you with the O.S.P., so long as Monteux remains the artistic director, and this title is not yours in the same way that, until now, it has been Monteux's.

"Awaiting the pleasure of reading a word from you," receive, my old friend, a brotherly kiss from your

Igor Stravinsky

STRAVINSKY TO ANSERMET   *Charavines-les-Bains*
September 6, 1930

Dear,

Very happy with your plan to come here. Come as soon as possible, whenever you wish, after next Wednesday. But remember that we will not stay here long; we are returning on September 16 or 17.

You can take the train to Grenoble and we will pick you up* at the station and bring you back here to Charavines, 50 kilometers from Grenoble. Could you perhaps get off the train before Grenoble? We are very near Voiron, Les Abrets, le Pont-de-Beauvoisin, and I think that all of these small villages are on your Geneva-Chambéry-Grenoble train route. The most convenient would be Les Abrets or Voiron.

Don't forget to telegraph the exact hour and, of course, the date of your arrival. You may telegraph: Stravinsky Charavines Isère. That suffices as an address. Joyfully awaiting to embrace you in the flesh. I already envision it.

Your   I Stravinsky

P.S. It would be best for you simply to consult the Michelin map no. 74, at the bottom of which you will find Lake Paladru, and Charavines along the lake; then you could choose the most convenient place to get off.

*By car

STRAVINSKY TO ANSERMET   *September 24, 1930*

Geneva

My dear,

On the 29th, at 9:46 in the morning, I will pass through Geneva on my way to Basel. I would be very happy to see you at the station, even if only for a moment.

It seems that I have an hour's wait, because the train leaves Geneva for Basel at 10:55. When the train arrives, I will head directly for customs, as you know, and you will find me there. Send a word in reply. I would so much like to see you.

STRAVINSKY TO ANSERMET

Geneva

167 bd. Carnot
January 2, 1931

HAPPY NEW YEAR, *mon vieux*, and thank you for your tender lines. My new year begins with an overload of correspondence that is driving me crazy; with the correcting of the orchestra score of the Capriccio, in which uncorrected mistakes abound despite my instructions and corrections;[277] and with a terror of seeing the already printed (!!!) parts of *Le Baiser de la fée*.[278] I can imagine what I will find in them.

It is impossible for me to answer your questions about the orchestra score of the Four Etudes,[279] because I do not have it here. Perhaps we will be able to consider these questions together in London. Obtain a copy from Païchadze and bring it to London. I will arrive there on the evening of the 26th on the Golden Arrow from Paris. Here is my itinerary: arrive in Berlin (Fürstenhof) on the morning of the 13th, arrive in Winterthur on the 17th, in Lausanne on the 23rd and 24th (probably at Ramuz's), leave Lausanne for London via Paris on the night of the 25th. Will you stay at Albemarle Court* in London, as we agreed?

Evans is annoying me with requests for information about the Capriccio, Four Etudes, and the Concerto.[280] I referred him to Cuvelier, presenting your wishes for our Brussels programs,[281] and I advised him to address himself to you about the Concerto since I do not have it. What a nuisance! I embrace you, *mon vieux*, very tired.

Your   I Str

*Answer this please.

---

[277] On January 5, Stravinsky filled a notebook with a list of 154 errors in the orchestra score. At the end he wrote: "Review the orchestra parts, which have plenty of faults, in addition to those which can be found in this extremely defective score. May God protect me from ever again falling into the clutches of this new printing process, and from such a caliber of worker."

[278] The copyright of *Le Baiser de la fée*, by the Edition Russe de Musique, is dated 1928.

[279] The Four Etudes for Orchestra were published in 1930 by the Edition Russe de Musique. The first complete performance took place in Berlin, conducted by Ansermet, on November 7, 1930.

[280] On January 28, the BBC recorded the following program, conducted by Ansermet in Queen's Hall: Overture to *Mavra, Apollo,* Concerto (first performance in England), *Le Sacre du printemps.* Stravinsky was the soloist in the Concerto.

[281] Soulima Stravinsky wrote to Evans on January 2: "... Ansermet wrote the notes, which my father approved."

STRAVINSKY TO ANSERMET

167 bd. Carnot
February 6, 1931

58 chemin de la Roseraie

Cher vieux,

I have just received the note you wrote yesterday and will hereby confirm both for you and for Georges Truc [?] the dates and times that were decided among us (Straram, Couesnon, and myself). They are as follows:

February 16 at 2 p.m.: Orchestra and then chorus and orchestra.

February 17 and 18 at 4 p.m.: Recording of the *Symphony,* and in case this recording is not finished on the 18th, February 26 at 2 p.m. has been set aside.

Now tell me, when might I be able to hear the chorus alone before combining it with the orchestra on February 16? Could it be done on the 15th? If so, I will come on the morning of the 15th. I beg you to arrange this for me because I would like to stay here, above all because I don't feel very well (influenza without fever), and would prefer not to advance my trip.

Please ask Vlassov[282] to arrange a rehearsal for me on the afternoon of the 15th and let me know about this subject.

I embrace you. Your   I Stravinsky

At home I found Catherine in bed with terrible pains—rheumatic flu. Happy to know that your mother is out of danger, and very sad for your mother-in-law.

STRAVINSKY TO ANSERMET

La Vironnière
Voreppe
October 5, 1931

58 chemin de la Roseraie

Cher vieux,

I will arrive in Geneva this Saturday, October 10, around 6 in the evening on the Grenoble-Chambéry train, and the next day I will continue my trip to Oslo.[283] As for the rest, I will telegraph in a few days to confirm the hour of my arrival, but you must not forget that there is a time change in France. Thus, I hope to be able to spend an evening with you, unless you have a rehearsal or concert that night.

May I ask a small favor of you? Scandinavian crowns are impossible to find here, and the purchase of foreign money in Berlin has been stopped. I must have about 50 Swedish and 50 Norwegian crowns. Would you buy them for me in Geneva? Thanks in advance, and a word in reply, please.

I embrace you, rejoicing in the anticipation of seeing you again and spending a few hours with you.

---

[282] Alexis Vlassov, a Russian choral conductor.

[283] Stravinsky's 1931 Oslo concerts took place on October 15 and 19. The program he conducted included *Apollo,* the Suites Nos. 1 and 2 for Small Orchestra, and the *Pulcinella* Suite.

Voreppe
July 14, 1932
[Letter with a picture of
Stravinsky in the corner]

STRAVINSKY TO ANSERMET

What has become of you, *mon cher?*

I have just heard Rimsky-Korsakov's *Dubinuchka*[284] conducted by you on the radio: a peculiar and academic German arrangement (harmonically and in its figuration) of a Russian revolutionary song.

Almost a month ago, I celebrated my fiftieth birthday.[285] Thanks for your kind telegram from Vienna, where, in that world of careerists and intriguers, you were the only one who thought of me.

Many letters and telegrams came from Germany—whence I have just returned after *Mavra* by Rosbaud[286] at the Funk in Frankfurt[287]—but only two from Paris, Pleyel[288] and Schaeffner! It is true, I forget that France is my second country. Send your news, and receive, dear Ansermet, my faithful affections.

I Str.

STRAVINSKY TO ANSERMET

Voreppe
November 17, 1932

Cher vieux,

I heard the quite defective Radio Paris broadcast of your London concert, from the last Nocturne by Debussy to the end.[289]

---

[284] A symphonic work composed in 1905. In spite of his criticisms of Rimsky-Korsakov, Stravinsky purchased a 4-hand piano score of *Sadko* on July 1, 1936.

[285] Stravinsky was born on June 5, 1882 (Old Style), the name day of Igor Olgovich, Prince of Novgorod and Grand Duke of Kiev.

[286] Hans Rosbaud (1895–1962), Austrian conductor, director of the Konzertverein in Munich from 1945 to 1948, when he became conductor of the Sudwestfunk in Baden-Baden.

[287] This performance took place on June 23, at the Sudwestdeutscher Rundfunk.

[288] Robert Lyon.

[289] This concert was given at Queen's Hall, London, with Ansermet conducting the orchestra and women's chorus of the BBC. The program consisted of the Overture to *Der Freischütz;* three lieder by Mahler; the three Nocturnes for orchestra by Debussy; "Et Incarnatus est," from the Mass in C minor by Mozart; *Le Sacre du printemps.*

By this time, Stravinsky had developed a distaste for radio concerts. He told *Paris-Soir,* December 6, 1932: "I perform too frequently on the radio and would like to play only in concert halls. The disposition of the orchestra is different for broadcasts. When an actual concert is being broadcast, the orchestra is seated to suit the public in the auditorium, and the microphones are placed anywhere, in such a way that certain instruments dominate everything, while others, essential to the harmony, completely disappear. The radio, in effect, is a cosmetic device, the microphones approaching a certain instrument, then another one. . . . A fine invention, the radio, but with something diabolical, and deceptive for the listener, the performer, and the composer."

I was *very satisfied* with the tempo of *Le Sacre,* in which I recognized you very distinctly; the tempo was the only thing that I could judge. One small reproach, concerning the nervousness in the first measures of the *Danse sacrale,* and later, at the reprise: it was too hurried at the beginning for the timpani to achieve their natural pace.

And you? Did you hear my Duo concertant and the remainder of the program (the new version of the Suite after Pergolesi, piano and violin,[290] and the Violin Concerto with orchestra) at the Studio of the Berlin Funk Stunde on October 28?

What are you doing and what has become of you since I last saw you?

I embrace you. Sincerely, your   I Stravinsky

STRAVINSKY TO ANSERMET   *Paris*
                                                December 20, 1933
58 chemin de la Roseraie   *[Postcard]*
Geneva
Switzerland

Well, what is the meaning of this gloomy silence?

These lines were written by someone who has lived in Paris, 21 rue Viète (XVIIe), since October 15 and who will stay there until June. Guess who and answer.

                                                [Ansonia Hotel]
                                            Broadway at 73rd St.
                                                New York City
STRAVINSKY TO ANSERMET   *February 2, 1935*

I am appalled by what you write, my very dear friend. To think that Gustave Doret, an old man belonging to the past, has not retired but still devotes himself to vile intrigues that will do nothing for him anymore.[291] What a miserable creature. . . .

---

[290] The Duo concertant for violin and piano in five movements, composed in Voreppe between December 1931 and July 1932, was published in 1933 by the Edition Russe de Musique.

[291] Henri Gagnebin's "Comment on a voulu tuer l'O.S.R.," *Journal de Genève,* March 15, 1935: "In February 1934, we learned, incredulous, that the committee of the Radio Suisse Romande planned to transfer the seat of the orchestra from Geneva to Lausanne, thereby compromising its collaboration with the Orchestre de la Suisse Romande. A committee to defend the O.S.R. set the Lausannais and Genevois newspapers against each other. . . . Meanwhile, the O.S.R. arranged to form its orchestra, excluding, without reason, the candidacy of M. Ernest Ansermet for the post of chief of musical broadcasting, and forming a committee composed of Doret, Denzler, and Balmer, one Romande musician and two German-Swiss, a slap in the faces of the Romandes. It goes without saying that a musician from Geneva was not chosen to play any part."

I will see Koussevitzky and speak to him. If only this were to lead to something, but you know as well as I do that he is a hypocrite, promising everything and doing nothing. Yesterday I saw Klemperer,[292] who is leaving for Italy (while I am going to Los Angeles). He received your letter, seemed very touched, and said that, from his side, he would do his best to help. It will be more difficult with Stokowski; I believe that he detests me, knowing what I think of him, thanks to many obliging tongues.

All of this is temporary, my friend, and you will come out of these difficult trials, I firmly believe (and feel). Don't lose courage.

I will be in America until about April 20. If you write to me—at the Musical Arts Management Corporation (cable: MUART New York), 30 Rockefeller Plaza.

I embrace you with all my heart.

Your   Stravinsky

The Powell
28 East 63rd Street
N.Y. City

STRAVINSKY TO ANSERMET   *April 4, 1935*

Thank you, my dear Ernest, for the good (less bad) news that you give me.[293] Glad to learn that the intrigues of Doret and his acolytes have been exposed.

The conservatives (*Journal de Genève*) love Doret, a Federal cadaver who believes himself to be alive (the reason for his intrigues). The conservatives are like Bolsheviks, who must love cadavers, since they have so many of them.

I spoke to Koussevitzky about you. Despite his answer, "[Ansermet's]

---

[292] After Stravinsky had conducted the Los Angeles Philharmonic in March 1935, Klemperer invited him to play his Concerto, or the Capriccio, on his next tour (1937). But as Stravinsky wrote to Dr. Alexis Kall, in December 1936: "Long ago I told Klemperer that I refuse to participate as a soloist because I have not played my own concertos for two years, and I do not have time now to try to refresh my memory. . . ."

[293] The good news was that the cabal to have Ansermet removed as conductor of the Orchestre de la Suisse Romande was defeated. A petition saved the post for him, as he explained to Stravinsky in a letter, January 12, 1935. Henri Gagnebin wrote: "At Chaux-de-Fond, thousands of signatures were collected in a few days to protest M. Ansermet's eviction. At Lausanne, as well, the committee received more testimony from people of all walks of life." But Stravinsky knew that Ansermet had had bad news as well as good. Catherine Stravinsky wrote to her husband, January 8, 1935: "Perhaps Vera has already written to you about the unfortunate Marguerite Ansermet? It seems that she tried to kill herself by taking veronal and turning on the gas, but they saved her and brought her to the clinic. She was screaming that she loves Ernest. How terrible it must be for her! Ira Urtado [Ansermet's mistress], who, for some reason, Ernest summoned, told me all this. I can't understand at all why her presence was needed at that time. What an unhappy woman Marguerite is! Now it will be even harder for her to live, and not easy for him either."

name is at the top of the list of guest conductors to direct my orchestra during my vacation," I think you would be wise not to believe a word of it. The same K., in a sudden moment of frankness, said to Lourié one day: "I am someone who has the weakness to promise everything, and the strength not to keep my promises." Well?

Catherine is ill again with tuberculosis. She is in the large sanitarium at Sancellemoz (Haute-Savoie). It is very sad and fills me with anguish. . . . The children and my mother are in Paris.

I leave, God willing, on April 14 or 15.

I heard *Lady Macbeth* by Shostakovich[294] conducted by Rodzinski with his Cleveland Orchestra. A well-organized advertising campaign bore its fruit, exciting all the N.Y. snobs. The work is lamentably provincial, the music plays a miserable role as illustrator, in a very embarrassing realistic style. It is in recitative form with interludes between the acts—marches brutally hammering in the manner of Prokofiev, and monotonous—and each time the curtains were lowered, the conductor was acclaimed by an audience more than happy to be brutalized by the arrogance of the numerous communist brass instruments. This premiere (and I hope *dernière*) reminds me of the performances of Kurt Weill[295] two years ago in Paris and all the premiere-goers and the snobs of my dear new country. Happily, this was the only event on this trip in the United States that did not make a very good impression on me.

Will I see you on my return? I must go to two concerts (with Nini playing the Capriccio), one in Copenhagen, May 8, and the other in Bologna, May 23, after which *Perséphone* is to be given again with Ida Rubinstein at the Opéra at the end of May or beginning of June.

I embrace you with all my heart.

Your   I Str

I regret being so hard on Shostakovich, but he has deeply disappointed me, intellectually and musically. I regret it the more because his Symphony [No. 1] favorably impressed me two years ago, and I expected something very different from a man of twenty-seven. *Lady Macbeth* is not the work of a musician, but it is surely the product of a total indifference toward music in the country of the Soviets. How good that I am not going there!

---

[294] The opera, *Lady Macbeth of Mtsensk,* composed in 1934, after the story by Leskov.
[295] Kurt Weill (1900–50), composer, pupil of Ferruccio Busoni, collaborator with Bertolt Brecht. He left Germany in 1933, and, after a long stay in Paris, moved to New York, where he wrote several works for Broadway. Stravinsky had been interested in an essay on Weill by Pierre Suvchinsky, written after the Paris performances of *Mahagonny, Jasager,* and *The Seven Deadly Sins,* which compared Weill's use of popular culture with that of Stravinsky in *Mavra.* Suvchinsky remarked "une parenté qui a ses racines dans la sociologie de notre époque entre Weill, Brecht, et Céline."

STRAVINSKY TO ANSERMET   *Paris*
                                                        October 26, 1935
In great haste.

Thank you for your note, my dear Ansermet, also for your card. Very happy about *Mavra,* which, alas, it was impossible for me to hear, since October 23 was Mika's wedding day.

I have been in Paris for ten days working on the second volume of my *Chroniques,* which I have just finished,[296] and on my Double Concerto, which I hope to finish very soon.

During the next few days I will record (conduct) my Violin Concerto with S. Dushkin.

I am staying in Paris until the end of December, when, God willing, I leave for the United States.

Very cordially yours,   I Stravinsky

Say *merde* from me to Geneva and its beautiful Freemasonic institutions, and I will be relieved.

STRAVINSKY TO ANSERMET   *Paris*
                                                        December 13, 1935
My dear Ansermet,

I am going with Nini to Mermod's house ("Fantaisie," Chemin de l'Elysée, Ouchy). Telephone me Monday night. We will await you for the rehearsal.

So pleased to see you again and also to hear such good news about your activities, which seem to be going well, even very well! So much the better.

I embrace you. Your   Stravinsky

STRAVINSKY TO ANSERMET   *Paris*
                                                        October 14, 1937
Geneva

In great haste, my dear.

There is absolutely no reason to make cuts in *Jeu de cartes* in concert performances, any more than, for example, in *Apollo.* Compositions of this type are a series of dances, rigorously symphonic in form. The public does not require any explanation, because there are no descriptive elements illustrating scenic action, and nothing to interfere with the symphonic evolution of the piece.

If you propose this strange idea of asking me to make cuts, the reasoning must be that the succession of movements in *Jeu de cartes* seems a little boring to you personally. I cannot do anything about that. But what amazes me more than anything else is that you try to convince *me* to make cuts in it—I, who just

---

[296] Stravinsky had begun the book in 1934, with the help of Walter Nouvel.

conducted it in Venice and who reported to you the enthusiastic reception of the audience. Either you forgot what I told you, or perhaps you do not attach much importance to my observations or to my critical sense, but I scarcely believe that your public would be less intelligent than the one in Venice.

And to think that it is you who proposed to cut my composition, with all the dangers of maiming it, in order that it might be better understood by the public—you, who were not afraid to play a work as risky in regard to success and audience comprehension as the *Symphonies of Wind Instruments!*

I cannot let you make cuts in *Jeu de cartes*! I think it is better not to play it at all than to do so reluctantly.

I have nothing to add. I have made my point.

Your   I Stravinsky

3 *Halkin Street*
London, S.W.1
October 19, 1937

STRAVINSKY TO ANSERMET

Two words in response to your strange note of the 15th, *mon cher.*

I am sorry, but I cannot allow you to make *any* cuts in *Jeu de cartes.*

The absurd* one that you propose *cripples* my little March, which has its form and constructive sense in the totality of the composition (*constructive sense* that you pretend to be defending). You cut only my March because its position and its development please you less than the rest. In my eyes, this is not sufficient reason, and I would like to say: "But you are not *chez vous, mon cher,* I have not said to you, 'Here, take my score and do with it whatever you please.' " I repeat: either you play *Jeu de cartes* as it is or you do not play it at all. You do not seem to have understood that my letter of October 14 was categorical on this point.

Last night I conducted *Jeu de cartes* in Queen's Hall: a triumphant success,[297] and there were no cuts. I will listen to you on the 27th.

Your   I Str.[298]

*You will excuse the word, but I cannot describe the cut in any other way.

On October 22, Ansermet answered this letter, but Stravinsky confined his reply to marginal comments that he never sent.[299] Strangely, Ansermet, in his first letter, October 12, proposed to play excerpts from the ballet, which is what Stravinsky himself later suggested as an alternative to making cuts. Then,

---

[297] This concert began the ninth season of the Courtauld-Sargent concerts. The program, repeated the next day, consisted of Beethoven's First Symphony, conducted by Sargent, *Jeu de cartes,* and Schubert's last C-major symphony, conducted by Sargent.
[298] Catherine Stravinsky wrote to her husband, October 27: "How unpleasant this correspondence you have with Ansermet is. What's the matter with him?"
[299] See *S.P.D.*, pp. 246–7.

after rehearsing the piece, Ansermet wrote, October 15, "You do not need to reply to my letter. I am convinced. . . . Jeu de cartes, *that beautiful marvel, must be done in its entirety. I ask only one thing: permit me to cut from the second measure of* 45 *to the second measure of* 58. *I have sufficient rehearsal time, and I count on being able to give you a jewel of a performance. You can hear it on the radio on October 27 at 7:30 Paris time."* (Stravinsky, in Amsterdam on the 27th to conduct Jeu de cartes *himself the next day, did not hear the broadcast.)*

The tone of Stravinsky's letter of the 19th, forbidding the cut, is harsh, but Ansermet's answer, hysterical and full of irrelevant arguments, reveals that the quarrel had deeper roots—as does Stravinsky's letter to Strecker, January 8, 1938: "After a bitter exchange of letters, in which I told him exactly what I thought, and after I forbade him to give Jeu de cartes *with cuts, he did so anyway. He confessed this to friends, who reported the whole conversation to me and presented his point of view (if only it could be called a 'point of view'). The megalomania that has obsessed poor Ansermet for some time is responsible for his absurd attitude toward my new score, with which he wanted to do his Bach-Busoni (Bach-Salabert, if you will). In order to forewarn the Swiss symphonic organizations, which, I hope, have not yet been the victim of his caprices, I am sending copies of this letter to Winterthur and Zürich." The letter for Winterthur and Zürich states, in part: "I allow my* Jeu de cartes *to be performed in two ways: either complete or as separate fragments. In the second case, the title in the program should read: 'Fragments of* Jeu de cartes, *ballet in 3 deals,' indicating, of course, which fragments are to be presented. . . . I would also like you to know that . . . I have not extracted a special suite for concert performance from this ballet because I deem it useless and in no way advantageous. The work itself, composed for dance, is equally suitable, without changes, for dance or concert performance. . . ."*

*On January 3, Stravinsky wrote to Reinhart: "I have learned that [*Jeu de cartes] *is on next season's program in Zürich and Winterthur and that Ansermet is to conduct it. In his recent performances with the [Orchestre de la] Suisse Romande, he introduced cuts in the ballet despite my categorical interdiction (two months ago we had a rather painful exchange of letters on this subject). I do not have time to elaborate on this strange obsession which has gripped him for some time now . . . but you will find attached a copy of my letter to [the Zürich] Tonhalle in which I give my instructions for performance of the piece. . . ." Reinhart answered on January 5 that he had heard Ansermet conduct* Jeu de cartes *in Zürich on November 16, and, not having had the score, did not realize that cuts had been made: "Ansermet was here last month and spoke to me about the whole matter. The work will be given in Zürich as a ballet, conducted by Hans Swarowsky."*

On January 5, Strecker wrote to Stravinsky: ". . . I find Ansermet's attitude regrettable, and I fail to comprehend it. The set of parts that he used was sent directly to the theater in Zürich, since they needed it in a hurry for the ballet performance. I wrote to them, suggesting that they exchange the score for another one, but I doubt that the conductor and the musicians, who are now familiar with the score, will want to do so. . . . In the future I shall inform prospective concert organizations of your specific wishes before the parts are sent out. I find it irresponsible for conductors to take liberties. You will not have to fear such behavior in Germany. . . ."

On October 27, 1938, Elie Gagnebin wrote to Stravinsky asking him to participate in a "Homage to Ernest Ansermet," celebrating the twentieth anniversary of the Orchestre de la Suisse Romande. The project was canceled, as Stravinsky learned from Dr. F. Blanchod (letter of November 8). Stravinsky wrote in the margin of Blanchod's letter: "A good thing, because I was proposing to send my homages, not like those in the Chroniques de ma vie, *but rather in the form of the fragments of* Jeu de cartes *that Ansermet sees fit to omit in his performances of the work."*

When Stravinsky's daughter Mika died, November 30, 1938, Ansermet sent a telegram to the composer, and Marguerite Ansermet sent a note of condolence to Catherine Stravinsky. On March 1, 1939, Ansermet sent Stravinsky a reconciliatory note: "I will be here in Paris until Saturday morning and would like to see you. Aside from Thursday (2–5) and Friday (9–12 and the evening), I am free at any time to meet with you when you say. From a distance I testify to the old friendship which I feel for you alone. . . ." Stravinsky's wife died March 2, however, and the meeting did not take place.

During World War II, Stravinsky received another request from Gagnebin to contribute to a homage to Ansermet. The composer replied as follows (in part): "Ansermet's name is intimately associated with my music, and I feel great gratitude to the musician who during so many years showed so lively an understanding of my musical ideas and brought them to life with as much talent as enthusiasm. . . . The brevity of my words does not affect the sincerity of my sentiments. I want these lines to restore our old relationship. I send them with my most affectionate wishes for him, for his art, and for the prosperity of his fine orchestra, which I had the privilege of seeing as it first came into the world." (May 11, 1942)

Nevertheless, the correspondence between the two musicians did not resume until three years after the war, when Ansermet came to New York as guest conductor of the NBC Symphony. English is the language of Stravinsky's remaining communications.

STRAVINSKY TO ANSERMET

Essex House
160 Central Park South
New York

*Los Angeles, California
January 13, 1948
[Telegram]*

Be welcome, dearest friend, so sorry not seeing you because I myself on concert tour starting February San Francisco, Mexico, Dallas, Los Angeles and only

April Washington and New York. Let me hear from you, affectionately.[300] Stravinsky

STRAVINSKY TO ANSERMET   *Los Angeles, California*
                                    January 17, 1948
Essex House   *[Telegram]*
Central Park South
NYC

Greatly enjoyed your masterful performance. Wish I were there to join your
warm audience in applauding you.[301] Cordial greetings.   Igor Stravinsky

STRAVINSKY TO ANSERMET   *[After January 23, 1948]*
                                    [Draft of a telegram]
Essex House
Central Park South
NY 19 NY

Many thanks letter.[302] Why use old instrumentation *Wind Symphony* when
new one technically superior? Not required alto instruments also easier reading. Naturally prefer it. Rejoice hearing you tomorrow Saturday. Cordially.

STRAVINSKY TO ANSERMET   *January 25, 1948*[303]
                                    [Draft of a telegram]
Essex House
Central Park South
NY City

Horn melodic line in **51** etc. changed. First second trombone G-sharp in **54** as
right as CDF-naturals of the third one. Greetings.   I Str.

---

[300] In the draft of this telegram, Stravinsky first wrote: "*Am* myself *in* concert
trip. . . ."
[301] The reference is to Ansermet's concert with the NBC Symphony on January 17.
The program consisted of one of the *Leonore* overtures by Beethoven, the *Symphonie
concertante* by Frank Martin, and the second *Daphnis et Chloé* Suite.
[302] Of January 23.
[303] This telegram is in reply to Ansermet's of January 24.

STRAVINSKY TO ANSERMET

1260 N. Wetherly Drive
Hollywood 46, California
January 26, 1948

Essex House
New York

My dear Ernest,

This very brief note in reply to your letter of Jan. 28, which deeply touched me. Poor friend, I am with you with all my heart, and Vera too, we know how dear the little departed one was to you.[304]

Here are my answers to your questions concerning the new version of my *Symphonies of Wind Instruments:*

1. At **15,** both the G-natural in the flute and the F-sharp in the clarinet are correct.
2. The measure before **17** should be $\frac{3}{8}$, not $\frac{2}{4}$; this mistake was corrected in my score but forgotten in yours.
3. Same as **15.**
4. Four measures after **29,** the new version is correct: B instead of G-sharp in the flute.
5. Last note in the clarinet before **35** is a G-sharp, and the last note in the clarinet before **36** is a D-sharp; these two notes sound, respectively, F-sharp and C-sharp. Both errors were corrected in my score and neglected in yours.
6. You are wrong; there was never an F on the first eighth of the third measure of **45.**
7. The last note of the 1st trumpet (in B-flat) before **43** is obviously a written D, not a written C. Please correct it; my score has been changed for a long time.
8. The passage of the clarinets in fourths at **60,** or rather after **60,** is no longer staccato, as it was in the old score.
9. From yesterday's telegram you know that I have changed the melodic line in the horns at **51, 52,** and **53** (sounding D instead of E) and that the trombones (with tuba and bassoons) now play major thirds in opposition to the minor thirds of the trumpets; the G-natural of the first trombone in the old version is less consistent. I refer to the trombones at **54** and **55.**

That's all for today. I will listen to you Saturday, with all the more interest because this Friday I conduct the same *Symphonies* in a private session with musicians from the film studios here [Hollywood].[305] Good luck and may God help you.

Your   I Stravinsky

---

[304] Ansermet's grandchild.

[305] Stravinsky gave a reading of his *Symphonies* on Friday, January 30, in the John Burroughs Junior High School Auditorium. William Malloch made a recording of this performance of the *Symphonies* on a "brush" sound mirror with paper tape. In spite of a non-concentric capston "wow," Stravinsky's voice is remarkable, singing and giving directions. As early as 1940, Stravinsky had been conducting private "rehearsal orchestras," as they were called. On September 30 of that year, he wrote to E. R. Voigt

STRAVINSKY TO ANSERMET   *NLT*
                                                   January 28, 1948
Essex House   *[Draft of a telegram]*
Central Park South
NY City

Beginning bassoons B-flat as written. English horn before C-flat. First trumpet in **44** A-flat same level as horns motif **48.**

STRAVINSKY TO ANSERMET   *1260 N. Wetherly Drive*
                                            Hollywood 46, California
Essex House   *Crestview 1-4858*
Central Park South   *January 30, 1948*
New York City 19 NY   *[Telegram]*

Second trumpet at **66** G-sharp. Third trombone **66** E-flat. Fourth horn notes before **48** certainly wrong they are same E as **48.**[306]   Igor Stravinsky

STRAVINSKY TO ANSERMET   *January 31, 1948*
                                                    10:30 a.m.
Essex House   *[Telegram]*
NY.

First trombone **66** and **67** completely wrong, take it away.   I. Str.

STRAVINSKY TO ANSERMET   *January 31, 1948*
                                                    [Telegram]
Essex House
Central Park South
NY City

Thousand thanks for wonderful performance. Glad you received timely my wire today. Do you really think I am a good businessman composing such music?[307] Cordially,   Igor Stravinsky

---

of Associated Music Publishers: "There has been formed an important group of musicians here (instrumentalists who play in film studios) to organize a symphony orchestra which is placed at the service of composers and conductors wanting to hold readings of their scores. The orchestra comes together twice a month, and the other day they told me that they wanted very much to play under my direction a work of my choice and, if possible, my Violin Concerto. . . . I promised them to write to you on this subject. . . . I would be much obliged to you if you would send a free set of the Concerto (normal strings). These readings are not concerts—there is no public—but merely 2-hour rehearsals where one works at the readings in shirtsleeves."

[306] This telegram replies to Ansermet's letter of January 29.

[307] *Time* magazine had quoted Ansermet's remark.

STRAVINSKY TO ANSERMET   *February 4, 1948*
                                                                  [Telegram]

Essex House
Central Park South
NYC

Glad to have received your touching letter.[308] Too bad no more time left for correspondence, leaving for concerts in two days. Wish see you Europe. Warmest
greetings.   Igor Stravinsky

STRAVINSKY TO ANSERMET   *1260 N. Wetherly Dr.*
                                                      Hollywood 46, Cal.
My dear Ansermet,   *November 27, 1948*

Your letter of November 20 (from Geneva) arrived today. Alas, it contained
nothing that I had not already found out from others. Such a shame that this
Mass, conceived in the modest tradition of Flemish motets, with a small choir of
children and men, had to have its premiere at the Scala in Milan. That sumptuous place is the last one I would have considered for this music. And I
understood that in these inconvenient circumstances, you renounced your participation in the performance.

As regrettable as these circumstances were, I would have liked at least to
have heard about public opinion, as well as your personal reactions.

As for the F-sharp at Discanti, a measure before the end of the Kyrie, you
are absolutely right. I noticed it the other day while going over the score that
just appeared. How could Erwin Stein,[309] who is always so reliable, let such a
fault go by? Better still, I see that in the "vocal score" they are just about to add
the precautionary parenthesis above that unfortunate F.[310]

Looking at my "schedule" and knowing yours, I doubt that we will be able
to see each other this year.

Wishing you every possible success, I send you my regards.

                                                          Igor Stravinsky

P.S. I appreciate your proposition concerning the establishment of a list of errata in *Le Sacre*. You would be very kind to deliver it to Boosey & Hawkes,* in
the name of my young friend Robert Craft, who will look it over closely with the
proofreaders and myself, when I am in New York.

*moved to 30 West 57th Str. NY., 19

---

[308] Of February 1.

[309] Erwin Stein (1885–1958), Austrian critic and publisher. He had been a conductor
in Europe until 1938, when he became one of the senior editors of Boosey & Hawkes in
London.

[310] Ansermet had conducted the premiere of the Mass in Europe.

STRAVINSKY TO ANSERMET

My dear Ansermet,

Hotel Pierre
New York, N.Y. 10021
July 15, 1966

Your letter[311] touched me. We are both too old not to think about the end of our days; and I would not want to finish these days with the burden of a painful enmity.

Your letter completely cleared it up for me. I am grateful to you.

Your   Igor Stravinsky

Hollywood

STRAVINSKY TO ANSERMET

August 6, 1966

Thank you, dear Ansermet, for what you have written to me about *Perséphone* and about *Zvezdoliki* (the absurd French title of *Roi des étoiles* when it is *Face de l'étoile*). This letter gave me immense pleasure. Thank you. The too-long pause about which you notified me in the clarinet music in this piece is not found in the orchestra score, but probably only in the parts for clar., since the orchestra score that I have in front of me is correct. All of my best wishes end this hurriedly written note.[312]

Cordially,   I Str.

ANSERMET TO STRAVINSKY

1260 North Wetherly Drive

My dear Igor,

Geneva
June 16, 1967
[Telegram]

On this day of your anniversary I send you with my best wishes the expression of my old friendship.

---

[311] Of July 13.

[312] In a draft of this letter, Stravinsky wrote: "Dear Ansermet, I just received your interesting letter of the end of July and I am thrilled by what you tell me about *Perséphone,* which I conducted many times last year."

LETTERS TO

NADIA BOULANGER

1938 ⁓ *1964*

63 Garden St.
Cambridge, Mass.

Very dear Nadia,

Your cable came this morning. Last night I received from Strecker the proofs of pages 27–37 of my Concerto in E flat.[1] I have just corrected and sent them to you, on the S.S. *Europa*. Only the last seven or eight pages remain to be sent, and I will do this as soon as I have time—next week. You can already extract the parts from the pages you have received. It would be difficult to make a correct score from the manuscript, which lacks many of the bowings and contains numerous mistakes that I did not have time to correct. I will try to get a special copy for you from Strecker. In making the copy of the orchestra parts, use only what I have sent (the corrected proofs of the first and second parts) and am sending to you today.

Changing the date of the concert to May 1 was truly unexpected and caught us off guard. I hope all will work out well, especially when I think that everything has fallen into your hands.

Have you spoken to Mrs. [Robert Woods] Bliss on the subject of our last conversation?[2]

I embrace you very affectionately.

Your Stravinsky

63 Garden St.
Cambridge, Mass.

Very dear friend,

Here are the mistakes that I discovered after having sent the first pages of the third part of the Concerto. I hope that you have received that package and that you have sent the copy.

Today I am sending the last pages of this movement (by the S.S. *Aquitania*, which does not leave until the 13th—no boat before then). So now you have the complete work, and I hope that you will have the time to finish the copying and rehearse the musicians. What folly, nonetheless, to have advanced the date so abruptly (May 1!) without finding out if it were physically possible to make the copies and rehearse in that period of time. As it turned out, Schott

---

[1] The *Dumbarton Oaks Concerto*. See the correspondence with B. Schotts Söhne in *S.S.C.* III for Strecker's objections to this title.

[2] Born Mildred Barnes, in New York, she married diplomat Robert Bliss. Stravinsky had wanted Mrs. Bliss to purchase the manuscript of the Concerto. She did so in the autumn of 1938 and presented the score to the Library of Congress.

was in the process of printing my manuscript, and Strecker returned it to me April 9, with the proofs of the last pages, which I will send to you the day after tomorrow. (The S.S. *Deutschland* embarked on the 8th; imagine, there is not another boat until the 13th.)

I embrace you, dear Nadia. All the best to you.

Istr

STRAVINSKY TO BOULANGER

My very dear Nadia,

Barbizon Plaza Hotel
101 West 59th Street
New York
December 4, 1940

I was so happy to have word from you.[3] We hope to see you soon, in January, when we plan to be in Boston for the week of my concerts. The Forbeses[4] have very kindly invited us to stay at their house. I am writing a note of thanks. I will accept their invitation, which will enable us to see a little more of you.

How I regretted your absence in Chicago (and Cincinnati), where I had beautiful performances of my Symphony [in C]. Koussevitzky wanted me to conduct it in Boston, repeating *Oedipus Rex* with it, but I was asked to furnish the orchestra parts, which is to say, in plain English, pay the rental, and I fear that this unexpected condition makes the performance almost impossible. Never, anywhere, have I paid for the rental of my compositions, and to do it with Koussevitzky's Boston Symphony, where I have always been considered a "member of the family," would be that much stranger. Probably the orchestra tried to impose this ridiculous condition without Koussevitzky's knowledge, hence I will wait for him to intervene and to cancel it. . . .

STRAVINSKY TO BOULANGER

My dear Nadia,

Chateau Marmont
Hollywood
March 3, 1941

Almost a month has passed since we have had news from you. It would be very nice of you to send us even a postcard, which is not always simple to do, I know. Nevertheless we await it, and in the hope that everything continues more or less normally for you.

I have discussed the Symphony with Mr. Ernest A. Voigt (Associated Music Publishers, Inc., 25 West 45th Street, New York City), and he has promised, as soon as he receives the parts from here, to send you the orchestra score and a part for each instrument. The parts will be new, which is to say full of mistakes, and the orchestra score will be the gray one that you already know. If

---

[3] Boulanger had written from Cambridge, Massachusetts, telling Stravinsky that she had seen his younger son at Vichy.

[4] Edward Forbes was director of the Fogg Museum at this time and had arranged for Stravinsky to give the Charles Eliot Norton Lectures for 1939–40.

you want mine, the black one, I will send it to you, but I prefer to keep it here in case I need it myself.

We have already been here for three weeks. My concerts here and in San Diego (after some very hard work, similar to that in Boston and complicated by a head cold) were quite successful. It is not until July that I conduct my Symphony in Mexico City.

It is crowded here and we are having a great deal of difficulty in finding a house for a permanent residence. Everything decent is taken and even the horrors that remain can be had only for very inflated prices. Since it is advantageous to buy one with a good, small mortgage this is probably what we shall do.

Will it be absolutely impossible to see you again this year, out here? Dear Nadia, I embrace you very affectionately.

Your   I STR

Please send Credo, Ave Maria, Pater Noster.[5]

STRAVINSKY TO BOULANGER

My dear Nadia,

1260 N. Wetherly Drive
Hollywood 46, California
May 19, 1941

Once again it is a long time since I have heard anything from you. Are you still in Cambridge? Are you on vacation (rather unlikely)? An eternity has passed since March 17, when you sent your, alas, very sad news.[6]

It grieves me to know that your health is bad, and I beg you to give me the details, even if only this once. Is it nerves, insomnia, or something still more serious? I am very troubled.

On April 1, A [ssociated] M [usic] P [ublishers] wrote to me that they had sent the Symphony parts to you for correction, but that the work has been delayed because you were "rather busy at this time." Is this time over? I ask this with a certain amount of anxiety for two reasons: 1. My concert in Mexico, in which I play my Symphony, is approaching, and I wonder if I can count on having the new score with your corrections; 2. If you received, together with the new parts, the set that was used when I conducted (to facilitate your job of correcting the parts). I am afraid that the Associated Music Publishers will be

---

[5] This sentence is in Russian in the original.

[6] On April 30, Stravinsky wrote to unidentified "Dearest friends," but obviously Mr. and Mrs. Bliss, who were then residing in Santa Barbara: "I reread the letter from my son Theodore. In effect, it is as I told you the other day: he asks me to find someone in France to help him in this difficult situation. As always, he is in his town (Villemur, Haute-Garonne), unable to do even the most ordinary work to earn his food and the daily needs of life. Do you know, my dear friend, to whom I must address myself, to a Minister of the Interior, or perhaps of Justice, in order that they give him his liberty— as before they gave him his captivity? Perhaps Nadia, who also wanted to intervene to assist Theodore, could give you some useful advice. Again thank you both for those good days spent with you." (Original in French)

obliged to take the corrected set from you in order to deliver it to the Philharmonic of Mexico for my concerts at the beginning of July (allow 10–14 days for transportation from New York to Mexico). This will interrupt your precious work unless you could continue with the corrections, some written on the gray score, others on pieces of paper. As you see, I am in complete ignorance about what is happening, and a word from you, if reassuring, would restore my nerves.

I have just had a letter from Theodore, who, poor thing, was taken by two policemen to a concentration camp near Toulouse, where he spent four days dying of hunger. This was the result of measures that the government took against all Russians, Red or White, after the rupture in diplomatic relations with the Soviets, measures taken against individual refugees from all countries, probably to please Hitler. If the Swiss Consul in Toulouse had not vouched for Theodore, he would still be imprisoned like the others. And to think that at the beginning of the war Theodore offered his services to the French army! The other day in Mexico someone asked me if I supported Pétain or, like many French people here, de Gaulle. I answered that I am "De*gueu*liste."[7]

1260 North Wetherly Drive
Hollywood 46, California[8]
June 12, 1941

STRAVINSKY TO BOULANGER   *[Fragment of a letter]*

. . . My poor Nadia! Your letter has greatly afflicted me. One consolation is your project to come to Santa Barbara—providing that events do not intervene and change this plan. I embrace you very affectionately. How is your arm? Have you arranged your trip to Canada? My thoughts to Sister Edward,[9] I beg you.

---

[7] On August 31, 1945, Gretl Urban, of Associated Music Publishers in New York, wrote to Stravinsky: "When General de Gaulle was in the city, he made a telephone call to us for two-piano copies of your *Circus Polka* and *Danses concertantes,* and also for the miniature score of your *Four Norwegian Moods.* We sent them with our compliments and are telling you this because it gives us pleasure and because we think that this will interest you." Stravinsky replied on September 6: "It seems really extraordinary that a man of state as busy as General de Gaulle would think of taking my recent scores back with him to France. That could not but cause pleasure. Apropos of that, I have just received word from Darius Milhaud telling me that Francis Poulenc begs me to send to him everything that I have published in the last years—sent by the intermediary of Foreign Affairs, M. Jacques Roche, Service de la Valise, Quai d'Orsay, Paris, or else by the French Embassy in Washington."

[8] All of Stravinsky's subsequent letters were sent from this address, unless otherwise stated.

[9] A pupil of Nadia Boulanger, Sister Edward taught at Edgewood College of the Dominican Sisters, Madison, Wisconsin. Stravinsky lectured there in January 1944, and on August 2, 1944, his Sonata for two pianos had its first public performance there.

STRAVINSKY TO BOULANGER   *July 29, 1941*

I received your letter of June 29 in Mexico and have not replied with a few words to thank you for it until now. *Answer me quickly by return mail* if you are coming here, or to Santa Barbara,[10] where Mrs. Bliss awaits you. If the former, it would be simpler to examine my Symphony together and to make our decisions verbally. (It is so complicated to correspond about such matters.) I am aware of the time that you give to this work, and I thank you with all my heart! I came back from Mexico with the two orchestra scores, mine and the gray one, which we will try to correct after mine. Imagine, the idiots at Associated Music Publishers have sent off the complete Symphony to London (for eventual performances) before receiving your corrections.

I have received a letter from Mr. Forbes informing me that his committee refuses to publish my lectures[11] in two languages. I was expecting as much. Now the committee proposes to issue them only in the original language, that is, in French. I consented, but to me the reasoning is incomprehensible. If an edition with the two texts together seemed risky because of the high costs of the volume with, at the same time, little hope of a large sale, I wonder what would be the advantage of publishing only in French?

I am frightened by the troubling news about Vichy.

STRAVINSKY TO BOULANGER   *March 12–13, 1942*
                                                          [Telegram]
c/o Mrs. Forbes   *[Original in English]*
Gerry's Landing
Cambridge, Mass.

Your November December letters never received (stop) for me utterly impossible (stop) please take all necessary steps to rush publication my lectures (stop) have complete confidence in your judgment thanks warmest greetings (stop)   Igor Stravinsky

STRAVINSKY TO BOULANGER   *May 18, 1943*
                                                          [Original in English]
Dearest Nadia,

As agreed, in the next few days you should receive the photostats (negatives and positives) of the orchestra scores of *Oedipus* and *Apollo* from the Economy Blue Print Co. They are sending this music C.O.D., meaning that immediate reimbursement is necessary. Despite the exceptionally low price (25 cents for each page of *Oedipus* and 16 cents for each of *Apollo**), the total sum is

---

[10] Boulanger spent the month of September 1941 in Santa Barbara, where Stravinsky saw her many times.

[11] The Charles Eliot Norton Lectures, 1939–40, were published by Harvard University Press in French in 1942, and later in English as *The Poetics of Music*. (See the correspondence with Roland-Manuel in *S.S.C.* II.)

significant, since each page is double (positive and negative). I hope that the large expense does not divert you from my music for a long time, and I give you my word of honor that I do not receive anything for this. And it is you who wanted it.

A hot wind blows from the desert, and after forty days in New York, with its spring showers, this makes one ponder the imperfection of human physiology. To return to work is difficult.

How happy I was to see you again and to know that you were in the hall when I was conducting *Apollo.* I am in the process of rehearsing the *Dumbarton Oaks* Concerto for the modern music concerts of the First Congregational Church of Los Angeles. Today the two horns and the contrabass were absent, tomorrow others, probably, and the concert is May 22—how pleasant!

Merritt[12] wrote a very nice letter about my concert at the Fogg Museum. Did you hear anything about it there?

Love and Kisses,   ISTR

*approximately

STRAVINSKY TO BOULANGER   *October 25, 1945*

Dear Nadia,

Just this word in reply to your telegram of October 24. Glad to know you are in possession of the score of *Scènes de ballet* and that it will be played (by Desormière[13]) shortly, in December. Here is the note which I placed in the program when I conducted the piece for the first time with the New York Philharmonic, February 2, 1945. I send the original English text since I have no time to translate it into French; you will change it, won't you?

---

[12] Tilman Merritt, professor of music at Harvard University.

[13] Roger Desormière (1898–1963), conductor. On November 10, 1945, Stravinsky wrote to Gretl Urban of A.M.P.: "Roger Desormière, who conducted my *Danses concertantes* so brilliantly last season in Paris, is an excellent conductor and musician, and an old friend of mine and of my music. For this reason he asks you for my new symphony and I ask you to send the parts to him as soon as possible, perhaps once again via the French Embassy in Washington." (Original in French)   Early in 1952, Desormière suffered a stroke, as Stravinsky learned from Darius Milhaud, to whom Stravinsky wrote on April 2, 1952: "My dear Darius, Upon my return to Hollywood after the concerts in Mexico, I found your letter containing the sad news of the attack suffered by poor Desormière. . . . How horrible!!! Is there any hope of recovery? That is what I wonder. I am doubly saddened because I had just asked Lehmann [of the Paris Opéra] to invite Desormière to conduct my opera, which we were planning to present in May. Perhaps I will hear good news from you about Desormière's health before my departure on April 22. I will fly from New York to Geneva . . . and then I will go to Paris (Plaza-Athénée) around May 8 to begin my rehearsals. Keep me informed. Affectionate thoughts to the three of you from the two of us." Desormière did not recover.

SCENES DE BALLET, a classical ballet which I composed in the summer of 1944. This music is patterned after the forms of the classical dance, free of any given literary or dramatic argument. The parts follow each other as in a Sonata or in a Symphony, in contrasts or [in] similitudes. The eleven parts of the score, played without pause, are: 1—Introduction, 2—Corps de Ballet Dances (Moderato–Più Mosso–Moderato), 3—Variation of the Ballerina (Allegretto), 4—Pantomime (Lento), 5—Pas de Deux (Allegretto-Adagio), 6—Pantomime (Agitato), 7—Variation of the Dancer (Risoluto), 8—Variation of the Ballerina (Andantino), 9—Pantomime (Andantino), 10—Corps de Ballet Dance (Con Moto), 11—Apotheosis.

That's all.

Very cordially yours.

[*In the margin*]: Tell Deso [rmière]: 1. In the variation of the Ballerina (96 and what follows), no vibrato in the 2 V-C solo; in the records, the miserable people added it; 2. In the recording of the Corps de Ballet Dances, I had to slow the tempo in order to permit the elderly clarinetist to play the notes properly between 108 and 111.

STRAVINSKY TO BOULANGER   *November 4, 1945*

Nadia, dear,

And now you too? So much the worse. When is your departure? I received the program for the Fauré centenary, November 27. So you will go in December, perhaps with Arthur Sachs?[14] I cannot tell you what an unpleasant surprise this is for me. You know my selfishness, especially since you will leave just before my Symphony [in Three Movements] in Boston. Better not to think about it.

I enclose the photostats of the first two parts of the Symphony, as you requested.

Please give the details of your nomination to the Paris Conservatory. Georges [Mrs. Arthur Sachs], who recently saw Nini and Françoise,*[15] tells us that you were named Professor of Accompaniment. What is the meaning of the title?[16]

---

[14] Arthur Sachs, a retired partner in the banking firm of Goldman, Sachs & Co., played an important role in Stravinsky's early years in America. In August 1924, as an emissary from the New York Philharmonic, Sachs visited Stravinsky in Biarritz and invited him to conduct the orchestra in January 1925. Sachs commissioned the Symphony in Three Movements.

[15] Soulima ("Nini") Stravinsky and Françoise Blandlat married in 1946, after Mme Blandlat's divorce.

[16] Before World War II, Nadia Boulanger had taught at the Ecole Normale de Musique in Paris, where she invited Stravinsky to "supervise" her course in analysis. A letter from Alfred Cortot, September 17, 1935, confirms the appointment. Stravinsky came

Needless to say, both of us were deeply touched by the packages you sent from Paris. How can we thank you! All our gratitude, too, for your car. We have had it with us for a week now. Vera needs a car badly, and your present will be a great help to her, especially for short trips and also during the inevitable repair of our Dodge, which has become old and a little tired after five years of continual use.

I am composing a short concerto (with the title *Ebony Concerto*) for the Woody Herman Band (New York), decently paid and published according to our contract by their ASCAP editor. Woody Herman will record the music in February, under my supervision, and it will be done on two sides of one record: 1st side: Moderato (2½ minutes) and Andante (2 minutes); 2nd side: Theme and Variations (3 minutes). The orchestra will consist of: oboe, clarinet, 5 saxophones, 5 trumpets, horn, 3 trombones, contrabass, harp, piano, guitar, and percussion. It should be completed by the end of December. I am somewhat unnerved by the short time that remains, and by my lack of familiarity with this sort of thing.

I beg you to send news, even if only a brief note about your activities.

* We now await their cable announcing the birth of the baby. Madubo[17] left Milene's house to be with Nini for the delivery and Françoise's convalescence.

STRAVINSKY TO BOULANGER   *December 1945*
                                                                [Telegram]
c/o Marcelle de Manziarly
304 East 66 Street
New York 21, NY

May your return France give much happiness to you dearest friend. Tell Nini agree entirely christen Jean Catholic.   Happy New Year.   Bon Voyage. Love, kisses,   Igor Vera Stravinsky

---

only once a month. Maurice Perrin, one of the twelve student composers, recalled that "under the influence of Mlle Boulanger our admiration for Stravinsky was quasi-religious, and when he first came into the room we were all petrified. Stravinsky was a bit embarrassed. . . . He told us that at the first rehearsal of *Perséphone* the chorus sang '*Reste avec nous*' sentimentally. When he asked why, they said that 'the music seems particularly expressive.' His response was: 'Then why do you want to *make* what already *is*?' One student composition was obviously influenced by the *Sacre*. Stravinsky said: 'It is important to know *how* to be *méchant,* but one should be *méchant* only when absolutely necessary. We must also know how to be *aimable. . . .*' Occasionally he went to the piano himself, played a chord, listened to it, changed a note, listened again, changed another note . . . , modified a voice, always keenly listening. . . . He said little, but his every remark opened a horizon: 'Never use folklore in a symphonic work. Folklore is for a single voice or solo instrument. We can add to it quantitatively, but not qualitatively. Folklore impedes the construction of form. . . .' "
(*Les Feuilles Musicales,* Lausanne, December 1951)

[17] Mina Svitalski, governess to Stravinsky's children since 1917.

STRAVINSKY TO BOULANGER   *April 19, 1947*

Dearest Nadia,

Here we are embarking not for Paris but for Washington, where Mrs. Bliss
awaits me for my *Dumbarton Oaks* Concerto. I will conduct it at Dumbarton
Oaks itself. Nine years ago you directed the premiere there. Your shadow, or
rather your light, will be respectfully evoked. We go by way of New York, where
I will rehearse the musicians. The Dumbarton concert will take place on April
25, and the program, as follows, will be repeated publicly the next day:

Vivaldi's Concerto in D minor
Mozart's Divertimento in D major (No. 11) with oboe and 2 horns
D.O. Concerto
Falla's Concerto for Harpsichord
D.O. Concerto (2nd time)

The decision to postpone our European trip was advantageous for me, although I had to spend some rather painful days before regaining my equilib-
rium and continuing my work. This work, as you probably know, is *Orpheus.*
Balanchine will mount it in the autumn, probably with the premiere at the end
of November. I have already finished two-thirds, including the orchestration,
and I have the greatest hopes that you will like the music.

Very glad to have Milene here, finally, and to see her so happy; all three[18]
are radiating happiness.

I enclose two documents that require your signature, without which it is
impossible to renew the license for your car. Vera, who is packing at this very
moment, and who sends her love, has lent the car to a young man, who is home
from the war, and now has a wife and two children but not a sou. You will make
him happy by returning these two pieces of paper to us armed with your sympathetic autograph, if possible by return mail, air mail.

I will write to you after Washington, that is to say, after May 4, and in the
meantime you might want to find here, *carissima* Nadia, my affectionate love
and many, many kisses from,

yours always

Did you receive my *Ode,* finally released? I am not fishing for your thanks, but
just want to know if it reached you.

STRAVINSKY TO BOULANGER   *March 18, 1949*

Dearest Nadia,

Just a note to accompany this Latin version of my a cappella choruses, Pater
Noster and Ave Maria, with which you are familiar. I have arranged this version

---

[18] Milene and her husband, André Marion, had arrived with Mina Svitalski from
France at Russian Easter.

for use by a Catholic group, but it is to be hoped that Protestant churches will use it as well.

Have you heard my Mass by Ansermet in London (BBC)? He is also playing *Orpheus** there. I just recorded both (Mass and *Orpheus*) in New York (Victor). *Orpheus* will be released in September and the Mass at Christmas. I did the latter with children rather than women (Ansermet used women). Unfortunately, they were not all first-rate, for, unlike in Europe, no tradition exists here in the training of discanti and alti. I chose the children, nevertheless, because the presence of women in the music of the Mass, no matter how perfect they might be, would be a more serious mistake for the sense and spirit of this music than the imperfection of a chorus of children.

LOVE

*I tremble at the thought of what could happen to the music of my poor *Orpheus* in the hands of M. Lichine and the Ballets des Champs-Elysées!

STRAVINSKY TO BOULANGER   *September 16, 1950*

36 rue Ballu
Paris 9ᵉ

Very dear Nadia,

Be assured that I am experiencing the same feelings and difficulties as you. I, too, would like to be able to write everything to you at length, as I would like to be able to speak with you, but I am so consumed by my work that I must limit myself to the imperative occasions, like the one with which you provided me in your letter of September 1, and for which I thank you with all my heart.

Indeed, long drawn-out projects are hazardous at present, but I am much in favor of the idea of having Monte Carlo give my opera [*The Rake's Progress*]. The size of the theater is particularly suitable, corresponding to the chamber-music character of my work. My instrumentation is similar to that of *Così fan tutte* or *The Marriage of Figaro* (woodwinds by twos, 2 horns, 2 trumpets, timpani, and strings).

Unfortunately, my enthusiasm for the Monte Carlo project is not unadulterated. The first problem is to translate the work into French without mutilating the vocal parts. The whole work—its musical prosody—is calculated to display Wystan Auden's magnificent English text. You know as well as I do the insurmountable difficulties of French translation, especially vis-à-vis Auden's brilliant poetry, which, with regard to my music, will already and inevitably undergo unforeseen modifications.

As for my financial interests, these are the same as those of my publishers, Boosey & Hawkes, who must negotiate and make the decisions. Ralph Hawkes[19] had the issues well in hand. Unfortunately, he died suddenly eight

---

[19] Ralph Hawkes (1898–1950), director of Boosey & Hawkes. He purchased Stravinsky's Edition Russe publications from Koussevitzky in 1946 and later signed an exclusive contract with the composer for his future works.

days ago in New York, and I still do not know how the company will reorganize and who will take care of my business. That is the situation.

I do not mention the French title to you because it must be translated, like the names of the characters, to preserve the unifying idea inherent in its—and in their—nature and their parts in the play. For this reason I doubt that a good translation can be made without collaborating directly with Auden. (His address is: Mr. Wystan Auden, 4 Cornelia Street, New York 14, New York.)

If I had an extra copy at hand of the two acts (350 pages) that I have already composed, I would send it to you right away. But all of my copies are now in use because of current discussions here. The easiest thing would be for you to stop at Boosey & Hawkes on your next trip to London. Then you can ask Mr. Erwin Stein* to allow you to see the first two acts on my word.

I work incessantly in the hope of finishing before spring but am not sure I will succeed.

Vera and I are physically well but we are uneasy about the present and future; Hollywood is without interest and California has changed substantially since you left.** The Sachses, who have decided to return to France, share our opinion.

We have had little time to see the Soulimas during their academic sojourn [this summer] in Santa Barbara,[20] where they were very busy. They are in the process of settling in Urbana (Department of Music, University of Illinois, Urbana, Illinois).

The only consolation is that the ménage of Milene, André, and the good Madubo is near us.

I expect to see your two pupils tomorrow and next week.

We will see the Sachses in three days, and I shall ask them to deliver the records of my Mass to you, assuming that you do not have them yet. I made these recordings with the male choir (children and adults) of a Catholic church in New York at the time of the American concert premiere. I do not say that these children have been ideally trained, but, even so, I prefer their timbre to that of the female voice, which is always too passionate for liturgical chant.

Do not forget me: even brief letters from you always give me immense pleasure.

*The editor
**Even the climate

STRAVINSKY TO BOULANGER   *November 27, 1950*

36 rue Ballu
Paris 9ᵉ

Very dear Nadia,

Only a few lines. I know that the Sachses have arrived safely in Paris but am slightly worried about the recordings that I entrusted to them for you. Please be

[20] At the Music Academy of the West.

so kind as to reassure me, or to remind them if they have forgotten to give them to you.

I am all the more anxious that these records not be misplaced because they are "standard" (78 revolutions a minute) and will soon disappear, available now only until the "long-playing" type (33 revolutions a minute and lasting about 30 minutes, or, in the case of RCA Victor, 45 revolutions a minute) [completely replaces it]. On this subject, could you tell me if the "long-playing" (33 revolutions) is now in use in France or whether you are still limited to the old model (78 revolutions)? This interests me because I want to know if I should send long-playing records when asked for technical information about the performance of my works.

Nothing new for the time being; I am immersed in my work. Give me your news and tell me if your Brussels concerts took place. If so, how did they go?

In a letter just received from Boosey & Hawkes, I learn that they have signed a contract for *The Rake* with two French theaters. I wonder if these would be the Paris Opéra and Monte Carlo. London offers no details.

I am far from reassured about the French and Italian translations for which Boosey & Hawkes is responsible. I have neither the time nor the means to apply myself to the matter, and I foresee the difficulties which will arise in making the French and Italian agree with my music, composed for a text in eighteenth-century English and, above all, in verse. . . .

I impatiently await a word from you. Vera and I embrace you affectionately.

STRAVINSKY TO BOULANGER   *April 27, 1951*

36 rue Ballu
Paris 9ᵉ

Dear Nadia,

A thousand thanks for your wonderful letter of April 2 (from Cap d'Antibes).

I have signed a contract with the Biennale to conduct the premiere of *The Rake's Progress* at the Venice Festival on September 10. It seems that Boosey & Hawkes was somewhat premature vis-à-vis La Scala, and, to avoid annoyances (which should not affect me personally), a compromise is sought that would satisfy the Biennale, the Scala, and myself. The way to satisfy me is for the Scala to participate in the Festival, since I do not want to change the time of my stay in Italy, and Venice is essential [to me], not Milan.

I have heard about Markevitch's[21] success with *Le Sacre,* of course, but I was not aware that he had also done *Mavra* and *Perséphone;* and though I knew that he had conducted *Orpheus* at the Biennale in Venice in 1949, I did not realize that he had given concert performances.

---

[21] See n. 227 on pp. 200–1.

The opera is finished, except for the short Prelude, which I am composing now; there will be no overture. I still have much work, because Boosey & Hawkes is engraving the piano score, and I continually receive proofs to correct from Germany.

I count on seeing you in Venice . . . but what a tumultuous time awaits us there!!! The Theodores will come from Switzerland with Kitty,[22] and Milene and André (who are in Nice this summer) will also be there.

Keep writing, dear Nadia, telling me a little more about yourself. I embrace you, as always, and, unfortunately, in great haste.

STRAVINSKY TO BOULANGER   *June 13, 1951*

36 rue Ballu
Paris 9ᵉ

Dear Nadia,

Your lines have deeply touched me; we were all equally affected by the sudden, practically unexpected death of Koussevitzky. At the request of *Time* magazine, I wrote the following lines about him:

> That Serge Koussevitzky was a great celebrity, everybody knows; but that many careers were created by his generosity, very few know.
>
> When a man passes away, those wishing to pay tribute to his memory recollect his good deeds, the things he did most ostensibly.
>
> Let us dwell today on those things that Serge Koussevitzky did for others without telling anyone about it. And for these secret things let him be rewarded infinitely.

I think my homage, limited to the truth, is thus more sincere than many of those which are being published.

What is this pessimistic news, of which you have transmitted only a few hints? You, in France, seem to know more about the Italian premiere of *The Rake* than I know here. For my part, I have a solid contract with the Biennale in my pocket, and I will be in Italy on the anticipated dates (middle of August) to fulfill it. A few days ago, I learned that La Scala will prepare the Venetian production in conjunction with the Biennale. But I have no other details—the Italians seem not to like to write—and I would be happy to know more from you, as your letter implies, when you gather information from various sources. *Who* in Italy and elsewhere is saying *what* about my *Rake*???? . . . Don't leave me in suspense.

Vera and I embrace you very affectionately.

---

[22] Catherine Stravinsky, the composer's granddaughter.

STRAVINSKY TO BOULANGER   *July 27, 1951*

36 rue Ballu
Paris 9ᵉ

Dear Nadia,

A few lines in reply to the questions in your letter of the 21st from Fontaine-bleau, just received.

I leave here on July 30 and will be in New York (Lombardy Hotel, 111 East 56 Street, New York 22, NY) from August 2–7, on which date I embark on the S.S. *Constitution* (American Export Lines), arriving in Naples on August 15. I will be in Milan until September 3 (c/o La Scala or the Hotel Duomo), then to Venice (c/o the Biennale or the Hotel Bauer-Grünwald). I conduct the pre-miere on September 8. On the 10th and the 12th, it will be repeated by an unknown conductor; I had recommended Markevitch, but this, it seems, is impossible.

After the performances I will most likely record *The Rake*.[23] But where? Venice or Milan? And when exactly? I know nothing about it. After that I have a couple of concerts at La Scala on September 27 and 28, *Oedipus Rex* in Cologne on October 8, a concert in Baden-Baden on October 14; *Oedipus Rex* again, with Cocteau, in Munich on October 21. Then I must catch the S.S. *Constitution* in Genoa or Naples on the 29th or 30th to return to New York on November 7.

See you soon. In great haste, I embrace you very affectionately.

STRAVINSKY TO BOULANGER   *January 8, 1952*

36 rue Ballu
Paris 9ᵉ

Dear Nadia,

I have just received your charming note with Gavoty's request. Here is a little choral theme which I beg you to transmit to him.[24]

Delighted that you have the orchestra score of *The Rake*. . . . But I am curi-ous to know how you were able to obtain it since, as yet, it is neither published nor for sale. You probably will receive 3 volumes from Milan. These are photo-copies of my summary sketches, bearing numerous (though never sufficient) corrections in my hand. I leave it to you to keep them for yourself or to entrust them to the Bibliothèque, as you suggested.

---

[23] The *Rake* was not recorded until 1953, in New York, with the cast, chorus, and or-chestra of the Metropolitan Opera, and the composer conducting.

[24] Under the pen name "Clarendon," Bernard Gavoty (b. 1908) was the music critic for *Le Figaro*. Stravinsky always referred to him as "Govnoty" (*govno* in Russian = *merde*). He wrote to the composer on December 22, 1951, asking for a theme on which Marcel Dupré, organist at Saint-Sulpice, could improvise.

I await [Nicolas] Nabokov's reply to know if my conditions for conducting *The Rake* myself [in Paris] have been accepted—by Nabokov and by his Congress of Cultural Freedom.

Always eager for your news, I embrace you affectionately.

I Str

"To Marcel Dupré, this chorale theme which I surrender to its improvisation with only one regret, that I will not be there to hear it. Igor Stravinsky, Hollywood, January 1952." (See letter of January 8, 1952.)

STRAVINSKY TO BOULANGER   *January 22, 1952*

36 rue Ballu
Paris 9ᵉ

Dear Nadia,

Thank you for the touching letter of January 17.

You were right to have kept a copy of the little chorale melody, since one of the two was destined for you, while the other, care of you, should have been delivered to Gavoty at *Le Figaro,* which you will surely have done.

I am pleased and reassured that finally you have received the three volumes of *The Rake* (photocopy of my summary sketches).

Do you know a professor (of what subject I am not certain) by the name of Leon Oleggini? Recently I received a letter from the Lausanne publishers Maurice and Pierre Foetisch, saying that they have purchased the manuscript of a book about me by this professor. They asked me to provide photographs to illustrate the book which they plan to publish along with a catalogue of my works!!! Knowing neither the author nor the work, and having no time to devote to it, I delayed. Also, I myself am in the process of making, little by little, a complete catalogue of my works, and for the first time a *correct* one.

Nabokov writes that it has been agreed in principle that I conduct *The Rake* at the Opéra, but that Lehmann can decide nothing for 3 weeks. On the other hand, Dr. Roth[25] writes from London that the Opéra is now in the hands of [Emmanuel de] Bondeville. Ultimately, I do not understand who commands whom and what. Nabokov mentions singers with whom I am not familiar: Janine Michaud [sic; Micheau] (Anne) and Roger Bourdin (Shadow). Do you know them? Have you seen the French translation, and, if so, what do you think of it?

Be an angel and answer me as soon as possible; you will make me very happy.

STRAVINSKY TO BOULANGER   *March 3, 1952*

36 rue Ballu
Paris 9ᵉ

Dear Nadia,

Very touched by your two letters, to which I must reply in a hurry.

1. Translation: Dr. Roth wrote that the translator is collaborating with Desormière to straighten out the rough parts. Since I doubt that you will be able to take charge of this work yourself, I prefer to let Dr. Roth direct and arrange it. If I participated at all, I would be obliged to start at the beginning, and I have no time for that.
2. Score of *The Rake:* According to Ghiringhelli[26] himself, the Scala is in possession of my three volumes of summary sketches. I wrote to him with instructions to send them to you, and if something unforeseen had come up, he would certainly have informed me.
3. Fragments of *The Rake* in concert: I am strongly opposed to this and in agreement with Dr. Roth. Recently I wrote to him again about [Elisabeth] Schwarzkopf, who, it seems, was going to perform fragments in London. When all of the opera has been played, this will be a different question.

---

[25] Ernst Roth (1896–1971), director of Boosey & Hawkes.
[26] Antonio Ghiringhelli (d. 1979) played a large role in re-establishing La Scala after the war.

4. Your invitation: Do not ask me to do it, first because I already have too much to do in Paris, where my time will be very taken up, and second, because I have no opportunity to exercise my fingers sufficiently. I beg of you, dear Nadia, do not insist.

I sign off today saying, in any case, *"à bientôt"* and embracing you.

STRAVINSKY TO BOULANGER   *April 14, 1952*

36 rue Ballu
Paris 9ᵉ

Dear Nadia,

This last word to answer your note of April 9.

We leave New York Monday, April 28, 5 p.m., on TWA flight 922. We have a short stopover in Paris at Orly Airport, Tuesday, April 29, at about 1:25 p.m. Without changing planes, we continue to Geneva, where we will attend performances of *The Rake* in French on May 2 and 4. On May 8 we return to Paris.[27]

I cannot yet give you an answer regarding the small reception after *Oedipus Rex.* We must discuss it again in Paris and see how things present themselves.

Finally, I do not know whether *The Rake* will be done in Paris in May. After what happened to poor Desormière, it seems doubtful to me. But you must know more about it than I do.

I embrace you. See you soon.

STRAVINSKY TO BOULANGER   *October 11, 1952*

36 rue Ballu
Paris 9ᵉ

Dear Nadia,

A few days ago I received your letter of September 20, which affected me very much. As always, I answer in haste. The fastest way for you to obtain my Cantata is to address yourself directly to Dr. E. Roth. London has already done the printing, I have corrected all the proofs, and I myself wait from day to day for the full and vocal scores.

Thank you for having sent the numerous signatures of your students and for their kind thoughts.

Very affectionately,   I Str

---

[27] Stravinsky left Geneva for Paris on May 3 in order to attend the Vienna Opera performance of *Wozzeck* at the Théâtre des Champs-Elysées.

STRAVINSKY TO BOULANGER   *June 17, 1953*

36 rue Ballu
Paris 9ᵉ

Very dear Nadia,

Received your very nice note on my return from Cuba/Venezuela/Boston. I spent three exhausting weeks doing *The Rake* with the students of Boston University. It was immensely successful, in spite of the malevolent press. But the two performances were done with different artists, which made everything twice as trying and difficult. The first group was good, the second very much worse. In fact, I was ill afterward, with an attack of colitis, which obliged me to cancel a concert in Chicago (an uninteresting one, though) and to return here and resume my customary activity.

You and others have mentioned the Paris performance of the Cantata, but without telling me where it was done and by whom. . . . On the radio, I assume? . . . Who were the singers, what were the reactions? Will you no longer tell me how you are doing personally? Try to answer me quickly.

I embrace you.   I Str

STRAVINSKY TO BOULANGER   *September 28, 1953*

36 rue Ballu
Paris 9ᵉ

Dear Nadia,

We are happy to have news from you finally. Thanks for your commentaries on *The Rake* and the Opéra-Comique. I did not know that Beydts[28] had died. Who will succeed him?

I had always thought that the French version would be the hardest to establish and, assuredly, the present translation has not helped to overcome the problems: on the contrary. As you foresee, we hope someday to succeed in doing a better translation.

Soulima, on his return to Urbana, told me that Swarsenski (of Boosey & Hawkes, rue d'Anjou) had organized a company to take *The Rake* to the [French] provinces. Were you referring to this in connection with tours? Big success [of *The Rake*] in Edinburgh, from which I've had many reports.

As for your "entreaty," attractive to me though it is, I can only answer you negatively, alas, for I am absolutely flooded with work and overburdened with engagements. After having lost about two months this summer because of my operation[29] and recovery, I have just accepted the composition of a ballet[30] for

---

[28] Louis Beydts (1895–1953), French composer.

[29] Stravinsky had had a prostatectomy in July.

[30] *Agon*.

Kirstein-Balanchine (City Center, New York). Furthermore, I am in the middle of another project, and I have a two-month American tour followed by one of two and a half months in Europe (Rome at Easter, then Turin, Switzerland, Germany, England, Lisbon). Thereafter I must attempt to make up for the backlog that will have accumulated. Thus, dear Nadia, do not ask it of me, and understand me.

I embrace you affectionately.

STRAVINSKY TO BOULANGER   *June 15, 1954*

Nadia, dear,

Thanks for your very nice letter of June 10. We have just arrived from Lisbon with Milene and André; what a flight! Both fast and calm. I will not forget the Webern instrumentation of the Bach Ricercar,[31] and will make a photocopy for you as soon as I recover.

I understood nothing of what you wrote to me on the subject of the *Scherzo à la russe* at Lugano, where I conducted a program of *chamber* music. You must have heard [the *Scherzo*] from Rome, where I conducted the piece in my *symphonic* concert on April 15, and, of course, without cuts. I suppose that the idiotic cut in the first Trio (the canon for piano and harp) was made by the broadcasting station, for reasons that I can guess: they either were short of time (to cut the canon would save one minute), or did not like the music, or a combination of the two. In any case, I had nothing to do with it at all.

It was good to have had you in London.[32] How was your performance of the Septet?

Love, kisses

STRAVINSKY TO BOULANGER   *November 14, 1954*

Dearest Nadia,

Your very sympathetic letter gave me great pleasure. Since I have been without news from you for a long time, and since you say nothing about yourself, I will be discreet, not ask any questions, and try to convince myself that all is well. Am I right? R.S.V.P.

We go to Europe again in the spring, this time at the end of March because Vera will have the first exhibition of her paintings at the beginning of April in Rome in the Obelisco Gallery. Exciting news, isn't it?

... Happy to have your kind words about my *In Memoriam [Dylan*

---

[31] Stravinsky is referring to the manuscript copy that he had made of Webern's instrumentation.

[32] Boulanger was in London when Stravinsky received the Royal Philharmonic's gold medal.

Thomas].[33] I have already recorded it (Columbia)—yes, just a few hours before the premiere, in a concert conducted by Bob Craft in which this piece was played next to unforgettable pages by Purcell, Gabrieli, Schütz, and Bach. Aldous Huxley took part, very graciously rendering his homage to the great poet. I will conduct *In Memoriam* in Rome. . . .

STRAVINSKY TO BOULANGER   *November 22, 1954*

36 rue Ballu
Paris 9ᵉ

Dear Nadia,

Received your charming letter. . . . I am rather disturbed not to be able to respond favorably, but this jury business in Monaco is completely impossible for me. I want to stay in Rome to rest for a few days before going directly to Baden-Baden, where I will have more work than usual because of Rosbaud's momentary absence. On the other hand, I count on seeing you in Rome, where I will be at the Hassler, as always. We will arrive there on March 31.

All of my felicitations for your 50 years of teaching . . . what a significant number! I, who am older than you, cannot claim as much, since my career as a composer began in 1907 with the premiere of my Symphony and my Suite for voice and orchestra, *The Faun and the Shepherdess,* the performance of which Rimsky had arranged in a concert for the Imperial Court.

See you soon. I embrace you very affectionately.

STRAVINSKY TO BOULANGER   *December 13, 1954*

Dear, dear Nadia,

Here is the reply to your letter of the 7th. 1. Tell Félix Passerone[34] that the difficulty is not with me (I would give it to him with pleasure) but with my agreement with Boosey & Hawkes (Dr. E. Roth in London). I therefore advise him against keeping the source anonymous. (He writes to me: ". . . these 'rhythms' are taken from the repertory *without an indication of their source.*") He would be more prudent to obtain a guarantee or an O.K. from Boosey & Hawkes. 2. Despite your hesitations I still hope to see you in Rome or elsewhere in Europe.

---

[33] On November 7, Boulanger had written to Stravinsky: "What music! Everything is there. I would like to talk to you about every note. . . . All of us here have a terrible need of you, but, in spite of my selfishness, I leave you to your work. We had a festival recently—a great many notes, 'impressions,' 'emotions,' very little music, many 'systems' but no true technique, and what one sees is that this genre of complications is actually extremely facile."

[34] Félix Passerone (1902–58), French percussionist. He had prepared a rhythmic exercise based on the *Danse sacrale.*

STRAVINSKY TO BOULANGER   *February 5, 1955*

Very dear Nadia,

Thank you for your letter of January 27, which awaited me on my return here
from a concert tour. . . . Now I begin my preparations for our European expedi-
tion next month (leaving here March 4).

Concerning the project with Venice, I think that Nabokov is a little too
caught up in his own enthusiasm. The truth is that ten months ago the Biennale of Venice submitted a proposal to me to compose a work of a religious nature which would have its premiere at the Cathedral of St. Mark under my
direction in 1956. I am very interested in this proposal, but nothing will be
done, nor even begun, until the contract with the Biennale has been signed. . . .
I had proposed a short Passion according to St. Mark, which pleased them very
much. But what the unions say here goes for me as well: "No contract, no
work . . ." We hope to see you somewhere during our European trip.

STRAVINSKY TO BOULANGER   *February 27, 1956*

Very dear Nadia,

I just read your kind letter of February 21 and thank you with all my heart for
having thought of March 2.[35]

What Halffter[36] solicits is touching and at the same time unrealizable for
me. If you only knew how much I have to do before my mid-June departure for
Europe—Greece and Constantinople for vacation, then the concerts: Venice,
Switzerland, Germany, Vienna, London, then New York at Christmas for a tri-
ple concert at the Philharmonic of *Le Sacre* and *Perséphone* and the recording of
the latter with Columbia.*

I have finished my *Canticum Sacrum.*[37] It is short, 16 minutes, and rather
difficult; now for the proofs, and corrections! Having finished the *Canticum,* I
have set to work on an instrumental version with choir of J. S. Bach's canonic
variations on *"Vom Himmel hoch da komm' ich her."* I have decided to do this
and my *Canticum* in Venice, together with other works of a religious character:
Andrea Gabrieli, Schütz, Monteverdi, Gesualdo. . . .

*At the beginning of January 1957. An exhibition of Vera's paintings will take
place in New York at the same time. Tomorrow is the opening of her exhibition
at the Santa Barbara Museum.

---

[35] The date of Catherine Stravinsky's death in 1939.

[36] Ernesto Halffter (b. Madrid, 1905), Spanish composer.

[37] Stravinsky conducted the first performance of his *Canticum Sacrum* at St. Mark's
Cathedral in Venice, September 13, 1956.

STRAVINSKY TO BOULANGER

Easter 1956 (Good Friday)
[Fragment of a letter]

[The *Canticum* is] rather difficult (especially as to the pitch of the singers). . . . The vocal score will probably be released in May, the full score after Venice. Ask Dr. E. Roth . . . to send you the 2nd proofs, which I have just corrected; this will be simpler because I have only the manuscript here.

I have just finished and sent back to London an important arrangement for an instrumental ensemble, with choirs, of the chorale and 5 canonic variations of J. S. Bach: *"Vom Himmel hoch da komm' ich her."* Bob will conduct it in Ojai in May, and I will do it in Venice with my *Canticum*.

Poor Marie-Blanche![38] Was it a stroke?

Love

STRAVINSKY TO BOULANGER   *May 16, 1956*

Dearest Nadia,

Excuse my silence—it is the fault of the Biennale. No one knows the date of my concert, only that it will not be later than September 20. I have not even managed to obtain the slightest detail about the choirs, orchestra, soloists. The correspondence has dragged on for months! It is appalling. I changed the entire program, because they did not want to simplify my job by letting Bob Craft conduct the old Venetian masters, though he certainly knows them better than I do. I cabled that I will conduct the following program at La Fenice, and not at St. Mark's*:

> *Canticum*
> Mass
> *Canticum*
> *Choral und Variationen* (*"Vom Himmel hoch"*) of J. S. Bach in my arrangement for choir and orchestra. Boosey & Hawkes is in the process of printing it.

We will be staying at the Bauer-Grünwald, as usual. In a month we leave for New York by train, then embark on the S.S. *Vulcania* for Athens.

I will conduct *Les Noces* at Ojai on May 27, and Bob will do my Bach arrangement.

I embrace you affectionately.

*Because one does not give a *concert* performance in church of a Mass intended to accompany a divine service.

---

[38] Countess Jean de Polignac. The count was a nephew of Princess Edmond de Polignac, Stravinsky's patron. The countess was an excellent singer who can be heard in Boulanger's recordings of Monteverdi madrigals.

STRAVINSKY TO BOULANGER   *May 12, 1957*

Dear Nadia,

This is to inform you that I have received your note of April 16, and that, as always, I have no time for letter-writing.

Boulez made an excellent impression on all of us: a musician of the first order and highly intelligent. . . . His *Marteau sans maître,* which he conducted so well here, is an admirable, well-ordered score despite all the aural and written complications (counterpoint, rhythm, length). Without feeling close to Boulez's music, I frankly find it preferable to many things of his generation.

I never received the microfilm (Isaac-Webern) that you promised to send through Georges Sachs, who was supposed to come to the United States at Easter. I have heard nothing from her.

I just spoke to Nika Nabokov, who should be back in Paris by the time you read these lines. Telephone him for fresh news.

R.S.V.P.

Love,   I STR

STRAVINSKY TO BOULANGER   *March 2, 1958*

. . . We go to Venice . . . on July 29, leaving from New York aboard the S.S. *Cristoforo Colombo* (which very recently collided with a whale between Genoa and Naples). *Threni* (or Lamentations, according to the Vulgate), the composition of which is nearly finished, will be heard at the Scuola di San Rocco under my direction around September 20. Then I conduct *Oedipus* and *Le Sacre,* and, on September 24, leave for Switzerland with the entire ensemble, where I will conduct *Threni* from September 24 to 29 in Geneva, Bern, Basel, and Zürich. Permission granted to the Lili Boulanger Fund in respect to the requested privilege.

Poor Marie-Blanche. I think of her and I sympathize with your sorrow, knowing that you were very good friends. I have also just had news of a death that has greatly afflicted me, that of Alessandro Piovesan[39] of the Biennale, who was only forty.

STRAVINSKY TO BOULANGER   *April 14, 1960*

. . . Much activity: composing, treatments for my blood and arteries (to insure against new surprises!?), a concert here (Mass and *Noces* in June), conducting elsewhere (*Oedipus* in Santa Fe in July). Then we fly to South America for a concert tour (sharing the program with Bob) in Mexico, Bogotá, Lima, San-

---

[39] Stravinsky had met Piovesan at the time of the *Rake* in 1951. The first performance of *Threni* was dedicated to his memory.

tiago, Buenos [Aires], Rio, Caracas, from August 1 to September 17.[40] Then to Venice, where I conduct half the program, Bob the other half, on September 26 at the Biennale.[41]

Bob and I are publishing the second volume of our conversations, under the title *Memories and Commentaries*. This volume is dedicated to you.

I embrace you with all my heart. Continue to write: I do not budge from here until the beginning of July.

STRAVINSKY TO BOULANGER   *July 30, 1964*

36 rue Ballu
Paris 9ᵉ

Nadia, dearest,

Thank you for the affectionate letter. Don't worry about me, for I am quite well. I think that Nabokov misinformed you; in London, a month ago, I had an ear infection, and the doctors advised me not to fly too often, for which reason I considered canceling my concerts in Israel and Berlin at the end of August and September. Having learned that Israel was basing its whole festival on my appearances, however, and that everything had already been sold for welfare and for the benefit of clinics and hospitals, I decided to fly there and not to Berlin. Nabokov was in a state of despair, and he telephoned from Paris, begging me to come to Berlin as well. I refused, with much regret, but I did not want to risk an additional flight. That is all. Certainly hundreds of letters and telegrams did come from all over wishing me quick recovery, but it is hardly to be expected that newspapers would correct their mistaken statements, since there is nothing sensational to sell in that. From Israel (a concert in Jerusalem and two in Caesarea) we go to Rome for two days (at the end of August), two days in New York, then to Hollywood.

We have bought the house of the late Catherine d'Erlanger and it is being reconstructed, furnished, and arranged for us to live there. We will put Bob Craft in the old house.[42] He is now in Santa Fe conducting *Lulu* and will join us in New York for the flight to Israel.

Thanks again for having written, I am very touched.

Your   I Str

[40] The concerts in Caracas and Rio de Janeiro did not take place at this time but in the autumn of 1962 and the autumn of 1963, respectively.

[41] In this concert Stravinsky conducted the world premiere of his *Monumentum pro Gesualdo*. Craft conducted music by Alban Berg.

[42] 1260 North Wetherly Drive. Craft lived there until the spring of 1965, when the house was sold.

STRAVINSKY TO BOULANGER   *November 17, 1964*
                                                [Telegram]

36 rue Ballu
Paris 9ᵉ

Regret infinitely but charge 10,000 [dollars] to conduct in a concert today and no less than 25,000 commission for a short piece. Thank you so much nevertheless. How sad the death of Pierre of Monaco. Affectionately,   Igor

STRAVINSKY TO BOULANGER   *[End of December 1964]*

36 rue Ballu
Paris 9ᵉ

Dear,

Please excuse me but I have no time to write a proper letter.

1. The *Variations,* dedicated to the memory of Aldous Huxley, has no connection with his work. I was composing it during the months in which dear Aldous was dying of throat cancer. Thus it was only natural that I dedicate this work to his memory. Furthermore, I am certain, though it does not discourage me, that this music would mean nothing to him or that it would displease him, because he liked romantic and classical music very foreign to my composition.
2. I will not give any more concerts in Paris after the outrage of the audience and of the press at the premiere of my *Threni,* conducted by myself in one of the Boulez concerts. That decision is final.
3. Besides, we have not forgotten that André Malraux—who, quite reasonably, organized an official demonstration for the centenary of the great Baudelaire—declared not long ago that he considers music a secondary art. On such an important occasion, therefore, it would be ridiculous to impose on him, the Minister of Public Education, examples of a secondary art.

    Those are the three things that I had to tell you in reply to your kind letter of December 4.

CORRESPONDENCE   WITH

LINCOLN   KIRSTEIN

1946   1966

LINCOLN KIRSTEIN[1] TO STRAVINSKY   *May 7, 1946*

Dear Mr. Stravinsky,

I am enclosing a check for twenty-five hundred dollars, which I understand from Mr. Balanchine is one half the payment for a ballet [*Orpheus*] to be written by you for the School of American Ballet. . . .

As you perhaps realize, our school is a non-profit making corporation, and we enjoy no government or private subsidy. The school is literally supported by the students who come to it from all over the country to learn the classic theatrical dance. This is the first commission the school has ever given, and it marks an important step in our development to feel that we are undertaking the creation of so important a ballet with our own resources. . . .

KIRSTEIN TO STRAVINSKY   *May 20, 1947*

. . . The Metropolitan is the only theater in New York which can hold the orchestra of 60 men that you want. . . . An evening at the Metropolitan will cost about $15,000, exclusive of the cost of production of the scenery and costumes, your fee for conducting, the fee to Tchelitchev[2] and to Balanchine. It would be wonderful if you could score a version for smaller orchestra. . . . Otherwise, the chances for a stage presentation limit themselves drastically.

Our idea is to have a two week season in New York, if not at the Metropolitan, then at another house. We can get the City Center [on Fifty-fifth Street], and while its acoustics are not bad, and the orchestra pit is large, the place itself is rather undistinguished. The audience is good, but the prices are very low, due to the fact that it is a municipally supported auditorium. In the two week season we should like to present *Orpheus* as often as it is possible, but the large orchestra again makes it hard. I wish you would think of some way out of our problem. It is the oldest problem in ballet.

I am trying also to think of other works on the same program with *Orpheus*. Balanchine would like to do *Apollo* with the sets and costumes by Tchelitchev that we used in Buenos Aires at the Colón Theatre. The third ballet would probably be the Mozart *Symphonie concertante* that he will compose in the fall. . . .

---

[1] Lincoln Kirstein, poet and author of many books on dance, editor of *Dance Index* (1942–48). In 1933 he brought Balanchine to the United States and, with E. M. Warburg, founded the School of American Ballet. In 1946 Kirstein formed Ballet Society, which two years later became the New York City Ballet, with Kirstein as General Director. All of his letters were sent from New York and all of Stravinsky's from Hollywood, unless otherwise indicated. All letters on both sides were written in English.

[2] Pavel Tchelitchev (1898–1957), painter and stage designer; decorated *Ode* for Diaghilev (1928). For Balanchine he designed *Errante* (1933), the ballet in the Metropolitan Opera's production of Gluck's *Orpheus and Eurydice* (1936), and *Balustrade* (1941), Balanchine's first ballet to Stravinsky's Violin Concerto.

STRAVINSKY TO KIRSTEIN

May 25, 1947
[Telegram]

Orpheus requires only 43 musicians altogether including 24 strings, but *Apollo* played same program requires 36 strings. If still difficult fix exact date, tell me at least time limits in April. . . .

KIRSTEIN TO STRAVINSKY

July 15, 1947

Dear Mr. Stravinsky:

. . . Balanchine has not been happy in Paris; there was a cabal against him, supporting Lifar; Toumanova did not handle herself very well. The atmosphere in the Opéra is the usual French bureaucracy. He could never get to see Hirsch, the director of the National Theaters; he was forced to use students in the school for *Serenade,* due to the restrictions against rehearsals imposed by the unions, etc. etc. He is longing to return here after the production of *Le Baiser de la fée* on the 25th of this month. He will come back here to plan our season, and will telephone you. . . .

Balanchine and I wish to present your ballets in the best possible way. We want to be the repository of the classic productions of your works, done by George and you. I suggested to Lucia Chase[3] that she revise her *Petrushka,* giving it to George, but she already had promised it to Jerome Robbins, who has his own ideas about it. We want to have in our permanent repertory *Apollo, Jeu de cartes, Baiser de la fée, Renard, Balustrade, Orpheus,* those other ballets of yours which you wish revived, and, we sincerely hope, new works when you write them. I feel that Balanchine is the Petipa *de nos jours;* he alone has brought the great tradition of western theatrical dancing to its possible high peak. His repertory, and that is largely based on your scores, is the single stable repertory. He deserves a frame where it can be well presented, and all my efforts are toward securing it.

. . . Corrado [Cagli] left for Italy, but before going he designed a lovely Mozart *Symphonie concertante* for violin and viola, which George did [once] before . . . but we will present it. I told Lucia that she must wait until Balanchine returns, as I cannot speak for him. . . . [Her] dancers dislike Balanchine's work because it is technically difficult, and gives as much interest to the corps de ballet as to the soloists. . . .

Pavlik [Tchelitchev] adores Arizona and wrote me a fascinating letter about his ideas for *Orpheus.* I am so happy he is having a good summer, as it makes all the difference in the world to his work for the winter. [Alexei] Haieff is at work on *Beauty and the Beast,* to be a classic ballet in two acts, with Esteban Francés. Vittorio Rieti is doing his Lorenzo de' Medici *Bacchus and Ariadne,* with Corrado. We are talking also to Harold Shapero,[4] but [his Symphony] will be [for] next year, I think, as we have to watch ourselves very carefully. . . .

---

[3] Lucia Chase (b. 1907), co-founder (1940) and patroness of Ballet Theatre.

[4] At this time, Stravinsky regarded Shapero (b. 1920) as the most talented American

STRAVINSKY TO KIRSTEIN   *July 18, 1947*

Dear Lincoln,

Glad to have your circumstantial message (of July 15) because of a letter I just received from Lucia Chase in which she [mentioned] something which, I must confess, puzzled me. I quote: "I have talked a great deal with Lincoln, who has been most enthusiastic in helping us, and he has even said he might let us do your new ballet for him next spring. (???)—This, of course strictly *entre nous.*"

Now, having your letter, I see the whole thing better.

Am entirely absorbed by *Orpheus* and hope to finish it by the beginning of September.[5]

Anxiously awaiting George back from Paris (I knew that he was not very happy) and badly need to get in touch with Pavlik. What is his Arizona address? Please, let me know it by return mail. When exactly do you expect George in N.Y.?

Don't be lazy, *écrivez-moi toujours.*

KIRSTEIN TO STRAVINSKY   *July 22, 1947*

Pavlik wrote me two weeks ago, about his ideas for *Orpheus*, but either he feels that I am incapable of understanding them, or because he wishes to speak about it later, in person, he only managed to cast a very intense spell of mystery over his work. I think that Pavlik feels the essence of the *Orpheus* legend is understood only by him; certainly it is so understood by him, as he understands it. It is most important that he communicate with you, as I am terrified lest he dream up a whole production which has nothing to do with your score; he is quite capable of so doing, and then you would not want it, or he would not— and then the wonderful collaboration that Balanchine imagined goes to pieces. I gather he feels that *Orpheus* is the essence of the artist, the creative impulse, who will not be forgiven since he penetrates the mysteries of life; that he creates without the benefit of women, not children, but art; and that the Bac-

composer of his generation. On May 18, 1945, answering a request from the music section of the Office of War Information, 224 West 57th Street, Stravinsky sent a list of ten composers of "the younger generation" whose music he recommended: "Copland, Shapero, Diamond, Schuman, Piston, Roy Harris, Haieff, Theodore Chanler, Robert Delaney, Lockwood."

[5] When the score was finished, Stravinsky gave an interview to the *Los Angeles Times* (September 21, 1947), describing the Furies as "the Gestapo of Hell. [The music is] dark and menacing but always soft, because the scene is dark." He also said that at the death of Eurydice on the path back to Earth, "Nothing in the music has foreshadowed the oncoming tragedy. At the climactic moment I have written only a long measure of silence, following the tradition of the Chinese and oriental theater that certain things are beyond the power of human expression."

chantes destroy him for his essential independence. I probably explain this badly; and I know Pavlik has thought a great deal about it; far more than I.

It is our greatest wish to bring him back into the theater, which he says he hates, because in it, one can never achieve a small percentage of what one wishes, and while the score lasts and can be performed in concert, the stage designer's work is lost, dependent upon theatrical caprice. But he must do it; and you are the only person who can make him. I am taking the liberty of sending you a poem by the California poet Yvor Winters; it is an elegy he wrote in memory of the American poet, Hart Crane, who killed himself in 1932. I came across it recently; I think it embodies something of what Pavlik was trying to tell me; but he will be able to tell you much better. . . .

KIRSTEIN TO STRAVINSKY   *July 28, 1947*

I have taken an option on the Ziegfeld Theater for *Orpheus,* for Sunday, April 24; this does not exclude the possibility of the Metropolitan, but Hurok's plans are obscure; he is now abroad and says he is trying to get the Leningrad ballet; I doubt if he does but he will have something, and if he cannot break the season at the Met, then at least we have a theater with first-class acoustics and a very large stage. In this we are at least assured of a house. Haieff's ballet *Beauty and the Beast* is very lovely, what I have heard so far. Esteban Francés is designing it in the spirit of the Unicorn Tapestries; the beast is a *licorne.* Rieti is doing his choral work on the Carnival Songs of Lorenzo the Magnificent with decor by Corrado Cagli; Cagli has done a lovely drop for the Mozart *Symphonie concertante* for violin and viola that George will do. [Emanuel] Balaban is conducting this summer in New Orleans; Barzin[6] is in Maine, vacationing. Maria Tallchief, Magallanes, Bliss, Bolender, Moncion and a lot of good dancers will be with us. In a bookstore here, I found a picture of you that I have never seen before, taken in Switzerland around the epoch of *Renard,* which we will use for *Dance Index* (Minna Lederman's issue). Did you see the Petipa article by Slonimsky?

With best wishes to Madame Stravinsky.

KIRSTEIN TO STRAVINSKY   *October 16, 1947*

First I wanted to thank you for the copies of the score of *Orpheus.* . . . It is a very great honor to be able to present it. It is the most important thing Balanchine and I will be doing; I hope we will be worthy of your confidence and your genius.

Second, I apologize for not having paid you the rest of the commission. Either I get the money this week, or I will obtain it in another way. . . .

There is much interest in Balanchine's ideas for a permanent company in

---

[6] Leon Barzin (b. 1900), chief conductor of Ballet Society, and of the New York City Ballet until its move to Lincoln Center.

New York that would belong to the City and get civic support; that would not travel at all, but have a home like Bernstein's orchestra [at City Center] and the opera company of [Laszlo] Halász. . . . The worst blow of the year is Tchelitchev, who is refusing to do *Orpheus* at all; he says that the idea is wrong (from his point of view); that we are a poor little group; that he has advanced into a different *niveau*, the range of coloratura, and that it would cost *cent mille dollars* to do what he wants. He resents what he considers George's inability to think in mystical terms; he sees the drama of *Orpheus* as the story of man and his soul; Orpheus as Bacchus, as Apollo, as the artist-scientist-magician; and here we are, making it into a ballet-ivanich. I have had two very long and painful talks with Pavlik; he says he is through with the theater forever; that it is a waste of time. . . .

A quoi faire? I am thinking of André Beaurepaire, a very fine French designer who has done *La Princesse de Clèves* as a film for Cocteau, and also *L'Aigle à deux têtes*. Cocteau admires him beyond any younger artist; I have seen his designs and they are astonishing, new, but in a great classic French spirit, pure and simple. If not Beaurepaire, then perhaps Corrado, but I had hoped for something more substantial, larger, less of a pastiche. Also, Corrado is in Rome and I don't know when he comes back. . . .

Wystan Auden spent the evening with me talking about *The Rake's Progress*. He has wonderful ideas. I am so glad you are working with him; for me, he is the greatest English poet of our time. He is not only a superb technician, an amazing mind on a purely intellectual level, but a very passionate and touching lyric poet as well. He adores opera; he spends half his time playing records of Mozart and Verdi; for him opera is a ritual. You can tell him just what you want, and you will get it, but to a degree of intensity and perfection that is quite stupendous.

KIRSTEIN TO STRAVINSKY   *December 26, 1947*

I wanted to wish you and Madame Stravinsky a very happy new year, and hope that all your projects, the Mass, *Orpheus,* and *The Rake's Progress,* will be crowned with the success they deserve. For me it is wonderful to know that you exist, as an island of genius and integrity, like Balanchine and Tchelitchev and Auden, in this disastrous world, and people like you prevent everybody else from becoming ill over politics, over the present horrors. . . .

Auden and I went up to Boston to hear Goldovsky's[7] production of *Idomeneo;* the opera was quite heavenly, and the performance no worse than at the City Center; but the form of the entire work is rather diffuse, and there is a terrific aria introduced just before the final curtain for the villainess, who has not been seen since Act 1, which is really impossible; but the choruses are lovely and it is certainly as effective as lots of other things done more often. Auden is so enthusiastic about working with you; he has wonderful ideas, and is so much

---

[7] Boris Goldovsky (b. 1908), Russian-born opera director and conductor.

inspired already that I think he is eager to do a second opera on an idea of his own, which is also most interesting.

Balanchine has had a vast critical success with his *Theme and Variations* to the 3rd suite of Tchaikovsky. In my opinion, and also that of Pavlik, it is not at all a first-class work, compared to the two Mozart concerti he did, but it appeals madly to the public, and I think now George has become recognized . . . after 15 years of work in this country.

Pavlik has done the greatest painting of his life, and I earnestly believe that he is the greatest painter of his generation. He is in good health and in good humor, but he is very much more removed from his former social life, his younger friends, and he stays alone and works on the insanely elaborate systems of poetical anatomy, which grow all the time more and more beautiful and majestic. He is having a show of his early work (1925–1933) in January. . . .

Ballet Society will open a big show at the Museum of Modern Art of all its stage designs on January 20; at least we are recognized as the principal spur to artistic creation in the non-realistic field in the country; meanwhile we exist miserably enough, and every week there is a major crisis, each month a disaster. I have no gift to inspire confidence in people; they think I am a profligate *qui jette les galettes de son père;* and since this is what they think, they won't help.

We hope that you will be able to conduct *Orpheus:* I thought that on the same program we would do *Renard*, the Mozart *Symphonie concertante* and, maybe, Haieff's *Divertimento*, to open. Balanchine would conduct the Haieff; he conducted the Tchaikovsky very well, and had a real success in the musical press. Of course, the orchestra knew the piece, but he really directed; it was not a fake, and he was very elegant, and has a real allure, *en chef d'orchestre.* . . .

KIRSTEIN TO STRAVINSKY   *January 4, 1948*

Balanchine tells me that you have talked about *Orpheus,* and that we are more or less all in agreement.[8] That is, with Tchelitchev out of the picture, it will not be a job for a painter but for lights and certain sculptured forms, and for this we believe that Isamu Noguchi is the man. I have worked with him before, and he has a charming delicacy and justice of handling forms; they are not wildly original, but he creates space and airiness, and this is what Balanchine wants. We will begin to talk to him soon.

You have made us very happy by being willing to take less than your formal price for conducting the ballet. . . . I have started a small silk-screen press

---

[8] Balanchine gave an interview to the *Los Angeles Times* (January 4, 1948) in Stravinsky's home: "Stravinsky beams with pride, and gently prods his friend and collaborator to remember [his own] musical achievements. . . . [Balanchine said] 'Now Stravinsky and I are discussing only the main details and working out the timing. . . . I do not like to have music written to fit predetermined action. I prefer to work directly from the music. My choreography is done entirely during rehearsals. . . .'"

which is doing very fine work, an example of which Balanchine showed you with the Berman[9] gouache. Now, Tchelitchev, Max Ernst, and many other artists are creating for the press, directly; not reproductions of existing works, but new works done for Ballet Society. . . .

We are presenting a new lyric-drama, like Menotti's *Medium,* called *Far Harbour,* by two young American boys. . . . Balanchine thinks the music for it is very bad, but I do not think of the music as anything more important than another element in it. Auden says it is hopeless to create in the tradition of *verismo,* and this new work has no set pieces except some songs, but I actually believe it has considerable theatrical power.

Tomorrow Tchelitchev opens his one-man show of pictures 1925–1933. They are very lovely, and while quite different from anything he does now, nevertheless have a great dignity and beauty of ideas, texture and design. . . .

KIRSTEIN TO STRAVINSKY   *April 29, 1948*[10]

Ballet Society wants to thank you for the wonderful evening of *Orpheus.* We have been working towards preparing ourselves for it for two years, and in spite of the inevitable trials of a first-night performance, we hope you were not too disappointed. It will get better with every performance, and I have no doubt but that it is a work which will last a very long time. We are proud to have been able to present it.

So far I have told you nothing about my own personal admiration for your wonderful music. *Apollo* was actually my start in musical education; it was a door through which I passed into the music of the past, and out of which I heard the music of the present and the future. *Apollo* gave me confidence in the line of the academic classic dance, and on it our school has been founded. To me *Orpheus* is the second act of a great lyric-drama.

Which leads me, on the day after the second act, to ask you to write a third act. I know that you are working on *The Rake's Progress,* and that it will take three years, but would you consider, after that, doing another piece, which can be a third act, which would perhaps show the maturity of Apollo? Balanchine and you will celebrate the Silver Anniversary of *Apollo* in 1952: perhaps as a surprise to him it could be ready then. At least let us talk about it.

It is given to few people to be able to work with the greatest artist of their epoch, so that is why we are very happy today.

With affectionate regards to Madame Stravinsky.

---

[9] Eugene Berman (1899–1973) was one of Stravinsky's closest friends.
[10] On May 31, 1948, *Time* magazine published the following letter from Kirstein: "In describing Igor Stravinsky at the triumphant premiere of his new ballet *Orpheus* . . . you say that the greatest living composer of ballet scores 'took his bows onstage with the dancers, his feet crossed in his best Position III.' Mr. Stravinsky, who has been writing ballets since 1909, . . . knows very well the logical anatomical basis of the Five

STRAVINSKY TO KIRSTEIN   *October 23, 1948*

Much enthusiasm from everywhere about *Orpheus*. Bravo, arcibravo.

From reports George looking badly. Tired? Watch him and try to send him out here, at least for Christmas. . . .

KIRSTEIN TO STRAVINSKY   *October 28, 1948*

. . . I had a long talk with Robert Craft yesterday; he will prepare *Mavra* as an unstaged work, and Ballet Society, if we are still in existence, would like to stage it . . . next spring in the City Center. We would like to revive *Jeu de cartes,* for which Balanchine has the material, and introduce *Pulcinella*. Also there would be *Renard* and *Orpheus* for a different program. I would like to do *Mavra* as a mimed work, like *Renard,* but using the music as a very literal sound track, and the dancers would actually pretend they were singers; it might be a very happy solution. Craft seemed enthusiastic. . . . We see lots of Auden, and he shares our place at the sea. He is working hard at a course on prosody; he has a house in the Bay of Ischia, and I think he wants to live in Italy more or less permanently. I long to hear *The Rake's Progress*. I hope you are thinking about the third act of *Apollo–Orpheus–* . We should do it in 1950 perhaps. Balanchine is terribly upset that *Orpheus* was badly done in Italy and Vienna and now [Jean] Babilée or [Aurel von] Milloss is doing it for Paris. I hope they will not do it in Covent Garden before our production is seen. . . .

KIRSTEIN TO STRAVINSKY   *January 11, 1949*

Dear Mr. Stravinsky:

I was so very touched by your lovely Christmas greeting; *Orpheus* is for me a part of life; it is my greatest artistic experience, and we all await, impatiently, for the sequel.

This is just to say that we hope surely to see you by the end of February; the rehearsal time has been reserved for you; the orchestra which Barzin has very well trained is virtually the same as before, and they play excellently. We do *Firebird* the first night, *Orpheus* the second. We are already in rehearsal; as usual we are attempting too much, but otherwise we would not do enough. We are very heavy on choreography and music and very light on scenery and costumes; but they can always be added, and the base cannot. . . .

As ever, faithfully.

Absolute Ballet Positions. In the Third Position (the heel of one foot locked against the instep of the other, weight equally distributed, with complete turnout), Mr. Stravinsky would have found it awkward to execute the traditional stage bow derived from the imperial Russian theater. He took it in the Fourth Position (with weight equally divided, the forefoot is twelve inches in advance of the back)."

KIRSTEIN TO STRAVINSKY   *November 28, 1949*

Cher Père Igor Stravinsky:

I wanted to report to you that *Firebird* had the most extravagant success imaginable last night.[11] I longed for you and Madame Stravinsky to have been here. Only once in a lifetime does something like this happen. Hurok sold us the Chagall decor, and it was wonderfully used by Balanchine, who re-created the ballet with no trace of Fokine. Maria Tallchief was absolutely miraculous, really a bird-of-fire. The reviews only give you an indication of what the effect on the audience was. . . . We hope to revive *Apollo* with the Buenos Aires decor of Tchelitchev. George will do *Fils prodigue* and one other work. The premiere of his big new Chabrier ballet [*Bourrée fantasque*] is next Thursday.

I hope you have not forgotten the idea of making a new ballet, the third act of *Apollo–Orpheus–* ? . . . I think that the story of Euripides' *Bacchae* is a wonderful thing, and Bacchus–Dionysus is in the absolute line of *Apollo–Orpheus*. But perhaps you have other ideas. Perennial homage.

STRAVINSKY TO KIRSTEIN   *December 2, 1949*

Dear Lincoln,

Thanks for writing me about the triumph of the new *Firebird*. . . . I plan to be in New York before Wystan Auden leaves for Italy (March 13), and I hope I will not miss at least one performance of the *Firebird*. Please let me know the schedule and the date of its last performance.

Regarding the plans for a *Third* Ballet, I always keep them in mind, but I am still so overloaded with *The Rake's Progress,* which will take me one more year to compose, that I prefer to talk the matter over again when my mind will be a little more free.

Most of all do not think I am trying to escape. . . .

KIRSTEIN TO STRAVINSKY   *December 5, 1949*

Firebird continues to be better danced, and each performance brings more people. Balanchine has done the last scenes not as an operatic coronation, but like a village marriage, and it is very pretty and impressive. Maria Tallchief is beyond description.

We have been asked to go to Covent Garden in 1951; I hope we may yet be asked to the Edinburgh festival, so we can be at the premiere of the *Rake*. We are opening our Winter season on February 21, and it will run four weeks, so you will certainly see at least one performance of *Firebird*. Balanchine is going

---

[11] In response to this letter, Stravinsky telegraphed to Balanchine on November 30: "Happy to learn new marvel with old *Firebird*. . . ."

to do . . . Prokofiev's *Fils prodigue* for Maria and Jerry Robbins.[12] Robbins will do Bernstein's orchestral work on Auden's *Age of Anxiety*. We will have 5 weeks of rehearsals before.

We hope to have 30 weeks of work next year. I think we are on our way to becoming solidly established. It has been already fifteen years. Balanchine is very tired. . . . He needs Hollywood sunshine, and relaxation.

KIRSTEIN TO STRAVINSKY   *August 23, 1950*

Cher Père Igor, et Madame:

You must have thought it very strange that I never wrote again after the fiasco of my attempts to get the [*Rake*] produced. I was terribly depressed by all the horror with Billy Rose, etc., and then our own preparations for our London season involved me, then the season itself; now I am free to report on what happened.

At Covent Garden we had the greatest artistic, social, and financial success of any foreign company since the last Diaghilev season in 1929. This success was entirely POPULAR, that is from *le peuple*. *Le monde* either was absent from London or had not been schooled either by our Embassy or by Royalty as such to treat us seriously. I think we were accepted at Covent Garden originally since it was thought we were no threat to the established order, we were cheap by contrast, and it would be no possible disturbance. . . . All I am attempting to describe to you, and this long letter is important for you to digest, since it will be the background of our future work together, is that what we did, we did on our own.

The press was unanimously against us from the start, as soon as it was seen that we were going to DANCE. They liked the fact that we had no scenery, which proved that Americans who are so rich in money are poor in culture. They hated us as soon as they saw the Rouault decor for *Fils prodigue* (which we had done new in London; very good), and then, the disaster of *Firebird*. It turned out that Fokine (God rest his soul) was a national asset, like Henry Moore, Benjamin Britten, and cricket. . . . *Firebird* had an overwhelming triumph in the theater, and it was—excuse me, as Pavlik would say—peed on in every part of the intellectual press. . . .

My wife and I were presented to her Altesse Grecque Marina Duchess of Kent; she hated everything. There was a huge party at Lady Rothermere's afterwards; everyone there hated everything. . . . Well, I got upset. Balanchine was naturally very calm and said, "What difference does it make as long as people pay to come and to see it, and they applaud?" The next night I was dining with E. M. Forster, and I described to him the reception, which surprised him,

---

[12] Earlier that year Robbins had left Ballet Theatre to become Associate Artistic Director of the New York City Ballet.

as he had gone with me, but he had not seen the papers. I had tried to get various distinguished friends all day to write a letter to the *Times,* but my two hundred closest friends among the artists and, yes, intellectuals, were either busy or relieved that the press was so bad. Forster and I wrote the enclosed letter.[13] He did the tone of it, and he gave it the particular concentration that made the *Times* print it in a very good spot, and everyone saw it, and when I dined at King's College, in the Great Hall, with Mr. Forster, some days later, seated next to the Provost, Forster said, "Well, I see that you trounced the critic of the *Times.*"

The criticisms of *Orpheus* were about on the same level. Virgil Thomson and Olin Downes are Daniels-Come-to-Judgement, in comparison to the roaring Oxford-trained idiots on the *New Statesman* and *Nation.* They said it was acrobatic, nervous, not lyrical, not soft, why don't they do *Giselle* and *Swan Lake*? Why don't they do *Sylphides*: finally, why do they *dance* so much? Because they can, and because they like to dance and because Balanchine has the naive idea that the ballet is about dancing and not about revolting pastiche or self-pity.

The Earl of Harewood was the exception; he was terribly sweet, a good friend, and he will be our chief aid in the Battle of Britain. . . . I talked at length to [Erwin] Stein, who is very sweet but so scared he doesn't know which way is up. But his heart is in the right place. He is so diffident about his daughter having married into the exalted classes that he never makes a peep.[14] However, I think that Harewood is very ambitious and that sooner or later he will turn up in a very responsible position. . . .

Also, I made friends with the Right Rev. Dean A. S. Duncan-Jones, who is a Welshman and the Dean of the very beautiful Cathedral of Chichester, which has the death-watch beetle in the roof and which Edward James,[15] who lives seven miles away, is interested in restoring.

Now, here is our schedule: we are a First Rate Ballet Company, and I am not even worried too much about money. I have decided not to put any more of my family money into the running expenses, as the City cannot avoid the responsibility any longer. I will save all my money for commissions to you. . . .

November 17–December 25, we dance at the City Center. Would you want to come for this and conduct (if I can get them to pay for it, and I think I can)?

---

[13] The letter in Stravinsky's archives is signed, in ink, by E. M. Forster.

[14] By the date of this letter, Stein was Stravinsky's editor at Boosey & Hawkes. Marion Stein, Lady Harewood, later married Jeremy Thorpe. Stein was a pupil of Schoenberg's—with Webern, one of the musicians closest to the master. Stein was extremely short in stature, and after his daughter married into the royal family, Schoenberg used to refer to him as "the *Erlkönig.*"

[15] Edward James, one of the last great eccentrics, was a close friend of the Stravinskys in California in 1952–54. The London *Times,* March 31, 1981, states that James was Edward VII's godson: "He is credited with being either the king's son or grandson on the wrong side of the blanket." James's 6,000-acre estate was at West Dean in Sussex.

It will be important, because we must talk at once with Pavlik about the new *Petrushka*.[16]

T. S. Eliot adored *Orpheus:* he said it was the most wonderful stage experience he has had since he could not remember when. I asked him to suggest a third part, *Apollo, Orpheus,* What??? (*Amphion, Bacchus???*), but he was very shy, and said, no, he could not exactly do that, but later he let me know that if it was interesting to you, he would like to begin to talk, possibly even, toward plans for a project for, maybe ideas around the ultimate eventual, even probably collaboration of (without the use of any spoken words) his *Sweeney Agonistes*; Eliot is coming to Chicago for two months in October–November, and you can talk to him, in any case; he is eager to do a ballet; *Sweeney Agonistes* (the two parts as one) could be marvelous. . . .

May 10–July 4: London, not at Covent Garden, but at Drury Lane or at the Prince's, where we will do a straight commercial enterprise. The Sadler's Wells Ballet will be on vacation, and unless something disastrous, like Serge Lifar or Dolin, happens, and I doubt it, we will have the field to ourselves, and offer a vindictive and triumphal season of late Stravinsky works plus the renovated *Firebird, Renard, Apollo* and—what will kill them, lacking Nijinsky, Benois, and Fokine—the new *Petrushka;* how they will howl; they may howl a good deal less, however, if you are there politely to remind them that you only wrote the music for these immortal masterpieces and possibly you should have some say as to how they should look. . . .

I realize that this may conflict with the *Rake.* Now Harewood, I think, as well as Boosey & Hawkes, would not be averse to producing the *Rake* also in England; I know Wystan admires Tyrone Guthrie, and I saw a superb performance of Verdi's *Falstaff* at the Sadler's Wells, which Guthrie did. . . . I do not *know what has happened to the Rake,* but I am sure that it could be done in London, if not when you were there, with the Ballet, then later. . . .

I submit that a Stravinsky Festival, with you there to be icy and polite, and have those dead eels and kippered herrings come around and say well, maybe you have some rights even in your, alack-a-day, non-Russian scores, well: I am sure we would all do well financially. I am so certain of it, that if the City Center will not let me do it, I will go out on my own and raise the money myself, and it will not be MY money either. I am certain now that our fifteen years of work together has not been in vain; that it is not by mistake or by coincidence that I met Edward James and Pavlik in 1933, and that Edward James, for whatever reasons, is WHO he is; and *il est un très grand monsieur (par naissance, je veux dire)* and that he lives seven miles from the Cathedral Church of Chichester, and that Sussex is where Christie has Glyndebourne and they want us there,

---

[16] Pavel Tchelitchev exposed his conception of a new staging of *Petrushka* to the composer in a long letter sent from Grottaferrata in May 1950. Since it would be impossible to summarize the metaphysical arguments that the painter sets forth in a mixture of Russian, French, German, and English, a single excerpt must suffice: "I see this fairy tale as subject to the universal symbolic laws. All fairy tales originate in the magico-

too, to do small works in July when we will be through in London, since the Sadler's Wells company will be back in London to feast the visitors to the Festival of Britain. So we can spend happy days in the country at Edward's divine West Dean Park, which is the most glorious house and garden I have ever seen. . . .

Now, there is a great deal that has not been decided; I have not even seen [Morton] Baum or the City Center people, but they are breathless to know what is next, since . . . the Opera under Halász and the Drama under Maurice Evans are really nothing . . . but within a little time, they will have a *very great* ballet company, with an expanding program of commissions, a strong artistic direction, and brilliant collaborations.

Please think about *Sweeney Agonistes*. Please write me if you are inclined to do this; we can wait for the third part of *Apollo–Orpheus*–Architecture????, because if Eliot is here for two months and he will come to our performances, then you can talk to him. . . .

I came home, as I became overtired from overwork and worry, and so I am being very quiet, at Fire Island, waiting for Wystan, who comes here in three weeks.

Give my love to Bob Craft, and please show him this letter and the clippings, as I would like him to assist Leon Barzin in all this. . . . You do not have to answer this, but ask Bob to, please, if you want to conduct *Baiser* and *Jeu de cartes* in November; *Petrushka:* March; London: May–June.

With love and admiration. . . .

STRAVINSKY TO KIRSTEIN   *August 25, 1950*

Such a thrilling letter! I was indeed very anxious to have detailed news about your new English experiences; fortunately they are very comforting and you and George come out as the happy winners, despite all traps laid in your path by the old London press idiots and the new British chauvinists.

Too busy right now to be able to go through all the fascinating things you mention. I shall limit myself to the points on which you need an urgent answer, i.e., my tentative conducting for you in New York. . . .

As you know, I am devoting all my time to the *Rake,* and for that reason I have had to cancel all concert tours. If I accept your proposition, it would be only on the basis of its unique and isolated character; and precisely for the same reason I am afraid it is going to mean too much money for you, as each conducting means a special trip to New York for which I have to ask your company to pay my expenses. This will cost them $1,500 for one performance or two, with

---

religious. The conflict between the body, the soul and the spirit is always the issue. . . . The Moor is the Body, the Ballerina is the Anima, Petrushka is the Spirit. The Magus (the Mountebank) is like all such people (as Rilke says, *'Gebunden ist er auch'*). The surprise of this Merlin is in seeing the triumphant liberation of that which he believes he has killed."

rehearsals of course, plus $500 for my expenses Los Angeles–New York–Los Angeles. . . .

You know how enthusiastic I feel about Tchelitchev. But he has sent me a letter from Rome, and, to tell you the truth, this has left me under the impression that his concepts will be very hard to mold to my own projects for a new setting of *Petrushka*. I [go] further: his concepts have very little to do with what I told you in New York last spring. Of course there is no doubt that he will show us new marvels, and I will let him have all of the credit for them. But I have to limit myself to music, in the present case conducting: as author, my concept of the staging is different. . . .

KIRSTEIN TO STRAVINSKY   *August 30, 1950*

Yesterday I saw Mr. Baum, the executive director of the New York City Center of Music and Drama. He definitely asked me to invite you to conduct your own works, at the City Center, in our Spring 1951 season, which would mean that, if you wanted to do it, you should be in New York by the 15–20 February, and we would schedule your conducting as premieres. We would have in the repertory by that time: *Firebird, Orpheus, Apollo, Jeu de cartes,* and *Baiser de la fée. Apollo* and *Baiser* we would keep for then so they would be premieres. I should like to do one program with an opening ballet, then *Apollo* and *Orpheus,* with Pavlik's designs for *Apollo,* which he did for the Colón and which are marvelous. I do not know if you will want to conduct twice; I hope so, but the *Rake* is of primary importance, and you do what you want. . . . Baum is making an onslaught on our orchestra; he thinks it's good, but too good, in comparison with the opera of Halász, and he wants to make everything equal.

I hear from Osbert Sitwell that Goncharova and Larionov are destitute. Larionov has had a stroke and has to go to a sanitarium for a year. Would you want them to do *Petrushka,* aside from the act of charity? I do not know if he can work, and he is far better than she, in the last years, at least, but if Balanchine spoke to them? Would you ask your wife to let me know? . . .

T. S. Eliot will be in America for some time. I hope it would interest you to talk to him about a possible future collaboration.

STRAVINSKY TO KIRSTEIN   *September 16, 1950*

You are asking me if I would want to conduct twice. I should say: yes, provided the interval between the two appearances is not too long; it should not exceed a week, as my time is too limited. But the price which your company has accepted covers the conducting of one or two performances of the same program. If the second program is different, this means extra rehearsing and . . . a fair price in this case would seem to be $1,000 for each program. . . .

Apollo: Delighted as I am to have the famous setting by Tchelitchev, I must warn you of some difficulties concerning the group of cellos. In your regular Ballet Orchestra you have 3 (at the most 4) cellos, but *Apollo* requires 4 first and 4 second cellos. . . . I do not see any possibility of cutting down on those because it would throw everything out of balance. The cello music is written in two separate parts, like that of the first and second violins. If you can afford it for the *Apollo* performances, all right, otherwise I suggest that we do *Scènes de ballet* instead. I have always wanted Balanchine to stage this. If you cannot afford to commission new decors for it (Pavlik would be ideal) you can always do it in regular classical costumes (tutus).

If you want to make an act of charity, I sympathize with your suggestions concerning Larionov. Is he really in such bad shape both physically and financially? If so it is a great pity. On the other hand it is hard for me to have any solid opinion of his work and his present abilities as I have not been able to follow his progress during the last 15 years. Should circumstances have to keep Tchelitchev out of the project, I think your first artistic choice should be Chagall.

As you are worried about the tentative reduction in size of your orchestra, I wonder if you should not keep on the safe side by forgetting all about *Petrushka,* which, even in the new, reduced version, requires 59 musicians at least. . . .

Bob Craft has just told me you are nourishing the good idea of staging *Pulcinella.* On this I agree 100 percent, first because it will be a complete novelty; a premiere for this country, and if you care to know my opinion about the staging I believe the best you can do is to get Esteban Francés. I already spoke with George Balanchine about the combination.

KIRSTEIN TO STRAVINSKY   *September 22, 1950*

Cher Père Igor:

Thank you for your very sensible letter. I have far too grandiose ideas. We have to do what we *can* do, and we cannot do *much.* . . .

In February, Balanchine wants to do, at once, the whole of Tchaikovsky's *The Nutcracker,* as close to the Maryinsky production as the City Center permits. . . .

In addition to *The Nutcracker,* we will do the regular repertory, but cannot think of *Apollo, Petrushka,* or *Pulcinella.* If this works, and we make our fortune, then we will produce *Pulcinella* for May. I want to do *Petrushka* in the fall of 1951, without fail. If you don't want Tchelitchev, as I now understand, nor Larionov, would you consider Chagall? Please tell me, so that we can think how this can get itself done.

Baum has agreed to the extra orchestral size for *Jeu de cartes.* But just barely. Balanchine has returned, resting a little with the blessed *durak* Volodin, but he is in New York. . . . Wystan is fine, longs to know what will happen, post Hawkes.[17] I daresay he has written you. I can see this year will be one of re-

---

[17] Ralph Hawkes, of the publisher Boosey & Hawkes, had just died.

trenchment, *pour sauter mieux.* I am too impatient. Thank you for slowing me down.

STRAVINSKY TO KIRSTEIN   *September 26, 1950*

I see you have to give up *Apollo*. . . . But what about *Orpheus*? You don't mention it at all and I wonder why?

Please make it clear to me what your choice is: are you able to afford me for one program (to be performed twice at close intervals for a total fee of $1,500) or for two different programs (for a total fee of $2,000)? Of course, in both instances you still have to pay me the extra $500. . . .

KIRSTEIN TO STRAVINSKY   *September 30, 1950*

We are having a serious crisis with the ballet; they have arrived at a disastrous decision about cutting us down, and we may not have a fall season at all. . . .

I will not be able to make any commitments of any sort for a month. If we get our money, we can continue somehow, though curtailed. Balanchine is naturally very nervous and upset. . . .

In fifteen years of work we have had many trials and tribulations; but this is the worst, coming as it does on top of the very good season at Covent Garden. Balanchine says if worst comes to worst, he will go to Italy for two years and reorganize the Scala. This would be a tragedy for me. . . .

KIRSTEIN TO STRAVINSKY   *February 9, 1951*
                                                [Telegram]

Strong possibility have found complete financing opera New York October 1951. Could you send Craft New York next week to arrange audition and play score. His expense is paid but hesitate to ask you to come also. When can I call you [at] Crestwood. Premiere *Card Party* [*Jeu de cartes*] Thursday next. Excellent advance for our season. Love to Vera and yourself.

STRAVINSKY TO KIRSTEIN   *February 9, 1951*
                                                [Telegram]

Am most interested. Your new project should be American premiere. Will be back end October from Venice world premiere. Unfortunately auditioning now impossible since am motoring to Cuba with Bob and have to complete composition and score.

KIRSTEIN TO STRAVINSKY   *February 16, 1951*

There is a man called Anthony Brady Farrell who has three children and $285,000,000. He became interested in the theater . . . and bought a large Broadway house which he re-christened the Mark Hellinger. It seats 1600 people; it has been entirely redecorated with some taste; its pit seats 45. His adventures in the theater so far have been regrettable; he knows nothing about art, literature, or music. . . . He has a new girl friend who has heard of Igor Stravinsky, the composer, just heard. . . . Well, anyway, Farrell came last night to *Jeu de cartes,* which was well done, the decor apart, and he liked it; today he is being taken to the Philharmonic to hear *Sacre* with Bernstein; and next week *Baiser de la fée, Oiseau de feu, Orpheus.* I told him the *Rake* would put his theater on the map, and he seems to believe me; I further told him it would cost $150,000, which does not trouble or much interest him. . . . A big expensive Bert Lahr musical is going into the house in April, but it can be thrown out at will, although naturally the theater-manager thinks Farrell is mad, particularly if the Bert Lahr show makes money; but this will have been there for six months, or in any case by the time the *Rake* is ready. Balanchine must be in Hollywood in December; the *Rake* should open in New York by November 15 in order to ensure the best possible chances for an extended run. If you can cast the opera for La Fenice and use the same principals in New York, much would be saved. I suppose you have promised the decor to Berman,[18] who is here and with an atmosphere of unparalleled gloom and dreariness. . . . Maybe Genia is alright, but he tends to overawe everything and overdress everything. . . . Here are some questions which I must know:

1. How much must you get for conducting the first performance in New York, for preparing the orchestra, etc.?
2. Would you agree that Balanchine does the direction and ballets?
3. What is the date of the [Venice] opening?

I have not spoken to Betty Bean [of Boosey & Hawkes], who behaves like a deserted virgin in regard to your ignoring her over La Fenice.

Finally, would you accept a $5,000 commission for Balanchine and myself for the third act of *Apollo–Orpheus,* subject to be determined? Wystan has suggested the Hero as Builder of Cities; Aesculapius, the doctor; or Amphion the architect? I suppose this could not be done before winter 1952–53, but would you consider it, as I want to allocate the money and the time?

STRAVINSKY TO KIRSTEIN   *February 19, 1951*

Your millionaire sounds very exciting indeed. . . . I will land back in New York on the S.S. *Independence* October 15. For my conducting the last rehearsals and the New York premiere altogether with my supervising the whole thing for a month I shall ask $5,000. . . .

Venice is still unclear as to singers. They have to select and submit for my approval a cast "able to give a fair performance in English"; where are they going to find it? Are they going to get an English, or American, or Italian cast (which should be coached)??? . . . An Italian cast might give a satisfactory per-

---

[18] Berman's set designs for *The Rake's Progress* were never used.

formance in Venice but one that would prove unsatisfactory for an appearance in an English speaking country.

Don't forget to get Kopeikin[19] for the piano rehearsals and the piano part in my orchestra, as the part will be of importance. (It could be an upright piano to save space.)

As to the Third Act of *Apollo–Orpheus,* I very much like the idea, as I have told you previously, but we should discuss it at length whenever you will come here to see me. . . . I am leaving tomorrow until March 13. . . . In Havana, Hotel El Presidente, February 28 to March 6.

KIRSTEIN TO STRAVINSKY

April 1, 1951
[Telegram]

Would you be kind enough to receive Chandler Cowles the producer and Anthony Brady Farrell his backer in Hollywood Wednesday to discuss opera? Please wire me. Things here look very hopeful.   Love

STRAVINSKY TO KIRSTEIN

April 1, 1951
[Telegram]

Will positively not play my opera but am ready to chat with them though rather useless.

KIRSTEIN TO STRAVINSKY

April 18, 1951
[Telegram]

Would you authorize use Basler Concerto ballet title as *Arioso.* . . .

STRAVINSKY TO KIRSTEIN   *April 18, 1951*

I do not understand whether you plan to use the music of the Basler Concerto in full (i.e., its 3 movements) or only the second, slow movement (andantino), which is entitled *Arioso.* If you are planning to limit yourself to the *Arioso,* this lasts only two minutes. On the other hand, if you are planning to label the whole three movement [s] *Arioso,* it will certainly sound most funny because movements I and III are definitely fast in tempo, especially the last one, and the concluding impression given the audience would of course not be that of the second, slow movement, but of the final, fast one.

Therefore I do not approve of the *Arioso* title for anything but the *Arioso* part, which in itself is too short to be produced as a ballet.

Now about Berman. . . . I am being asked only to give my suggestions, and this is what I did with La Biennale and Cowles. But the decision is not mine and they are free to make the choice . . . a suggestion cannot be called a commit-

---

[19] Nicolas Kopeikin worked for Stravinsky as rehearsal pianist in the last decade of Diaghilev's Ballets Russes and continued with Balanchine through *Agon.*

ment. Please drop me a [line] about your Basler Concerto project. I hope Balanchine is in it and I will be very happy, of course, if he stages the whole piece; besides, he was the first one to whom I played the work and his [first] reaction was to stage it as a ballet; I remember also his special enthusiasm for the first movement.

KIRSTEIN TO STRAVINSKY

April 19, 1951
[Telegram]

Balanchine and I request use of complete Basler Concerto for Jerome Robbins's excellent idea and choreography the story of Hippolyta and the Amazons. Understand perfectly your objection to *Arioso*. May we call ballet *Hippolyta* or *The Amazons*?

STRAVINSKY TO KIRSTEIN

April 19, 1951

Jerome Robbins's idea seems very good and I entirely approve of it. As far as the title is concerned you may use either *Hippolyta* or *The Amazons* as you like.[20] But I have two absolute conditions. The music should be kept entirely as is, i.e., no changes, no alterations. Moreover, you must mention in the programs . . . that the music is that of Stravinsky's String Concerto in D.

When you [ask] for the orchestra parts you should specify the set which includes my own alterations (some repeats and "reprises" I made in the last part of the Concerto). . . . Tell George we are going through very sad days here as our friend Adolph Bolm just died. . . . I think it would be nice of George to send a telegram to Mrs. Bolm, who is at our house. . . .

KIRSTEIN TO STRAVINSKY

June 25, 1951

Robbins's ballet, to your beautiful Basler Concerto, has been the conspicuous success of our June season. I hope you will be able to see it in the fall. Nora Kaye was quite marvelous and the visual aspects of the decor, dance and costume made a whole. Tchelitchev thought it was the best thing we have done this year; he said it made him want to work in the theater again, which, of course, he will never do.

Agnes de Mille thinks she wants to do the *Dumbarton Oaks* Concerto as a ballet. I visualized the big room at Dumbarton Oaks: an evening party; Mildred Bliss the hostess, the manager, the diplomat, the woman, the aging woman. George wants also to do *Pulcinella*, but since he has to be in Hollywood at that time in order to do the life (?) of Hans Christian Andersen for Goldwyn,[21] I do not know what he can do, practically.

---

[20] The title eventually chosen was *The Cage*.
[21] The film was released in 1952, with choreography by Roland Petit.

I am trying to make Cowles commit himself to producing *The Rake's Progress* with Farrell's money at the City Center. I doubt if the Mark Hellinger Theater will ever be free, Farrell's business-manager disapproves of art ventures in the house. Farrell has money. The manager wants to make it. . . .

STRAVINSKY TO KIRSTEIN   *June 30, 1951*

Thank you very much for your nice letter of June 25 and for the clippings. All this is very interesting indeed. . . .

I was glad to hear from you after rather a long silence. Your plans for next season are quite attractive. I think we should talk it over at length not by letter but when I will be in New York in a few weeks. I will arrive at the Lombardy Hotel Thursday, August 2, and I will stay there until the *Constitution* sails Tuesday August 7.

KIRSTEIN TO STRAVINSKY   *July 18, 1951*

. . . Chandler Cowles married an absolutely impossible woman; I take a dim view of his seriousness at this juncture due to the caprice of this appalling act, but he has been married before and seems to be able to control large sums of money still. I think that, if you want it, there's a fairly good chance of *The Rake* being done, partly with Farrell's money and partly with City Center money, in the Spring of 1952, but more of this when I see you around August 2. . . .

KIRSTEIN TO STRAVINSKY   *November 28, 1951*

Hotel Gladstone
52nd Street

It is wonderful to have you back in America. Thank you so very much for immeasurably aiding the brilliance of our present season by conducting *Le Baiser de la fée* last Sunday night. We apologize for various technical slip-ups which will be corrected when we have the time to use the stage. . . . I know how busy you are with plans for *The Rake,* but I hope, before you leave for the Coast, you will speak to Balanchine about plans for *Terpsichore:* I hope we can present it a year from now. Is this too early to make plans for it? I want to ask Pavlik to re-design *Apollo* and *Orpheus,* and do the new ballet, as a consecutive three-act spectacle. Pavlik is very remote from the theater at the moment, but I know he will do this.

Draft sketch for *TERPSICHORE*

Scene: a vast ballroom in space, between the stars. Music of the spheres.
  1. Entrance of ZEUS: a reception of the gods (Pavane)
  (Order not necessarily the one Balanchine will use)
  2. (?) Apollo and Terpsichore

3. (?) Cupid
4. (?) Pegasus
5. (?) Prometheus chained
6.   Orpheus and the Bacchantes
7.   Venus and Mars

leading up to the final dance when the previous pavane, rigaudon, men-uet, waltz, tarantella, polka, develops under Jerome Robbins as Mer-cury. . . .

Balanchine, Robbins, and myself consider you our father and our future. Gratefully. . . .

KIRSTEIN TO STRAVINSKY   *February 11, 1953*

I was more touched than I can well say by your thoughtfulness (in the middle of *The Rake* rehearsals, as well) in sending me the charming note and drawing. It made up entirely for the savage attack in the newspapers against our violation of the sanctity of Shakespeare. The fact that you (and Wystan and Balanchine) liked *Love's Labour's Lost* makes it love's labour's gained.

The music of the *Rake* is so marvelous; I hope it goes on Saturday as well as it sounded today. But of course, there is never enough time, and singers won't act (and actors can't sing). But even so, it's quite wonderful; it is like meeting a new friend you are sure will be with you the rest of your life. . . .

                                               August 27, 1953[22]
KIRSTEIN TO STRAVINSKY   *[Air-mail special-delivery letter]*

I saw Balanchine, and he asked me to write you. I hesitated up to now, but maybe you won't mind hearing from us.

We received a grant from the Rockefeller Foundation to commission new works for the opera and ballet. The conditions of the grant are strict; nothing for production or performance. . . . We have heard various rumors as to your next work. However, Balanchine and I would like to ask you as the first of our pro-spective commissionaires, and long-time collaborator, to do a ballet for us. We are authorized to pay $10,000, exclusive of parts, for a work of not more than forty-five minutes, and as much less as you see fit to write.

Balanchine and I still have the old idea of a third act for the Apollo-idea:

1. *Apollon Musagète*
2. *Orpheus*
3. Apollo Architectons: builder of shelters and bridges

We would like to have the three works re-designed by Pavlik Tchelitchev and presented on a single evening. This year, when the company returns from

---

[22] On May 17, 1953, Kirstein had come to Boston to see Sarah Caldwell's production of *The Rake's Progress,* with Stravinsky conducting.

Milan, we do a full-length *Casse-Noisette*. We will return to Hollywood next summer for at least six weeks. Please give my love to Madame Stravinsky and to Bob.

STRAVINSKY TO KIRSTEIN   *August 28, 1953*

I am glad to be able to give you a favorable answer this time. I am quite willing to compose a ballet for you to complete the Apollo-idea. Your suggestion for Apollo Architectons only needs being described to me in detail.

As with *Orpheus*, Balanchine and yourself should put down at once and send me the outline of the scenario; the title is not enough for me to start with. I hope George is still in New York, but if he is not, please ask him to do this immediately. . . . The reason for my insisting on this is that I want to start working on this ballet right away instead of starting on some more intricate projects which can wait. . . . So let us not waste any time. Only three full months are available to me before my concert season, which will be followed by a European tour in the early spring of 1954. I cannot afford to lose any time. . . . Dear Lincoln, please do not drag and let me hear from you at once. . . .

STRAVINSKY TO KIRSTEIN   *August 29, 1953*

Since I wrote to you yesterday I gave more thought to this future ballet of ours, and I hasten to let you know how I visualize what should and should not be done.

The pleasure of working with you again at first took my attention away from the subject itself. But the subject is most important. . . . *Apollo* and *Orpheus* are already works progressing with "slow motion," and if we build a program including them both, we will find it impossible—whatever Apollo Architectons may be—to overcome or counterbalance this dominating slowness.

Therefore I suggest something entirely different . . . the Nausicaa episode of *Odyssey*. It is not the first time I [have thought about this subject] and no other is more suited to the ballet. . . .

I would like you to make me a draft of this Nausicaa episode as you see it yourself. . . . I doubt [our conceptions] will be far apart. . . .

Again, please do not drag and let me know your reactions *"par retour de courrier."*

KIRSTEIN TO STRAVINSKY   *August 31, 1953*

We were delighted to know that you were interested in an idea for a commission. Balanchine left today with the company, for La Scala, and he will be gone until the beginning of December. We talked about ideas for the ballet. He agrees with you that a third act of the *Apollo–Orpheus* might seem too slow motion, although personally, I should have liked it.

We both felt that while the story of Nausicaa has charm, the end is hard to find; what becomes of her? Ulysses returns to Penelope, and nothing at all becomes of Nausicaa; George was at first amused by the idea of a dance of the laundry baskets, but he said there were neither variations nor finale.

What he wants (as usual) is a ballet-ivanich. He would like a ballet which would seem to be the enormous finale of a ballet to end all the ballets the world has ever seen, mad dancing, variations, pas d'action, pas de deux, etc., with a final terrific and devastating curtain when everyone would be exhausted. He suggested a competition before the gods; the audience are statues; the gods are tired and old; the dancers re-animate them by a series of historic dances, the correct tempi of which you can quite ignore, but they are called courante, bransle, passepied, rigaudon, menuet, etc. etc. It is as if time called the tune, and the dances which began quite simply in the sixteenth century took fire in the twentieth and exploded. It would be in the form of a *suite de danses,* or variations, numbers of as great variety as you pleased.

I am sending you a book which may possibly interest you along these lines.[23] There are others like it, the Arbeau and the Rameau (no relation to the composer), and I can get them for you; but certainly you do not need them. Balanchine sees a marvelous theatricalized cosmic space in an architectural frame, more like Palladio than baroque; your music is the drama; his dances would attempt to stage dramatic tensions entirely in terms of dancing, but the characters would be dressed with some reference to historic styles. But you are the boss.

STRAVINSKY TO KIRSTEIN   *September 9, 1953*

. . . Your objections to Nausicaa are quite right. On the other hand, the idea you and George have of doing "a ballet to end all ballet"—well, limits are precisely what I need and am looking for above all in everything I compose. The limits generate the form.

I will compose a "Concerto for the dance" for which George will create a matching choreographic construction. He is a master at this, and has done beautifully with Bizet, Tchaikovsky, Bach, Mozart in music not composed for the dance. So, we can well imagine how successful he will be if given something specially composed for the ballet. . . . I would like to start working without further delay. This would enable me to deliver the new ballet to you sometime in November or December 1954.

KIRSTEIN TO STRAVINSKY   *September 23, 1953*

. . . Balanchine and I will be pleased to have whatever you will write for us. The company has had an enormous success at La Scala and La Fenice; they have

---

[23] *Apologie de la danse,* by F. de Lauze, 1623. Stravinsky underlined several places in the text, and rephrased and reaccented the musical examples by Mersenne.

gone back to Milan for an extra week, then Turin, Naples, and Rome. *Orpheus* was a big hit, and everything was made fresh and clean for Italy. We hope to continue to Sweden, then open here with the complete *Casse-Noisette* in January.

Jerry Robbins has asked me for your permission to do the Symphony in Three Movements as a ballet; he wants to call it *Procession*. It would be a dramatic continuous procession embodying a variety of marches—bridal, funeral, battle, etc. I think he sees it very clearly, but he does not want to start unless you like the idea and bless it. . . .

With love to Madame Stravinsky, yourself and Bob.

STRAVINSKY TO KIRSTEIN   *September 25, 1953*

. . . Let me tell you frankly how I feel about the Symphony in Three Movements as a ballet. I am against it. As a symphonic composer as well as a ballet composer, I always feel uneasy at the idea of using my straight symphonic forms on the stage. I let the experiment be tried with the Basler Concerto and, to tell you the truth (*confidentially*), I feel somewhat unhappy and uncomfortable about it.

Not that Jerome Robbins has not done well. On the contrary, I think he is a very talented man and he is still proving it in *The Cage*. But it is simply a matter of "plastic" incompatibility. This one experience has only confirmed me in my opinion and cautiousness.

KIRSTEIN TO STRAVINSKY   *October 24, 1953*

. . . *The Trial*[24] was a terrific trial; but it received a very handsome production, and I was proud of the staff at our opera-house, which achieved an absolute scheme and worked it out to perfection.

In the spring we will do Aaron Copland's opera,[25] and, if I have my way, *L'Italiana in Algeri*.

The ballet, with Balanchine, has had a great success in Italy and are on their way to Germany. . . .

STRAVINSKY TO KIRSTEIN   *October 27, 1953*

. . . I am back to my desk [after influenza] and "our" work is getting its start. I will not be able to do [much] because my concerts start already in two weeks. But we will be able to chat when I will see you in New York in late December and January.

When do you expect George back? . . .

---

[24] Opera by Gottfried von Einem.
[25] *The Tender Land.*

KIRSTEIN TO STRAVINSKY   *October 29, 1953*

Here is a notice from the BBC publication about *Oedipus.* I hope one day we can do it at the Center; we are trying to organize a chorus, now. Balanchine returns on the 19 of November to prepare *The Nutcracker*. . . .

STRAVINSKY TO KIRSTEIN   *August 13, 1954*[26]

During George Balanchine's stay here for his Greek Theater engagement I had several meetings with him during which we established the whole structure of my new ballet. George will give you all details when he will see you back East. He is flying to New York tomorrow.

And now I wish to tell you that I have already started work on the ballet and that from now on I shall be working exclusively on it until completion.

It has been a real delight to all of us to see your brilliant company and its accomplishments. What a real marvel, this first act of *The Nutcracker*!!!

. . . How marvelous it would be to have one program with *Apollo,* the new Ballet (I have named it *Agon*[27]—contest—Ballet for twelve dancers), and *Orpheus.*

KIRSTEIN TO STRAVINSKY   *August 24, 1954*

I had to clear the plans for the Stravinsky Festival with Mr. Baum, the chairman of our finance committee. He has been in Europe, and I could see him only yesterday. I proposed that we do the Festival in the early part of February. He agreed, and has asked me if you will conduct whatever you want to do. Balanchine and I particularly want *Pulcinella,* with decor by Esteban Francés. *Apollo* will be done with stark simplicity for Jacques d'Amboise and will be a revelation. . . .

The plans for the new ballet sound marvelous, and Balanchine is wildly enthusiastic. I don't suppose you will be able to give it to us for another year? I got a notice of the Ojai Festival but it did not give much idea of what actually happened aside from Bob's usual efficiency.

STRAVINSKY TO KIRSTEIN   *August 26, 1954*

Now that you have Mr. Baum's backing for a Stravinsky Festival to be held in February 1956, I assume that you plan to produce the new ballet (*Agon*) at this

---

[26] Stravinsky and Kirstein had seen each other in the interim, notably on April 2, 1954, for a lunch in the Gladstone Hotel.

[27] A note in the present writer's diary, August 12, 1954, says that Stravinsky chose the title that morning and that he went to a rehearsal of Balanchine's *Ivesiana* at the Greek Theater in the afternoon. One year later to the day, Stravinsky revealed his choreographic conception of *Agon* to his wife and the present writer.

[time]. Considering the whole project centers around *Pulcinella, Apollo,* and—I guess—*Agon,* I would suggest to break the whole thing in two programs as follows:

First Evening:		Second Evening:	
Renard	15 minutes	*Pulcinella*	43 minutes
Agon	26^{28}	*Apollo*	30
Baiser de la fée	45	*Agon*	26

. . . All this, dear Lincoln, I leave to your meditations. . . .

STRAVINSKY TO KIRSTEIN   *December 16, 1954*

I plan to be in New York for a few days between my engagements in Birmingham and Atlanta.

I arrive at the Gladstone Hotel from Birmingham sometime in the afternoon of Friday, January 21, and leave for Atlanta Tuesday, January 25. Please reserve some of your time to have lunch with us Saturday the 22nd, Sunday the 23rd, or Monday the 24th, and ask George Balanchine to join us. We must discuss some important technical problems in connection with my *Agon*. . . .[29]

KIRSTEIN TO STRAVINSKY   *December 21, 1954*

We are very eager to talk about *Agon,* and to make plans for the Stravinsky Festival of 1956. Balanchine will be here; he has had a hellish time with the Truman Capote musical called *House of Flowers;* a little group of dwarves and monsters has succeeded in ruining it by this time, and he has bowed out. But he is tired. Balanchine will end up doing Bizet's *Roma,* and the Harold Shapero Symphony. We both like the last piece very much, [a combination] of you and Beethoven, but, as George says, at least the models are okay. . . .

Wystan is back home, and has finished a wonderful new book of poems, *The Shield of Achilles;* very, very beautiful things. Our *Nutcracker* ran for seven weeks; we had two sets of children, and they had two sets of mothers and fathers. The company goes to Europe in April for three months and will be a month in Los Angeles, as usual in July–August.

We all hear Willie Walton's *Troilus and Cressida* is so good, but I have not yet talked to anyone who is not English who has heard it. With love and a Merry Xmas to you and Madame Vera and Bob Craft; show them this.

---

[28] The timing of *Agon* is three minutes too long, but since so little of the music had been composed by this date, one wonders how Stravinsky determined this figure.

[29] Stravinsky, Kirstein, Balanchine, and Eugene Berman met for lunch on January 24, 1955, and an agreement was reached to postpone *Agon* until 1957. In the evening the Stravinskys saw *House of Flowers* (see following letter).

KIRSTEIN TO STRAVINSKY   *May 3, 1956*

Balanchine and I are making a Mozart Festival at the Festival Theater in Stratford this month, a sort of Festivalette—rather than a Salzburg or Glyndebourne—but we had to start somewhere. Balanchine and I live less than half an
hour from the theater. Chester [Kallman] has done a wonderful job with the
words for *Entführung,* and we think Basil Rathbone is playing the Pasha.

We open on Wednesday, May 30, at 5:30 with the Austrian Ambassador,
etc. We should appreciate a telegram of God Bless from you, Bob, and Vera, to
whom George and I send our best love.

KIRSTEIN TO STRAVINSKY   *December 9, 1957*[30]

Agon has become a real popular success; we have changed our program to accommodate six additional performances; we really cannot do more, even though
we would like to. We have a lot of *Nutcrackers* for the Christmas holiday, and
Balanchine has completed a lovely *ballet de l'opéra,* quite a big one, on the First
Symphony of Charles Gounod, upon which Bizet based the Symphony in C.

For the first time in twenty years *Apollo* has had a major popular success; . . . it's the first time anybody really listened to it, or looked at it. . . . The
Stravinsky evening, with *Apollo, Orpheus, Agon,* and *Firebird,* was the most
thrilling evening of my life; it was an enormous demonstration of the historical
position, both in the hearts of the audience and in their niches in the grand tradition of the two greatest artists of their epoch.

With all my thanks, and love to Vera and Bob.

KIRSTEIN TO STRAVINSKY   *December 27, 1957*

. . . We were not entirely happy about the telecast of *Nutcracker,* but it paid . . .
for the rehearsals of *Agon.*

On next Thursday we have the premiere of the Gounod First Symphony,
which Bizet studied as a model for the Symphony in C. Balanchine has made a
grand ballet de l'opéra, which Karinska has dressed, à la Winterhalter-Frago-
nard, to look like a garden of flowers smothered in butterflies. It is very pretty.

With love to you and Vera and Bob for 1958, from all our company.

KIRSTEIN TO STRAVINSKY   *March 3, 1958*

The concert at St. Thomas went wonderfully well. You would have been very
proud of Bob; Balanchine said he never heard the *Symphonies of Wind Instru-*

---

[30] On January 1, 1957, Kirstein escorted Stravinsky through the Balthus show at the
Museum of Modern Art, and at lunch on January 12, the approximate date for the premiere of *Agon* was set.

ments played better and the *Psalms* were absolutely marvelous.[31] The people were wildly enthusiastic; hundreds were turned away.

Wystan and Chester have an idea about an opera which is based more on an English pantomime idea than on anything else—in the spirit, and even in the manner, of Aristophanes. The *Ice Maiden* is not the *Snow Queen,* and could not be further from *Baiser de la fée;* Wystan is very excited about it. I think it should be commissioned for the opening of the new opera in Lincoln Square [Lincoln Center], for 1962.

Balanchine has had a dreadful winter. Tanny[32] is home after a very serious operation; she seems alright but her morale is low; she woke up after the operation and had quite forgotten that she was paralyzed. The ballet goes to Japan next Sunday, but he will stay in New York with her.

STRAVINSKY TO KIRSTEIN   *March 5, 1958*

Thank you, dear Lincoln, for your nice note after the church concert. I am very glad it went so well. I know Balanchine is not going to Japan, but I wonder if you are going with your ballet or staying in New York.

Bob writes me he is expecting a letter from you at my address. Till now I received nothing.

KIRSTEIN TO STRAVINSKY   *February 9, 1959*

George is perfectly fine; he was in the hospital, in great pain, only for a short time; he passed the stone from his kidney; there has been no recurrence and none is expected. He is going to Paris on the 20th for two weeks, to mount the Gounod Symphony for the Grand Opéra; it may amuse you to know that there is no set of orchestral parts of this work in France, although the autograph score has long been in the archives of the Conservatoire. We did this lovely work again at the end of our present season, and while it is rather mild, it is one of Balanchine's finest "late" works.

We are fortunate in securing permission from the Japanese Foreign Office to bring the dancers and musicians of the Imperial Household in mid-May, 1959. I have to go to Tokyo on the 23rd of this month to make the final arrangements. I hope to see you, possibly there. . . .[33]

Balanchine is planning the Webern [*Episodes*] for May; also a Gabriel

---

[31] St.-John Perse wrote to Stravinsky, March 2, 1958: "L'exécution de la Symphonie de Psaumes était particulièrement émouvante."

[32] Tanaquil LeClercq, the wife of Balanchine and formerly a leading dancer of the New York City Ballet, had been stricken with polio in 1956. A note in Stravinsky's papers reads: "I gave the Sibelius medal, June 19, 1957, to Balanchine—the National Foundation for Infantile Paralysis, New York Chapter, in the name of Tanaquil LeClerq.   IStr."

[33] Stravinsky was in Japan in April 1959.

Fauré ballet in an upside-down ballroom in Genoa; also a Gershwin piece, on point. For the opening of the Lincoln Square Dance Theatre [New York State Theater], I hope you will write us a piece: anything you want . . . for 1962–63. Wystan and Chester are trying to think of something wonderful and hideous for Lotte Lenya; maybe about Circe or Morgan la Fay.

KIRSTEIN TO STRAVINSKY   *Sunday December [?] 1960*

Dear Mr. Stravinsky:

This is poor thanks for all the marvelous things you have done for us and for keeping our company alive by giving Balanchine the only new scores that inspire him to equivalent work.

                                                                        With love

STRAVINSKY TO KIRSTEIN   *[No date]*

We were delighted by your Washington report, and glad not to have been there.

   And I am also delighted by the idea of the *Rake* in the spring of 1962 in New York. What can I do to help this project? Letters to foundations or individuals? I write enough of them for *other* people. No work of mine has been treated so unjustly as the *Rake*, and no work of mine am I more eager to see performed in New York. . . .

On March 5, 1964, Lincoln Kirstein wrote to the present writer: "We open the new theater on April 23, with Movements *and* Agon. . . . *I don't suppose Igor would give us a fanfare lasting 30 seconds to be played from the top balcony of the foyer to summon people into the Festspielhaus; for $1,000. Or even 15 seconds; I am quite serious; it would be paid for by me as a present to Balanchine for the opening of his new house; maybe silver trumpets. . . ."*

STRAVINSKY TO KIRSTEIN   *March 21, 1964*

Dear Lincoln,

If only you had asked me sooner, I would have been delighted to do it, and for nothing, of course, but I go on tour soon and am using every minute until then to compose something for Wystan's beautiful poem.[34] Yet. . . .[35]

---

[34] *Elegy for J.F.K.*
[35] On March 23 Stravinsky composed the "Fanfare for a New Theater to Lincoln and George."

294   *Stravinsky: Selected Correspondence*

March 30, 1964

Dear Mr. Stravinsky:

THANK YOU

But how can we thank you; with all the other things you have to do, with Wystan's beautiful text, with Life, with everything else. . . .

Balanchine says it sounds like two golden cockerels speaking the fables of La Fontaine to each other; we want to have it played from the top of the third balcony of the big foyer on one side, and then answered on the other side. Then we want to have it played from the orchestra pit, just before the lights go down, and then the "Star-Spangled Banner," in your orchestration.

The theater is beautiful beyond anything. The fact that you gave us this beautiful fanfare makes the whole thing absolutely perfect. Balanchine tried to call you.

With love and *thanks*.

And *The Last Savage:*[36] Mercy! *Merci.*
The show of Pavlik is wonderful!

STRAVINSKY TO KIRSTEIN

April 8, 1964

How to thank you for this beautiful Pavlik album and your brilliant article! You made me very happy.

Too bad I will not be in New York soon and will not see Pavlik's show: concert in Ann Arbor, recordings in Toronto, and back home where we have worries—our housekeeper sick and Vera, so busy with the house we bought (that of the Baroness d'Erlanger), has now all this work at home. *Merde!!!*

KIRSTEIN TO STRAVINSKY

February 26, 1966[37]

Cher maître:

I was touched more than I can say with your more than generous words about the undersigned in the February number of the *London Magazine*. The greatest part of our collaboration since 1933 has been those parts where Balanchine has worked with you, and I have touched on the connection.

I would love to give George a surprise present; would you consider a commission, from myself and my sister, for anything you would care to do, of any length, for any date, of dance-work, in the line of your recent compositions that he has undertaken? This calls for no immediate reply, but do think of it.

---

[36] Opera by Gian Carlo Menotti.
[37] Kirstein lunched with Stravinsky at the Hotel Pierre on January 15, but the composer's tribute had been written some weeks earlier.

George has done a beautiful solo for Suzanne[38] (Dulcinea, Eloise, Helen of Troy, Beatrice, Venus) and seems to be working well, in spite of his health, which seems to me disastrous. He has done two movements of quite fantastic complexity and splendor of the *Brahms-Schoenberg [Quartet]* .[39]

We have launched a subscription-campaign to support the week-nights of the ballet season, and have over twenty-one thousand subscribers, which is quite fantastic. It means we can plan and pay for new sceneries for the Mozart and other older but useful ballets.

The New York City Opera opened with Ginastera's *Don Rodrigo,* a synthetic dodecaphonic "opera," full of dramatics, but without drama. . . . The premiere of [your] Aldous Huxley *Variations*[40] is Thursday evening, 31 March. It will be a big night. I hope your schedule permits you and Vera and Bob to come.

With love and thanks to you all.

---

[38] Suzanne Farrell, a leading dancer of the New York City Ballet. Stravinsky was especially fond of her, and after seeing her in his *Variations,* considered her the most musically intelligent dancer he had ever observed. On April 29, 1965, CBS Special Reports filmed her with Stravinsky and Balanchine on the stage of the New York State Theater.

[39] Schoenberg's orchestration of Brahms's G-minor Quartet. The present writer had suggested this score to Balanchine for a ballet.

[40] Balanchine presented the piece three times in succession, each time with different choreography.

CORRESPONDENCE WITH

W. H. AUDEN

1947 ↄ 1965

STRAVINSKY TO W. H. AUDEN

1260 N. Wetherly Drive
Hollywood, Calif.[1]

7 Cornelius [*sic*] Street
New York City
October 6, 1947

Dear Mr. Auden:

Mr. [Ralph] Hawkes wrote me of his interview with you and your enthusiasm to write the libretto to my projected opera and to start working right away. But how to go about it—you in New York, I here until spring? Corresponding on such [an] intricate matter, of course, [is] quite arduous, but what is there to be done?

At any rate, I believe, the first thing is that you prepare a general outline of *The Rake's Progress.* I think at the moment of two acts, maybe five [*sic*] scenes (five for the first and two for the second act). I also plan to incorporate a Choreographic Divertissement in the first act's finale. Chamber music orchestration of which [the] dimension [is] not yet established. Mr. Hawkes suggested about ten characters, but I believe seven soloists a good number.

After the outline is completed, I suggest you prepare a free verse preliminary for the characters (arias, duets, trios, etc.), also for small chorus. Bear in mind that I will compose *not* a musical drama, but just an opera with definitely separated numbers connected by spoken (not sung) words of the text, because I want to avoid the customary operatic recitative. Please, do feel absolutely free in your creative work on the chosen theme. Of course there is a sort of limitation as to form in view of Hogarth's style and period. Yet make it as contemporary as I treated Pergolesi in my *Pulcinella.* As the end of any work is of importance, I think that the hero's end in an asylum scratching a fiddle would make a meritorious conclusion to his stormy life. Don't you think so?

Am grateful to Aldous Huxley who suggested you to me as a prospective collaborateur. Not so long ago I heard with delight your brilliant commentary verses in an English travelogue film. The more I am glad that you can undertake this work. Looking forward to your reaction to all the above said.

Sincerely

AUDEN TO STRAVINSKY

7 Cornelia Street
New York 14, New York
October 12, 1947

Dear Mr. Stravinsky,

Thank you very much for your letter of October 6th, which arrived this morning.

As you say, it is a terrible nuisance being thousands of miles apart, but we must do the best we can.

As (a) you have thought about the *Rake's Progress* for some time, and (b) it is the librettist's job to satisfy the composer, not the other way round, I should

---

[1] All of Stravinsky's letters to Auden were sent from this address, unless otherwise indicated.

be most grateful if you could let me have any ideas you may have formed about characters, plot, etc.

I think the Asylum finale sounds excellent, but, for instance, if he is to play the fiddle then, do you want the fiddle to run through the story?

You speak of a "free verse preliminary." Do you want the arias and ensembles to be finally written in free verse or only as a basis for discussing the actual form they should take? If they were spoken, the eighteenth-century style would of course demand rhyme, but I know how different this is when the words are set.

I have an idea, which may be ridiculous, that between the two acts, there should be a choric parabasis as in Aristophanes.

I need hardly say that the chance of working with you is the greatest honor of my life.

In addition to Aldous Huxley, I think we have another mutual friend, Nicholas Nabakov [sic].

Yours very sincerely,   Wystan Auden

P.S. I hope you can read my writing. Unfortunately I do not know how to type.[2]

STRAVINSKY TO AUDEN   *October 23, 1947*
                                                          [Telegram]
7 Cornelius [sic] Street
New York City

Thanks kind letter. All things considered, find impossible discuss this important matter by letters. Could you spend few days my home? Gladly take care your airplane expenses. Please wire. Greetings,   Igor Stravinsky

                                                          October 24, 1947
AUDEN TO STRAVINSKY   *[Telegram]*

Many thanks for wire and generous offer shamefacedly accepted. Suggest leaving New York November tenth if convenient for you.   Wystan Auden

STRAVINSKY TO AUDEN   *October 27, 1947*
                                                          [Telegram]
7 Cornelius [sic] Street
New York City

Delighted you are coming. Kindly let me know time arrival on November 11th. If in the morning will expect you for breakfast. Best wishes,   IStr

---

[2] Except for his letters of January 24, 1952, c. March 1, 1964, and March 6, 1964, all of Auden's letters are handwritten.

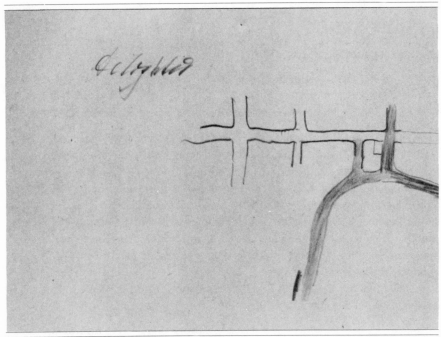

Stravinsky's map on a draft for the telegram to W. H. Auden, November 10, 1947. Sunset Boulevard is the horizontal street; moving from left to right, the third turn-off to the right is North Wetherly Drive, and the line shows the location of the Stravinsky home.

AUDEN TO STRAVINSKY

November 10, 1947
[Telegram]

Flight cancelled arriving 7:40 p.m. Tuesday [November 11].[3]   Auden

---

[3] Auden stayed in the Stravinsky home from 10:00 p.m. on Tuesday, November 11, to the evening of November 18. While there, he diverted the composer by writing examples of verse forms, without regard to content. Stravinsky kept one of these, a scheme for a sestina, and the following, a version of a poem written a few months before, and published later under the title "Nursery Rhyme":

> *Cantiga d'amigo*
> Their learned kings bent down to chat with frogs
> That was before the Battle of the Bogs
> *The key that opens is the key that rusts.*
>
> Their cheerful kings made table on their stoves
> This was until the Rotting of the loaves.
> *The robins vanish when the ravens come.*
>
> This was until the coaches reached the bogs
> Now woolly bears pursue the spotted dogs
> *A witch can make an ogre out of mud.*

AUDEN TO VERA STRAVINSKY

7 Cornelia Street
New York 14, New York

Dear Mrs. Stravinsky,

November 20, 1947

First, an account of my stewardship. I have

a) Posted the letter to the Guggenheim Foundation.
b) Called Miss Bean.
c) Called Mr. [Hans W.] Heinsheimer [of Boosey & Hawkes].

The journey was a nightmare. The flight was cancelled; I was transferred to an American Airlines local which left at 7:00 a.m., stopped *everywhere* and reached New York at 4:00 a.m. this morning. The meals, as usual, would have tried the patience of a stage curate, so you can imagine what I felt, after a week of your luxurious cuisine. And finally, of course, I got back here to a pile of silly letters to answer, a job I loathe. The only consolation is the pleasure of writing you this bread-and-butter letter (How do you say that in Russian?). I loved every minute of my stay,[4] thanks to you both, and shall look forward with impatience to the next time we meet.

Greetings to Vassily, *Das krankheitliebendes Fräulein,* Popka, Mme Sokolevsky [*sic*], *La Baroness des Chats,* etc.[5]

Yours ever,   Wystan Auden

P.S. Could you give the enclosed note to the maestro?

That was before the weevils ate the loaves
Now blinded bears invade the orange groves
A witch can make an ogre out of mud.

The blinded bears have polished off the dogs
Our bowls of milk are filled with drowning frogs.
The robins vanish when the ravens come.

The woolly bears have rooted up the groves
Our poisoned milk boils over on our stoves
The key that opens is the key that rusts.

[4] Like almost everyone who ever saw Stravinsky's workroom, Auden wrote about it: "To achieve anything today, an artist has to develop a conscious strictness in respect of time which in former ages might have seemed neurotic and selfish, for he must never forget that he is living in a state of siege. His workroom has also to be a fortress; the stop-watch and the metronome are his shield and buckler. Similarly, in a howling storm, a theatrical and purple artistic style is ridiculous; only clarity and economy will work as charms against the void. Intervals, as Stravinsky says, must be treated like dollars." (From the *New York Times,* February 4, 1951)

[5] "Vaska," or Vassily, was the Stravinskys' cat. The illness-loving Fräulein was the Stravinskys' cook, Yvgenia Petrovna; "Popka" was the favorite parrot; Mrs. Sokolov was the co-owner with Mrs. Stravinsky of an art gallery; the Baroness was their neighbor Catherine d'Erlanger.

Du syllabiste
Au compositeur

Cher Igor Stravinsky,

Memo. Act I, Sc. I, *Je crois que ça sera mieux si c'est un oncle inconnu de l'héro [sic] au lieu de son père qui meurt, parce que comme ça la richesse est tout à fait imprévue, et la note pastorale n'est pas interrompue par le [sic] douleur, seulement par la présence sinistre du villain. En ce cas, la* girl *possédera un père, pas un oncle.*

    Etes-vous en accord? Je tiendrai silence pour Oui,

Wystan Auden

P.S. I can't tell you what a pleasure it is to collaborate with you. I was so frightened that you might be a prima donna.

Salut au "making."

STRAVINSKY TO AUDEN   *November 25, 1947*

Dear Wystan Auden,

Many thanks for your nice letters and for "running" my phone errands.

    OK for the uncle of the girl now becoming instead her father (*quelle histoire!*) and OK for the father's death of our hero to be replaced by his uncle's death. *Bonne trouvaille! A vrai dire, je comprends notre pauvre héro [sic], il y a, en effet, de quoi de [sic] venir fou.*

    Enclosed a clipping from *Los Angeles Times*—this article of A. Goldberg after his informal interview with us the other day.[6]

    Warmest greetings from both of us and from Vaska too.

Cordially,   IStravinsky
Sincerely,   Vaska

---

[6] On November 18, the composer and the librettist made a few general statements to Albert Goldberg of the *Los Angeles Times;* some of these remarks appeared in an article on November 23. Stravinsky is quoted as saying that the opera "will be tragic only in the sense that *Don Giovanni* is tragic." The *New York Times* obtained a further comment from Boosey & Hawkes to the effect that the librettist intended to use Pope and Congreve as models, and that the composer intended to study the settings of English in the operas of Purcell and Handel. In July 1949, Goldberg borrowed the libretto from Stravinsky, and on August 1 he returned it with an enthusiastic letter.

STRAVINSKY TO AUDEN   *December 5, 1947*

Dear Wystan Auden,

What a delight your Collected Poetry! Many, many thanks.

Je ne me répond [sic] *plus de votre poésie, je l'aime, je l'aime, à l'infinie.*

Don't worry about Handel's *Messiah*. I finally got it in Novello's publication.

All best. Cordially,   IStr

AUDEN TO STRAVINSKY   *7 Cornelia Street*
                                                        New York 14, New York
Dear Igor Stravinsky,   *January 16, 1948*

Herewith Act I. As you will see, I have taken in a collaborator [Chester Kallman], an old friend of mine in whose talents I have the greatest confidence.

We are in the middle of Act II now, which I will send as soon as it is done.

I've marked places where cuts in the text can be easily made if you want to, but of course, don't hesitate to make cuts of your own.

I'm seeing Nicholas [Nabokov] on Sunday; he's been quite ill again, poor thing.

With warmest remembrances to Mrs. Stravinsky and everyone else.

Yours ever,   Wystan Auden

STRAVINSKY TO AUDEN   *January 23, 1948*
                                                        [Telegram]
7 Cornelia Street
New York 14, New York

Read your wonderful first act many times. Foresee however some musical difficulties repeating sentences traditionally. Consider therefore our meeting essential. Are you still sailing April seventh? Greetings.

                                                        January 24, 1948
AUDEN TO STRAVINSKY   *[Telegram]*

Many thanks for wire. Will mail Act Two Monday. Do not worry about excessive length which can be cut ad lib when we meet. Hope you come in March before I leave April seventh.   Wystan Auden

AUDEN TO STRAVINSKY   *7 Cornelia Street*
                                                        New York 14, New York
Dear Igor Stravinsky,   *February 9, 1948*

Here is the last act (& an insert for Act I to explain Act III, scene 2). We will send you a proper whole copy in covers as soon as the typist is ready with it.

I have been down for the last ten days with trigeminal neuralgia which is hell.

Nicholas Nabokov is sitting here as I write and sends his love, so do I to all.

Wystan

STRAVINSKY TO AUDEN   *February 19, 1948*

Mon cher Auden,

Fly out tomorrow to Mexico, coming back March 3d. So glad to have read your whole book. When time permits will go over and mark all things to let you know (while in NY, Apr. 5 or 6) my observations.

    1,000,000 thanks for your beautiful work.

All best,   IStr

AUDEN TO STRAVINSKY   *7 Cornelia Street*
New York 14, New York

Mon cher Igor Stravinsky,   *[Postmark: March 5, 1948]*

Many thanks for your letter. I hope you had an enjoyable time in Mexico.

As you know I am sailing on April 7th. Could you possibly arrive a few days earlier than you planned as you know how difficult it will be to discuss any alterations while packing?

Greetings to all.   Wystan Auden

P.S. I hope the suggestions of Ralph Hawkes etc. about the contract are OK with you.

STRAVINSKY TO AUDEN   *March 8, 1948*

Dearest Auden,

Thanks for your note (March 5). Back from Mexico with a cold (*schnuppfen*). The next week I am conducting here a pair of concerts. Going to Washington D.C. March 27, where conducting Apr. 4 at 4 p:m. Will try to catch the train at 9 p.m. to be in the same night in N.Y. In other words, the earliest I can see you is April 5. I will stay at the Ambassador Hotel. Hope we can go over the whole book in one day. If there should be some alterations to be carried out, I think we have to postpone it until your return from Europe, because it could not be done, of course, in one or two days.

As to the suggestions of Ralph Hawkes concerning a "contract" with you, they are not yet quite clear to me; besides he will write to my lawyer, A. Sapiro,[7]

---

[7] Aaron Sapiro commented on the libretto in a letter to Stravinsky, August 29, 1948: ". . . I do not think it is necessary to provide Baba with a beard which is unwholesome

about it and I am sure he will bring the whole matter to our mutual satisfaction.

All best. Hasta luego,   I Stravinsky

AUDEN TO STRAVINSKY   Firenze

Mon cher Igor Stravinsky,   May 15, 1948
                                                         [Postcard]

Arrived safely after a fortnight in England, which is much more expensive than U.S. I hope your son has got over by now[8] and that Act I *va bien.*
    Off this evening to see *I Lombardi.*

Love to all.   Wystan Auden

P.S. Have just been to Rome to hear *I Puritani.* A heavenly work.

STRAVINSKY TO AUDEN   October 25, 1948

Dear Auden,

Happy you like my *Orpheus.* Would love to show you my "progress" in our *Rake*—Hope in Febr., while in NY.

All best whatsoever,   IStr

STRAVINSKY TO AUDEN   November 17, 1948

Dear Auden,

I need to repeat the music of the attached verse. Be an Angel and compose four new lines of same length and rhythm to fit with the already existing music. It will be up to you to decide (for the sense) which one of the two groups of your verses is to be sung . . . first. . . . Please, please, answer as soon as possible.

Cordially

[*Original verse enclosed*]

ROARING BOYS and WHORES

    While food has flavor and limbs are shapely
    And hearts beat bravely to fiddle or drum
    Our proper employment is reckless enjoyment
    For too soon the noiseless night will come.

---

and which pushes the opera into slapstick farce. . . . A great many of the speeches are exceedingly long, [but] my disappointment is in Baba. . . ."

[8] Soulima Stravinsky arrived from France in June.

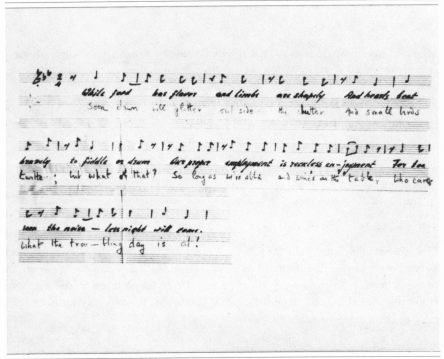

The manuscript of some measures of the chorus part of The Rake's Progress, Act One, Scene 2, *with added verse (in pencil) in Auden's hand. (See letter of November 23, 1948.)*

AUDEN TO STRAVINSKY   *November 23, 1948*

Dear Igor Stravinsky,

I got back from Washington yesterday afternoon to find your letter. I enclose another verse which should, I think, come first. It is difficult in this metre to get an *exact* rhythmical identity—e.g., *Who cares what* is slightly different from *For too soon,* but they are, I hope, near enough. In case you can't read my pencil on the score, here is the verse in printed caps:

> SOON DAWN WILL GLITTER OUTSIDE THE SHUTTER
> AND SMALL BIRDS TWITTER; BUT WHAT OF THAT?
> SO LONG AS WE'RE ABLE AND WINE'S ON THE TABLE
> WHO CARES WHAT THE TROUBLING DAY IS AT?[9]

I'm very excited about what I hear of the music from Robert Craft. Very mozartian, he says.

                                       Yours ever,   Wystan Auden

[9] Seeing that his original stanza was inappropriate, Auden wrote new words better suited to Stravinsky's music—e.g., "troubling" perfectly fits the octave, whereas "noiseless" sounds like two words.

STRAVINSKY TO AUDEN   *November 27, 1948*

Dear Auden,

Many, many, many thanks—That is exactly what I need. Don't worry about a slightly different rhythm which occurs from time to time—the music smooths it down.

Looking forward to show you (in February) the first act, which I hope will be completed before going East (end of January).[10]

All best.   Cordially

Via Santa Lucia 22
Forio d'Ischia
Prov. di Napoli
April 26, 1949
AUDEN TO STRAVINSKY   *[Postcard]*

The sirocco is blowing, which makes it a good day to write letters. Arrived after a *very* boring voyage just before Easter when the Madonna ran down the street to meet her son to the sound of explosions. Your photo is up in the kitchen. Hope that Act II is going well. I keep nagging at St. Restituta about it.

Love to all.   Wystan

STRAVINSKY TO AUDEN   *May 8, 1949*

Glad to have your nice card. Hope sirocco will soon blow again and bring us fresh news from you. Though slowly, *Rake*'s progressing well.

Love,   IStr

Via Santa Lucia 22
Forio d'Ischia
Prov. di Napoli
July 2 [1949?]
AUDEN TO STRAVINSKY   *[Postcard]*

Many thanks for your card. Hope *R.P.* is progressing well. Mr. Kallman and I are writing a comic libretto about the Muse and her relations with Berlioz, Mendelssohn and Rossini. Heard *L'Assedio di Corinto* in Florence and thought it wonderful.

Love to all.   Wystan

---

[10] The act was completed January 16. The following is a list of all of the dates in Stravinsky's "summary sketch score" of the opera:

December 11, 1947	Completes the Prelude to Act III, scene 2, in sketch and in full scores.

ACT I

May 8, 1948	Begins the opera at 2. (The Prelude, not dated, was written after the Epilogue.)

STRAVINSKY TO AUDEN   *October 18, 1949*

7 Cornelia Street
New York 14, New York

Dear Wystan,

I have not heard from you for a long time but I suppose, and I hope, that you are
in New York now, because I need your help badly and urgently.

I have just driven my music to the Trio (Act II, Scene II) and my composing is stalled because any music I might compose for Anne and Rake will be
drowned under Baba's comic interference and the audience's laughs (I am positive about this).

My first move has been to reunite Anne's and Tom's verses by staggering
their lines until the very end when I let them sing twice together (please check
with the enclosed pattern). [But] my efforts to hold the audience's attention
focused on a single action are [in] vain, as long as Baba keeps interfering by
inserting her parlando monologue while Anne and Rake sing. I cannot figure
any other way out but for you *to compose verses for Baba's grumbling.* The
verses that I want you to compose should match those of Anne and Rake, and
might stagger with them most of the time, except when you would find it possible to melt them with the words of Anne or Rake, without, of course, drowning
any of them.

Be an angel and send me this overhauled trio as soon as possible. It will
then be a genuine trio and not a duo with a third person's intervention. My

July 17, 1948	Completes the music through "You are a rich man."
September 13, 1948	Completes Duettino.
October 3, 1948	Completes scene 1 (except for the repeat in the Terzetto, which was added at a later date).
October 5, 1948	Begins scene 2.
January 16, 1949	Completes Act I.

ACT II

April 1, 1949	Begins Act II with "Vary the song."
August 29, 1949	"O Heart be stronger."
"End October 1949"	Begins Terzetto ("Could it then?").
November 3, 1949	Completes Terzetto.
December 18, 1949	Begins Baba's "As I was saying . . ."
December 29, 1949	Completes Baba's D-minor aria.
January 10, 1950	"Oh Nick, I've had the strangest dream."

ACT III

"End May 1950"	Begins "What curious phenomena . . . ?"
October 29, 1950	Completes scene 2.
January 28, 1951	Completes the opera through "Madmen, where have you hidden her?"
April 7, 1951	Completes the Epilogue.

suggestion would be to reduce Baba's words to not more, and even rather less, than either Anne's or Rake's.

Give me some news concerning [yourself] and your plans. I shall be in New York on March 20, and it is impossible for me to be there before.[11] I hope you will not leave as early as you did this year, because it is important to both of us to go through everything regarding Act III.

As ever, affectionately yours.

AUDEN TO STRAVINSKY

Dear Igor,

7 Cornelia Street
New York 14, New York
October 24, 1949

Many thanks for your letter. In order to distinguish Baba in character and emotion from the two lovers, it seems to me that her rhythm should be more irregular and her tempo of utterance faster. In writing her part, therefore, I have given any line of Baba's twice the number of accents as compared with the equivalent line of Anne or Tom's. If you find I have given her too many lines,[12] cuts are easy to make, e.g.

v. 1 can become: Why this delay . . . Away . . . O. Who is it pray
He prefers to his Baba on their wedding day.

v. 2 An ancient flame? I'm quite perplexed
And more, I confess, than a little[13] vexed.

v. 3 Here there is a succession of short phrases, which can be used or not ad lib.

I hope you had a good summer and am longing to hear the new scenes. I had a wonderful time in Italy and managed to get a lot of work done.

Bob Craft's concert last Saturday went quite nicely with the usual impatience of the management to throw us out. The voices in *Renard* were a bit frightened.

---

[11] Shortly after this letter, Stravinsky accepted invitations to conduct in New York in February.

[12] Auden also enclosed the following new verses for Baba:

Why this delay? Away, or the crowd will . . . [she sees Anne] O!
And why, if I may be allowed to inquire, does my husband desire
To converse with this person? Who is it, pray,
He prefers to his Baba on their wedding day?

A family friend? An ancient flame?
A bride has surely the prior claim
On the bridal night! I'm quite perplexed
And more, I confess, than a little vexed.

[13] The original libretto has "a trifle."

Am seeing Hawkes this afternoon who has schemes, I understand, about the Edinburgh Festival, which sound rather good.

Much love to you and Vera and come east soon.

Wystan

STRAVINSKY TO AUDEN   *November 15, 1949*

7 Cornelia Street
New York 14, New York

Dear Wystan,

Pardon me for being so late in thanking you for your brilliant versified version of Baba's interfering recitative. I am delighted, and I have already composed the trio.

In Baba's first two interferences I dropped only the alternate words as per your advice;[14] I kept the whole of her babbling in the third one.

And you sent it to me so quickly! Thanks so much.

I am composing now the end of that scene, which is a chaconne; even when the crowd greets Baba, the chaconne continues, thus ending the whole scene.

After that I shall carry on without respite until I finish the third scene, before next March, as I want not to miss you in New York.

Bob Craft just writes me that you have booked passage for March 13. This shortens my deadline by a fortnight. Nevertheless I hope I will finish the second act and be able to show it to you. Please keep the dates of March 11 and 12 free for me as we have so many things to decide together concerning Act III.

Will be glad to hear from you soon.

As ever, cordially yours.

AUDEN TO STRAVINSKY   *7 Cornelia Street*
                                       New York 14, New York
Dear Igor,   *November 15, 1949*

If you haven't yet composed the Trio in Act II, Scene 2, here is an alternative version of Baba's part where the rhymes fit the others, which you may prefer to what I sent you.

BABA

I'm waiting, dear. . . . Have done
With talk, my love. . . . I shall count up to ten. . . .
Who is she? *One* . . .
Hussy! . . . If I am found
Immured here, dead,
I swear . . . *Two* . . . I'll haunt you . . .

---

[14] Stravinsky used the short version indicated by Auden in his letter of October 24.

Three . . . You know you're bound
By law, dear . . . *Four* . . . Before I wed
Could I . . . *Five, Six* . . . have . . . *Seven* . . . then
Foreseen my sorrow? . . . *Eight, Nine* . . . *Ten* . . .
O never, never, never . . .
I shall be cross, love, if you keep
Baba condemned to gasp and weep
Forever.[15]

Looking forward to hearing *Perséphone* on Monday.[16]

Love to you both.   Wystan

December 31, 1949
AUDEN TO STRAVINSKY   [Telegram]

Love and all wishes for another great year.   Look forward seeing you February.[17]   Wystan

[*At a meeting in the Lombardy Hotel, New York, March 1, 1950, Auden composed the following draft of bids for the Auction scene.*]

    2   3   3   2   2   3   2   3
    50 51 52 60 80 85 89 100

1)   7. 11. 17. 19. 20. 21./

2)   14, and ½, ¾, 15

AUDEN TO STRAVINSKY   March [3?] 1950
                                             [Hand-delivered note]
Hotel Lombardy

Dear Igor,

Sorry about the delay with these.

                                                         Wystan

ACT III SCENE I.
p. 3 after first verse of Sellem's song. (Aha! the what.) [*In Stravinsky's hand: "what" is circled, "pike" written above; line drawn from "what" leads to note by Stravinsky: "later on."*] Members of crowd speak in turn each higher bid, which Sellem repeats.

---

[15] Auden's letter crossed with Stravinsky's and the trio had been completed before Stravinsky saw this new text.
[16] In a concert conducted by Robert Craft in Carnegie Hall, in which Auden read a selection of his poems.
[17] Stravinsky was in New York from February to May.

[*"bid" in Stravinsky's hand*]

Crowd member	7	
Sellem	7	
C.M.	11	
S.	11	
C.M.	14	
S.	14	
C.M.	19	
S.	19	
C.M.	20	
S.	20	
C.M.	23	
S.	23	Going at 23, going, going, gone.

Verse II. p. 4. Aha! the palm.

C.M.	15	
S.	15	
C.M.	And ½	
S.	And ½	
C.M.	¾	
S.	¾	
C.M.	16	
S.	16	
C.M.	17	
S.	17	Going at 17, going, going, gone.

Verse III. p. 6. Aha! the what.

C.M.	50	
S.	50	
C.M.	55	
S.	55	
C.M.	60	
S.	60	
C.M.	61	
S.	61	
C.M.	62	
S.	62	
C.M.	70	
S.	70	
C.M.	90	
S.	90	Going at 90, going at 90
C.M.	100	
S.	100	Going at 100, going at 100, going, going, going, going, GONE.

Forio d'Ischia
July 6, 1950
[Postcard]

AUDEN TO STRAVINSKY

Hope A and P[18] not discouraged. *Auguri* for Act III.

Wystan Auden

STRAVINSKY TO AUDEN   *November 27, 1950*

7 Cornelia Street
New York 14, New York

Dear Wystan:

Just to say: "Hello" and "How are you"?

Also to tell you that Boosey & Hawkes are having *Rake's* translations made in French and Italian. Do not ask me what [they are] going to be like; I prefer to ignore it.

In my opinion Betty Bean is doing her best, now that she has taken over the directorship. Maybe you could get in touch with her and see if you can at least *"limiter les dégâts"* by showing her kindly where discrepancies are far too obvious.

What do you think of it all? Please mail me a few lines before long.

Cordially as ever.

AUDEN TO STRAVINSKY   *8 Park Street*
                                        South Hadley, Massachusetts[19]
1260 N. Wetherly Drive   *December 5, 1950*
Hollywood, CA

Dear Igor Stravinsky,

Many thanks for your letter which arrived just as I had to be off to N.Y. to give a lecture.

Am teaching here till the end of Jan. Poor Betty Bean is in a tizzy, I gather, trying to deal with everything; I hope she doesn't have a breakdown.

How is Act III? Am longing to hear. The ideal premiere would be La Fenice, don't you think.

I'll write next week when I start Christmas Vacation.

Love to you and Vera and hope you have plenty of Scotch.

Wystan

---

[18] "A and P" is a reference to Huntington Hartford, heir to the A & P fortune. At the time that Auden left New York, Hartford had been approached to sponsor a limited run of *The Rake's Progress* in a Broadway theater.

[19] Auden was teaching English at Mount Holyoke College.

AUDEN TO STRAVINSKY

Happy Christmas. Love,   Wystan

STRAVINSKY TO AUDEN   *January 4, 1951*

7 Cornelia Street
New York 14, New York

Dearest Wystan:

How to thank you for your wonderful poetic present? We are awfully glad to include this brilliant anthology[20] made by yourself in our library. No one could be
a better judge than you in this matter.

   Rake is progressing well though this last act takes more time than the
others. The vocal score of the first two scenes of Act 3, which I have just finished, is twenty pages longer than the whole three scenes of Act I.

   When will I see you now? For the moment I have no plan to be in New
York. Some months ago Kirstein had invited me to conduct the Ballet in February,[21] but owing to his silence since then, I doubt it will materialize.

   I am going to Havana for conducting during the first week of March.

   When do you intend to sail to Italy this year?

All best as ever.

AUDEN TO STRAVINSKY

Dear Igor,

I was so delighted to hear from Bob Craft the good news about La Fenice. I
would have written before but the last fortnight at Mount Holyoke was hectic.

   Are they doing the *Rake* in English or Wop? Because I imagine we shall
now be having to think seriously about the singers.

   Who is going to direct?

   I do hope the last scene is progressing well; am dying to hear it.

   I may possibly be sent to India in the middle of March for four days; a nuisance but it means that my fare to Italy and back will get paid for.

Love to all.   Wystan

---

[20] Stravinsky's next work, the Cantata (1952), resulted from his reading the five-
volume anthology edited by Auden and Norman Holmes Pearson, *Poets of the English
Language,* from which he selected four anonymous Elizabethan lyrics.

[21] See Kirstein's letter to Stravinsky of August 30, 1950, p. 278.

STRAVINSKY TO AUDEN   *February 10, 1951*

7 Cornelia Street
New York 14, New York

Dear Wystan:

What a surprise! When are you planning to take that India trip? Will you be flying through here?[22] In that case it will be a great joy to us all to see you and you
can share Bob Craft's home,[23] where you will have plenty of room.

I want only to let you know that we will be away from home from February
20 to March 13, as I have concerts in Cuba and we go from there motoring to
Florida.

Yes, the premiere of *Rake* will take place at the Venice festival in September. Everything is arranged in principle; I am only waiting [for] them to sign
and return the contract.

But keep it for yourself as the contract gives Venice the privilege to announce it first, after they meet the terms.

I am finishing the last pages of Bedlam before going to Cuba, and upon my
return here I will work on the epilogue. Hope to be through by April 15.

I do not know yet who will direct; I have recommended Dr. Carl Ebert,
who masterminds the Edinburgh festival.

Love from both of us.

AUDEN TO STRAVINSKY   *7 Cornelia Street*
                                                  New York 14, New York
Dear Igor,   *February 14, 1951*

Many thanks for your letter.

Delighted to hear that Act III, Scene 3 is nearly finished.

Mr. Kallman and I are a bit worried about the prospect of Ebert directing.
We saw his *Così fan tutte* and thought it was much too refined and "minia-
turized." As you can imagine, we, as librettists, are as concerned about the
stage goings-on as you are about the singing.

If it can possibly be arranged, Kallman and I would like to be present in an
advisory capacity when rehearsals start.

Hope you have a lovely time in Cuba.

Love to all.   Wystan

---

[22] As Auden's letter explains, he went from India to Italy, but Nicolas Nabokov, who
was in India with him, returned by way of Los Angeles and the Stravinsky home.
[23] 8624 Holloway Drive, a few blocks from the Stravinsky home.

STRAVINSKY TO AUDEN   *February 16, 1951*

7 Cornelia Street
New York 14, New York

Dearest Wystan:

Nice to have your lines; but you forgot to tell me when you will be away on your India trip.

Don't worry so much about Ebert. . . . Maybe he was not at his best in *Così fan tutte,* but as a whole he is the most experienced opera stage director we can find at present. Of course, it is up to the Italians to close the deal with him but, as far as I am concerned, he is my choice, and I selected him because they asked me to give my suggestion.

His assets (most important to me) are that he is an experienced musician and also he is already familiar with my score. Besides I will be on the spot for my rehearsing (from August 15), and this will give me all chances to cooperate with him.

You should be there too, for some time at least; but, unfortunately, it is not my responsibility to provide for your active role with Kallman.

I have not sold La Biennale anything but my conducting[24] and musical supervision of the performance, and most of your problems are off bounds to me.

I strongly wish you would immediately contact Ferdinando Ballo[25] at La Biennale as I am sure he will be most willing to do his utmost to be able to use your advice.

Furthermore, my particular arrangements with La Biennale (conducting) do not interfere in any way with the provisions of any contract you may have with the publishers Boosey & Hawkes. Anything you are expecting to get from them you should get, and anything I am entitled to get from them I should get too.

Don't be lazy; write me soon again.

Much love.

AUDEN TO STRAVINSKY   *April 23, 1951*
                                                      [Cable]

Is Berman doing *Rake* sets?   If not, Balthus interested.   Please cable me Forio d'Ischia. Love,   Wystan

---

[24] Stravinsky is pretending that the $20,000 for the opera, procured for him from the Italian government by Nicolas Nabokov, was not a commission (which he would have had to share with the librettists) but a fee for conducting the premiere.
[25] Director of the Biennale in 1951.

STRAVINSKY TO AUDEN   *April 26, 1951*

Forio d'Ischia

Dear Wystan,

I have found your cable of April 23 upon my return home from a short trip. I prefer to write you as the situation is not clarified yet.

Neither Berman nor Ebert (who just came back here from Italy and whom I just saw) [has] received any definite answer one way or another from Ballo. Before speaking of replacing them we should know first if they are out. . . .

I have written Ballo exactly the same thing I am writing you, and I still have no answer from him. I believe the dragging is the result of the pending negotiations between La Biennale and La Scala, the outcome of which will most likely command all decisions including the singers who, anyhow, are out front in any operatic production. Don't you think so? . . .

Glad you are back in Italy and hope you are well. Would like to have a word from you.

Cordially

AUDEN TO STRAVINSKY   *Via Santa Lucia 14*
                                                             Forio d'Ischia
Dear Igor,   *June 9, 1951*

Thank you for your letter of April [26]. Everything still seems in a terrible muddle here and I hope that we aren't going to have a scratch performance with last-minute singers, designers, etc.

Mr. Kallman, who has been proof-reading the vocal score in New York, writes me that in Act II, Scene 1 (p. 85), stage directions prior to no. 48, the stage direction now indicates that the broadsheet of Baba should be visible to the audience—the face, that is. Did you mean this, because there seem to me two serious objections:

1) It is physically impossible to show the broadsheet in such a way that it is equally visible in all parts of the house. Those of the audience who can't see it will be irritated.

2) More importantly, the revelation that Baba has a beard at this point will ruin the dramatic effect of the finale to Act II, Scene 2.

I know you must be frightfully busy, so don't bother to answer this, unless you violently disagree.

Looking forward to seeing you in Italy.

Love to all.   Wystan

STRAVINSKY TO AUDEN   *July 18, 1951*

Forio d'Ischia

Dear Wystan,

I am writing you today to keep you posted on my planned activities. I am leaving here July 30 and I will stay in New York (Hotel Lombardy, 111 East 56th Street, New York 22, N.Y.) from August 2 until my sailing on board the S.S. *Constitution* (American Export Lines) on August 7. I will land in Naples August 15.

We will no doubt meet somewhere in Italy though I do not know yet what my schedule of rehearsals will be. So far, I have been informed officially only that the premiere will take place under my direction at the Fenice on September 8. The Scala has finally agreed to take responsibility for the production.

Though the Scala never asked me about the staging (*metteur en scène*) I understand that they [have] already contracted Ebert. Ghiringhelli[26] (Scala) wired me asking whom I wanted as painter (Berman no longer available), and I recommended John Piper, whom you know well, and who happened to be in the best position to work at once with Ebert in England. But another telegram from Ghiringhelli was asking me [for] another suggestion. I immediately wired (July 14) recommending Balthus. I made it clear that Balthus—if contracted—should see Ebert at once. Still no answer, and at the present time you may know more than I do about it.

I did not answer your letter concerning the broadsheet as it was clear that no answer meant my approval of your [reasoning].

Last week I spent [an] evening with your fellow college professor, Passinetti; we discussed the matter of the title of *Rake's* in Italian. I liked very much his suggestion:

Carriera d'un Libertino.

What do you think of it?

By the way, have you seen the Italian translation? Who has done it? The German translation is outstanding and amazingly close to the English.

Will be glad to have even a line from you in New York before sailing.

Most cordially

AUDEN TO STRAVINSKY   *Via Santa Lucia 14*
                                                        Forio d'Ischia
Dear Igor,   *July 25, 1951*

Many thanks for your letter of July 18. Delighted to hear you are at Naples Au-

---

[26] See n. 26 on p. 252.

gust 15 and will be on the dock to meet you.[27] Rehearsals, I understand, start in Milan (hope it will be) about the 16th or 17th.[28]

Everything seems to be in rather a muddle because La Fenice and La Scala were so long in coming to terms. I have seen Oldani, the General Secretary of La Scala, who is in Ischia, and am seeing him again on Friday.

Neither Piper nor Balthus, it seems, is likely to accept doing sets. Ebert has asked too much money for the direction, etc., etc. As to the latter, it sounds rather conceited to say so, I know, but I believe that I and Kallman could do an adequate job; at least we shouldn't sacrifice the music to the action, as most modern operatic directors do, in my opinion.

Passinetti's Italian title sounds fine. Ballo still hasn't told me if they have an Italian translator.

Longing to see you.

Love to you and Vera.

STRAVINSKY TO AUDEN   *January 7, 1952*

235 Seventh Avenue
New York, New York

Dear Wystan,

A few words only to forward to you the letter I have just received from Italy. It concerns you and it is better to let you handle the matter by yourself.

Is Chester back at last? If so what news is he bringing with him? Where does our new project [*Delia*] stand? Have you been progressing forward?

About the *Rake's*, Betty Bean writes me the following:

> *The Rake's Progress* vocal score—I have just had a note from [Dr. Ernst] Roth [Boosey & Hawkes] in which he indicates that the new print of the *Rake* is now in progress and will probably be available within the next three to four weeks. This will be confirmed to me at a later date from our German office.

You should contact Betty Bean or Dr. Roth directly but *at once* in order to be able to have them enter the last few corrections made at your suggestion in the vocal score. You have them, I do not. *Please don't delay* otherwise the score will bear the "misaccentuating" forever. . . .

Affectionately

---

[27] Auden and Kallman were there on the dock.

[28] Stravinsky was still in Naples on August 18. His draft of the following telegram, sent to Boosey & Hawkes in Bonn on that date, is in Auden's hand: "Act III, Scene 2. Figure 197. Between bars four and five, two newly added bars not in any score we have. Please send immediately." On July 9, Stravinsky discovered that he had overlooked two phrases in the text, and on July 10, he sent his setting of them to his publisher.

AUDEN TO STRAVINSKY

Dear Igor,

Just a line to say:

1) Thank you for your letter. I had already given La Bean all the corrections in the vocal score. The only one I'm not sure about is your musical correction of "initiated."

2) Chester arrived two days ago, and we have begun discussing the "Project," which, D.V., we hope to have ready for you by April.

3) How are you & Vera & the calcium shots?

4) The Armstead [*sic*] sketches for sets are beginning to shape up nicely.

Much love.   Wystan

STRAVINSKY TO AUDEN

March 28, 1952
[*Telegram*]

AUDEN TO STRAVINSKY

Libretto finished this instant. Love,   Wystan and Chester

STRAVINSKY TO AUDEN AND KALLMAN   *Tuesday, April 1, 1952*
                                                          [Telegram]
235 Seventh Avenue
New York City

Happy hear you completed libretto for project, which I hope will not be stillborn. When are you leaving for Europe? Affectionately,   Igor Stravinsky

STRAVINSKY TO AUDEN   *October 14, 1952*

235 Seventh Avenue
New York City, New York

Dear Wystan,

Hope you are back and well.

On the *Rake*'s first birthday I got a very nice telegram from Chester, and I am sure all our thoughts were together then. I hope Chester received my "musical drawing" in answer to his telegram.

I had a letter from the League of Composers inviting me to be "honored." Your participation was mentioned.

You know how I feel about these things, and I am sending you a copy of my answer to them. Moreover I am not in favor of giving excerpts from my music before the premiere in this country.

The broadcast of Markevitch's performance with Schwarzkopf (CBS a month ago) was very well received, but nevertheless I think it would have been better to keep the opera intact until the premiere.

Please drop me a line or two. Love to you and Chester.

AUDEN TO STRAVINSKY   *Northampton, Mass.*
                                                      May 17, 1953
Sheraton Plaza Hotel   *[Telegram]*
Boston

Best wishes for tonight. Wish I could be there [for the *Rake* in Boston]. Much love to all.   Wystan

AUDEN TO STRAVINSKY   *77 St. Mark's Place*
                                            New York City 3, New York
Dear Igor: *[c. October 19, 1955]*

Harper's Bazaar asked me to do something for the Mozart Bicentenary. Hope it will amuse you.[29]

                                                            Wystan

---

[29] Near the end of the poem, "Metalogue to *The Magic Flute*," Auden wrote the follow-

STRAVINSKY TO AUDEN   *October 22, 1955*
                                                           [Telegram]
77 St. Mark's Place
New York 3, New York

Hope to see you in Dec. at Gladstone and to tell you my enthusiasm for your
most wonderful Metalogue. Much thanks for sending it. Love,   Igor

                                                              London
                                                          June 12, 1961
AUDEN TO STRAVINSKY   *[Postcard]*

I have just been to the North Cape or, as the Norwegians say, "above the Moral
Circle."

                                                   Love,   Wystan

AUDEN TO STRAVINSKY   *[c. March 1, 1964]*

Dear Igor:

Many thanks for the birthday telegram. I'm so sorry I [have] been so dilatory
about your Elegy,[30] but I have been immersed in translating the Hammarskjöld
diary. I hope it will do.

   Formally, the stanzas are haikus, ie, the number of syllables in any one
line can vary, but the total number of syllables when the three lines are added
together must be seventeen.

                                             Love to all.   Wystan

STRAVINSKY TO AUDEN   *March 4, 1964*

Dear Wystan,

What a marvel your *Elegy for J.F.K.!*
   Delighted to work on its so beautifully set words. Thank you, dear Wystan,
thank you so much.

                                             Yours as ever,   IStr

AUDEN TO STRAVINSKY   *77 St. Mark's Place*
                                                       New York City 3
Lieber Meister: *March 6, 1964*

Journalists must listen under beds. How they got wind of the Elegy I cannot
imagine. I gather they bothered you as well as me. I'm so sorry. *Newsweek* had

---

ing couplet: "Nor, while we praise the dead, should we forget/We have *Stravinsky*—
bless him!—with us yet."

[30] This letter contained Auden's *Elegy for J.F.K.*

the nerve, when I asked them what they proposed to pay for printing the piece, to say that, since they would use it in the *news* section, they didn't think they should pay anything, so I told them where to put it.

Stanza 4. line 3.

For *Sadness* read *Sorrow*. Fewer s's and more sonorous. As I expect you saw, this last stanza is *disponable* [*sic*] : it can be used at the beginning, at the end, as a refrain, *wie Sie wollen*.

Love,   Wystan

AUDEN TO STRAVINSKY

Dear Igor:

77 St. Mark's Place
New York City 3, New York 10003
November 22, 1965

Bob has just sent me a copy of your contribution to the B.B.C. film about me.[31] That you should have taken the time and trouble to say *anything* would have been overwhelming enough, but that you should say what you do—well! I am speechless with gratitude, my head is swelling, my boots are too tight, and I am walking on air. Thank you, my dear.

I didn't see the production of the *Rake* in Vienna, but Chester did, and wrote a long letter of denunciation to *Die Presse* which they printed. The so-called "stage director" slashed it to ribbons so that often it made not only no dramatic sense, but no musical sense either. What is one to do under such megalomaniacs *ohne Talent*? Would it be legally possible to demand that no cuts be made without the composer's consent?

Delighted to hear that you will be here at Christmas time, and shall much look forward to seeing you.

Much love to you and to Vera.   Wystan

---

[31] On June 28, 1965, Christopher Burstall, a BBC Television producer, wrote to Stravinsky asking him to participate in a documentary program about Auden, "answering an unseen questioner." Stravinsky wrote back on July 8 that he would be "pleased to contribute to the program" but that the filming would have to be done in his Hollywood home. He asked for a "question from Mr. Auden himself. I would then compose an answer of ca. two minutes duration and read it from . . . 'idiot cards.' " The film was made in the latter part of August and aired in England on November 28, 1965. Stravinsky saw it in New York in October 1965.

LETTERS TO

ROBERT CRAFT

1944 ～ *1949*

Though Stravinsky dominated modern music in America in 1947, perform-
ances of his later compositions were comparatively rare. This helps to explain
his remarkably cordial response to the letters of a young musician evidently
immersed in the music and intent on presenting it. Other factors contributed to
the relationship that developed between Stravinsky and me, the chief one being
his decision to write an opera in English, for he must have thought that I could
assist with questions that might arise involving the language. He also under-
stood that I was conversant with new tendencies in music from which he felt
isolated, including the awakening interest in Schoenberg and his school. Still
another consideration was that Stravinsky was at the very moment deciding to
settle in California and resolving to become more "American," while his friends
and fellow refugees in the United States were returning to Europe.[1] Finally, like
everyone who has ever been close to him, I was a factotum. As Soulima Stra-
vinsky wrote to me, December 8, 1949: "Father says he does not trust anybody
except you. As such a compliment cannot be received just gratis, he would
ask you to. . . ." But I did not mind this, for I had also become Stravinsky's
Achates.

Like others who were surprised at the confidence that Stravinsky placed in
me, I continue to speculate as to the reasons. My musical background and
training were unexceptional. My parents were ordinary opera and concert
goers, who occasionally took me to the Metropolitan and the New York Phil-
harmonic, and amateur pianists, though my mother had been encouraged to
become a professional one. They opposed even the thought that I might become
a musician, yet when musical aptitudes were discovered in me, by a choir-
master to whom I owe an early appreciation of Bach and Mozart, I was given
lessons in harmony, counterpoint, orchestration, and "form." But my quest for
knowledge about great music and my discoveries were entirely my own, and
certainly no one led me in the direction of Stravinsky.

By the time I entered the Juilliard School of Music (1941), at age seven-
teen, the pillars of my musical world were Le Sacre du printemps *and* Pierrot
Lunaire. *The logical path of study for an aspiring composer, I believed, was to*
be found in the works of the masters of modern music. Hence my disappoint-
ment in those superconservative classrooms where Stravinsky was mentioned
only derogatorily, Schoenberg was unknown, and Hindemith was considered a
reckless radical. (I received extra demerits for choosing to play a Hindemith so-
nata at a school audition.)

In order to learn contemporary music, therefore, I studied conducting, but
had so few opportunities to practice that before the concert that I shared

---

[1] Stravinsky's decision not to return to Europe dates from 1942. On February 20 of
that year he wrote to Ernest Voigt, of Associated Music Publishers, "I have decided to
remain [in the United States]. I have purchased a house here in Hollywood, and, already two years ago, I took out my first papers. My musical activities have been transferred here by events, and there seems to be absolutely no reason to hope for a return
to a normal life in Europe when this gigantic conflict ends."

with Stravinsky in April 1948, my total experience with an orchestra consisted of a fifteen-minute rehearsal of the Oberon Overture *with the Juilliard ensemble. Stravinsky was aware of my lack of technical expertise, if not of its extent. But no matter. I managed to perform his* Symphony in C *by the grace—as he recognized—of a profound love of the music.*

In February 1944 I sent a letter to Stravinsky in Hollywood,[2] asking a few general and several technical questions, one of which concerned the articulation of the cornet-à-piston groups-of-fives in the Royal March from Histoire du soldat. *On February 27 he dictated a reply to his secretary, Mrs. Adolph Bolm, and corrected it in pencil. He had not understood the question about the* Soldat *(". . . I am completely baffled by it"), and as for the scores that I had hoped to borrow, he said that he was looking for them himself and would "like to purchase any extra copies you might find." He added:*

My son Sviatoslav, according to latest news received through his brother Theodore who is in Switzerland, is, as before, in Paris teaching my music. . . . My youngest daughter, Milene, from the last letter by Theodore, has returned to the health clinic in the Upper Savoie, France, for further treatment of her lungs. . . . I did not attend the reception you mention for Proust. . . .

Sincerely,   Igor Stravinsky

P.S. Enclosed your letter of which you have no copy for your guidance.[3]

He then decided not to post the two letters. Giving them to me as a memento years later, Stravinsky recalled that he had not mailed them at the time because, assuming that I had no copy of my (February 22) letter, he feared that it might be lost.

 I wrote again on March 29, reporting on performances of his music in New York, as well as on the lack of them at Juilliard,[4] "except for the Serenade, which the Lhevinnes teach to their better pupils." I also expressed the hope that

---

[2] With the exception of the letter of March 9, 1949, all Stravinsky's communications published here, entirely or in part, were sent from 1260 North Wetherly Drive, Hollywood 46, California.

[3] My letter was handwritten.

[4] A change of attitude toward Stravinsky came about in 1946 with the presidency of William Schuman, who, on June 28, 1947, wrote to Stravinsky inviting him to accept a commission to compose a quartet for the Juilliard ensemble. Stravinsky answered on July 10, saying that he would "love to do the work for Juilliard," but that he was "overcrowded with work" at present. On September 26, Schuman wrote that a Stravinsky Festival would be held at the school in 1948–49, and that "we should like to have you with us . . . to conduct one concert, or portion of a concert. . . . Obviously, the

he would include Oedipus Rex *or* Perséphone *in the programs for his forth-coming appearances with the New York Philharmonic. To my next letter, August 15, 1944, requesting the loan of a score, the composer replied on August 19:*

I am sorry not to be able to give you a satisfactory answer about the orchestra score of my Capriccio. I am exactly in your case.

One reason for the composer's tardy acknowledgment of my next letter is that it had been misaddressed to him in New York:

Hollywood
February 10, 1947

Dear Mr. Craft:

Returning home from my concert tour I hasten to answer your very kind letter of December 21 (!!). Sorry for this delay.

I have recently signed a long-term contract with Boosey & Hawkes (668 5th Ave.), who are preparing to publish the works you mention in your letter. I advise you to contact Mr. H. W. Heinsheimer, who, I am sure, will be helpful in the matter.

Wishing you the very best of success.

Sincerely

The letter that led to our close relationship was the one I wrote on August 20, 1947, asking for assistance in procuring the score and parts of the Symphonies of Wind Instruments *and offering to send a new French recording of his Piano Concerto in exchange for comments on tempi and other matters. I had been invited by the pianist Elly Kassman[5] to conduct the piece in her Town Hall recital, December 28, 1947. In the meantime, Stravinsky had apparently heard favorable reports of my broadcast performances of his Octet at the Brooklyn Museum (February 2) and at Juilliard (May 2). He answered on August 29:*

---

pleasure of having you here could not be measured in money." Stravinsky answered on October 6, placing the emphasis of his letter on Juilliard's agreement to a postponement of the quartet. In the last week of January 1948, Schuman visited Stravinsky in Hollywood, at which time Stravinsky revealed that he was working on an opera and that the quartet would have to be put aside indefinitely. Then, on May 22, 1950, Stravinsky wrote to Juilliard, withdrawing all hope for the quartet.

[5] I had met Miss Kassman's sister Vera at Tanglewood in 1946, Elly Kassman Meyer (mother of Nicholas Meyer, the future author of *The Seven Per-Cent Solution*) in New York later that year.

41 Johnston Avenue
Kingston, New York[6]

Dear Mr. Craft:

Just read yours of August 20.

You will be disappointed to know that at present it is impossible to get the orchestra material of the *Symphony for Wind Instruments*. All I have of this work is a very dirty proof of the orch. score in the last revision made before the war, sent to me by my son Sviatoslav upon my request. I have my doubt that it ever was published.[7] As to its last movement, the Choral, I reorchestrated it omitting clarinet group for the special purpose to be played in addition to *Psalms* broadcast[8] in order to use the same instruments as in this symphony.

I shall be more than glad receiving Sviatoslav's record of my Piano Concerto, which you so generously offer me. Concerning the orch. score of this Piano Concerto, I corrected the very poorly published old score of which I have a photostatic copy here.

Surprised that you do not know of the change of date in *Orpheus* premiere. Instead of October or November, it will be given in the early spring (probably about the end of April at the City Theater Center).

What is *Speculations* by T. E. Hulme, have no idea. And Suvchinsky's new essay on me, do you mean his article of the last year in *Contrepoint*? This latter, I read it. Do you know Gisèle Brêlet's *Esthétique et création musicale*—an important essay [that] recently appeared in the Presses Universitaires de France? I recommend you this work.

All best sincerely,   Igor Stravinsky

---

[6] Unless otherwise indicated, all Stravinsky's letters were sent to me at this address.

[7] Stravinsky wrote to Païchadze, May 28, 1932: "Ansermet managed to call about the *Symphonies of Wind Instruments* before his departure for Switzerland. He asks that you immediately send the proof sheets, which he will soon have corrected for you." On July 4 Stravinsky reminded Païchadze that Ansermet kindly agreed to correct the proofs of the *Symphonies of Wind Instruments*, but on August 11 the composer was still asking the publisher to "send the *Symphonies of Wind Instruments* to Ansermet immediately. This is the only time that he can work on it and it would be a pity to let the opportunity pass." More than a year later, Stravinsky wrote once again: "Ansermet asks me a number of questions concerning the *Symphonies of Wind Instruments*, which means that he has agreed to correct [*korrecturit*, a nonexistent form of the verb] it." (Originals in Russian)   Still, the score was not published, and soon the Edition Russe de Musique, having declined an offer in April 1932 to be bought out by Schott, virtually ceased to function, other than to rent music.

[8] CBS's "Invitation to Music," New York, January 30, 1946. Stravinsky conducted *Perséphone* in the same series on January 15, 1947, and in the interval between the dress rehearsal and the broadcast, he was photographed on the podium flanked by several younger musicians, including Walter Hendl, Lukas Foss, and myself. In a book

I replied on September 5, saying that I had obtained the Piano Concerto records through friends in Paris and London, and that the discs had survived a very long odyssey. I also asked permission to send W. R. Inge's Plotinus, *in addition to the Hulme, as well as one of Mannheim's books of sociology and some English commentaries on Bossuet, whose* Méditations sur l'Evangile *(in a 1922 edition published by the Librairie Garnier Frères) was always at Stravinsky's bedside. The composer replied as follows:*

October 7, 1947

Dear Robert Craft,

I apologize for my long silence. Your good letter of Sept. 5 received and also Sviatoslav's records [of the Concerto] and also Hulme's *Speculations.* Thank you heartily. I was overcrowded with thousand matters. Happy to have these records and this so important book. *Tell me by return mail how much I owe you for all that.*

Although Sviatoslav records (his playing) are good on the whole, there are many things to say about—correctness for tempis (too hurriedly), the balance of wind instruments (Oubradou),[9] and the technical side (engineering) of the records. I already wrote Sviatoslav about it.

As to the *Symphony for Wind Instruments,* I already started to rewrite it, as I am far from satisfied with the one I have here in proofs. When this will be done, I hope not far away, I shall then be ready to have it performed.

I heard here the test of L.B.[10] recordings to *Octuor* and *Histoire du soldat.* I wonder why he did not follow the very good cutting of my own European Columbia records. The only explanation for his odd cutting is that he took in various parts of these two works absolutely arbitrary tempis against my indications and against already established tradition. You are right, he used the pedal drum (*H. du soldat*) to ease the job of the percussion; that is, of course, not a solution of the problem. Wrong also—the whole drum's coda, the pitch of the different drums—entirely entangled! I am praying those records would never be published. I spoke to Mr. Gilbert of RCA Victor who understands my worry, but he is the only one in this Company and I am afraid he would be not able to impede the publication of these records of which L.B. is so proud. What an intolerable situation for a living author!

---

about Stravinsky that appeared in 1972, one of these pictures is misleadingly captioned "Historic Encounter." I did not meet or in any way "encounter" Stravinsky at that time. I had been in closer proximity to him during a rehearsal of *Renard* at Hunter College Playhouse on January 13, as well as at rehearsals in Carnegie Hall for the premiere of the Symphony in Three Movements in January 1946. At no time before March 31, 1948, did I present myself to Stravinsky, not even on the day after the *Perséphone* broadcast, when Mark Schubart, Dean at Juilliard, arranged for me to borrow the handwritten score from which Stravinsky had conducted the performance.

[9] Ferdinand Oubradou (b. 1903), who conducted the recorded performance.

[10] Leonard Bernstein.

I heard about Mrs. Tangeman's[11] excellent Jocasta performance, but what can she do alone to save *Oedipus* this fall while under K.'s[12] baton?

Have you heard my *Dumbarton Oaks* records (Keynote Corporation)?[13] Why is it so difficult to get it in retail shops? Can you investigate?[14]

Would be glad to hear from you soon.

All best sincerely,   Igor Stravinsky

P.S. No, the last 8th in the 5th measure after **86** in my Piano Concerto is a G-sharp, only in the next bar comes the G-natural.

My October 11 answer describes a performance of Oedipus Rex *in a Stravinsky concert at City Center as "maudlin," a word he evidently did not know, since he wrote "affecté, sentimental" in the margin. (He also provided the Russian equivalent for my word "fixation.") And on October 18 I sent a report on the Keynote mystery, telling Stravinsky that the first records, issued six weeks before, "were made of pure vinylite, some of which [had] developed boils and cracks. They will be reprocessed with an alloy. . . ." I also tried to explain that the RCA employee's job was to "understand Stravinsky's worry and to sympathize with him," but the logical-minded composer never grasped the reasons for the conflicting positions taken by the public relations and budgeting departments of the same company. His next communication was a telegram:*

---

[11] Four years later, Nell Tangeman sang the part of Mother Goose in the first performance of *The Rake's Progress*. Her husband, Robert Tangeman, wrote to Stravinsky, March 9, 1958: "Robert Craft was in one of my most interesting classes as its most interesting student the first year I taught at Juilliard."

[12] Serge Koussevitzky. Stravinsky wrote to him on March 15, 1948: "Your telegram touched me deeply and made me happy. I have just received words from friends in Boston of the brilliant performance of *Oedipus Rex,* and I am sincerely sorry that I was unable to be there and to thank you in person. But I thank you from here. After much fluctuating and fretting, I have decided not to go to Europe this year. I cannot risk it. The situation is too uneasy, and who can assure us that we can get out in the event of an emergency. . . . This week I conduct the Philharmonic here [Los Angeles] and then am in Washington and all of April in New York."

[13] The Concerto was recorded in New York between April 27 and 30, 1947. John Hammond, president of Keynote, promised test pressings by May 14, but they did not come until late June. (Stravinsky had known Hammond since 1925, when Koussevitzky took the composer to the Hammond house in Gloucester, Massachusetts.) The album was released in early September. On October 3, Stravinsky wrote to David Diamond: "Am delighted you like my *Dumbarton Oaks* records. Are they now on sale, because Alexie Haieff could not get them recently when leaving for Rome." Diamond answered (on October 9) that he had found a copy "at Rabson's." Diamond was the Stravinskys' first guest I met while living in their house in the summer of 1949. "I remember that Friday, June 3, 1949," Diamond wrote to me recently. "Mme Stravinsky's delicious [kulebiaka], . . . the Master as we listened to his music, he conducting quietly. . . ."

[14] On December 8, 1947, Stravinsky wrote to Nicolas Nabokov: "Bring three albums of

October 21, 1947 (8 a.m.)

Many thanks, could you get *Dumbarton Oaks* album for my son handing it over to Arthur Sachs Waldorf Astoria who leaves October 22 for Paris. Greetings.   Igor Stravinsky

I delivered the Dumbarton Oaks *album to Sachs at the Waldorf and described this adventure to Stravinsky on October 24. Sachs, engaged in an extramarital liaison, suspected that I was a private detective and did not remove the chain on the door of his hotel room; I had to pass the recording through the narrow opening.*

My letter also mentions that I had just heard an air-check recording of Leopold Stokowski's attempt to conduct Stravinsky's Symphony in C[15] with the NBC Symphony, in which two flutes (instead of one) had been used at 75, the bassoon solos were impeccably played but in the wrong clef, and the third movement was unrecognizable. Sachs, meanwhile, had telephoned to Stravinsky, who sent the following telegram to me:

October 26, 1947 (7:43 a.m.)

Thousand thanks for *Dumbarton Oaks* records. Will write you next week hoping to finish before that time reorchestration of my *Wind Instrument Symphony.* All best   Igor Stravinsky

On November 1, I wrote inviting him to conduct the new version in a program of my "Chamber Arts Society"[16] in Town Hall, New York. Stravinsky immediately telegraphed a reply to my proposal:

Dumbarton Oaks Concerto, which, so far, has still not arrived here in stores. Tell this to Sasha Schneider, who so zealously defends Keynote."

[15] Air-check recordings were acetate recordings of broadcasts. Hundreds of small companies made them at the time. When Samuel Dushkin telegraphed Stravinsky after hearing Stokowski's broadcast performance of the Symphony in C, the composer answered, on February 23, 1943: "*Mon cher* Samsky: . . . I ask only what anyone could understand in this performance. . . . The first movement—well, he got through that. But with the second, he began to spoil everything (pitilessly dragging in spite of all my verbal instructions and against the evidence of the music itself): the music was deformed because of the insensitivity to tempo that is innate in this man. As for the third movement, this was simply beyond his technique, and instead of going to the source of the problem (rhythmic relationships), he plunged the music into a chaos of disordered sounds. I tell you that by this time my patience was a little tried, and it is not necessary to tell you that although the last movement was less badly presented, this by no means made me forget the torture of the two preceding ones. . . ."

[16] This was founded in New York City in 1947 by Eugene Kassman, brother of the pianist, and me.

November 4, 1947

Washington Concert April fourth. Could conduct *Wind Symphony* your request after Washington. Advise contact Columbia Concerts for arrangement. Two-Piano Concerto recorded in Paris Columbia before war my son and myself try to get them. Glad friends my music not fooled by Broadway music merchants. Greetings.   Igor Stravinsky

The reference to "Broadway music merchants" is explained by a clipping from the Los Angeles Times, *November 9, 1947, which Stravinsky sent later, together with some comments. Headed "A Run of Half Notes," the article, heavily underscored by the composer, says, in part:*

> Igor Stravinsky is "very much disturbed" over reports that he has sold out to the juke boxes. The fact of the matter is that the original version of *Firebird*, from which the Ronde des princesses was drawn to make a popular song, has always been in the public domain in the United States. The only existing American copyright is that of the revised version, to which all rights are held by the Leeds Music Corp., which exercised its privilege to use the material for a popular song. Stravinsky did not write the popular arrangement, known as "Summer Moon," nor did he see it until after it was printed.[17]

On November 19, 1947, Stravinsky wrote to Louise Frey of Columbia Concerts:

Please tell the Chamber Arts Society that I accept the sponsorship and would be glad to conduct my *Wind Instrument Symphony* for nothing provided it does not interfere with my engagements in April, "Invitation to Music" and Pittsburgh, if any.[18] Up to you to arrange the dates.

On November 24, at Hunter College Playhouse, my Society's chamber orchestra concert included the second Brandenburg Concerto and Mozart's Serenade (K. 388), as well as the Dumbarton Oaks *Concerto and* Histoire du soldat. *Evidently some of Stravinsky's friends in the audience reported back to him enthusiastically, since, on December 10, he informed Ralph Hawkes of a promise*

. . . to conduct this Symphony [*Symphonies of Wind Instruments*] on the program of my works in April, when in N.Y. I am doing this gratis to help that

---

[17] Stravinsky sued Leeds for $250,000 on the grounds that "Summer Moon" was "devoid of musical merit" and that Lou Levy, president of Leeds, had remarked in an interview that Stravinsky was "making a bid for juke-box popularity." On July 30, 1948, the *New York Times* published Murray Schumach's detailed account of the suit on the front page.

[18] Neither engagement took place.

young and gifted Robert Craft and by the way to hear myself how it sounds. You will understand that in such a case even Ansermet, who used to be a faithful interpreter of my works, conducting the same piece and preceding me, is out of the question. . . .

Stravinsky's publishers, unaware of the ten-year-old rift between Stravinsky and Ernest Ansermet, had chosen the Swiss conductor to give the premiere of the new version of the Symphonies *(although Ansermet greatly preferred to play the old one, with which he was familiar).*[19] *The composer was angry that he had not been consulted.*

Stravinsky's next letter to me turns down my request to include the Kyrie and Gloria from the Mass in the program with the Symphonies, *although these two movements had already been performed in Boston, on February 26, 1947, under the direction of Irving Fine,*[20] *in an arrangement of the wind parts for two pianos:*

December 10, 1947

Dear Mr. Craft:

Just a short note concerning your April program of my works.

I would prefer that fragments from my Mass yet not finished (I have now completed the Credo) would not be played before the whole work is ready, and that is precisely what I don't know. Before April, after April?—*aucune idée.*

The entire Orchestra material of the newly revised and reorchestrated version of my Wind Instruments Symphony will be available at Boosey & Hawkes in about 10 days. Will you enquire? Bear in mind—it lasts about 9 minutes *only.* The Mass numbers excluded, you have only 20 minutes of the Piano Concerto and 22 or 23 minutes of *Les Noces*—total 51 or 52 minutes. What will you do with the 40 min. missing? Because you told me the concert will last 1½ hour, I suggest to play twice the Wind Symphony with the addition of the Octet and *Dumbarton Oaks* Concerto, which I shall do with pleasure. Do you really intend to come here? This will be nice.

Sincerely,   I. Stravinsky

The composer's next message was a Christmas greeting, forerunner to a gift:

---

[19] When Stravinsky refused Ansermet's request to play the "original version" of the *Symphonies* on his January 31 NBC Symphony broadcast, the composer was inevitably "preceded" in performing the new version. Ansermet wrote to Stravinsky from the Essex House, New York, January 13, 1948: "Mr. Craft has given me to understand that this does not make any difference to him, since he will have the first public performance."

[20] Irving Fine (1914–1962), professor of music at Harvard and later at Brandeis.

[December 1947]

Merry Christmas, dear Mr. Craft. I sent you some days ago for this occasion the summary sketches of *Orpheus* which you will receive probably with some delay.[21] Hope you will like it.

On December 26, New York was paralyzed by the largest snowstorm in its history. I was stranded on a bus in New Jersey and missed the rehearsal of the Piano Concerto. Fortunately, another rehearsal could be arranged for the morning of the day of the concert, which had a considerable success, in spite of the references by Stravinsky in the third paragraph of his next letter to reviews of the Concerto performance sent to him by his friends:

January 5, 1948

Dear Robert Craft,

Many thanks for your telegram and New Year wishes (your letter of Jan. 1 I just received). Glad you have my *Orpheus* and you like it.

As to the April concert settled for the 14th, it seems to me all right. But concerning the program (*Mavra* or String Concerto in D), let me think it over, I shall write you later on. At any case I do not think it is a good idea to perform *Pribaoutki* in this concert, because these three very short pieces will be completely lost in the vicinity of their neighbors. For the chorus of *Les Noces* I always had a number not exceeding the modest figure of 30, sometimes less (24). Are you singing it in English?

The discovery of my Piano Concerto after my own and multiple performances in this country (NY Phil.—twice, Boston—twice, Chicago—twice, Cleveland, Detroit, Philadelphia . . .) twenty-three years ago and at the NY Philharmonic with B. Webster[22] three years ago, as it appears, does not disturb the ignorant press at all. An old story, indeed. Glad you had a personal success with this "intricate" (as always) and "full of barbaric rhythms" (as always) score. How was Miss Kassman in your opinion, and who is she?[23]

I heard about the English *Horizon* of November, but I did not get this issue. Kindly send for my information, although it already causes me a nausea.

Please, give me news about the K.[24] performance of Nabokov's *Elegy*. Nabokov spent here the Christmas week and played me his charming work. Get

---

[21] On January 2, 1948, Stravinsky wrote to Nabokov: "If you see Harold Shapero, ask him whether or not he received my *Orpheus,* which I sent to him as a present. . . . [Vittorio] Rieti and Craft got them and answered me, but not Shapero. . . ." (Original in Russian)

[22] The pianist Beveridge Webster was a close friend of the Stravinsky family from the mid-1930s.

[23] See n. 5 above.

[24] Koussevitzky.

in touch with him, you will not regret. His address is: 1350 Madison Avenue New York 28, NY, ph.: SAcram. 2.5782.

I wrote from Florida on January 21, asking Stravinsky if he still approved of the very fast tempo in the first movement of his Duo Arte piano-roll perform-ance of the Piano Concerto, and proposing a change of program for Town Hall. The composer replied to the second question by telegram:

February 1, 1948 (9:07 a.m.)

22 North Lakeside
Lake Worth
Florida

Danses concertantes preferable but only if you prepare it in order not to lose time with musicians in reading the music during my rehearsals. Greet-ings.   Igor Stravinsky

After conducting concerts in San Francisco on February 12, 13, and 14 and in Mexico on February 27 and 29, Stravinsky flew to Los Angeles on March 2, where my next letter, sent from New York on February 27, awaited him. It con-tained examples of English word-setting by Purcell, and Purcell's Funeral Music for Queen Mary, *a piece that must have impressed Stravinsky, since he made his own copy of it. He telegraphed:*

March 3, 1948

Halmans Agency
119 West 57 Street
New York New York

Accept new dates rehearsals and concerts April 9 to 11.   IS

His next letter contained a clipping from Time *magazine about Ansermet in which the composer had underlined the following lines:*

Between premieres and table-pounding talk with Picasso, Diaghilev, Prokofiev, and Stravinsky ("a man of great culture—and the best businessman I ever knew"[25]), Ansermet mastered the classics—without losing his appetite for the moderns.

Stravinsky wrote again on March 9:

[25] See Stravinsky's second telegram to Ansermet of January 31, 1948, p. 231.

Dear Robert Craft,

Just to thank you for your kind letter of February 27 (also for the previous one from Palm Beach).

Arriving in Washington D.C. on Tuesday, March 30 at 8:25 a.m. Staying there at the Hotel Raleigh.

Will be nice to see you on the same day, a free day, because the rest of the week—working every morning (four rehearsals all together), unless you planned to come later in the week.

Delighted you enjoy reading dictionaries, so do I. I found the other day in a French dictionary the following definition of *sex*: "*Conformation particulière de l'être vivant, qui lui assigne un rôle spécial dans l'acte de génération.*"

OK for the change of dates (rehearsals and concert April 9 to 11)—I wired March 3 to the Halmans Agency, as you asked.

All best,   Igor Stravinsky

I had copied out some of Samuel Johnson's most eccentric definitions. Later I sent Johnson's dictionary itself.

On March 15 Stravinsky completed his Agnus Dei and on March 19 conducted the Los Angeles Philharmonic. He wrote to me a few days before leaving for Washington via Chicago:

Dear Robert Craft:

Since my letter of March 9, some changes have occurred, first—I am arriving in Washington only on March 31 (Hotel Raleigh), then Wystan Auden coming expressly to work with me on his libretto for *Rake's Progress,* very urgent in view of his departure for Europe on April 7.

In spite of all this rush I hope to have time for you too, but want to let you know of all this.

Have you attended the so "reputed" Boston performance of *Oedipus* am curious to know your own reaction?

Sincerely,   Igor Stravinsky

In Washington I accompanied Stravinsky to and from his National Symphony Orchestra rehearsals, to a concert of Mozart chamber music at Dumbarton Oaks on April 1, and to parties and receptions—one of them by the director of the Byzantine collection there, Dr. John Seymour Thatcher, whom I nicknamed "Chicher-Yacher" (after the song "Chicher yacher soberalaya vecher" in Stravinsky's Souvenirs de mon enfance[26]*), a soubriquet that Stravinsky never for-*

---

[26] Composed ca. 1906, rewritten in 1913, these songs were orchestrated between 1929 and 1931 (the first instrumental sketch is found in a notebook following the Capriccio) for an animated cartoon. This specific use was "indicated by the manuscript heading," Stravinsky wrote to Païchadze on March 29, 1931, "but I am not thinking

*got. Following one of Stravinsky's rehearsals, I also was present with him at an
interview, the first of hundreds that I was to hear him give:*

> ... Mr. Stravinsky poured himself a [whiskey] and soda. ... Someone
> suggested he hide the pint of [whiskey] so as not to afford any free adver-
> tising. He obliged, caressing his drink: "My friend," he said meaning-
> fully. ... He admonished the photographer not to photograph him with an
> open mouth. "I look terrible photographed with an open mouth—like a
> tenor. ... I studied under Rimsky-Korsakov. He taught me everything—
> even how to erase. ..." (*George Washington University Hatchet,* May 6,
> 1948)

*I returned to New York, but was back in Washington for the concert on April 4
(Scènes de ballet,* Symphony in Three Movements, Divertimento from *Le
Baiser de la fée, the "Dance, Lullaby, and Finale" from* Firebird). *Meanwhile,
Stravinsky had drafted a program note for the* Symphonies of Wind Instru-
ments, *postdating it April 10, the day before our Town Hall concert:*

> The Wind Instrument Symphony was composed during the season
> 1920–21 in France and thereafter was played very little, mostly by Anser-
> met who performed it last January at NBC. I don't know if there was any
> concert performance in this country before this NBC broadcast.[27]
>
> This work was composed to the memory of Debussy who died in 1918.
> The title "SYMPHONY" given to this short composition must not be taken
> in the usual sense of the word. There are various short sections,
> a kind of litanies in close tempo relations succeeding one another; and
> various instrumental groups (woodwinds and brasses) succeeding one
> another; and some rhythmical dialogues between separate woodwind in-
> struments, such as flute and clarinet.
>
> The whole peculiar structure of this work required a special title. This
> title is very easily rendered in French—*Symphonies* (in plural) *d'instru-
> ments à vent*—but in English we can find only an approximate translation,
> which is *Symphonies of Wind Instruments,* the togetherness of wind in-
> struments.

The next four weeks in New York, as I wrote to a friend, were

> ... the most exciting in my life. I was with Stravinsky every day, early
> morning to late night, at rehearsals for *Orpheus* as well as for our concert. I

---

along such lines anymore and, for practical reasons, therefore we will have to change
the title in the printing." Another letter to Païchadze, April 7, 1932, refers to the proofs
for "Three Songs, Memories of the Youthful Years"—and to the completion of *Otche
Nash* (Pater Noster)—and a letter, July 20, 1932, refers to correcting the orchestra
score of "the children's songs."

[27] The *Symphonies of Wind Instruments* was performed in New York and Philadelphia
in 1924 and 1925 by Stokowski with the Philadelphia Orchestra.

absorbed his talk with Balanchine,[28] Kirstein, and others, accompanied him to the theater and to parties, went with him and Nicolas and Patricia Nabokov to a debate at the Rand School (Mary McCarthy was brilliant), ate multiple-decker sandwiches with the composer at Reuben's, but, chiefly, basked in the man himself, whose energy, alertness, and vivacity left everyone else behind. He dominated not only gatherings of people, but even his physical surroundings. . . . One obstacle was that before meals he obliged me to join him in swallowing large, straight slugs of *eau de ginèvre,* which made rehearsing the Symphony in C, with a scratch orchestra and with the composer sitting directly behind me, difficult indeed.

On Saturday night, April 10, Stravinsky, Balanchine, Kirstein, and I were interviewed by Abram Chasins on radio station WQXR. On the 20th, I went with Stravinsky to watch and hear Balanchine conduct the orchestra in his Tchaikovsky ballet Theme and Variations *(Ballet Theatre, Metropolitan Opera).*[29] *On April 21 I accompanied the Stravinskys to a staged performance of* Oedipus Rex *at Juilliard and on April 27 stayed with Stravinsky in his dressing room before he conducted* Apollo *for Ballet Theatre. The premiere of* Orpheus *took place on April 28, on a program that began with* Renard *and the* Elegy *for solo viola (two ballerinas), and concluded with the Mozart* Symphonie concertante.

Meanwhile, on April 12,[30] the day after our concert in Town Hall, Stravinsky wrote a letter to Virgil Thomson, which was published in the New York Herald-Tribune *on Sunday, April 18:*

Dear Virgil Thomson,

In your review of the concert of my music last Sunday night, in which I took part conducting the first half, you, unfortunately, did not remark upon young Robert Craft's performance of my Capriccio and the Symphony in C. I do not think that you failed to notice the accomplishments of this talented musician, but, I presume, time and space prevented you from writing about it. Yet, he certainly deserves thorough consideration, for his performance was valuable in many, many respects.

Cordially, as always,   Igor Stravinsky

Stravinsky returned to California on May 4, after inviting me to stay with him there. Five days later I conducted Histoire du soldat *in Times Hall (44th Street), and on May 12 I wrote to accept the invitation and to send reading*

---

[28] Stravinsky and Balanchine habitually conversed in Russian, but Maria Tallchief, wife of the choreographer at that time, had begun to insist that he speak English.

[29] My friends in the orchestra thought Balanchine "the most musical conductor we have ever had."

[30] That same day Stravinsky also wrote to his Los Angeles lawyer, Aaron Sapiro: "Yesterday—a very brilliant Town Hall concert. Today—a very prosaic rainy day. . . ."

lists that both Stravinskys had requested. I wrote again on May 18, describing Stokowski's performance of the String Concerto, and on May 30 told of an afternoon spent with Goddard Lieberson[31] of Columbia Records listening to test pressings of Stravinsky's Ode.

The composer's next messages, a telegram and a covering letter, are both dated June 1:

Can you be New York to meet and help my son arriving with wife and baby by plane June 17 at 11 a.m. Air mailing details. Greetings.   Igor Stravinsky

Dear Bob,

Too bad. I had no time at all these last weeks to answer your letter of May 12 and to thank you for the "Concert Hall" album.[32] So I do it now in this short note which will let you know that my son Sviatoslav with his wife and their baby arrive at LaGuardia field on June 17 at 11 a.m., NY time, airplane No. Af-009.

It would be wonderful if you could meet them there and help them at their arrival. Am afraid our friends V. Rieti and S. Dushkin will be not in New York to meet and help them, as they planned to do, the former coming here the next week and the latter—probably in Paris, by now.

Could you also ask Mr. W. E. Brown, the Manager of the Ambassador Hotel, to make a reservation for them, one room with a double bed and a small one for the baby (two years old).

Enclosed a pocket score of my Symphony in C[33] which, as you see, finally arrived from Mainz after four months of traveling.

Don't pay attention to the gossips about Sviatoslav; fortunately I know too well what they are worth and their source.[34]

Thanks again and let me know if it is OK. 100,000 cordialities from both of us.

ISTR

P.S. They will stay till Tuesday June 22 in NY.

---

[31] I had met Lieberson two years before. In 1948 Stravinsky was under contract to RCA, and because of this I was asked to edit the composer's CBS recording of the Ode.

[32] Of Stravinsky's Concertino and Three Pieces for String Quartet.

[33] See Appendix L.

[34] The reference is to Soulima Stravinsky's activities during the Occupation, and in particular to his ambition to give concerts in Germany in 1941; the "sources" were Pierre Suvchinsky, Nicolas Nabokov, and French friends of Stravinsky's. At the end of the war, a U.S. government official gave the composer a letter, found in the files of a Nazi musician, Hans Gebhardt (b. 1895), and dated April 17, 1941. The author was Willy Strecker, who wrote that he had received a request from Soulima Stravinsky to arrange concerts for him in Germany. Strecker asked Gebhardt to reply and explain that this was not possible at present.

I met Soulima Stravinsky and his wife and son on June 17 and, five days later, helped them entrain for California. Meanwhile, a note had come from Mrs. Stravinsky:

June 2, 1948

Dear Bob,

Thank you for your nice letter. I am waiting for the book list. Please write me the next time who is who in "Lions and Shadows," and if Homer Lane really existed. You know everything—that is why I ask *you*. At this moment we are terribly busy and happy with the arrival of Sviatoslav (Soulima, Nini, Svetik— his other nicknames), his wife and the baby. My husband will ask you to help them on their arrival, just to find them a room in the Ambassador and show them the Italian restaurant Maria (on the 52 Str?). I hope they speak almost fluently english and you will enjoy to meet them.

It would be nice if you can come to Hollywood this summer. The Denver concert will be July 23. Before and afterward we are in Hollywood.

With all my best wishes, dear Bob,   Vera Stravinsky

Then Stravinsky wrote:

June 6, 1948

Thank you, dear Bob,—very, very kind of you. Am so glad you can meet Sviatoslav at his arrival.

In saying "Brahms has more feeling than Beethoven" the ridiculous old man[35] seems to be for once right, but beware—*unfortunately* for Brahms and *fortunately* for Beethoven. However, doubtful he, the old man, had exactly that in mind.

Miteleuropulos[36]—I already heard about his charming behavior in *Histoire du soldat*. Disgusting, including his conducting without music.[37] Mass— am also a little bit distrustful as to Westminster Choir or the Washington Cathedral project. You are right in mistrusting the ppppp-fffff technic of this kind of organization.

No more time to write—so long.[38]

Best wishes,   ISTR

---

[35] Koussevitzky. The quotation is from an interview with him in the *Los Angeles Times* that Stravinsky had clipped and enclosed.

[36] Dimitri Mitropoulos (1896–1960) conducted the Minneapolis Symphony Orchestra from 1937 and the New York Philharmonic from 1950 to 1958.

[37] Stravinsky always distrusted conductors who performed from memory.

[38] By 1948, Stravinsky had acquired an extensive vocabulary of such American expressions from orchestra musicians, the cinema, and his reading.

June 24, 1948

Dear Bob,

Today, the evening of Sviatoslav's arrival, we were at the funeral of our best friend, Mrs. Lisa Sokolov, who died from a heart attack two days ago.
    It is terrible.

Affectionately,   ISTR

Lisa Sokolov, wife of the actor Vladimir, was co-owner with Mrs. Stravinsky of La Boutique, an art gallery on La Cienega Boulevard. In February, the Sokolovs had accompanied the Stravinskys to Mexico, where Lisa contracted jaundice. She recovered and was with the Stravinskys in New York in April; her death came unexpectedly. From January 1950 to April 1952, I rented the widower's guest house at 8624 Holloway Drive, a few blocks from the Stravinsky home; the Soulima Stravinskys had lived there from the summer of 1948 to December 1949.
    On July 3, 1948, Stravinsky telegraphed:

Arriving Denver 7:50 a.m. July 20 morning. Rehearsals the following three days. Leaving Denver July 25 evening. Longing to see you. Affectionately, Igor Stravinsky

On July 7 the Stravinskys, Schoenbergs, and Thomas Manns, among numerous other notables (see the Los Angeles Times, *Thursday, July 8), attended a dinner in honor of Alma Mahler-Werfel at the Beverly Hills Hotel. On July 20, the Stravinskys were in Denver, at the Brown Palace Hotel. I was there, too, and in the following days spent many hours with the composer poring over the libretto of* The Rake's Progress; *he had already written the music for much of the first scene. On July 24 we attended a University of Colorado performance of Virgil Thomson's* The Mother of Us All, *and on July 22, a performance of Stravinsky's favorite opera of the time:*

> *July 22.* Saul Caston, now conductor of the Denver Symphony, does not remember me from the Curtis Institute a decade ago. He drives us to Central City for *Così fan tutte,* and, on the way, manages to prise an answer from I.S. as to how he composed *The Rite of Spring:* "My ear was experienced." (Thanks.) (Robert Craft diary)

On July 23 Stravinsky led the Denver Symphony in a concert in Red Rocks, an open-air theater about twenty miles from the city. The program consisted of the Overture to Glinka's Ruslan and Lyudmila, *Tchaikovsky's Second Symphony,*[39]

---

[39] A letter from Païchadze to Stravinsky, April 25, 1939, reveals that the composer had paid the publisher to have the parts extracted for both the first and the second symphonies of Tchaikovsky.

the Capriccio (with the composer's son at the piano), and the Divertimento. The Stravinskys left for California on July 25, and I joined them there a week later, by way of Mexico City. The composer's letter to Ralph Hawkes, August 2, is the first that may show traces of having been written with my assistance, as in the following passage:

. . . In my whole career I have never been so concerned about launching a work [the Mass]. This is why I am so cautious about a possible wrong presentation for the huge NBC radio audience. This is, of course, nothing deprecatory in reference to our friend Ansermet, but even he cannot be aware of my incommunicable intentions. . . .

From New York, on August 16, I thanked my hosts for "every gilded moment" with them. I also enclosed a copy that I had made of Bach's fughetta "Christum wir sollen loben schon," drawing attention to

. . . the entrance on the subdominant in the fifth measure; the 6th-chord on the downbeat of measure 9 and the relation to the same chord in measure 17 (first beat); and the cadence from the diminished chord to the final E major—in a very short piece that begins in D minor!

Stravinsky's next communication consisted of only three lines:

August 30, 1948

Dear Bob,

Can you answer this letter if you have time?
    Thanks 100,000 times for the scrap book which I will send back at my earliest. No answer yet from Hawkes!!

But he wrote again on September 8:

Dear Bob,

Nini will see you in NY next week and discuss with you all details of the Mass premiere on which I shall roughly write you now.
    What you say about Detroit, primarily the absence of a children's Choir and also the fact that they have not yet written me formally, makes a Detroit premiere doubtful. As time is short, other decisions must be made, and here is what it is.
    Between Kirstein's Ballet Society Productions and your Chamber Art Society Concerts I prefer the latter as a strictly musical event. So it would be your production. We will start our program with the Octet conducted by you, followed by Soulima's solos. After the intermission the Choir master presenting

the three Russian Church choruses and finally the Mass conducted by myself. It goes without saying that none of us, neither I nor Soulima, expect any financial remuneration. Should there be any profit (let us hope) it will go toward your musical production fund.

Here is another thought. I am informed that soon things will get going with Petrillo.[40] So I suggest that you see Richard Gilbert of RCA Victor.[41] They ought to be interested to take advantage of the occasion and make records of the already prepared Mass and also to help you with the actual concert of the premiere.

As to Detroit, it can be done later with the "handsome fee," if such it would be without a world premiere.

Try to prepare all dates, Town Hall (last week of February), Westminster or other Choir, Boosey & Hawkes material (hope gratis for premiere); to discuss and settle as much as possible details with Nini to save time.

Glad you are doing *Mavra* (and what else in this your opening concert) and blessings for successful translation by the brother . . . of NN[42] "the Bulwark of Baltimore" and the taming of the brother . . . Ralph Hawkes if he kicks about a $75 translation. Keep me abreast.

Love–kisses,   ISTR

September 13, 1948

Nini arriving this Friday 1 p.m. New York time La Guardia his plane is Air America please fix with Baldwin for afternoon going there directly from air field.

Stravinsky

Soulima came to New York to play Mozart's Concerto K. 503, with the CBS Symphony conducted by Alfredo Antonini. On September 23 Stravinsky wrote to Nicolas Nabokov that "[Soulima] couldn't bring the conductor, Antonini, evidently rather a primitive gentleman, to see any reason for avoiding a Strauss [doubling] of instruments to play Mozart; additional rehearsals would also have been useful." (Original in Russian)

---

[40] James C. Petrillo, president of the Musicians Union, which was on strike against the recording companies.
[41] Richard Gilbert was director of Artists and Repertory at RCA.
[42] Nicolas Nabokov, who was teaching at St. John's College in Annapolis. By "the brother of NN" Stravinsky means Nicolas's cousin, Vladimir, who had been suggested as a possible translator for *Mavra*.

September 25, 1948

Dear Bob,

This is just to inform you about my correspondence re: Mass with this people (am writing Betty [Bean] also). But are you or not in touch with the Westminster Chorus?

All best,   ISTR

[*Enclosure: the carbon copy of a telegram from Stravinsky to Eugene Ormandy, saying that the American premiere of the Mass had already been promised.*]

September 27, 1948

Dear Bob,

Is it too much to ask you to fill up these forms[43] (with Betty if you cannot do it yourself) and send them back for signature. Many thanks.

Love,   ISTR

October 8, 1948

Hallo, Bob,

Yes, am glad to hear from you for I too miss you greatly. Please, do come at Christmas, please please! Please answer YES.

Minna Lederman[44]—On Oct. 3 there was a wire from her: "Working hard on book full cooperation of Rieti Berger Balanchine *Craft* All *feel material about new opera vitally important for book.* Urgently need reply to my questions of Sept. 18. . . ." And here is my answer which I did not wire her: "Air mailed you yesterday (Oct. 3) regret not able collaborate for absolute lack of time. Dont find expedient to speak about my opera before completely finished." So you see, I am in complete agreement with you NOT TO SPEAK AT ALL ABOUT RAKE. You better show her this not wired telegram.

What are the "important things you learned by being in the B & H vicinity"? What happened? Am somewhat troubled.

Very interesting (and important) what you say about Olivier's *Hamlet.* Hope they are coming here.

Nini gave his greatly successful recital (Evening on the Roof on Sept. 27) well packed small hall (Wilshire Ebell Theater) and a very enthusiastic audience and critics. And one week later he took part in a whole Stravinsky program (same place but the big hall) playing with Ingolf Dahl the two-piano concerto and with Sol Babitz the Duo concertant.[45]

---

[43] I.e., to update his curriculum vitae.

[44] Lederman, editor of *Modern Music,* was preparing her book *Stravinsky in the Theatre* (New York: Pellegrini and Cudahy, 1949).

[45] Ingolf Dahl and Sol Babitz were the first of Stravinsky's friends to whom the composer introduced me in the summer of 1948.

My *Rake* makes progress (starting the 2nd scene), but not as fast as Ralph Hawkes wants it.

Love–Kisses,   I Str

P.S. A letter from Charles-Albert Cingria with this "P.S.": *"Ansermet est l'être le plus faux du globe."*

P.S. No. 2. No broadcasts this year for the Boston Symphony. So much the better for composing programs, but the worse for Basler Concerto and also for my and Nini's pockets. Airmailed R. Gilbert asking him to get in touch with Boston to record *Orpheus*. Wonder if Mass will prevent it. Try to see Gilbert and write to me about it. That is important.

October 9, 1948

Dear Bob,

Just to tell you that Richard Gilbert is no longer at RCA Victor. Too bad! I wrote him the other day about the necessity of the *Orpheus* recordings during my performances with the Boston Symphony and received today an answer from a certain Richard A. Mohr[46] (Artists & Repertoire Department) that he thinks a "definite decision could be reached within the next two weeks" by his (Gilbert's) successor, who is not yet named. Am worried. Wonder if the Mass recording still holding. Please check up and advise me quickly (see my last letter of Oct. 8—the P.S.).

In hurry—no time to speak with you about interesting things in your letter to Vera (Oct. 9th) [*sic*] just received.

Houston concert—on January 31. Program not yet discussed (!?) February 1 leaving for NY. Boston rehearsals will start February 7, on Monday as usual.

Affectionately,   ISTR

As Stravinsky's next letter shows, he had not yet changed his mind about Falstaff, *nor did this happen until the early 1950s.*

October 20, 1948

Dear Bob—Greetings!

Heard yesterday Verdi's *Falstaff*—a very discomfortable sensation feeling myself *a poor cretin in what I* am able to give the crowd, sensation which does not exist when *listening to Traviata* or *Trovatore*. Hope will be happier today with *Elexir* [*sic*] *of Love* (Donizetti).

Now expecting news after your visit to RCA Victor Monday.

Love,   ISTR

---

[46] Richard Mohr, the new director of Artists and Repertory at RCA, succeeded Gilbert.

P.S. The lady you often see with Rieti is la Marquise de Casafuerte she is a violinist.

October 28, 1948

Dear Bob,

Enclosed a new nonsense from B. & H. which they probably call *catalogue*. Even as a proof it is not acceptable. In order to avoid writing them a letter with high words which they deserve, please explain them, as you can, their utmost stupidity and neglect. You will be an Angel! Please send me back this "catalogue" with my remarks.

Good news—at last the Petrillo ban lifted. Many thanks for your phone the other day. Will it be possible to record as well my Basler Concerto (13 minutes)?

In a big hurry—going down-town to hear *Don Giovanni*.

Love,   ISTR

This San Francisco Opera performance of Don Giovanni *in the Los Angeles Shrine Auditorium was the first of three that Stravinsky attended. The conductor, Paul Breisach,*[47] *made a good impression, and he became the composer's first choice to conduct* The Rake's Progress. *Breisach died before the opera was completed, however.*

Stravinsky wrote again on November 3, 1948:

Dearest Bob,

Thanks a lot for your nice letter (Sunday–Oct 31).

Am a little bit worried about the fate of my thin sheet of music with a few bars of the Jocasta aria's ending for Nell Tangeman. Did you receive it? How was her performance?[48]

Delighted you are hopeful not only for RCA recording of my Basler Concerto but also they are willing to record *Apollo* too. Provided they agree!

OK with your schedule for my recordings and my Mass rehearsals. Provided R. Shaw[49] will be ready before my starting rehearsals (Feb. 23, 24, 25)!

Just received the published vocal (and when the full?) score of my Mass. As was to be expected, B. & H. disfigured my original (black) negative and

---

[47] Stravinsky had been introduced to Paul Breisach at the home of Eric Zeisl (whose daughter Barbara later married Ronald Schoenberg, the composer's son; she had been tutored in French by Mina Svitalski, governess to Stravinsky's children from 1917). A letter from Willy Strecker to Stravinsky, August 7, 1930, referring to Breisach as a *"sehr gute, bisher Dirigent,"* implies that Stravinsky knew him at that date.

[48] Stravinsky composed a concert ending for Jocasta's aria and sent it to me to give to Mrs. Tangeman for a recital performance in Town Hall.

[49] Robert Shaw (b. 1916), choral director, later conductor of the Atlanta Symphony.

printed under its *Instrumentation*—"Duration: 17 minutes"! Where comes this figure from? My timing was, as you remember, 23 minutes and I recollect (unfortunately too late) I never was asked about it by them. Is it possible to print the right timing in the orchestra score?[50] Please, inquire.

Sorry a healthy lady died from a heart attack listening to a Mitteleuropulos performance of Arnold Schönberg's music. I did not know the 12-tone system were not good for the healthy people neither.[51]

More than glad to meet Evelyn Waugh in February. Delighted he is coming. What a marvel his *Scott-King's Modern Europe!*

Please do write, don't be lazy—write or typewrite, as you want.

Grüss aus Hollywood.   ISTR

November 9, 1948

Dearest Bob,

Your good letter concerning the Milan premiere of my Mass somehow confused me. The discrepancy between the enclosed cables I received a week ago and *Time*'s report seems rather complete.[52] Hawkes and Ansermet suspiciously silent. Is there the key to this riddle? Who, good heavens, provided *Time* reporter with this ridiculous (and useless for the public) information about 17 min., and why?

Better I keep silent and answer by my own performance* with children (am sure Ansermet had female voices) on February 26, 1949, and by my own

---

[50] Stravinsky was obsessed with determining the exact timings of his music, before as well as after he composed it. In the case of the Mass, he calculated the duration from his reading at the piano, which was six minutes longer than any performance that he ever conducted. Although he admitted that performances inevitably vary in length, he continued to plan programs based on the timings given in his scores. When his late-in-life recordings lopped minutes from these earlier estimates, he would write in the score, parenthetically: "Today I do it in . . ." and give his latest timing, as if the discrepancy required an explanation. No less peculiar was his inability to foresee the approximate amount of music still to be composed in a work-in-progress. On February 11, 1955, he wrote to Nicolas Nabokov: "I have composed barely half of *Agon*." Yet only the first two numbers had been composed, and not in final form. Writing again to Nabokov, February 19, 1958, Stravinsky said: "The composition of *Threni* is slowly coming to an end, but the length of what is already composed is not so great as Bob tells you, as he always tends to exaggerate." At that time, however, and though Stravinsky estimated that the piece would not last more than twenty minutes, it was already considerably longer. On March 27, he wrote to Nabokov: "The *Threni* are finished. The music lasts longer than I had thought, 35, not 20 minutes."

[51] An elderly woman had died of a heart attack at a New York Philharmonic Friday matinee subscription concert during Mitropoulos's performance of Schoenberg's Five Pieces for Orchestra (which, of course, are not "12-tone").

[52] *Time* had reported that Ansermet conducted the Mass on the stage of La Scala with a chorus of a hundred and twenty.

records, provided RCA Victor not impressed *Time*'s jeer and not renounced to record it.

If possible, send me two or three clippings of the *Time* issue and its date.

Love,   ISTR

*of 23 minutes duration

One of the cables enclosed was from the Sovrintendente of La Scala, Antonio Ghiringhelli, who still held that position three years later when La Scala provided the chorus and orchestra for the Venice premiere of The Rake's Progress.

November 10, 1948

Dearest Bob,

Please check up immediately at Boosey & Hawkes *whether orchestra parts of my Piano Concerto* (with winds) which were made here by my copyist and after which I conducted the work with B. Webster at piano in Carnegie Hall, Febr. 1 and 2, 1945, *are still at B. & H.*

A year ago I sold B. & H. this my material. Now I need it in Boston for my performances of it with Soulima. So, please, see to it that B. & H. deliver to the Boston Symphony *precisely this corrected set* and not an old one (from Galaxy[53] or London-Paris) which will undoubtedly cause me much trouble.[54]

Thank you a million.

Love,   ISTR

On November 12, Stravinsky wrote to Ralph Hawkes:

. . . I continue to receive from everywhere (England, Switzerland, France) very enthusiastic letters about my Mass heard in the broadcast from Milan. From everybody except Ansermet. . . . I do not approve this La Scala performance. . . . This large opera-house was no place to present an absolutely liturgical piece of chamber music proportions. . . .

At Boosey & Hawkes in New York, I was shown a letter from Ansermet to Erwin Stein, the firm's principal editor, saying that some hissing was heard in Milan and explaining that "I can teach the chorus pitches, but, after years of Aida, *not the whole style of singing a motet." The letter also quoted a phrase from a review by Domenico de' Paoli: "A work of humility and submission and diabolical pride."*

---

[53] Galaxy Music Corporation, the New York branch of the Edition Russe de Musique. On June 25, 1945, Stravinsky wrote to Koussevitzky: "Dear Sergei Alexandrovich, I have just finished my new *Firebird* ballet suite. . . . Galaxy paid an advance of $1,000 in January 1940, the last and only payment received from them."

[54] A note in Stravinsky's archives reads: "Piano Concerto orch. score and parts; Ralph Hawkes took it for revision and publication May 1, 1948, NY City."

November 27, 1948

Dearest Bob,

How to thank you for Lorenzo da Ponte's Memoires. Exceedingly happy to have it. Thanks also for your Kingston Nov 24 letter. No time to answer these days: Nov 29 & 30—Ralph Hawkes visit, Dec. 1 & 2—Poulenc, Bernac, Dec 3—Ald. Huxley.

Today only to complain: a very bad mistake in my Mass—Kyrie, No. 9, 4th measure, Discanti, on the 3rd beat a sharp is missing at F (see Trumpet) in the full score. In the vocal score also, which makes it worse because London editor put (in plus) a precaution at F. Really too bad!

Finally—a letter from Ansermet (from Geneva). A very empty letter, indeed, excuses for writing so late, not a word, of course, about his personal reaction to the work (neither about that of the public). The only thing he said was: "singers, instrumentalists, and the conductor did their best" (*sic*). How very kind of them![55] All best for you and *Mavra* (who will be the tenor, Hess?).[56]

Love,   ISTR

Ansermet had written to Stravinsky on November 20 with questions about the pitches at several places in the Mass, and Stravinsky answered in the margin of the letter. On November 30 I sent copies that I had made of Purcell's catches. But the next letter to me was from Mrs. Stravinsky:

December 1948

We were terribly busy all this last time. People was (or were?) coming in and out. Sometimes boring, sometimes amusing. We saw the whole Orchestre de Paris, a lunch with them in a French restaurant, garden party with them, organized by the French Consul, with Charlie Chaplin, the Robinsons and movie people. Poulenc and Bernac had lunch in our garden. Sun and strawberries in December! Their concert had a continental style, like a concert in a *salon de la princesse de Polignac*. We also had a party for Charles Bayly.[57]

Finally, we were so tired that we went with Nini *et* Françoise for two days to Palm Springs and I send you a picture. Also to have a little rest before Ralph Hawkes' arrival. Huxleys are here now, but he has bronchitis and teeth troubles, so we did not see them.

The composer wrote shortly thereafter:

---

[55] See Stravinsky's answer to Ansermet, November 27, 1948, on p. 232.

[56] On November 29, 1948, I conducted a concert performance of *Mavra* at the Y.M.H.A., 92nd Street and Lexington Avenue. William Hess had sung Eumolpus in *Perséphone* in Stravinsky's January 1947 broadcast, but Robert Harmon was the tenor in *Mavra*. He had sung the role of Oedipus at Juilliard in April 1948.

[57] Stravinsky had met Charles Beyly, a descendant of Henri Beyle (Stendhal), in 1935, when the composer and Samuel Dushkin gave a recital in Denver.

December 4, 1948

Greetings, dearest Bob,

Have a letter from Mr. Mohr and yours of Nov. 30 and your books—*The Steps of Humility*[58] and the *Sewanee Review*[59]—many, many thanks. When will I only have time to read all this. Just finished to read P. Valéry's remarkable *Faust*. Is it translated? You must read it.[60]

Orpheus—of course it would be a suicide to rehearse and record it in one four-hour session. So tell Mr. Mohr that I agree for Feb. 22 but need another date (Feb. 23 or 24) to let the musicians and myself do the job in more human conditions. *Danses concertantes* (19 minutes) was recorded a year ago in 2 three hours sessions, the same for Divertimento (23 minutes), and everybody agreed that it was a *tour de force* on my part to do it in such a short time.[61]

Mass—that is quite different, because we will use the last rehearsal (Feb. 25) of our February 26 concert. O.K. But what can I put on the sixth side? Mr. Mohr suggests one or two of my a cappella choruses. I suppose Pater Noster and Ave Maria will not exceed 4'25", so let us go ahead. By the way, in what language will it be sung? It is my feeling that the original Russian text must be used, this text being printed in Latin letters. Please airmail me an immediate reply on this. No more time except for

Love,   ISTR

Please explain all this to Mr. Mohr—have no time to typewrite for him a new letter.

Played what is composed of *Rake* to Ralph Hawkes—he is enthusiastic about it. I told him I heard in July a very good performance of *Così fan tutte* in Center [Central] City, Colorado, and we conceived the project to give the world premiere-preview *there*. Am sure of your reaction to this.

December 14, 1948

Dearest Bob,

Received your letters (Dec. 10 & 11)—will answer in a few days (Auden—a good idea).[62] Maybe the Mass—twice?

Read the inclosure and tell him (Gary Graffman)[63] I have absolutely no

---

[58] Bernard of Clairvaux's classic, in Latin with facing English, in a recent edition by Harvard University Press.

[59] This issue contained Eliot's "Poe and Valéry."

[60] In 1958 Stravinsky wrote a preface to a volume of Valéry's plays that included *Mon Faust*.

[61] Stravinsky recorded *Danses concertantes* and Divertimento in Hollywood in 1947, but a recording of *Danses concertantes,* made at a performance in the Museum of Modern Art by Vladimir Golschmann, had already been issued by Mary Howard Recordings, 37 East 49th Street, and Stravinsky was intent on quashing this because "the tempi are often too nervous and unsteady." (Letter to Nabokov, October 5, 1943)

[62] I had suggested that Auden read three of his new poems in our February 26 concert.

[63] The second half of Graffman's program began with Stravinsky's Serenade and two Rachmaninov preludes. Stravinsky wrote in the margin: "What a neighborhood!"

time to correspond. Why not use my records? He surely can ask Arthur Berger[64] to let him hear them. . . . Just typewriting these last words I received his [Graffman's] records which I immediately played. Not bad the whole thing, but why not follow my records? The degree of closeness to my records—as follows: 4th part, 2nd part, 1st part, and 3d part (too turbulent indeed).*

OK for *Orpheus* recording on Feb. 22 in two 3½ hour sessions.

Will check Mass's timing again; afraid you are right—we made a wrong estimation of the duration of each number and in plus we made a wrong total (with wrong figures). What a shame! Ansermet will be delighted with R. [alph] H. [awkes] triumphant. What a shame!

Love, ISTR

*and too *fast*

December 15, 1948

Dearest Bob,

Enclosed a letter from Merle Armitage[65] which I ask you to send back after reading it. Try, if possible, to bring up the matter with this, although nice, but rather unreliable man.

Nini is writing to you. Please send us the photos of the *Harpers Bazar* [*sic*] (Zizi[66] & family) impossible to find the right issue. What is the date of it?

Pre-Christmas love, ISTR

[Here is] my answer to Mr. Eric Walter White about Beethoven (his article* in *Tempo*, Summer 1948—London)

1—It is wrong that I do not like Beethoven.

2—The reference to Ramuz is rather a weak argument, because Ramuz, who was not a musician, meant what he said about it quite differently.

3—After all, is it really obligatory for any composer to like Beethoven and what exactly does it mean? Also, I would like to know the reason Mr. White is so interested in it. What will be his reaction if I tell him, for example, that I cheer the influence of Beethoven in Harold Shapero's work, and that I feel more than a little bit embarrassed by his influence in Romain Rolland's work.   ISTR

*"Stravinsky as a Writer"

The next letter, of December 22, 1948, was from Mrs. Stravinsky:

---

[64] Arthur Berger (b. 1912), composer, critic for the *New York Herald-Tribune*.

[65] Merle Armitage, the book designer, had published a volume of articles about Stravinsky in 1935, and was bringing out a revised edition which Stravinsky described to Nabokov in a letter of December 15, 1949: "The general appearance of the book, with its importunate, cheap, and provincial illustrations and vignettes, is as unacceptable as the price. . . ." (Original in Russian)

[66] John Stravinsky, the composer's grandson (b. 1945).

Dear Bob,

I send you all the beginnings of my letters to you. The collage I made for you of the opening of the Philharmonic season to show you what kind of menagerie we have here and how S. is getting inspired by reading the dictionary.

I make miles and miles now before Christmas and my legs are now "strictly ornamental."

I wish you a nice Christmas time and the most successful 1949. It would be so nice to have you here for Christmas but I understand that you are very busy. We ordered for you some books but I am afraid that they will not get there on time. Forgive us the delay, but you will have it one day. It is Mozart, *Letters*.

Give our best wishes and greetings to your parents and your sisters. And our love to yourself

Vera Stravinsky

Mrs. Stravinsky's collage-menagerie was made up of clippings from the society pages of the Los Angeles Times. *"Making miles" was her way of saying that she had been driving a great deal. "Strictly ornamental" was Aldous Huxley's expression, coined by him after he had been apprehended by the Beverly Hills Police on suspicion of vagrancy while walking in a residential neighborhood in that village of many automobiles and few pedestrians. The three volumes of Mozart's letters, sacred books for Stravinsky, arrived on December 25.*

Stravinsky's next note was inscribed on the carbon copy of a telegram he had sent to Richard Mohr:

December 26, 1948

Mr. Mohr in his letter to A. Sapiro asked for Manhattan Center, gave only 3½ hours for each session, did not speak about a good rest between, and finally mentioned Mass recording on 4 *sides* (*sic*). Is it a trick or a mistake, I wonder. Please clear it up dear Bob. We missed you yesterday.

Love,   ISTR

Stravinsky's next three messages were telegraphed:

December 28, 1948

Town Hall, 113 West 43 St.[67]
NYC

Dearest Bob,

If you have time please call collect after the concert. Longing to have immediate news. Needless to say how intensely we are with you.   The four Stravinskys

---

[67] Stravinsky had failed to notice that the concert took place in the Y.M.H.A. Auditorium and not in Town Hall.

January 2, 1949

Perplexed your silence after *Mavra* performance wired you Tuesday Town Hall. Best wishes for success asking to phone me collect. Have you ever received it?   Stravinsky

January 3, 1949

Happy your *Mavra* success. Congratulations. Delighted Auden participation and your program suggestion. Just yesterday wired Richard Mohr my acceptance to record Mass on five sides with Russian choruses on the sixth one. Now if these choruses eliminated wonder how to cut Mass without harm otherwise than if five sides.   Igor Stravinsky

Each movement of the Mass was composed to fit a record side (four to five minutes).

The next two envelopes from Wetherly Drive contained one request and two clippings:

January 5, 1949

Dear Bob,

Please send me the program of your Dec. 29 concert (*Mavra*).

Love,   ISTR

[Enclosure: a photograph from the Los Angeles Times, *Tuesday morning, January 5, 1949, of five-year-old Marjoe Gortner signing a marriage license after performing a wedding ceremony. Stravinsky has written in the upper margin: "for the Evelyn Waugh collection, ISTR."]*

[Enclosure: In an article from the Los Angeles Times, *Friday, January 7, 1949, entitled "Orchestra Welcomed After Month's Rest," Stravinsky underlined the following sentence: "David Diamond's Symphony No. 4 had a bit of rough going in meeting the competition of Mozart's masterpiece [the Sinfonia concertante in E-flat major] and Tchaikovsky's overwhelming 'Pathétique' Symphony which ended the concert, though Mr. Wallenstein, with his usual discretion in programming, gave it first chance on the auditors' approval and spared no pains in giving the new work an illuminating performance."]*

January 10, 1949
[Telegram]

Received yours, sixth and eighth. Airmailing you Betty's letter just received strictly confidential. Wired her there is no question to renounce Mass premiere February 26.   Igor Stravinsky

January 10, 1949

Dearest Bob:

Just sent you a Night Letter; herewith are copies of the letters from Betty Bean and Andrew Tietjen [of Boosey & Hawkes].

Why did Tietjen write to Betty Bean (who understands nothing about technical matters) and not to you? What a shrewd people all those Betties & Boosies! Unhealthy atmosphere indeed.

Have you obtained with Tietjen the number of soprano boys to get a good balance? I guess you did. Otherwise you would not write me (Jan. 8) "Notified both, Mohr and B. Bean." Please reassure me.

LOVE LOVE LOVE,   ISTR

[Enclosures: (a) copy of a letter from Betty Bean regarding the forthcoming recording of the Mass; (b) program of a Carnegie Hall piano recital by Gary Graffman and letter from him inviting Stravinsky to attend.]

My letter of January 11 discusses the distribution of singers in the Mass, cites a report by J. S. Bach on the numbers of sopranos, altos, tenors, and basses in his Leipzig churches, and goes on to say that "polyphonic singing is unknown here. The soprano line, the only one that anyone expects to hear, is always overloaded. . . . Furthermore, plainsong has been shoe-horned into $\frac{4}{4}$ hymn-tunes."

January 22, 1949

Dearest Bob,

Yours Jan. 20 at hand. Thanks.

We will stay in Houston at Rice Hotel. Ave Maria and Pater Noster without Credo under [Robert] Shaw's baton perfectly all right.

Have no opinion concerning your *Renard* project. We will speak about it Feb. 3. However, I think Octet more fitting.

Do your best in casting Ballet Society musicians for Victor recording of *Orpheus*. I trust you will.

Nini's concerts very successful. He called yesterday from San Francisco. We will see him today at 11 p.m.

Happy to see you soon.

Love,   ISTR

The Stravinskys left Los Angeles for Houston on the Sunset *Limited the morning of January 23, 1949, and Soulima Stravinsky wrote to me the same day:*

Dearest Bob,

. . . Father will play *Rake's* score to you and Auden, *nobody* else. So keep it in absolute secret, don't tell anybody (even Rieti or Nabokov . . .).

In the Rice Hotel, on the afternoon of January 25, Stravinsky gave an interview to Hubert Roussel:

> "Neo-classicism?" he scoffed. "A label that means nothing whatever. I will show you where you should put it"—and he gave his derrière a firm pat. . . . "The only dance company in the United States is Lincoln Kirstein's Ballet Society in New York and it doesn't travel. The Ballet Russe? Many excellent dancers, but the music. . . . Who could make music with that orchestra? At the premiere [of *Danses concertantes*], they did it right. Never since. I heard it in Los Angeles recently and I took my head in my hands." (*Houston Post,* January 26, 1949)

On January 31 Stravinsky conducted the Houston Symphony in a concert consisting of the String Concerto, Apollo, *the Divertimento, and the* Firebird Suite.
     The Stravinskys arrived in New York on February 3, dined with Auden and myself that night, with Evelyn Waugh on the next, and on February 6 went by train to Boston (the Sheraton Hotel), always with me in tow. Stravinsky conducted the Boston Symphony Orchestra in Sanders Theater, Cambridge, on February 10 (Ode, Capriccio, String Concerto, Divertimento); in Symphony Hall, Boston, on February 15 and 16 (Ode, Capriccio, String Concerto, Orpheus); *Carnegie Hall, New York, on February 16 and 19 (same program as in Boston); in the Mosque Theater in Newark on February 17; and in the Brooklyn Academy of Music on February 18 (Overture to* Ruslan and Lyudmila, *Tchaikovsky's Second Symphony, the Capriccio, and the Divertimento). On February 22 and 23 he recorded* Orpheus *in Manhattan Center (West 34th Street), not with the Boston Symphony but with an orchestra of free-lance musicians. On February 24 and 25, he recorded his Mass and the new Latin versions of the* Pater Noster *and* Ave Maria *in Town Hall. At the performance of the Mass on February 26, Dame Edith and Sir Osbert Sitwell sat in a loge with Mrs. Stravinsky, and on March 5 Dame Edith wrote to the composer:*

> My brother and I will remember the evening of the 26th of February for the rest of our lives. . . . It was a great privilege to us to meet the man whom we know to be the greatest living creator in any of the arts.

The Brown Palace
Denver, Colorado
March 9, 1949

O Bob!

Two (2) wonderful concerts: Urbana[68]

---

[68] The concert, March 3, consisted of the String Concerto, *Apollo,* the Suite from *Pul-*

Denver[69]

See you June 1, 1949. Going home.

Love, kisses,   ISTR & family

June 1 had been set as the date on which I would begin to work regularly for Stravinsky, as well as to live in his house.

March 13, 1949

Dearest Bob,

I'll write you soon. 1000 thanks for yours of March 8.

Love Kisses Love Love,   I Str

[*Enclosure: Address of Victoria Ocampo.*[70]]

March 16, 1949

Dearest Bob,

I wanted you to know that I received the following wire from Olin Downes: "Will you join with other outstanding American musicians in sending the following cable of greetings to Dimitri Shostakovich:[71] 'We are delighted to learn of your forthcoming visit to the United States and welcome you as one of the outstanding composers of the world. Music is an international language and

---

cinella, and the Piano Concerto. On the afternoon of March 2, Stravinsky gave a press conference at the Urbana-Lincoln Hotel.

[69] Stravinsky conducted the Denver Symphony on March 8 in the String Concerto, *Apollo,* the Piano Concerto, and the *Firebird* Suite.

[70] Argentine writer and publisher (1890–1979). She and Stravinsky were close friends, and he had asked me to invite her to narrate the part of Perséphone.

[71] On March 6, the U.S. State Department had granted permission for Shostakovich and twenty-one other delegates from Russia and the Soviet bloc to attend a peace conference in New York. On March 13, Stravinsky received the telegram from Downes. Stravinsky's telegram was published in the world press on March 18, and the next day, the Soviet paper *Red Star* condemned the composer as a "traitor and enemy of our fatherland. . . ." This, too, appeared in the world press and among other reactions divided Americans into supporters either of Shostakovich or of Stravinsky. On March 25 reporters converged on Stravinsky in his Beverly Hills home and asked if he would debate with Shostakovich on political or artistic issues. Stravinsky replied: "How can you talk to them? They are not free. There is no discussion possible with people who are not free." On March 27, Shostakovich played a piano transcription of the second movement from his Fifth Symphony in Madison Square Garden. Nicolas Nabokov, who was in the audience of 19,000, asked Shostakovich from the floor if he were in agreement with "the denunciation by Soviet critics of the works of Stravinsky, Hindemith, and Schoenberg." Shostakovich replied: "I am in accord with the denunciation of Stravinsky and Hindemith . . . and Schoenberg, too."

your visit will serve to symbolize the bond which music can create among all peoples. We welcome your visit also in the hope that this kind of cultural interchange can aid understanding among our peoples and thereby make possible an enduring peace.' Please wire me. . . .   Olin Downes."[72]

The old fool! (*Rake's Progress*)

I answered him as follows:

Regret not to be able to join welcomers of Soviet artists coming this country. But all my ethic and esthetic convictions oppose such gesture.   Igor Stravinsky.

Love, kisses,   I Stravinsky

March 22, 1949

Bob dearest,

Yours of March 18 at hand. Strangely enough—not a word in it about your good wire you sent me the very same day. From this wire I only learned that Olin Downes [gave] my answer (to him) to the A [ssociated] P [ress]. Do you know where it appeared?

Best thanks to Auden for his touching interest in this unsuccessful, alas, trial.[73] Of course Sapiro will retake it on a more solid basis this time. He is now in Chicago for a week, where he met R. Hawkes. The latter, stubborn as ever,

---

[72] Olin Downes (1886–1955), music critic for the *New York Times* from 1924 to 1955, was not held in high regard by Stravinsky, who wrote to Nabokov on December 15, 1949: "I heard Prokofiev's Sixth Symphony. Nothing justifies its dullness and it shows neither esthetic nor technical novelty. This is clear to everyone except comrade Olin Downes." (Original in Russian)

[73] See p. 334 and n. 17. On March 9 Los Angeles Judge Joseph Vickers ruled that Stravinsky's lawyer, Harold Fendler, should have brought the action against the Leeds Music Corp. "not on tort but on contract." According to the *Los Angeles Daily News*, February 18, 1949, F. F. Spielman had testified that the Leeds Music Corp. hired him to make the arrangement published as "Summer Moon." He added: "I didn't want to use hillbilly harmonics [*sic*] because I wanted to come as close as possible to the master's feelings in the music." Max Fink, attorney for Leeds, contended that the company was trying to "bridge the gap" between the classical and the popular. "Experts say it's a void, not a gap," Judge Vickers answered. The experts were Eric Zeisl, who said that "in the classical world, Igor Stravinsky is the greatest living composer," and Ingolf Dahl, who said that "Stravinsky is the greatest contribution to modern musical culture." The newspaper report continues: "The judge grabbed his dictionary, read definitions of harmonics, started on 'harmonica,' but ruled this out as irrelevant and immaterial. 'I did my best, as I thought it would be shown to Stravinsky whom I hope to meet sometime,' [Spielman said] . . . . [He] da-daed a few bars [from his and Stravinsky's versions] . . . . 'By the way,' the Judge said, 'you've never sung professionally, have you?' . . . The arranger admitted he changed the . . . harmonies . . . but [claimed] that his adaptation still conveyed the same feelings."

proved once more to be the less accommodating person Sapiro met in his life. Disgusting!

Wise arrangement for singers and instruments of *Les Noces*.

Ocampo! She planned to be again in NY only at Christmas and, as she cannot dispose of her Argentine money in USA, I wonder if she will be able to come here at all. Who else, in this case, could be the lady narrator? Madeleine Milhaud?[74] But she too cannot do it for nothing.

Second act of *Rake* not yet started—till now am really overloaded by so many things in hand. Just made a final Latin version of Pater Noster and Ave Maria, now in B. & H. hands. Sent them a corrected score of my Mass with a newly photographed cover and the Basler Concerto with all my corrections in the full score and in the newly engraved pages (additional measures) I received from London. Lots of things, as you see.

Vera busy with flowers in the garden after her cold (two weeks). Nini-Françoise for two days out (pleasure trip). Milene-André every day here. André very helpful (correspondence).

Thanks also for clippings (in your previous letter). Convey my sincerest sympathy to Harold Shapero.[75] His contact with the "pompiers" of the "radicalism" of the "20s" is as symptomatic as this old, very old story.

And what about Dr. Koussevitzky and his enthusiasm for Shostakovich?

I Stravinsky

[Enclosure: A clipping from the Los Angeles Times, *Tuesday, March 22, 1949, of Stravinsky's corrections of that newspaper's misprinted version of his telegram to Olin Downes: "I said it was against 'my ethic and esthetic convictions.' Ethic was omitted." The quoted phrase is underlined by Stravinsky.]*

April 2, 1949

Dearest Bob!

100,000 thanks for your wonderful Feb. 28 letter.

Please send me your full score *Perséphone* (Nini's letter). Almost finished the corrections on the proofs.

Please ask Nabokov to write me a letter.

Love, kisses,   ISTR

[Enclosure: A letter to Stravinsky from Vladimir Horowitz, President of an Artists Committee for Koussevitzky: "Dear Mr. Stravinsky: . . . You belong to the group of artists who have had the great privilege of working with Dr. Kousse-

---

[74] Wife of the composer Darius Milhaud.

[75] I later sent Stravinsky another clipping, from the *New York Herald-Tribune*, March 13, 1949, which reported that while Henry Cowell was reminiscing about the radical music of the 1920s in one New York concert hall, in another one, Harold Shapero's "half-hour long sonata in F minor was being hissed . . . for daring to attempt a rein-

vitzky. . . ." (*Underlined thus in red and blue, by Stravinsky, who has written in the margin: "!!!!!!????? How polite!"*)]

Stravinsky's next note was attached to the new Boosey & Hawkes catalogue of his works:

April 5, 1949

Dear Bob,

Have you or Betty my old *corrected* copy?—Because the new copies I just received are absolutely identical to the old stuff full of mistakes. Please answer, I am disturbed.

Love,   ISTR

At Town Hall on April 19 I conducted Les Noces, Histoire du soldat, *and the Pastorale for violin and wind quartet, on a program with Bartók's Sonata for Two Pianos and Percussion. I wrote two days later, mentioning a letter from Lincoln Kirstein stating that Baba the Turk was modeled on Christian Bérard. Stravinsky answered:*

April 27, 1949

Dearest Bob:

So glad to have at last your letter. 2 days ago—a very nice one from E. Berman, who was enchanted by your concert. But there never was a call from Nabokov.

Am enthusiastic about your November program (*Perséphone, Pulcinella* & Violin Concerto).

Heard Robert Shaw's Mass performance by transcription.—Chorus from beginning to the end covered by instruments. A very bad balance, indeed, and annoying lack of reasonable stoppages between phrases. Disappointed.

When exactly will you do this Mass? Don't know the date.

Everybody here eager to see you soon, very soon. Hope not later than June 1. Yes.

Love, kisses by millions,   ISTR

What a wonderful book that of Bernard de Clairvaux.

[*Enclosure: A clipping from the* Los Angeles Times, *the "Music Mail Box," Sunday, April 24, 1949, containing a letter from Arnold Schoenberg. The editor has divided Schoenberg's text into three parts, subtitling the second "Very Characteristic," and the third "Happened Rather Often." Stravinsky has circled these editorial headings in red pencil, added question marks, and inscribed the whole: "Most idiotic titles I read in my life."*]

statement of late Beethoven principles, instead of adding to musical evolution with new sonorities." Stravinsky underlined the statement in red and blue pencil.

May 5, 1949

Dear Bob,

Enclosed a sample of Hawkes's stupid and mean behavior, as well as my answer to him.

Thank you so much for yours of Tuesday a.m.:

1. [The orchestra] parts of *Babel* are probably with Nathan Shilkret.[76] Where is he now? . . .
2. Your brilliant article I had already read in *Musical America*. Has it been printed in full there? . . . I doubt it. Remember—June 1st.

Love,   ISTR

[*Enclosure: A copy of Ralph Hawkes's letter to Aaron Sapiro—"I am disturbed to hear that Mr. Strawinsky authorized the free performance of his works recently at the Town Hall concert given by Robert Craft at which Mr. Strawinsky also conducted. . . ."—and of Stravinsky's reply: ". . . Your grievances against me seem to be rather directed against Robert Craft who, though not a 'star' (God forbid), is regarded by myself and by many pure bred and really 'éprouvés' musicians as a most excellent, reliable and devoted interpreter of my music. This of course is, unfortunately, and very often, the contrary of 'big money.' . . ."*]

May 10, 1949

Dearest Bob,

How very consolatory an attitude like yours (the only one possible) in front of this ludicrous celebration of an old, experienced megalomaniac[77] by his fellow-travellers of the younger generation.

Eagerly expecting news after this Saturday's Mass performance.

Much thanks for this letter.

League of Composers condition (in buying tickets for your concert) is no surprise to me. I know them well already twenty-five years; it is why I never accepted their membership.

Does really exist a portrait of me by Shagal [*sic*] ? I never heard about it.[78]

Praising *Mavra* reprise with Monteverdi's *Orfeo*.

Love, love,   ISTR

[*Enclosure: An article about Sartre and Existentialism.*]

---

[76] Nathaniel Shilkret (b. 1895), Hollywood film composer who had commissioned Stravinsky, Schoenberg, and other composers to contribute short pieces to a *Genesis* Suite.
[77] Serge Koussevitzky.
[78] Chagall's portrait of Stravinsky, dated 1949, had been drawn from memory and a photograph.

The League of Composers had agreed to buy a block of tickets on condition that a work by another composer besides Stravinsky be included in the program. My performance of the Mass on Saturday, May 14, was at the McMillin Theater, Columbia University, on a program with Stepan Wolpe's Palestinian Songs, and some pieces by John Cage for prepared piano.

May 29, 1949
[Telegram]

Happy to see you, dearest Bob. Please come directly Wetherly Drive for early breakfast with us.   Stravinsky

I arrived in Los Angeles in the evening of June 1. Throughout the summer I kept a diary, portions of which are published in Stravinsky in Pictures and Documents. *I returned to New York on September 7, and Stravinsky wrote on the 10th:*

Dearest Bob:

Happy to have your wire—1000 thanks. Provided you keep your word and *we see you here in Dec.*

Enclosed an incredible letter from an unknown old idiot after the *Orpheus* broadcast. Send it back for my collection, please.

Expecting now your letters.

Much love,   ISTR

[Enclosure: An article from the Los Angeles Times, *Wednesday, September 7, 1949, in which Stravinsky underlined the following comment on a speech by Koussevitzky at the Beverly Hills Hotel: "As is always the case with great men, his message was concise and asked no quarter . . . for it had a warning, too. . . . All those here must work together and without thought of personal gain or aggrandizement. . . ."]*

Stravinsky's next message was written in the margins of his carbon copy of a letter to Boosey & Hawkes regarding their receipt of the score of Act Two, Scene 1, of The Rake's Progress:

September 13, 1949[79]

Dearest Bob,

Please see to it that they send me a *decent acknowledgement.* Also, inquire at AMP if Hugo Winter[80] is coming here (he wanted to be here Sept. 10). Just received yours of Sept. 11. How disgusting!

---

[79] This letter and those of September 18 and 20 were addressed to me c/o Boosey & Hawkes, 30 West 57th Street, New York.

[80] Hugo Winter, publisher and friend of Stravinsky and Webern for many years.

[*Enclosure: An announcement from the* Los Angeles Times *of a forthcoming performance of* Pierrot Lunaire *at Evenings on the Roof, and an article from the same newspaper, Sunday, September 13, 1949, about Koussevitzky's twenty-five years with the Boston Symphony.*]

September 18, 1949

Bob dearest,

Hope we'll hear from you (your impressions) before Nini's arrival.[81] How was it? Eager to know. L.K.[82]

ISTR

[*Enclosure: The* Los Angeles Times *review of* Living Music of the Americas *by Lazare Saminsky and* Music to My Ears *by Deems Taylor. These books, targets of Stravinsky's scorn, received the* Los Angeles Times's *highest accolades.*]

The "impressions" that Stravinsky wanted before his son's return to California were of a ballet that Soulima Stravinsky had "pieced together . . . from his favorite Scarlatti sonatas for a revised version of choreographer Antonia Cobos' . . . The Mute Wife." (Time, *September 26, 1949) Stravinsky was anxious about the Scarlatti, fearing that comparisons would be made with* Pulcinella. *At the last minute, he telephoned me asking for a report. I wrote that the*

choreography has some good points, hampered by idiotic costumes; the choice of the sonatas is discriminating, and the orchestrations are simple. The question is whether these keyboard pieces can be transferred so literally, since the even and continuous keyboard line is difficult to reproduce in the strings unless they are reapportioned. . . .

The reviews condemned the performances as "ragged." As Time *noted, "About the most charitable word the critics could find . . . was 'drab.'" Nevertheless, it was after this engagement—according to Vera Stravinsky's diary (October 5)—that the Soulima Stravinskys decided to move to New York.*

On September 20 Stravinsky sent me a clipping of Leonard Lyons's column in the Daily News, New York, *September 17, 1949, on which he had marked and queried the following statement: ". . . Judy Garland promised to return to New York for a Carnegie Hall appearance, and recite Stravinsky's* Perséphone *with Leonard Bernstein conducting the New York Philharmonic. . . ."*

October 7, 1949

Dearest Bobsky,

Today just this: By now you must have received the *Pribaoutki* material I sent you one week ago via B & H. Please acknowledge!

---

[81] I.e., before Soulima's return to California.

[82] Not L[incoln] K[irstein], but L[ove] K[isses].

Paul Sacher (of Basel) was here the other day—on his way (from Mexico) to New York. He will be there on October 10 at the Ambassador Hotel. I promised him to write you—he wanted so much to get in touch with you and to come at your concert. He leaves New York on October 26.

Let us hear from you very soon.

ISTR

[*Enclosure: The* Los Angeles Times *obituary for Richard Strauss, September 25, 1949.*]

On October 7, Ralph Hawkes wrote to Stravinsky inquiring about the Praeludium and Canon announced for my October 22 concert. Stravinsky replied on October 17.

. . . The "Preludium" is a 1-minute piece of music which I composed in 1937 at the request of a certain Reichman (jazz leader). . . . I made a piano solo reduction of this music which Bob wanted to be played at his concerts. As to the "Hommage à Nadia Boulanger," this is just a very short canon (just a few measures) which I sent her for her birthday and I did not intend to be publicly performed. I know Bob liked it very much. That is why he will probably try to squeeze it between other short vocal pieces in one of his programs. . . .

Stravinsky's next two communications were telegrams:

October 13, 1949

Dearest Bob,

What a joy for us you're coming here December hope for a long time. Soulimas definitely leaving Hollywood for New York mid December. Affectionately, Stravinsky

October 21, 1949

Care Mrs. Frederick Hyde
Morningside Dr., NY

Happy birthday to you dearest Bob, wishing you heartily a very very successful concert, all the Booseys, Beans, Betties, and Hawkes notwithstanding. Love kisses,   Stravinskys

My Town Hall program on October 22 included Stravinsky's Renard *and Suite No. 1 for Small Orchestra, Mozart's Clarinet Concerto (with Reginald Kell), Falla's Harpsichord Concerto (with Sylvia Marlowe), and Berg's Chamber Concerto (with Isidore Cohen, violin, and Robert Cornman, piano). The Praeludium and Canon were not performed because the program was already too long. After the concert, I dined with Auden, then flew to Los Angeles for four days.*

October 29, 1949
[Telegram]

Delighted record *Orpheus* with Victor orchestra. Finishing my Boston Symphony tour in New York Feb. 19. Can start rehearsals next day. Try arrange Basler concerto too.   Igor Stravinsky

November 14, 1949
[Telegram]

Glad am able to give you good news. Money at your disposal. Where to send it and to whom exactly? Shall write my bank on hearing from you. Affectionately, Stravinsky

In an effort to raise money for my Perséphone *performance,*[83] *Stravinsky wrote on November 1, 1949, to Arthur Sachs, then in Faugeras, Corrèzes, asking him for*

. . . the sum of $900.00 to permit me to keep my word *vis-à-vis de Robert Craft, qui a organisé ce concert en tablant sur mon aide.* . . . I will reimburse you from the receipts, or, if these are not sufficient, I will make up the balance by giving one of my manuscripts to you. . . .

Sachs answered on November 9: "I accept your proposition cheerfully, in the way that you have indicated," but he inquired if the gift would be tax-deductible. Stravinsky replied on November 15 that his lawyer, Aaron Sapiro, had given assurances that the money for the purchase of the manuscript could be deducted. The letter went on to say that

. . . *Hollywood est devenue si mort* . . . because the economic prosperity created by the war has given place to a *marasme* . . . and because all of the most interesting people whom we knew and frequented had come to California only as a temporary residence and have now returned to Europe. . . .

November 15, 1949

Here is the check dear Bob, just received yours of Sat. Nov. 12.

Will write you today or tomorrow—*tell me your address in NY*—have your dates but not the address.

Love,   ISTR

---

[83] Even though Stravinsky had a reputation for haggling about fees, he was thoughtful in trying to procure better wages for his associates. Here, for example, is an excerpt

November 15, 1949

Dear Bob,

1. I sent you this morning a check of $900.00 because Sachs answered me in the way we all expected—i.e., he will transfer the money to my bank. One point has yet to be cleared in order to help Sachs get the most out of his gesture in relation with his taxes. That point is: are you or are you not a "Non-Profit Organization"? Just let me know by return mail.

2. I hope that you are not too worried regarding your Carnegie Hall-*Perséphone* finances. Have you to wait until your father returns to get that money from him? Or did you find some other way out?

3. If Auden leaves on March 13 I figure I shall arrive in New York on the 10th in order to be able to work with him the 11th and 12th. This means that we will have to start from here on March 1, so that we do not get too tired driving too fast across the country.[84]

4. If you think that my bad terms with Toscanini would not become an obstacle to his consent to invite you, I am quite ready to write him.[85] I'd like you to suggest the best argumentation to convince him: your talent as a young American conductor or my wish of having a good and correct performance of my Symphony.

5. As to the concert planned for April, I think it is better not to start worrying about it until you are through with *Perséphone*.

6. Of course if you have the possibility to do *Pulcinella* I will be delighted.

Please answer me immediately before going to New York.

Love to you dearest Bob,   ISTR

---

from a letter to Nicolas Nabokov, June 16, 1958: "Hamburg refused Bob the 750 dollars and offered him only 500. With this money he'll pay for the trip, Venice to Hamburg, and rehearse [for two weeks]. These conditions seem to me very poor. . . . Is it possible that [Rolf] Liebermann did not agree, or else that you forgot to ask him about it? I told Bob that I would write to you. If this does not bring results, I will pay the 250 dollars to him from my own pocket, since he is doing this Hamburg business only for me, and, what is more, he would be paying for it."

[84] The Stravinskys and I had planned to drive from Los Angeles to New York, where he had conducting engagements. We left Hollywood on February 6, 1950, stayed in El Centro, Las Cruces, Del Rio, Beaumont, New Orleans, Tallahassee, Sarasota, Miami, Daytona, Charleston, Williamsburg, and Philadelphia, arriving in New York on February 18.

[85] Stravinsky's desire to have his Symphony in C performed was such that he went to the length of writing to Toscanini, November 28, 1949: "Dear Maestro, . . . I would like to recommend to you a very talented, cultured, young musician and conductor, Mr. Robert Craft. . . . He knows my music so well . . . he is able to handle any of my works. . . ."

November 20, 1949
[Telegram]

Carnegie Hall NY

Our thoughts are with you ever and especially this evening. Convey best wishes to Zorina[86] and Hess. Please call us collect after concert. With love,   The Stravinskys and Max[87]

The complete Pulcinella, *Four Etudes for Orchestra, and* Zvezdoliki *had not been performed before in America, and Harold Schonberg's review of the concert, in the* New York Sun, *November 22, 1949, emphasized these novelties in programming, while acclaiming* Perséphone *to be one of Stravinsky's greatest works.*

November 28, 1949

Dearest Bob,

I have your 3 letters (Nov. 22, 25, 26).

Poor Bob! . . . I prefer to talk all this over with you when you will be here again.[88] Today only these lines.

1. Enclosed a copy of my letter to Toscanini to which I shall await the reply anxiously.[89]
2. What happened with Berger?[90] He was the only friendly critic of your activities; and what is your trouble with him? I'd like to know all about it as soon as possible.
3. RCA Victor. Tell Mohr that it is imperative to make *Apollo* and Basler Concerto in one single album as the cutting of the Concerto in four sides would be a real mutilation to which I shall never agree. It is also imperative I do it before others would.
4. If you don't need the *Pribaoutki* material anymore, please bring it with you or send it back.
5. The Mass yesterday with Byrnes[91] was very good and attracted a good public.

---

[86] After hearing Vera Zorina in Honegger's *Jeanne d'Arc au bûcher* at Hollywood Bowl in the summer of 1949, I invited her to narrate the part of Perséphone.

[87] Dr. Maximilian Edel, Stravinsky's physician for many years.

[88] I had lost $3,000 on this concert.

[89] Toscanini did not reply.

[90] Berger had criticized the performances in the *New York Herald-Tribune*, saying that they should have had more rehearsal time. This was true, but the dress rehearsal had had to be canceled because Toscanini commandeered the hall for a recording session.

[91] Harold Byrnes, German-born conductor who lived in Hollywood during the war.

Goldberg very elogious,[92] the others not mean, but stupid. What a terrible hall that Wilshire Ebell Theatre! . . . All the voices sounded like behind the curtain.

6. Did you go to the premiere of the City Center *Firebird* with new setting of Balanchine? He called me up yesterday night just while I was at the Mass and I received a very enthusiastic telegram from Berman. That's all for today.

Love

[*Enclosure: An article from the* Los Angeles Times, *November 25, 1949: "Britten Conducts Own and Purcell's Works."*[93]]

Stravinsky wrote on December 2 to thank Arthur Sachs:[94]

. . . All musical enterprises here are in an ultraprecarious situation at the moment. Only large and long-established organizations, with their committees, patrons and subscriptions, can survive. And, unfortunately, these societies offer only the most popular repertory: *Ceci nous oblige à compter sur le sacrifice héroïque de quelques apôtres du genre de Robert Craft.* . . .

On December 8, I conducted the New York City Ballet in Orpheus, *but without a rehearsal in which to correct a serious mistake. As I wrote to Stravinsky on December 6, "Barzin conducts the music between 77 and 79 not as equal measures but as three-eighths and two-eighths."*

Then, on December 10, I conducted Mavra *and Monteverdi's* Orfeo *in Town Hall, and a few days later disbanded my New York concert organization and boarded a bus for Los Angeles, where Stravinsky presented me with the most marvelous gift I have ever received, a copy of his only unpublished major*

---

[92] This was one of Stravinsky's favorite words.

[93] On December 15, 1949, Stravinsky wrote to Nicolas Nabokov: "All week here I've listened to aunt Britten and uncle Pears. . . . Britten himself makes quite a favorable impression as a performer, especially at the piano." (Original in Russian)

[94] On December 2, Stravinsky also wrote to Vittorio Rieti, who had expressed disappointment in my last two concerts. Stravinsky asked for a frank explanation: *"J'aime trop Bob et apprécie trop votre jugement pour ne pas m'inquiéter de cette phrase énigmatique."* Rieti replied on December 6 that "the tempi . . . seemed to me rigorously exact and how you want them. On this point one cannot do better. But *Renard* was dead. *Pulcinella* and *Perséphone* were better." The letter continued: *"Pour terminer, un interminable Concerto de Alban Berg . . . les gens s'en allaient, pendant que Craft continuait à battre la mesure de Berg. . . . Craft s'est arreté, on n'a jamais compris si le morceau de Berg était fini. . . ."* (Rieti did not know the Berg Concerto?) Stravinsky never mentioned this letter to me, but his relationship with Rieti became more distant.

composition, the Dialogue Between Joy and Reason.[95] *This marked not an end but the beginning of my twenty-three years of friendship and collaboration with Igor Stravinsky.*

---

[95] The text is that of an early French translation (No. 244, Bibliothèque Nationale, Paris) of Petrarch's most popular Latin verse dialogue (from *De Remedii utriusque fortunae,* 1358). After Stravinsky and Dushkin played the Duo concertant in the Salle Pleyel on December 8, 1932, C.-A. Cingria wrote to the composer: "... What a triumph, the Cantilène, Eglogue I, Eglogue II! The music is wise ... in a way achieved by no one before.... It is Petrarch. You have captured the equivalence. Set Petrarch in the same voice as that of the Duo concertant. Perhaps that title would even make people understand.... How good the music was! It absorbs me entirely.... My *Pétrarque* has been published. It will be sent to you from Lausanne."

Stravinsky read Cingria's *Pétrarque* in January 1933, and was profoundly influenced by it, particularly the passage, which he underscored, beginning: *"Le lyrisme n'existe pas sans règles.... autrement ce n'est qu'une faculté de lyrisme et elle existe partout."* Stravinsky was also influenced by the book's musical examples, which range from a sestina by Arnault Daniel (the manuscript, in the Ambrosiana, was transcribed, in lozenge notes, by Johann B. Beck) to pieces by Bardi, Caccini, and Gluck. Cingria inscribed Stravinsky's copy of the book: *"A l'auteur du Duo concertant qui va si bien avec Pétrarque...."*

Stravinsky conceived the *Dialogue* for two voices and a keyboard instrument, but interrupted it to compose *Perséphone,* which was commissioned. The text, as transcribed by Cingria, is as follows:

Joye   *Je me délecte en chant et en cordes d'instruments.*
Raison *Mieux te serait réjouir en larmes et en soupirs, car il vaut mieux par pleurs venir en joye que par joye venir en pleurs et en gémissements.*
J.   *Je suis adoulci et réconforté par la doulceur de la musique.*
R.   *L'araignée ainsi que disent les naturiens, adoulcit devant qu'elle morde, et le barbier devant qu'il frappe, et l'oiseleur devant qu'il preygne, et le larron devant qu'il tue ... et plusieurs hommes ne sont terribles, ne dangereux que quand ils se monstrent estre bien doulx ...*
J.   *Je m'esjouis en chant.*
R.   *Garde-toi car il est écrit que pleur est fin de joye et que souvent l'esprit s'esjouit devant la ruine.*
J.   *Je chante doulcement.*
R.   *Tu ne sais ci c'est le dernier chant. Le cygne chante doulcement à l'eure de sa mort. Nous trouvons que plus de gens sont morts de joye que de tristesse et que plusieurs sont morts en chantant ...*

this is an exact copy.
(made by myself)
of a *Dialogue between*
JOY and REASON — my
Sketches in a book
bound in pig skin $9\frac{1}{2}$ by $7\frac{1}{4}$
under № 46 of the cata-
logue of my manuscripts

I St
Hollywood
July 21/49

Merry Christmas
to dearest Bob (CRAFT)

I St
Dec 25/49

Dialogue de la
Joye et de la Raison

J. - Je me délecte en chant et en sons
d'instruments.

R. - Mieux te serait réjouir en larmes
et en soupirs, car il vaut mieux
pas pleurs réduis en joye que pas
joye venir en pleurs et en gémisse-
ment.

J. - Je suis adoulci et réconforté par la
douleur de la musique.

R. - L'araignée, aussi qui ourdit les matériaux,
adouloit devant qu'elle morde, et le
barbier devant qu'il frappe, et l'
oiseleur devant qu'il preygne, et le
larron devant qu'il tue...
et plusieurs hommes ne sont terrible,
ni dangereux que quand ilz se monstrent estre bien doux.

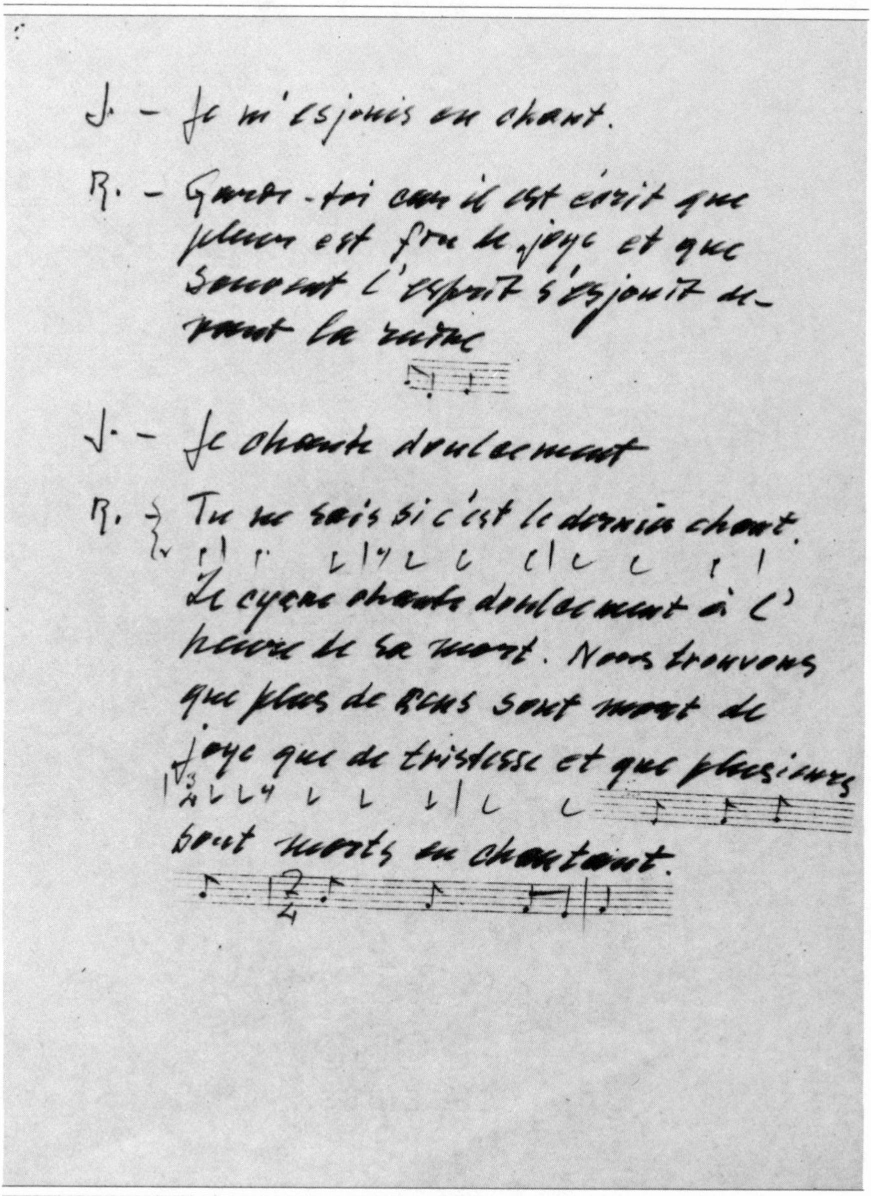

J. — Je m'esjouis au chant.

R. — Garde-toi car il est écrit que pleurer est fin de joye et que souvent l'esprit s'esjouit devant la ruine

J. — Je chante doulcement

R. — Tu ne sais si c'est le dernier chant. Le cygne chante doulcement à l'heure de sa mort. Nous trouvons que plus de gens sont mort de joye que de tristesse et que plusieurs sont morts en chantant.

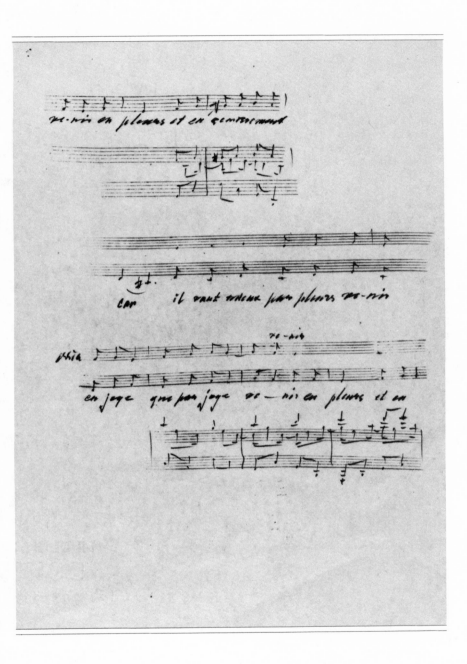

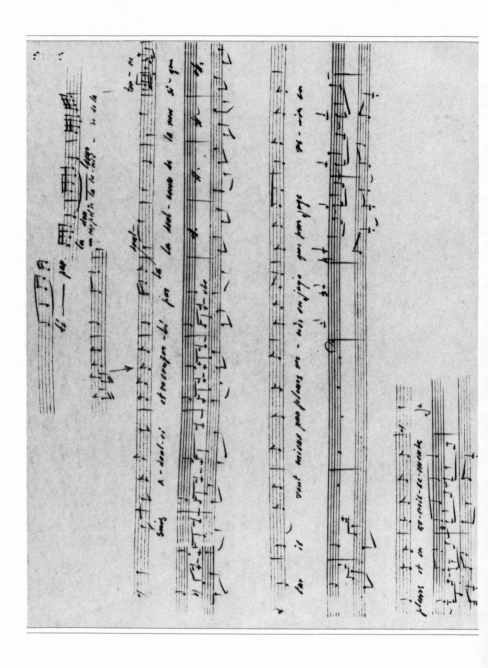

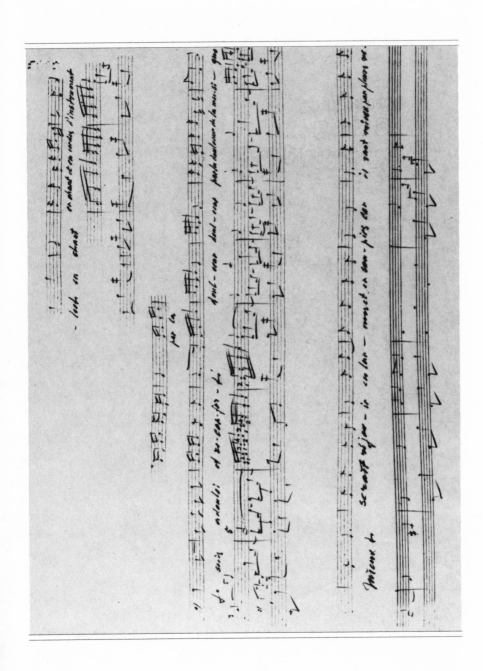

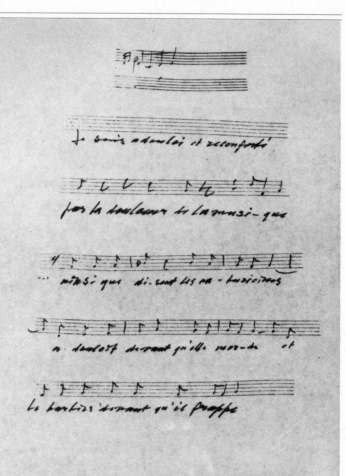

APPENDIXES

APPENDIX A

Family Documents

CERTIFICATE
[*of Catherine's birth*]

By decree of HIS IMPERIAL HIGHNESS, The Minsk Church Registry hereby certifies, through the undersigned and the Church stamp, that the Birth Register of the Gorval Church, in the Rechitsky district, contains the following entry, No. 2, for the year 1881: Born on January twelfth,[1] and christened on the fifteenth, of the year one thousand eight hundred and eighty-one, Ekaterina, the daughter of the College Counselor Gavril Trofimovich Nossenko,[2] who is temporarily residing on the estate of the Kholodovsky heirs, in Gorval, in the Rechitsky district of the Minsk Church, and of his legal wife, Maria Kirilovna. The Godparents were: Architectural Consultant Alexander Frantsevich Yelachich[3] and Ekaterina Kirilovna, widow of Medical Doctor Lazarenko. The christening was performed by Father Stepan Teravsky, with the assistance of Psalm-reader Fyodor Golubovich. The duty fee was paid. Minsk District, December 2, 1882.

Parish member	Archpriest Nikanor Smolich
Secretary	A. Lukashchevich
Clerk	A. Lukashchevich

November 17, 1942[4]

CERTIFICATE

[French stamp]

By decree of HIS IMPERIAL HIGHNESS, the St. Petersburg Ecclesiastic Registry hereby gives notice of the following entry, No. 128, in the 1882 edition of the Birth Register of the St. Petersburg Marine Nikolaevsky Cathedral of the Epiphany: That, to the Artist of the IMPERIAL St. Petersburg theaters, nobleman Fyodor Ignatievich Stravinsky, and to his legal wife, Anna Kirilovna, both of whom are Orthodox and first-married, a son, Igor, was born on the fifth, and christened on the twenty-ninth of June, in the year one thousand eight hundred and eighty-two. The Godparents were: Lieutenant-Colonel Alexander Ignatievich Stravinsky and nobleman's wife Olga Ignatievna Dimaevskaya. The duty fee has been paid, March 3, 1892. Registry Representative—Father N. Drozdov. Secretary—Kamchatov. Chief of Department—Al. Briantsev / M.P. /

[1] All dates on the certificates are Old Style.

[2] Other documents indicate that Catherine Stravinsky's father was also a doctor for the Kiev City Prison System.

[3] "My favorite uncle," Stravinsky wrote on a photograph of A. F. Yelachich. He married Sofya, the sister of Stravinsky's mother, and his eldest son, Nikolai, married the daughter of the poet Jakov Polonsky.

[4] On this date Soulima Stravinsky presented this certificate to the Occupation authorities in Paris as proof of his Aryan descent.

I, the undersigned, attest to the validity of this copy and the original, which were presented to me, Ivan Ivanovich Strumilo, as the St. Petersburg Notary of the Baron Nikolai Alexandrovich Rausch von Traubenberg, in his office in the Admiralty sector, on the Nevsky Prospect No. 12, by Fyodor Ignatievich Stravinsky, gentleman by birth, resident of the Kazansky sector, on the Kryukov Canal, House No. 6. At the time of my signing this copy and the original, there were no additional underlined words or peculiarities of any other kind; this copy was certified for presentation to an educational institution on March 7, 1892, according to register No. 2242.

Notary   Ivan Strumilo

[*Notary's stamp*]

CERTIFICATE

June 30, 1890. I do hereby certify that Ekaterina Gavrilovna Nossenko, daughter of College Counselor Gavril Trofimovich Nossenko, has been found, upon examination by me, to be completely healthy, suffering from no contagious illness which might prevent her from being accepted to the Institute for Young Ladies, and that she has received her inoculations.[5]

Kiev City Doctor   S. Zaslavine

[*Seal of
Kiev City
Doctor*]

NOTICE

M.V.D. [?]

St. Petersburg
City Office
for
Military Service
May 3, 1903
No. 2373

The St. Petersburg City Office for Military Service informs nobleman Igor Fyodorovich Stravinsky that, if he is at the present time enrolled in an educational institution and would like a postponement for reasons of study, then, in accordance with articles 143 and 145 of . . . he is required to inform this Office accordingly and to present proof of enrollment before August 15, 1903; and if, in addition, Stravinsky is due preferential consideration for reasons of family position, then he must present this Office with appropriate family information before conscriptive action is taken, i.e., before October 15, 1903.

Office Representative   P. Zhukovsky
Clerk   N. O. [signature illegible]

---

[5] Catherine Stravinsky apparently inherited tuberculosis from her mother, who died of the disease at age 35.

MARRIAGE CERTIFICATE

This copy, which was certified in the Office of the St. Petersburg Notary for the Baron Nikolai Alexandrovich Rausch von Traubenberg on May 7, 1892, is based on register No. 2442, and is being given to Mr. Stravinsky on May 20, 1906. . . .

The said Igor Fyodorovich Stravinsky was on this day of January 11, 1906, married in the Novoderevensky Church of the Annunciation, in the district of St. Petersburg, to Ekaterina Gavrilovna Nossenko, daughter of the retired College Counselor, 24 years of age and of Orthodox denomination.

> Father Afanasy Papov
> Psalm-reader Pavel Beliayev

The said Ekaterina Gavrilovna Nossenko was on this day of January 11, 1906, married for the first time, in the Novoderevensky Church of the Annunciation, in the district of St. Petersburg, to Igor Fyodorovich Stravinsky, student of the Imperial University of St. Petersburg.

> Father Afanasy Papov
> Psalm-reader Pavel Beliayev

PASS

The bearer of this pass, a student of the_____class _____of the Faculty of___Law___of the IMPERIAL University of St. Petersburg___Igor Fyodorovich Stravinsky__,__24__years of age, and of ___Orthodox___denomination, is hereby released on holiday to___Kiev and other cities in Russia___until the date of August 20, 1906._____This notice should be returned to the Inspector by the above-stated date.

St. Petersburg,___April 21, 1906.__

> For the Inspector of students
> of the Imperial University of
> St. Petersburg . . .   A. [signature illegible]
>
> Secretary of student affairs . . .   [signature illegible]

In accordance with page 327 of vol. XIV of passport regulations, any individual who is absent from one sector for reasons of travel to another sector must, upon arrival at the place of holiday, notify the local authorities.

Note: Re. item 20 of the regulations governing students of the Imperial Russian Universities. Any student who is not able, for reasons of illness or for any other valid reason, to return from holiday by the indicated date must notify the Inspector accordingly, and not initiate correspondence regarding postponement.

account of births		month, day, year		name of newborn	nicknames, given names, patronymics, and family names of parents, and their denomination
male	*female*	*birth*	*christening*		
I		March 2 1907	April 29 1907	Fyodor	Hereditary nobleman Igor Stravinsky and his legal wife, Ekaterina Gavrilovna, both of Orthodox denomination Archpriest Alexander Preobrazhensky Deacon Konstantin [Portanov?] Psalm-reader Nikolai Petropovlovsky
			(stamp)		
I		Sept. 10 1910	Jan. 8 1911	Sviatoslav	Nobleman Igor Fyodorovich Stravinsky and his legal wife, Ekaterina Gavrilovna, both of Orthodox denomination Father Superior of the Church, Archpriest Sergei Livbimov Deacon Alexander Pobedonostsev
			(stamp)	No. 5 1911 January 11	
	I	Jan. 2 1914	Dec. 3 1914	Maria, after the Saint Mother Maria, whose name day is celebrated on October 29	Nobleman Igor Fyodorovich Stravinsky and his legal wife, Ekaterina Gavrilovna, both of Orthodox denomination
			(stamp)		

The sons' dates are New Style, the daughter's, Old Style.

nicknames, given names, patronymics, and family names of godparents	who performed the christening	signatures of witnesses, if desired
Student of the Imperial University of St. Petersburg, Gury Fyodorovich Stravinsky, and widow of the artist of the Petersburg Imperial Theatres, Anna Kirilovna Stravinskaya	Archpriest Alexander Preobrazhensky with Psalm-reader Dmitri Grechaninov	
Naval Engineer Grigory Pavlovich Beliankin; wife of the Kiev merchant of the 2nd guild Anna Ivanovna Beliankina	Father Alexander Selivanov with Deacon Alexander Pobedonostsev	
Nobleman Yuri Fyodorovich Stravinsky; Fyodor Igorievich Stravinsky; Lyudmila Gavrilovna Beliankina and Anna Mikhailovna Nachaev	Archpriest Sergei G. Orlov and the clergy of the parish	

The authenticity of this excerpt is evidenced by the signature of the clergy and the stamp of the Church. 7/20th of December, 1914 Father Superior of the Geneva Holy Cross Church, Archpriest Sergei G. Orlov
No. 122   Deacon [signature illegible]

CERTIFICATE

Volunteer

Of Reporting For Military Service

(permanent)

[Igor Fyodorovich Stravinsky]_____presented himself for military duty on March 11, 1908, as a volunteer,_____subject to conscription into the army; but upon examination he was declared completely unfit for military service and is thus permanently exempted from said service.

Issued by the St. Petersburg City Office for military service on_____ March 11, 1908 . . .

Representative Office, Colonel . . . [signature illegible]

Clerk . . .   [signature illegible]

January 25 [1911?] [6]

1. Any person who has taken part in the induction process, but who has been recognized as completely unfit for military service, will be given a permanent certificate regarding presentation of himself for military service and his *permanent* exemption from said service (p. 182, No. 1).

2. The certificate regarding reporting for military service is to be presented by those people who have passed the age for military duty, upon the occasion of their marriage or of the entry into civil or social service (pp. 185 and 188).

RELIGIOUS OBJECTS BELONGING TO ME—

IGOR FYODOROVICH STRAVINSKY

1. The Cross behind the Altar
2. The Image of the Resurrection behind the Altar
3. The Holy Shroud of Christ[7]
4. The Image of the Savior "Bright Eyes" . . . right side of iconostasis
5. The Image of the Holy Mother Tenderness . . . left side of iconostasis
6. The Image of John the Baptist . . . right side of iconostasis
7. The Image of St. Panteleimon . . . right side of iconostasis
8. The Image of St. Nikolai the Miracle-Worker . . . left side of iconostasis
9. The Image of St. Sergei Radonezhsky . . . left side of iconostasis
10. The Image of St. Vassily the Great, Grigory the Holy, John the Golden-Haired, and John the Great . . . upper right side of iconostasis
11. The Image of the Holy Men and Women Martyrs . . . above image of St. Panteleimon

---

[6] Stravinsky apparently requested a copy of the document in 1911.

[7] A framed photograph of the Turin Shroud.

12. The Image of the Holy Moscow Metropolitan . . . upper left side of iconos-tasis
13. The Image of Holy Venerable Women . . . above image of St. Sergei Radonezhsky
14. The Image of the Secret Evening . . . above the Holy Gates, tryptich
15. The Image of St. George the Victorious, embroidered in silk in icon-case, under glass
16. The Image of the beheading of John the Baptist, embroidered in silk
17. The Image of the Holy Serafim Sarovsky the Miracle-Worker . . . in icon-case on the left
18. The Image of St. Dmitri Rostov . . . in gilded frame on right wall
19. The Image of the Savior and the Holy Mother in medallions on the Holy Gates
20. The Image of the Holy Mother of the Annunciation and Four Evange-lists, Holy Gates
21. The Image of the Holy Mother of the Annunciation and Four Evange-lists*
22. The Image of the Holy Baptism*
23. The Image of the Holy Ascension*
24. The Image of the Birth of Christ*
25. The Image of the Feast of the Presentation of the Blessed Virgin*
26. The banners
27. Four large wooden candlesticks and a small one
28. A bronze chandelier
29. Priest's robes: white silk
30. Priest's robes: yellow (half of this belongs to O. I. Beliayevaya)
31. Priest's robes: Lenten, violet, of paper
32. Altar robes: white silk
33. Altar robes: violet satin
34. Lectern robes: two yellow ones
35. Canonical robes: white satin
36. Altar coverlets: white silk
37. Altar coverlets: crimson velvet
38. Altar coverlets: violet velvet
39. Altar coverlets: black velvet
40. Altar cloths: white velvet
41. Altar cloths: white silk
42. Altar cloths: black satin
43. Altar cloths: light blue material
44. Cover for desk: light blue material
45. Cover for little table: light blue material
46. Cover for Shroud of Christ: red satin

* Items 21–25 were painted by Theodore and Milene Stravinsky on thick wooden plates which are located on the Sacrificial Altar.

47. Cover for table for blessing bread: crimson and white satin
48. Patens in white silk with embroidered cherubs
49. Patens in black velvet
50. [Illegible] for the Altar: yellow flowers and gold satin

All of the religious objects that I have mentioned in this list were lent temporarily to the Ecumenical parish of Nice on various occasions. I give the parish the right to continue using them as long as the Archpriest Nikolai Podosonov, under whose spiritual leadership the parish was educated, remains its Father Superior.[8] Igor Stravinsky, Voreppe (Isère), May 4, 1932.

---

[8] A letter from Catherine to Igor Stravinsky, November 31, 1931, explains something of the background of this inventory and of the composer's concluding statement. Father Nikolai, the parish priest of the Stravinskys' church in Nice, had been suspended by the Metropolitan Vladimir in Paris, and Catherine urged her husband to come to Nikolai's defense. Catherine wrote that the Metropolitan "is without character. . . . You must write a protest to him, and it must be you, since he has failed to reply to either of my last two letters . . . This is a terrible affair . . . and you will be needing a rest for your nerves, not another test of them. . . . I kiss Vera affectionately, and I hope that she received my letter in Cologne. . . ." In fact, the original of Stravinsky's letter to "his Holiness the Superior" is in Vera's hand: "I have just learned of the Episcopal Council's decision, of November 10 of this year, concerning the religious objects that I and my family lent on a temporary basis to the parish of our church in Nice. I read with much surprise in the [November] resolution: 'due to the fact that a written agreement concerning the temporary loan of these objects to the church was not submitted on time' (is this reason enough to begin appropriating such objects?), 'said objects are to be considered the property of the Nice parish.' I must in good conscience contest this conclusion on the following grounds: 1. I never received an official confirmation that my possessions were only being lent out temporarily, nor did I ask for one, being myself a member of the parish and therefore considering a receipt unnecessary. But this circumstance does not imply that, following my departure from Nice and from the parish there, these objects were to become the property of that parish automatically, without any agreement on my part. 2. The mention of these things in the inventory book of the parish is of no consequence, since this book did not exist at the time, but only a project notebook compiled by the Church watchman. A Council representative entered various remarks in the notebook regarding Church property, one stating that I was not actually donating those objects, but only temporarily lending them. I intended eventually to build a chapel at my home, after which I would want these objects restored for my own use there. This was well known among the parishioners. I have not abandoned my project; indeed, if circumstances work in my favor, I still hope to realize it. 3. I consider it my duty to bring to your attention that the statement in the Nice Council's record of October 8/21 of this year regarding the entry of the list of my possessions in the 'book of inventory' is not entirely proper, because the record of that meeting underwent certain editorial changes during the Council meeting of November 2, at which time the new edition of the record was confirmed by the Council. Hence it is only logical to assume that the record of the first version (i.e., of October 8) need not have been sent to you for confirmation. Having no desire to burden you with

APPENDIX B

Stravinsky's French Citizenship

December 27, 1933. 21 rue Viète, Paris. Writes to M. Jean Chiappe, Prefect of Police, thanking him for his assistance.

January 10, 1934. The Prefecture of Police sends a form listing the documents that Stravinsky must attach to his application—marriage license, proof of three years' residence, etc.

January 11. Writes to the Prefect of Police, Grenoble, for a "statement of character" that must accompany the citizenship application. Stravinsky gives his address as La Vironnière, Voreppe.

January 18. Writes again to Grenoble, giving his address as "care of Mme Ollivier, 21 rue Viète, Paris."

January 19. Nice. A certificate is issued confirming Stravinsky's residence in Nice, October 1924 to October 1931, and a letter is sent from the Ministry of the Interior, Nice, requesting 9 francs for this document.

February 28. André Ribaud, of the Cabinet of the President of the Chamber of Deputies, informs Stravinsky that his dossier has been submitted to the chancery.

May 11. Receives seal and stamp from the chancery.

June 4 (Monday). Becomes a naturalized French citizen. *Excelsior* publishes an article entitled "The Illustrious Composer Stravinsky Becomes French," and a photograph of Stravinsky's head, with the caption "Stravinsky conducting a rehearsal of one of his works at the Opéra last month." Stravinsky has penciled over this: "Myself at the piano at Pleyel in 1925."

Le Journal publishes an interview by Ruth Léon, entitled "A decree of the President of the Republic, affirmed by the keeper of the seal, that Igor Stravinsky has become a French citizen":

> I left Russia long before the war. . . . Why, therefore, since Paris is my intellectual climate, am I so late in taking this new step? It is because of a deep feeling for my motherland, Russia. But my conscience, my Orthodox Faith, and the classical but individual character of my music do not correspond to the collective emotion required today in the music of the Russian people. . . .

June 7. Maison de Santé, 29 avenue Junot (Butte Montmartre). Stravinsky undergoes an appendectomy.

---

expressions of the bitterness I feel at the moral injustice of the actions of my former fellow parishioners, I still cannot restrain myself from saying that I hope you will correct the November resolution peacefully and recognize me as proprietor of my belongings. I will shortly be returning to Paris from travels abroad, and I hope to be able to see you there at that time. Requesting your pastoral blessing, I remain fondly and devotedly yours,   Igor Stravinsky."

June 10. The *Journal Officiel de la République Française* announces Stravinsky's naturalization.

June 11. Mainz. Willy Strecker writes, expressing his pleasure in the visit of Mika, and regretting that she was not permitted to leave Germany with Stravinsky's money.

June 12. Ivan Thiele writes, reminding Stravinsky that he painted his portrait "in Paris, twenty years ago, at the same time that I made the one of Debussy."

June 13. From the publication *Marianne:*

> Events of the week, looking throughout Europe: A meeting between Hitler and Mussolini; the English refuse to pay America; Hitler's representatives come to Paris to protest the publication of a French translation of *Mein Kampf;* Igor Stravinsky, born in Russia, becomes a French citizen. . . .

June 15. Stravinsky is discharged from the Maison de Santé.

June 16. Excelsior publishes a photograph of Stravinsky with his physician, Georges Pascalis, and an article:

> The great musician Stravinsky, operated on eight [*sic;* nine] days ago, was discharged yesterday. "I have two anniversaries,"[1] he told us, smiling. . . . "Twenty-four years ago, to the day, before this operation, I arrived in France.[2] . . . I had long since been attached to France by many things, . . . and by ties both spiritual and intellectual. . . . The French are the greatest Latin people, and my education was Latin. . . . I love the country of my birth, but so much has changed in Russia that I would feel like a foreigner there. . . . Ever since I became conscious of the spiritual life, I could breathe only in France. Every man has two countries, his own and France. . . ."

June 19. Bern. André Ribaud writes that Herriot was responsible for obtaining the citizenship with such speed, but in the margin of Ribaud's letter Stravinsky has penciled: "It was Berthelot and not Herriot who arranged it."

---

[1] The reference is to his fifty-second birthday, June 18, 1934.

[2] I.e., Stravinsky arrived in Paris for *Firebird* rehearsals on June 7, eighteen days before the premiere.

APPENDIX C

PETRUSHKA: *Revisions, Early and Late*

The labor of alteration and improvement which he ex-
pended in giving perfection and polish to his work: he
would have continued to revise and alter with every
new edition.—T.S. Eliot on Ben Jonson

Publishers' royalty statements, among other gauges, indicate that prejudice against the revised version of *Petrushka* is disappearing. The purposes of the present commentary are not to argue the merits of the later score, however, but simply to point out that many of its improvements had already been introduced in approximately the same ways in 1912, and that while writing out the 1947 score, Stravinsky modified some of the most extreme changes that he had worked out in his sketches.

A misconception to be corrected at the outset is that apart from making *Petrushka* accessible to smaller orchestras, Stravinsky revised it with concert, rather than ballet, performances in mind, this because the music is thought to be more "theatrical" in the original. The new version reduces the number of players by only six, and was undertaken during a time when Stravinsky frequently conducted the piece for ballet, while he seldom played more than fragments in concert. *Petrushka* was rewritten because the composer was dissatisfied with and wished to make improvements to its orchestration. Furthermore, he intended the new version to supersede the old one, even suggesting to his publisher that the original be withdrawn. In a letter to Ralph Hawkes, October 12, 1947, Stravinsky wrote: "My new orchestration . . . is a *full orchestra* version, and, in addition, an *improved one,* so I do not really see any reason to reset the old one (undoubtedly less perfect) 'in case [as you say] it is wanted.' "

Shortly after the publication of the full score in 1912 (Russischer Musik Verlag, No. 127), Stravinsky began to make revisions. An errata of 156 items, both large and small, was prepared and eventually supplemented by a number of corrections by an editor, F. H. Schneider, at the time of its printing in 1922. But by June 1914, a "second, corrected edition" of the full score had been prepared, and on the 16th of that month, Nicolas G. Struve wrote to Stravinsky from Berlin, "We have now finished the proofs of the score, but, before we print, it is essential that you examine them, so be good enough to tell us when and where we can send the score to you for proofreading. There will be inquiries about the score, and during the summer there will probably be many.[1]

---

[1] The first inquiry had come in September 1911, from Jan Torzhanowski, ballet master of the Dresden Opera: ". . . At the end of June, in Paris, I saw your ballet *Petrushka. . . .* I do not seem to be able to get your address, and do not know whether, as before, I will get my letter back, which proves how difficult it is to find someone in Russia, even a famous composer. . . . *Petrushka,* in my opinion, would be tremendously successful at the Dresden Opera. . . ." (Warsaw, September 19, 1911; original in Russian)

Finally, we will have to put the *Petrushka* score into a corrected and present-able form." But the war intervened, and the corrected edition was not pub-lished.

Almost every page of Stravinsky's personal copy of the first score contains alterations in pencil and red ink that would multiply the supplemented errata list tenfold. That these were never incorporated in any reprinting is mysterious, though the explanation is probably an economic one. They are not found in the 1947 edition for the reason that Stravinsky's copy of the 1912 score was in Eur-ope and unobtainable at the time that he began the revised score (1945). Errors of oversight, such as the missing cello notes at 1^2 and the next measure, are due to this circumstance, for though Stravinsky had inserted the phrase in his 1912 score, and though the part is complete in the 4-hand piano reduction,[3] he forgot, while writing out the new version, that the phrase had been inadver-tently truncated.

A complete survey of Stravinsky's early changes in the original score is not within the scope of this essay, whose principal aim is to point out that many of the 1947 revisions actually date from 1912. Already at that time, for example, Stravinsky added the first violins to the first oboe part in the second, third, fourth, and sixth measures after **7** and in the corresponding places (at **10**, be-fore **18**, and at **22** and **24**), since the single woodwind is scarcely audible without support. At the corresponding places in the 1947 version, the string music, apart from the violin doubling, has been entirely reworked, with new parts for piano and second horn to clarify the design. As early as 1912, too, Stravinsky corrected a number of editorial errors in the First Tableau that still survive un-corrected in reprinted and pirated editions. The most important of these is his addition of a beam to the triplets in measures 5 and 6 (first violins), and, in the same two measures, the shifting of the basses from the second to the first part of the triplet.

In the original, but not the 1947, score of the Second Tableau, the left hand of the piano part at **54** (**104**) is marked "8" (i.e., 8va bassa), and whether

---

[2] Here the rehearsal numbers in boldface refer to the 1912 version, those in boldface in parentheses to that of 1947.

[3] Stravinsky's notations for the pianola transcription, written on the 4-hand score, are too extensive to be described or even catalogued here, but a facsimile edition would be useful in that these markings provide a guide to emphasis, dynamics, and articulation. (The piano duet of the 1947 version does not indicate the earlier changes.) At the end of 1936, Stravinsky wrote to "My dear, fat, kind friend, Dr. Kall," in Los Angeles, apropos of a stage production of *Petrushka* there, to be choreographed by Theodore Kozlov and conducted by Stravinsky: "Kozlov should immediately get my Columbia records of *Petrushka*. . . . Tell him to check his record-player to see that the pitch of the first measures of the score agrees with piano pitch, for if the pitch of the recording is higher, the tempo will be too quick. This is very important. Also tell him not to pay at-tention to the discrepancy between the tempi in the records and the metronomes in the score, the latter sometimes being misprinted in *Petrushka*. And tell him to be

the omission in the later version is intentional or a slip is unclear.[4] In the first orchestration, Stravinsky seems to have wanted the piano to double the E of the basses and to play the three successive notes of each beat loco. Ernest Ansermet's recording supports this interpretation, an almost certain indication that he was following an early instruction from the composer, since the conductor abominated the revised version, and his performance is in agreement with it only in this particular. Moreover, if the piano were playing in the wrong octave, Ansermet would certainly have detected the error, particularly in music of such transparency and with which he was so familiar (having conducted it more than anyone else). As for the 4-hand piano reduction of the 1912 full score, the first chord of each beat is in the lower octave, while the voicing of the other notes reveals that Stravinsky intended the bassoon music to be more prominent than that of the piano. At the same place in Three Movements from *Petrushka*,[5] the left-hand part resembles the piano part in the 1947 version—but, then, Stravinsky could scarcely have used the lower octave and left the middle register empty.

In the Second Tableau, Stravinsky's corrections of simple mistakes in the 1912 score, not adjusted in pirated editions, include the change from "bouchés" to "con sordini" in the horn parts in the last three measures, and the addition of a beam to the eighth-notes, third beat in the penultimate measure. In the Third Tableau, the final chord was changed to "arco" in 1912 when

---

careful about the metronomic marks in the 4-hand version, since this too is full of errors."

[4] On December 4, 1916, Stravinsky wrote to Gabriel Pierné answering some of his questions concerning this section of the score. The letter suggests that in his earlier years, Stravinsky may have favored more rubato in the performance of his music. It is also worth remembering that even his good friend Pierné, who had conducted the first performance of *Firebird*, could not induce Stravinsky to spend four days away from his work. Here is the full text of the letter: "Very dear friend, Here are the answers you await: 1. The dance of the nurses (at **90**) should be conducted as a subdivided $\frac{3}{2}$. It has always been done this way, which creates the correct rhythmic emphasis. 2. The tempo $\quarternote = 84$ (**53**) is a typographical error and should read $\eighthnote = 84$. 3. The eighth at **53** equals the eighth at **54**. 4. The metronomic indication $\quarternote = 72$ before **56** is also a misprint and should read $\eighthnote = 72$. A rallentando is required not only in the last four eighths of the second measure $\left(\frac{3}{4}\right)$, but also in the final quarter of the third measure before **56**. As for your January concert, I do not think it will be possible for me to attend, let alone to participate. Here is the reason: the performance [of *Les Abeilles*] at the Opéra will take place on January 12, thus I would be obliged to stay in Paris four more days. . . . I cannot do this because of work which I must complete by the end of January. I need every hour, and four days is enormous for me! I had thought that we could arrange to do this concert while I was in Paris. I am very sorry, my dear friend; I would so much have liked to hear you do *Petrushka*. . . . I will bring you the *Firebird* parts. Yours as always, I. Stravinsky."

[5] Stravinsky completed the arrangement in the summer of 1921, but it was not sent to the printer until about May 1922. On June 12, 1922, E. A. Oeberg wrote

Stravinsky also revoiced it, giving quadruple stops to the violins, violas, and cellos, and lowering the bass an octave. The absence of this "arco" in the 1947 version is a proofreading error, since the next entrance of the strings is marked "pizzicato," and since, when he remembered, Stravinsky asked that the chord be played "arco" in his performances.

Many of Stravinsky's early corrections in the Fourth Tableau were never entered in reprinted and pirated scores. Beams are missing from the groups of fives in the two measures before **100**, the basses should play F-sharp on the fifth quarter of the fourth measure of **100**, the first flute's F should be F-sharp in the second measure after **117**, and the C and A are missing in the trombones in the third measure after **119**. In 1912, Stravinsky added celesta, piano, and harp parts in the measure before **122**, parts that were undoubtedly played thereafter in Diaghilev's performances.

Stravinsky deleted the slurs in the bass clarinet part at **130** in 1912, but the elimination of this instrument at (**260**), with its contrasting color and character, is a debatable "improvement." The sketches for this passage in the new version are of interest in that Stravinsky eventually did not follow his drafts but chose a compromise solution, closer to the 1912 score. The composer's mind can be followed in the illustration, as he attempts to avoid the risk of late entrances by the contrabassoon (third staff) and assigns the music to two ordinary bassoons:

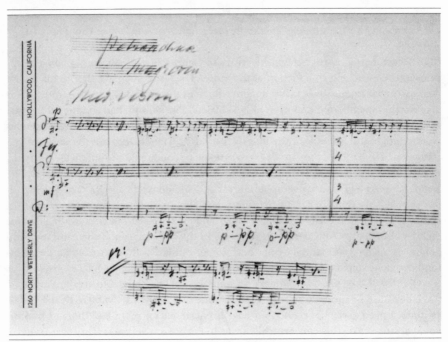

to Stravinsky from Berlin: "You will receive the proofs in two weeks. I beseech you not to delay with it, and let me know whether all three numbers are to be released

On the other hand, the 1947 orchestration of the music at the entrance of the Bear is an incontestable improvement, clarifying the linear construction by strengthening the ascending figures of fives and fours in the first part of the measure. In the original score, a horn, nearly obliterated by a trombone chord, is followed by a bassoon. In 1912 Stravinsky transferred the horn part to the first trombone, but the sharing of the line between trumpet and trombone, in the revised score, is a superior solution.

Ernest Ansermet deprecated the 1947 orchestration of the Wet Nurses' Dance because the original accompaniment of four bassoons playing legato seemed to him more aptly suited to the nurses than the staccato articulation and greater volume, with added trumpets and clarinets, of the later instrumentation. And though the new scoring, with its mixed timbres and crossing voices in real contrapuntal parts, provides richer textures than the simple measured trills of the original, Ansermet, nurtured on the original, may understandably have found the revision less wet nurse–like. Similarly, the addition of triplets— in a clarinet, then in flutes, and, finally, in horns—from the end of **190** to **192** (six measures before **101** in the 1912 score) stresses the pulsation, as do the scale-like passages replacing measured trills in the second measure after **192** (**101**).

A major alteration occurs at (**167**) **88**, where Stravinsky evades the messy doubling of strings and winds of the original by confining the sixteenths to the woodwinds, the eighths to piano and horns. The composer's experience as a conductor may account for this change. Having mentioned this, one should add that the failure to preserve other aspects of his performance practices is regrettable; even the bowings that he added during rehearsals were not incorporated in either of the published scores.[6] For only one instance, he always instructed the first violins at (**175**) **92** to phrase the measure in three groups of two beats, and to begin the second measure with an up-bow, followed by a down-bow on the second beat, an up-bow on the third (and fourth), a down-bow on the fifth, and an up-bow on the sixth.

As for the discrepancies between the revised version as published and Stravinsky's sketches for it, two examples must suffice. First, his draft for the section at (**184**) (four measures before **98**), shows that he wished to strengthen the F-sharp on the third beat, yet the final score, in which the principal revision is the addition of sixteenth-note figuration, does not accomplish this. Second, at

---

together. Or would it be better to do each one separately? . . . I am just back from Dresden, where I had to see Rachmaninov. . . ." The Three Movements were published in November 1922, and Stravinsky received his copy in Berlin, while awaiting the arrival of his mother from Petrograd.

[6] A study of Stravinsky's articulation markings is urgently needed, especially since some of his own definitions are misleading. Thus he wrote to Otmar Nussio, conductor of the Swiss-Italian Radio Orchestra in Lugano: "The sign ♪ or ♪̂ indicates a clean entrance (not quite an accent, but a secco entrance on the note). Once the note sounds, it is to be sustained, just as the pedal sustains a note played on the piano." In practice, however, Stravinsky always asked for a sharp edge to a note marked ♪ ,

(**22** to **28**) **12** to **16**—one of the passages altered most radically in the 1947 score—Stravinsky's first sketch for the new flute-piccolo figure proposes a six-note pattern for the four-note one, and eighth-notes for triplets. He must finally have decided, however, that this change was too remote from the *Petrushka* with which audiences were already familiar.

In April 1932, Tonfilm, Berlin, opened negotiations with Stravinsky to record twenty minutes of *Petrushka* for a soundtrack, but nothing came of the proposal.[7] Then in January 1956 he received an offer of $10,000 to make a tape of slightly less than fifteen minutes of the music for synchronization with an animated cartoon. On January 16 and 18 Ned Hertzstam and John Wilson, the producers, displayed the artwork and a score indicating the musical excerpts to be recorded. The composer objected to some of these, but since the piece was in the public domain in the United States and could be used without his permission, he accepted the proposal (on January 31), hoping to improve the shape of the excerpts by composing new beginnings and endings. On February 2, when it was agreed to use the 1947 version, the contract was signed. After further conferences (February 15, 25, and 26), thirteen segments were recorded in one three-hour session (March 2) at the Warner Brothers sound studio on Santa Monica Boulevard. The tapes were edited by Stravinsky himself (March 5). The excerpts form a new "Suite," of sorts, and though Stravinsky was far from de-

---

which resulted in an accent. As far back as the early 1930s, Prokofiev wrote to him: "Dear Igor Fyodorovich, For God's sake, shed some light on the following: What is the meaning of the sign – in the string instruments? Is it 'portamento,' whether for the piano or for the wind instruments, or is it, rather, a very sustained note? For example: should the cello play this:

like this:

Or, as one musician explained it to me, should it be played like this,

as though the sign in the strings meant legato [in one phrase]? I embrace you affectionately. Don't neglect to send me just a word. Yours,   Serg." (The music examples are facsimiles of Prokofiev's originals.)

[7] The *Petrushka* Suite that Stravinsky himself performed most frequently lasts about twenty minutes and is described in a letter from him to his publisher, F. V. Weber, on March 2, 1931: "That Furtwängler will play the *Petrushka* music on his tour around Germany is good news for you but not for me, since I am not an admirer of this conductor. Nevertheless, I shall mark the small score according to the sections that make up the so-called 'Suite'—something that all conductors except Furtwängler have known for twenty years. The 'Suite' is made up of the Hocus-Pocus, the Russian

lighted with it, and never performed it again, he enjoyed telling the story of how he received as much money for the mutilation of his masterpiece, requiring only a slight effort, as he had earned for the composition of *Threni*. As he wrote to Nadia Boulanger on February 27, 1956:

> The Bach Variations [*"Vom Himmel hoch"*] are taking more time than I had anticipated; I am going to have Bob conduct them in May at the Ojai Festival, when I conduct my *Noces*. This work is interrupted by all sorts of things—at the moment, and for at least a week, by an abbreviated version of *Petrushka* for a TV cartoon. I am using the beginning episodes, Petrushka's cell, the Moor, part of the Masks, and the death of Petrushka. In short, a potpourri. What is more, I am doing it for money!!!![8] Yes sir! [These two words are in English.] Work of this kind is certainly reprehensible, but understandable, too, considering the taxes that are so pitilessly gouged from us. [Original in French]

The order of the soundtrack is as follows:

1. The beginning through the brass chord one measure before (13).
2. From the triplet upbeat to (19) through the final three notes of the triangle at (23).
3. From one measure after (28) through the measure before (33).
4. From (53) through the first beat of the measure after (72).
5. (82) to (95).
6. From (100), with an upbeat from part of the piano and clarinet music, through the measure before (104), with a new ending for the flute.
7. (106) to (114).
8. From (148) to the end of the second bar of (160).
9. (234) to (240), with a new part for the trumpets at the end.
10. (252) to (258).
11. The two measures before (262).
12. From two measures before (264) through the second measure of (267).
13. From (167) to (169), with ending. This music was used for the film's titles.

Dance, the entire second scene, and the fourth scene ending in a specially orchestrated trill by the full orchestra on F-sharp. . . . Be certain that this trill is clearly marked in the orchestra parts, which is not always the case; the last time on the London radio, I had to play the piece through to the end. Direct Furtwängler's attention to my metronomic indications and advise him to get my Columbia recording."

Stravinsky wrote to Païchadze on February 15, 1932: "When is *Petrushka* finally going to be published for popular orchestra?" This evidently refers to a jazz-band arrangement of certain selections, similar to the arrangement of *Mavra*, May 1930, for the Jack Hylton band.

[8] Stravinsky received $10,000 but was warned that the film would be made even if he did not give his name to it, since the music was in the public domain. Stravinsky, the present writer, and the producer, Ned Hertzstam, planned the episodes, and the present writer conducted.

APPENDIX D

LE SACRE DU PRINTEMPS: *A Chronology of the Revisions*

To the memory of Abdon Laus, first bassoonist in the
first performance of Le Sacre du printemps, *May 29, 1913.*

The publication of the *Sacre du printemps* sketches[1] in the André Meyer collection enables us to correct Stravinsky's long-accepted statement, quoted in André Schaeffner's biography of the composer, that the eleven measures from rehearsal number **86** to **88** were added on March 29, 1913 (three weeks after the score had been completed, on March 8). The sketches show that this section was fully composed and in proper sequence by March 1912, while the manuscript of the full score reveals that the measures inserted on March 29, 1913, were the four *before* **86**. But even without the aid of sketches, a comparison of the two passages should have disclosed that the four measures, rather than the eleven, are the ones that were added. A letter to Stravinsky in Clarens from Pierre Monteux in Monte Carlo, April 15, 1913, confirms this:

> It would be helpful if you would send right away the *Sacre* score containing your changes to be copied into the parts. I would like to take advantage of my stay here to correct all the parts, in order not to lose time when I return to Paris. I have already given the copyist the four added measures, which I received from Berlin.

The confusion in identifying the added music was probably due to Stravinsky's transferal of the eleven-measure page to the blank verso of page 43 (the recto of which contains the conclusion of Part One) and replacement by the page with the four added measures. He signed his name in Latin letters in the lower right corner of his new page,[2] noted the place and date ("Clarens, 29 III 1913"), and drew an arrow directing the reader to turn back for the music at **86** to **88**. Another indication that the eleven-measure page formerly occupied the place of the four-measure one is that in the new positions of the pages, Stravinsky forgot to connect all of the ligatures from the notes in the measure before **88** to the same notes at **88**—which explains the missing flats, in his manuscript, before the B, D, and A in the strings at **88**. Furthermore, the words "con sord [ine] "

---

[1] Boosey & Hawkes, 1969. At first, Stravinsky did not want these sketches to be published, but he changed his mind. He wrote to Suvchinsky on October 7, 1964: "As you see, I have agreed to publication, which, earlier, I had not wanted to do. After all, why not? My attitude toward my first period has changed radically, and it is as though someone else had composed [the early music]. My present musical interests are completely different, so let the sketches be published if this will bring anyone any pleasure."

[2] Numbered 44D. The music of Part Two begins on 44A, and the eleven-measure page is 44E.

and "senza sord[ine]" are rubber-stamped[3] on the page containing the four extra measures, but handwritten everywhere else in the score, meaning that the Berlin editor corrected the composer's oversight omission in the four measures, but would not write on his manuscript.[4] Before sending the manuscript to the Berlin publisher, Stravinsky wrote a note on the title page of Part Two to the effect that he was sending pages 43 to 68 now, pages 69 through the *Danse sacrale* at a later time. The note also points out that pages 44A, 44B, 44C, 44D, and 44E follow page 43.

The four measures in question, dated March 29, 1913, were the last to be composed and the music between **28** and **29** the last to be reorchestrated,[5] but Stravinsky reworked pages 85 and 86 at a still later date. Monteux wrote on April 2, 1913:

> I am returning the score which I used in the [Paris] rehearsals. This morning I received another score from your publishers in Berlin. The last twenty measures are missing, but this does not matter, since, for the moment, I do not have any more rehearsals.

Monteux used Stravinsky's first-draft score for the Paris rehearsals of Part One, while the composer continued to work with his master score for the entire piece, which contains the rearrangement of the pages at the beginning of Part Two. Thus the score that Monteux returned on or about April 2 is the same one that Stravinsky sent to Miaskovsky to proofread.[6]

---

[3] That Stravinsky did not use rubber stamps is especially curious, since, in the same year, he applied for a patent for a "note-writing machine." Struve wrote to him from Berlin on November 14: "I have made inquiries at Röder, who told me that such machines have existed for a long time but are no longer manufactured because of the small demand for them." On January 6, 1914, Struve said that he had "obtained all the necessary information, and there is hope of getting the patent since no such instrument is in circulation; but it will not be cheap to make, and no more than about 300 or 400 should be made. For a small number of individuals, however, this appliance will be desirable and useful. . . . You will have to add to the 'Stravinsky note-writing machine': 1. a spare reel with larger lines; 2. an ink-pad with ink; 3. a ruler. . . . And all of this will have to be put in a box." Stravinsky's invention was a stylus (for drawing staves, not notes), a modern version of the rastral.

[4] Regrettably, conductors did not exercise similar restraint, every page of the original manuscript being marred by their reminders to give cues, by large redrawings of the meters, and by such expressions as *"très tranquille"*—where Stravinsky merely gives a change of tempo.

[5] Two sets of Stravinsky's two manuscript pages exist for the music at **28**, one in the holograph of the score in the Sacher Collection, the other in the copy made by "O. Th." in Leipzig and completed May 1, 1913. This score, used by Monteux for the first performance, contains numerous corrections in Stravinsky's hand, and is signed by him at the end, "completed at Clarens, March 8, 1913" (original phrase in Russian). See the correspondence with Monteux in *S.S.C. II.*

[6] See Miaskovsky's letter to Stravinsky of August 7, 1913, n. 16 on p. 53.

The score—lacking "the last twenty measures"—that Monteux received from Berlin on April 2 was the manuscript of the complete work,[7] except that the twenty missing measures were not the "last" ones, but those on manuscript pages 85 and 86 (*not* 87, the final page). Pages 85 and 86 were inserted at a later date, and obviously written in great haste, for which reason the present writer naively interpreted the penmanship here as evidence of Stravinsky's impatience to reach the end.[8] The actual end, page 87, is calligraphic, and in this sense differs from pages 85 and 86, which contain the most often revised music in *Le Sacre* and may not have been finished until after April 15.

The orchestra score of *Le Sacre* was not engraved after the 1913 performances for the reason that Diaghilev did not decide to drop the piece from the repertory until November 1913,[9] by which time Stravinsky and his publishers were occupied with *The Nightingale*. In January 1914, when Monteux announced his intention to present *Le Sacre* in concert form,[10] the publisher and the composer welcomed the opportunity to make further changes. On March 16, the Russischer Musik Verlag sent the parts to Monteux, and in a letter from Struve to Stravinsky on April 4 (one day before the Paris performance), the publisher stated that the manuscript score had been sent to Paris for the composer's use.

Stravinsky received the first proofs before the end of the year, corrected and returned them, and in March 1915 recovered his manuscript, which was still with him at the end of the war, along with the unique set of orchestra parts, and, as he informs Struve in a letter dated April 6, 1919, "a *copy* of the orchestral score. The only printing of *Le Sacre*, engraved just before the war, is also

---

[7] In a letter to Stravinsky on December 8, 1921, Eric Zingel of the R.M.V. says that "your corrections have been inserted in the two manuscript scores."

[8] *Stravinsky: Chronicle of a Friendship, 1948–1971*, New York, 1972.

[9] Struve, in Berlin, to Stravinsky, in Clarens, November 23, 1913: "Diaghilev told us that he is unconditionally postponing *Le Sacre* for at least a year." This and many other steps in the chronology of the revisions are either omitted or erroneously presented in *S.P.D.*, but the book's most important mistake is the statement (p. 531) that the music at 57 and in the measure before 59 was rewritten in 1929. In fact, the alterations at these places were made in 1922 and were *not* included in the 1929, or rather 1930, edition of the pocket score, even though Stravinsky wrote "corrected version" on the spine of his copy of this. (The pirated scores, of which the Kalmus edition, "copyrighted" in 1933, is the best known, follow the 1930 R.M.V. score, but do not include the Russian titles.) Other errors concerning *Le Sacre* in *S.P.D.* are: on p. 101, twelfth line from the end, the text should read, "June 5. M. D. Calvocoressi writes . . ." (*not* Ravel, and *not* June 6); on p. 517, Diaghilev *did* telegraph to Stravinsky in Ustilug after the London performances of *Le Sacre* ("*Quand comptes-tu terminer opéra? Amitiés, Serge, Hôtel Crillon, Paris, August 1, 1913*"); also, the dates of the performances of *Le Sacre* in Paris in 1913 are May 29 and June 2, 4, 6, and 13.

[10] On January 21, 1914, Monteux wrote to Stravinsky: "Dear friend . . . Undoubtedly you know that I am no longer with the Ballets Russes. I will be giving concerts in Paris on Sunday afternoons with a very fine orchestra, and I intend to play *Petrushka* and

here with me." Other exchanges between composer and publisher confirm that the engraving took place during, not before, the war, and that the "printing" in Stravinsky's possession was a set of proofs. Stravinsky wrote to Struve on December 11, 1919:

> A year ago I gave you a detailed account of my difficult material situation, with a wife, four children, and now the family of my sister-in-law—five people—in my care. I assumed that in view of all this you would not be surprised by my request to sell the *Sacre* manuscript, which, by the way, is here with me and not in America, as you mistakenly suppose. As it turns out, you have had a completely different reaction to my proposal . . . and, naturally, I am surprised. . . . Really, it is as though nothing had happened these past few years . . . whereas all Russia is ruined and all of us Russians are robbed blind. The only thing that anyone thinks about now is how to keep . . . alive. And at a time like this, you, a representative of the Edition Russe de Musique, a company created solely for the authors whom it publishes, you, the owners of a manuscript whose sale could be invaluable to me, have preferred to act according to the letter of the law and hold on to the manuscript for "bibliographic reasons," placing museum-related interests above those of my material well-being. . . . If you had overlooked the rules, in this instance, and taken world events into account, none of the members of the Edition Russe de Musique committee (if they still exist) would have criticized you for it. Nor am I convinced by your argument that selling the manuscript in America is doubly dangerous. Russian authors are not protected there, and *Petrushka* is played in the United States without permission, yours or mine. The Americans will publish whatever they please without asking either of us.[11]

Early in 1920, Stravinsky sent the manuscript to Berlin so that the publication of the score could be completed. But the first edition did not appear in time for the revival of the ballet in December 1920, and, in fact, Stravinsky was still writing to the R.M.V. a year later, demanding to make more corrections. Zingel answered on December 15, 1921:

> . . . The score is at the printer and almost finished, incorporating, it is hoped, all the corrections from the two corrected manuscripts. The edition is not large; but before we undertake a new printing, whether of the large

Le Sacre. Would you be so kind as to send the music to me?—and as soon as possible, since I plan to present these pieces in my first concerts, beginning February 8, in an excellent hall seating 2,000. . . . Quickly, write a note, my dear friend, because I am preparing my programs now, and I want to reserve a good place for you. Also send news of yourself and your entourage. My wife joins in sending our best wishes to you as well as to Madame Stravinsky. Your cordially devoted　Pierre Monteux."
[11] In this same letter, Stravinsky says that he has given permission to the Aeolian Co. in London "to put out the entire *Petrushka* and *Sacre* in piano rolls, because Zingel told me that the rights belong to me."

score or of the one in pocket format, we must have the third score back from London.[12] Our proofreader can then collate all three scores, if you will leave your manuscript score with us so that we may compare it with the printed one. We are very sorry to say that we can do nothing more with this edition, which we hope to have from the printer very soon.

But the large score did not come from the printer until February 1922, and the pocket score not until May, by which time Stravinsky had entered numerous corrections in the former. On May 26 he wrote to the R.M.V. insisting that new orchestra parts be prepared to include the changes. Oeberg replied on May 31 that Diaghilev had the only parts, and that as soon as these were available from him

> I will send them to Germany to have several copies made, since Brussels and Madrid have requested the piece for the fall season. But I cannot ask to have the parts copied from the score because, as you say, there are still many errors to correct.

Oeberg wrote again on June 12, insisting that to make new parts would be too expensive, and that the best that could be done would be to insert the changes in the existing set and eventually to issue a revised pocket score—though eight years were to elapse before this happened! Meanwhile, since Ansermet was to conduct the Berlin premiere of *Le Sacre* in November 1922, Stravinsky sent his pocket score—"containing my corrections in red ink and pencil"—to him with a request to copy the changes, but adding that "these are by no means all." By August 15, the date of this letter, Stravinsky had made alterations on every page of the music, as well as rewritten whole sections of the piece.

Only two editions of the score of *Le Sacre du printemps* were published by the R.M.V., the first dated 1921 (but not released until 1922), and the second dated August 1930 and incorporating the changes made in 1922 and in January 1926. Païchadze wrote to Stravinsky on August 7, 1930:

> The orchestral score of *Sacre* is in its second week of printing and will be finished in about ten days, except for the timpani parts, which we had engraved again. Jean Morel, whom we approached in your name and at your suggestion, extricated us from all of those difficulties magnificently. Konius is delighted with the way in which Morel did the first and second timpani parts so clearly and intelligently. He rewrote the introductory explanation so that this too became a model of lucidity, and he even gave a schematic picture of the distribution of the timpani between two musicians; we reproduced this in the timpani parts. Morel really knows his business and we would not have gotten out of the technical labyrinth of these parts without his help. It would be appropriate, unless you disagree, to print a statement in these two parts, "Distribution and technical indications by Jean Morel," which I am sure would please him. Since these parts

---

[12] *Le Sacre* had just been performed in London by Eugene Goossens, who presumably conducted from the copy that Monteux had used in April 1914.

must soon go to print, let me know by return whether you have anything against the idea so we can propose it to him.

Whether or not Morel is responsible for the inauthentic timpani notes at **146** and **171** the present writer cannot say.

Stravinsky answered on August 9:

> Very pleased to hear that the problem of the timpani parts is finally resolved. We should certainly put Morel's name in the music as the author of the technical indications as well as of the distribution of the timpani parts. Thank him very sincerely for me.

The 1926 revisions were immediately made available. Stravinsky wrote to Païchadze, October 17, 1926:

> Make a copy of the pages of *Le Sacre* that I recomposed, place them in a score, and send this score and parts to Stokowski. New York does not have these changes, which are not only very important, but which also facilitate the conductor's job.[13]

Stravinsky had no doubt reasoned that since the score would be pirated anyway, a correct version would be preferable to an incorrect one. Whether these pages bore the name of F. H. Schneider as "editor," the present writer has not been able to discover, but the method of trying to obtain copyright protection by means of an editor from a member country of the Bern copyright convention irked Stravinsky, who wrote to Païchadze, April 17, 1928: "It is perfectly idiotic to write 'edited by Albert Spalding.' But what can we do when the American laws openly protect the theft?"

In January 1926, Stravinsky rewrote the entire *Evocation des ancêtres* and much of the *Danse sacrale,* adding lower brass (bass trumpet, trombones, tubas) between **186** and **190**; canceling the bassoons, flutes, and horns between **186** and **189**; introducing alternating pizzicato and arco articulation (except for the basses) in the first and corresponding sections; adding the second contrabassoon to the first from **190**; changing the penultimate and antepenultimate measures to $\frac{3}{4}$; eliminating the fermatas on the violin tremolo and the English horn trill in the third measure from the end; deleting the guero part at the end and at **70**; correcting the first note of the double appoggiatura at **3** (from A to B—a mistake still found in the Boosey & Hawkes 1965 "corrected" reprint); adding crescendo and decrescendo markings for violins and violas at the fifth measure after **133**; combining the two measures at **39** into one $\frac{9}{8}$ measure;

---

[13] As late as January 7, 1930, however, Païchadze wrote to Stravinsky: "Please let me know, if only on a postcard, whether I can make arrangements to have the corrected, written orchestral score of *Sacre* sent to Stokowski. You had told me that I could, but I would like to have you confirm this once again." Stravinsky's next letter to Païchadze, dated January 13, does not seem to answer this question: "I almost forgot to reply to you on the subject of *Le Sacre*. Certainly you can use the orchestra parts, to which you refer, because this season I will not conduct the piece. Only keep my orchestra score and do not give it to anyone."

indicating in a marginal notation that the triplet figures in the strings from **86** to **89** are to be played as two thirty-second-notes and a sixteenth-note (as in the 4-hand score); correcting the second note of the fourth trumpet at one measure before **109**; doubling the first two trumpets with the third and fourth, an octave lower, at one measure before **109**. Since Stravinsky made changes in the large score up until April 1940, when he recorded *Le Sacre* with the New York Philharmonic, many of their dates cannot be precisely determined.

Stravinsky instructed Païchadze to keep the new manuscript pages "for the engraving of the new edition. Explain to the copyist that the red lines in my manuscript must be copied as dotted lines, since they indicate the divisions within the measure." Yet three years later, this new edition had still not appeared. "I understand your annoyance concerning the printing of *Le Sacre*," Stravinsky wrote to Païchadze on August 13, 1929, and, on August 20, "Only yesterday I received the newly engraved plates of *Le Sacre,* together with my score." On October 23, the composer said: "I sent the second proofs of the *Danse sacrale* to Weber a week or two ago, while I was still in Paris," but on November 7, Röder, the Leipzig printer, complained to the R.M.V. that Stravinsky had returned the corrected first proofs but not the second. On November 15, he sent his score and the second proofs from Nice to Paris by Messageries Rapides, and on November 21 he wrote to A. L. Rabenek of the R.M.V. :

> The score of *Le Sacre* that I sent to you contains my own revised pages, after which the new ones will be engraved. As Koussevitzky knows, since he himself copied them a few years ago, these manuscript pages are mine. Thus it is quite out of the question to paste in the engraved pages, and to substitute them for the manuscript;[14] the publisher must make a special copy. But why, in the first place, did Weber—on behalf of Païchadze—ask me to send my *Sacre* score? I do not understand it. . . . I myself will be in Paris in a few days, probably on Tuesday morning. [Original in Russian]

Apart from the large score, Stravinsky's other revisions are found in two pocket scores, the one identified by "red ink," the other by "blue pencil" (used for the bar lines in the *Evocation des ancêtres*). The "red ink" changes were entered in 1922. Since the "blue pencil" changes supersede some of the "red ink" changes, especially in the *Evocation des ancêtres*[15] (where the "red ink"

---

[14] Here Stravinsky is challenging the rule that the manuscript is the property of the publisher.

[15] In the manuscript of the full score, the title of the *Evocation des ancêtres* is *Azklynanya Mista—Purification du Sol*. Stravinsky must have changed this not later than April 1913, since the Evocation title appears on the 4-hand piano score, published at the end of May. The engraving of this score was begun in January 1913. Struve wrote to Stravinsky in London on February 2: "Regarding the title page in *Le Sacre,* we notified the printer in Leipzig immediately, but I cannot promise that everything will be done as you now wish, since the engraving and all the preparation has already begun." A second printing of the 4-hand piano score was issued on January 1, 1914, and be-

score employs meters of $\frac{7}{4}$, $\frac{8}{4}$, and $\frac{10}{4}$), the revisions in the "blue pencil" score must have been made after 1922 and before January 1926. The metrical recasting of the *Ancêtres* in the "blue pencil" score marks a great advance in the direction of the 1926 version.

The most important changes in the "red ink" score occur in the following places: at **51** (clarinet in E-flat an octave lower in the first measure); at **53** (the addition of two piccolos); in the sixth measure after **53** (the addition of two flutes); at **57** (the timpani part); in the fourth measure before **59** (the rewriting of all the parts); in the fourth and fifth measures after **59** (the timpani parts); between **104** and **121** (the deletion of the first two notes of the flute and piccolo appoggiaturas); at one measure before **114** (the D trumpet part is rewritten a major second lower, an error in the original manuscript not corrected until 1967[16]); the rebarring and the deletion of the fermatas throughout the *Ancêtres*; the transferal of the fermata at **142** from the first to the third sixteenth; and at **175** and two measures before **175**, the addition of horn parts. Yet Stravinsky did not extensively alter the meters in the *Danse sacrale*, and he had second thoughts about some of the few changes that he did make. The *Danse sacrale* as it is now known dates from January 1926.

Every page of the "red ink" score contains minor revisions. These include: a breath mark in the bassoon part after the second fermata in the first measure; the cancellation of the dynamic markings for the clarinet in D at **8** and two measures after; the instruction that the two clarinets in A continue to play the same music in the three measures before **9**, as in the first three measures of **8**; and at **10**, the notation of the first bass's harmonic in the bass clef (D on the third line, to sound two octaves higher). But a complete list is beyond the scope of this brief investigation.

The most important revisions in the "blue pencil" score are found in the *Ancêtres*, where Stravinsky retains the fermatas but adds a third trombone part from **123** to **124**, and, at **128**, doubles the violas with cellos an octave lower. In the *Glorification de l'élue,* the first violin and viola parts are renovated throughout, and short measures are grouped to form larger ones—changes not incorporated in any later score. In the *Danse sacrale,* the meters have been changed from **186** to the end, but the main revisions amount to little more than forming $\frac{3}{8}$ measures out of four sixteenths and two sixteenths.

---

tween this date and December 31, 1920, the edition earned 338 marks of the 440 marks advance that Stravinsky received for this arrangement.

[16] Among the many mistakes in the Boosey & Hawkes score 16333, one of the most puzzling is that of the bass drum part in the measure before **118**. In the original manuscript, the drum part in this measure, unlike that in the corresponding ones, is not written on the staff, but simply as a rhythm, which suggests that, after finishing the page, Stravinsky added it without having left room for it, misplacing the notes in his haste. When listening to recordings, in any case, he would protest at this point, yet let the error pass while conducting the piece himself, as he did in the case of many other errors in his music.

Stravinsky did not correct the trombone parts (which lacked flats) in the second measure after **62** until after the publication of the 1930 score. After 1930, too, he changed the C-flat to C-natural in the second and fourth horns on the last beat of **134** and on the last beat of the measure after **134**, and changed the instruction for the cellos in the last measure from "descordez" to "descendez."

In a letter to Païchadze, July 20, 1932, Stravinsky refers to additional corrections, by Roger Desormière, that he, Stravinsky, has verified. In a letter to Molinari on August 1, 1938, replying to a number of questions from the Italian conductor concerning discrepancies between the 4-hand piano score and the orchestra score, Stravinsky authorizes—surprisingly—the change to a slower tempo at **174** that he was later to reject:

142   *est juste*

174 ♩ = 116   *est juste*

181   *est juste*

201   *pas besoin d'accelerando ni de "lunga ad libitum"—tout doit être joué régulièrement dans le tempo indiqué au **186** et au début de la* Danse sacrale **142** *en gardant la pulsation de 126 à la croche (=126).*

The most important "revision" of all, the completely rewritten *Danse sacrale* of 1943, would require an extended study in itself.

APPENDIX E

Three Pieces for String Quartet: The Revisions

The publication of the Three Pieces for String Quartet, like that of the orchestra score of *Le Sacre du printemps,* was interrupted in 1914 by the start of World War I. In consequence, the original version remained in manuscript and was withdrawn after Stravinsky revised the pieces in 1918 (No. 1 on December 2, No. 2 on December 6, and No. 3 a few days later; Stravinsky sent the new score and parts to London on December 16 for three performances by the London

Philharmonic Quartet).[1] The revised version of the score and parts (Russischer Musik Verlag 401), published in 1922 (Stravinsky dated his copy February 1, 1923), differs from the original in almost every measure.

From Salvan on July 26, 1914, Stravinsky wrote to Eric Zingel in Berlin:

> I am sending three pieces from my new chamber-music album, which will consist of five pieces in all. I ask you to make a copy of the parts immediately, as well as a copy of the score. This album must be ready by August 20 for the famous Lausanne Quartet, "Quatuor du Flonzaley." . . . They will make a world tour, as they do each year—Berlin, London, Paris, New York, Boston, Chicago, Philadelphia, Washington, and many other cities, where they will play my work. I also ask you immediately to tell Herr von Struve . . . that I need my honorarium now—200 rubles for each piece, or 1,000 rubles in all. Please take care of this question as soon as possible. *Hochachtungsvoll,*   I. Stravinsky [Original in German]

The publisher assigned separate numbers to each of the Three Pieces (R.M.V. 272, 273, and 274), and on August 15 Zingel wrote to say that the music had been sent to Leipzig for engraving. (Zingel mentions that he has learned from Frl. Eichelberger[2] that Stravinsky and his family are in good health.) Another message from Zingel, on August 26, confirms that work has already begun. Then, in December, Zingel wrote that the printing had stopped; and on December 23 Stravinsky's manuscript was returned to him. (Stravinsky wrote to Struve, April 6, 1919: "Zingel managed to get the quartet pieces engraved,[3] but I was not able to get the score; I got only the manuscript back.") His arrangement of the music for piano 4-hands, probably completed in August 1914,[4] and still showing the name "Alexander Cingria" as the original dedicatee, was not sent to Berlin and was never published, for the reason that the pieces were drastically revised after the war.[5]

When Stravinsky was in Paris in January 1914, Misia Sert asked him to compose a work for performance in her "Chinese room." By March, a rumor had circulated that he had written a "dance," or "dances," and on March 14

---

[1] The performances were on February 13, March 27, and April 9. A page of notes by Ansermet was inserted in the program: "The first [piece] represents a group of peasants singing and dancing against the monotonous setting of the steppes. . . . The second [piece] represents an unhappy juggler, who must hide his grief while he performs his feats before the crowd. . . . The third [piece] represents priests chanting in church, now in plainsong, now with a suggestion of the Dies Irae. . . ."

[2] See *S.P.D.*, p. 658, n. 49.

[3] Stravinsky did not know about the engraving until the end of the war.

[4] The Ansermet archives contain a 4-hand piano score of the first piece, dated Leysin, April 1914.

[5] The parts of the 1914 Quartet survived in copies made by the American composer Templeton Strong (1856–1948) in January–February 1915, for a private concert in Geneva. The bowings and other markings are surely Stravinsky's own.

Pierre Monteux wrote to him, requesting the first performance of the new opus: "Nothing could please me more, dear friend, than if you would reserve the premiere of your *Trois Danses* for me. Approximately when do you think that they will be ready? I can hardly wait to become acquainted with them." By this date, Stravinsky had no more than sketched the first of the pieces, the only one that was to become a dance.

The main differences between the 1914 and 1918 scores in No. 1 are that in the solo violin part in the early version, the phrases are clearly separated but marked "legato," "ponticello," and "on the G string," whereas in the later version, each note is separately articulated, the player being directed to use the full length of the bow throughout. In the 1914 score, the sustained D is in the second violin and the figure of four eighth-notes is in the viola, while in the 1918 score, the viola and second violin parts are switched; also in the 1918 score, when the quarter-notes are sounded only once, they are played with separate up-bows, but, when the figure is immediately repeated, with four down-bows followed by four up-bows.

The most striking discrepancy between the 1914 and 1918 versions of No. 2 is that the opening two-note figure (originally two eighth-notes) was changed to triplets and marked "quasi glissando" and "crescendo" from the first to the second note. The motif in measures 4 and 5 of the original, given to the first violin and cello alone, is played by all four strings in the 1918 score, thereby sounding in three octaves instead of in two. In Stravinsky's sketchbook, this motif first appears designated "for cornet" with bassoon accompaniment. On a detached sheet, next to another draft of the "cornet" tune, Stravinsky wrote: "a female dancer on horseback." Although it might be concluded that he made the notation after a visit to a circus, another sketch reveals that the motif is derived from a "Breton song given to me by Shura [Alexandre] Benois. A clarinetist, sitting on a stone during a strong rain, played full force and the music was danced." Benois had visited Stravinsky at La Baule, Brittany, in August 1910,[6] and Stravinsky copied the song on a piece of music paper. The "cornet" tune used in measures 4 and 5 is an extract from this folk melody, and in the first sketch for the second of the Three Pieces, Stravinsky combined the tune with the music of the beginning.

The first notation in No. 3 is for the music that begins in the third measure (published score), but the sketch is for violin and viola alone, playing in parallel fourths and in triplet rhythm, the cello entering only at the end. The first notes of the violin and viola are the same as in the final score, and, in contour and rhythm, the melody is close to the final form but within the compass of a major, instead of a minor, third. The next sketch, for the passage beginning twenty measures from the end, is substantially the same as in the finished version. In the third sketch, Stravinsky discovered the final versions of the melodic and harmonic progressions that begin in the third measure of the piece. The music of the opening measures, and of the refrain, was the last to be composed.

---

[6] In an interview in *The Latest News,* a Russian newspaper in Paris, Friday, March 21,

"Lied ohne Name"

Stravinsky added the German title and the instrumentation to this brief duo in July 1949. The sketches date from the end of December 1916:

Sometime before October 1918, Stravinsky expanded this music into a song that apparently became the source of the first of the Three Pieces for Clarinet

1930, Benois says that "Diaghilev and Stravinsky turned to me in the autumn of 1910, asking me to compose a plot for a ballet of which they had a vague vision, and for which Stravinsky had already composed two amazing pieces. . . ." Stravinsky has circled this and written in the margin: "A blatant lie." The plot of *Petrushka* was purely Stravinsky's, and it occurred to him in Switzerland, after he had left La Baule. The pieces that Benois heard, played to him by Stravinsky, in St. Petersburg in November 1910, were from the second tableau of *Petrushka* and should not be confused with the string quartet pieces.

Solo (in which opus see measures 2–3 and 7–9; and 15–16, 18, and 20–21—the four descending-scale eighth-notes):

APPENDIX G

Easy Pieces

"Valse des fleurs," the first "easy piece" that Stravinsky completed,[1] is a surprising creation, contemporary with *Pribaoutki* and *Les Noces,* but utterly different from them in character, as well as simple in form and slight in content to a degree unprecedented in his work. Stravinsky always anticipated new compositions before completing those in hand, and the "Valse des fleurs" and Three Easy Pieces (1914–15) point to *Histoire du soldat* and beyond.

---

[1] "September 30, 1914, Clarens," Stravinsky wrote after the last measure. At the time, he was living in the Villa La Pervenche, rented from Ansermet, who had written to the composer in August, "I have just seen Rambert; the German demoiselles have occupied your old apartment in Les Tilleuls, but the apartment above, *1er étage,* is free." This statement confirms Stravinsky's recollection, during a visit in May 1965, that his

Erik Satie may have inspired the "Valse des fleurs," as he did the Valse, which Stravinsky dedicated to him. Fragments of both pieces are found on the same sketch page, along with drafts for a third:

In December 1915 and June 1916 Stravinsky began to sketch two other Valses for piano 4-hands, the first of which is designated—though the original is in Russian—"four hands, for children":

Why did Stravinsky publish only one of these "Valses"? Possibly because he had used an identical harmonic construction in two of the others, or because the music of all five is similar, or simply because the one for Satie is the most developed and substantial. In any case, the Three Easy Pieces (Marche for Casella, Valse for Satie, and Polka for Diaghilev) are landmarks in Stravinsky's art, which cannot be said of the national songs and dances ("Napolitana," "Española," and "Balalaika") in the Five Easy Pieces (1917). Nevertheless, the earliest sketch (1913) for any of the easy pieces belongs to the latter type:

---

studio and apartment had both been on the *rez-de-chaussée*. (See *Stravinsky: Chronicle of a Friendship*, pp. 265–6.)

Writing to Ansermet in care of the Ballets Russes, New York, late in March 1916, Stravinsky described the Marche, Valse, and Polka as "music-hall" numbers. The conductor had cabled from Boston, February 10, asking the composer to "send piano pieces and terms publication." Stravinsky replied that he would send the music with Mrs. Adolph Bolm, who was to sail from Bordeaux on March 12.[2] But the Polka had not been transcribed for chamber ensemble, and if Stravinsky made a 2-hand version of the Marche, this has not been found. Ansermet wrote from New York on April 7: ". . . I regret not having the orchestrations, because I have an idea that would have quickly resolved the affair. But with Mrs. Bolm's arrival, it was too late to ask you for them."

The 2-hand score of the Polka, first of the Three Easy Pieces to be completed, would appear to have preceded the 4-hand score, if only because all the C-flats in the former are changed to B-naturals in the latter. (Stravinsky's alterations from draft to draft in the orthography of accidentals and in the elimination of key signatures would provide the subject for a thesis.) The 2-hand version lacks the heading for the 4-hand: "Dedicated to Sergei Pavlovich Diaghilev." Whether or not the music was inspired, as Stravinsky wrote, by a vision of Diaghilev as a whip-cracking ringmaster,[3] the 4-hand transcription, with a very simple part for one of the players, seems to have been a later idea. On March 23, 1915, Stravinsky began to rewrite the Polka for a single player,[4] substituting a glissando from the A to the F-sharp in measure 7, and harmonizing the upper note and subsequent A and G with major thirds below.

When the Polka appeared—probably in 1915—in an unidentified French-language periodical, p. 137—the dedication to Diaghilev was missing, but the metronome mark ♩ = 96, and legato, staccato, and dynamic indications not found in the manuscripts, were included. Stravinsky seems to have ad-

---

[2] See Stravinsky's letter to Ansermet of February 14, 1916, p. 130.

[3] At the beginning of October 1914, just before composing the Polka, Stravinsky visited Diaghilev in Florence. (Ansermet wrote to Catherine Stravinsky on October 7, asking her to inform him as soon as her husband returned.) The 4-hand score was completed in Clarens on November 15, and a few days later Stravinsky and his wife were in Leysin, where Ansermet visited them, probably on November 22. Misia Sert wrote to Cocteau in the latter half of 1915: "Diaghilev is getting fatter and fatter, his clothes tighter and his hat smaller, rather 'circus director' as Igor says. . . ."

[4] The verso of this draft contains notations for the fanfare that begins the second piece in *The Five Fingers*.

justed the dedications as occasion moved him, and, after orchestrating the Eight Easy Pieces and regrouping them in two Little Suites, sometimes omitting the names of all of the dedicatees. Nor was the composer consistent in using the title Little Suites. He presented the orchestra versions no less frequently as Eight Easy Pieces, and, at the premiere of all of them together—under his baton in Haarlem (*not* Amsterdam), March 2, 1926—as "Huit pièces enfantines." In a concert in Biarritz on August 25, 1932, he authorized a note in the program, *"Dédiées à Mme Eugénie de Errazuriz"*—to whom he had inscribed the Five Easy Pieces in 1917.

Stravinsky embellished the first page of the earliest manuscript of the 4-hand Marche with wartime illustrations. One cannon belches orange fire, another pink flames—in cartoon style, like the music, for the Marche and Polka are his first essays in caricature. The letters of the name "Alfredo Casella," at the top of the page, tumble as if from the detonations, while the "R" in "MARCHE" rolls in diminuendo ("R R R R R R"), and the title "MAR—CHE" has been blown in half. (Stravinsky also wrote the name of one of the Five Easy Pieces pictographically—"GALOP P P P P"—to suggest receding movement.) The brightly colored Marche manuscript, its staves drawn with Stravinsky's stylus, is dated December 19, 1914. On the same day, he made a fair copy on printed music paper, adding a measure (sustaining the C and G in measure 4), changing flats to enharmonic sharps, repeating the dotted rhythms in measure 4 (replacing the sixteenths), and implementing other improvements as well. The earlier score contains his penciled indications for the 12-instrument transcription, which also lacks the extra measure.

Like the Polka, the Valse, completed March 6, 1915, in Château-d'Oex, appears to have been conceived for a single player, to judge by the much-corrected manuscript of the 2-hand score and the comparatively clean 4-hand one. Neither of these autograph scores justifies any change of tempo in the second section. The Trio is marked simply "rubato" (not "rit."), and Stravinsky's metronomes in the instrumental version verify that $\downarrow$ = 56 for the second section (i.e., three times as slow as the first) cannot be correct.[5]

The "Valse pour les enfants" may be classified as an "easy piece." Although published[6] in facsimile in *Le Figaro, Supplément Littéraire*, May 21, 1922, with Stravinsky's handwritten dedication and date, *"pour les petits lecteurs du Figaro, mai 1922,"* the music was in fact composed in December 1916 or the beginning of January 1917. A complete draft, using an alphabetical shorthand for repeated measures (A, B, C, D, E), is found on a sheet containing two notations for the "Lied ohne Name," which, although canceled, are melodic sources for the Valse.

Why did Stravinsky date the Valse May 1922? The answer may be that *Le*

---

[5] Cf. *Stravinsky: The Short Piano Pieces*, Boosey & Hawkes, New York, 1977.

[6] Answering a letter of January 21, 1961, from E. W. White, Stravinsky wrote that he did not want the "Valse pour les enfants" and the "Souvenir d'une marche boche" to be republished.

Figaro had offered him money for a *new* piece. But surely the agreement did not include the right to claim, as the newspaper did, that he had "improvised" the work on the premises. He wrote in the margin of one copy of the newspaper score, *"Mensonge, ce n'est pas une musique improvisée! IStr.,"* and, in another copy, *"Quelle blague! Je n'ai jamais improvisée cette Valse [;] au contraire, elle est tout ce qu'il y a de composée [,] et non pas au Figaro mai [s] c'est chez moi à la maison.   IStr."* Whether or not *Le Figaro* had many *"petits lecteurs,"* one of Stravinsky's aims in all of the easy pieces was to disguise pedagogy. The bass part in each of the Three Easy Pieces, and in the "Valse des fleurs" (where the same three notes are repeated in every measure), can be played by someone sitting at a piano for the first time—if she or he can *keep* time. Hence the easy pieces afford both untrained adults, and not especially precocious three-year-olds, the experience of performing music of considerable sophistication, instead of struggling with technical exercises.

A complete Stravinsky album of easy pieces would include three leaves of arrangements for piano 2-hands. In the summer of 1940, he arranged the final song from *Berceuses du chat* and the Andante of the Five Easy Pieces (from the orchestra version and retaining its tonality), intending both pieces for children. The third leaf—a transcription of the chorus from the Prologue to *Boris Godunov*—probably dates from August or September 1918, since the music is found on the same page as one of the final sketches for a passage in the Triumphant March of the Devil from *Histoire du soldat*. Stravinsky transposed Mussorgsky's chorus from F minor to A minor, added the metronome marking $\downarrow$ = 92, and placed the open fifth of the accompaniment before the music of the chorus. Both the bass and the treble parts were designed for small hands. At the head of the manuscript, Stravinsky wrote the words of the first line of the chorus, "Why have you forsaken us, our father?" perhaps expressing his own sentiments about the plight of Russia.

In conclusion, it should be said that *The Five Fingers* (1912) are not easy pieces in the same ways as the others, although the first edition (J. & W. Chester, 1922) is subtitled on the flyleaf "8 Very Easy Pieces on Five Notes." Even if "notes" are understood to mean "pitches," both descriptions are misleading: the melodies sometimes shift into the bass, thereby requiring "The Ten Fingers," and in the last piece the right hand must play nine different pitches. But even when the melody is confined to a range of five pitches, these are the same in only three of the pieces.

APPENDIX H

RENARD: *Sketch for an Instrumental Version;*
the Piano Transcription of the Cimbalom Part; Stravinsky's Revisions

In October 1940, Stravinsky signed an agreement with the Walt Disney studios
for the right to make an animated cartoon of *Renard*. In the same month, the
composer began work on an arrangement of the piece for instruments only. In
the one section that he completed, from **41** through the fourth measure after **46**,
the tenor parts are assigned to the trumpet and the first bass part to the bassoon
(and later to a combination of English horn, French horn, cello, bass, and
trombone). That he did not finish the arrangement of the entire opus for this
instrumentation is regrettable, if only because the music would have been more
frequently performed. (See above.)

Stravinsky's transcription of the cimbalom for piano dates from March 12
to 16, 1953. He had finished recording *The Rake's Progress* in New York on
March 10 (2:00–7:30 p.m.), seen *Guys and Dolls* that evening, and flown to
Los Angeles the next day. He was present at rehearsals of *Renard* in the new
instrumentation on March 17 and 20, and he heard the premiere at a Monday
Evening Concert on March 30 (sitting between Gertrude Schoenberg and
Darius Milhaud). Although the substitute piano part makes the piece available
to performing groups that would otherwise be unable to program it, Stravinsky
preferred the light and springy cimbalom to the piano, for which, nevertheless,
he wrote full, uncimbalomistic chords.

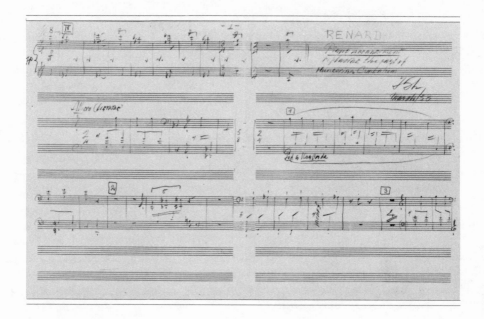

Stravinsky conducted the 1953 version in a concert in Royce Hall (UCLA) on November 20, 1955. (His program also included the *Ragtime* with the cimbalom part transcribed for piano.) The plan for the positions of the performers in *Renard,* reproduced here in facsimile, was drawn by the composer in the present writer's copy of the miniature score.

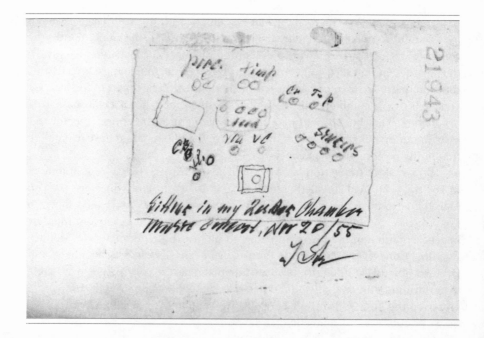

In January 1962, preparing to record *Renard,* Stravinsky made a number of revisions, adding the bassoon at measures 21 and 55 to double the Bass II for four measures, rewriting the bassoon figure in measure 145 as five notes (deleting one of the D's) in the time of a quarter (not three eighths), and, in measure 147, deleting the last bassoon quintuplet. At measure 144, he changed the time values to " ♩. in measure 143 = ♩. in measure 144," but this was done hastily, during the actual recording session; the notation in the printed score, " ♩. in measure 143 = ♩ in measure 144," must stand as correct, not only because Stravinsky had always performed it this way in the past but, also, because he is unlikely to have written *any* proportion if he had intended the values to be simply ♩. = ♩. , which implies no change. Some vocal doublings were introduced in January 1962. He added the second bass and the two tenors on the first note of the first bass at measure 166 and at measure 168; at measure 291, he joined the second bass to the first for the first eight notes, and again from the second note in measure 321 through the first in measure 322, and for the first three notes in measures 325 and 329. In measure 354, Stravinsky changed the bassoon's sixteenths to a quintuplet and in 354 and 355, doubled the first three notes of each bassoon quintuplet with cimbalom. In measures 448–51 and measures 452–55, he added a muted trumpet sustaining D (same pitch as the second violin), and in measures 204, 209, 215, and 224, he altered the triplet in the flute part to a triple-tongue D without the octave and rewrote the first violin in the same places as follows:

The following errors are among the many still found in the *Renard* score:

ms. 137: The trumpet-note belongs on the fourth eighth-note of ms. 136. (The same correction should be made in measure 347.)

ms. 155: The first note of the 2nd horn should sound B-natural.

ms. 157: The last note of Bass II should be B-flat.

ms. 318: A sharp is missing before the C in the trumpet.

ms. 348: The tenor clef is missing in the bassoon part (and the bass clef at ms. 354).

ms. 407: The second note in the horn part should sound A (not G-sharp).

ms. 423: The first note of the viola should be E (not E-sharp).

At four measures from the end of the piece, the second horn should double the first (i.e., the score is wrong).

In January 1947, *Renard,* newly choreographed by George Balanchine, was presented by the Ballet Society at Hunter College Playhouse. The composer supervised the staging as well as the musical preparation, and, wanting the piece to be sung in English, he sent a translation, made by Gregory Golubev, his agent at the time, to Balanchine (letter of October 30, 1946). Lincoln Kirstein commissioned another translation, however, by Harvey Officer, which Stravinsky liked, and for which he rewrote the rhythms and phrasings in the vocal parts at some places. (Stravinsky's final corrections in the English text are preserved in the present writer's score.) At others, where the words had previously been freely spoken, he added rhythmic notations, as in ms. 504:

You,   Scoundrel!   Let the beasts   tear you to   bits!

Stravinsky's correspondence with his publisher J. & W. Chester Ltd, London, reveals that as early as 1923 he had intended to rewrite *Renard* using only two singers. In New York, on April 14, 1950, he listened to the test pressing of the Dial recording of *Renard* and decided that the music from **81** to **90**—the *"pribaoutki,"* as he called it—should be lighter and clearer in the vocal parts. Furthermore, no longer caring for the Harvey Officer translation, Stravinsky rewrote the text. At this period he was a devotee of Broadway musicals, which explains some of the rhymes: time/dime, happy/snappy.

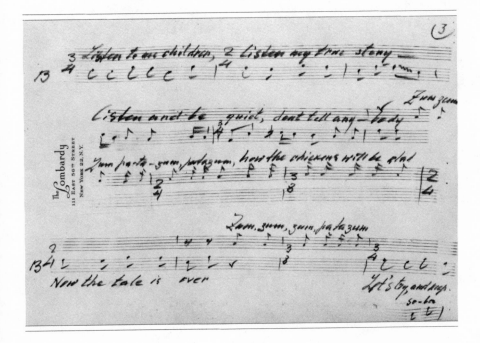

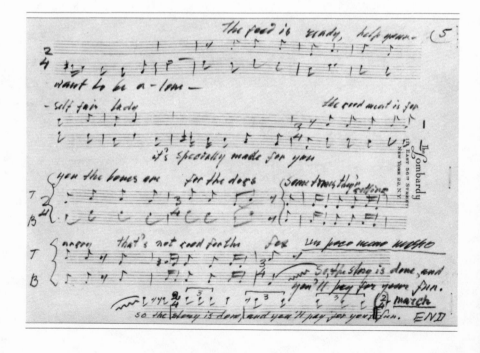

APPENDIX I

"Sektanskaya"

The most serious lacuna in the Stravinsky literature is an adequate study of his use of Russian folk texts, music, drama, and the traditions of folk entertainers.[1] His early song "The Mushrooms Going to War" (1904), based on verses extracted in part from Kireyevsky, may not testify to an abiding interest in the subject, since Tchaikovsky set the same text, but late acquisitions do, especially of such collections as Rubyetz's *Russian Folk Songs,* Vorotnokov's *Russian Folk Songs,* and Lysenko's *Ukrainian Songs,* all purchased in February 1926.

Stravinsky employed Russian sectarian verse in the "Mystic Song of the Ancient Russian Flagellants" (1908), although the text in this case is not pure but an adaptation by Serge Gorodyetsky, and in a song, "Sektanskaya" (February–March 1919). Sectarian music is used in two other Stravinsky pieces, his composition of the final chorus of *Khovanshchina* (1913), and of an incomplete work, "Khlyst" ("Flagellant"), which is without text, and for which only two sketches have been identified (Examples 1 and 2).

Example 1

---

[1] Professor Simon Karlinsky, in a brilliant chapter on "Pre-Literate Russian Theater," remarks that "none of the book-length studies of Stravinsky published in the West ever tells its readers the obvious fact that *Renard* is a work that portrays a group of itinerant *skomorokhi* who don animal masks, perform a satirical, anti-clerical skit for a rural audience in pre-Petrine Russia and demand a payment in barter at the end of the performance: 'Well, here is a tale for you and I get a crock of butter!' ... The entire text is permeated with familiar Russian nonsense rhymes, proverbs and parodies of ecclesiastic diction and Orthodox prayers. But since singing translations are concerned

Example 2

The Khlysts, who were orgiasts as well as demonists, believed that Christ's spirit did not leave the earth when he died, but was reincarnated in saintly people. Though persecuted by the government and church in the eighteenth century, the sect persisted into the twentieth, and produced at least one considerable poet, Nikolai Klyuev (1887–1937).

"Final chorus of *Khovanshchina* composed by Igor Stravinsky after Mussorgsky's own and authentic sectarian themes," Stravinsky wrote (in English) late in life on the cover of his copy of the *Khovanshchina* piano score.[2] But his chorus is an elaboration of a single theme, the sectarian one employed by Rimsky-Korsakov, in whose own version the opera ends at a point corresponding to only the twenty-fifth measure of Stravinsky's 116-measure chorus. Stravinsky's composition, dedicated "To Sergei Pavlovich Diaghilev," emulates the simplicity of Mussorgsky. The opening theme is exposed by the chorus, a cappella. The orchestra enters with a bass accompaniment figure derived from the theme, and the instrumentation is remarkable in the use of tremolo, particularly at the perdendosi ending, and in some skillfully voiced and transparent wind chords in an orchestral interlude. One obvious imitation of Mussorgsky is in the bell-like alternating of treble and bass chords. (Shostakovich's version, in contrast, concludes with other melodic material and a long orchestral postlude, orchestrated in a "modern" fashion, with piano, harp, percussion, onstage trumpets and trombones, and busy violin figures in a high register.)

In the first sketchbook for "Sektanskaya," Stravinsky identifies the text as "No. 351, p. 445, from songs of Russian sects." This corresponds to the num-

---

with syllable count and stresses, very little of all this native lore is ever conveyed to non-Russian listeners of *Renard*."

[2] The orchestra score was apparently never published, but the manuscript is known to be in a private collection in Europe. On October 22, 1913, the publisher V. Bessel

bering in Rozhdestvensky's and Uspensky's *Pesno russikh sektantovmistikha* (St. Petersburg, 1912). But in the third line from the end Stravinsky substitutes the words "Jesus Christ" for the word "honor."

In proportion to the brevity of the music, the abundance of sketches for the song is unprecedented in Stravinsky's oeuvre. These are found in three books—No. 1 with eighteen pages, No. 2 with two pages, and No. 3 with twelve. Stravinsky did not make a fair copy of the completed score, and the facsimile reproduced here has been pieced together from the final drafts in book No. 3, which, however, do not occur in the sequence of the song as published. (Stravinsky's calligraphic copy of the flute part for a performance in Paris—letter to Jean Wiéner, December 3, 1923—is intended for the piano version of the song, not the cimbalom version.)

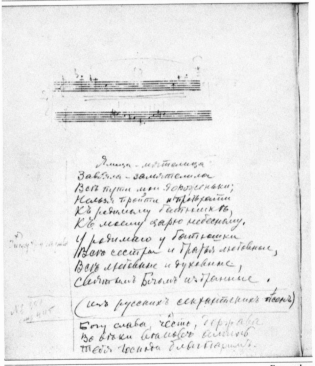

Example 3

wrote to Stravinsky from St. Petersburg complaining that the package which Diaghilev sent from London "did not contain the score of the final chorus, nor even one of the 78 choral parts." On November 24, Bessel wrote again: "I still have not received the orchestration of the concluding chorus from *Khovanshchina*. . . . Please write to Diaghilev again, for although he is here, I have tried in vain to reach him, both by telephone and by letter. I want to publish your score in the near future." Bessel moved to Paris after the Revolution and continued to publish there, but his correspondence with Stravinsky in the 1920s does not mention the *Khovanshchina* chorus.

The first entry, the thirteen-note palindrome[3] and final E (above the text), is the source for many of the basic intervals of the song (Example 3).

The diminished fifth, transposed, is the nucleus of the accompaniment for the first section of the piece, while the uppermost note of the first chord, C-flat (B-natural), becomes the principal melodic note at the start of the vocal part. The groups of five notes and nine notes are converted into figures for the flute obbligato, while the $\frac{6}{8}$ and $\frac{7}{8}$ measures form the basis of the beginning of the piece (Example 4).

Example 4

Having found the frame of the beginning, Stravinsky immediately turned to the second section, to which he did not give a meter (Example 5).

In the next several pages, Stravinsky explored the combination of flute and voice in close harmony (featuring thirds), and imitating the contour of the vocal part. He later transferred the five-note cimbalom accompaniment figure, with changes, to the flute part. The bass notes in the cimbalom, starting in the third measure, form a half-cycle of fifths, repeated in palindrome. Stravinsky has faintly penciled in his name and the date—"March 1, '19"—at the end (Example 6).

---

[3] Palindromes occur with some frequency in Stravinsky's sketchbooks, beginning in 1917.

Example 5

Example 6

In the next sketch (Example 7), Stravinsky discovers the rhythm of the vocal part in measures 10–11 (of the published song), for although the notes beneath the verse lack stems and beams, the distancing is similar to that in the voice part in the score at the bottom of the page.

Example 7

Here is the complete song:

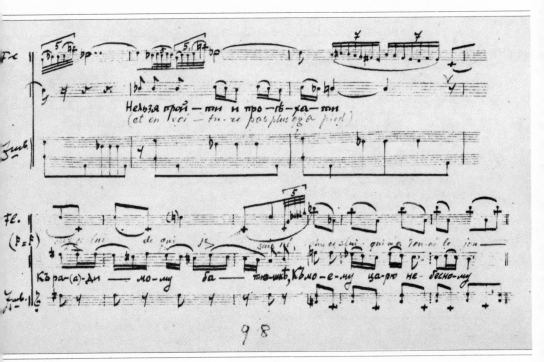

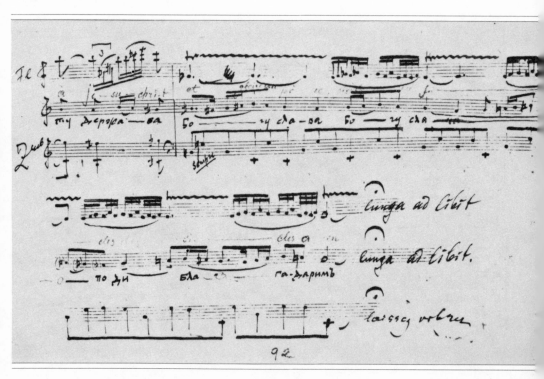

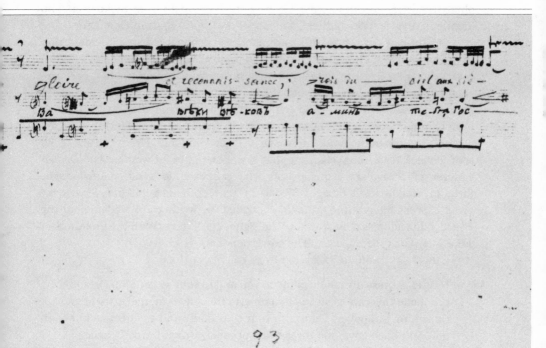

APPENDIX J

Stravinsky, Stokowski, and Madame Incognito

In July 1923, Leopold Stokowski became the intermediary—or so he said—for a woman who wished to make a semi-annual gift of money to Stravinsky for a period of three years. The events that followed form one of the stranger chapters in Stravinsky's biography, partly for the reasons that his benefactress insisted on remaining anonymous, did not commission any music with the money, and never met the composer or answered his letters. The $6,000 that Stravinsky eventually received is a larger sum than he would have earned from concerts with the Philadelphia Orchestra that Stokowski had already invited him to conduct.

The story of "Madame," as Stokowski referred to her, and as Stravinsky addressed her in letters of thanks, must be told against the background of the composer's negotiations for an American tour. These had begun in August 1921, when Walter Damrosch asked Stravinsky to conduct programs of his works with the New York Symphony. Whatever the reasons, for this correspondence Stravinsky used the address of Mme Sudeikina, Hôtel Elysée, 100 rue de la Boëtie. Stravinsky refused Damrosch's proposal, but another one soon came from Stokowski, who, in May 1923, discussed with Stravinsky, in Paris, the possibility of conducting a series of concerts in Philadelphia. The terms are found in a letter of September 29, 1923, from Arthur Judson, manager of the Philadelphia Orchestra, and in another letter of the same date from Stokowski, who mentions that he will conduct *The Song of the Nightingale* in October.

On June 3, 1923, Stravinsky and Stokowski concluded an agreement that gave Stokowski the rights to the American premiere of the *Symphonies of Wind Instruments* for $100. Stravinsky invited Stokowski to attend the first performance of *Les Noces* (June 13), but the conductor telegraphed from Bordeaux, saying that he was ill and would come later, and telegraphed again, on June 25 from Quimper, saying that he would arrive in five or six days. On July 5 he deposited the $100 in the Bankers Trust Co., Place Vendôme. Then, on July 14, he sent a check for $1,000, claiming that it was the gift of a woman who was an admirer of Stravinsky's music and who promised to send, anonymously, through Stokowski, a total of $6,000 in six-month installments. Stravinsky could express his gratitude, Stokowski added, by writing to "Madame" at the Philadelphia address of Stokowski, who signed his letter, "With the profoundest admiration for your music." (The correspondence is in French.)

Stravinsky wrote to Stokowski from Biarritz on July 21:

> How to express my appreciation to you and to your so generous friend, who has made this rare gesture of coming to the aid of another person and yet remaining unknown! Thanks to your so friendly and so effective intervention, you have given me three years of relief, which I greatly need.

A letter was enclosed for "Madame":

Monsieur Stokovsky [*sic*] has forwarded $1,000 to me, saying that you wish to give a sort of pension to me of $2,000 a year for three years ($1,000 every six months, of which I have had the first installment) and that you are doing this to procure for me the tranquillity indispensable for my work and for the realization of my artistic ideas.

I cannot convey to you, Madame, all the gratitude that I owe you, and my appreciation, not only of your so generous gesture, but also of the way in which it was made, which is to say, without self-interest. . . . For my part, I will not conceal from you the very strong desire that I have to know you and to thank you in my own voice, if I ever have the opportunity of meeting you. . . .

On September 13, Stravinsky sent the orchestra parts of his *Symphonies* to Stokowski, with a letter asking for news of the American audience's reaction to the piece.

Stravinsky soon began to suspect that the mysterious donor was actually Stokowski, who was subsidizing him to secure American premieres of his new works, as well as his approval. A letter from Carlos Salzedo in Maine to Stokowski in Paris, June 26, 1923, may be interpreted as supporting this theory. Salzedo explains that the International Composers' Guild in New York, of which Edgard Varèse was the founder and chairman, intends to perform Stravinsky's *Renard* but lacks the money to meet his conditions:

> . . . As our principal offering last year was *Pierrot Lunaire,* so this year we would like to give *Renard.* Would you intercede with Stravinsky and find out his terms for [exclusive rights] for the American premiere? . . . We could organize a tour for him, but, as you know, we are beholden to two parvenues, Mrs. Reis and Mrs. Wertheim, whose only interest is in social climbing, who understand absolutely nothing in contemporary music, and who support only what that boring Louis Gruenberg writes. . . . I thank you in advance for your ambassadorship.

In view of Stokowski's meetings with Stravinsky at this time, and of the circumstance that Salzedo's letter could not have been received much more than a day or two before July 14, the sudden appearance of a wealthy enthusiast for a composer still scarcely known in America, and certainly not popular in Philadelphia, is suspect. Stokowski *does* seem the most probable source for the stipend.

On September 8, Salzedo wrote directly to Stravinsky, saying that the scores and parts for *Renard* had come from London, and that the important question of the conductor must now be decided—either Stokowski or Monteux, since Ansermet (who had led the premiere) was unavailable. Whether or not Stravinsky realized that Stokowski had been the foregone choice, the composer learned that Stokowski would conduct the piece when Salzedo sent the program (November 9), and learned, too, that the concert would take place in the Vanderbilt Theater, New York, on December 2, and that in addition to *Renard,* music by Schoenberg, Bartók, Hindemith, Lourié, and Delage would be heard.

"Stokowski gave a marvelous performance of *The Song of the Nightingale* and he will give a perfect one of *Renard,*" Salzedo added. But Stravinsky had already received the first part of this news from Stokowski himself, in a letter dated October 27. The conductor, however, attributed the "decided success of the piece with the public—far more than the newspaper clippings that I am sending would indicate"—to the many extra rehearsals. "The performance of *The Nightingale* was a good one."

Stravinsky was more interested in "Madame." He wrote from Paris on November 4, mentioning the "very lively success" of his Octet, and the composition of the Piano Concerto, the first performance of which, in Paris in the spring of 1924, he invited Stokowski to attend; but the purpose of the letter was to ask Stokowski to arrange for the second installment to be sent in dollars to Lloyds' Banque [*sic*], Biarritz. Writing again on November 15, Stravinsky expressed his "great pleasure in the success" of *The Song of the Nightingale,* and announced that, since his prior obligations to his American manager, A. F. Adams, no longer obtained, the Philadelphia engagements in January and February 1925 could now take place. He waited four days before writing to Stokowski asking him to arrange an earlier payment of the January installment from Madame.

This November 19 letter crossed with one from Stokowski which was dated November 24 and which revealed that at the premiere of the *Symphonies* the day before, the audience had been very antagonistic, even though

> I conducted a great many rehearsals . . . and I feel that it was a good performance. The public was simply unable to understand the music at a first hearing. . . . I am conducting [the piece] again tonight. . . . Your letter to Madame was placed faithfully in her hands, and she was happy to hear from you. . . . She is most enthusiastic about *The Nightingale* and the *Symphonies.*

This report also describes rehearsals for *Renard,* and the difficulties with the cimbalomist—"I am searching all over America to find a better man in time for the concert"—concluding with the statement, "I have had the most profound musical pleasure in studying your work this season, and although the public is hostile, I shall continue to perform it."

Stravinsky's next letter, on November 30, reveals that he had asked his now ex-manager, A. F. Adams, to guarantee twenty-five American engagements, at $1,000 each, as soloist in the Piano Concerto, and ten conducting engagements, at $500 each. That Stravinsky's fee for conducting an entire concert was half of that for a quarter of an hour of piano-playing is less surprising than his in-principle acceptance of a new proposal from Judson (December 1) offering a mere $5,000 for six concerts with the Philadelphia Orchestra. But on December 22, Stravinsky sent a counter-offer—repeated in a letter directly to Stokowski on January 1, 1924—demanding that his travel expenses be paid, not only from Europe and back, but also within the United States. Judson did not respond until March 12, and whatever the new proposition, Stravinsky refused it in a one-word cable, writing later to Stokowski: "I prefer to talk about the matter with you in Paris, where I hope to see you in May or June."

Stokowski had sent the January 1924 installment on December 14, which again suggests that the money was at his immediate disposal, since Stravinsky's request could hardly have reached Philadelphia more than a day or so before. Stokowski's accompanying letter characterizes the *Renard* performance as a sensational success, even though the cimbalom part had to be played on the piano by Salzedo, whose own account of the event, on December 17, confirms the conductor's and informs Stravinsky that *Renard* and Schoenberg's *Herz-gewaechse* had had to be repeated, that Stokowski took seven curtain calls after *Renard,* that friends who heard the Paris performance have attested to the superiority of the one in New York, and that "the occasion was a triumph for contemporary music."

The failure of the audience to understand the *Symphonies* did not dampen Stravinsky's enthusiasm for his new champion:

> Your letter referring to my *Symphonies* has given me very great pleasure. It is of no importance that a symphony-concert audience has received this work badly. With a man such as yourself, I have nothing to fear. You will finish by convincing these good people. Nevertheless, I wait impatiently for news of the second performance. Thank you for having given my letter to Madame. Tell her how happy I was to know that she likes not only my *Nightingale* but also my *Symphonies.* . . .

No doubt because of this encouragement, Stokowski decided to play the *Symphonies* again in Philadelphia on February 1 and 2, and in New York on February 5 (letter of January 11). But the Orchestra Committee unanimously vetoed his plan to repeat the piece locally, and, according to a letter from Stokowski on February 26, after the New York performance

> there was a great deal of hissing and a great deal of applause. But although the reception was only half good, I feel that your music is gaining in understanding in America. In a few weeks I am going to play your *Renard* twice in Philadelphia and once again in New York.

Writing on April 14, Stokowski expressed his desire to conduct the *Scherzo fantastique,* and, on April 20, his hopes of giving *Les Noces.* Stravinsky replied on May 3, asking the conductor to bring the parts of the *Symphonies* with him to Europe, for the reason that "the work has not yet been published and there are many difficulties with it." Stravinsky also explained that his publisher, J. & W. Chester, neglected to ask for his author's rights for the New York performance of *Renard,* and, since he received nothing from this "sensational premiere," he asks for Stokowski's help. Whatever the outcome of this request, when the conductor arrived in France, Stravinsky taught him *Le Sacre du printemps.*

On September 2 Stravinsky wrote that he had signed a contract with Bottenheim for an American tour, in the period January–March 1925, and was therefore free to appear with the Philadelphia Orchestra during that time as guest conductor and pianist. In the same letter, Stravinsky also asked Stokowski to try to procure the January installment from Madame on October 1, "my expenses having been augmented because of my forthcoming move to Nice"—except that neither in this nor in any subsequent letter does he refer to "Madame." The money, sent on September 16, was tied to a request by Stokowski to conduct *Le Sacre* in Philadelphia, unless Stravinsky intended to do so himself. The composer answered on October 8:

> . . . As for *Le Sacre,* knowing the great desire that you have always had to conduct it, and also knowing the zeal with which you studied the score with me, I really do not have the courage to take the lead from you and to conduct the work myself. Therefore I will not conduct it this year with your orchestra, but instead, as they say, pass the baton to you. . . . I hope that my guest tour with your orchestra has been well arranged for me. Waiting for your good news, I send you, dear Mr. Stokowski, *amitiés.*

In his next letter, July 20, 1925—more than a year after the American tour—Stravinsky asked Stokowski to pay the January 1926 installment together with the current one,

> so that I can draw on the sum of $2,000 by the first of September, on which date I have very large financial obligations to meet. These two payments will be the last from the generous unknown person for whom I will always feel the greatest gratitude. Permit me to tell you, with the frankness that has always existed between us, that despite my profitable tour in America, I must again, this last time, ask for the help that has been so generously given me these three years. It is because I must liquidate, as quickly as possible, the numerous debts that I have accumulated during the last years, and because I must give the money that I earned in America to my numerous family. . . . Hoping you will understand the reasons that have forced me to write this letter, and that you will not condemn me, I send you, dear friend, my most devoted regards.

Stravinsky understood that he was in a position to request the remainder of his "pension" a half-year in advance as the result of a letter from Louis Bailly of the Flonzaley Quartet, sent from Corsica on June 20. Bailly wrote that Stokowski "would be infinitely pleased to have the red ribbon of the Legion of Honor." But a campaign to gain support for this, launched in November, had come to nothing, Alfred Cortot having complained that "too many Americans had received the ribbon recently." According to Bailly, Stokowski believed that a few words from Stravinsky would accomplish the desired result. Stravinsky wrote to Stokowski, on July 6, 1925:

> Recently I saw M. Bailly, who told me that there was a question of the Legion of Honor being awarded to you, but that the matter has been dragging since November. Since you are an American citizen, the question is in the

hands of the Minister of Foreign Affairs. Knowing many people in this ministry, and knowing that to receive this award would please you, I spoke to one of the most important functionaries and asked him to speed the process. I am happy to tell you that he received my request very favorably and promised to see to it immediately. . . . Hoping to have good news from you, I send you, dear Mr. Stokowski, my best *amitiés*.

Stokowski acknowledged this letter on July 16, and on September 8 he wrote to say that he was hoping for a reply from Madame "in about two days." Stravinsky did not write again until Christmas day, however, at which time he excused his long silence because of a concert tour:

Returning from this trip, I push myself to reply to your nice letter with the check and to send great thanks to you and to the person who has so generously supported me through these three years. . . .

Surely this person was Leopold Stokowski.

APPENDIX K

Text of the Brochure "The Tomb of F. I. Stravinsky"[1]

Department of Culture of The Executive Committee of the Lengor Soviet

STATE MUSEUM OF CITY SCULPTURE

Statue to F. I. Stravinsky in the Necropolis of the Great Masters[2]

In Leningrad, in the southeastern corner of the Necropolis of the Great Masters, to the left of the entrance, Fyodor Ignatievich Stravinsky lies buried. He was one of the most brilliant representatives of Russian operatic art, and the father of the prominent contemporary composer I. F. Stravinsky. F. I. Stravinsky, endowed with a bass voice of tremendous range, was a singer of exceptional musicality. During a period of twenty-five years of work on the stage of the Maryinsky Theater (1876–1901), he played approximately seventy roles in almost sixty operas, and, in all, appeared on stage nearly fifteen hundred times.

Artistically, Fyodor Ignatievich Stravinsky was multi-gifted. A man of great culture, a bibliophile, and an exacting connoisseur of art, he was also a most tal-

---

[1] Published by the Soviet government in 1935.

[2] In the chronicle of events of the magazine *Theater and Art*, No. 48 (1902), it was announced that the cause of F. I. Stravinsky's death was a sarcoma. He was buried in the Volkov Cemetery. Then his remains were moved to the Novodevichy Monastery. In 1936 the remains were reinterred in the Necropolis of the Great Masters.

ented and skillful graphic artist and make-up man. All these talents helped the singer to create artistically masterful scenes on the opera stage. He was the first to realize the importance of words and gestures as a means for conveying a scene in the musical theater, and was thus a forerunner of the genius Chaliapin. The latter pronounced Stravinsky "a great artist who has triumphed over the routine." P. I. Tchaikovsky also praised the "beautiful voice and lively acting" of this singer.

F. I. Stravinsky died on November 2, 1902. On July 23, 1936, the singer's remains, as well as a monument to him, were moved from the Novodevichy cemetery to the fields of the Necropolis of the Great Masters.

The monument to F. I. Stravinsky was built according to the design of the sculptor V. A. Beklemishev. Carved into the face of a tall, granite obelisque is a bas-relief portrait of the singer, the work of the sculptor L. V. Pozen. This is executed in a realistic manner and with great likeness. The left side of the bas-relief is framed by a wreath of laurel and palm branches. On the right, attention focuses on the figure of a Muse of sadness who is holding a lyre with a broken string in her left hand, as if to indicate that it had pronounced the final chord. The slender figure of the Muse, also the work of V. A. Beklemishev, reflects a tragic theme of sorrow: the right arm is lowered in a gesture of helplessness, the head is slightly raised and turned away in profile, the expression on the face is one of thoughtful sadness. The whole figure of the Muse is reminiscent of the weepers depicted in monuments of the Classical period.

Certain characteristics of early–twentieth-century art are visible in the composition of the statue and in its plastic realization: a certain affected grace and asymmetry in the posture of the Muse, the lovely manner of the modeling, and the contrast between the sculpture and the architecture of the monument.

The monument to Fyodor Ignatievich Stravinsky was unveiled on November 21, 1908. Present at the unveiling were members of the family, friends, admirers of the talented singer, representatives of the world of art, the Maryinsky Theater's leading actors I. V. Ershov and I. V. Tartakov, the monument's authors—the sculptors V. A. Beklemishev and L. V. Pozen—and others.

APPENDIX L

The Manuscript of the Larguette concertante

The manuscript of the full score of the second movement of the Symphony in C in the Library of Congress is not the original but a copy. The provenance of the true autograph score is as follows:

March 15, 1939. Cambridge, Massachusetts. Nadia Boulanger writes to Stravinsky in Sancellemoz, Sallanches, Haute-Savoie, saying that Mrs. John Alden Carpenter and Mrs. Robert Woods Bliss guarantee the commission of the Symphony for the premiere in Chicago.
March 25. Mainz. Willy Strecker, director, B. Schotts Söhne, writes, referring to

> the mourning felt in your last letters, and . . . this unhappy time in your family. . . . I am aware that you are working on an orchestra piece and beg you to write to me about it. . . . Do you think that this new work will be finished in time for the London concert?

March 28. Sancellemoz. Stravinsky's daughter-in-law writes to a concert agent in Milan:

> My father-in-law is unable to reply himself . . . scarcely three months after the death of his daughter, his wife has died. He left Paris abruptly, on the advice of his doctors, in a state of complete exhaustion, after months of anguish.

April 1. Stravinsky to Strecker:

> Knowing of my pecuniary difficulties this year, friends in America had the idea of procuring a sum of money in return for which I would give my manuscript to the National Library of the White House [Library of Congress]. There is still a question of presenting the world premiere of my work in Chicago under my direction.

April 17. Stravinsky completes the first movement in short-score form.
May 1. Stravinsky writes to Edward Forbes, Cambridge, Massachusetts:

> I cannot guarantee more than six lectures [at Harvard], for the reason that for some time I have been occupied with a very important work that has already been interrupted by the tragedies that have struck me, but that must be finished in the next season. You will understand that . . . I am obliged to be a little stingy with my time. . . . I must tell you that it is indispensable to my work to have a place where *"je puisse travailler la musique"* in the most complete isolation.

May 16. Florence. Stravinsky gives the full score of the first movement of the Symphony to Strecker.
May 29. Paris. Vladimir Golschmann writes: ". . . I have your news from Roland

[-Manuel]. Everything that he tells me about your new work gives me a great desire to hear it soon."
June 9. Mainz. Strecker promises "to return the original manuscript of the first movement with a photocopy."
July 9. Sancellemoz. Stravinsky writes to Strecker acknowledging

> . . . the magnificent photographic reproduction (first part of my Symphony). . . . It is only now that I answer your letter of June 9, my new sorrow[1] having interrupted our correspondence. . . . As for the world premiere of my new Symphony with the BBC, I must see what is happening on this subject in America. N. Boulanger, who has just arrived, will surely inform me.

July 10. Stravinsky signs the contract for the Symphony and sends it to Strecker.
July 19. Stravinsky finishes the second movement in short-score form.
July 19. Mainz. Strecker inquires whether the second part of the Symphony will be finished before Stravinsky leaves for America: "The engraving of the score will start at the beginning of August; the extracting of the parts of the first movement is virtually complete."
July 29. Stravinsky to Strecker:

> I have completed the second movement . . . a *Larguette concertante.* I am orchestrating it and will send it as soon as this work is finished, probably toward the middle of August. Since you will be on vacation again, please give the order to photograph the manuscript in exactly the same manner as was done for the first movement. The manuscript will contain either 33 or 33½ pages. I will stay here until August 31, then go to Venice.[2] On September 4, at the Biennale, I will conduct my opera *Mavra* and the *Dumbarton Oaks* Concerto. On September 6, I should be in Paris, where you can write to me c/o Mme Sudeikina. . . . I embark for New York September 27 on the S.S. *Ile de France.* . . . The Symphony is not commissioned, and, contrary to what I had thought about the American affair (about which I told you in Florence), when my engagement by Harvard became known, all the do-gooders backed out. We can envisage something interesting with

---

[1] Stravinsky's mother died on June 7, 1939.
[2] Stravinsky had asked Païchadze to procure Italian visas for him and for Mme Sudeikina. But on August 1, Païchadze answered that a new rule had gone into effect that anyone seeking a visa would "have to come for it personally. . . . I told [the official] that this was impossible since the person involved was in the Haute-Savoie in a sanitarium, and could not come to Paris. . . I had not imagined that, in spite of the frightening political situation, there could be so many people going to Italy. I took on the official again [and] to his question as to why an exception should be made, I explained that Il Duce knew you personally and has often given you an audience. That made an immediate impression and instead of replying, the official gave me a form to fill out and

London, therefore, and on a larger and more interesting scale, giving the world premiere with the BBC.

August 22. Strecker goes to Sancellemoz and leaves on the same day with the manuscript of the second movement.

August 28. Mainz. Strecker to Stravinsky:

> I was with Hindemith for only two days, having been obliged to return home sooner than expected. . . . The manuscript of the *Larguette* has already been photographed. This music is an absolute masterpiece. . . . After the political crisis, I will return your manuscript, or perhaps send only the photocopy.

September 9. Strecker writes:

> The second movement of your Symphony is finished. I will keep the manuscript here and send the photocopy until receiving further instructions from you.

October 13. Strecker writes to Stravinsky, c/o Harvard University, saying that a photocopy of the second movement of the Symphony has been sent and asking him to deliver the remaining movements to Associated Music Publishers, New York, so that photocopies can be forwarded to Alsbach (Amsterdam).

October 29. The *New York Times* publishes a photograph of Stravinsky working on the Symphony in C at a piano in Cambridge.

October [?]. From an interview with Stravinsky in a Boston newspaper:

> My new Symphony is going to be classical in spirit, more concise in its form than Beethoven. . . . Instead of all chords gravitating toward one final tonic chord, all notes gravitate toward a single note. Thus this Symphony will be neither a Symphony in C major nor a Symphony in C minor but simply a Symphony in C.

January 10, 1940. Alsbach. Strecker writes to Stravinsky (who receives the letter in Pittsburgh on January 31) saying that his November 29 letter has been received, via Alsbach, but as yet no way has been found to send the manuscript of the second movement.

February 2. New York. Paul Stoes, Stravinsky's concert manager, writes to him

---

said that the visa would be granted the next day. I have just returned from the consulate, where they delivered your passport to me with a kind smile. I am enclosing it here. But I could not have gotten a visa for Vera Arturovna in her absence." The full story of Stravinsky and fascist Italy has yet to be written, but it can be noted here that by the end of 1935, he was defending the country against the "misunderstanding democracies." For example, in a letter to Yakov Lvovich Lvov, in Trieste, December 5, 1935, Stravinsky says: "It is a great pity that I cannot accept the kind invitation of the Ministry of Propaganda for the performance of *Oedipus* set for March 15," and he goes on to express sympathy for "the difficult position that Italy, glorious and unique, now rejuvenated and thirsting for life, has been put in by worldwide obscurantism. . . .''

c/o Dagmar Godowsky, saying that Stravinsky must write a few words to announce the premiere of the "New Symphony which he is writing in honor of the 50th Jubilee Celebration of the [Chicago] Orchestra."

March 29. Stoes writes to Stravinsky in Cambridge:

> Concerning the world premiere of your new Symphony in Chicago, I understand that because of the interest of Mrs. [Robert Woods] Bliss and Mrs. [John Alden] Carpenter, certain people have contributed the necessary funds. In the case of Chicago, I believe that $1,000 has been given through the efforts of Mrs. Carpenter . . . with the definite understanding that your new work was written in honor of the Fiftieth Anniversary of the Chicago Orchestra.

April 9. New York. Ernest Voigt of Associated Music Publishers writes Stravinsky that the photostat of the second movement of the Symphony is not clear enough to be reproduced photographically.

April 13 (Saturday). Boston. Stravinsky to Voigt:

> The manuscript of the second part of my new Symphony is in Europe and I cannot get it from Mainz because of the war. . . . It is absolutely necessary, therefore, to make new photostats, even if they are not good. . . . I need them to recopy my handwritten manuscript for the Congress Library, which has purchased the manuscript.

April 14. Boston. Stravinsky writes to Frederick Stock, Chicago:

> . . . my contract for the next season in Chicago has not yet been signed [because] of my failure to dedicate this composition to the Chicago Symphony Orchestra. . . . No one has ever mentioned this stipulation to me. . . . It has always been my intention to dedicate my symphony to the Chicago Orchestra, only I did not wish to have it publicized before the actual signing of the contract, as that would have lessened my chances of a world premiere in another city (i.e., in which case the piece would be dedicated to another orchestra).

April 15. New York. Voigt writes: "I still feel that we ought to make an attempt to get your manuscript from Schott."

April 16. Chicago. Mrs. Charles Goodspeed writes: "Dear Igor . . . We are all looking forward to your return here and to your conducting your new symphony."

April 17. Contract signed by Chicago and by Stoes.

April 20. Boston. Dr. Alexis Kall, Stravinsky's secretary,[3] writes to Voigt reiterating Stravinsky's belief that the second photostat should be made for the reason that parts would soon have to be extracted.

April 24. New York. Voigt informs Stravinsky of a cable from Schott saying that Mrs. Paul Hindemith will bring the manuscript.

---

[3] On arriving in Los Angeles at the beginning of June, Stravinsky discharged Kall and engaged Gregory Golubev, from August to November 1940.

May 8. Voigt acknowledges the receipt of the manuscripts of the first and third movements.

May 14. Voigt acknowledges the receipt of Stravinsky's copy of the *Larguette*.

June 7. New York. Voigt sends photostats of the first three movements to Stravinsky, now in California.

July 16. Beverly Hills. Stravinsky to Voigt:

> The last movement of my Symphony is very far advanced but not yet completed. I will send it to you at the end of July if my trip to Mexico does not interrupt my work. At this moment I have begun to work again, and I strongly hope to be able to send the complete orchestra score by the end of August. You will have two full months in which to extract and correct the orchestra parts. . . . I can tell you that the orchestra score of the last movement will have about 50 pages with 4 to 5 measures per page. But if two months seem like too short a time for work on the whole Symphony, why not do the first three movements now? . . . I am sending . . . the photostats of the first two movements, received from Strecker, so that you may insert the corrections in your new parts, as well as the corrections (slurs, bowings, etc.) that I have marked in colored pencils, and that are also marked in the margins of the score. . . . The terrible events in France, and the anguish in which I have been living, have slowed my work, which otherwise would have been completed a long time ago.

July 29. Voigt telegraphs to Stravinsky in Mexico City, acknowledging the receipt of the photostats but adding that "Gertrude Hindemith has not yet arrived."

August 23. Beverly Hills. Stravinsky sends the last movement to Voigt, asking him to make photocopies and then to send the manuscript directly to the Library of Congress: "Ask the librarian to send $1,000, according to the conditions stipulated in the letter of July 8, 1939, by Mr. Herbert Putnam, Chief, Division of Acquisitions, to Mrs. Robert Woods Bliss."

August 29: New York. Voigt writes that he did not send the photostats of the last two movements to Schott, because "Clipper Mail costs 30 cents a half ounce. [Moreover] I have written to Strecker saying that the work must be published in New York."

September 3. Stravinsky to Voigt:

> . . . As you know, the Symphony is dedicated to the Chicago Symphony on the occasion of its fiftieth anniversary. This organization had expressed the desire to see me conduct the premiere myself at the beginning of the next symphony season during a week of guest conducting beginning November 7. . . . I have not made any special arrangements with the Chicago Orchestra concerning rental fees. I simply told Dr. Frederick Stock that this question must be resolved between the Chicago Symphony and your company, this being a business matter that does not concern me. All that I did was to indicate that the sum of $250 for the first performance was suggested by Willy Strecker when I last saw him in France, ten days before the

war. . . . But it is also evident that my engagements as a guest conductor this season have been based on the novelty of the new Symphony. . . . I will conduct it with the Boston Symphony. . . . I ask you not to give the Symphony to other conductors, at least for the season of 1940–41.

September 4. Stravinsky writes to Voigt, discussing a proposition from Columbia to record the Symphony in Chicago. The composer asks whether he can accept a royalty of 2 cents per side, noting that "the piece lasts about 28 minutes and will fill seven sides. Of course, this is far from an appropriate remuneration for serious music, which can never sell like pieces of light music." He discusses the rental of the music to Columbia and his conductor's fee for the recording, mentioning Bruno Zirato in the latter regard, and the recent New York Philharmonic recordings of *Le Sacre* and *Petrushka*. The letter ends with a request for the photostat of the last movement, and with the notice that "I am going to San Francisco by car and will be there between September 6 and 13."

October 12. 124 S. Swall Drive, Beverly Hills. Writes to John Alden Carpenter accepting invitation to stay in his home in Chicago at the time of the Symphony in C premiere.

November 2. Leaves for Chicago by train.

November 7. Chicago. First performance of the Symphony in C, repeated on November 8 (matinee) and 12. Telegraphs to Mrs. Robert Woods Bliss, Dumbarton Oaks, on the 8th, "I was in my thoughts with you, with whom this work is closely united."

November 22 and 23. Cincinnati. Conducts Symphony in C.

April 10, 1941: Writes to Victoria Ocampo in Argentina:

> These few lines are to inform you that we have settled here in Hollywood, 1260 North Wetherly Drive (telephone, CRestview 1-4858). We have bought a ravishing little house. . . . In mid-February I was conducting a series of concerts with the Philharmonic in Los Angeles and San Diego. Now I shall stay here for a while, after four months of rather hard work in the East, interrupted by interminable illnesses. The winter was bad. My next engagements are in Mexico for the second half of July, a week in Mexico City where I conduct my new Symphony, which I played everywhere this season.

Stravinsky conducted the Symphony in Boston in January 1941, in Mexico in July, and in St. Louis in December. On June 2, 1942, Voigt telegraphed that the BBC had cabled requesting the Symphony, which it performed under Adrian Boult later in the year. On October 13, Stravinsky wrote to Voigt expressing the hope that the parts of the Symphony were corrected, because the parts of this work were "the most abundant in mistakes of any [example] I have ever met at any time in my musical career." The next performance anywhere was Stokowski's broadcast with the NBC Symphony on February 21, 1943. On February 15 Stravinsky had written to Voigt's secretary: "Mr. Stokowski called on me, and I indicated all the necessary directions of performance of my Symphony. At the same time, I gave him my own and only copy of the orchestra score. . . ."

Stravinsky conducted the Symphony in Boston again, in January 1944. On February 11, in Hollywood, he wrote to Hugo Winter of A.M.P.:

> In my last telephone conversation with Boston, [Koussevitzky] spoke to me with great enthusiasm about my Symphony (which he heard for the first time). . . . You would be wise to send the recordings . . . so that he can have the document of my own performance in hand, which will leave nothing to conjecture. Why did you send *my* score of the Symphony to him and not one of the new copies? . . . Is it Alexei Haieff, about whom I spoke to you, who made this copy so quickly and so well, and have you abandoned your idea to publish pocket scores after this copy?

On March 27, Stravinsky wrote to Winter again:

> Do you still intend to recopy my Symphony, photostating it for a provisional edition, as we had proposed to do with the help of A. Haieff? If his writing does not inspire confidence in you, do you have someone else in view? It seems to me absolutely indispensable to have some sort of publication of my Symphony.

Stravinsky's next communication with Willy Strecker was a letter, July 11, 1946: "I would very much like to have an impression of the proofs of the finale of my Symphony in C before you bring it out. Will this be possible?" Not Willy Strecker, but his son, Hugo, answered five weeks later (August 20), from London: "Your request to see a final proof of your engraved score of the Symphony in C has been forwarded to my father in Mainz." Proofs were sent from London on September 2, and Stravinsky cabled to Schott in London on September 29: ". . . unfortunately great many important corrections mailing . . . directly." On October 2 Stravinsky wrote to Gerhard Singer, c/o Wiesbaden Outpost:

> I am taking advantage of your offer [and] am mailing to you . . . the proofs of my Symphony in C. . . . I have made many corrections and would like very much that [Schott] gets them as soon as possible.

The next day, Stravinsky wrote to Schott, explaining that the proofs could not be sent by airmail, and that regular mail "takes from 7 to 8 weeks, which is certainly a lot of time." He requested that Schott be "in touch with Mr. Gerhard Singer, who is in charge of the theater and music branch for the American Military Government for Greater Hesse." Stravinsky says of the corrections, "unfortunately they are many," and "I am mailing the proof to you under separate cover."

January 6, 1947. Philadelphia, Hotel Warwick. Stravinsky receives a telegram from A.M.P. saying that Hugo Strecker received the corrected proofs on October 5. The composer wrote on this message: "And his father . . . received them in Mainz December 1!!!" The score was not published until the summer of

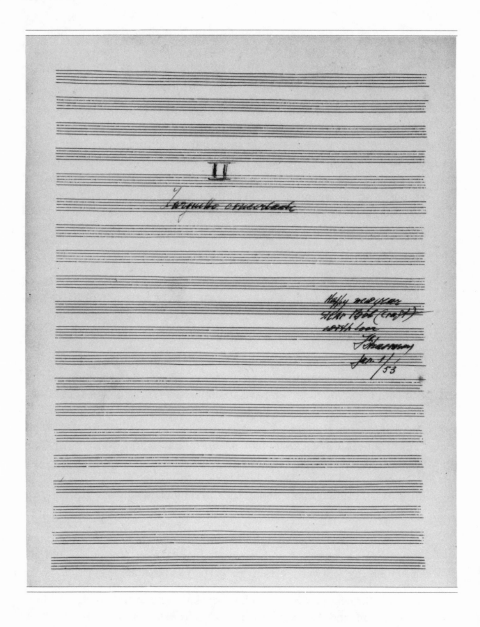

1948, however, and the present writer conducted the performance in Town Hall on April 11, 1948, from a photostat of the Library of Congress manuscript.

The autograph of the Second Movement had been in Mainz throughout the war and was brought to Stravinsky in the Gladstone Hotel in New York in December 1952 by Paul Hindemith. Stravinsky gave it to the present writer on January 1, 1953, as a souvenir of the concert of April 11, 1948.

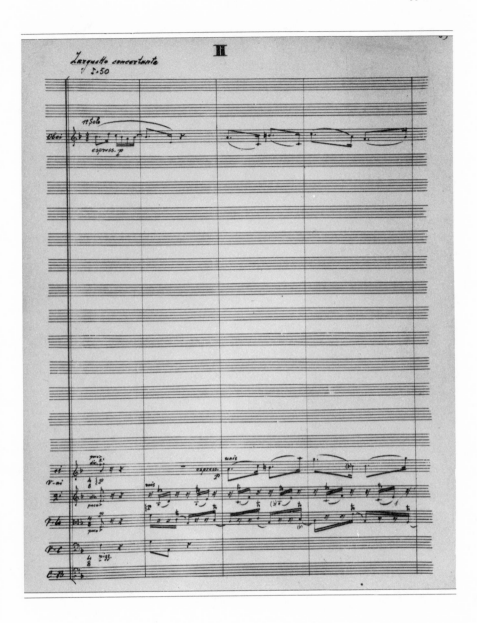

INDEX

A NOTE ON THE TYPE

This book was set via computer-driven cathode ray tube in a face called
Primer, designed by Rudolph Ruzicka (1883–1978). Ruzicka was earlier responsible for the design of Fairfield and Fairfield Medium, faces whose vir-
tues have for some time been accorded wide recognition.
The complete range of sizes of Primer was first made available in 1954,
although the pilot size of 12-point was ready as early as 1951. The design of
the face makes general reference to Century—long a serviceable type,
totally lacking in manner or frills of any kind—but brilliantly corrects its
characterless quality.

Composition by American–Stratford Graphic Services, Inc.,
Brattleboro, Vermont.
Printing and binding by American Book–Stratford Press,
Saddle Brook, New Jersey.
Title-page calligraphy by Golda Fishbein.
Design by Betty Anderson